INTERVIEWING
AND
INVESTIGATING

ESSENTIAL SKILLS FOR THE PARALEGAL

INTERVIEWING
AND
INVESTIGATING

ESSENTIAL SKILLS FOR THE PARALEGAL

Second Edition

STEPHEN P. PARSONS, J.D.

ASPEN
PUBLISHERS

1185 Avenue of the Americas, New York, NY 10036
www.aspenpublishers.com

Permissions
Aspen Publishers
1185 Avenue of the Americas
New York, NY 10036

Printed in the United States of America.

1   2   3   4   5   6   7   8   9   0

ISBN 0-7355-4067-5

Library of Congress Cataloging-in-Publication Data

Parson, Stephen P.
    Interviewing and investigating: essential skills for the paralegal / Stephen P. Parsons.—
    2nd ed.
      p. cm.
    Includes bibliographical references and index
    ISBN 0-7355-4067-5 (alk. paper)
    1. Interviewing in law practice—United States.   2. Attorney and client—United States.   3. Legal assistants—United States—Handbooks, manuals, etc.   4. Investigations.   I. Title.

KF311.Z9P37 2003
340'.023'73—dc21

                                      2003052426

About Aspen Publishers

Aspen Publishers, headquartered in New York City, is a leading information provider for attorneys, business professionals, and law students. Written by preeminent authorities, our products consist of analytical and practical information covering both U.S. and international topics. We publish in the full range of formats, including updated manuals, books, periodicals, CDs, and online products.

Our proprietary content is complemented by 2,500 legal databases, containing over 11 million documents, available through our Loislaw division. Aspen Publishers also offers a wide range of topical legal and business databases linked to Loislaw's primary material. Our mission is to provide accurate, timely, and authoritative content in easily accessible formats, supported by unmatched customer care.

To order any Aspen Publishers title, go to *www.aspenpublishers.com* or call 1-800-638-8437.

To reinstate your manual update service, call 1-800-638-8437.

For more information on Loislaw products, go to *www.loislaw.com* or call 1-800-364-2512.

For Customer Care issues, e-mail *CustomerCare@aspenpublishers.com*; call 1-800-234-1660; or fax 1-800-901-9075.

Aspen Publishers
A Wolters Kluwer Company

To Marcia, Andrew, and Emily Grayce:

abeatus ter

(I am thrice blessed)

Summary of Contents

Contents

List of Illustrations

Preface

Approach

As with the first edition, one underlying premise to this text is that interviewing and investigating are *skills* to be mastered, rather than a unit of information to be memorized. A second is that interviewing and investigating are *essential* skills for the well-trained paralegal, every bit as critical as legal research skills.

As a consequence, the approach taken in the text is two-fold. First, textual discussion of the subject matter is joined with hands-on learning activities in the Learn by Doing exercises. Like any skill, interviewing and investigating can only be effectively learned by practice. Second, varied and realistic legal scenarios are provided in which the student applies the principles studied. With that in mind, the Illustrations, Examples, Hypotheticals, and Learn by Doing exercises used throughout the book, and the Case Studies provided in Appendix A, present a variety of civil and criminal, and litigation and non-litigation scenarios.

A multi-layered approach is utilized in each chapter of this book. First, numerous brief Examples are sprinkled through the text of each chapter along with frequent Illustrations. Then lengthier Hypotheticals, typically three to six in number, are positioned at key points throughout each chapter. The Hypotheticals present a specific factual and legal context, complete with characters, in which the student can see the application—or misapplication—of the concepts being studied. Discussion Questions accompany the Hypotheticals rather than being collected at the end of the chapter, so the student, or the class as a whole, can engage in immediate analysis to reinforce the lessons taught by the Hypotheticals.

In most chapters, the Hypotheticals are serial in nature. They follow the exploits of a single paralegal character or set of characters working on a particular case. This allows the students to see how an investigation progresses over time in a real case. It also allows them to see the various responsibilities of the paralegal involved in investigation. And it allows them to see the consequences of decisions made and actions taken—for good or ill—as a legal matter moves along.

At the end of each chapter, numerous Learn by Doing exercises (LBDs) are presented, designed to be selectively assigned by the instructor. The LBDs require the student to close the book, go out, and engage in some hands-on learning activity related to the subject covered in the chapter. The LBD activities range from having the student determine their state's requirements for becoming a licensed private investigator (LBD 1–2); to interviewing an experienced trial attorney or litigation paralegal concerning the importance of using verbal and nonverbal communication skills to evaluate clients, witnesses, jurors, judges, and opposing counsel (LBD 8–4); locating and evaluating actual experts in various disciplines (LBD 15–2); touring the local or regional office of a federal or state agency to learn how the agency collects and maintains records and how it handles requests for information (LBDs 16–3 and 17–5); and performing a factual investigation of a large local business using the Internet and other resources (LBD 18–4). Although the LBDs are collected at the end of each chapter, references to them are made at relevant points throughout the text.

Additionally, the text provides four detailed Case Studies (Appendix A), complete with characters, designed to be assigned to the students individually or in small groups. The Case Studies present realistic scenarios (a murder case, a personal injury case, a domestic relations case, and a real estate development project) and provide a vehicle for the student to put in practice the skills being learned. As the student moves through the text with an assigned Case Study, the LBDs at the end of the chapters are keyed to each of the Case Studies and require the student to identify and evaluate evidentiary questions based on the facts in the case (Chapter 7); prepare a complete investigation plan for the case (Chapter 9); schedule, prepare for, and conduct the interview of a person role-playing as the client in the Case Study (Chapters 10 and 11); schedule, prepare for, and conduct the interview of a person role-playing as a witness in the case (Chapters 12 and 13); prepare investigation reports, authorizations, witness statements, and correspondence related to the case (Chapters 10–13); identify potential witnesses and determine how to locate missing witnesses in the case (Chapter 14); locate and evaluate qualified experts who might be needed in the case (Chapter 15); and determine how they would go about seeking relevant factual information in the case from federal, state, and local government sources and private sources (Chapters 16–18). In short, to learn by doing.

Great emphasis is placed on resources available to the investigator, particularly Internet resources. Appendix E, Resources for the Investigator, provides a rich, diverse source of investigation tools along with information on how to locate and access them. In Appendix E, the student will find online and other resources for locating experts; online resources and an extensive bibliography on alternative dispute resolution; extensive reading lists for developing good communication skills in verbal, nonverbal, and written communication; online sources for accessing information from state and local governments and all three branches of the federal government; written and online resources for utilizing the Freedom of Information and Privacy Acts; citations to the open records acts of all fifty states; people-locating resources, from online people search services to genealogical resources; extensive lists of records search companies and online database vendors; and even a comprehensive section on resources for and about private investigators. References to Appendix E are made at relevant points throughout the text and a number of LBDs require the student to utilize the resources found there.

New for the Second Edition

For the second edition, the citations to all Web sites have been updated, references to many new Web sites and court decisions included, more Learn by Doing exercises added, and the Hypotheticals and Examples refined. Both the text of the second edition and the Learn by Doing exercises reference important new federal statutes and regulations that will impact the paralegal's investigation task significantly, including the Homeland Security Act, the E-Government Act of 2002, the Federal Financial Modernization Act ("Gramm-Leach-Bliley Act"), and the new health-privacy rules promulgated by the Department of Health and Human Services.

Two brand new features for the second edition, designed to make the book a more effective and enjoyable learning tool, are the *Sleuth on the Loose* exercises and a Glossary of important words and phrases. *Sleuth on the Loose*, appearing two or three times in each chapter in the margin of the page, provides the student an opportunity to use the Web to perform a quick factual investigation on an interesting subject related to the material covered in the chapter. The Glossary collects in one convenient place the definitions of key words and phrases defined throughout the text.

Organization of the Book

The text is divided into two parts:

Part 1: Foundations for Interviewing and Investigating (Chapters 1–8)

Part 2: Formulating and Executing a Plan of Investigation (Chapters 9–18)

Part 1 introduces the student to the legal contexts in which interviewing and investigating skills are utilized. Based on 20 years of experience as a trial attorney, the author firmly believes that in order to assist an attorney effectively in case or project investigation, paralegals must:

(1) understand the critical connection between law and fact;
(2) be able to engage in effective factual analysis;
(3) have well-developed communication skills;
(4) be knowledgeable and *committed* to the highest standards of legal ethics; and
(5) be well grounded in the adversarial system, the formal discovery rules in civil and criminal cases, the distinctions between formal and informal investigation, and the basic rules of evidence.

Accordingly, those subjects are covered in Part 1 of the book. They are studied from the viewpoint of the investigating paralegal with emphasis on practical application in real-life scenarios reinforced by the Learn by Doing exercises. The Appendices supplement the material covered in Part 1, providing selected Federal Rules of Civil Procedure (Appendix B), Federal Rules of Criminal Procedure (Appendix C), and Federal Rules of Evidence (Appendix D).

Part 2 of the book walks the student step by step through an investigation. We begin with how to plan an investigation and how to properly handle documents and physical evidence uncovered in an investigation (Chapter 9). Then we consider how to schedule, prepare for, and conduct a client interview (Chapters 10 and 11), and a fact witness interview

(Chapters 12 and 13). Next we learn how to identify potential witnesses and how to locate the missing witness (Chapter 14). Chapter 15 is devoted to the important topic of locating, evaluating, and working with expert witnesses. The text concludes with three chapters devoted to the myriad sources of information available to the investigator, including information available from the federal government (Chapter 16), state and local governments (Chapter 17), and private sources of information (Chapter 18).

Because of the emphasis in Part 1 on the legal context in which interviewing and investigating is done, including the emphasis on the adversarial system, civil and criminal procedure, formal discovery, and the supporting Appendices and Case Studies, this text can be used for a litigation course as well as an investigation course. The Instructor's Manual provides a sample syllabus and suggested chapter sequencing for teaching the course over one or two academic terms, and for using the text for both a litigation course and an investigation course.

Key Features

Among the many learning tools which distinguish this book are those multi-layered features discussed above:

Brief Examples
Illustrations
Hypotheticals
Discussion Questions following the Hypotheticals
Key Words and Phrases
Learn by Doing exercises
Case Studies

In addition, the text contains occasional Ethical Notes and Career Tips for the student. And new for the second edition are the Sleuth on the Loose feature and the Glossary of important words and phrases.

The Instructor's Manual for the text contains detailed Character Descriptions for each of the clients and witnesses mentioned in the Case Studies; Instructions for persons role-playing as clients or witnesses; and an Evaluation Form for those persons to complete for each interviewer and return to the instructor. The Instructor's Manual also contains suggested procedures for video taping and critiquing student interviews; a model syllabus; comprehensive examination questions covering all of the chapters, with answer keys; and a comprehensive section containing suggested approaches to teaching with the text including testing and grading, how to use the LBDs in each chapter, how to use Appendix E effectively, and how to best utilize the Hypotheticals, Examples, and Illustrations in each chapter. The complete text of the Privacy Act and the Freedom of Information Act are also set out in the Instructor's Manual.

An Internet Web page will be maintained by the author to update the materials in the book including the resources presented in Appendix E to update users of changes in law or practice affecting the concepts and skills taught here and to advise instructors of new ideas or methods for teaching the subject. The http address for the Web page will be distributed with the Instructor's Manual.

Finally, a word about the alliterative and other fictitious names used in the Hypotheticals. These names are not used simply to be clever. The author has developed these materials over five years of teaching an interviewing and investigating course for paralegal students, and there are calculated pedagogical goals involved in the name selections. Some Hypotheticals use names keyed to the factual context. For example, in Chapter 6 we learn the importance of knowing the basic rules of evidence by following a dispute between a professional golfer, Snap Hook, and his caddy, Teed Off, over an alleged promise to share the winnings in a major golf tournament. In Chapter 7 we review the specific rules of evidence by focusing on a fraud allegation made by Gulli Bull against Smooth Talker. In Chapter 9 we learn how to prepare a plan of investigation by working on an automobile accident case involving Speed Freak and Granny Puttalong. And in Chapter 14 we learn how to identify witnesses and locate missing witnesses when Turnme Loose dumps her boyfriend, Getta Life, and then turns up dead.

Other Hypotheticals use names keyed to the lesson to be learned. For example, in Chapter 2 paralegal Sally Oops teaches us the consequences of mishandling client funds, even inadvertently. The experiences of paralegal Ned Newatit demonstrate why new paralegals need to be familiar with the dangers of unauthorized practice of law (UPL) and disclosing client confidences. In Chapter 8, paralegal Dis Tracted illustrates the perils of not using good communication skills with co-workers. In Chapter 12, paralegal Dee Termined demonstrates how to handle the hostile witness and the skeptical witness. And in Chapters 10–13, paralegal Paul Perfect does a, well, perfect job of preparing for and conducting client and witness interviews.

Thus the names serve not only to catch and hold the *attention* of the student, but to constantly *remind* the student of what the Hypothetical is about, and to *reinforce* the concept being taught. Of course, the names might also make the learning experience a little more enjoyable for the students and even for the instructor.

In Appreciation

The author has had the good fortune to be ably assisted by a number of people at Aspen Publishers in the production of this second edition. Special mention among those goes to Elizabeth Kenny whose sound judgment and steady hand always made the task easier. And thanks to Suzanne Rapcavage for her excellent text editing work. Appreciation is expressed to my wife, Marcia, and to my son, Andrew, for their help with the citation updates and taking care of so many messy details. And, finally, a special thanks to the legal assistant students at Walters State Community College and the law students at Appalachian School of Law who are the continuing inspiration for this project and have served as its willing crash dummies: thanks guys, and bless your hearts.

Stephen P. Parsons

Acknowledgments

The author is grateful to copyright holders and others for providing permission and assistance in using the following materials:

American Arbitration Association, Dispute Submission, form GIA. Reprinted with permission of the American Arbitration Association.

Johnny Hart and Creators Syndicate, Inc., Wizard of Id cartoon dated 9-2-96. Copyright © 1996, Creators Syndicate, Inc.

Lyndon Baines Johnson Library, Austin, Texas, for assistance in locating and using the LBJ/Abe Fortas photograph. From the LBJ Library collection. Photographed by Yoichi R. Okamoto.

Phillip Margolin, excerpt from *The Last Innocent Man.* Copyright © 981, 1995 by Phillip Margolin.

INTERVIEWING
AND
INVESTIGATING

ESSENTIAL SKILLS FOR THE PARALEGAL

FOUNDATIONS FOR INTERVIEWING AND INVESTIGATING

PART OUTLINE

Chapter 1

Introduction to Interviewing and Investigating

CHAPTER OBJECTIVES

In this introductory chapter you will learn:

- Why lawyers do interviewing and investigating work and need assistants skilled at these tasks.
- Why it is important for the paralegal investigator to also be skilled at legal research and writing and to know the rules of evidence and procedure, basic substantive law, and principles of legal ethics and professionalism.
- The role of the paralegal in interviewing and investigating.

A. ▶ Why These Skills Are Important to the Lawyer

"You ever play any sports in high school or college?"

David shrugged.

"I ran a little track in college and wrestled some."

"Okay. Why don't you tell me how trying a case compares to the feeling you get just before a sporting event. How's that?"

David thought for a few minutes before answering.

"I don't think they're that similar," David said. "Winning or losing at sports depends on your performance during the sporting event, but a lawyer can't win a case at trial. Or, anyway, not usually."

"What do you mean?"

"Well, the facts of each case are determined by the time the case gets to you. All the facts might not be revealed, but they're there. So a lawyer wins his case before trial by finding out, through investigation, what the facts are. A lawyer can't change the facts, but once he knows what the facts are, he can deal with them. Try to get the jury to look at them in a certain way. And there is usually more than one way to look at the facts.

"A few years back I represented a man who tried to hold up a minimart. He walked in with a shotgun and told the manager to give him the money or he would kill him. The manager was a feisty little guy, and he whipped out a handgun and shot my client through the neck. When the police arrived, my man was lying in a pool of blood holding the gun, and there were five eyewitnesses who swore that he tried to rob the place. The DA charged my client with armed robbery. Those were the facts I started with. Want to guess the verdict?"

Gault smiled.

"It has to be not guilty, but how did you do it?"

"There were other facts we didn't know about when we started. When they took the defendant to the hospital for surgery, they took a blood sample. One of the routine checks the hospital makes before performing surgery is to find out how much alcohol a person has in his system. My man was loaded. He had consumed so much alcohol that I was able to get two prominent psychiatrists to testify that a person in his condition would not be able to form the intent to commit the crime, and the district attorney must prove intent as one of the elements of the crime of armed robbery.

"The next step was to find out why my client drank like that. It turned out that his wife had died and he had gone to pieces. When I got him, he was already an alcoholic.

"Finally, we had to figure out why he had been at the minimart in the first place. My investigator asked around, and it turned out that our boy had been blotto that day. Two of his buddies had planned the robbery and sent him inside. He was so drunk, he didn't know what he was doing. In fact, he doesn't remember what happened to this day.

"When we presented all the facts to the jury, they acquitted. It wasn't what we did at trial, but the investigation before trial, that mattered. Getting the facts, then presenting them in a favorable light at trial."

—Excerpt from *The Last Innocent Man,*
Copyright © 1981, 1995 by Phillip Margolin.

Investigation is the process by which attorneys, and those assisting them, gather relevant information from a variety of public and private sources in order to successfully represent the interests of their client. The ability to effectively interview clients, potential witnesses, and other persons who may have helpful information is a critical part of the investigation process. These skills are essential in criminal and civil litigation matters and in all other types of legal representation as well.

1. The relationship between law and fact

The law does not exist in a vacuum. In every matter that a lawyer handles for a client the **facts** that are discovered will determine what **law** controls. Even a slight change in the facts can result in a change in the controlling law. When facts are disputed as between parties to a lawsuit, that dispute will give rise to competing arguments by the attorneys for those parties as to which facts are more believable and, consequently, as to what law should control the dispute. And if the dispute is litigated in a civil or criminal lawsuit, the judge or the jury, sitting as finder(s) of fact, will have to make a decision as to what the actual facts are before applying the applicable law to those facts to reach a decision. **Interviewing** and **investigating** are the means by which lawyers identify and gather the facts that will control the law of the case.

HYPOTHETICAL 1-1

Assume that in your state the criminal homicide statutes permit the state to charge and convict a person for first degree murder based on proof of the willful, deliberate, and premeditated taking of a human life; for second degree murder based on proof of the willful taking of human life but without deliberation or premeditation; for manslaughter based on proof of reckless behavior (including sudden passion) that foreseeably results in the taking of a human life; and for negligent homicide based on proof of negligent behavior that foreseeably results in the taking of a human life. The use of reasonable force in self-defense or in defense of a third party are recognized in your state. This is the law of the case. The attorney you work for is representing Quick Temper, who is charged with first degree murder in the shooting death of his neighbor, Hi Fi. The indictment alleges that Quick Temper told a friend the day before the killing that he hated Hi Fi because he played loud music all night long, that Quick Temper purchased a rifle the day of the murder, that he laid in wait in the darkness outside Hi Fi's door, and that he shot Hi Fi as the victim entered his apartment.

What difference might it make to the outcome of this case if your investigation turns up the following facts?

1. Quick Temper had abandoned his plan to kill Hi Fi but dropped the rifle on the ground as he was leaving the scene. The gun discharged, and the bullet struck and killed Hi Fi.
2. Quick Temper had been adjudicated mentally incompetent a week before the shooting.
3. The neighbor living on the other side of Hi Fi also hated him and had fired a rifle at him at the same time as Quick Temper.
4. Quick Temper fired the shot that killed Hi Fi but was actually trying to hit the neighbor who was aiming her gun at Hi Fi.
5. Quick Temper had fired at Hi Fi only when he saw Hi Fi kissing his (Quick Temper's) wife.
6. Hi Fi had threatened to kill Quick Temper and in fact had a gun in his hand at the time of the shooting. (But what if it was a sling shot and not a gun?)
7. Quick Temper thought the gun was not loaded and only intended to scare Hi Fi.
8. The rifle discharged not because Quick Temper pulled the trigger but because of a defect in the firing mechanism.
9. Although the bullet fired by Quick Temper did strike Hi Fi, the actual cause of death was a massive heart attack that occurred immediately before the shot was fired.
10. Quick Temper did tell the friend of his hatred for Hi Fi but said this five years before the shooting.

> What other facts can you hypothesize that, if discovered, would change the application of the law to Quick Temper's situation?

None of the facts in Hypothetical 1-1 change the law. But they do dramatically change the application of the law to the case and thus the potential outcome of the case. Factual investigation is an essential skill for those involved in the legal system.

2. Factual analysis

Think for a moment about the process your mind went through as you considered whether and how each of the facts given to you in Hypothetical 1-1 impacted on the legal issue of whether Quick Temper should be charged or convicted under any of the criminal homicide statutes. We call this process **factual analysis.** Factual analysis is a critical thinking skill. It is the process of taking information, making sure that you understand it, evaluating it in order to determine if it is reliable, and then applying it to determine the impact or difference it makes on your legal question. From that definition, we can see that there are three steps involved in the process of factual analysis:

- *comprehension* of the law and of the facts discovered;
- *evaluation* of the facts discovered to see if they are reliable; and
- *application* of the facts to the legal issues.

Let's consider each of these three steps in turn.

a. Comprehension

You must **comprehend** or understand the law you are dealing with in a given case and the facts that you discover in the investigation. For example, if the investigator does not understand that in order to convict Quick Temper of first degree murder the state must prove that he took the life of Hi Fi willfully, deliberately, and with premeditation, then the investigator will be unable to see the relevance of fact no. 1 in Hypothetical 1-1—that Quick Temper had abandoned his plan to kill Hi Fi, but dropped his rifle on the ground with the result that it fired and killed Hi Fi anyway.

Once we do understand the law—that *willfully* means that Quick Temper must have intended Hi Fi's death when he dropped the rifle; that *deliberately* means he must have acted with the purpose of taking Hi Fi's life when he dropped the rifle; and that *premeditation* means that he must have acted with forethought in taking Hi Fi's life—then and only then are we able to recognize that this fact, if true, means that Quick Temper did not take Hi Fi's life willfully, deliberately, or with premeditation.

Unless the paralegal investigator has a basic understanding of the law at issue in a client's case, she will be unable to do effective investigation. She won't know what factual information to look for and she won't recognize relevant information even if she stumbles over it!

And, of course, the investigator must be able to understand the factual information she discovers as well. That may sound simple enough when we are talking about someone who tells us they accidentally dropped a rifle. But factual information sometimes comes in such great volume that it is difficult to assess. And factual information also comes to us in more complex forms, such as the financial statements of a corporation that we must be able to read with comprehension. And often factual information comes to us in technical jargon that we must be able to interpret, such as when a computer expert throws out terms like *URL, HTML, digital subscriber loop,* or *arithmetic logic unit,* and expects the interviewer to understand them.

b. Evaluation

By **evaluation of information** we mean that every piece of information discovered in a legal investigation has to be examined carefully. We have to test it and compare it to other information we have, in order to determine whether and to what extent it is *reliable.*

The first commandment in interviewing and investigating work is: **DON'T ASSUME ANYTHING.** In particular, don't assume that everything you are told by a client or witness or everything you read in a document is automatically true, accurate, complete, or trustworthy.

SLEUTH ON THE LOOSE

Have you been Googled yet? *Go to www.google .com*, one of the most popular search engines. Enter the name of someone you want to know more about and see what information this comprehensive engine can locate for you. Try entering your own name or someone in your family.

- Sometimes people lie.
- Sometimes people tell half-truths.
- Sometimes people are mistaken in what they thought they heard or saw.
- Sometimes people guess but don't tell you they're guessing.
- Sometimes people forget or misremember what they heard or saw in the past.
- Sometimes people make unwarranted assumptions and pass those assumptions off as fact.
- Sometimes people speak in conclusions that are not supported by fact.
- Sometimes people allow their prejudices to color what they "know."
- Sometimes people have only second- or third-hand information rather than first-hand information but leave it to the interviewer to figure that out.
- Sometimes people confuse their opinions with facts.
- Sometimes people are reluctant to tell what they know.
- Sometimes two people can hear or see the same event and each describe it differently from the other while both swear they are telling the truth.
- Sometimes the same types of inaccuracies and falsehoods get included in documents.

Welcome to the real world! We assume nothing in legal investigation. Instead, we follow the second commandment of interviewing and investigating, which is: **VERIFY EVERYTHING.** That means we evaluate information that comes to us by testing it. We take it apart and put it back together. We sift it and shake it and turn it on its head until we can reach a conclusion regarding its accuracy and reliability. More specifically:

- We attempt to determine if the source of the information is competent, honest, reliable, and objective.
- We try to filter out opinions, assumptions, and statements of prejudice to get to the real provable facts.
- We distinguish between first-hand information and second- or third-hand information.
- We work to verify the information by seeking corroboration (information that tends to confirm or verify other information).
- We seek details and leads to other sources of information.
- We seek clarification of confusing or incomplete information.
- We compare the information to other information we have found and see how the different pieces of information fit together.
- We look for contradictions and inconsistencies.
- We look for gaps in information and seek to fill them in.
- We draw reasonable inferences from the information we locate but seek confirmation nonetheless.
- We resist the urge to draw unwarranted conclusions from information and look for hard evidence.

This is factual evaluation and it is at the heart of the interviewing and investigating process.

EXAMPLE

Assume that our source for the information that Quick Temper abandoned his plan to shoot and kill Hi Fi but dropped the gun as he was leaving, is Quick Temper himself. How reliable is that source? Not very reliable, is it? Why? Because Quick Temper has a strong motive to lie—to save himself! But what if the source of that information is a bystander who says she was there and saw Quick Temper walk away from Hi Fi's house and drop the gun? More reliable? Yes, but remember the first commandment—don't assume anything. If the prosecutor's paralegal investigator follows that commandment, he may discover that the bystander is actually Quick Temper's sister, or is legally blind, or was actually driving by in a car at 90 mph at the time, or is mentally insane, or has a history of telling lies to the police to get attention. Attorneys, and those who assist them, are constantly searching for new factual information relevant to the legal issues in the client's case. And they are constantly evaluating and testing the facts discovered to determine their accuracy and reliability.

c. Application

The final step in factual analysis is the determination of whether the information we locate, regardless of its reliability, is **legally relevant.** By that we mean, does the information matter? Does it arguably impact or make a difference on the legal issues we are considering? Could it be significant in any way for the legal problem we are handling for the client?

EXAMPLE

> You may discover in the course of your investigation for the attorney defending Quick Temper that he is 45 years old and still lives with his mother. You may be able to verify that information as absolutely true. But so what? Are those facts relevant to whether Quick Temper violated any one of the homicide statutes? They don't appear to be. So what will we do with these facts? We will categorize them as irrelevant to any legal issue we have and set them aside—at least for now.

This **categorizing of information** is an important part of the factual analysis process. It is the ability to look at information from all different sides and angles and to recognize what information is relevant—is significant, and makes a difference—and what information is not. If information is not relevant to any legal issue before us, we cull it out.

We not only categorize factual information according to whether it is legally relevant but we also consider which legal issue(s) it is relevant to.

EXAMPLE

> The information contained in fact no. 4 of Hypothetical 1-1, that Quick Temper fired his rifle not at Hi Fi but at a neighbor who was aiming a gun at Hi Fi, is not legally relevant to the question of whether Quick Temper "willfully" took a human life—he admits he shot to kill. But it is relevant to the legal defense he will assert—using reasonable force to defend the life of a third person. The paralegal investigator must be able to categorize information in order to understand why it is relevant and where it fits in among all the legal issues and other facts.

Not only is the information we gather in a factual investigation usually relevant to different legal issues, sometimes the information appears to be irrelevant to any issue, then later becomes relevant because a new issue arises.

EXAMPLE

> Remember those facts we established, that Quick Temper is 45 years old and still lives with his mother? Not significant, until his mother testifies that her son couldn't have killed Hi Fi because at the time of the shooting he was with her at the mall! Now those facts become very relevant. The prosecution will bring those facts out in order to show that the mother is close to the son and thus is biased in his favor and has a strong motive to lie for him.

Go through the factual statements set out in Hypothetical 1-1. For each fact given, identify every legal issue, if any, to which you think that fact is legally relevant. Be prepared to explain why you think that fact is (or isn't) relevant to that issue.

Factual analysis is central to the interviewing and investigating tasks. It is a learned art. It takes work and practice. The paralegal investigator gets better at it with practice, and we will attempt to give you plenty of practice in succeeding chapters.

3. The role of factual investigation in civil litigation

a. By the attorney for the plaintiff

In **civil litigation** (the distinction between civil and criminal law is discussed in detail in Chapter 3), the attorney who is retained by the potential plaintiff will engage in factual investigation *before* filing a complaint initiating the lawsuit. This **pre-filing investigation** is done in order to determine:

- if the client has a valid cause of action on any legal theory;
- if the client has a timely cause of action in light of the controlling statute(s) of limitation and repose;
- the likelihood that the client will be able to prevail if suit is brought;
- the existence and relative strength of any defenses that may limit or defeat the client's recovery;
- the identity and availability of all potential defendants;
- the likelihood of a counterclaim being filed against the plaintiff;
- the solvency of potential defendants and the existence of insurance or indemnity agreements as sources to satisfy a judgment;
- the identity, availability, and value of potential witnesses; and
- the existence and value of all documentation and physical proof that may tend to support or defeat the client's claim.

All of this will go into the decision to file the lawsuit and, if so, against whom and on what theories.

b. By the attorney for the defendant

The attorney retained to represent the defendant in a civil suit will need to do investigation prior to filing an answer or other response to the complaint in order to determine:

- whether to admit or deny the allegations in the complaint;
- whether any factual or affirmative defenses are available;
- whether a motion to dismiss or for summary judgment is advisable;
- whether a counterclaim against the plaintiff exists on behalf of his client;
- whether a cross-claim against a third party exists on behalf of his client; and
- how to evaluate the case for his client, i.e., the likelihood and cost of winning or losing and thus the advisability of attempting to settle out of court and, if so, on what terms.

HYPOTHETICAL 1-2

Assume you work for an attorney specializing in plaintiff's personal injury work. A potential new client, Road Rage, meets with you and the attorney and tells you he was involved in a car accident when another driver, Lead Foot, ran a red light at an intersection and collided with his car.

Also assume that in your state, to recover on a theory of negligence a plaintiff must allege and prove that the defendant owed a duty of care to the plaintiff; that the defendant breached that duty; that the injuries of plaintiff were in fact and foreseeably caused by that breach of duty; and that the plaintiff was in fact injured. Your state is a pure comparative fault jurisdiction, which means the plaintiff's ultimate recovery will be reduced by any percentage of fault the jury attributes to him rather than the defendant. The statute of limitations for filing a personal injury action is one year. This is the law of the case.

What factual investigation will your supervising lawyer probably want you to do before deciding to file suit on behalf of Road Rage? What kind of questions will you ask Road Rage? Who else do you want to interview? What documents or physical evidence do you want to locate and view? Consider how what you find out in your investigation will affect your lawyer's decision to take this case.

If you work for defense counsel representing Lead Foot when Road Rage files suit, what factual investigation will she want you to do before responding to the complaint filed by Road Rage?

4. The role of factual investigation in criminal litigation

In **criminal litigation** (the distinction between civil and criminal law is discussed in detail in Chapter 3), the prosecution will engage in pre-filing investigation for the same reasons that the civil plaintiff's attorney does, except that the legal theories explored will be criminal rather than civil. Likewise, the criminal defense attorney will engage in investigation in order to:

- evaluate the government's charges against his client;
- advise his client how to plead and whether to defend the charges or plea bargain; and
- prepare the defense for trial.

HYPOTHETICAL 1-3

Using the facts set out in Hypothetical 1-1 involving Quick Temper and the death of Hi-Fi, assume you work for the state prosecutor. What, if any, homicide crime would you recommend Quick Temper be charged with in connection with each of the assumptions set out in Hypothetical 1-1?

If you worked for counsel defending Quick Temper on a first degree murder charge, what recommendation would you make regarding a plea bargain versus trying the case in connection with each of the assumptions set out in Hypothetical 1-1?

And, as with civil litigation, factual investigation continues in a criminal case after the case is commenced up until the time of trial.

5. The role of factual investigation in other legal representation

Interviewing and investigating skills are also vital to the lawyer engaged in representing a client in a non-litigation matter. In any commercial, corporate, or private legal matter the lawyer must determine:

- what options are available to the client based on the available facts;
- what risks and rewards there are for the client with regard to each such option;
- the advisability of pursuing one available option over another; and
- how best to put together the information necessary to accomplish the goals selected.

HYPOTHETICAL 1-4

Assume that you work for an attorney specializing in business and commercial law. A husband and wife and their two adult children come to see your attorney, and tell him that they have come up with a sensational recipe for cinnamon rolls. They have been selling their rolls (which they call Sinfully Cinnamon Sensations) in their neighborhood with great success. The feedback has been so positive and the demand so great that the four have decided to quit their other jobs and go into business full time producing the cinnamon rolls and distributing them regionally at first and then perhaps nationally.

During the conference you hear your supervising lawyer tell the clients that, from a legal standpoint, they will have to make initial decisions regarding securing product and name protection; whether to do business as a corporation, partnership, or limited liability company, including tax considerations; how to raise necessary financing; whether and when to franchise or license the product to others; where and how to initially market their product; compliance with federal, state, and local regulations or ordinances governing food production, packaging and distribution; distribution agreements; and liability insurance.

What questions would you want to ask these clients or others on each of these topics?

B. ▶ Other Skills and Areas of Knowledge Related to Interviewing and Investigating

Interviewing and investigating are not isolated skills. Legal assistants undertake these activities on behalf of lawyers for specific reasons and with particular goals in mind. And to be successful, the person undertaking this work for the lawyer must have a number of related skills and be knowledgeable in other areas related to the law.

1. Substantive law

It is critical that the legal assistant engaging in interviewing and investigating on behalf of a lawyer have a firm foundation in various areas of **substantive law.** Substantive law is the law that defines the rights and duties of persons with respect to each other, as opposed to **procedural law,** which defines the manner in which those rights and duties may be enforced. Examples of substantive law include constitutional law, contract law, the law of business associations, tort law, criminal law, real property law, and so on. Knowledge of substantive law is essential in order for the paralegal to:

- understand why and for what purposes the investigation is being done in a particular case;
- plan a successful investigation; and
- identify all sources of information available regarding a particular legal matter.

EXAMPLE

If the paralegal is asked to investigate a corporation as a potential defendant in a civil lawsuit, it will be critical for the investigator to understand how corporations are created under the law, how they function, how they are organized, the records they must keep or usually keep, the sources of public and private information about corporations, etc. Without such knowledge no plan of investigation will be successful.

2. Legal research and writing

Interviewing and investigating are sister skills to legal research and writing. Facts that are gathered in the investigation must be fitted into civil causes of action and defenses, criminal charges and defenses, legal business arrangements, or whatever the subject matter of the representation is. The paralegal must have the ability to locate and understand the law and the ability to apply the facts discovered to the law involved in the representation.

Using the situations described in Hypotheticals 1-1, 1-2, and 1-4, what legal issues might you be asked by your supervising lawyer to research? Other than your research memorandum, what legal documents might you be asked to draft in those various hypothetical situations?

3. Rules of evidence

In litigation matters, the legal investigator must have a knowledge of the fundamental rules of evidence that will govern in the trial of the matter, whether civil or criminal. (See Chapters 6 and 7.) Such knowledge not only has an impact on the decision of what evidence to pursue, but the form in which evidence must be obtained in order to be admissible in a court of law, as well as the importance of properly storing and preserving evidence in such a way as to prevent attack on its authenticity or reliability.

EXAMPLE

If the state charges Quick Temper with first degree murder as suggested in Hypothetical 1-1, there may be evidentiary questions of relevance and hearsay raised at trial regarding the statement of Quick Temper to the friend concerning his hatred of Hi Fi, and questions of authenticity and hearsay regarding the sales receipt for the rifle. What other evidentiary questions can you foresee based on the various factual findings set out in Hypothetical 1-1?

4. The adversarial system and rules of procedure

In litigation matters, the legal investigator must have an understanding of the adversarial system, knowledge of various statutes of limitation and repose (see Chapter 3), and knowledge of the rules of civil or criminal procedure that will govern the proceeding (see Chapters 4 and 5). This will determine the form and the timing of the investigation, as well as the procedures that must be followed in order to accomplish formal discovery.

EXAMPLE

We have already seen in Hypothetical 1-2 that the date of an event needs to be factually determined as early as possible to determine if the client can now bring an otherwise valid cause of action.

5. Ethics and professional responsibility

The legal investigator must be knowledgeable of and comply with all ethical obligations (see Chapter 2). If the investigator is working on a matter as the employee or contract agent of an attorney, she must know and comply with the ethical rules that govern that attorney. In particular, the ethical rules governing client confidentiality, conflicts of interest, the unauthorized practice of law, how to contact a party already represented by counsel, the duty of competence, and the handling of client funds and other property should be well known and observed.

Keep in mind too that ethical and legal requirements frequently overlap. In other words, behavior that is unethical may also be criminal. The unauthorized practice of law is a good example. It is not only unethical for an unlicensed person to engage in the practice of law, it is likely to be a crime as well. Another example is the mishandling of client funds. There are not only strict ethical rules governing this but, in addition, to mishandle those funds may constitute a theft crime or some type of criminal fraud.

C. The Role of the Paralegal in Interviewing and Investigating

1. Definition of a paralegal

The widely accepted definition of a **paralegal** is that developed by the American Bar Association's Committee on Ethics and Responsibility:

A person qualified by education, training or work experience who is employed or retained by a lawyer, law office, corporation, governmental agency or other entity and who performs specifically delegated substantive legal work for which a lawyer is responsible.

In most jurisdictions, and for our purposes in this text, the terms **paralegal** and **legal assistant** are used interchangeably.

2. The paralegal as an agent of the attorney

In the eyes of the law, a paralegal working with an attorney is an **agent** of that attorney and a **subagent** of the attorney's client. That has many ramifications, including:

a. The actions of the paralegal may be legally binding on the attorney and the client

EXAMPLE

Assume a paralegal is authorized by her supervising attorney to set up a deposition for the client. The paralegal is told to set up the deposition for a time *after* the opposing party is deposed. If the paralegal ignores or forgets those instructions and agrees for the client to be deposed before the opposing party, that agreement may be enforced against the supervising attorney by the court under principles of agency law.

b. The attorney may be liable for damages caused to another by the paralegal

Under the doctrine of *respondeat superior* (Latin for "let the master respond"), also called **vicarious liability** (when legal responsibility is placed on one for the acts of another), the attorney who employs and supervises the paralegal may be liable along with the paralegal herself for damages incurred by the client or others due to the negligent and sometimes even the fraudulent or intentional acts of the paralegal.

c. The attorney may be sanctioned for actions of the paralegal

The attorney employer of the paralegal who engages in unethical or unprofessional conduct while acting for the attorney may receive sanctions from the state body that regulates attorney behavior. These sanctions are enforced as if the attorney himself had engaged in the behavior or for the attorney's failure to properly supervise the paralegal.

3. Paralegals as licensed private investigators

Attorneys and paralegals should check the **private investigators** licensing statute in the state(s) where they practice (see LBD 1-1, 1-2, 1-3, and 1-6). The wording of these statutes as to what constitutes engaging in private investigating (and thus requires a license from the state for that purpose) varies widely, as does the wording of exceptions to the licensing requirement. For example, under some statutes, one engaging in this work on behalf of an attorney need not secure a private investigator's license but must be careful not to identify themselves or hold themselves out as a private investigator.

Some attorneys may prefer that paralegals engaging in investigation work on their behalf on a regular basis obtain a private investigator's license. The procedure for that is also controlled by state law, but is typically not difficult or expensive.

CAREER TIP

Obtaining one's private investigator's license may also be a smart career move for a paralegal. It may make your credentials more appealing to a hiring attorney, and may qualify you to work for an experienced private investigator as an alternative career. It is also a step toward working for yourself if you truly enjoy this kind of work.

4. What attorneys expect from paralegals

Though specific expectations and ways of doing things will vary from attorney to attorney, it is safe to say that attorneys utilizing paralegals to engage in interviewing and investigating work will expect the paralegal to have, in addition to the related skills discussed in this chapter, a professional attitude, good people skills, and highly developed investigative skills. More specifically that means:

a. The willingness to work under the supervision of the attorney

It is one thing to understand that a paralegal is defined as one who performs certain tasks under the supervision of an attorney. But it is another to *accept* that limitation and be willing to abide by it every day in the law office.

SL)EUTH ON THE LOOSE

Identify an attorney or law firm you would like to know more about then access the Martindale-Hubbell Law Directory at *www.martindale.com* and see what information you can locate concerning that attorney or firm.

b. The initiative to clarify assignments

Sometimes the assignment the paralegal receives will be unclear in scope or purpose. It is critical in those situations for the paralegal to know that she should go back to the supervising attorney and clarify the assignment rather than making a guess and proceeding on it.

c. Good judgment

For example, you need the judgment to know when to use your own initiative to complete an assignment already given, and when to come back to the attorney for further authority—not always easy. Good judgment comes from experience in doing this kind of work, experience in working with a particular attorney, and common sense. A good rule of thumb here for the paralegal is *better safe than sorry!*

d. The discipline to keep the supervising attorney well advised

In investigating, it is critical for the paralegal to report back promptly to the supervising attorney, to keep him thoroughly and regularly advised regarding the status of the investigation. Keep in mind that the attorney's ethical responsibility is to supervise the paralegal's work and it is the attorney who maintains the direct relationship with the client. The attorney must be kept advised to fulfill both these responsibilities.

e. The ability to work well under pressure

There is tremendous pressure in a law office. Heavy work loads, pressing time deadlines, and demanding clients are the stuff our days are made of. But the work is challenging and rewarding—for those who can handle the pressure.

f. Good communication and people skills

Communication skills are essential to the paralegal to work effectively with the assigning attorney, other staff in the office, opposing counsel and her staff, the client, witnesses, and other information sources (see Chapter 8).

g. Objectivity

It is easy for the attorney or the paralegal to identify emotionally with the problems or position of a client or witness (or in some instances, the position of an adverse party). That is a very human instinct that you do not want to extinguish. However, part of being a professional is the ability to set those feelings aside and *do your job.*

The affirmative ethical obligation of the attorney (and her agents) to represent the interests of a client demands objectivity. This may mean asking tough questions to someone obviously upset by them. It may mean digging up and reporting negative information about likeable or pitiable people. It may also mean resisting the urge to sugarcoat your analysis of the damage that a witness is going to do to the position of a client you like very much. The possibilities are endless. The paralegal, like the lawyer, must learn to set certain feelings aside and do the job.

h. Thoroughness

Unlike the preparation of a document that the attorney will review and correct after the paralegal has drafted it, when the paralegal investigator interviews a potential witness and reports back that the witness has no helpful information, the attorney may rely on that report and make no further contact with the witness. Or if the investigator is assigned to locate factual information the attorney may rely on the accuracy of the information produced by the paralegal. The nature of interviewing and investigating work is such that the paralegal is often the only person to make certain inquiries and the supervising attorney and ultimately the client depend on the work to be done thoroughly.

EXAMPLE

A paralegal is asked by his supervising attorney to contact the secretary of state's office to obtain the name and address of the registered agent for service of process for a corporation that is a potential defendant in a civil suit. The clerk in the secretary of state's office supplies the paralegal with that information but the paralegal neglects to confirm that the corporation is in good standing with the state. In fact, it is not and its charter has been revoked by the state. Only after the supervising attorney files suit against the corporation for her client does she learn that the corporation is defunct.

i. Creativity

There is no substitute for an investigator who can think through a problem, overcome obstacles, and find a way to get the job done. Nowhere is there more opportunity for creative thinking than in legal investigation. Information that we thought would be available from one source isn't so we have to think of another place to find it. A critical witness we thought would cooperate won't so we have to find a way to convince him to talk with us. A witness we expected to say one thing says another during a taped interview and we have to revise our planned questions on the spot. The creative juices have to be constantly flowing to excel at this work. But that's what makes it challenging and fun.

j. Sound interviewing and investigating skills

It is difficult to overstate the importance of the paralegal engaged in interviewing and investigating work for an attorney KNOWING HOW TO DO IT AND DO IT WELL. The paralegal who can competently prepare for and conduct the interview of a client or witness, who knows how to locate witnesses and factual information, who knows how to preserve evidence, who is honest and ethical, who is resourceful and dogged, will find herself indispensable to the attorney for whom she works. And it is not going too far to say that the interviewing and investigating skills of the paralegal can make all the difference in a case won or a case lost for the client.

KEY WORDS AND PHRASES TO REMEMBER

abuse of process	informal investigation
agency	investigation
application of information	law
categorizing of information	legal assistant
cause of action	legally relevant information
civil litigation	malicious prosecution
comprehension of information	paralegal
criminal litigation	pre-filing investigation
critical thinking	private investigator
evaluation of information	procedural law
facts	*respondeat superior*
factual analysis	subagent
formal discovery	substantive law
informal discovery	vicarious liability

LEARN BY DOING

LBD 1-1. Locate the statute(s) in your state setting forth the definition of a private investigator. Prepare a memorandum summarizing whether, and under what circumstances, a paralegal performing interviewing and investigating work for an attorney as an employee or on a case-by-case basis, will need to obtain a private investigator's license.

LBD 1-2. Locate the statute(s) in your state setting forth the requirements for obtaining a private investigator's license. Contact the agency or administrative board that regulates issuance of the license in your state and obtain an application and other relevant information.

LBD 1-3. Arrange and conduct an interview with a licensed private investigator in your area who works frequently with attorneys on civil and/or criminal cases. Your questions should focus on:

- the process of becoming a licensed private detective;
- the skills and procedures routinely used by private detectives;
- the role of ethics in the profession; and
- the importance to the private detective of understanding litiga-

tion procedure, the rules of evidence, legal ethics, and any other areas indicated by your instructor. Prepare a memorandum summarizing your interview.

LBD 1-4. Locate the most recent case(s) decided by the highest court in your state setting forth the elements of an action for malicious prosecution and abuse of process. Prepare a short memorandum distinguishing the two causes of action in your jurisdiction.

LBD 1-5. Determine whether your state has adopted any formal guidelines for attorneys licensed in the state governing their supervision of paralegals. (Such guidelines may have been adopted by statute, court rule, case law, or by the state bar association.) Prepare a memorandum summarizing how those guidelines apply to a paralegal involved in interviewing and investigating work under the supervision of an attorney.

LBD 1-6. Locate and review the materials on private investigators in Appendix E, Resources for the Investigator. Then do the following:

a. Using the online resources for locating a private investigator set out in Appendix E, locate a private investigator in your area who specializes in (1) domestic relations investigation; (2) employment background checks; and (3) locating missing persons.

b. Using the Web site for Investigative Reporters and Editors, Inc., at *www.ire.org*, determine what special interest groups have made political donations to the person who represents your district in the U.S. House of Representatives or to one or both of your state's U.S. Senators.

Chapter 2

Ethical and Professional Responsibilities in Interviewing and Investigating

CHAPTER OUTLINE

A. Sources of Ethical and Professional Responsibility
B. Consequences of Unethical Conduct
C. Specific Ethical and Professional Concerns for Paralegals Engaged in Interviewing and Investigating

CHAPTER OBJECTIVES

This chapter introduces you to the important ethical and professional responsibilities that rest on one involved in legal interviewing and investigating. You will learn:

- The various ethical rules and guidelines that have been promulgated by the American Bar Association for attorneys and paralegals, and by the NALA and NFPA for paralegals.
- The various civil, criminal, and career-ending consequences that may be suffered by attorneys and paralegals who engage in unethical or unprofessional conduct while engaged in interviewing and investigating work.
- The specific ethical and professional concerns that arise regularly in interviewing and investigating work including unauthorized practice of law (UPL), maintaining client confidences, conflicts of interest, and improper communications.

A. Sources of Ethical and Professional Responsibility

The various ethical and professional obligations imposed on the paralegal investigator arise from a number of sources.

1. State statutes which prohibit the unauthorized practice of law (UPL)

Attorneys are licensed to practice law by the states. Engaging in the practice of law without a license is known as the **unauthorized practice of law** or **UPL**, and most states have statutes in effect that make it a **misdemeanor** (a crime punishable by up to a year in jail). Some of the UPL statutes purport to define what constitutes the practice of law in that state but, surprisingly, many do not, leaving it to court decisions to flesh out. It is important for the paralegal to become familiar with the existing UPL statute in the state(s) where she practices and to be familiar as well with court decisions that may have construed and applied the statute to particular factual situations. (See LBD 2-1.)

2. Mandatory ethical rules governing attorneys

In each of the fifty states the governing body for attorneys has adopted ethical rules that are binding on attorneys licensed to practice in that state. These ethical rules carry the force of law for attorneys bound by them which means that the failure of an attorney to comply with them can result in a variety of **penalties** or **sanctions** including the revocation of his license to practice law in that state. Forty-five states have adopted some form of the **ABA Model Rules of Professional Conduct** (ABA Model Rules) to govern attorneys. All others, except California, have adopted some form of the older **ABA Model Code of Professional Responsibility** (ABA Model Code). California's ethical code is not based on either set of model ABA rules (see LBD 2-8).

It is important for the paralegal to determine which ethical rules govern attorneys in the state(s) in which she practices and to become familiar with them. The attorney with whom the paralegal works will expect her, as the attorney's agent, to know and comply with those rules.

3. Ethical rules promulgated for the paralegal

Both the **National Association of Legal Assistants** (NALA) and the **National Federation of Paralegal Associations** (NFPA) have promulgated ethical codes purporting to define the ethical responsibilities of paralegals. NALA has its **Code of Ethics and Professional Responsibility** (NALA Code of Ethics) and NFPA has its **Model Code of Ethics and Professional Responsibility** (NFPA Model Code) (see LBD 2-9). The ethical rules of these organizations do not currently carry the force of law in any jurisdiction. However, members of each organization pledge to comply with the respective ethical rules adopted by the organization and both of these ethical codes have come to be recognized by attorneys as setting the standard for expected professional conduct by paralegals.

4. Guidelines for attorneys and paralegals working together in the law office

In 1984 NALA promulgated its **Model Standards and Guidelines for the Utilization of Legal Assistants** (NALA Guidelines) which summarize the specific types of activities that a paralegal can (and cannot) engage in legally and ethically. In 1991 the ABA adopted its **Model Guidelines for the Utilization of Legal Assistant Services** (ABA Guidelines) which set forth ten specific guidelines for attorneys utilizing paralegals followed by a lengthy comment concerning the origin, scope, and application of the Guidelines. The bar associations or highest appellate courts in a number of states have adopted their own guidelines based on the NALA or ABA Guidelines. The paralegal should determine whether the state in which she works has adopted such guidelines and become familiar with them (see LBD 2-2).

5. Advisory ethical opinions

For many years the ABA has issued **advisory ethical opinions** on a large range of topics. The bar associations or the highest appellate courts of most states, and some local bar associations, have a procedure in place to issue advisory opinions as well. These opinions do not typically purport to establish new ethical requirements but, as the word "advisory" suggests, attempt instead to clarify questions that arise regarding the application of established ethical principles to specific fact situations or to provide guidance on the propriety of some anticipated course of conduct.

It is the obligation of the paralegal engaged in interviewing and investigating work not only to know and comply with existing ethical requirements, but to stay updated on changes in such requirements. This can be done by regularly reading professional journals for both paralegals and attorneys, reading advance sheets containing new court opinions and new advisory opinions, and by attending seminars providing ethics updates.

B. Consequences of Unethical Conduct

1. To the lawyer

a. The lawyer may be fired by the client

The lawyer/client relationship is a contractual one in which the lawyer acts as the agent of the client. The relationship is a terminable one. An unethical act by the lawyer or the paralegal working for the lawyer in the course of the representation of a client may well be deemed by the client a reason to terminate the relationship.

b. The lawyer may be sued by the client damaged by the unethical behavior

Because the attorney is a licensed professional and the client must rely on the attorney's training and expertise, and because the client entrusts the attorney with his confidences and, in many cases, his property as well, the law imposes on the attorney a **fiduciary duty.** Not only must the attorney use reasonable care in handling the client matter, she must be scrupulously honest and loyal to the client in all matters related to the representation and must keep the client fully advised regarding developments in the matters being handled.

If the unethical behavior of the lawyer or the paralegal working for the lawyer in the course of the representation causes harm to the client, the client may sue the attorney for breach of this fiduciary duty. Such a suit against an attorney is referred to as a suit for **legal** or **professional malpractice.** As discussed in Chapter 1, the paralegal should never forget that he acts as the agent of the supervising attorney and the law may impose vicarious liability on the attorney for the paralegal's wrongful acts that result in harm to the client.

c. The lawyer may be sanctioned

The lawyer may be subject to an investigation by the state authority charged with the regulation of legal ethics. Depending on state law, the **sanctions** may range from private or public reprimand to temporary license suspension to license revocation. (See LBD 2-3.)

d. The lawyer may face criminal prosecution

If the unethical act involved fraud or the misappropriation of client funds or other property, the attorney may face criminal fraud or theft charges. And in some states it is not only a crime for an unlicensed person to engage in the practice of law (see discussion below), it is also a crime for anyone—including an attorney—to aid or assist another in engaging in the unauthorized practice of law.

e. The lawyer's reputation may be damaged

To the extent that an ethical violation is known to others, it typically damages the reputation of the lawyer among his peers, with other clients, and with the public. This could lead directly to a loss of existing clients and future business for the attorney.

HYPOTHETICAL 2-1

Assume that Johnny Go-Gettum is a prominent plaintiff's personal injury lawyer in your area. Last year he obtained the highest jury verdict in the history of your state and now has all the lucrative plaintiff's work he could desire. Every week he turns down cases, which other lawyers would consider the case of a lifetime. Then Johnny hires Sally Oops as his new paralegal.

One of Sally's responsibilities is to handle the funds that come into the office on settlements and collected judgments. Since Johnny Go-Gettum handles almost all his plaintiffs' cases on a contingency basis, his office processes a lot of settlement funds. When a settlement check is received, Sally's job is to deposit the check in Johnny's trust account, wait for the check to clear, and prepare a final bill to the client showing the gross settlement amount received, the deduction of Johnny's contingency fee amount, the deduction of Johnny's out-of-pocket expense charges, and the net amount payable to the client.

Unfortunately, Sally Oops concentrated more on her law classes in paralegal school than she did on her math and accounting courses and she regularly makes errors in the calculations contained in the final bills she prepares. She also has a lazy streak, which causes her to regularly put off preparing the final bill and pay-out until weeks after the settlement checks are received and deposited.

One client, Phil Finicky, already upset by the delay in distribution of his settlement funds, looks over Johnny's final bill very thoroughly, finds an error in the bill that resulted in his receiving $200 less than he should have, and calls the state body charged with disciplining attorneys. In the ensuing investigation, it is discovered that Sally Oops has made errors resulting in underpayments to more than 100 clients and that she has regularly held client funds too long, depriving them of interest they could have been earning.

Do you think the authorities who enforce the ethical standards for attorneys in your state will find that Johnny Go-Gettum was ethically and professionally responsible for Sally's mishandling of the funds? What specific provisions of your state's ethical code for attorneys might he have violated?

List all the negative consequences that could reasonably occur to Johnny Go-Gettum as a result of this situation. (Hint: The last we heard of Johnny, he was operating a hot dog stand across from the court house.)

What do you suppose may have happened to Sally Oops?

2. To the paralegal

a. The paralegal may lose her job

Few attorneys would consider keeping an employee who committed a serious ethical breach or a series of minor ones. The risk to the attorney is too great, as is the potential damage to clients.

b. The paralegal may lose her certification

If the paralegal is certified by the NALA or NFPA, or by a state certification authority, that certification may be suspended or lost.

c. The paralegal may lose her right to appear before administrative agencies

If the paralegal is authorized to appear before a state or federal governmental agency on behalf of claimants (see discussion of the unauthorized practice of law below), that authorization may be revoked as a result of unethical conduct.

d. The paralegal may be sued by the client damaged by the unethical action

Paralegals can be named as defendants in legal malpractice suits growing out of unethical conduct, and plaintiffs also will seek to impose vicarious liability on the attorney under principles of agency.

e. The paralegal may be subject to criminal prosecution

If the unethical conduct involves the practice of law, the paralegal may be subject to criminal prosecution under the state UPL law. (See

LBD 2-1.) If it involves the mishandling of money or other property belonging to another, she may face a theft or criminal fraud charge.

f. The paralegal's reputation may be tarnished

To the extent that an ethical violation is known to others, it may damage the reputation of a paralegal both among her peers, in the community at large, and with other prospective employers.

HYPOTHETICAL 2-2

Here's what happened to Sally Oops following the disclosure of her mishandling of client funds. Johnny Go-Gettum fired her immediately. No one else in town would hire her. Phil Finicky named her as a defendant in the class action suit he initiated on behalf of all of Johnny's clients. And her CLA certification was suspended by the NALA. (The last we heard of Sally, she had gone into politics.)

What specific provisions of the NALA Code of Ethics and the NFPA Model Code did Sally Oops violate?

As a client, would you hire an attorney who had Sally working for her?

C. Specific Ethical and Professional Concerns for Paralegals Engaged in Interviewing and Investigating

1. The unauthorized practice of law

Reference should be made to the UPL statute in the state(s) where the paralegal practices and other related state materials for the prevailing definition and interpretations. But, in general, the following often-quoted definition of the practice of law stated in *Davies v. Unauthorized Practice Committee of State Bar of Texas*, 431 S.W.2d 590 (Tex. Civ. App. 1968) is helpful:

> According to the generally understood definition of the practice of law, it embraces the preparation of pleadings and other papers incident to actions of special proceedings, and the management of such actions and proceedings on behalf of clients before judges in courts. However, the practice of law is not confined to cases conducted in court. In fact, the major portion of the practice of any capable lawyer consists of work done outside of the courts. The practice of law involves not only appearance in court in connection with litigation, but also services rendered out of court, and includes the giving of advice or the rendering of any service requiring the use of legal skill or knowledge, such as preparing a will, contract or other instrument, the legal effect of which under the facts and conclusions involved must be carefully determined.

431 S.W.2d at 593.

It is fairly well settled that *only* licensed attorneys can perform the following acts and, consequently, that they *cannot be properly delegated* to others by the attorney:

a. *Establishing an attorney-client relationship*

This means that the paralegal cannot say or do anything in dealing with a potential client that amounts to reaching an agreement for the attorney to undertake the representation of that potential client. It also means that the paralegal cannot say or do anything in dealing with an existing client that amounts to an agreement for the attorney to undertake a different or additional representation for that client.

Paralegals involved in interviewing and investigating will work closely with potential and existing clients of the attorney. They will frequently develop familiar and even friendly relationships with these persons and may feel strongly about helping them. Nonetheless, this important decision must be left to the attorney. And the paralegal must not create expectations or assumptions concerning representation in the mind of the existing or potential client.

b. *Setting legal fees*

Clients often ask many questions of the paralegal regarding charges and billing procedures. Some attorneys have established fixed fee schedules and billing and payment procedures for many legal services, and those attorneys may authorize their assistants to communicate these scheduled amounts and procedures to inquiring persons. That appears to be permissible so long as the paralegal limits the communication to decisions the attorney has made and authorized her to communicate. But even here the paralegal and attorney must exercise caution because the discussion of established charges may be construed by the lay person as an acceptance of their representation. For that reason, many lawyers have established procedures in their office that preclude non-lawyers from discussing fees at all.

c. *Giving legal opinions or legal advice*

These activities are at the heart of the practice of law and cannot be performed by unlicensed persons. Nor can the authority to perform these functions be delegated by the attorney to the paralegal. See NALA Guideline VI. Problems in this area typically arise in four different contexts for the paralegal engaged in interviewing and investigating work:

1. **When interviewing a prospective client.** Paralegals frequently screen calls or visits from potential clients when the attorney is unavailable. These persons are typically quite anxious to get quick answers to their legal questions and will assume the paralegal must know the answer because she works in a law office. And frequently the paralegal may know (or think she knows!) the answer to the legal question being asked. In those situations, and especially when the paralegal identifies closely with the anxiety of the potential client, the paralegal must resist the temptation to answer the legal questions being asked.

   Paralegals must remember that, in the law, what appear to be simple questions may not be so simple at all. While compassion for a troubled and anxious person is understandable and even appropriate, a professional detachment must be maintained.

2. **When interviewing witnesses.** During interviews with witnesses and other information sources, the paralegal will frequently be asked questions about the case at hand or about other legal matters of interest to the witness or source. Again, the paralegal may think she knows the answer and reason, "What's the harm?" She may also feel pressured to help in order to ensure the cooperation of the witness or source. Such temptations must be resisted.

3. **When dealing with clients in the course of a case.** The paralegal will often become the primary contact person for the client. Trust, familiarity, and even friendship may develop between the paralegal and the client. But the legal questions must still be deferred to the busy or absent attorney.

HYPOTHETICAL 2-3

Assume that Ned Newatit has just finished his formal paralegal training. He lands his first paralegal job with a two-lawyer firm specializing in domestic relations work. The firm has an established fee schedule for certain kinds of legal work including separation agreements ($500), uncontested divorces ($750), and name changes ($250).

Sue Debum, who is not currently a client of the firm, calls to speak with a lawyer, and since both lawyers are in court (aren't they always?) the call is referred to Ned. Sue says she and her husband Iam Debum are getting a divorce and she wants to know how much it will cost if the firm handles it. Is it okay for Ned to tell Sue that the firm will charge $750 if the divorce is uncontested? What should he tell her about how much it will cost in legal fees if the divorce is contested?

During the conversation, Sue says that she is not sure if her husband will agree to a divorce but she wants to go ahead and file anyway. Can Ned tell her that the firm will "probably" handle the case since that is the kind of work it does? Can Ned go ahead and set up an appointment for Sue Debum to come in and meet with a lawyer to discuss the case? If he does the latter, what explanation, if any, do you recommend he give Sue about the firm's representing her?

During the conversation, Sue tells Ned that her husband is still in town where they have been living for the past five years, but he may be moving to another state soon. She asks if the divorce suit can still be filed against him in this state even if he moves before it is filed. Ned knows the answer to this question. He made the high grade in his domestic relations course in paralegal school. He has also heard the attorneys he works for answer this question dozens of times. Under those circumstances, can he answer Sue's question?

4. **When family or friends ask for help.** Everyone knows that lay persons share legal opinions and give each other advice regarding legal matters all the time, especially in friendship and family contexts. Why does it become inappropriate for a paralegal to do that? Because with greater knowledge comes greater responsibility.

When a friend or family member knows that you have received legal training and work with an attorney, they may well rely on that training and experience, trusting your advice and judgment. And that is the essence of legal practice. It is never easy, but in those situations the paralegal must explain to friends and family members that she cannot offer legal advice or opinions. The only recommendation that should be made to avoid the danger of UPL is to advise the person to speak with an attorney.

HYPOTHETICAL 2-4

Assume that all of the family of Ned Newatit has come into town to attend his graduation. Afterward his tightwad grandfather even springs for lunch for everybody at the most expensive restaurant in town. Ned is enjoying himself until his grandfather sidles up to him and says in a low voice:

"Say Ned, you may know the answer to this. My neighbor planted some trees along our property line a few years ago and I didn't like it but I hated to say anything to him. You know how it is. But now the trees are getting bigger and the branches have grown over onto my side of the property line. Seems like after every storm I'm finding limbs I've got to pick up and in the fall the leaves blow onto my side. What do you think I should do? I'm probably never going to do anything anyway but I'd just like to know what my rights are. And I hate to take a little ol' piddling thing like this to an expensive lawyer."

What ethical danger(s) are presented to Ned by this development? What harm could occur if he answers his grandfather's questions? How would you suggest that Ned respond to his grandfather (and get his grandfather to go ahead and pay the lunch bill!)?

d. Representing a client before a court or tribunal

This is forbidden to the unlicensed person unless such representation is expressly authorized by the rules of that court or tribunal. Reference should be made to the local rules of some state courts, which allow non-licensed persons to appear in court on behalf of a client for very limited reasons, for example, to set a hearing date. In addition, increasing numbers of federal and state administrative agencies (e.g., the United States Social Security Administration and many state welfare agencies) are allowing paralegals to appear and represent the interests of claimants. This may be a growing trend reflecting both the increased professionalism of paralegals and the higher standard to which they will consequently be held. But the attorney and paralegal should be careful to check the rules and regulations of the court or tribunal before sending a paralegal there on behalf of a client.

e. Negotiating a legal matter on behalf of a client

Closely related to the concepts of giving legal advice and representing a client before a court or tribunal is negotiating legal matters on behalf of a client. Since this would amount to the exercise of legal judgment on behalf of a client, it is also prohibited to the unlicensed person.

f. Attorneys must be aware of the dangers of UPL as well

Not only must paralegals be careful about UPL, attorneys too must be sure that proper training and procedures are in place in their offices to avoid the occurrence of UPL. Ethically, lawyers are obligated to avoid aiding another to engage in UPL. See ABA Model Code DR-3-101(A) and

ABA Model Rules 5.5(b). And many state statutes impose criminal liability on one who aids another to engage in UPL.

Both attorneys and paralegals should be familiar with the ethical rules regarding the proper delegation of tasks by the attorney to the paralegal and the adequate supervision of that work to avoid committing UPL. In general, other than the five matters mentioned above, the paralegal may perform any task that would otherwise constitute the practice of law so long as certain conditions are satisfied. See EC 3-6 of the Model Code and Rule 5.3 of the Model Rules. Generally, those conditions are:

- The attorney must properly supervise the paralegal's work.
- The attorney must maintain a direct relationship with the client.
- The attorney must assume full responsibility for the paralegal's work product.

Assuming those conditions are satisfied, the paralegal can interview clients and prospective clients, witnesses, and other information sources; investigate legal and factual claims; draft contracts, pleadings; memoranda, discovery documents, and other legal documents for the attorney's review and signature; prepare correspondence; and perform many other related tasks that would otherwise constitute the practice of law.

2. Maintaining client confidences and secrets

The basic ethical obligation imposed on lawyers and legal assistants to maintain client information as confidential is the evidentiary privilege commonly known as the **attorney-client privilege.** But the ethical duty of maintaining client confidentiality is much broader than the evidentiary privilege.

a. The attorney-client privilege

This is an **evidentiary privilege** (a privilege relating to what information can be offered and received in evidence in a court of law, see Chapter 6), which applies to communications in any form (oral, written, electronic, body signal, etc.) between an attorney and her client that are deemed confidential in nature and that relate to the subject matter of the representation. Such information is privileged from discovery or involuntary disclosure in a trial or other proceeding. In other words, the client cannot be compelled even under oath to disclose the confidential communication and can also prevent the attorney from disclosing it without the client's consent. All fifty states recognize the attorney-client privilege by **statute** (act of the legislature), **court rule** (rule of procedure or practice adopted by a court), or **common law** (court decision in a contested case).

Confidential communications that occur between a client and agents of the attorney, such as paralegals, are protected as are communications between the client and the attorney with those agents present (see LBD 2-6). Communications made by the client in the presence of persons not working as employees or agents of the attorney may *not* be deemed privileged even though the attorney or the paralegal is present as well.

The attorney-client privilege belongs to the client, not the lawyer, and it is up to the client to waive it. The privilege, if not waived by the client, lasts indefinitely which means that it survives the end of the attorney-client relationship and usually even the death of the client.

The attorney-client privilege is generally construed very broadly by the courts to protect confidential communications from disclosure. For example, confidences disclosed in consultations between a lawyer and a prospective client are protected by the privilege even when the lawyer does not undertake the representation.

Some types of information divulged to the attorney by the client are generally not protected by the privilege including, for example, the identity of the client or his whereabouts or the fee arrangement. The privilege cannot be properly asserted to conceal physical evidence of the client's crime from the authorities.

Moreover, there are various **exceptions to the attorney-client privilege,** the most notable of which for our purposes is that the privilege is deemed **waived** if the confidential communication is disclosed to others by the client or by the client's representatives, including his attorney or the paralegal working for the attorney. Some courts have held that even inadvertent disclosure of confidential information by the client or the client's representatives waives the privilege.

b. The broader ethical duty of confidentiality

To be distinguished from the evidentiary rule of attorney-client privilege is the broader ethical obligation imposed on attorneys and their assistants to keep confidential *any and all information* they have obtained from or about a client. Indeed, there is no rule of attorney-client relations older or more sacred than the duty imposed on the attorney to maintain the **confidences and secrets** of the client. DR 4-101 of the ABA Model Code requires attorneys to preserve the confidences and secrets of the client and defines **confidences** to mean information protected by the attorney-client privilege. It defines **secrets** to mean "other information gained in the professional relationship that the client has requested to be held inviolate or the disclosure of which would be embarrassing or would likely be detrimental to the client."

Rule 1.6 of the ABA Model Rules contains a more expansive definition of the obligation of confidentiality. It prohibits attorneys from disclosing "information relating to representation of a client."

Thus the ethical obligation to maintain the confidences and secrets of a client is much broader than the evidentiary rule surrounding the attorney-client privilege. Information obtained by the attorney or her assistants from or about a client must not be disclosed without the client's knowledge and consent even though it does not rise to the level of a confidential communication protected by the attorney-client privilege.

The duty to protect client information from disclosure is imposed on the attorney, the paralegal, and anyone else working with or for them on client matters. Canon VII of the NALA Code of Ethics and Canon V of the NFPA Model Code both require the paralegal to preserve and protect client confidences.

DR 4-101(D) of the ABA Model Code requires lawyers to exercise reasonable care to ensure that their employees and others do not disclose or use client confidences and secrets. Rule 5.3 of the ABA Model Rules and the Comment to it impose on attorneys the duty to supervise their legal assistants and other employees to ensure their compliance with the lawyer's ethical obligations, "particularly regarding the obligation not to disclose information relating to representation of the client." Moreover, Guideline 6 of the ABA Model Guidelines provides: "It is the responsibility of a lawyer to take reasonable measures to ensure that all client confidences are preserved by a legal assistant."

c. Protecting client information from disclosure

The broad scope of the duty to maintain all client information as confidential, the ease with which confidential communications can lose their privileged evidentiary status if made in the presence of unauthorized persons, and the fact that even privileged information can be waived inadvertently has a number of practical implications for the paralegal doing interviewing and investigating work:

1. **When speaking on the phone.**   Care must be taken by the paralegal in speaking with the client (or other privileged agent) about client matters in person or by phone. Always be sure no third person is present or can overhear verbal communications. Close the door to your office when you are on the phone regarding client matters. Ask the party to whom you are speaking if they are alone.

   Speaker phones pose special problems on either end of a conversation because another person may be in or near the room and able to hear. So, on your end of the conversation, close the door and turn the volume down so it can't be heard outside the door. Then ask the person(s) on the other end to do the same.

   Calls made via **cellular phones** are susceptible to interception. It is better to avoid making calls regarding client matters by cellular phone unless you have no alternative. Get direction from your supervising attorney before using a cellular phone for those calls.

2. **When sending letters.**   When anyone in the law office corresponds with the client by mail, or with an expert or private investigator working with you on a client matter, it is good practice to place the words *Confidential* or *Personal* on the letter and the envelope in a prominent place (see Illustration 8-4). Remember that many people do not open their own mail. We must endeavor to prevent unauthorized persons from opening or seeing confidential communications.

3. **When sending communications by FAX.**   Care must be taken in sending written communications by facsimile (FAX) to ensure that no unauthorized person receives or handles the FAX message.

4. **When sending e-mail messages.**   Communications sent or received by electric modem (e-mail) are not secure and privacy cannot be guaranteed. Such communications are not secure, privacy cannot be assured, and the communications sent that way may not be impressed with confidentiality at all. E-mail communications appear on a computer tape and can be shared on a network, copied, stored, or forwarded to others. Currently, the only way to assure a measure of

privacy in e-mail communications is to send encrypted (coded) messages.

5. **When interviewing a witness.**   The paralegal engaged in informal investigating must not disclose client confidences in the process of explaining to a witness why she is seeking information (see Chapters 12 and 13).

6. **In the office.**   Confidential client information must be kept in a safe and organized fashion in the office so that it isn't lost or inadvertently seen by visitors. In many law offices, the policy is to prevent even other office employees without a need to know from seeing confidential client information. Attorneys and those working for them should show zeal in protecting client information. It is a mark of professionalism and an expression of genuine client concern that can increase the public's respect for the legal profession.

7. **At home.**   Outside the office the paralegal must avoid discussing specific client matters with family, friends, or others.

8. **In working with opposing counsel and paralegals.**   Over the course of a case, the paralegal will have numerous occasions to speak with personnel from the offices of opposing attorneys. The paralegal must exercise discretion in what information she discloses about the client and the case and in what she allows those persons to see.

9. **In responding to formal discovery requests.**   Care must be taken too in answering formal discovery requests such as interrogatories and document requests (see Chapters 4 and 5) not to disclose confidential information that is not discoverable.

HYPOTHETICAL 2-5

Assume that during the course of the phone conversation between Ned Newatit and Sue Debum mentioned in Hypothetical 2-3, Sue mentions the following things to Ned in no particular order:

- She is 35 years old and her husband, Iam Debum, is 36.
- She is a wonderful cook.
- Her husband has been guilty of numerous extramarital affairs.
- She is a registered Democrat who sometimes votes Republican.
- She wants to keep the marital home after the divorce.
- Her father killed Jimmy Hoffa and she helped him dispose of the body.
- Her sister is coming to stay with her this week.

Assume further that Ned makes an appointment for Sue Debum to come in and meet with an attorney but she fails to keep the appointment and he never hears from her again.

Which item(s) of information that Sue gave Ned qualify as "confidences" and which as "secrets" within the meaning of the ABA Model Code? Which items would be subject to the confidentiality provisions of the ABA Model Rules?

Under the ethical rule governing attorneys in your state, *must* or *may* Ned or the attorneys he works for disclose the information regarding the crime(s) related to the murder of Jimmy Hoffa to the authorities?

If Ned were called to testify at some later time in a criminal proceeding against Sue Debum and her father in connection with the death of Jimmy Hoffa, could Sue successfully assert her attorney-client privilege to keep him from testifying to her statements on that subject?

3. Competence

The paralegal has an affirmative ethical duty to seek and maintain what Canon VI of the NALA Code of Ethics calls ''a high degree of competency.'' Paralegals should think of themselves as professionals and be proud of that standing.

a. Seek good education and training

Access *www.tile.net/lists/* and look over the various listservs that you can sign up for. Choose three you think might be useful to you as an investigating paralegal.

One seeking a career as a paralegal should seek the best education and training available and do her best while pursuing that education.

b. Seek certification

The paralegal should make it a professional goal to seek and obtain the highest level of certification available to her in her field by private paralegal organizations or the state(s) in which she practices.

c. Stay informed concerning changes in the law and the profession

The paralegal should conscientiously and regularly read professional journals, case summaries, and other legal publications to keep abreast of changes and developments in the law and the paralegal profession. Attending seminars and workshops in substantive law areas and professional skill areas is another means of keeping up with changes and developments.

d. Stay on the cutting edge of technological advancements

But that is the world in which we live and no professional can afford to be behind the curve technologically. Fifteen years ago it was the facsimile machine that revolutionized communications in law offices. Today, FAX machines are taken for granted and we are now challenged to learn to utilize computers, the Internet, e-mail, and distance communication tools. This is not easy in a world where such advances are coming with mind-boggling speed.

e. Commit yourself to excellence

The paralegal should dedicate herself to achieving the best possible result in every single client matter on which she is called to work. Competence is not just having knowledge and skills, it is applying them on a daily basis in each individual case. This is where competence becomes professionalism. Thoroughness, consistency, perseverance, and hard work on every single file—this is the stuff of which competence is made.

4. Integrity

The legal field is like most others in that the persons who achieve the highest level of respect from their peers and who enjoy the greatest success professionally and monetarily are those who are known for their integrity.

a. Truthfulness in dealing with clients, co-workers, and others

In the course of her work, the paralegal will work with many different kinds of people every day, including clients, co-workers, witnesses, other attorneys and their staff, and court personnel. The paralegal should never use deception or misstatement in her work.

EXAMPLE

> Never tell a client you haven't received something on their case when you have it but it's still sitting in your in-box waiting for you to get around to it. Never tell a court clerk you need something immediately if you don't. Never tell an attorney desiring to assign you work that you are too swamped to take it on if you aren't. Never promise a witness you will take only a few moments of their time for an interview if you know it's going to take longer.

b. Fidelity in handling client funds and other property

The paralegal should be familiar with the specific ethical rules and office policies regarding the requirements for handling, depositing, and accounting for funds and other property that pass through a law office. For example, it is fundamental that monetary funds that come into the possession of the law office for use in client transactions must be placed in **trust accounts** separate from the lawyer's accounts and strictly accounted for. See DR 1-102 of the ABA Model Code and Rule 1.15 of the ABA Model Rules. The paralegal should be familiar with the specific ethical rules and office policies regarding the recording of billable time, the charging of expenses, and collection practices.

c. Loyalty

A key ingredient of integrity is loyalty. That includes loyalty to the attorney for whom the paralegal works, loyalty to the client, and loyalty to the legal profession.

5. Diligence and communication with the client

In most states, the most frequent ethical complaint made against attorneys is the failure to adequately communicate with a client regarding the status of their case. In client relations, there is simply no substitute for regular, thorough communication with clients (see Chapter 8). Attorneys and paralegals are required to be zealous in their representation of client interests. Keeping every client file current, responding to client inquiries promptly, and keeping the client fully informed regarding the status of their case is the essence of diligence.

6. Conflicts of interest

A **conflict of interest** is anything that compromises or which could reasonably appear to compromise the loyalty of the attorney or paralegal to the client. One important aspect of conflicts of interest is that they need not be actual conflicts in order to cause problems. Even a potential conflict of interest must be identified, disclosed, and dealt with as discussed below. In this area, as in all areas of ethical concern, attorneys must avoid even the **appearance of impropriety.** (Canon 9 of the ABA Model Code.) And paralegals are called upon to do "all things incidental, necessary, or expedient for the attainment of ethics." Canon VIII, NALA Code of Ethics.

In the legal profession, conflicts can arise in a number of ways, including:

a. Simultaneous representation

This occurs when the attorney represents the interests of two or more clients simultaneously in the same transaction or case. The inherent danger is that at some point in the representation the attorney may feel compelled to take some position or action for the benefit of one client that will work to the detriment of the other. It is not always easy at the outset of a representation, when the interests of the multiple clients seem identical and feelings are amicable, to anticipate future events that may make the clients' interests diverge and feelings between them grow hostile, leaving the attorney in a compromised position.

Most attorneys try to avoid placing themselves in this position by declining simultaneous representation when there is any possibility of such a conflict developing. And many jurisdictions have local rules that prohibit simultaneous representation in certain areas fraught with likely conflicts, such as divorce proceedings. However, where it is not barred by such rule, simultaneous representation can be undertaken by the attorney who concludes it will not prejudice the interests of either client, but only if potential conflicts are fully disclosed to both clients and the consent of both is obtained.

Paralegals working in the interviewing and investigating area need to be especially sensitive to this rule when the supervising attorney is representing more than one client in a single matter. The paralegal will frequently be the one having the most contact with those clients and should immediately communicate to the attorney all evidence of hostility or disparate interests reflected by the clients. And, in gathering information related to the case, the paralegal should be aware of the implications of any discovered information that creates or could create a real or potential conflict and report that possibility to the supervising attorney immediately.

b. Representing an interest adverse to a former client

Rule 1.9 of the ABA Model Rules states "[a] lawyer who has formerly represented a client in a matter shall not thereafter represent another person in the same or substantially related matter in which that person's interests are materially adverse to the interests of the former client unless the former client consents after consultation." This ethical concern arises out of the obligation to preserve the confidences of a client and the climate of trust that is critical to the attorney-client relationship. Confidences of a client must remain confidences even after the attorney-client relationship has ended or otherwise no client can have trust in the attorney-client relationship at all. There are a number of times and situations when this conflict can arise:

(1) Before accepting representation

Before agreeing to represent a new client or to take on a new matter for an existing client, there should be a procedure in place within the law office to check for potential conflicts. The parties adverse or potentially adverse to the client may be former or current clients or be employed by or otherwise related to former or current clients. The attorney and the paralegal should make sure, in every instance, that a thorough conflicts check is done before the attorney accepts the new client or matter.

(2) After representation has begun

Conflicts of interest can arise throughout the representation with important consequences. Sometimes all potential adverse parties have not been identified when a case is accepted by a lawyer and it is left to the investigation process to identify such additional adverse parties. And sometimes the employment or other relationship of known adverse parties to other persons or entities that can create a conflict are not known until some point in the investigation process. Consequently, the paralegal involved in the investigation must always be alert to potential conflicts and report them to the supervising attorney immediately upon their discovery.

(3) Job changes

EXAMPLE

Suppose you are working as a paralegal for a plaintiff's personal injury firm and get a much better offer to work for an insurance defense firm. You accept the offer but then remember that your new employer is defending one or more cases brought by plaintiffs represented by your old employer. And you were working on those cases when you switched jobs. As you might expect, the clients of your former employer may be quite upset that you have "gone over to the enemy camp," taking with you knowledge about their case. Obviously, anyone working in the legal field (attorney, paralegal, and possibly the legal secretary or office manager) who changes employment cannot ethically work on behalf of the new employer against the interests of the former client. But should you be prevented from changing jobs due to the potential conflict?

The typical solution in these situations is for the new employer to implement policies that effectively screen or wall off the new employee from having anything to do with cases in which there might be a conflict. (Thus this arrangement is sometimes called an *invisible wall* or an *ethical wall*.) For example, the paralegal working under such an arrangement in the Example would not have access to any files involving those cases or be routed any memos dealing with them or be involved in the billing of such work. If computers in the new office are networked it typically is necessary to flag screened files with warning messages.

Note that everyone involved in this potential conflict has a real motivation to ensure that the interests of the clients of the former employer are protected. Both the employee who has made the move and the former employer may be sued by a client if in fact client confidences are compromised, resulting in harm to the client. The employee and the new employer may face an ethical complaint if they fail to establish and implement appropriate screening procedures.

(4) Personal relationships

EXAMPLE

> Suppose you are a paralegal working for that same plaintiff's personal injury firm mentioned above and you plan to marry (or just become involved in a dating relationship with) that cute paralegal working for the defense firm that just happens to be defending one or more cases brought by your firm. Might the clients of both your firms be a little curious about what you two lovebirds discuss at dinner?

SLEUTH ON THE LOOSE

Identify a well-known corporation or corporate executive, then access the Wall Street Research Network at *www.wsrn.com* and see if you can locate stories concerning that company or executive.

One option, of course, is life-long celibacy. But a more practical solution is full and prompt disclosure of the relationship by both persons involved to their respective supervising attorneys. The attorneys will then disclose the relationship to their respective clients and either obtain the clients' consent (preferably written) for the paralegals to continue working on the case (with appropriate assurances of client confidentiality being preserved) or remove them from working on those cases.

(5) Recognizing potential conflicts

Anything that does or could reasonably be seen as affecting your impartiality and loyalty to a client is a conflict of interest. It may be discovering that a witness in a case is a friend of yours. If the statement that witness/friend gives you about the case later comes under attack by the opposing party, that friendship may be the basis on which the other side attempts to undermine its integrity, by showing either that the witness was biased because of the friendship or that you unfairly traded on the friendship to obtain a favorable statement.

The possibilities are endless. If at any time during investigating or interviewing the paralegal becomes aware of a real or potential conflict of interest involving the financial, business, property, or other personal interest of themselves or anyone else involved in representing the client, that conflict should be immediately reported to the attorney.

HYPOTHETICAL 2-6

> Assume that a year after his conversation with Sue Debum outlined in Hypotheticals 2-3 and 2-5, Ned Newatit leaves the domestic relations firm and goes to work for a larger firm specializing in defending employers against employment discrimination charges. On his first day at work with the new firm, Ned is called into a new client conference and there sits Sue Debum, who is telling one of the lawyers that she was fired from her job due to unlawful age discrimination and that she is 45 years old. Ned recognizes Sue's voice from their prior conversation and recalls that she told him then that she was 35 years old. Ned realizes that if Sue is under 40 years of age she has no standing to bring an age discrimination complaint under federal or state law. What, if anything, should Ned do with his information and why?
>
> Assume instead that when Ned enters the conference room at the new firm for the new client conference, he is introduced to Iam Debum who wishes to engage the firm to defend a lawsuit recently filed against his

company by a former employee who also happens to be his former wife, Sue Debum. What should Ned do and why?

Assume that Iam Debum wants to retain Ned's new firm to represent his company in an employment suit brought by someone other than Sue Debum. Should Ned disclose anything about his earlier contact with Sue Debum and why?

7. Disclosure of status in verbal and written communications

The paralegal is required to disclose her status as a paralegal in all verbal and written communications (see Canon V of the NALA Code of Ethics). That means, in phone conversations, introducing yourself by both name and paralegal status. That means, in written correspondence, making sure your signature is followed by the designation of paralegal or legal assistant. In jurisdictions that allow paralegals to have business cards or to have their name appear on firm stationery, it means being sure that the title appears with your name. One major reason for these requirements is the need to avoid UPL since, unless the paralegal status is properly disclosed, lay persons may assume they are dealing with an attorney.

8. Improper communications

Both attorneys and paralegals are prohibited from communicating or causing another to communicate with persons known to be represented by counsel about matters related to the representation. All communications, in that event, must be with the attorney for that person unless the attorney for that person consents to direct communication. Paralegals involved in interviewing and investigating work will frequently have reason to inquire of potential witnesses whether they are represented by counsel and must be careful to comply with this rule.

9. Discovery of client misconduct

SLEUTH ON THE LOOSE

Identify a physician you want to learn more about, then go to *www.knowx.com* and see if you can determine whether that physician has been sued for malpractice.

The paralegal involved in investigating work will typically have considerable client contact or will be gathering considerable information regarding the client. There are several categories of client misconduct that have ethical consequences and should be reported immediately to the supervising attorney.

a. Intent of the client to commit a criminal act

This is a grounds for the attorney to withdraw from representing a client. See DR 2-103 of the ABA Model Code. And if the criminal act threatened is one the attorney believes could result in imminent death or substantial bodily harm, the attorney-client privilege does not prevent the attorney from disclosing it to proper authorities. See Rule 1.6 of the ABA Model Rules.

b. Fraudulent claim or malicious harassment

If the client is making a false, fraudulent, or frivolous claim or is undertaking litigation against another merely to harass or maliciously injure another, the attorney must decline employment or must withdraw from employment if it has already been undertaken. See DR 2-109 and 2-110 of the ABA Model Code and Rule 3.1 of the ABA Model Rules. For the attorney to undertake or continue in such representation may cause the attorney to run afoul of Rule 11 and subject both the client and the attorney to potential tort liability for malicious prosecution.

c. Commission of fraud on the court or perjury

An attorney cannot knowingly use perjured testimony in a trial or proceeding. In some cases, the attorney may have a duty to disclose the use or intended use of perjured testimony or the perpetration of a fraud on the court to the court or tribunal. See Rule 3.3 of the ABA Model Rules and DR 7-102(A) and (B) of the ABA Model Code. Such conduct by the client is also a grounds for the attorney to withdraw from representation. See DR 2-110(B) and (C) of the ABA Model Code.

KEY WORDS AND PHRASES TO REMEMBER

ABA Model Code of Professional Conduct
ABA Model Guidelines for the Utilization of Legal Assistant Services
ABA Model Rules of Professional Responsibility
advisory ethical opinion
adverse interest
American Bar Association
appearance of impropriety
attorney-client privilege
client confidences and secrets
client misconduct
common law
conflict of interest
court rule
Disciplinary Rule
Ethical Canon

evidentiary privilege
fiduciary duty
improper communications
invisible (ethical) wall
legal malpractice
NALA Code of Ethics and Professional Responsibility
NALA Model Standards and Guidelines for the Utilization of Legal Assistants
NFPA Model Code of Ethics and Professional Responsibility
professional malpractice
sanctions
simultaneous representation
statutory law
trust account
unauthorized practice of law (UPL)

LEARN BY DOING

LBD 2-1. Locate the statute(s) in your state governing the unauthorized practice of law and prepare a memorandum summarizing how your state has defined the practice of law and the penalties for engaging in the unauthorized practice of law.

LBD 2-2. Determine if the authority that governs attorneys licensed in your state(s) has adopted guidelines for attorney utilization of paralegals and, if so, prepare a memorandum comparing such guidelines to the NALA and ABA Guidelines.

LBD 2-3. Locate the rules regarding authorized disciplinary measures, both public and private, that may be taken against attorneys in your state(s) for unethical conduct. Prepare a memorandum summarizing those measures and the existing procedure for imposition of such measures.

LBD 2-4. We have been asked to render an ethical opinion based on the following facts. Please review the facts of the case, research the governing ethical rules in your state, and draft an opinion letter with your conclusions for your instructor's review.

Mary Bryant was employed as a legal assistant by the law firm of Rock, Roll, and Remember. Ms. Bryant had a friend, Ruth Jones, who wanted to divorce her husband, Ralph Jones. Ms. Jones, however, did not feel she could afford to hire an attorney. Knowing that Ms. Bryant's law firm did divorce work, she asked Ms. Bryant for assistance in filing her divorce suit. Ms. Bryant explained to her friend that she was not a lawyer and could not represent her. However, Ms. Bryant did agree to copy certain forms in her employer's office and provide them to Ms. Jones so Ms. Jones could fill them out and file them *pro se* with the appropriate court. Ms. Bryant proceeded to do this without the knowledge of her employer. She provided the papers to Ms. Jones and explained to her how to fill them out and that was the extent of the assistance she rendered to her friend. However, to her surprise, Ralph Jones retained Rock, Roll, and Remember to represent him in the divorce action filed by Ms. Jones. Ms. Bryant did not work on the case and decided to say nothing about her assistance to Ms. Jones. This all came to light in the course of Ms. Jones's discovery deposition. The law firm was fired by Mr. Jones. Ms. Bryant was fired by the law firm. An ethical complaint has now been filed against the law firm by Mr. Jones. Ms. Bryant has filed for unemployment compensation which is being opposed by the firm on the grounds that she was fired for cause.

Please address the following questions in your draft opinion letter:

a. Did Ms. Bryant violate any legal or ethical rules by assisting Ms. Jones in the way that she did?

b. Did Ms. Bryant violate any ethical rules by remaining silent when her employer agreed to represent Mr. Jones in the divorce?

c. Can the law firm be held responsible for any ethical violation or liable for any tortious conduct committed by Ms. Bryant in this matter?

d. What kind of punishment or sanction can the law firm expect to receive if it is found to be responsible for unethical conduct with respect to Mr. Jones?

LBD 2-5. Read, then prepare a memorandum summarizing Wade, *Tort Liability of Paralegals and Attorneys Who Use Their Services*, 24 Vand. L.

Rev. 133 (1971). Read and brief one of the following cases: *Musselman v. Willoughby Corp.*, 230 Va. 337, 337 S.E.2d 724 (1985); *State ex rel. Oklahoma Bar Assn. v. Braswell*, 663 P.2d 1228 (Okla. 1983); *Florida Bar v. Lawless*, 640 So.2d 1098 (Fla. 1994).

LBD 2-6. Read *People v. Canfield*, 12 Cal. 3d 699, 117 Cal. Rptr. 81, 527 P.2d 633 (1974), *Makita Corp. v. U.S.*, 819 F. Supp. 1099 (CT 1993), and *People v. Mitchell*, 86 A.D. 976, 448 N.Y.S.2d 332 (1982). Prepare a memorandum summarizing what these cases say about the applicability of the attorney-client privilege to nonlawyers. Read *In re Complex Asbestos Litigation*, 232 Cal. App. 3d 572, 283 Cal. Rptr. 737 (1991) and *In re American Home Products*, 985 S.W.2d 68 (Tex. 1998). In your memorandum, summarize what these cases say about conflicts of interest involving nonlawyers. Read *Akron Bar Assn. v. Green*, 673 N.E.2d 1307 (Ohio 1997); *In re Hessinger & Assocs.*, 192 B.R. 211 (N.D. Cal. 1996); *UPL Committee v. State Dep't of Workers' Comp.*, 543 A.2d 662 (RI 1998). In your memorandum, summarize what these cases say about the unauthorized practice of law by nonlawyers.

LBD 2-7. Arrange and conduct an interview with a representative of the entity in your state charged with investigating or prosecuting charges of unethical conduct by attorneys. Your questions should focus on:

- the most common ethical and professional violations and what could be done to avoid them;
- any disturbing trends in ethical and professional violations; and
- the role of paralegals in causing or preventing ethical violations by the supervising attorneys;

and any other matters as assigned by your instructor. Prepare a memorandum summarizing your interview.

LBD 2-8. Determine what ethical code for attorneys has been adopted in your state and prepare a memorandum discussing the provisions of that code that speak to the attorney's proper use of paralegals or other support staff.

LBD 2-9. Visit the Web site of NALA (*www.nalanet.org*) and NFPA (*www.paralegals.org*). Locate the code of ethics of each organization posted there and prepare a memorandum noting the topics both codes address and any topics addressed by the code of one organization but not the other.

Chapter 3

The Adversarial System and Pre-filing Investigation

CHAPTER OUTLINE

A. The Adversarial System
B. Distinguishing Between Formal Discovery and Informal Investigation
C. Pre-filing Procedures

CHAPTER OBJECTIVES

This chapter provides an overview of the adversarial system in our country, including

- The civil and criminal court process
- Federal and state court systems
- The role of the rules of procedure and evidence in that adversarial system
- Concepts important to the interviewing and investigating tasks such as substantive law and the civil and criminal cause of action

This chapter also provides an overview of administrative procedures and various forms of alternative dispute resolution and considers the role of the paralegal investigator in those areas. Finally, the chapter discusses the specific goals of pre-filing investigation.

A. ▸ The Adversarial System

In the United States, we have an **adversarial system of justice.** This means that when disputing parties are unable to resolve the dispute themselves there is a system in which those parties can present their dispute as adversaries before a court or tribunal empowered to resolve the dispute for them. The parties to the lawsuit present, or *plead,* their side of the case to the judge or jury. They also attack the opponent's presentation with a view toward convincing the judge or jury to decide in their favor rather than the opponent's. The courtroom becomes a legal battlefield bounded by well-defined rules of procedure and proof in which both sides seek to win and cause the other side to lose. The process is sometimes referred to as *civilized warfare.*

1. Civil and criminal law

In the adversarial system, cases are broadly classified as either civil or criminal. **Criminal law** involves a prosecution by the government, either federal or state, which seeks to punish by fine or imprisonment, or both, one accused of violating societal laws as codified in criminal statutes passed by the U.S. Congress or a state legislature. Criminal laws are typically classified as crimes against the person, crimes against property, or crimes against the public.

Civil law involves the determination and enforcement of all private or public rights—essentially all law that does not involve a criminal matter. Civil disputes involve claims between persons that one party has engaged in conduct injurious to the person, property, or personal rights of the other. Examples of civil areas of the law include torts, contracts, business associations, estate planning and administration, and domestic relations.

2. The court systems

In the United States, because of the doctrine of **federalism** (the division of power between the U.S. government and the various state governments), we have a two-tiered court system—a single federal court system for the entire country and fifty separate state court systems. Illustration 3-1 charts the U.S. government court system.

The court systems of the various states are diverse but most are modeled on the federal system with one or more trial courts, one intermediate appellate court, and a supreme appellate court. Illustration 3-2 charts a typical state trial court system. The paralegal should be thoroughly familiar with the federal court system and the state court system for the state(s) in which she practices. (See LBD 3-1.)

Illustration 3-1   THE COURT SYSTEM OF THE U.S. GOVERNMENT

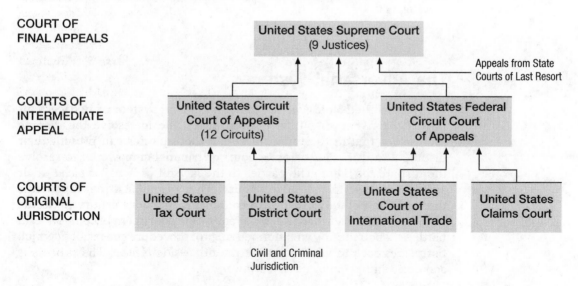

Illustration 3-2
A TYPICAL STATE
COURT SYSTEM

State Supreme Court
(Court of final resort. May be
called Supreme Judicial Court *or*
Supreme Court of Appeals.)

Decisions of a state supreme court
may be appealed directly to the
U.S. Supreme Court if an issue of
federal law is involved.

Intermediate Appellate Courts
(37 of 50 states—usually larger
States—have these courts. Most
cases reach final decision here
because the parties choose to seek
no further appeal *or* the State
Supreme Court refuses to hear it.)

Trial Court of General Jurisdiction
(May be called Circuit Court,
Superior Court, District Court, *or*
in New York, Supreme Court.)

Specialized Courts of Limited Jurisdiction,
e.g., Probate, Domestic Relations, Small
Claims, Juvenile, or Municipal.
(Appeal from decisions of these courts may
be to the trial court of general jurisdiction
or to the intermediate appellate court.)

3. Rules of procedure

An adversarial system that encourages hostility to an opposing position is bounded by many rules. The rules that govern the adversarial process in our courts are called the **rules of procedure.** In civil cases, these rules are called **rules of civil procedure.** In criminal cases, these rules are called **rules of criminal procedure.**

Because of the two-tiered court system, there are different rules of procedure governing the proceedings in the different courts. The **Federal Rules of Civil Procedure (FRCP)** govern civil proceedings in all federal district courts across the country (see Chapter 4). The **Federal Rules of Criminal Procedure (FRCrP)** govern criminal proceedings in all federal district courts (see Chapter 5). Each state will have rules of procedure that govern civil and criminal proceedings in that state's courts, and these rules of procedure may be quite different from the federal rules and from the rules of other states.

For appellate proceedings in both the federal and state court systems, there are separate rules of procedure. In the federal system, the **Federal Rules of Appellate Procedure (FRAP)** will govern, and each state will have its own rules of appellate procedure to govern proceedings in its courts. For our purposes, we will concentrate on the federal rules of civil, criminal, and appellate procedure.

Illustration 3-3   STAGES OF A CIVIL TRIAL

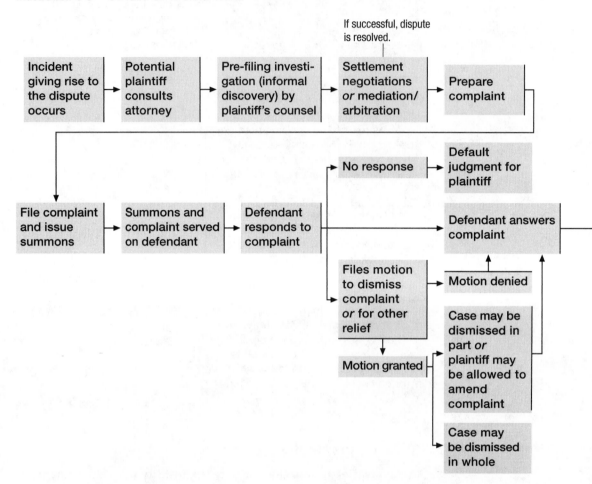

Illustration 3-3 demonstrates the stages of a civil lawsuit as it moves from the time of the incident giving rise to the dispute through trial. Illustration 3-4 demonstrates the stages of a criminal lawsuit from the time of the crime giving rise to the prosecution of the accused through trial.

As was discussed in Chapter 1, to be effective at investigation, the paralegal must be thoroughly familiar with the basic rules of procedure in the civil and/or criminal cases that his supervising attorney handles and with the trial process.

4. Rules of evidence

In the actual trial of a civil or criminal case there are also rules that strictly govern what evidence the judge or jury may hear and consider in order to make a decision in a case. These are known as the **rules of evidence** and, again, due to our two-tiered court system, the paralegal must become familiar with the **Federal Rules of Evidence (FRE)** (see Chapters 6 and 7) and the rules of evidence that govern in the state courts of the state(s) where the paralegal works. (Selected FRE are set out in Appendix D.)

5. Court rules

In addition to the rules of procedure and evidence, each individual court typically will have adopted its own **local court rules** governing certain procedures in that particular court. Local rules may cover matters such as particular days when the court hears argument on various kinds of motions, whether a legal brief must be submitted along with a motion, how long before trial subpoenas must be served on witnesses, and so forth. These rules are typically available from the clerk of the court that propounds them. The paralegal must be familiar with local rules of the courts in which the supervising lawyer practices.

6. The cause of action

a. In a civil suit

In the adversarial system, parties cannot make any allegation they wish against another in court and expect to be heard by a judge or jury.

Illustration 3-4   STAGES OF A CRIMINAL TRIAL

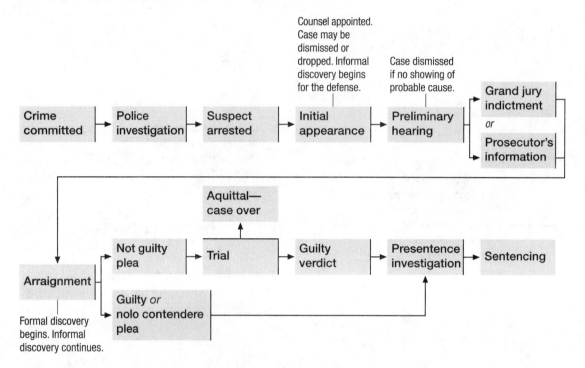

Our laws have developed in such a way that, in civil law, we identify certain theories or **causes of action** that a private party may bring against another and that the courts will entertain. Some of these causes of action have been developed by court decisions (**common law**) and others have been enacted by legislation passed by Congress at the federal level or state legislatures at the state level (**statutory law**). Still other causes of action arise from the United States Constitution or a state constitution (**constitutional law**).

A recognized cause of action is made up of certain **elements** or parts that must be pled and proven by the party making the allegation.

EXAMPLE

If one wishes to sue another for **breach of contract,** the elements of that cause of action will typically be:

- the existence of a valid contract;
- the material breach of that contract by the defendant; and
- provable damages sustained by the plaintiff because of the breach.

If one seeks to allege a cause of action in **negligence** against another, the elements of that cause of action will typically be:

- a duty of care owed by defendant to plaintiff;
- a breach of that duty by defendant;
- damages sustained by plaintiff; and
- legal and proximate causation between the breach of duty by defendant and the damage sustained by the plaintiff.

Unless every required element of a cause of action is proven by the **plaintiff** in a civil suit, the case will be dismissed by the judge on motion of the **defendant** (see Chapter 4). And, of course, what lawyers use to prove the cause of action for their client is **facts**, gathered through interviewing and investigating.

b. In a criminal prosecution

Neither the federal government nor state governments can prosecute a person criminally for just anything. The government must prosecute for a crime already recognized by the state or federal government. And the alleged criminal act will also have **elements** that the government must allege and prove to the requisite degree (usually beyond a reasonable doubt—see Chapter 6) to prevail.

EXAMPLE

> Take a look back at Hypothetical 1-1 and note the various elements of each of the homicide crimes mentioned there.

In both civil and criminal cases, the investigating paralegal must be able to determine and understand the elements of the cause of action involved in the client's representation in order to know what factual information to seek. (See the discussion of factual analysis in Chapter 1.)

7. Remedies

a. In a civil suit

In a civil suit, the plaintiff will seek some type of **remedy** from the defendant(s). Most often the remedy sought is **money damages.** Money damages sought may be either compensatory or punitive. **Compensatory damages** are money damages that *compensate* the plaintiff or make the plaintiff whole. Compensatory damages may be **general** (compensation for pain and suffering) or **specific** (out-of-pocket expenses such as medical bills, lost wages, etc.). (Lawyers sometimes refer to specific compensatory damages as the *specials* in a case, as in "What are his specials?".)

EXAMPLE

> If Road Rage sues Lead Foot for negligence in causing the automobile accident described in Hypothetical 1-2, Road Rage, as plaintiff, may seek compensatory damages for his past and future pain and suffering, permanent disability, loss of enjoyment of life, past and future medical expenses, past and future lost income, and travel expenses to and from the doctor. All of these would be considered compensatory damages. Which would fall into the category of general compensatory damages and which into the category of specials?

Punitive damages, sometimes called **exemplary damages,** are damages which are meant to "punish" the wrongdoer for his conduct. In most states, such damages can only be recovered against a defendant whose actions are proven to have been willful, reckless, or malicious.

EXAMPLE

> If Road Rage can prove that Lead Foot deliberately (willfully) ran the red light in order to strike his vehicle, he may be awarded some amount of money as punitive damages in addition to his compensatory damages.

In some types of civil actions, **equitable relief** may be sought instead of or as an alternative to money damages. There are a number of different kinds of equitable relief but two of the most common forms are **injunctive relief** and **declaratory relief.** An **injunction** is an order by the court directing a party to do or refrain from doing something.

EXAMPLE

> If Road Rage is able to show that Lead Foot is stalking him by car and attempts to cause a collision with him every time Road Rage takes to the streets, Road Rage may be able to secure an injunction from the court enjoining Lead Foot from coming around or about him in a vehicle.

Declaratory relief is a remedy sought when the plaintiff is uncertain of what action is proper to take and seeks the court's "declaration" of what is proper.

EXAMPLE

> If Road Rage was killed in the car accident with Lead Foot and had a life insurance policy covering his life at the time of his death, the life insurance company will want to pay the proceeds of the policy to the beneficiary. If both the wife and adult child of Road Rage claim to be the sole beneficiary and the insurance policy is unclear, the insurance company may file a lawsuit seeking a declaration from the court as to which of the claimants is the proper beneficiary.

And, of course, the remedies available in a civil suit depend on the **facts** gathered through interviewing and investigating.

b. In a criminal prosecution

In criminal proceedings, the government usually seeks the incarceration of the criminal defendant or a monetary fine or both. A crime may be a **misdemeanor,** which is punishable by incarceration for up to one year, or a **felony,** which is punishable by incarceration for more than one year.

Civil law and criminal law sometimes overlap. Criminal charges may be filed by the state for actions that also give rise to a civil suit by the victim for money damages.

EXAMPLE

> If it is shown that Lead Foot did in fact run the stop sign and strike the car driven by Road Rage, Lead Foot may not only be sued for damages in a civil action for damages by Road Rage, he may also be prosecuted for the misdemeanor of reckless driving. If Road Rage is killed in the accident, Lead Foot may be prosecuted for a homicide offense.

In both civil and criminal cases a major focus of factual investigation is on matters relating to the remedies sought. The paralegal investigator must be able to determine and understand the law regarding remedies in a particular case.

8. Defenses

a. In a civil suit

For every civil cause of action that may be alleged, the defendant may merely **deny** the allegations and force the plaintiff to carry his **burden of proof** on all the elements of the cause of action (see discussion of the burden and degree of proof below). But in addition, the defendant may allege **affirmative defenses** which, if proved, will defeat plaintiff's right to recover in whole or part even if the plaintiff does prove all the elements of his cause of action (see extended discussion in Chapter 4). For these affirmative defenses, there are recognized elements that must be properly pled and proven by the defendant who asserts them.

EXAMPLE

If the defendant in the negligence action wants to raise the affirmative defense of **assumption of risk,** he will have to allege and prove:

- that the plaintiff was injured while voluntarily engaging in risky behavior;
- that the plaintiff knew and appreciated the risk of the behavior;
- that the plaintiff's undertaking of the risky behavior was unreasonable; and
- that the injuries sustained by plaintiff were caused by his voluntary and unreasonable undertaking of the known risk.

b. In a criminal prosecution

To every crime with which one may be charged, there are recognized **defenses** that may be available to the criminal defendant beyond a simple denial of guilt. These defenses, like the alleged crimes themselves, will have elements which the criminal defendant will typically have the burden of alleging and proving (see Chapter 5).

EXAMPLE

If Quick Temper from Hypothetical 1-1, is charged under one of the homicide statutes for killing Hi Fi, it may be a defense to him if he can show he fired at Hi Fi because he thought Hi Fi was about to shoot him. Depending on the laws of the state, to make out a case of self-defense, Quick Temper might have to show:

- that he reasonably believed himself to be in mortal danger from Hi Fi;
- that the mortal danger he perceived was imminent; and
- that he used reasonable force under the circumstances to protect himself.

In both civil and criminal cases a major focus of **factual investigation** is on matters relating to the defenses that are or might be raised.

9. The burden and degree of proof

a. In a civil suit

In a civil case, the **burden of proof** is initially on the plaintiff to prove all the elements of her cause of action. The **degree of proof** required in civil cases is typically by a **preponderance of the evidence.** This means the plaintiff, in order to prevail, must convince the trier of fact that it is *more likely than not* that her allegations regarding the elements of her action are true and that she is entitled to prevail. If the defendant in a civil action asserts an affirmative defense, the defendant will have the burden of proving all the elements of that defense, typically by a preponderance.

In some civil actions, the degree of proof required may be slightly higher than the preponderance. For example, in some court states, civil fraud must be proven by **clear and convincing evidence,** not by a mere preponderance.

b. In a criminal prosecution

In a criminal case, the burden is on the prosecution to prove all the elements of the crime alleged. The degree of proof required in a criminal case is greater than in a civil case, for the government must prove its case **beyond a reasonable doubt.**

In both civil and criminal cases, where the burden of proof lies and what the degree of proof is both have significant impact on the factual investigation that must be done to carry the burden of proof by the requisite degree.

10. Means of proof

SLEUTH ON THE LOOSE

Identify a prescription medication you or someone you know has taken recently, then access the Web site of the American Society of Health Systems Pharmacists at *www.safemedication.com* to learn more about that medication including its chemical makeup, side effects, and contra-indications.

As is discussed in more detail in Chapters 6 and 7, in both civil and criminal cases, the proof of facts relevant to the issues is controlled by the rules of evidence (see Appendix D). Evidence may be presented to the court in several different ways:

- **Testimonial evidence** is evidence received from the sworn testimony of witnesses.
- **Documentary evidence** is evidence received from properly admitted documents.
- **Real or physical evidence** is evidence in the form of properly admitted objects (e.g., the weapon in a murder case).
- **Demonstrative evidence** is evidence in the form of properly admitted charts, graphs, diagrams, etc., that illustrate something for the court.

Understanding the rules that govern the kinds of evidence that can be received in court is critical to the investigating paralegal who seeks that kind of information on behalf of the supervising attorney.

11. Statutes of limitation and repose

The rules of procedure and local rules of court mentioned above contain many time limitations and deadlines with which the paralegal must become familiar. In addition, state and federal statutes and regulations set forth time periods in which a civil cause of action or criminal prosecution can be brought. These are referred to as statutes of limitation or statutes of repose. If the civil case or criminal prosecution is not instigated within the designated time, it is typically barred forever.

A **statute of limitation** states the time in which a lawsuit must be commenced against a defendant. The time limitation varies depending on the cause of action and typically begins to run from the date the particular cause of action arose. For example, in many states a lawsuit seeking damages for personal injury based on a negligence cause of action must be commenced within a year from the date the cause of action arose, which usually will be the date of the negligent act itself.

A **statute of repose** places an absolute limit on the time in which a lawsuit must be commenced without regard to when the cause of action arose. For example, some states have statutes providing that a suit alleging an injury due to a defect in a product be commenced within some number of years from the date the product was first offered for sale regardless of when the defect was discovered or when the injury occurred.

HYPOTHETICAL 3-1

Assume that in your state the statute of limitations for commencing a personal injury action in negligence is one year from the date the cause of action arose. For causes of action in strict liability, the statute is three years from the date the cause of action arose. And for causes of action in breach of warranty, the statute is four years from the date of purchase of the product. Your state also has a ten-year statute of repose for products liability actions, which commences on the date the product was first offered for sale to the public.

Today a client comes into your office and meets with you and your supervising attorney. The facts you elicit in the initial interview are that two months ago the client was badly injured when the riding lawn mower she was using to mow her lawn failed to slow down when she engaged the clutch, causing the mower to go over a steep slope. She also says she bought the mower two years ago from a dealer specializing in reconditioned yard equipment. Your lawyer comments that the client may have a valid cause of action in negligence, strict liability, and breach of warranty. He assigns you the factual investigation.

Your investigation confirms that the mishap and injury occurred two months ago and that she bought the mower a little over a year ago, but you also learn that this particular mower was first sold and put in service eleven years ago. Absent other facts, what should your supervising attorney advise this client regarding her potential causes of action?

Assume your investigation reveals that the product was first sold and put in service five years ago, but that the accident and injury actually occurred fourteen months ago. What should your supervising attorney advise this client regarding her potential causes of action?

The failure of lawyers to initiate actions within a statute of limitation or repose may constitute legal malpractice. And in most jurisdictions there are many different statutes of limitation and repose for the various causes of action that may be brought. (See LBD 3-2.)

12. Administrative procedures

Because of the plethora of **administrative agencies** (governmental bodies charged with administering legislation in specific areas) at both the state and federal levels, much litigation today occurs in the administrative context rather than in a civil or criminal lawsuit. Governmental agencies are engaged in rule making, investigation, and adjudication. Many paralegals today work for attorneys involved in administrative law—social security appeals, workers' compensation claims, environmental violations, health care regulation, and employment discrimination are examples. Whenever an agency action is to be challenged or appealed, it is necessary to be familiar with:

- the **enabling legislation** (the statute that created and controls the agency);
- the **rules and regulations** promulgated by the agency that define the perimeters of its authority and the procedures by which it acts; and
- the **Administrative Procedures Act,** which, in most cases, governs the procedures by which agency action may be challenged or appealed.

Illustration 3-5
PROCEDURAL
STEPS IN AN
ADMINISTRATIVE
ADJUDICATION

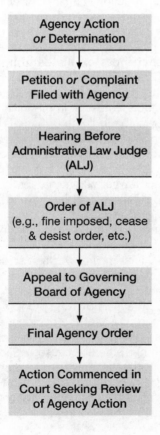

Agency Action
or Determination

↓

Petition *or* Complaint
Filed with Agency

↓

Hearing Before
Administrative Law Judge
(ALJ)

↓

Order of ALJ
(e.g., fine imposed, cease
& desist order, etc.)

↓

Appeal to Governing
Board of Agency

↓

Final Agency Order

↓

Action Commenced in
Court Seeking Review
of Agency Action

Generally, no suit may be brought in a court of law challenging agency action until the required administrative procedures have been exhausted (called the **exhaustion of remedies**). Illustration 3-5 sets out the procedural steps involved in an administrative adjudication.

Interviewing and investigating skills are just as important in an administrative proceeding as in traditional litigation. Differences will arise in the procedure and, sometimes, in the form in which factual information must be placed for evidentiary purposes.

13. Alternative dispute resolution (ADR)

Because of the growing expense of litigation, the crowded court dockets, the time it takes to move a suit through the court system, growing disenchantment with the hostile nature of the adversarial process, and the problem of attorney abuse of the adversarial system, there has been a growing interest in providing disputing parties an alternative means of resolving their dispute. The most common methods of ADR are as follows:

a. Negotiation

Negotiation is the process by which the adverse parties, either before or during the litigation process, talk informally, usually through their attorneys, to try and work out a compromise settlement of the dispute. Today, more than 90 percent of all civil suits settle out of court before trial by negotiation and the vast majority of criminal cases are plea bargained the same way.

The great weakness of negotiation, however, is that it usually does not take place until the parties have retained attorneys, suit has been filed, much formal discovery has taken place, and pretrial motions have been filed and ruled on with the attendant expense and delay. Many conscientious attorneys attempt to resolve disputes prior to filing a lawsuit. Too often, however, time does not permit this because a statute of limitations is about to run, or the opposing party decides to engage in discovery in order to determine the merits of the claim prior to negotiating. In addition, some less scrupulous attorneys still avoid or delay negotiations to give themselves an opportunity to *churn the file* and earn more fees.

Judges will frequently inquire of the parties to a pending suit whether settlement negotiations have taken place and encourage the parties to attempt them. Of course, the judge cannot order parties to settle. However, FRCP 26(f) now authorizes the U.S. District Courts to require the parties to meet and discuss a number of things about the case including "the possibilities for a prompt settlement or resolution of the case." This procedure is frequently used in the federal courts.

b. Mediation

A **mediator** is a neutral third party who seeks to facilitate a voluntary settlement between disputing parties. The mediator will listen to both sides, serve as a communication link between the disputing parties, and will encourage both sides to be reasonable and move toward a realistic

---

CAREER TIP

The growing popularity of mediation as an alternative to litigation may present a career opportunity to paralegals. Where mediation is not yet regulated by the state or where nonlawyers are expressly authorized to act as mediators, paralegal training and experience provide excellent background for those wishing to provide mediation services. Those services may include, subject to the laws of your state, offering private mediation services, working for a mediation center, or serving on a panel of court-approved mediators **("court-annexed ADR").** In addition, many types of businesses are developing in-house mediation services in connection with their human resources departments, to resolve various employee, customer, or supplier disputes before litigation results. More attorneys in private practice are recognizing the value of mediation training for their paralegals. All federal agencies have now been mandated by the President to develop and use ADR procedures and many state agencies are following suit.

Graduate programs in ADR have grown rapidly in the last decade, as have baccalaureate, associate, and certificate programs in mediation training. Adding such training to your formal paralegal studies may enhance your qualifications and make you more appealing to all kinds of potential employers. Resources available to those interested in investigating possible career opportunities in this area are collected in Appendix E, Resources for the Investigator.

---

settlement. The mediator has no authority to compel a settlement or to make any ruling in the favor of either party, nor does the mediator report the content of the discussions to the judge.

Mediation is proving to be a popular and successful ADR tool. Some states have begun to adopt rules giving trial judges the authority to mandate mediation and to select the mediator. Some federal district courts have adopted similar procedures by local rule. It is expected that this trend will grow and time will tell if mediation proves to be a significant means of resolving cases short of the courtroom. (See the various resources on ADR available in Appendix E, Resources for the Investigator. See also LBD 3-9 and 3-10.)

c. Arbitration

In **arbitration** the parties agree to submit their dispute to a disinterested person (or panel of persons) other than a judge or jury. The arbitrator(s) will listen to both sides and then render a decision. That decision may be binding or non-binding, depending on the nature of the dispute and the terms of any agreement between the parties. Disputing parties may voluntarily agree to arbitrate after a dispute arises (*voluntary arbitration*). Or contracting parties may agree at the time the contract is entered into that in the event of a dispute they will submit it to arbitration rather than litigating (*mandatory arbitration*). Many contracts today routinely contain clauses requiring arbitration in the event of a dispute and designating it as *binding* or *non-binding*. The decision of the arbitrator in binding arbitration may not be set aside by a court unless it is determined that the arbitration award was not made in good faith or that the arbitrator was guilty of misconduct.

The federal government and a number of state governments favor arbitration over litigation. The Federal Arbitration Act of 1925 (FAA), 9 U.S.C. §§1-15, provides that courts must give deference to all arbitration agreements in cases governed by federal law.

Procedures in an arbitration often are governed by the Uniform Arbitration Act (UAA) formulated by the National Conference of Commissioners on Uniform State Laws in 1955 and adopted by 34 states and the District of Columbia.

Arbitration services are available from numerous private organizations and from various government agencies. The American Arbitration Association (AAA) (online at *www.adr.org*), a non-profit corporation, is the largest provider of arbitration services, including assisting in locating qualified arbitrators, suggesting appropriate language for an arbitration agreement, and providing helpful forms for the arbitration process. Illustration 3-6 sets out the AAA form for submission of a commercial dispute to arbitration resolution. (See Appendix E for additional resources on arbitration. See LBD 3-10.)

B. ▶ Distinguishing Between Formal Discovery and Informal Investigation

The distinction between formal and informal discovery is important and should always be kept in mind when planning and undertaking investigation.

1. Formal discovery

Formal discovery is that discovery governed by rules 26 through 37 of the rules of civil procedure or by applicable rules of criminal procedure (see Chapters 4 and 5). Such discovery, with very limited exceptions, occurs *after* a civil lawsuit has been filed or a formal criminal prosecution has begun and requires notice to and the right to participation by all parties to the lawsuit or their legal representatives.

Often it is necessary to do investigation through the formal rules of discovery. For example, the only way to compel an opposing party to give a statement or provide documents in a civil case may be by formal deposition and document requests submitted after a lawsuit is started. Likewise, an uncooperative witness sometimes may be compelled to talk only by subpoenaing that witness to a deposition after the lawsuit has been filed.

2. Informal investigation

Informal investigation is private investigation that may be undertaken by an attorney on behalf of a client either before (**pre-filing investigation**) or after a lawsuit is commenced and which need not follow the formal rules set forth in the rules of civil or criminal procedure. There is no legal or ethical prohibition on continuing to engage in informal investigation after a lawsuit has been commenced. Illustration 3-7 highlights the important distinction between formal discovery and informal investigation.

Illustration 3-6 AMERICAN ARBITRATION ASSOCIATION FORM FOR SUBMISSION OF DISPUTE TO RESOLUTION BY ARBITRATION

American Arbitration Association
SUBMISSION TO DISPUTE RESOLUTION

Date: _____

The named parties hereby submit the following dispute for resolution under the _____

_____ Rules* of the American Arbitration Association.

Procedure Selected: ☐ Arbitration   ☐ Mediation Settlement

☐ Other _____

(Describe.)

Nature of Dispute (Attach additional sheets if necessary.):

The Claim or Relief Sought (the Amount, if Any):

Type of Business: Claimant _____ Respondent _____

Place of Hearing: _____

We agree that, if arbitration is selected, we will abide by and perform any award rendered hereunder and that a judgment may be entered on the award.

To Be Completed by the Parties

Name of Party	Name of Party
Address	Address
City, State, and ZIP Code	City, State, and ZIP Code
( ) Telephone Fax	( ) Telephone Fax
Name of the Party's Attorney or Representative	Name of the Party's Attorney or Representative
Name of Firm (if Applicable)	Name of Firm (if Applicable)
Address	Address
City, State, and ZIP Code	City, State, and ZIP Code
( ) Telephone Fax	( ) Telephone Fax
Signed† (may be signed by a representative) Title	Signed† (may be signed by a representative) Title

Please file two copies with the AAA.

* If you have a question as to which rules apply, please contact the AAA.
† Signatures of all parties are required for arbitration.

Form G1A-3/99

*Reprinted with permission of the American Arbitration Association.

Illustration 3-7
COMPARING
FORMAL
DISCOVERY AND
INFORMAL
INVESTIGATION

* Must follow formal procedural rules of notice to and participation by all parties.
** Need not follow procedural rules. No notice to or participation by other parties.

3. The advantages of informal investigation

Where possible, it is usually preferable to engage in informal investigation before beginning formal discovery and to do so as early in the representation as possible. There are several reasons why this is true.

a. Early investigation produces more information

Documents do get changed, lost, or destroyed. Witnesses move, die, forget. Accident scenes change. Physical evidence can change form or disappear.

b. Information located early is more reliable

Statements of witnesses taken a week after an accident are likely to be more reliable than statements taken nine months later.

c. Information sought informally is more easily obtained

Many witnesses tend to be less cooperative if they know a lawsuit is pending. Many information sources tend to want to share the information with the other side to be "fair" if they know a lawsuit is pending.

d. Information sought informally is less expensive

The formal discovery process can be quite expensive. Informal investigation need not be. For example, taking a witness's statement informally will take less time and involve a lot less expense than waiting for a formal deposition after a suit is filed.

e. No opposing party is present for informal investigation

Formal discovery requires notice to all other parties and they have the right to be present and participate in the discovery event. In contrast, when the investigator undertakes informal investigation, no notice need be given to adverse parties of informal investigation and they have no right to be present or participate.

f. The first side to locate relevant information gains advantages in litigation

This is true for all the reasons considered in *a* through *e* above. The side obtaining relevant information first can better evaluate the case, plan strategy, and seize the initiative.

g. *Prompt investigation enhances settlement prospects*

Litigation is expensive and time consuming. There also is emotional stress for the parties involved in a lawsuit. Early settlement of a dispute avoids these problems for the client and prompt investigation leads to early settlement.

Informal investigation is limited only by:

- the parameters of what is legal;
- the ethical rules that govern lawyers and those that work with them;
- the scope of authority given to the investigator by the client; and
- the investigator's imagination and industriousness.

HYPOTHETICAL 3-2

Assume the attorney you work for undertakes representation of Road Rage from Hypothetical 1-2. You learn that the accident occurred only last week so your lawyer has nearly a year to prepare and file the suit for Road Rage against Lead Foot. Road Rage says that not only did Lead Foot run the red light, but the brakes on Road Rage's car failed to work when he braked. Your lawyer says this is worth investigating since it could produce a second defendant. Road Rage also tells you that he thinks Lead Foot will claim that he (Road Rage) actually ran the red light rather than Lead Foot but that there were two other witnesses to the accident whose names are on the accident report who should confirm his version of the incident.

Your lawyer assigns you the task of interviewing the two known witnesses to the accident and of taking your consulting expert out to inspect the brakes on Road Rage's car which was totaled in the accident and is now stored at Biff's Garage. He expresses the hope that your investigation can confirm Road Rage's allegations and lead to a settlement without even having to file suit.

Since you have plenty of time on this file you let it slip to the bottom of your work pile and don't get around to it for six months. When you finally contact witness number one to set up an interview you learn that the witness was an elderly man who died two months after the accident. His widow says somebody from an insurance company did interview him before he died though. You conclude this must have been the insurance adjuster from Lead Foot's insurance company. When you contact the second witness she grants you an interview but says the cars were both blue and she can no longer recollect which car ran the red light. When you call Biff's to set up a time for you and the expert to inspect Road Rage's car you learn that the insurance company has already authorized it to be sold as junk and it's gone. When you get back to the office you learn that Road Rage has just been sued in negligence by Lead Foot who is alleging that Road Rage ran the red light.

You decide to go home and update your resume on the assumption you may soon be in the market for a new job! Before you leave for good though, you might want to suggest to your attorney employer that he notify his professional liability carrier of a potential malpractice claim!

Identify each of the reasons for doing informal investigation early, as listed in 3(a) through (g) above that you have ignored. What could you have done differently and what difference might it have made to Road Rage, your attorney, and to you?

C. Pre-filing Procedures

1. The mandate for pre-filing investigation

The days when a competent lawyer would file a lawsuit and then begin to look into the real merits of it are long gone. Today, for several reasons, the attorney must do a legitimate and adequate investigation prior to filing the lawsuit to determine that it has merit. The consequences of failing to do so can be quite serious.

- The mandates of FRCP 11 and similar state rules may be violated, resulting in fines and penalties assessed against the client and the lawyer. (See Chapter 1.)
- Filing a frivolous or insupportable suit may result in ethical sanctions against the attorney. (See Chapter 2.)
- Filing a frivolous or insupportable suit may result in the client and the lawyer both being sued by the adverse party for malicious prosecution or abuse of process. (See Chapter 1.)
- Doing an inadequate or untimely pre-filing investigation, or filing a frivolous or insupportable suit may result in the attorney being sued for legal malpractice by the client for whom he filed the suit. (See Chapter 2.)

2. Objectives of pre-filing investigation

a. To determine if there are facts sufficient to state one or more causes of action

It is the responsibility of the attorney to determine what, if any, valid causes of action exist and to direct the paralegal in her search for facts to support potential causes of action. Even so, it is critical that the investigating paralegal has a sufficient understanding of the elements of the different causes of action or defenses considered by the supervising attorney. Only then can the paralegal plan and execute an investigation that seeks legally relevant information (see Chapter 9). Only then will the paralegal recognize the relevance and value of information she obtains in her investigation. Only then will the paralegal know what leads to follow to locate more helpful information.

The paralegal should also be able to recognize potential causes of action not yet being considered by the supervising attorney but which may be supportable by new information the investigating paralegal discovers.

Identifying provable causes of action in pre-filing investigation is critical too because of the various statutes of limitation and repose that may be running on each cause of action. Woe to the lawyer who fails to identify a cause of action which could have been identified in pre-filing investigation and files the lawsuit without alleging that cause of action. And discovers its existence only later. Subject to the rules on amending pleadings contained in the rules of civil procedure (and the tender mercies of the presiding judge), the attorney may have committed malpractice by this inadequate pre-filing investigation.

b. To determine provable damages

Closely related to the decision on what causes of action are available to a client is the decision on what damages may be successfully recovered in a given action. Plaintiffs' attorneys learn quickly that a case may be a good one on liability but not be worth filing because of little or no provable damages, as shown in Hypothetical 3-3.

HYPOTHETICAL 3-3

Assume that Clum Zee works as a clerk in a discount retail store. One busy Saturday, while stocking shampoo on the shelves of the store, Clum Zee drops a bottle on the floor and sees it burst, spreading a slick white puddle across the white tiled floor in the aisle. Clum Zee goes off to get a mop to clean up the spill but he does not place any warning sign or barrier at the spot of the spill. Clum Zee intends to come right back and clean the spill, but when he gets to the back of the store he finds some of his friends on break watching a soccer match on TV and decides to join them. Thirty minutes later, a customer in the store, Born Toshop, is walking down the aisle where the spilled shampoo is with her hands full of merchandise. She would have used a shopping cart or a hand shopping basket but there were none at the front of the store. Born Toshop does not see the spill, steps in it and slips, falling on her backside and spilling the merchandise she was holding. Just as Born Toshop sits up, Clum Zee returns to the aisle and says, "Oh my gosh, I knew I should have gotten back here sooner. This is all my fault." Two other shoppers hear him say this and provide Born Toshop with their names and addresses. One of them retrieves a video camera from her car and videotapes the spill with Clum Zee standing proudly beside it with his mop explaining how and when he had caused the spill, apologizing to Born Toshop, and saying repeatedly that it was his fault.

Born Toshop contacts an attorney the next week, thinking she has hit the jackpot and can now put her daughter through college. She relates the facts to the attorney and his paralegal, both of whom try to keep from salivating on the table while they watch the videotape of Clum Zee. When it is over, the attorney, giddy with anticipation, tells Born Toshop he will take her case. The paralegal, slightly more in control of his emotions, whispers to the attorney, "Don't you want to ask her if she was hurt?" The attorney nods and asks Born Toshop how she was injured in the fall. "Oh, that's the most amazing thing about all this," she replies. "I wasn't hurt a bit. In fact it was really sort of fun. I almost felt like I was snowboarding down that aisle. And no one saw me fall so it wasn't even that embarrassing. How much do you think we can get?"

Do you think the attorney might change his mind about taking Born Toshop's case? Why?

c. To determine if there are facts sufficient to assert a valid defense

On the defense side of a civil or criminal action, once the plaintiff or prosecutor has filed the initial pleading containing the allegations, an investigation must occur prior to filing an answer or responsive motion. Remember that the dictates of Rule 11 and the relevant ethical rules apply not only to complaints that initiate civil lawsuits, but to all pleadings, motions, and discovery papers filed in a civil or criminal action by any party.

The initial investigation done by the defense counsel will not only enable counsel to decide whether and what to plead in the client's defense but will assist in making other critical recommendations to the client regarding, for example, whether to seek an early settlement in a civil case or to plea bargain in a criminal case.

d. To satisfy special pleading requirements

Not only must the defense conduct a pre-filing investigation to determine how to respond to the complaint, it must also determine the existence of affirmative defenses. FRCP 8(c) mandates that in a civil case, *affirmative defenses* asserted by the defendant, such as the running of the statute of limitations, release, satisfaction, etc., must be set forth affirmatively in the responsive pleading. The consequence of failing to do so may be the permanent waiver of such defenses that could have been discovered in pre-filing investigation.

And FRCP 9 allegations require that the facts supporting some types of allegations, such as fraud, be pled *with particularity.*

e. To identify all potential defendants

Frequently the client may be able to identify only one potential defendant in a case. That known defendant may be **judgment proof** (having insufficient assets to pay any judgment rendered). It will be up to the attorney and paralegal, in pre-filing investigation, to identify other defendants. In fact, it is part of the attorney's duty to the client to identify all potential defendants. Defendants considering a counterclaim or third-party claim in response to a suit filed against them will also look for potential defendants to such claims.

Identifying potential defendants frequently requires an understanding of various other areas of the law that render persons other than the wrongful actor liable for the consequences of the wrong. The investigating paralegal must understand and be able to see the potential application of:

1. **The law of agency and principle of** *respondeat superior.* In the law of **torts,** one who commits a wrongful act that injures another while acting as the **authorized agent** of another may not only be liable himself to the injured party, but may render the principal for whom he was acting liable as well.
2. **The principle of indemnity.** Sometimes the law recognizes that a party is legally responsible for an obligation, but the party liable is able to place the obligation on another. This is the concept of **indemnity.** It is common in the business world for one person or entity to agree to be liable for the debts or obligations of another. This is **contractual indemnity.** The policy of liability insurance that you (hopefully) carry on your automobile is an example of contractual indemnity. If you operate your vehicle in a negligent manner and cause the injury of another, your liability carrier agrees by contract to indemnify you for the liability up to the limits of the policy.

Sometimes the law implies the existence of indemnity (**implied indemnity**) without regard to the existence of a contract. Usually this has to do with the relationship or dealings between two parties. The first party may commit the wrongful act but have been so controlled or directed by the second party that the law implies that the second party is liable for the harm done by the first party. It is a well-established principle of agency law, for example, that the principal must indemnify the agent for liability imposed on the agent for torts committed by the agent in the course and scope of the agency and for liability on contracts entered into by the agent on the principal's behalf.

Another frequent application of implied indemnity is seen in the products liability area when suppliers of defective products may be found strictly liable to persons harmed by the defective product even when the defect is attributable to the design or manufacture of the product by a party other than the supplier. In those cases the supplier, though properly found liable to the injured party, may obtain indemnity against the party who had the higher duty and greater responsibility for causing the defect. This branch of the implied indemnity doctrine is sometimes called active-passive indemnity.

SLEUTH ON THE LOOSE

For current business information and economic statistics check the Web site of the Department of Commerce at *www.doc.gov.*

3. **The law of business organizations.** The way that people organize themselves to carry on business can have significant consequences on their legal liability. The paralegal involved in pre-filing investigation must have a fundamental understanding of the various business organizations and the rules of liability that apply to a particular business entity, its owners, employees, and other representatives. And the paralegal must know where and how to locate information on such business organizations (see Chapters 16 through 18).

HYPOTHETICAL 3-4

Assume that the law office where you work as a paralegal represents Ben Runover, who was badly injured one morning last month when a truck driven by Needa Floorit crossed lanes and struck Ben Runover's new Cadillac head-on. Runover's injuries from the collision were worsened by the fact that the air bag in the steering column of the Cadillac failed to deploy until seconds after the collision. It also didn't help that the city-licensed ambulance crew transporting Runover to the hospital following the accident stopped for pizza on the way because it was nearly lunch time. You have been assigned to investigate the facts and identify all potential defendants.

Ben Runover has told you and your supervising attorney that he purchased the Cadillac brand-new two months ago from a local Cadillac dealer here in town. The local dealer had custom-ordered the car for Runover from the manufacturer.

According to the accident report and your interview with the investigating officer, Needa Floorit said she was making deliveries for Funny Bread at the time of the accident and the truck she was driving is titled jointly in the names of Funny Bread, Inc. and a Mr. Big Hurry. Needa Floorit also told the officer that her boss, whom she referred to as Mr. Hurry, had told her to finish her deliveries by noon that day or she would be fired.

Based on these facts, what potential defendants can you identify for Ben Runover's personal injury suit?

Based on what you know so far, what additional information do you want to obtain to possibly identify other defendants?

If Ben Runover sues the local Cadillac dealer and obtains a judgment against it, could that local dealer seek indemnity against anyone else? Who and on what basis?

Assume it is learned that the contract between the local Cadillac dealer and the manufacturer contains an indemnity provision pursuant to which the local dealer agrees to indemnify and hold harmless the manufacturer from all claims and awards related to vehicles provided to the dealer by the manufacturer. Will this provision prevent Ben Runover from suing the local dealer? Will it prevent Ben Runover from suing the manufacturer? Both of them? What other effect(s) might it have?

Assuming that your investigation determines that Funny Bread Inc. is a corporation organized and existing under the laws of your state and that Big Hurry is the sole shareholder and director as well as president of the corporation, can he be sued by Ben Runover based on the facts you have so far?

Assume that your investigation determines that all of the potential defendants you have identified so far are insolvent and have no insurance. In desperation, your supervising attorney tells you to take a close look at the pizza place where the ambulance crew stopped for pizza on the way to the hospital. (Or did you already think of it?) This sounds like a long shot to you but you begin to think of questions you could ask to determine if the pizza place might actually be a potential defendant in this suit. What are your questions?

f. To determine the assets of identified defendants

It does a plaintiff no particular good to identify numerous potential defendants if none of them have sufficient assets to pay any judgment that may be rendered against them. Such a defendant is judgment proof. Pre-filing investigation may involve determining the existence of policies of insurance, their coverage and limits, and checking a number of public records to determine assets, the equity in assets, and any recent transfer of assets held by potential defendants. (See Chapters 16 through 18.)

g. To determine questions of personal jurisdiction

The paralegal engaged in pre-filing investigation must understand the requirements of **personal jurisdiction** (also called *in personam* **jurisdiction**). Personal jurisdiction concerns the power of a court to enter an order binding on a defendant. It does little good to locate potential solvent defendants if they are not subject to the jurisdiction of the court in which the attorney wants to bring the action.

Making a determination regarding whether a particular defendant is subject to the personal jurisdiction of the court will require a combination of fact investigation and legal research. For potential defendants that are residents of the state where suit is to be brought (the **forum state**), this will not be a problem. For defendants that reside out of state, we frequently must fall back on due process concepts of *minimum contacts* with the forum state to determine if the courts of that state can obtain and keep personal jurisdiction.

States have **long-arm statutes** that set forth the factual criteria for determining when a non-resident defendant has sufficient contacts with a forum state to satisfy due process and justify the assertion of jurisdiction e.g., using the roadways of the state, entering into contracts to be performed in the state, etc. A factual investigation must be made using those criteria and the attorney will make a determination regarding the likely outcome of a challenge to jurisdiction if suit is brought in that state. (See LBD 3-3.)

h. To determine questions of subject matter jurisdiction

Subject matter jurisdiction concerns the power of a court to hear a particular kind of case. Questions of subject matter jurisdiction are fact-sensitive. In other words, the decision regarding which court may have jurisdiction to determine a particular dispute has to do with facts regarding the identity of the parties, their residence, and the causes of action to be alleged, all factual matters to be determined in pre-filing investigation.

All states have one or more trial courts of **general jurisdiction,** authorized to hear most kinds of civil lawsuits. But all states also have specialized courts of **limited jurisdiction** in which matters of a particular kind of dispute or matters involving a particular sum of money can or must be brought. A simple example is what many states call their small claims court, or municipal court, or justice of the peace court. These courts typically have subject matter jurisdiction over some kinds of civil and criminal cases but not all. They may, for example, be able to hear civil disputes involving relatively small sums at issue, say $25,000 or less, or disputes involving contracts but not personal injuries, and so forth.

Of course, most states have specialized courts in which certain types of suits *must* be brought. For example, in some states, all matters regarding wills, administration of estates, and guardianship of minors must be brought in probate court. In some states, all divorce actions must be filed in domestic relations court. The paralegal must be familiar with the court system of the state(s) in which she practices to understand the significance of the pre-filing investigation that she is involved in and how it affects the choice of forum. (See LBD 3-5.)

Federal court jurisdiction is uniform across the country and more limited than state court jurisdiction. The basic concepts of federal court jurisdiction with which the paralegal engaged in pre-filing investigation must be familiar are:

1. **Federal question jurisdiction.**   28 U.S.C. §1331 allows U.S. district courts to have original jurisdiction of civil actions arising under the Constitution, laws, or treaties of the United States.
2. **Diversity jurisdiction.**   28 U.S.C. §1332 allows U.S. district courts to have original jurisdiction of civil cases between citizens of different states where the amount in controversy exceeds $75,000, exclusive of interest and costs.

3. **Removal jurisdiction.**   28 U.S.C. §§1441-1452 set forth a procedure where a case filed in a state court may be removed by the defendant to federal court if the case is one which could have been brought originally in federal court and if notice of removal is filed by the defendant within 30 days of the receipt by the defendant of a copy of the initial pleading.
4. **Pendent jurisdiction.**   This concept allows a plaintiff having a federal question claim to join other claims with it in a federal court action if the other claims (which, by themselves, would not trigger federal court jurisdiction) "derive from a common nucleus of operative fact" with the federal question claim. *United Mine Workers of America v. Gibbs*, 383 U.S. 71 (1966).
5. **Ancillary jurisdiction.**   This concept allows a party other than the plaintiff, in a case properly filed in federal court, to file a counterclaim, cross-claim, or third-party complaint even though the latter claim does not have an independent jurisdictional basis that would have allowed it to be initiated in federal court. Such ancillary claims will be allowed where there is a "logical basis" between them and the plaintiff's original claim that does have independent jurisdiction. *Owen Equipment Co. v. Kroeger*, 437 U.S. 365 (1978).

i. *To determine the proper venue for a case*

Unlike subject matter jurisdiction, which has to do with the power of a court to hear a particular kind of case, **venue** has to do with the most appropriate geographic location for the case to be heard. For example, the general trial court of a state clearly may have subject matter jurisdiction of the controversy, but there still may be a question regarding in which county of the state the case should heard. Or a case may clearly have federal jurisdiction, but a question may remain regarding in which federal district the case should be heard.

Like jurisdictional questions, venue issues are fact-sensitive. In most states, venue is properly laid in the county in which the cause of action arose or in which the defendant resides.

EXAMPLE

If a contract is negotiated between parties in two different counties, signed in a third, and performance undertaken in several counties, when breach is alleged, where did the cause of action arise?

Or, if a defective product is advertised across the state, sold in one county, and hurts the consumer in another, where did that cause of action arise? To resolve such questions, reference must be made to the venue statutes of the particular state but the decision regarding venue begins with pre-filing factual investigation.

All states have special venue statutes for particular kinds of actions. Divorce cases (venue in county of separation) and suits brought against the state government or its agencies (venue in county of state capital) are examples of kinds of cases that may have specialized venue requirements. (See LBD 3-6.)

In federal court suits, the general venue statute is 28 U.S.C. §1391, and venue depends on whether the jurisdictional basis is diversity of citizenship or some other basis. The federal statutes also contain many specialized venue provisions that will sometimes take precedence over §1391.

j. To determine questions regarding governmental immunity

Any time the state or federal government or one of their agencies is a potential defendant in an action, consideration must be given to **governmental immunity** (also called **sovereign immunity**). Historically, the sovereign cannot be sued unless it consents and waives its immunity. In such cases, reference must be made to federal or state statutes in which the government has consented to be sued in particular matters to determine if the facts of the case satisfy the statutory waiver of immunity.

There are a number of federal statutes pursuant to which the U.S. government has waived immunity in certain matters. The three most commonly used statutes are:

- The Federal Tort Claims Act, 28 U.S.C. §1346(b);
- The Court of Claims Act, 28 U.S.C. §1491; and
- The Tucker Act, 28 U.S.C. §1346(a).

Similarly, every state will have statutes providing for waiver of its immunity from suit in limited areas. Such statutes not only define the scope of the waiver but set forth the procedures for bringing such a claim. (See LBD 3-7.)

KEY WORDS AND PHRASES TO REMEMBER

Administrative Procedures Act
adversarial system
affirmative defense
alternative dispute resolution
ancillary jurisdiction
arbitration
assumption of the risk
breach of contract
burden of proof
cause of action
civil law
clear and convincing evidence
common law
consequential damages
constitutional law
contractual indemnity
court-annexed ADR
criminal law
declaratory judgment
defense's degree of proof
demonstrative evidence
diversity jurisdiction
documentary evidence
elements of a cause of action
enabling legislation
equitable remedies
exemplary damages
exhaustion of remedies
Federal Rules of Appellate
    Procedure
Federal Rules of Civil Procedure
Federal Rules of Criminal
    Procedure
Federal Rules of Evidence
federal question jurisdiction
federalism
forum state
general damages
general jurisdiction
implied indemnity
injunctive relief
in personam jurisdiction

judgment proof	preponderance of the evidence
limited jurisdiction	punitive damages
local rules of court	real evidence
long-arm statutes	remedies
mediation	removal jurisdiction
mini-trial	sovereign immunity
misdemeanor	special damages
money damages	statute of limitations
negligence	statute of repose
negotiation	statutory law
pendent jurisdiction	subject matter jurisdiction
personal jurisdiction	testimonial evidence
pre-filing investigation	venue

LEARN BY DOING

LBD 3-1. Prepare a diagram of the court system in your state and summarize the subject matter jurisdiction of each court.

LBD 3-2. Locate the statutes of limitation in your state for the following civil causes of actions and prepare a memo summarizing them and your sources of authority. Also indicate if there is a statue of repose which relates to any of these.

negligent personal injury	slander
medical malpractice	libel
negligent injury to personal property	fraud
	products liability
legal malpractice	assault
outrageous conduct	

LBD 3-3. Assume your client was injured by a product she ordered from a shop-at-home catalog distributed by a company in a distant state. Your client did not receive the catalog directly from the company but borrowed it from a friend who also lives in another state. You wish to file a product liability suit in the state where your client resides and was injured by a defect in the product purchased out of the catalog. Locate your state's long-arm statute and prepare a memorandum stating an opinion as to whether the civil trial court(s) of your state courts will be able to assert personal jurisdiction over the nonresident catalog company. Include in your memo other facts that you might want to determine in order to form a better opinion.

LBD 3-4. Determine whether your state has a rule with language similar to FRCP 11. If so, research the decisions of your state courts regarding what constitutes a "reasonable inquiry" sufficient to satisfy the rule's requirements and prepare a memorandum summarizing your findings. Or, locate and read Nelken, *Sanctions Under Amended Rule 11*, 74 Geo. L. Rev. 1313 (1986), and summarize the various sanctions that different courts have imposed for Rule 11 violations.

LBD 3-5. We wish to file a lawsuit in state court alleging breach of contract and fraud in connection with a land sale transaction. We wish to demand a jury and will also be seeking immediate injunctive relief in the complaint because we have information that the defendant is removing assets from the state for the purpose of defeating our client's ability to satisfy any judgment that may be awarded. Locate the following information and prepare a memorandum summarizing what you find:

a. Which trial court(s) in your state will have subject matter jurisdiction to hear this suit?

b. What rules govern proper preparation of the complaint for filing in that court and its service on the defendant?

c. Does that court have any local rules that pertain to the proper preparation of the complaint or its service?

d. Are there any special rules or statutes that come into play since we will be seeking injunctive relief in the complaint?

e. What rules govern how quickly we can get a hearing on our request for injunctive relief after we file the complaint?

f. Do the rules of procedure or the local rules of the court tell us when the court conducts hearings on motions for injunctive relief and whether a legal brief is required in support of the motion?

LBD 3-6. Locate the venue statute(s) for the civil and criminal trial courts of your state and prepare a memorandum summarizing them.

LBD 3-7. Determine whether and to what extent your state has waived sovereign immunity for the following wrongful acts and prepare a memorandum summarizing your findings:

negligent operation of a vehicle by state employee on the job
failure to properly maintain a state road right of way
physical assault by state employee while on the job
theft of property by state employee while on the job
negligent procedures by medical staff in a state hospital

LBD 3-8. Research the three federal statutes mentioned in the last section of this chapter and prepare a memorandum summarizing the scope of the governmental waiver of immunity in each.

LBD 3-9. Determine if your state has adopted by statute or court rule a mandatory or discretionary mediation procedure for civil actions. If so, obtain the text of the rule and any governing procedures and prepare a memorandum summarizing them. Be sure to cover whether, and under what circumstances, a paralegal or other non-licensed person can act as a mediator. If your state has not adopted any such procedure, determine if the U.S. district court in your federal district has done so.

LBD 3-10. Using the online resources provided in Appendix E for alternative dispute resolution, locate a qualified mediator to help resolve a dispute in your state regarding (1) a commercial construction contract; (2) alleged race discrimination in the work place; (3) a stock transaction; and (4) distributions to withdrawing partners in an engineering firm.

Chapter 4

Formal Discovery in Civil Litigation

CHAPTER OUTLINE

A. Introduction
B. The Scope and Purposes of Formal Discovery in a Civil Case
C. Methods of Formal Discovery in Civil Litigation
D. Drafting Guidelines for Discovery Documents
E. The Order of Discovery

CHAPTER OBJECTIVES

In this chapter you will learn:

- The procedural rules that govern formal discovery in a civil case.
- The kinds of information that are discoverable in civil litigation.
- The various methods of formal discovery including depositions, interrogatories, document requests, requests for physical or mental examination, and requests for admission.
- The order in which formal discovery ought to be conducted.
- The role of the investigating paralegal in each method of formal discovery.
- How to draft the various kinds of discovery documents and related motions.
- How to index or summarize a deposition.

A. Introduction

Once the pre-filing investigation has been completed and decisions made concerning appropriate causes of action, defendants, forum, defenses, etc., the lawsuit will be initiated and the issues joined in accordance with Rules 2 through 25 of the FRCP or applicable state rules of procedure. Keep in mind that informal investigation does not end with the institution of formal litigation. It may continue throughout trial preparation and even during the time of trial (see Illustration 3-7). Institution of formal litigation does, however, bring into play the formal rules of discovery available under the governing rules of procedure. The attorney will continue with informal investigation while initiating formal discovery.

The paralegal may be heavily involved in assisting the attorney in planning and implementing discovery accomplished through the formal rules and must be well acquainted with those rules and skilled in their use. In this chapter we will summarize the discovery rules under FRCP 26 through 37. Remember, there may be important differences between the discovery rules under the FRCP and applicable state rules of civil procedure.

The specific FRCP referenced in this chapter are set out in Appendix B. The full text of the current FRCP can be viewed online at *www.cornell.edu* (see Appendix E, Resources for the Investigator).

B. ▶ The Scope and Purposes of Formal Discovery in a Civil Case

FRCP 26(b)(1) provides in pertinent part:

> Parties may obtain discovery regarding any matter, not privileged, that is relevant to the claim or defense of any party, including the existence, description, nature, custody, condition, and location of any books, documents, or other tangible things and the identity and location of persons having knowledge of any discoverable matter . . . Relevant information need not be admissible at the trial if the discovery appears reasonably calculated to lead to the discovery of admissible evidence . . .

The **scope of permissible discovery** is thus quite broad. This is consistent with the overall purposes of the federal discovery rules—to facilitate the flow of information between the parties, to avoid trial by surprise, and to encourage settlement.

1. The relationship between the scope of formal discovery and the rules of evidence

Rule 26(b) says that the information sought in discovery need not be admissible at trial. Information is discoverable even though inadmissible at trial if it appears to be reasonably calculated to lead to the discovery of admissible evidence. Thus the discovery permitted under the rules of civil procedure is not governed by the evidentiary rules (see Chapters 6 and 7), which strictly limit and control what can be testified to or presented at trial. Another way to say this is that the discovery rules permit broader factual inquiry before trial than do the evidentiary rules at trial.

HYPOTHETICAL 4-1

Assume that you are working as a paralegal for the attorney representing Ben Runover from Hypothetical 3-4. A suit has been filed on behalf of Runover against Needa Floorit and her employer, Funny Bread, Inc. In her FRCP 30 deposition, Needa Floorit has denied that she was speeding and lost control of her truck at the time of the collision with Ben Runover. Your supervising attorney deposes the investigating officer and asks her if she has any reason to believe that the Funny Bread truck had been speeding. The officer responds that she has no information of her own but that one bystander told her after the accident that he "saw the truck flying down the road like a bat out of hell before it crossed the median and hit the Cadillac." The attorney for Funny Bread, Inc., makes no objection to this question or the answer.

After the officer's deposition you excitedly ask if the statement by the bystander witness won't help win the case for Runover. The attorney replies that unless you can locate this bystander to testify, the statement of the officer will do Ben Runover no good. He tells you that the statement of the officer about what the bystander witness said is probably inadmissible at trial because it is hearsay. You reply, "But if it's inadmissible hearsay, why didn't the Funny Bread lawyer object during the deposition?"

Why is your supervising lawyer giving you a disgusted look?

Could the attorney for Funny Bread, Inc., have properly objected to the question asked of the investigating officer at the deposition on the grounds that it was not reasonably calculated to lead to the discovery of admissible evidence? Could he have properly objected to the answer given?

2. Privileged materials not discoverable

Though the scope of permissible discovery is broad, it is not unlimited. **Privileged material** such as attorney-client correspondence and attorney work product (see full discussion in Chapter 6) is rarely discoverable.

3. Discovery of experts

Rule 26(a)(2) requires the disclosure to opposing parties of the identity of persons who may provide **expert testimony** at trial and Rule 26(b)(4)(A) allows discovery to be had of such experts. Discovery of experts retained by parties for consultation only and not for testimony is strictly limited by Rule 26(b)(4)(B) and usually cannot be had except on a showing of exceptional circumstances under which it is impracticable for the party seeking the discovery to obtain facts or opinions on the same subject by other means.

HYPOTHETICAL 4-2

Assume that you are working as a paralegal for the attorney representing Ben Runover from Hypothetical 3-4. As part of the pre-filing investigation, you take your consulting expert to inspect the wrecked Cadillac. The expert identifies the air bag in the car as a Safe Bag 1000 designed and manufactured by a company called Soft Landing, Inc. The expert also takes notes, draws diagrams, and snaps some pictures of the car and the air bag apparatus, then tells you and your supervising attorney verbally that in his opinion the air bag installed in Ben Runover's Cadillac did in fact malfunction due to a design defect.

Three months later your supervising attorney files suit on behalf of Runover against Soft Landing, Inc. Your lawyer does not intend to use the expert who inspected the car with you as a testifying expert because he is vacillating and does not handle the pressure of cross-examination well. After the suit is commenced, Soft Landing files a FRCP 34 request to inspect the Cadillac. However, you learn that the car has been sold for scrap since the inspection by you and your expert and is no longer available.

Might Soft Landing prevail on a request to the court to obtain discovery from your consulting expert under FRCP 26(b)(4)(B)?

What arguments could you suggest to your supervising attorney to prevent such discovery on these facts?

4. Required voluntary disclosures

FRCP 26(a), now requires voluntary disclosures by the parties to each other without waiting for formal discovery requests. These disclosures include:

- the identity and location of persons likely to have discoverable information relevant to disputed facts;
- a copy or compilation of all documents and things relevant to the disputed facts;
- a computation of damages claimed and allowed inspection of supporting documents;
- the inspection and copying of any insurance agreement that may reflect that the insurer is liable for part or all of any judgment rendered; and
- a written report from each expert expected to testify containing all opinions expected to be offered, and the basis for them.

The timing of these disclosures is tied to the Rule 26(f) meeting of the parties. (See LBD 4-1.)

Pursuant to FRCP 26(a)(3), at least 30 days before trial or as set by local court rule, the parties must disclose:

- the identity and location of all anticipated witnesses;
- the designation of witnesses whose testimony is to be presented by deposition; and
- a listing of anticipated documents and other exhibits.

C. ▶ Methods of Formal Discovery in a Civil Case

1. Depositions (FRCP 27 through 32)

In a **deposition,** a lawyer asks questions of a party or witness (the deponent) who answers under oath. Depositions are typically oral interrogations, although FRCP 31 does provide a procedure for depositions by written questions. The questions, answers, and objections that occur during the deposition are transcribed by a **court reporter** and, on request of the lawyer taking the deposition, are typed up by the court reporter into a **transcript.**

a. Why lawyers take depositions

Lawyers take depositions for four primary reasons:

1. They wish to discover prior to trial what knowledge and information the deponent has.
2. They observe the deponent and make a decision regarding his effectiveness as a witness at trial.
3. They get the witness to commit to a version of recollected events prior to trial so that the witness can be impeached at trial with the deposition testimony if he deviates from that deposition in trial testimony. See FRCP 32(a)(1).
4. They wish to preserve and present the deposition testimony of a witness at trial when that witness cannot be present at trial. See FRCP 32(a)(2)(3).

b. The role of the paralegal in depositions

The paralegal may be given various responsibilities in securing deposition testimony. (See LBD 4-2 and 4-3.)

SLEUTH ON THE LOOSE

Identify a nearby nursing home then access *www.medicare.gov* and see what information you can find about the nursing home, including whether it has been cited for any violations of state or federal regulations.

1. **To help identify potential deponents.** The paralegal may be asked to help identify potential deponents in a case and gather pertinent background information on them.
2. **To help prepare questions.** The paralegal may be asked to help formulate suggested questions to be used by the attorney at the deposition, or questions it is anticipated opposing counsel may ask.
3. **To arrange the time and place of the deposition.** If the deposition is taken by agreement with opposing counsel the paralegal may be the one who arranges the time and place of such depositions. In that event, the paralegal should be careful to confirm arrangements made orally in a prompt letter to all concerned parties. As with all correspondence the paralegal generates on a matter, the supervising attorney, other office personnel working on the matter, and the file should receive a copy of the correspondence. (See Illustration 4-1.)
4. **To arrange for the court reporter.** The paralegal may be responsible for arranging for the court reporter to handle the deposition. The court reporter should be contacted as soon as the depositions are scheduled and such arrangements confirmed by a letter to the court reporter with copies to all concerned parties. (See Illustration 4-2.)
5. **To calendar the deposition dates.** The paralegal may be responsible for calendaring the deposition in her office and making sure the dates are properly recorded in the office's **docket control system.**
6. **To prepare and file the notice of deposition.** The paralegal may be asked to draft the required **notice of deposition** in compliance with FRCP 30(b). As with all other court filings after the original complaint, a copy of the notice of deposition must be served on every other party to the lawsuit because all parties and their counsel have a right to be present and participate in questioning the deponent. (See Illustration 4-3.)
7. **To prepare necessary subpoenas.** If a **subpoena** (a document issued by the court clerk ordering a person to appear at a deposition or trial) is necessary to secure the presence of a witness at the

Illustration 4-1   LETTER TO OPPOSING COUNSEL CONFIRMING DEPOSITION BY AGREEMENT

May 1, 2004

Hard Case, Esq.
Duck, Dodge & Deny
(Address)

Re: Runover v. Soft Landing, Inc.

Dear Mr. Case:

This will confirm our telephone conversation of today's date to the effect that we have agreed to schedule the deposition of Dr. Bright Idea, Chief Engineer for the Design/Build Division of Soft Landing, Inc., for Thursday, May 18, 2004 to begin at 10:00 A.M. in our offices. You have also agreed to accept service of the deposition subpoena duces tecum for Dr. Bright, which I will deliver to you this week.

We will make arrangements for the court reporter.

Thank you for your courtesies.

Sincerely,

Dee Pendable
Legal Assistant

cc: Mellow Fellow, Esq.*
    Mr. Ben Runover

(*In some offices it may be the practice to not show copies on the original. The file copy of the letter will show the copies as blind copies, abbreviated "bcc.")

---

deposition, the paralegal may be responsible for preparing the subpoena, having the clerk of the court issue it, and arranging for its service and return in compliance with FRCP 45 and 30(a)(1).

A subpoena that not only compels the presence of a witness but directs that witness to bring documents or things with him to the deposition is called a **subpoena *duces tecum.*** FRCP 30(b)(1). (See Illustration 4-4.)

The subpoena must be served on the named person as provided in FRCP 45(b) and the server of the subpoena (often the paralegal) must complete a certified **proof of service** (sometimes called a *return of service*) and file it with the clerk of the court that issued the subpoena. A typical proof of service form is shown in Illustration 4-5.

Some U.S. District Courts require the use of Administrative Office (AO) Form 90, a copy of which is set out in Illustration 4-6, for deposition subpoenas. Many state courts will have their own forms for the subpoena and subpoena duces tecum and may require their use.

8. **To help prepare the deponent.** The paralegal may be asked to help prepare a client or friendly witness for a deposition by commu-

Illustration 4-2   LETTER TO COURT REPORTER CONFIRMING ENGAGEMENT

May 1, 2004

Ms. Listen Close
Close Court Reporting Service
(Address)

Re: Ben Runover v. Soft Landing, Inc.

Dear Ms. Close:

This will confirm that you will be handling the court reporting duties for the audio-visual deposition of Dr. Bright Idea, Chief Engineer for the Design/Build Division of Soft Landing, Inc., which is scheduled for Thursday, May 18, 2004 to begin at 10:00 A.M. in our offices.

Please let me know if you have any questions.

Sincerely,

Dee Pendable
Legal Assistant

cc: Hard Case, Esq.
    Mellow Fellow, Esq.
    Mr. Ben Runover

---

nicating the supervising attorney's explanation of deposition procedure and areas of expected examination, or by participating in a mock examination.

9. **To copy and arrange exhibits.**   The paralegal may be asked to make a sufficient number of copies and organize documents the lawyer expects to use in the deposition.

10. **To assist at the deposition.**   If the paralegal attends the deposition, she may be expected to keep the documents used as exhibits organized and furnish them to the attorney at the appropriate time; to take extensive notes on the deposition; to make discreet, written suggestions to the attorney for additional or forgotten areas of inquiry; to observe, record, and advise the attorney at the appropriate time of the demeanor of deponents and parties present during the deposition.

11. **To arrange for the preparation of the transcript.**   The paralegal may have the responsibility of ordering the deposition transcript from the court reporter. She will then be expected to stay in touch with the court reporter regarding prompt preparation and delivery of the transcript, particularly if the depositions are taken close to a trial or hearing where the transcript will be needed.

12. **To help a client review the transcript.**   If signature by the deponent was not waived at the deposition, the paralegal may be expected to be sure the transcript is reviewed by the deponent, then signed and returned as required by FRCP 30(e).

Illustration 4-3 NOTICE OF DEPOSITION

IN THE UNITED STATES DISTRICT COURT
FOR THE EASTERN DISTRICT OF YOURSTATE
NORTHERN DIVISION

BEN RUNOVER, Plaintiff	)))	
v.	)	DOCKET NO. 03-00001
SOFT LANDING, INC., Defendant	))	

NOTICE OF DEPOSITION

To: Soft Landing, Inc.
    c/o Hard Case, Esq.
    (Address)

Plaintiff, Ben Runover, pursuant to Rule 30(b) of the Federal Rules of Civil Procedure, hereby gives notice that counsel for plaintiff will take the audio-visual deposition of Dr. Bright Idea, Chief Engineer for the Design/Build Division of defendant Soft Landing, Inc., on Thursday, May 18, 2004, at 100 South Main St., Capital City, Yourstate, beginning at 10:00 A.M. (EDST), before an officer duly authorized to administer oaths. A stenographic record of the deposition will also be made. This deposition may be adjourned from day to day until completed.

Mellow Fellow
Counsel for plaintiff Ben Runover
(Address)

CERTIFICATE OF SERVICE

The undersigned hereby certifies that a copy of the foregoing notice of deposition was served upon the following counsel of record by placing a copy in the United States mail, postage prepaid, addressed as follows:

Hard Case, Esq.
(Address)

This _____ day of May, 2004.

Mellow Fellow

---

13. **To file the transcript with the court.** The paralegal may be responsible for seeing to it that the transcripts of depositions are properly filed with the court as required by FRCP 30(f) or local court rule. In many jurisdictions, the court reporter does not file the deposition transcript, but only certifies it and delivers the original to the attorney who requested it. It is then up to that attorney to be sure the deposition transcript is properly filed with the clerk of the court.

14. **To review the deposition transcript for leads.** The paralegal may be asked to review deposition notes and/or transcripts for leads to additional information and witnesses.

15. **To prepare a summary or index of the deposition.** The **deposition summary** or **index** is prepared from the transcript. There

Illustration 4-4   DEPOSITION SUBPOENA DUCES TECUM

IN THE UNITED STATES DISTRICT COURT
FOR THE EASTERN DISTRICT OF YOURSTATE
NORTHERN DIVISION

BEN RUNOVER,   )
    Plaintiff   )
)   DOCKET NO. 03-00001
    v.   )
SOFT LANDING, INC.,   )
    Defendant   )

DEPOSITION SUBPOENA DUCES TECUM

To: Dr. Bright Idea, Chief Engineer
    Design/Build Division
    Soft Landing, Inc.
    c/o Hard Case, Esq.
    (Address)

YOU ARE HEREBY COMMANDED to appear and give testimony under oath at the law offices of Shake, Rattle & Roll, 100 South Main Street, Capital City, Yourstate on Thursday, May 18, 2004, beginning at 10:00 A.M. (EDST).

YOU ARE FURTHER COMMANDED to bring the following with you:

All written, recorded or graphic matter, however produced or stored, and specifically including copies of data stored on computer disk or by other electronic means, which refer or relate in any way to the development, testing, design, manufacture, production and/or distribution of the Safe Bag 1000 system including, but not limited to correspondence, notes, memoranda, interoffice communications, studies, analysis, reports, reviews, proposals, contracts, working papers, statistical reports, blue prints, sketches, drawings, drafts, or documents similar to any of the foregoing, however denominated.

Dated: May 1, 2004

_____
Clerk of the Court

---

are four different types of deposition summaries typically used by attorneys:

the **chronological summary**
the **subject matter summary**
the **topical summary**
the **narrative summary**

The four types of deposition summaries are shown in Illustration 4–7. Such summaries enable attorneys to use depositions effectively at trial for the impeachment of a witness or for the rehabilitation of an impeached witness. They are especially important when the depositions taken in a case have been lengthy and/or numerous. When asked by an attorney to prepare a deposition index, the paralegal should be sure to ask which type the lawyer prefers.

Illustration 4-5   PROOF OF SERVICE OF SUBPOENA

IN THE UNITED STATES DISTRICT COURT
FOR THE EASTERN DISTRICT OF YOURSTATE
NORTHERN DIVISION

BEN RUNOVER,
    Plaintiff
 	
    v.
 	
SOFT LANDING, INC.,
    Defendant
	)
	)
	)
	)
	)
	)

DOCKET NO. 03-00001

PROOF OF SERVICE OF DEPOSITION SUBPOENA DUCES TECUM

I, Patsy Paralegal, hereby declare under penalty of perjury under the laws of the United States of America that:

1. I am over eighteen (18) years of age.
2. On the 1st of May, 2004, I served a copy of the attached subpoena duces tecum on Dr. Bright Idea, Chief Engineer of the Design/Build Division of Soft Landing, Inc., by hand delivering a copy thereof, by agreement, to Mr. Hard Case, attorney for Soft Landing, Inc., at 123 North Tulip Street in Capital City, Yourstate.

Executed this 2nd of May, 2004.

_____

Patsy Paralegal

---

2. Interrogatories (FRCP 33)

Interrogatories are written questions submitted by one party to another, which must be answered in writing and under oath by the party being interrogated. Interrogatories have been the subject of much abuse by attorneys, because they can be extremely time consuming and expensive to have to answer numerous written questions. Consequently, FRCP 33(a) now limits parties to 25 interrogatories, including subparts, subject to the discretion of the trial court to limit or increase that amount by order or local rule. Many states have begun imposing similar restrictions by rule of civil procedure or by local court rule and care should be taken to consult such rules before posing or answering interrogatories.

a. Information to be sought by interrogatories

Interrogatories are primarily used to obtain basic background information from the opposing party; information that can provide leads for further informal investigation or provide the basis for more detailed deposition questions. Though the specific questions to be posed in interrogatories will vary depending on the facts and law of a particular case, there are some general areas of inquiry that should typically be covered:

1. **The identity and relationship of parties.**   Frequently there is a question regarding the correct identity and legal relationship of parties, potential parties, related parties, agents, and employees. We can-

Illustration 4-6   AO FORM 90: DEPOSITION SUBPOENA USED IN FEDERAL COURT

AO 90 (Rev. 5/85) Deposition Subpoena

United States District Court

DISTRICT OF _____

DEPOSITION SUBPOENA

V.

CASE NUMBER: _____

TYPE OF CASE	SUBPOENA FOR
☐ CIVIL ☐ CRIMINAL	☐ PERSON ☐ DOCUMENT(S) or OBJECT(S)

TO:

YOU ARE HEREBY COMMANDED to appear at the place, date, and time specified below to testify at the taking of a deposition in the above case.

PLACE	DATE AND TIME

YOU ARE ALSO COMMANDED to bring with you the following document(s) or object(s):*

☐ Please see additional information on reverse

Any subpoenaed organization not a party to this suit is hereby admonished pursuant to Rule 30(b)(6), Federal Rules of Civil Procedure, to file a designation with the court specifying one or more officers, directors, or managing agents, or other persons who consent to testify on its behalf, and setting forth, for each person designated, the matters on which he will testify or product documents or things. The persons so designated shall testify as to matters known or reasonably available to the organization.

U.S. MAGISTRATE OR CLERK OF COURT	DATE
(BY) DEPUTY CLERK	

This subpoena is issued upon application of the:

☐ Plaintiff   ☐ Defendant   ☐ U.S. Attorney

QUESTIONS MAY BE ADDRESSED TO:

ATTORNEY'S NAME, ADDRESS AND PHONE NUMBER

*If not applicable, enter "none".

Illustration 4-6   AO FORM 90: DEPOSITION SUBPOENA USED IN FEDERAL COURT *(continued)*

AO 90 (Rev. 5/85) Deposition Subpoena

RETURN OF SERVICE [1]

RECEIVED BY SERVER	DATE	PLACE
SERVED	DATE	PLACE

SERVED ON (NAME)	FEES TENDERED
	☐ YES ☐ NO AMOUNT $_____

SERVED BY	TITLE

STATEMENT OF SERVICE FEES

TRAVEL	SERVICES	TOTAL

DECLARATION OF SERVER [2]

I declare under penalty of perjury under the laws of the United States of America that the foregoing information contained in the Return of Service and Statement of Service Fees is true and correct.

Executed on _____
                    Date

_____
Signature of Server

_____
Address of Server

ADDITIONAL INFORMATION

---

(1) As to who may serve a subpoena and the manner of its service see Rule 17(d), Federal Rules of Criminal Procedure, or Rule 45(c), Federal Rules of Civil Procedure.

(2) "Fees and mileage need not be tendered to the deponent upon service of a subpoena issued on behalf of the United States or an officer or agency thereof (Rule 45(c), Federal Rules of Civil Procedure; Rule 17(d), Federal Rules of Criminal Procedure) or on behalf of certain indigent parties and criminal defendants who are unable to pay such costs (28 USC 1825, Rule 17(b) Federal Rules of Criminal Procedures)".

not always determine in pre-filing informal investigation all that we need to know about the organization of business entities and the relationships between such entities and their owners and agents. As we have seen, it is vital to be able to identify all potential parties before applicable statutes of limitation expire.

2. **The identity and location of witnesses.**   Although FRCP 26(a)(1)(A) now compels parties in civil litigation to voluntarily disclose information regarding persons likely to have knowledge of disputed facts, this interrogatory should still be posed. In state court actions, the governing rules of procedure may not have a voluntary disclosure requirement. And, even in federal litigation, there still are counsel who honor neither the letter nor the spirit of that rule and will not comply with it.

HYPOTHETICAL 4-3

   Assume that our pre-filing investigation on behalf of Ben Runover raises a serious question as to whether Soft Landing, Inc., is judgment proof. However, your attorney learns in the deposition of Dr. Bright Idea that at the time Dr. Idea tested and developed the Safe Bag 1000 system he was employed not by Soft Landing, Inc., but by a large conglomerate known as World Wide Discoveries (WWD). Dr. Idea thinks WWD created or spun-off Soft Landing, Inc., to market the Safe Bag 1000.
   Draft no more than two interrogatories that might be posed to defendant Soft Landing, Inc., to determine the details of this relationship.

3. **Information regarding documents and things.**   Interrogatories are ideal to learn the identity, location, and custodian of documents and things related to the case. Everything said of the voluntary disclosure required by FRCP 26(a)(1)(A) also applies to that required by FRCP 26(a)(1)(B). Why is it important to know where documents and things are and who is the custodian of them? (See Chapters 6 and 7.)

4. **Medical history and damages information.**   In any personal injury case it is important to obtain the plaintiff's complete medical history as well as information regarding the treatment of alleged injury as early as possible and, in any case, well before the deposition of the plaintiff. Asking for this early in an interrogatory gives the defendant time to do informal discovery into the medical history and current condition of the plaintiff to enable the attorney to thoroughly cover those areas in the deposition.

    Interrogatories posed by Soft Landing, Inc., to Ben Runover regarding his medical history might read as those in Illustration 4-8.

    In any suit for damages, details should be obtained by interrogatory regarding the factual basis and means of calculating such damages. In a federal court suit, do not rely exclusively on the voluntary disclosure requirement for this information.

5. **Defendant's ability to satisfy a judgment.**   It is important for case evaluation and possible settlement purposes for the plaintiff to determine early on as much as possible about the financial condition of each defendant. In many instances, informal investigation into public records can produce much helpful information regarding this

Illustration 4-7   DEPOSITION SUMMARIES

---

(1) The chronological summary digests the deposition in the order in which topics appear. A chronological summary might look like this:

Biographical Info.
P1-P4 L.12   Born 8-1-52 in Dodge City, KS. Through high school there. BA from U. Kansas, in Lawrence. Married '72.
                               No children.

Employment His.   P-T for father's drug store in H.S. Artist for Hallmark Cards 72-83.
P4 L.13-P.6 L.2   Self-employed commercial artist since.

(2) The subject matter summary organizes the deposition into subjects without regard to where in the deposition they may appear. That might look like this:

Negotiations re contract
P17, L.1-16   John Brown, Hallmark manager in June '99
P22, L.4-11   John Brown again in Dec. '99
P23, L.16-24   Carl Able, Co. president in Jan. '01

(3) The topical summary is identical to the subject matter summary except that it only covers selected topics in the deposition and is not comprehensive. The attorney will typically identify which topics he needs summarized from the deposition.

(4) The narrative summary is a condensed version of the deposition put in memorandum form. It is useful to give to the client and to help identify areas of additional investigation. A narrative summary might begin like this:

Peter Jesse James was born 8-1-52 in Dodge City, KS. He lived there through high school with his parents Paul and Peggy James and his younger brother Perry James. During high school Peter worked as a waiter at the Red Robin Cafe in Dodge City. . . .

---

matter. (See Chapters 17 and 18.) However, it will frequently be necessary to determine additional or more definite information through formal discovery.

FRCP 26(a)(1)(D) now requires the voluntary production of insurance policies that may be available to satisfy judgments. However, many states do not have a voluntary disclosure rule. In addition, some states will not require production of insurance information even upon request, considering it an improper violation of a defendant's privacy prior to a judgment being entered. (See LBD 4-5.)

In cases where the issues make the current financial condition of the defendant a relevant topic of inquiry, that information should be requested as well. In most states, such information is discoverable only in special situations, as where punitive damages are sought. (See LBD 4-5.)

6. **Details as to events and transactions.**   Asking an opposing party by interrogatory to explain an event or series of events in detail prior to their deposition can help the attorney prepare better deposition questions. It also provides time for informal discovery to test the

credibility of the details provided. It is also permissible to ask a party by interrogatory what the factual basis is for a legal position taken in a pleading.

EXAMPLE

If the plaintiff sues alleging the defendant breached a contract, the interrogatory may ask the plaintiff:

State in detail each and every action or inaction by defendant which plaintiff contends constitutes a breach of the contract at issue.

7. **Information regarding experts.**   Interrogatories are used to obtain the identity of experts who will testify for the opposing party, their opinions, and the basis of those opinions. FRCP 26(b)(4) allows this discovery and it should be obtained by interrogatory well before the discovery deposition of the expert. This allows the inquiring attorney ample time to prepare to examine the opposing expert.

EXAMPLE

An expert witness interrogatory might read like this:

Identify each and every expert witness you expect to testify at trial and for each one identified state:

1. all opinions the expert will offer;
2. the factual or other basis for each such opinion; and
3. all data or other information considered by the expert in reaching each such opinion.

b. The paralegal's role in discovery by interrogatories
The paralegal will typically be heavily involved in discovery by interrogatories (see LBD 4-4), including the following:

1. **Drafting interrogatories for the opposing party.**   (See the drafting guidelines below.)
2. **Helping the client compile information to answer interrogatories.**
3. **Drafting responses for the client's review.**   The wording of such responses can be just as important as the wording of the interrogatories themselves.
4. **Suggesting possible objections to the lawyer.**   If an interrogatory is so **vague** that it cannot be reasonably understood or requires guessing, or if it is so **over broad** that it requires an unreasonable amount of time and expense to answer, or if it inquires into privileged areas, or is outside the permissive scope of discovery, or is otherwise objectionable, the **objection** must be stated in writing in the response to the interrogatories. Since the paralegal will frequently take the lead in reviewing and preparing responses to interrogatories, the attorney will expect her to identify objectionable questions and draft or suggest objections for his review.

Illustration 4-8 INTERROGATORIES REGARDING MEDICAL CONDITION AND TREATMENT

IN THE UNITED STATES DISTRICT COURT
FOR THE EASTERN DISTRICT OF YOURSTATE
NORTHERN DIVISION

BEN RUNOVER,   )
  Plaintiff   )
)   DOCKET NO. 03-00001
  v.   )
SOFT LANDING, INC.,   )
  Defendant   )

DEFENDANT'S FIRST INTERROGATORIES TO PLAINTIFF

Defendant, Soft Landing, Inc., pursuant to FRCP 33, requests that plaintiff answer the following interrogatories under oath within thirty (30) days of service upon counsel for plaintiff.

Interrogatories

1. Identify each and every physician, osteopath, chiropractor or other health care provider or medical personnel of any kind who has treated or consulted with you as a result of the injuries alleged in your complaint and for each one identified state:

 a. the date(s) of such treatment or consultation;
 b. the medical or other condition for which the treatment or consultation was rendered;
 c. the diagnosis made and treatment rendered, including medication(s) and physical therapy;
 d. the amount charged for such treatment or consultation and whether such charges have been paid.

2. Identify each and every hospital, clinic or other health care facility of any kind where you have received treatment as an in-patient or out-patient for the injuries alleged in your complaint and for each one identified state:

 a. the date(s) of such treatment, including dates of admission and discharge;
 b. the medical or other condition for which the treatment was rendered;
 c. the treatment rendered, including medical procedures performed, medication(s) and physical therapy;
 d. the amount charged and whether such charges have been paid.

3. Identify each and every physician, osteopath, chiropractor or other health care provider or medical personnel of any kind who has treated or consulted with you as a patient during the last ten years other than those identified in response to No.1 and for each one identified state:

 a. the date(s) of such treatment or consultation;
 b. the medical or other condition for which the treatment or consultation was rendered;
 c. the diagnosis made and treatment rendered, including medication(s) and physical therapy.

4. Identify each and every hospital, clinic or other health care facility of any kind where you have received treatment as an in-patient or out-patient during the last ten years other than those identified in response to No. 2 and for each one identified state:

 a. the date(s) of such treatment, including dates of admission and discharge;
 b. the medical or other condition for which the treatment was rendered;
 c. the treatment rendered, including procedures performed, medication(s) and physical therapy.

EXAMPLE

If defendant Soft Landing, Inc., were to pose an improper interrogatory to plaintiff Ben Runover regarding his financial condition, the question and response might look like this:

15. State your current net worth.

   Response: Plaintiff objects to answering this interrogatory on the grounds that the information sought is not relevant to any issue in the case and the question is not reasonably calculated to lead to the discovery of admissible evidence.

5. **Drafting a motion for protective order.**   **Motion practice** is an important part of the litigation process including formal discovery. A **motion** is an oral or written application made by the attorney to the court asking for some kind of relief. In the event an objectionable question is asked in an interrogatory or a deposition, FRCP 26(c) permits the party to whom the discovery is directed to file a motion with the court for a **protective order** with regard to that discovery. FRCP 26(c) requires a certification that prior to filing a motion for protective order the moving party conferred or attempted in good faith to confer with the opposing side to work out the objection. The paralegal may be involved in this attempt to resolve conflicts or may be asked to draft letters for the attorney reflecting his attempts to work them out.

   If plaintiff Ben Runover decides to object to interrogatories nos. 3 and 4 served on him by Soft Landing, Inc., in Illustration 4-8 because they ask about his medical history unrelated to the injuries he is suing for in the present case, his FRCP 26 motion for protective order might look like Illustration 4-9.

6. **Drafting a motion to compel discovery.**   In the event an opposing party does not properly or timely comply with interrogatories posed (or other discovery as well), FRCP 37 authorizes a **motion to compel discovery** and, in certain circumstances, **sanctions** to be imposed on the other side. The paralegal may be asked to draft such motion and may be directly involved in the required pre-motion effort to resolve the conflict. In the event that Dr. Bright Idea refuses at his May 18, 2004 deposition to produce memorandum he sent to the legal department of Soft Landing, Inc., regarding the design of the Safe Bag 1000 System (see Illustration 4-4), counsel for Ben Runover might file a FRCP 37 motion similar to that in Illustration 4-10.

7. **Monitoring time deadlines associated with answering interrogatories.**   FRCP 33 imposes certain timing requirements regarding answering interrogatories. If the paralegal works with the attorney who has posed the interrogatories, this means calendaring the date when answers from the other side are due. If the paralegal works with the attorney who has received the interrogatories, this means calendaring the date when answers from the client are due. It can be severely damaging to the interests of the client to fail to meet a deadline for answering an interrogatory, and may constitute malpractice as well.

3. Requests for production of documents and things (FRCP 34)

Rule 34 permits a written request to be served on any other party to the lawsuit requesting documents for inspection and copying; tangible

Illustration 4-9 FRCP 26 MOTION FOR PROTECTIVE ORDER

IN THE UNITED STATES DISTRICT COURT
FOR THE EASTERN DISTRICT OF YOURSTATE
NORTHERN DIVISION

BEN RUNOVER,	)	
Plaintiff	)	
	)	DOCKET NO. 03-00001
v.	)	
SOFT LANDING, INC.,	)	
Defendant	)	

MOTION FOR PROTECTIVE ORDER AND
CERTIFICATION OF GOOD FAITH EFFORT TO RESOLVE DISPUTE

Motion

Plaintiff, Ben Runover, pursuant to FRCP 26(c), moves the court for an order providing that he not be required to answer interrogatories 3 and 4 from Defendant's First Interrogatories to Plaintiff served on counsel for plaintiff on May 10, 2004. The interrogatories objected to are as follows:

3. Identify each and every physician, osteopath, chiropractor or other health care provider or medical personnel of any kind who has treated or consulted with you as a patient during the last ten years other than those identified in response to No.1 and for each one identified state:

    a. the date(s) of such treatment or consultation;
    b. the medical or other condition for which the treatment or consultation was rendered;
    c. the diagnosis made and treatment rendered, including medication(s) and physical therapy.

4. Identify each and every hospital, clinic or other health care facility of any kind where you have received treatment as an in-patient or out-patient during the last ten years other than those identified in response to No. 2 and for each one identified state:

    a. the date(s) of such treatment, including dates of admission and discharge;
    b. the medical or other condition for which the treatment was rendered;
    c. the treatment rendered, including procedures performed, medication(s) and physical therapy.

Plaintiff objects to answering these interrogatories on the grounds that they are overly broad and burdensome and request information regarding medical treatment received by plaintiff unrelated to the injuries received by plaintiff in the instant suit.

Certification

Counsel for plaintiff, Mellow Fellow, hereby certifies that he has made a good faith effort to resolve this discovery dispute by placing a telephone call to Mr. Hard Case, counsel for defendant, on May 15, 2004. In that phone conversation Mellow Fellow explained to Mr. Case his objections to answering interrogatories 3 and 4. Notwithstanding that explanation, Mr. Case advised that he would take the position that the interrogatories must be answered.

_____
                                     Mellow Fellow
                                     Attorney for plaintiff Ben Runover
                                     (Address)

(Certificate of Service omitted)

things for inspection, copying or testing; and the entry on land or property for inspection and testing. Responses to these requests must be in writing but are *not* made under oath as with interrogatory answers. The attorney for the party served with the document request will sign the response but the client need not.

To obtain documents and things from persons who are not parties to the litigation, FRCP 34(c) permits the use of the subpoena power of FRCP 45. (See the subpoena *duces tecum* to Dr. Bright Idea in Illustration 4-4.)

The role of the paralegal in connection with document requests and the guidelines for drafting requests and responses is essentially the same as with interrogatories. However, there are some special considerations for document requests:

a. Serving document requests and interrogatories together

Document requests are frequently served along with interrogatories. It is good practice to have only one set of definitions or instructions (see detailed discussion in the section on drafting guidelines below) that are worded to apply to both interrogatories and document requests. That way they need not be repeated in the two documents. Thus the definition section of a document request may read, "The definitions and instructions contained in plaintiff's first set of interrogatories served on defendant are incorporated herein by reference." (See Illustration 4-11.)

Also, identify interrogatories and document requests as sequential sets—for example, *Plaintiff's First Set of Interrogatories and First Document Requests to Defendant.* In the course of extended litigation the parties may eventually serve two or more sets of interrogatories or document requests on each other. The identification of them as the first or second set, etc., helps avoid confusion, and things such as definitions used in the first set can be incorporated by reference in subsequent sets without having to be repeated. (See Illustration 4-11.)

As a time and space saving technique, have the document requests and interrogatories refer to each other by number.

EXAMPLE

If interrogatory number 5 asked the plaintiff to itemize all damages she is claiming to have sustained due to the accident, document request number 3 might simply ask for her to "produce all documents that refer or relate in any way to your response to interrogatory number 5 in Defendant's First Set of Interrogatories to Plaintiff." (See Illustration 4-11.)

b. Assisting the client to locate and review documents

When the client is served with document requests, it may be the paralegal's job to help the client locate, assemble, and prepare the documents for inspection by the opposing party. In performing this task, special considerations must be kept in mind:

1. **Review documents carefully before production.** Caution must be taken to review every one of the documents your client has *before* they are inspected by the other side to ensure that they are properly to be produced. Remember that your client does not know the rules

Illustration 4-10   FRCP 37 MOTION TO COMPEL DISCOVERY

IN THE UNITED STATES DISTRICT COURT
FOR THE EASTERN DISTRICT OF YOURSTATE
NORTHERN DIVISION

BEN RUNOVER,
     Plaintiff
 	
     v.
 	
SOFT LANDING, INC.,
     Defendant
	)
	)
	) DOCKET NO. 03-00001
	)
	)
	)

MOTION TO COMPEL DISCOVERY AND FOR SANCTIONS WITH
CERTIFICATION OF GOOD FAITH EFFORT TO RESOLVE DISPUTE

Motion

Plaintiff, Ben Runover, pursuant to FRCP 37(a), moves the court for an order compelling defendant Soft Landing, Inc., and Dr. Bright Idea, Chief Engineer of the Design/Build Division of Soft Landing, Inc., to produce for inspection all memorandum delivered by Dr. Idea to the legal department of Soft Landing, Inc., that discuss the Safe Bag 1000 System and to answer questions regarding those memoranda in his deposition which began on May 18, 2004 and has been continued by plaintiff pending the resolution of this motion.

Plaintiff further moves the court, pursuant to FRCP 37(a)(4), for an order directing defendant and/or defendant's counsel to reimburse plaintiff for the attorney's fees incurred by plaintiff for the preparation, filing, and hearing on this motion and for the additional *per diem* court reporter expense to be incurred in the continuation of the deposition of Dr. Idea.

In support of this motion, plaintiff would show that at his May 18, 2004 deposition, Dr. Idea, on advice of counsel for Soft Landing, Inc., refused to produce those memoranda or to answer questions concerning them. Plaintiff would also show that Dr. Idea was lawfully subpoenaed to the May 18, 2004 deposition and ordered to bring those documents with him. A copy of the subpoena *duces tecum* served on Dr. Idea on May 1, 2004 is attached hereto as Exhibit 1. A copy of the Return of Service executed by Patty Paralegal on May 2, 2004 showing service of the subpoena *duces tecum* on May 1, 2004 is attached hereto as Exhibit 2.

Certification

Counsel for plaintiff, Mellow Fellow, hereby certifies that he has made a good faith effort to resolve this discovery dispute by placing a telephone call to Mr. Hard Case, counsel for defendant, on May 19, 2004. In that phone conversation Mellow Fellow explained to Mr. Case the relevance of the subpoenaed documents and the inadequacy of the claimed attorney-client privilege. Notwithstanding that explanation, Mr. Case advised that he would take the position that the memoranda were protected by attorney-client privilege and that any questions put to Dr. Idea regarding the memoranda would be improper as infringing on that privilege.

Mellow Fellow
Attorney for plaintiff Ben Runover
(Address)

(Certificate of Service omitted)

---

surrounding formal discovery and probably does not understand the concept of privileged documents. It will be up to you to identify documents that are outside the scope of the request, or privileged from being disclosed, or the request for which is otherwise objectionable. This can be a time-consuming and challenging responsibility, particularly when the documents to be reviewed are numerous or detailed.

2. **Start early to comply with a document request.**   Because of the time involved in reviewing documents to be produced and the number of documents involved in many cases, you need to start early. The paralegal must work closely with the client to be sure the documents are located and assembled for review in ample time to allow the paralegal and the supervising lawyer to inspect them closely. This may mean making numerous reminder calls to a busy or procrastinating client.

3. **Sometimes parts of documents are discoverable and other parts are not.**   Sometimes the non-discoverable parts of a document must

Illustration 4-11   REQUEST FOR PRODUCTION OF DOCUMENTS

IN THE UNITED STATES DISTRICT COURT
FOR THE EASTERN DISTRICT OF YOURSTATE
NORTHERN DIVISION

BEN RUNOVER,
    Plaintiff

    v.

SOFT LANDING, INC.,
    Defendant

)
)
)
)
)

DOCKET NO. 03-00001

DEFENDANT'S FIRST REQUEST FOR PRODUCTION OF DOCUMENTS TO PLAINTIFF

Defendant, Soft Landing, Inc., pursuant to Rule 34 of the Federal Rules of Civil Procedure, requests that plaintiff, Ben Runover, produce the following documents for inspection and/or copying at 10:00 A.M. on June 1, 2004 at the offices of Duck, Dodge & Deny, 123 Tulip Street, Capital City, Yourstate or at such other place and time as the parties, through counsel, may agree.

Definitions

The definitions contained in Defendant's First Interrogatories to Plaintiff are incorporated herein by reference.

Requests

1. All medical reports, records, charts, x-ray reports, and all records regarding any and all medical examinations and/or treatment received by plaintiff as a result of the injuries alleged in the complaint.

2. All documents which refer or relate in any way to plaintiff's response to interrogatory no. 15 in Defendant's First Interrogatories to Plaintiff.

3. All documents which refer or relate to the service and/or repair history of the Cadillac.

4. All federal, state and/or local income tax returns filed by plaintiff for all tax years since 1998.

Hard Case, Esq.
Attorney for Soft Landing, Inc.
(Address)

(Certificate of Service omitted)

be blacked out on a copy before they are produced for inspection. A document produced for inspection by an opposing party which has non-discoverable information deleted from it might look like that in Illustration 4-12.

4. **Make sure the supervising attorney reviews documents to be produced.**   The ultimate decision as to what documents to produce or withhold from production lies with the supervising attorney. Your review of the client's documents should be reported to the supervising attorney. And your suggestions with regard to which documents to withhold or object to producing should be made known to her in plenty of time to allow the attorney's own review of them.

5. **Arrange the time and place for the document production.**   Frequently this job will fall to the paralegal. Depending on the number of documents, their sensitivity and the feelings of the client, the in-

Illustration 4-12   DOCUMENT MODIFIED FOR PRODUCTION AND INSPECTION

MEMORANDUM

FROM: Dr. Bright Idea, Chief Engineer, Design/Build Division
TO: Legal Department
DATE: September 4, 1998
RE: Safe Bag 1000 System

I have just been advised by Maka Quickbuck, head of Production, that a decision has been made by the board to suspend testing of the new Safe Bag 1000 Air Bag System effective September 10. It is my strong opinion that this decision is ████████████████████████████ ███ ██████████████████████████████████████. There are at least three reasons for this opinion as I have discussed with ██████████ ████████ at least three times:

1. In today's litigious climate it is important that our products be as fully tested as possible.
2. ████████████████████████████████████
3. ██

I am urging your department to take a similar position to that outlined here. If you would like to meet regarding this, I am available at your request.

spection may be allowed in your office or that of opposing counsel. You should discourage the idea of allowing a document inspection in your client's office since it encourages the other attorney to ask for more documents, which may be near by.

6. **Remain present during the inspection.**   The paralegal should remain present at all times that the opposing side is inspecting her client's documents and things. Though in the vast majority of cases trustworthiness can be assumed, your client may not share that view and even honest mistakes (lost documents, documents placed out of order, documents with new markings on them) can be made to look devious later. Better to be present at all times and watch after your client's documents and things.

7. **Keep a record of documents produced and withheld.**   Litigation drags on and, as it heats up, disputes can arise between attorneys as to what was or was not produced on a given day months or years ago. When the opposing party produces documents for you, keep a record of what was produced and copied by you. Keep a copy and a record of what your side produced or withheld from production to the opponent.

8. **Reviewing documents produced by the opponent.**   The paralegal may be asked to review documents produced by the opponent. If that responsibility falls to you, your review should be careful and thorough. Report to the supervising lawyer deleted pages or blacked out portions of documents or anything else that appears unusual or inappropriate.

4. Requests for physical or mental examination (FRCP 35)

This rule allows the examination of a person to be ordered by the court upon motion and a showing of good cause. In a personal injury case, particularly one involving a soft tissue injury, the defendant may want to have the plaintiff examined by a physician of the defendant's choosing. This is called an independent medical examination (IME) and usually will be agreed to by the plaintiff. The paralegal's role in arranging such an IME may be in locating or suggesting a qualified physician or psychologist to conduct the examination.

5. Request for admissions (FRCP 36)

Rule 36 permits parties to ask opponents in writing before trial to admit the truthfulness of facts or of the genuineness of documents or things related to the case. Responses must be submitted in writing and must fairly and in good faith respond to the substance of the request. For example, the answering party cannot simply give lack of knowledge or information as a reason for failing to admit unless they have conducted a reasonable inquiry into it. Failure of a party to respond to the requests to admit in a timely fashion or giving an insufficient reason for failing to admit the matter requested may result in the matter being deemed admitted against them. And if the answering party refuses to admit the matter requested and the asking party proves that matter as true at trial, the court has the discretion to impose the costs the asking party incurred in proving the matter on the answering party even if the answering party prevails at trial.

FRCP 36 is a useful tool to cut down on what has to be proven at trial. Getting the opposing side to admit what is undisputed means it need not be proven at trial, reducing the time and expense of the trial. It is also a useful tactical tool, causing a party confronted with a request to admit on an issue on which they are likely to lose at trial to run the risk of costs being imposed on them if they fail to admit prior to trial.

The role of the paralegal in connection with this Rule includes identifying factual and other matters that can be the subject of a request to admit, recommending its use to the supervising attorney, and then drafting the request. As with all discovery documents, careful, concise drafting of the requests to admit is critical to their successful use. (See Illustration 4-13.)

D. Drafting Guidelines for Discovery Documents

One of the most important skills that a paralegal can possess is the ability to draft legal documents well. Nowhere is this more important than in drafting discovery documents such as interrogatories, document requests, and related discovery motions. It is a skill that is developed over time from practice. Here are some general drafting guidelines in the discovery area. Keep in mind that these guidelines apply to the drafting of all kinds of legal documents.

1. Identify and organize the topics to be addressed

Start by brainstorming a list of the areas of inquiry and then rework that list into carefully worded questions placed in a logical order—what should be asked first, second, etc. By doing this you will eliminate duplicative questions that need not be asked in an interrogatory. (See LBD 4-4.)

2. Use clear and concise language

Avoid vague, unclear, or ambiguous terms or phrases. Remember our system is an adversarial one. That means the opposing party that receives your attorney's interrogatories will be scrutinizing them carefully to avoid answering any more than the interrogatory calls for—as your side will do for interrogatories served on your client. If a question contains a word or phrase that is vague or ambiguous, it may be objected to on that grounds rather than answered. Though you may eventually clear up the objection through negotiation or court order, the consequence is delay and additional time and expense that could have been avoided.

It may take several rounds of editing to make your interrogatories clear and concise but it is worth the effort. Read over your draft of interrogatories and ask yourself, "What am I really asking for here? Is

Illustration 4-13   REQUEST FOR ADMISSIONS

IN THE UNITED STATES DISTRICT COURT
FOR THE EASTERN DISTRICT OF YOURSTATE
NORTHERN DIVISION

BEN RUNOVER,
    Plaintiff
 	
    v.
SOFT LANDING, INC., and
WORLD WIDE INDUSTRIES, INC.
    Defendant
	)
	)
	)
	) DOCKET NO. 03-00001
	)
	)
	)
	)

PLAINTIFF'S FIRST REQUEST FOR ADMISSIONS FROM DEFENDANTS

Plaintiff, Ben Runover, pursuant to Rule 36 of the Federal Rules of Civil Procedure, hereby requests that defendants Soft Landing, Inc., and World Wide Industries, Inc., admit the following facts and genuineness of documents.

1. The Safe Bag 1000 car air bag system was designed by defendant World Wide Industries, Inc., between 1997 and 2000.

2. In 1999 defendant World Wide Industries, Inc., caused defendant Soft Landing, Inc., to be incorporated under the laws of the state of Delaware.

3. Defendant Soft Landing, Inc., was incorporated for the purpose of marketing the Safe Bag 1000 car air bag system to the American automobile industry.

4. At all times since its incorporation, all outstanding shares of stock in defendant Soft Landing, Inc., have been owned by defendant World Wide Industries, Inc.

5. The letter attached as *Exhibit 1* to this request for admissions is a true, genuine, and authentic copy of a memorandum dated September 4, 1998 from Dr. Bright Idea, Chief Engineer of the Design/Build Division of Soft Landing, Inc., to the Legal Department of Soft Landing, Inc.

6. The letter attached as *Exhibit 2* to this request for admissions is a true, genuine, and authentic copy of a letter dated September 22, 1998 from Marcus Jawosky, President of defendant Soft Landing, Inc., to John Brown, President of defendant World Wide Industries, Inc.

7. The letter attached as *Exhibit 2* to this request for admissions was written in response to the memorandum attached as *Exhibit 1* to this request for admissions.

_____
Mellow Fellow
Attorney for plaintiff Ben Runover
(Address)

(Certificate of service omitted)

it clear to me? Will it be clear to the one receiving it? Will they be able to object to it in good faith? Can I say this any better?"

HYPOTHETICAL 4-4

Assume that your supervising attorney has filed suit on behalf of Ben Runover against Needa Floorit and Funny Bread, Inc., alleging negligence by Needa Floorit in operating the truck on behalf of Funny Bread. The attorney for defendant Needa Floorit serves a set of interrogatories on Ben Runover, which you are assigned to review. The following questions are included in the interrogatories you are reviewing.

1. What were you doing before the accident happened?
2. State whether you have been injured and, if so, how.
3. List all medications you were taking prior to this accident.
4. Explain in detail how you can't do anything now that you could do before the accident.
5. List everybody who saw your car or might have seen it before or after the accident.
6. List all medical problems you had before this accident and the names of everybody who helped you with them and when.
7. Were you alone or by yourself when the accident happened and if you weren't who was with you?
8. List everybody you talked to after the accident.
9. List all your bills and how much they are.
10. Explain in your own words how this accident could have been avoided.

What, if any, objection would you suggest your supervising attorney make to each of these questions?

How would you word the objections if your supervising attorney asks you to prepare a draft response?

Try your hand at rewriting each question to make it clearer.

3. Be thorough

Be sure your questions cover all the areas you intended. And be sure they are worded well enough to cover all the information you want to obtain. Don't leave loopholes in your questions. The other side will find them.

4. Don't be wordy

Generally, the fewer and simpler words you use in your interrogatories, the clearer and more concise they will be. It is a real art to achieve the goals of clarity, conciseness, and thoroughness using the simplest words possible. Remember, practice makes perfect.

5. Use subparts carefully

In general, subparts should be used in a question only if the subparts are substantially related to the main question. The expert witness interrogatory is a good example:

Identify every expert witness that you expect to use at trial and for each one identified state:

1) all opinions they will offer;
2) the factual or other basis for each such opinion; and

3) all data or other information considered by the expert in reaching each such opinion.

Remember you are allowed only a limited number of interrogatories. Poorly worded subparts may be considered more than one question.

6. Use definitions

Good interrogatories contain definitions of words and phrases unique to the case or that might be objected to otherwise as vague or over broad. For example, in the Ben Runover case, you will be asking many questions about the accident. To avoid confusion over which accident or an objection for vagueness if you simply refer to it in your questions as "the accident," and to avoid needless repetition, define the phrase "the accident" before you ask any questions using it. (See Illustration 4-14.)

If you are going to ask the opposing party to "identify" witnesses or documents, which is regularly done in interrogatories, define that word before you use it in questions. What it means to you might not be how the opposing party chooses to interpret it. (See Illustration 4-14.) Other similar words and phrases that are often defined in interrogatories include **plaintiff, defendant, document(s),** and **person(s).**

Once you have defined a word or phrase, you need only use the word or phrase in succeeding questions and not the entire definition. For example, if you have defined "identify" when used in reference to a person to mean to state his or her entire name, current or last known home and business addresses, current or last known home and business phone numbers, etc., you don't have to repeat that entire definition in every interrogatory in which you ask the opposing party to identify someone.

In fact, once you have defined a word or phrase, you should be sure to use the word or phrase throughout the interrogatories. It may be confusing and possibly objectionable to fail to use the defined term.

EXAMPLE

In the Ben Runover case, if you have defined "Cadillac" to mean the car operated by plaintiff at the time of the accident, don't refer to it in the interrogatories as "the Cadillac automobile" or "plaintiff's car."

7. Use instructions with caution

Some attorneys like to use general instructions along with definitions in interrogatories. For example, there may be a general instruction that says: "For each answer provided, state the identity of each person known to have personal knowledge of the answer."

Instructions should be used with caution. First, there are already extensive rules regarding the answering of interrogatories set forth in the rules of procedure and it may be onerous and objectionable to attempt to add to those obligations with instructions.

Second, many instructions tend to be duplicative of requirements already set out in the rules of procedure and thus needlessly redundant.

Illustration 4-14 DEFINITIONS IN INTERROGATORIES

For purposes of these interrogatories the following definitions shall apply:

1. The word "plaintiff" shall mean plaintiff Ben Runover.

2. The word "Floorit" shall mean defendant Needa Floorit.

3. The letters "FBI" shall mean defendant Funny Bread, Inc.

4. The phrase, "the accident" shall mean that collision between the automobile operated by plaintiff Ben Runover and the truck operated by defendant Needa Floorit which occurred on April 1, 1999 at the intersection of Fifth Street and Vine in Harmony City, Yourstate and which is referenced in the original complaint filed in this cause.

5. The word "Cadillac" shall mean that automobile operated by plaintiff at the time of the accident.

6. The word "truck" shall mean that truck operated by Floorit at the time of the accident.

7. The word "person" shall mean all natural persons and entities, including, without limitation, all sole proprietorships, associations, companies, corporations, partnerships, joint venturers, limited liability companies, trusts, estates, agencies, licensing arrangements, franchise arrangements, and any other business arrangement.

8. The word "document(s)" shall mean all written, recorded or graphic matter, however produced, reproduced or stored, including, but not limited to, photographs, audio or video tapes, transcripts, data stored on computer disk or by other electronic means, correspondence, notes, memoranda, interoffice communications, studies, analysis, reports, reviews, proposals, contracts, working papers, statistical reports, blue prints, sketches, drawings, drafts, computer data, calendars, diaries, books of account, inventories, business records, financial records, or documents similar to any of the foregoing, however denominated.

9. The word "identify" when used with respect to a person(s) shall mean to:

   a. state the fullest known name, present or last known address(es), designating which, and telephone number(s) of such person;
   b. provide the name and address of the present or last known employer(s), place of employment, and job title of such person; and
   c. if such person was affiliated at any time with a party to this litigation by employment or otherwise, to state the nature (including job title, if any) and dates of such affiliation.

10. The word "identify" when used with respect to a document shall mean to:

   a. specify the nature of the document (such as, for example, letter, memorandum, etc.);
   b. state the date, if any, appearing on the document or, if none, the date upon which the document was prepared;
   c. identify each person who wrote, signed, dictated, or otherwise participated in the preparation of the document; and
   d. identify each person, if any, who was an addressee or recipient of the document.

This is especially true of instructions which purport to require the other party to supplement their responses at a later date if they discover additional information pertinent to an answer given earlier or if they discover their original answer was incorrect. FRCP 26(e) imposes an obligation on all parties responding to discovery requests to supplement their responses under certain circumstances. An instruction to do so is needlessly repetitive. And, if the instruction purports to impose an obligation on the other party in excess of that imposed by Rule 26(e), it will likely draw an objection.

Third, instructions tend to add to the complexity and difficulty of answering interrogatories, which are already burdensome enough. Thus, instructions should typically be used only in highly technical or complex cases when there is good reason to do so.

8. Avoid abusing discovery

Interrogatories historically have been the most misused discovery method. They are too often used merely to harass another party by keeping them busy, to increase the other lawyer's time spent on the case, or to run up the opposing client's bill. The wording of interrogatories can make them tricky, burdensome, or needlessly complex. Never do this on purpose. That is **sharp practice** (behavior that is on the fine line of being dishonest) at best and often unethical.

The courts generally do not favor interrogatories because they are subject to abuse and may accordingly be sympathetic to a motion for protective order and sanctions. Also, remember that what goes around comes around, and the law office that files needlessly lengthy, poorly worded, tricky, or burdensome interrogatories may see the same instructions coming back at them. Just try objecting to them then!

9. Before responding to discovery requests review them carefully for objections

Advise the supervising attorney as to your suggestions. See the discussion of objections above.

10. In responding to discovery requests, answer only what is fairly asked

It is a cardinal rule in responding to all formal discovery not to volunteer information. In answering interrogatories, help the client draft a truthful response, but one which gives no more information than is asked. And with document requests, produce the documents that fairly correspond to the request but nothing more.

11. Comply with all rules of procedure and local rules of court regarding discovery

For example, it is common in both state and federal courts for the courts to adopt local rules directing that interrogatories, document requests, etc., not be filed with the clerk but only the responses thereto or motions relating to discovery disputes. Know those rules and comply with them strictly (see LBD 4-7).

E.

The Order of Discovery

The rules of formal discovery in civil litigation provide for broad, comprehensive discovery from opposing parties and witnesses. To maximize their effectiveness and avoid wasted or duplicative effort and expense, the attorney and paralegal should carefully plan in what order the formal discovery tools will be utilized in a particular case. Every case will call for its own analysis but generally the formal discovery in a civil case should proceed in this order:

1. Interrogatories and document requests

Interrogatories and document requests should be utilized first, and simultaneously. If well planned and carefully worded, they will obtain the broad general information and documents needed to plan more detailed and specific formal and informal discovery.

2. Depositions

The depositions of parties and witnesses are taken after interrogatories have been answered and documents produced for inspection. The oral examination of a party will be much more comprehensive and effective if the attorney has background information from interrogatory answers and responses to document requests.

3. Requests for physical or mental examination

Requests for physical or mental exams can occur at any time during a civil case, but typically occur after the plaintiff's medical condition and history has been discovered and the plaintiff deposed.

4. Requests for admissions

This discovery tool can be used early on to clarify exactly what has to be proven and what doesn't. But generally it is used near the time of trial after other discovery has been completed. Or, it can be used to lay the groundwork for a dispositive pretrial motion such as a Rule 56 motion for summary judgment, to demonstrate conclusively that there is no genuine issue of any material fact.

KEY WORDS AND PHRASES TO REMEMBER

deposition
deposition index
deposition summary
docket control
document request
expert witness

independent medical exam
interrogatory
motion to compel discovery
notice of deposition
objection
over broad

proof of service
protective order
request for admission
request for physical or mental exam
request for production of
   documents and things
sanctions

scope of discovery
sharp practice
subpoena
subpoena *duces tecum*
transcript
vague
waiver of signature

LEARN BY DOING

LBD 4-1. Determine whether the rules of procedure governing civil actions in the state courts of your state or the local rules of your state trial court(s) contain a voluntary disclosure rule similar to FRCP 26(a). If so, prepare a memorandum comparing any differences in the state and federal rules.

LBD 4-2. Your instructor will provide you with the transcript of a deposition. You are to prepare a chronological index of the deposition, then a subject matter index of it, and finally a narrative summary of the deposition.

LBD 4-3. Arrange and conduct the interview of a trial attorney or a litigation paralegal regarding the importance of the paralegal being familiar with the adversarial system and the rules of civil and/or criminal procedure including, in particular, the discovery rules, to effectively assist the trial lawyer in pre-filing investigation, formal discovery, trial preparation, and trial.

LBD 4-4. Assume you are asked by your supervising attorney to work on a case involving the following facts. Your client, Big John, broke his leg while working for his employer Slim Jim, Inc., on a construction site. Big John's doctor, Dr. Jack, set the leg and sent him to Big Bargain Home Health Care, Inc. ("BBHHC"), to rent a crutch, instructing Big John to use it for two weeks before returning to see him. Big John, who is 6'3" and weighs 240 lbs., went to BBHHC and was fitted for a crutch by Sally Slack, a new, part-time employee of BBHHC. Ms. Slack had the owner of BBHHC, Little Jake, check the fitting of the crutch before Big John left the premises. Two days later the crutch gave way as Big John was coming down a set of stairs and he fell, breaking his other leg. The crutch has a sticker on it saying it was made by B & J, Inc., a corporation in your state. Suit will be filed by your supervising lawyer on behalf of Big John in the general trial court of your state. The theories of liability will include negligence and strict liability due to an inherently dangerous and defective crutch. Do the following:

(a) List prospective defendants in this suit.
(b) List prospective witnesses to be deposed in this suit.
(c) Select one of the prospective witnesses you listed in (b) and do the following:
   (1) Outline the questions your lawyer should ask that witness.
   (2) List the documents, if any, that should be requested or subpoenaed to the deposition of that witness.

(3) Prepare an appropriate notice of deposition to be served on opposing counsel in connection with the deposition of that witness.

(4) Prepare an appropriate deposition subpoena for that witness.

(5) Assuming suit has been filed, draft a letter to the opposing counsel confirming the agreed-upon date for the deposition and enclosing the notice.

(6) Assuming suit has been filed, draft a letter to the court reporter confirming the arrangements for the deposition.

LBD 4-5. Assume the same facts as in LBD 4-4 and assume further that suit is filed on behalf of Big John against defendants including BBHHC. Draft a set of interrogatories and document requests on behalf of Big John to this defendant.

LBD 4-6. Determine whether the rules of procedure governing civil actions in the state trial court(s) of your state or local court rules or case law authorize the discovery of (a) the existence and provisions of liability insurance agreements as is permitted by FRCP 26(a) and (b) the financial condition of a defendant. Prepare a memorandum summarizing the law in your state regarding these matters and detailing the circumstances under which such discovery is permitted.

LBD 4-7. Using the online resources for the federal judiciary and for state and local governments in Appendix E, Resources for the Investigator, see if you can locate online the local rules for (1) the U.S. District Court in your federal district and (2) the state courts of your state.

Chapter 5

Formal Discovery in Criminal Litigation

CHAPTER OUTLINE

A. The Scope of Formal Discovery in Criminal Litigation
B. Means of Formal Discovery Available to the Defense in Criminal Litigation
C. Means of Formal Discovery Available to the Prosecution in Criminal Litigation
D. The Resolution of Discovery Disputes in Criminal Litigation
E. The Role of the Paralegal in Formal Criminal Discovery

CHAPTER OBJECTIVES

In this chapter you will learn:

- The procedural rules that govern formal discovery in a criminal case.
- The kinds of information that are discoverable by the defense and by the prosecution in criminal litigation.
- The role of pretrial hearings in discovery in a criminal case.
- The use of motions in a criminal case to aid in discovery.
- The role of the paralegal in formal discovery in a criminal case.

A. The Scope of Formal Discovery in Criminal Litigation

At both the state and federal levels, formal discovery in criminal litigation is more limited than in civil litigation. Consequently, for both the prosecution and the defense, great reliance must be placed on informal investigation. Otherwise, **trial by ambush** is a possibility.

Still, there are a number of formal procedures in the criminal process that provide discovery opportunities. (It may be helpful at this time to review the stages of a criminal case as set forth in Illustration 3-4.) At the federal level, the scope and means of formal discovery in criminal cases is controlled by the Federal Rules of Criminal Procedure (FRCrP) and by certain constitutional rights as determined by the U.S. Supreme Court. Many states have modeled their rules of criminal procedure after the FRCrP, but the paralegal who works in the criminal area for either the prosecutor or defense attorney should be familiar with both the federal and state rules. (See LBD 5-1 and 5-2.)

Under the FRCrP and the procedure of most states, the scope and means of formal discovery available to the defense are different from those available to the prosecution. We will therefore address the discovery available to the defense and prosecution separately. The FRCrP referenced in this chapter are set out in Appendix C. (See Appendix E, Resources for the Investigator, for additional resource material related to criminal law.)

B. Means of Formal Discovery Available to the Defense in Criminal Litigation

HYPOTHETICAL 5-1

Aluh Bye is a paralegal working for attorney Plea Bargain who specializes in criminal defense. Plea Bargain has been retained to defend Yugotta Bekiddin, a thirty-year-old man who has been arrested and charged by the state with aggravated robbery. Bekiddin called Plea Bargain from jail following his arrest on the morning of January 6, 2004, and asked Plea Bargain to be present on his behalf later that day at the initial appearance.

The story the client tells is that on January 5 he took his girlfriend out to a fancy dinner at Gino's Italian Restaurant in Capital City. He planned to propose marriage to her during the dinner. Last Christmas Yugotta had been given a gift certificate by his mother, good for a dinner for two at Gino's. He presented the gift certificate to the hostess when he and his girlfriend arrived and they were seated at a private table in a quiet corner of the restaurant. They both ordered the house specialty, spaghetti with meatballs. Everything was fine until the couple began to try to eat the spaghetti. The noodles were tough as leather and the meatballs hard as rocks. The sauce had the consistency of motor oil. Yugotta says it was impossible to eat.

Frustrated, Yugotta called the waiter over and told him they could not eat the spaghetti. He requested that they be served something else. The waiter said that was fine and brought them both a seafood pasta that was delicious. Just as the couple was finishing their pasta and Yugotta was reaching into his pocket for the engagement ring, the waiter approached the table, presented a bill in the amount of $68.92, and asked if Yugotta would be paying with cash or credit card. Yugotta reminded the waiter about the gift certificate. The waiter responded by saying he knew about the gift certificate, but it only covered the spaghetti dinners, not the seafood pasta. Yugotta said that he was broke and asked to see the owner.

Shortly thereafter, another man came to the table who identified himself as Gino Maretti, owner of the restaurant. He asked what the problem was. Yugotta says he again explained that the spaghetti was inedible and that he and his girlfriend had asked to be served something else in its place and assumed the seafood pasta dinners would be covered by the gift certificate. Maretti replied that he was sorry for the apparent misunderstanding, but that the gift certificate would only cover the spaghetti dinners, not the seafood pasta and the bill for $68.92 would have to be paid.

Yugotta Bekiddin says that he told Maretti, "You gotta be kiddin me," but Maretti said he was entirely serious. Yugotta then told Maretti he refused to pay for the seafood pasta. His girlfriend intervened at that point and paid the bill in cash, saying she didn't want a nasty scene.

Everything would have been all right except that as Yugotta and his girlfriend were leaving the restaurant, Maretti spoke to his girlfriend and said, "You and Mr. Big Spender have a nice evening." Yugotta says he lost it at that point. He went back to the table where the cold spaghetti was still sitting, dumped a plate of it into a cloth napkin, twisted the ends of the napkin into a handle and came back to the cash register. He demanded the refund of the $68.92 and when Maretti refused, he banged the napkin with the spaghetti and meatballs inside against the counter several times, causing Maretti to back away. Yugotta says he didn't mean to frighten Maretti with the spaghetti, didn't ever strike him, and thinks Maretti only backed away so the spaghetti sauce wouldn't splatter on him. Yugotta told Maretti he wasn't leaving until the money was refunded, at which point Maretti opened the cash register and handed his girlfriend $68.92. Yugotta's girlfriend backs him up on his story.

Yugotta had no idea anything was wrong until he was arrested early in the morning of January 6 at his house. The arresting officer told him he was under arrest for aggravated robbery.

1. Review of the criminal complaint

SLEUTH ON THE LOOSE

Access *www.capindex .com/zipcode.htm* and check the criminal statistics for your ZIP code. Then try the same using a ZIP code where a friend or relative lives.

Under FRCrP 4 the **criminal complaint** may be used to obtain either an arrest warrant for a defendant or a summons ordering the defendant to appear before a magistrate. The criminal complaint is the initial charging instrument in a criminal case and, pursuant to FRCrP 4(a), it must establish "probable cause that an offense has been committed and that the defendant committed it." If the accused is arrested without a warrant, FRCrP 5(a) requires that a criminal complaint satisfying the probable cause requirements of FRCrP 4(a) "shall be promptly filed." The criminal complaint may also be used by the prosecution to establish probable cause at the preliminary examination under FRCrP 5.1. FRCrP 3 defines the criminal complaint as follows:

The complaint is a written statement of the essential facts constituting the offense charged. It shall be made upon oath before a magistrate judge.

Illustration 5-1 sets forth the form of the criminal complaint used in the federal courts. Illustration 5-2 sets forth the form of the summons in a criminal case used in the federal courts.

Reviewing the criminal complaint in a case is the first means of formal discovery available to the attorney representing the criminal accused. FRCrP 4(b) provides that the criminal complaint need not be written upon personal knowledge and the officer executing the complaint can rely on hearsay and inference from circumstantial evidence. However, the criminal complaint must set forth the facts alleged by the prosecution constituting the offense, and it may be supported by **affidavits** (sworn signed statements) of police officers, victims or witnesses with personal knowledge of the facts. Thus, reviewing the criminal complaint may provide the defense team with important information about the prosecution's case against their client.

HYPOTHETICAL 5-2

Before going to the initial appearance for Yugotta Bekiddin, Plea Bargain has asked Aluh Bye to do some legal research and factual investigation into the charges against the client. Aluh Bye goes first to the law library to locate the aggravated robbery statute and to determine the penalty for conviction under the statute. The aggravated robbery statute located by Aluh Bye in the criminal code for Yourstate provides as follows:

YS. Crim. Code §39-13-402: Aggravated Robbery.

(a) Aggravated robbery is robbery as defined in §39-13-401:

(1) Accomplished with a deadly weapon or by display of any article used or fashioned to lead the victim to reasonably believe it to be a deadly weapon; or
(2) Where the victim suffers serious bodily injury.

(b) Aggravated robbery is a Class B felony.

Since the statute refers to the crime of robbery, Aluh Bye also locates the robbery statute, which reads as follows:

YS. Crim. Code §39-13-401: Robbery.

(a) Robbery is the intentional or knowing theft of property from the person of another by violence or putting the person in fear.
(b) Robbery is a Class C felony.

Aluh Bye also checks on the definition of a "deadly weapon" under the criminal code and finds the following:

YS. Crim. Code §39-11-106: Definitions
(a) The following definitions apply in this title:. . .

(5) "Deadly weapon" means:

(A) A firearm or anything manifestly designed, made or adapted for the purpose of inflicting death or serious bodily injury; or

(B) Anything that in the manner of its use or intended use is capable of causing death or serious bodily injury.

Aluh Bye also determines that a Class C felony is punishable by up to 15 years incarceration and a Class B felony by up to 25 years incarceration.

Next, Aluh Bye goes to the Criminal Court Clerk's office and obtains a copy of the criminal complaint filed against Yugotta Bekiddin. The criminal complaint against Yugotta Bekiddin is set forth in Illustration 5-3.

1. Note that the criminal complaint in Illustration 5-3 is not accompanied by an affidavit of any eyewitness to the alleged crime. Does that make it defective to support an arrest warrant?
2. Does the criminal complaint in Illustration 5-3 allege sufficient facts to establish probable cause that Yugotta Bekiddin committed the crime of aggravated robbery as it is defined in YS. Crim. Code §39-13-402?
3. How complete a picture of what happened at Gino's Italian Restaurant can we gather from the criminal complaint in this case?

Illustration 5-1

CRIMINAL
COMPLAINT FORM
USED IN FEDERAL
COURT

AO 91 (Rev. 5/85) Criminal Complaint

United States District Court

DISTRICT OF _____

UNITED STATES OF AMERICA

V.

CRIMINAL COMPLAINT

CASE NUMBER:

(Name and Address of Defendant)

I, the undersigned complainant being duly sworn state the following is true and correct to the best of my

knowledge and belief. On or about _____ in _____ county, in the

_____ District of _____ defendant(s) did, (Track Statutory Language of Offense)

in violation of Title _____ United States Code, Section(s) _____ .

I further state that I am a(n) _____ and that this complaint is based on the following
                                    Official Title

facts:

Continued on the attached sheet and made a part hereof: ☐ Yes   ☐ No

_____
Signature of Complainant

Sworn to before me and subscribed in my presence,

_____ at _____
Date   City and State

_____   _____
Name & Title of Judicial Officer   Signature of Judicial Officer

2. The initial appearance

After an arrest, FRCrP 5(a) requires the accused be taken before a federal magistrate judge for an initial appearance, "without unnecessary delay." In most cases this **initial appearance** will be made within 24 hours of the arrest, unless the arrest is effected on a weekend in which case the initial appearance may be delayed to the following Monday. Little happens at the initial appearance that advances discovery. The judge will confirm the identity of the defendant as the one named in the criminal complaint, advise the defendant of his various rights and, if necessary, appoint counsel to defend the accused. The one exception

Illustration 5-2

SUMMONS IN A
CRIMINAL CASE
FORM USED IN
FEDERAL COURT

AO 83 (Rev. 12/85) Summons in a Criminal Case

United States District Court

DISTRICT OF ————————

UNITED STATES OF AMERICA
V.

SUMMONS IN A CRIMINAL CASE

CASE NUMBER:

(Name and address of defendant)

YOU ARE HEREBY COMMANDED to appear before the United States District Court at the place, date and time set forth below.

Place		Room
		Date and Time
Before:		

To answer a(n)

☐ Indictment ☐ Information ☐ Complaint ☐ Violation Notice ☐ Probation Violation Petition

Charging you with a violation of Title_____United States Code, Section(s)_____

Brief description of offense:

Signature of Issuing Officer   Date

Name and Title of Issuing Officer

---

involves the judge's decision on whether to grant a **pretrial release** to the defendant who is in custody (sometimes called the bail/bond hearing). The judge has the discretion to release a criminal defendant until trial on his personal recognizance, or upon posting cash **bail, surety bond,** or **property bond** in an amount set by the court.

The purpose of the bail/bond requirement is to ensure that the defendant will appear at trial—the defendant who does not forfeits the bail or bond posted. The judge also has the discretion to deny bail or bond and order the defendant held until trial if there is good reason to believe the defendant will flee before trial or that he poses a threat to the community.

The prosecution, if it is arguing for no pretrial release or for the setting

Illustration 5-2

SUMMONS IN A
CRIMINAL CASE
FORM USED IN
FEDERAL COURT
(continued)

AO 83 (Rev. 12/85) Summons in a Criminal Case

RETURN OF SERVICE

Date

Service was made by me on:[1]

Check one box below to indicate appropriate method of service

☐ Served personally upon the defendant at:_____
_____

☐ Left summons at the defendant's dwelling house or usual place of abode with a person of suitable age and
discretion then residing therein and mailed a copy of the summons to the defendant's last known address.
Name of person with whom the summons was left:_____
_____

☐ Returned unexecuted:_____
_____
_____
_____

          I declare under penalty of perjury under the laws of the United States of America that the foregoing
information contained in the Return of Service is true and correct.

Returned on _____   _____
                        Date   Name of United States Marshal

                                                                      _____
                                                                        (by) Deputy United States Marshal

Remarks:

(1)   As to who may serve a summons see Rule 4 of the Federal Rules of Criminal Procedure.

of a high bail figure, will have the burden of convincing the judge that there is good reason to believe that the defendant will flee or that he poses a risk to the community. There are some federal and state statutes which create a *presumption* of intent to flee or danger to the community. Serious drug charges may carry with them the former presumption and crimes of violence charged against someone with a prior conviction involving violence committed during a pretrial release often carry with them the latter presumption. In that case the burden will shift to the defense to rebut the presumption. To carry its burden on the bail issue, the prosecution may disclose information by way of oral argument or by calling witnesses. And that may provide the defendant more information about the case than appears in the criminal complaint. Thus the initial appearance may be a discovery opportunity for the defense.

Illustration 5-3   CRIMINAL COMPLAINT

IN THE CRIMINAL COURT
FOR HARMONY COUNTY, YOURSTATE

STATE OF YOURSTATE	)	CRIMINAL COMPLAINT
v.	)	
YUGOTTA BEKIDDIN	)	CASE NO. 2004-199CR

I, the undersigned complainant, being duly sworn according to law, state that the following is true and correct to the best of my knowledge and belief: On or about the 5th day of January, 2004, in Capital City, Harmony County, Yourstate, defendant did commit a robbery and accomplished same with a deadly weapon or by display of an article used or fashioned to lead the victim to reasonably believe it to be a deadly weapon in violation of YS. Crim. Code §39-13-402, Aggravated Robbery.

I further state that I am a Sergeant with the Capital City Police Department and that this complaint is based upon the following facts: At 9:15 P.M. on 1-5-2004 my partner and I received a call to respond to an assault in progress at Gino's Italian Restaurant, 533 West Main Street in Capital City. Arriving at 9:18 P.M. I was informed by the proprietor of Gino's Italian Restaurant, Gino Maretti, that the defendant had robbed him of $68.92 by threatening to strike him about the head and shoulders with a club.

_____
                                            Complainant

Sworn to before me and subscribed in my presence this _____ day of _____, 2004 at
_____.

_____   _____
Name and Title of Judicial Officer   Judicial Officer

At the initial appearance, the judge will also schedule the preliminary examination, to be conducted not later than 10 days following the initial appearance if the defendant is in custody and 20 days if the defendant is not in custody.

3. The preliminary examination

At the **preliminary examination** (usually called a **preliminary hearing** under state rules of criminal procedure) the judge hears proof to determine if there is **probable cause** to believe that the accused committed the crime alleged. If probable cause is found by the judge, the case is bound over to a grand jury or to trial. If probable cause is not found by the judge, the charges are dismissed and the defendant released.

The preliminary examination is adversarial with witnesses called by both the prosecution and the defense if it chooses to do so, and the attorneys make argument to the judge. Consequently, this hearing can be an important source of discovery for the defense in hearing at least part of the prosecution's case, and for the prosecution to the extent the defense calls witnesses or takes a position in legal argument. However, the preliminary examination has limitations on its usefulness as a formal discovery technique.

a. Frequently, no preliminary examination is held

There is no constitutional right to a preliminary examination. *Gerstein v. Pugh*, 420 U.S. 103 (1975). A few states do not have a preliminary examination procedure at all. In those that do, the prosecution can usually avoid the hearing by submitting the case directly to the grand jury for an indictment or by filing an information directly (see discussion below). In the federal system, if a grand jury indictment has issued, the preliminary examination can be dispensed with. 8 U.S.C. §3060(e). (See LBD 5-1.)

Grand jury proceedings are non-public, secret proceedings at both the federal and state levels, so they do not provide a discovery opportunity to the defense. Defendants can also waive their right to a preliminary examination where such right exists.

b. There typically is little time to prepare for the preliminary examination

Since the preliminary examination must occur within 10 days of the initial hearing, if the defendant is in custody and within 20 days if the defendant has been released, time to prepare is limited. Most states have similar time limitations for their preliminary hearings.

c. The prosecution need not present its entire case at the preliminary examination

The only burden placed on the government at the preliminary examination is to show probable cause that the offense occurred and that the defendant probably committed the offense. The probable cause threshold is far below the **beyond a reasonable doubt** burden that the government must meet to convict at trial. Accordingly, and since the prosecution knows that the preliminary examination often presents a discovery opportunity to the defense, the prosecution may not present its entire case or even its best proof. Instead it will usually rely on the same information set forth in the criminal complaint.

4. The information and the indictment

The **information** is the formal charging instrument filed by prosecutors. The **indictment** is the formal charge issued by the grand jury. The **grand jury** consists of 16 to 23 people selected from the community (the number may be different in state proceedings) to hear evidence of alleged criminal conduct, and it has the power to issue an indictment based on a finding of probable cause. Procedures before the grand jury are unique in our adversarial system for several reasons. First, grand juries are closed to the public; not even the defendant is entitled to attend. Second, only the prosecutor may present evidence to the grand jury; the defendant has no right to appear, testify, present proof, or cross examine prosecution witnesses. Third, the actions of the grand jury are secret; no one in attendance may disclose what transpired. Fourth, those who testify before the grand jury have no right to have an attorney present with them in the grand jury room. In most states, however, witnesses are permitted to leave the jury room to confer with their attorney before returning to answer.

The grand jury has the power to subpoena witnesses to appear, to subpoena the production of documents and things, to hold reluctant witnesses in contempt, and to grant immunity from prosecution. Illustration 5-4 shows the form of grand jury subpoena used in federal grand jury proceedings.

When an information is filed or an indictment issued, it will replace the criminal complaint as the formal charging document in the case. Note that the information and the indictment are *alternative* charging instruments. You would never have both issued in one case. The Fifth

Illustration 5-4
FEDERAL GRAND
JURY SUBPOENA
FORM

AO 110 (Rev. 12/89) Subpoena to Testify Before Grand Jury

United States District Court

DISTRICT OF

TO:

SUBPOENA TO TESTIFY
BEFORE GRAND JURY

SUBPOENA FOR:

☐ PERSON   ☐ DOCUMENT(S) OR OBJECT(S)

YOU ARE HEREBY COMMANDED to appear and testify before the Grand Jury of the United States District Court at the place, date, and time specified below.

PLACE	COURTROOM
	DATE AND TIME

YOU ARE ALSO COMMANDED to bring with you the following document(s) or object(s):*

☐ *Please see additional information on reverse*

This subpoena shall remain in effect until you are granted leave to depart by the court or by an officer acting on behalf of the court.

CLERK	DATE
(BY) DEPUTY CLERK	

This subpoena is issued on application of the United States of America	NAME, ADDRESS AND PHONE NUMBER OF ASSISTANT U.S. ATTORNEY

*If not applicable, enter "none"

Illustration 5-4

FEDERAL GRAND
JURY SUBPOENA
FORM *(continued)*

AO 110 (Rev. 12/89) Subpoena to Testify Before Grand Jury

RETURN OF SERVICE [1]			
RECEIVED BY SERVER	DATE	PLACE	
SERVED	DATE	PLACE	
SERVED ON (PRINT NAME)			
SERVED BY (PRINT NAME)		TITLE	

STATEMENT OF SERVICE FEES

TRAVEL	SERVICES	TOTAL

DECLARATION OF SERVER [2]

I declare under penalty of perjury under the laws of the United States of America that the foregoing information contained in the Return of Service and Statement of Service Fees is true and correct.

Executed on _____
              Date   Signature of Server

                                      _____
                                      Address of Server

Additional Information

[1] As to who may serve a subpoena and the manner of its service see Rule 17(d), Federal Rules of Criminal Procedure, or Rule 45(c), Federal Rules of Civil Procedure.

[2] "Fees and mileage need not be tendered to the witness upon service of a subpoena issued on behalf of the United States or an officer or agency thereof (Rule 45(c), Federal Rules of Civil Procedure; Rule 17(d), Federal Rules of Criminal Procedure) or on behalf of certain indigent parties and criminal defendants who are unable to pay such costs (28 USC 1825, Rule 17(b) Federal Rules of Criminal Procedure)".

Amendment to the United States Constitution requires that all prosecutions for capital and infamous crimes be by indictment. The Supreme Court held long ago that "infamous" means crimes punishable by imprisonment for more than a year. *Ex parte Wilson*, 114 U.S. 417 (1884). Today, FRCrP 7 provides as follows:

> An offense which may be punished by death shall be prosecuted by indictment. An offense which may be punished by imprisonment for a term exceeding one year or at hard labor shall be prosecuted by indictment or, if indictment is waived, it may be prosecuted by information. Any other offense may be prosecuted by indictment or information. An information may be filed without leave of court.

A defendant may waive his right to grand jury review in all federal cases except those involving the **death penalty** (*capital cases*) and consent to be prosecuted by information. Illustration 5-5 sets forth the **waiver of indictment** form used in the federal courts.

The Supreme Court has never held that the Fifth Amendment right to grand jury review is a **fundamental right** or a right *essential to an ordered liberty* and therefore has never said that it is applicable to the states under the Fourteenth Amendment pursuant to the **selective incorporation doctrine.** (See *Hurtado v. California*, 110 U.S. 516 (1884).) However, many states have the grand jury system and require that serious charges be prosecuted by indictment. (See LBD 5-1.)

Illustration 5-5

WAIVER OF INDICTMENT FORM USED IN FEDERAL COURT

AO 455 (Rev. 5/85) Waiver of Indictment

United States District Court

──────────── DISTRICT OF ────────────

UNITED STATES OF AMERICA

V.

WAIVER OF INDICTMENT

CASE NUMBER:

I, _____, the above named defendant, who is accused of

being advised of the nature of the charge(s), the proposed information, and of my rights, hereby waive in open court on

_____ prosecution by indictment and consent that the proceeding may be by information
Date

rather than by indictment.

_____
Defendant

_____
Counsel for Defendant

Before _____
Judicial Officer

FRCrP 7(c)(1) provides that: "The indictment or the information shall be a plain, concise and definite written statement of the essential facts constituting the offense charged." If more than one crime is charged, the indictment or information must satisfy those requirements as to all crimes charged.

Reviewing the information or the indictment can provide necessary and important information to counsel for the criminal defendant. Significantly, however, there is no requirement that the government disclose its entire case in an indictment or information and the government frequently will try to avoid doing so in order to deprive the defense of this discovery opportunity. On the other hand, many states require by statute of court rule that the names of witnesses appearing before the grand jury be endorsed on the indictment.

HYPOTHETICAL 5-3

Assume that at the initial appearance of Yugotta Bekiddin, his bond was set at $10,000, which he was able to post with a surety bond. The prosecutor for the state, Hangem High, made little argument on the bond amount and no evidence was presented. When the judge dealt with setting the date for the preliminary hearing, Hangem High announced to the court that the state would submit the case directly to the grand jury, thereby bypassing the preliminary hearing. Plea Bargain tells Aluh Bye that he was hoping for a preliminary hearing so he could get a chance to cross examine the witnesses for the state because all he has heard is the client's version of what happened that night. Plea Bargain tells Aluh Bye they will just have to wait to see if the grand jury indicts Yugotta Bekiddin and see what the indictment says.

Within days, Yugotta Bekiddin is indicted by the grand jury for aggravated robbery. (When the client is told of the indictment, he says, "You gotta be kiddin me!") Plea Bargain tells Aluh Bye to get a copy of the indictment from the court. The front and back pages of the indictment issued by the grand jury against Yugotta Bekiddin are set out in Illustration 5-6.

1. What facts and leads can Aluh Bye obtain from the indictment that were not available from the criminal complaint?
2. Can Aluh Bye and Plea Bargain feel confident that Gino Maretti is the only witness besides Yugotta Bekiddin and his girlfriend with first-hand knowledge of the incident since he was the only witness to appear before the grand jury? Why?
3. Does the indictment in Illustration 5-6 appear to satisfy the requirement that an indictment contain a plain, concise, and definite written statement of the essential facts constituting the offense charged?

5. The bill of particulars

In the federal system and in most state systems, a criminal defendant may ask the court by motion to compel the prosecution to provide a **bill of particulars,** the purpose of which is to make general allegations contained in the indictment or information more specific. However, the defendant has no absolute right to a bill of particulars; it is in the judge's discretion to grant such a motion. FRCrP 7(f). The test is whether the

Illustration 5-6   INDICTMENT

(front page)

IN THE CRIMINAL COURT
FOR HARMONY COUNTY, YOURSTATE

STATE OF YOURSTATE	)	INDICTMENT FOR
v.	)	AGGRAVATED ROBBERY
YUGOTTA BEKIDDIN,	)	
defendant	)	CASE NO. 2004-199CR

IN THE NAME OF AND BY THE AUTHORITY OF THE STATE OF YOURSTATE:

The Grand Jurors of the State of Yourstate, empaneled and sworn to inquire and true presentment made in and for the county of Harmony, upon their oaths, do present that

YUGOTTA BEKIDDIN

on the 5th day of January, 2004, in Gino's Italian Restaurant, 533 Main Street in Capital City, Harmony County, Yourstate, did then and there knowingly and intentionally steal and obtain property by theft from the person of Gino Maretti, by violence and threat of violence with a deadly weapon and the display of a deadly weapon used or fashioned to lead Gino Maretti to reasonably believe it to be a deadly weapon all with the intent to deprive said Gino Maretti of the property and without his effective consent, in violation of YS. Crim. Code §39-13-402, contrary to said statute and against the peace and dignity of the people of the State of Yourstate.

_____

Hangem High
District Attorney General

---

defendant needs more details concerning the charges to avoid prejudicial surprise at trial. *United States v. Diecidue*, 603 F.2d 535 (5th Cir. 1979), *cert. denied*, 445 U.S. 946 (1979).

HYPOTHETICAL 5-4

Assume that Plea Bargain, frustrated at his lack of information regarding the specifics of the prosecution's case against Yugotta Bekiddin, instructs Aluh Bye to draft a motion for a bill of particulars for his review. Aluh Bye drafts the motion you see in Illustration 5-7.

1. Are there any additional requests you would add to this bill of particulars?
2. Do you think Plea Bargain has a good chance of convincing the judge to grant this motion under the standard set forth in *United States v. Diecidue*?
3. Assume the motion for bill of particulars as it appears in Illustration 5–7 is filed by Plea Bargain and the court grants his motion and orders the State to provide responses to all the information requested. The bill of particulars filed by the State can be seen in Illustration 5-8.

Although a motion for bill of particulars is not routinely granted, criminal defense lawyers utilize the motion regularly to fulfill their duty of zealous representation to the client. And in those cases where the

Illustration 5-6   INDICTMENT *(continued)*

(back page)

TRUE BILL	NO. 2004-199CR	WITNESSES
	INDICTMENT	

1. *Edgar Boone*
2. *Wayne Moses*
3. *John Hargis, Sr.*
4. *Keneth Sells*
5. *Cecil Whitlock*
6. *Betty Cochran*
7. *Ron Hansen*
8. *Sylia Huff*
9. *Kathy Green*
10. *Velma Wright*
11. *Deborah Barnum*
12. *Jerry Mayes*
13. *Scott Ray*

THE STATE

V.

YUGOTTA BEKIDDIN

Aggravated Robbery

1. Gino Maretti

Prosecutor: Hangem High

Witnesses sworn by me in the
presence of the Grand Jury

*Jun. 30*_____, 20*04*
Edgar Boone
Foreman

Filed, *30* day of *Jan.*, 20*04*
Karen Shipley, Clerk

---

motion is granted, the information provided can greatly advance defense counsel's knowledge of the prosecution's case.

6. Rule 16 discovery

FRCrP 16 contains a laundry list of information discoverable by the defendant in a criminal case. The rules of criminal procedure in effect in most states track Rule 16. (An example of a discovery request made under a state rule that tracks FRCrP 16 may be seen in Illustration 5-9.)

a. Statements of the defendant

FRCrP 16(a)(1)(A) requires the prosecution "upon request of a Defendant" to allow the defense counsel to inspect and copy "any relevant written or recorded statements made by the defendant" which are in the possession, custody, or control of the prosecution or which the prosecution may discover through due diligence. This includes the defendant's testimony before the grand jury (though typically the defendant will not have been called by the prosecution to testify before the grand jury and, if called, will assert his Fifth Amendment right against self-incrimination). And, it includes all statements by the defendant relevant to the charges against him, not just the ones the prosecution intends to use at trial.

Illustration 5-7   MOTION FOR BILL OF PARTICULARS

IN THE CRIMINAL COURT
FOR HARMONY COUNTY, YOURSTATE

STATE OF YOURSTATE	)	
v.	)	CASE NO. 2004-199CR
YUGOTTA BEKIDDIN,	)	
Defendant	)	

MOTION FOR BILL OF PARTICULARS

The defendant, pursuant to Rule 7(c) of the Yourstate Rules of Criminal Procedure, moves the court for an Order directing the State to furnish a Bill of Particulars with reference to the indictment. The State should be compelled to provide the following particulars to counsel for defendant:

1. The exact nature and description of the "property" referred to in the indictment.

2. Whether Gino Maretti was the actual owner of the "property" referred to in the indictment.

3. The exact nature and description of each and every "deadly weapon" referred to in the indictment.

4. The exact manner and means by which the defendant is alleged to have used "violence" to obtain the "property" from the person of Gino Maretti.

5. The exact manner and means by which the defendant is alleged to have used "threat of violence" to obtain the "property" from the person of Gino Maretti.

_____

Plea Bargain
Attorney for defendant

(Certificate of Service omitted)

Under the same rule, the prosecution must provide the criminal defendant with the substance of any oral statement of the defendant that the government intends to offer in evidence.

b. The criminal record of the defendant

FRCrP 16(a)(1)(B) requires the prosecution, upon request, to furnish to defense counsel copies of the prior criminal record of the defendant that the prosecution has or that can be discovered by the prosecution through due diligence.

c. Documents and things

FRCrP 16(a)(1)(C) requires the prosecution, upon request, to allow defense counsel to inspect and copy or photograph documents and things (and places) that are within the possession, custody, or control of the prosecution and that are:

- material to the preparation of the defendant's case; or
- to be used by the prosecution in its case-in-chief at trial (as opposed to being used as rebuttal evidence); or
- items which belong to or were obtained from the defendant.

Illustration 5-8 BILL OF PARTICULARS

IN THE CRIMINAL COURT
FOR HARMONY COUNTY, YOURSTATE

STATE OF YOURSTATE	)	
v.	)	CASE NO. 2004-199CR
YUGOTTA BEKIDDIN,	)	
Defendant	)	

BILL OF PARTICULARS

The State, pursuant to Order of the Court, hereby furnishes the following Bill of Particulars to defendant:

1. The exact nature and description of the "property" referred to in the indictment.

RESPONSE: The "property" referred to in the indictment is $68.92 in cash.

2. Whether Gino Maretti was the actual owner of the "property" referred to in the indictment.

RESPONSE: No. The actual owner of the property referred to in the indictment was Maretti Enterprises, Inc., a corporation wholly owned by Gino Maretti.

3. The exact nature and description of each and every "deadly weapon" referred to in the indictment.

RESPONSE: The "deadly weapon" referred to in the indictment was a large mound of hardened spaghetti noodles and meatballs encased in a cloth napkin which had been twisted to enclose the spaghetti and meatballs and which was wielded as a club by the defendant by holding the ends of the napkin together.

4. The exact manner and means by which the defendant is alleged to have used "violence" to obtain the "property" from the person of Gino Maretti.

RESPONSE: The defendant used violence by swinging the above referenced deadly weapon over his head while advancing in a threatening manner toward Gino Maretti and demanding that Mr. Maretti turn over the property to him. In addition, the defendant repeatedly slammed the deadly weapon on the counter within inches of Mr. Maretti demonstrating its capacity to cause death or severe bodily injury to Mr. Maretti.

5. The exact manner and means by which the defendant is alleged to have used "threat of violence" to obtain the "property" from the person of Gino Maretti.

RESPONSE: The defendant used threat of violence to obtain the property by swinging the above referenced deadly weapon over his head while advancing in a threatening manner toward Gino Maretti and demanding that Mr. Maretti turn over the property to him. In addition, the defendant repeatedly slammed the deadly weapon on the counter within inches of Mr. Maretti demonstrating its capacity to cause death or severe bodily injury to Mr. Maretti all the while demanding that Mr. Maretti turn the property over to him.

_____
Hangem High
District Attorney General

(Certificate of Service omitted)

Illustration 5-9   DISCOVERY REQUEST

IN THE CRIMINAL COURT
FOR HARMONY COUNTY, YOURSTATE

STATE OF YOURSTATE	)	
v.	)	CASE NO. 2004-199CR
YUGOTTA BEKIDDIN,	)	
Defendant	)	

REQUEST FOR DISCOVERY, INSPECTION, AND
NOTICE OF INTENT TO USE EVIDENCE

The defendant, through his counsel of record, requests that the District Attorney for the State of Yourstate provide certain information which the defendant contends is material to the preparation of his defense.

Definitions

For purposes of this request, the defendant defines the "State" to mean and include the District Attorney General for Harmony County, the Capital City Police Department, the Harmony County Sheriff's Office, the Yourstate Highway Patrol, the Yourstate Bureau of Investigation, any agents or employees of those offices, any other law enforcement department or agency of Yourstate, any other law enforcement officer, and any other person acting in conjunction with, or in behalf of, any such law enforcement agency, including without limitation, the Federal Bureau of Investigation.

The defendant defines each of the requests to include items currently within the actual or constructive possession, custody, control, or knowledge of the State, and items which may become known, identified, or available through the exercise of due diligence by the State.

Requests

1. To receive a list of the names and current addresses of all witnesses the State intends to call to testify, whether or not they are listed upon the indictment.

2. To be provided with any police reports and witness statements to the extent they contain the defendant's prior criminal record, his statement, or the results of any tests or examinations.

3. To be provided with the statements and reports of any witnesses after the witness testifies, said production to be made outside the presence of the jury.

4. To inspect and copy any written or recorded statement, confession, or admission against interest made by the defendant.

5. To be advised of the substance of any oral statement, confession, or admission against interest made by the defendant, whether before or after arrest, in response to any person then known to the defendant to be a law enforcement officer.

6. To receive a copy of the defendant's prior criminal record, if any.

7. To be allowed to inspect and copy all books, papers, documents, photographs, tangible objects, buildings, or places or copies or portions thereof, which are intended for use by the State as evidence-in-chief at trial of this cause.

8. To be allowed to inspect and copy all books, papers, documents, photographs, tangible objects, buildings, or places or copies or portions thereof, which are material to the preparation of the defense in this matter.

9. To be allowed to inspect and copy all books, papers, documents, photographs, tangible objects, buildings, or places or copies or portions thereof, which were obtained from or belong to the defendant.

Illustration 5-9   DISCOVERY REQUEST *(continued)*

10. To be allowed to inspect and copy any results of reports or physical or mental examinations, and of scientific tests or experiments, or copies thereof, which are material to the preparation of the defense.

11. To be allowed to inspect and copy any results of reports or physical or mental examinations, and of scientific tests or experiments, or copies thereof, which are intended for use by the State as evidence-in-chief at trial.

12. To be furnished the names and addresses of all persons known to the State to have been present at the time and place of the alleged offense.

13. Pursuant to *Brady v. Maryland*, 373 U.S. 83, 83 S. Ct. 1194, 10 L. Ed. 2d 215 (1963) and *United States v. Agurs*, 427 U.S. 97, 96 S. Ct. 2392, 49 L. Ed. 2d 342 (1976), to be advised of and allowed to inspect and copy or photograph any and all evidence that might be fairly termed "favorable" to the defense, whether that evidence be completely exculpatory in nature or simply tending to reduce the degree of the offense or punishment therefore, or whether that evidence might be termed "favorable" in the sense that it might be fairly used by the defendant to impeach the credibility of any witness the government intends to call in this matter including, but not limited to:

    a. The nature and substance of any agreement, immunity promise, or understanding, between the State or federal government or any agent thereof, and any witness, relating to the witness's expected testimony, including but not limited to, understandings or agreements relating to pending or potential prosecutions.

    b. The nature and substance of any preferential treatment given at any time by any state agent, whether or not in connection with this case, to any potential witness, including but not limited to letters from State Attorneys or other law enforcement personnel to federal or state agencies, creditors, etc., setting out that witness's cooperation or status with the state, and which letter or communication might fairly be said to have been an attempt to provide some benefit or help to the witness.

    c. Any money or other remuneration paid to any witness by the State, including but not limited to rewards, subsistence payments, expenses, or other payments made for specific information supplied to the State.

    d. Any and all information in the possession of the State regarding the mental condition of the state's witnesses which would reflect or bring into question the witnesses' credibility.

    e. The original statement and any amendment thereto, of any individuals who have provided the State with a statement inculpating the defendant, who later retracted all or any portion of that statement where such retraction would raise a conflict in the evidence which the State intends to prove.

    f. Any and all interview memoranda or reports which contain any information, whatever the source, which might fairly be said to contradict or be inconsistent with any evidence the State intends to adduce in this matter.

    g. The names and addresses of any witnesses whom the State believes would give testimony favorable to the defendant in regard to the matters alleged in the indictment, even though the State may not be in possession of a statement of this witness and regardless of whether the state intends to call this witness at trial.

    h. The results of any scientific tests or analysis done on any person or object in connection with this case where the result of that test or analysis did not implicate, or was neutral to the defendant.

    i. Any documentary evidence which contradicts or is inconsistent with any testimony the State intends to introduce in this case.

    j. The statement of any individual who has given a description to any person of an individual involved in the perpetration of the charged offense, which person the State alleges to be the defendant, where such description might fairly be said not to match the defendant in characteristics such as height, weight, body build, color of skin, color of hair, etc.

    k. The name and address of any individual who has been requested to make an identification of the defendant in connection with this case, and failed to make such identification.

Illustration 5-9 DISCOVERY REQUEST *(continued)*

WHEREFORE, defendant requests as follows:

    a. That the State respond in writing to each and every request as soon as possible, but no later than fifteen (15) days prior to the scheduled trial of this case.

    b. That should the State be of the opinion that any item of information requested herein is not discoverable, is privileged, or is not relevant to these proceedings, that the State, for each such item of information, acknowledge whether that item of information exists, cite the authorities the State relies upon to refuse the request for such item of information, and produce the item of information under seal to the Court for *in camera* inspection.

    c. That the clerk of the court file this request within the record of these proceedings, but the defendant waives any present necessity for a hearing upon these issues until such time as a motion to compel production may be filed.

_____

Plea Bargain
Attorney for Defendant

(Certificate of Service omitted)

---

d. Reports of examinations and tests

FRCrP 16(a)(1)(D) requires the prosecution, upon request, to allow defense counsel to inspect and copy or photograph any results or reports of physical or mental exams, or scientific tests or experiments (autopsy, blood, fingerprint, drug, DNA, etc.) that are within the possession, custody, or control of the prosecution and that are material to the preparation of the defense or intended for use by the prosecution in its **case-in-chief** at trial.

e. Expert witnesses

FRCrP 16(a)(1)(E) requires the prosecution, upon request, to provide defense counsel with a written summary of expert witness testimony the prosecution intends to use in its case-in-chief at trial, including expert testimony the prosecution may offer to rebut the defendant's expert witnesses who testify regarding the defendant's mental state.

f. Procedure for conducting Rule 16 discovery

You may have noticed that the various forms of discovery allowed by Rule 16 are "upon request." Unlike the bill of particulars, which is sought by *motion*, Rule 16 discovery, like other means of discovery discussed below, is sought by *request*. See Illustration 5-9 for a typical **request for discovery** form under Rule 16.

7. Identity of witnesses

The Supreme Court has held that the defendant is entitled, upon request, to advance notice of the names of the witnesses to be called by the prosecution. See *United States v. Agurs*, 427 U.S. 97, 96 S. Ct. 2392,

49 L. Ed. 2d 342 (1976). This only applies to witnesses to be called by the government in its case-in-chief, not **rebuttal witnesses** (witnesses called to rebut the opposing party's proof). And, as discussed below, the right of the defendant to obtain pretrial statements of witnesses is very limited, as is its right to depose those witnesses prior to trial. Practically speaking, during the discovery phase of the criminal case, the defense team must attempt to obtain information from the government's witnesses by informal discovery, which usually means persuading those witnesses to consent to an interview (see Chapters 14 and 15 on interviewing witnesses).

8. Statements of witnesses

FRCrP 16(a)(2) states specifically that it does not authorize the discovery or inspection of statements made by prosecution witnesses or prospective witnesses except as authorized by 18 U.S.C. §3500. In the federal system and in most state systems, criminal defendants are not entitled to inspect or copy statements of witnesses the prosecution intends to call at trial. However, 18 U.S.C. §3500, commonly known as the **Jencks Act,** requires the prosecution to provide the defense, upon request, with prior written or recorded statements of witnesses *after* they have testified. This is an example of **trial discovery,** that is discovery that can only be made at or during the trial.

Note that while witnesses' statements are not generally discoverable before trial under this rule, they must be disclosed pretrial to the extent they contain defendant's statement, his prior criminal record, or the results of tests related to the investigation.

The procedure for obtaining witnesses' statements is governed by FRCrP 26.2, which provides that following the direct testimony of the witness at trial, the party who did not call the witness may make a motion to be allowed to examine and use any statement of the witness in the possession of the prosecution that relates to the subject matter concerning which the witness has testified. The prior statements, or material portions of them, are then produced, and the moving party may apply for a recess to allow time to inspect the statements. The types of statements that must be produced pursuant to this procedure are defined in FRCrP 26.2(f) and include written statements of the witness, recorded or transcribed oral statements of the witness, and the statement or transcript of the witness's grand jury testimony.

9. Exculpatory material—the Brady doctrine

Under the decisions in *Brady v. Maryland*, 373 U.S. 83, 83 S. Ct. 1194, 10 L. Ed. 2d 215 (1963) and *United States v. Agurs*, 427 U.S. 97, 96 S. Ct. 2392, 49 L. Ed. 2d 342 (1976), the prosecution in both state and federal proceedings must provide to the defense all evidence in its possession, custody, or control that is **exculpatory,** that is, favorable to the defense in that it tends to prove the defendant not guilty. Note there is no obligation arising from *Brady* for the prosecution to reveal **incriminating evidence** to the defense before trial.

10. Depositions

The FRCrP and most state rules of criminal procedure allow very little use of **depositions** for pretrial discovery. FRCrP 15 allows depositions to be taken only when "exceptional circumstances" exist and then the court may order it and the deposition may be used at trial. Exceptional circumstances might include impending death or the necessary (and permitted) absence of a witness from trial.

HYPOTHETICAL 5-5

Assume that, following the arraignment of Yugotta Bekiddin (at which the defendant, when asked to enter a plea said, "You gotta be kiddin me," which the judge accepted as a not guilty plea), Plea Bargain instructs Aluh Bye to draft a standard discovery request in the case for his review. Illustration 5-9 sets forth the discovery request drafted by Aluh Bye. Illustrations 5-10 and 5-11 set forth the letters drafted by Aluh Bye for Plea Bargain's signature forwarding the discovery request to the court clerk and to the prosecution.

1. Are there other discovery requests you would include in Illustration 5-9?
2. Notice the definitions included in the discovery request preceding the requests themselves. What advantages can you see in using such definitions in a discovery request?

Illustration 5-10   LETTER COMMUNICATING DISCOVERY REQUEST TO THE COURT CLERK

Date

Harmony County Criminal Court Clerk
(address)

Re: State of Yourstate v. Yugotta Bekiddin (Case No. 2004-199CR)

Dear _____:

Find enclosed a copy of our request for discovery in the above styled case which has been delivered to the State as of this date. Please mark the document filed with the Court. It is not necessary that it be set on the Court's motion docket since we are not requesting that this matter be treated as a motion at this time. The request is being filed simply to preserve the fact that the request for discovery has been made.

Very truly yours,

_____
Plea Bargain
Attorney for Defendant

cc: Attorney General Hangem High

Illustration 5-11   LETTER COMMUNICATING DISCOVERY REQUEST TO THE PROSECUTION

                                                                Date

Attorney General Hangem High
(address)

Re: State of Yourstate v. Yugotta Bekiddin (Case No. 2004-199CR)

Dear General High:

   Find enclosed our request for discovery in the above styled case. Please respond to the specific requests in writing. If there are physical items to be examined please let me know when it would be convenient to make the examinations.

                                                    Very truly yours,

                                                    _____
                                                    Plea Bargain
                                                    Attorney for Defendant

---

11. Motions as discovery devices

There are a number of **pretrial motions** that the defense may make in a criminal case. Although the primary purpose of such motions is not discovery, some of them may, in fact, aid defense counsel in learning more about the prosecution's case. Here are three such pretrial motions that may aid the defense in discovery.

a. *The motion to dismiss*

FRCrP 12 authorizes a pretrial **motion to dismiss** (sometimes referred to as a **motion to quash**) on various grounds. In fact, under FRCrP 12(b) and some state rules, the motion to dismiss on some grounds *must* be filed before trial. The motion may be directed at some defect in the institution of the proceeds or at the indictment or information. Examples of theories advanced by the defense in a motion to dismiss are:

- The court lacks jurisdiction.
- The facts alleged do not constitute a crime.
- An essential element of the crime is not alleged.
- The defendant has a complete legal defense such as double jeopardy or running of the statute of limitations.

Depending on the nature of the motion, the court may conduct an **evidentiary hearing** in deciding the motion, which may provide the defense an important discovery opportunity.

b. The motion to suppress

FRCrP 12(b)(3) authorizes the pretrial **motion to suppress evidence** (sometimes called a **motion to exclude evidence**). Like the motion to dismiss on various grounds, the motion to suppress *must* be filed before trial under the federal rules and some state rules. The motion to suppress is generally used by the defense to exclude unlawfully obtained evidence from trial. Examples of such unlawfully obtained evidence might include coerced confessions from the defendant or evidence seized in a warrantless search in violation of the Fourth Amendment.

When a motion to suppress is filed, the court will conduct an evidentiary hearing to decide on the motion, again allowing the defense a discovery opportunity. In particular, FRCrP 12(i) provides that Rule 26.2 applies in a hearing on a motion to suppress and that a law enforcement officer is deemed a government witness. This means that the defense may get an early, pretrial look at the statements of witnesses called at the suppression hearing, including law enforcement officers (e.g., investigation notes, police reports) who will later testify for the government at trial.

c. The motion in limine

The **motion *in limine*** is a request to the court prior to trial seeking to have the court order the other party not to question a witness about certain matters or not to allow a witness to mention certain inadmissible things while testifying. For example, if the defense believes that the prosecution plans to call a witness who will be asked to testify concerning the defendant's character before the defense has put that at issue (see Chapter 7), a motion *in limine* may be appropriate.

Depending on the nature of the particular case, defense counsel may be able to use the motion *in limine* to discover in advance what the prosecution does or does not intend to try to prove with a particular witness.

12. The Freedom of Information Act and The Privacy Act

The **Freedom of Information Act** (FOIA), 5 U.S.C. §552, is a federal statute allowing anyone to access certain files, documents, records, and other information in the possession of federal government agencies. **The Privacy Act,** 5 U.S.C. §552(a), allows an individual to obtain access to certain information maintained by federal agencies about themselves. Many states have their own **open records acts** allowing access to information held by state and local governments. (A full discussion of the scope and procedures for using the FOIA and Privacy Act is included in Chapter 16. A full discussion of state open records act is included in Chapter 17. A list of current citations to the state open records acts for all fifty states and the District of Columbia is provided in Appendix E, Resources for the Investigator, together with other resources related to the FOIA/PA.)

Not all information held by a federal agency is obtainable using the FOIA or Privacy Act. Both statutes contain exemptions which allow the government to withhold access to some information. For example, under the FOIA, there is an exemption for law enforcement records providing that they may be withheld from disclosure if they will:

- interfere with enforcement proceedings;
- deprive a person of a fair trial;
- constitute an unwarranted invasion into a person's privacy;
- disclose government investigative techniques and procedures; or
- endanger the life or safety of law enforcement personnel.

Similarly, not all information known to state and local governments is obtainable through a state open records act. But notwithstanding those limitations, there is a substantial amount of information about people, public and private organizations, and events that is obtainable through these statutes.

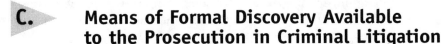

C. Means of Formal Discovery Available to the Prosecution in Criminal Litigation

1. The initial appearance

Although there are no witnesses called at the initial appearance, it does provide the prosecution with what may be its first opportunity to observe the appearance and demeanor of the defendant.

2. The preliminary examination

The defense may call witnesses to testify at the preliminary hearing if it chooses, including the defendant. As a practical matter, the defendant rarely testifies at this hearing, choosing rather to rest on his Fifth Amendment privilege against self-incrimination. But if he does testify, or if the defense calls other witnesses, the hearing provides the prosecution an opportunity to discover information known to those witnesses and get an early look at defense strategies.

3. Grand jury testimony

The grand jury proceedings, discussed earlier, provide the prosecution with an unchallenged opportunity to discover information known to witnesses. Because it is a process controlled by the prosecution, closed to the defense, and because the grand jury has the power to subpoena any witness the prosecution wishes to hear from (see Illustration 5-4), the grand jury process gives the prosecution a clear advantage over the defense in pretrial discovery.

4. Rule 16 discovery

FRCrP 16(b) allows the prosecution to engage in some limited discovery from the defendant. However, the right of the prosecution to obtain Rule 16(b) discovery from the defendant is conditioned on the defense having requested discovery *and* the prosecution having complied with those requests. Subject to those conditions, the prosecution may engage in the following discovery under Rule 16(b):

a. Documents and things

FRCrP 16(b)(1)(A) requires the defense, upon request, to allow the prosecution to inspect and copy or photograph documents and things (and places) that are within the possession, custody, or control of the defendant and that the defendant intends to introduce as evidence in its case-in-chief at trial (as opposed to being used as rebuttal evidence).

b. Reports of examinations and tests

FRCrP 16(b)(1)(B) requires the defense, upon request, to allow the prosecution to inspect and copy or photograph any results or reports of physical or mental exams, or scientific tests or experiments (autopsy, blood, fingerprint, drug, DNA, etc.) that are within the possession, custody, or control of the defendant and that the defense intends to introduce as evidence in its case-in-chief at trial.

c. Expert witnesses

FRCrP 16(b)(1)(C) requires the defense, upon request, to provide the prosecution with a written summary of expert witness testimony the defense intends to use in its case-in-chief at trial, but only when the defense has either made a similar request under FRCrP 16(a)(1)(E) or given notice under FRCrP 12.2(b) of its intent to present expert testimony on the defendant's mental condition.

The procedure followed by the government to obtain Rule 16 discovery is to make request for the discovery, in the same form as the defense (see Illustrations 5-9, 5-10, and 5-11).

5. Statements of witnesses

The prosecution may obtain the prior statements of witnesses called by the defense under the procedure set forth in FRCrP 26.2 as discussed above. And if the defense files a motion to suppress evidence, the prosecution may benefit from FRCrP 12(i) allowing the production of defense witness statements at the suppression hearing.

6. Prior notice of affirmative defenses

The defendant in a criminal case need not put on any proof at trial. He may simply put the government to its proof and hope to persuade the jury that the government has failed to prove all elements of the alleged offense beyond a reasonable doubt.

The defendant may also raise affirmative defenses such as **insanity, diminished capacity, justification** or **excuse** in the form of **self-defense** or **defense of a third person, alibi,** etc. FRCrP 12 requires the defendant to give the prosecution pretrial notice of some of these affirmative defenses.

a. Alibi witnesses

FRCrP 12.1 allows the government to serve on the defendant a written demand for notice of an alibi defense. The defendant must respond within 10 days with written notification to the government of its intent to rely on an alibi defense. The defendant's notice must state the specific place or places at which the defendant claims to have been at the time of the alleged offense and the names and addresses of witnesses on whom the defendant intends to rely to prove his alibi defense. The government then has 10 days to supply the defense with a written notice stating the names and addresses of the witnesses it intends to rely upon to place the defendant at the scene of the crime or to otherwise rebut the defendant's alibi witnesses.

b. Insanity defense

FRCrP 12.2 requires the defendant to give the government written notice of its intent to rely upon the defense of insanity and/or its intent to call an expert witness at trial to testify regarding the defendant's mental condition. Rule 12.2(c) then gives the government the right to ask the court for an order directing the defendant to submit to a mental examination.

c. Public authority defense

FRCrP 12.3 requires the defendant who intends to rely on the defense of having been acting with actual or believed public authority on behalf of a law enforcement or federal intelligence agency at the time of the alleged offense to give the prosecution written notice of that intended defense. The notice must identify the specific law enforcement or federal intelligence agency involved and the dates during which the defendant had actual or believed public authority to act. Within 10 days, the government must respond in writing by admitting or denying the defendant's claim of public authority.

The government may then serve on defendant, no later than 20 days before trial, a written demand for the names and addresses of persons upon whom the defense intends to rely to prove its defense. The defendant must respond within seven days. The government then has seven days to supply the defense with its list of witnesses who will be called to rebut that defense.

D. ▶ The Resolution of Discovery Disputes in Criminal Litigation

FRCrP 16(d) authorizes either the prosecution or the defense to file an appropriate motion with the court seeking a protective order from inappropriate discovery requests or seeking to compel the opposing party to comply with discovery requests. The form of the motion to compel or the motion for protective order is similar to those used in civil litigation (see Chapter 4). The FRCrP do not currently contain any requirement that the parties seeking to compel discovery or obtain protection from it, certify to the court good-faith attempts to resolve the dispute prior to filing the Rule 16(d) motion.

E. ▶ The Role of the Paralegal in Formal Criminal Discovery

1. Attendance at pretrial proceedings

SLEUTH ON
THE LOOSE

To learn more about the quantities of information now available online from the various agencies and departments of the federal government, access the government's new comprehensive Web site at *www.FirstGov .gov.*

The paralegal for both the prosecution and defense may be asked to attend all pretrial proceedings including, in particular, the preliminary hearing. She may not only assist the attorney as the attorney presents evidence, but may take exhaustive notes and observe the proceedings carefully to maximize the discovery opportunity.

2. Review and analysis of court filings

The paralegal for the defense may be asked to obtain and perform the initial review of the criminal complaint or the indictment or information in order to determine the legal sufficiency of the charging documents and to glean from them all information that can be discovered regarding the prosecution's case.

3. Drafting discovery documents and related motions

The paralegal for the prosecution may be involved in the initial drafting of the information or indictment. This is a critical step in the prosecution because, as we have seen, a defective indictment may result in a motion to dismiss or to quash. She may be asked to draft requests for discovery on behalf of the government or responses to discovery served on the government by the defense. She may be asked to draft or respond to the various motions commonly filed in a criminal case.

The paralegal for defense counsel may be asked to draft the motion for bill of particulars, the defendant's request for discovery, responses to discovery requested by the prosecution, and the same types of motions as the prosecution paralegal.

Good writing skills are critical to the paralegal working in the criminal law area. Careful, thorough drafting by the paralegal will help ensure that her supervising attorney is able to obtain all discoverable information from the opposing party. And when the paralegal is drafting a document responsive to a discovery request, careful drafting is important to ensure good-faith compliance with the request as well as that no disclosure is made of unrequested or non-discoverable information. (See Chapter 4 for drafting guidelines.)

4. Familiarity with discovery procedures

It is precisely because the paralegal in the criminal law area is involved in reviewing and analyzing court filings and in drafting all kinds of documents relevant to formal discovery that it is critical for the paralegal to be thoroughly familiar with the FRCrP and the rules of criminal procedure in the state(s) where she practices. The scope of permitted discovery and the procedures for obtaining discovery vary widely among the states in the criminal law area. In addition, in some states, criminal procedure is still based to some extent on case law as well as statutes or court rules.

The court, by standing rule or scheduling order made on a case-to-case basis, will establish time frames in which permitted formal discovery must be initiated and complied with. It will typically fall to the paralegal to know these time frames, calendar them as they arise in the office, and make sure that her office complies with all discovery deadlines and that the supervising attorney is advised of the adversary's failure to comply with any discovery deadline.

5. Familiarity with forms

In both civil and criminal discovery, familiarity with forms plays a large part in the work of the paralegal because she may be asked to prepare the initial draft of discovery documents. In using forms for discovery documents, the paralegal must be sure her forms are current, that is, that they comply with the requirements of the applicable rules of procedure. The paralegal must also avoid the temptation to be too dependent on forms in drafting discovery documents for the attorney's review. Every case is different. And the forms we use for discovery requests or responses or motions must be customized to suit the particular case.

6. Reviewing documents, reports, and summaries

The paralegal may be expected to review carefully all information produced by the opposing side by formal discovery, or pursuant to the Jencks Act or the *Brady* doctrine, to confirm that party's compliance with the discovery requests and to identify leads for additional formal discovery or informal investigation.

7. Assisting the client in responding to discovery requests

The paralegal may be expected to review documents to see if they fall within the scope of requested discovery or are privileged, or to interview witnesses to see if they should be identified in response to discovery requests as having particular knowledge, or to assist in preparing the summary of an expert's opinions for production to the opposing party.

The ability to read and understand the scope of a discovery request, an understanding of the law of privileges (see Chapter 6), and the discipline to review numerous documents carefully are just some of the skills needed by the effective paralegal in this area.

HYPOTHETICAL 5-6

Assume the case of *State v. Yugotta Bekiddin* goes to trial.

1. What do you consider the defendant's best argument against conviction? What do you consider the State's best argument for conviction?
2. Based on the facts as you know them, what verdict do you think a jury would return on the charge of aggravated robbery? Why?

3. What witnesses do you think the prosecution would call at trial other than Gino Maretti?
4. What witnesses do you think the defense would call, if any?
5. Would you recommend that Yugotta Bekiddin testify at trial on his own behalf? What other information might you want to have before you make that decision?
6. If Yugotta was convicted, what do you think the first thing he said was?

KEY WORDS AND PHRASES TO REMEMBER

affidavit
affirmative defenses
alibi
bail
beyond a reasonable doubt
bill of particulars
Brady doctrine
case-in-chief
criminal complaint
defense of third person
diminished capacity defense
evidentiary hearing
exculpatory evidence
fundamental right
grand jury
in camera
incriminating evidence
indictment
information
initial appearance
insanity defense
Jencks Act
justification defense

motion for protection
motion *in limine*
motion to compel
motion to dismiss
motion to exclude evidence
motion to quash
motion to suppress evidence
open records acts
preliminary examination
preliminary hearing
pretrial motions
pretrial release
probable cause
property bond
public authority defense
rebuttal evidence
request for discovery
Rule 16 discovery
self-defense
surety bond
trial by ambush
trial discovery
waiver of indictment

LEARN BY DOING

LBD 5-1. Locate the rules of criminal procedure for your state. Prepare a memorandum comparing the scope and procedures for discovery allowed under those rules with the scope and procedures allowed by the FRCrP.

LBD 5-2. Read *Brady v. Maryland*, 373 U.S. 83, 83 S. Ct. 1194, 10 L. Ed. 2d 215 (1963) and *United States v. Agurs*, 427 U.S. 97, 96 S. Ct. 2392, 49 L. Ed. 2d 342 (1976). Then research the case law of your state to see how your courts have construed and applied the Brady doctrine to specific discovery requests. Prepare a memorandum summarizing your findings.

LBD 5-3. Review the Jencks Act at 18 U.S.C. §3500. Prepare a memorandum discussing whether you agree or disagree with the limited procedures allowed there to obtain statements of witnesses and why. How, if at all, would you change that procedure?

LBD 5-4. Arrange and conduct the interview of an attorney who specializes in criminal defense work, a prosecuting attorney, or an experienced paralegal who works in that area of the law. In your interview, ask questions about the importance of formal pretrial discovery to their work, whether they think the rules favor the prosecution or the defense or neither, and the role they believe the paralegal can play in assisting with formal discovery. Prepare a memorandum summarizing your interview.

LBD 5-5. Assume that Rowdy Outlaw (see Case Study No. 1 in Appendix A) is going to be charged with first degree murder under the homicide statutes of your state. Draft the indictment for that charge.

LBD 5-6. Using the online resources for criminal law provided in Appendix E, Resources for the Investigator, see if you can locate current crime statistics for your state for the past five years.

Chapter 6

Rules of Evidence for the Investigator—Part 1

CHAPTER OBJECTIVES

The rules of evidence control the proof that can be admitted in both civil and criminal trials. Knowledge of the basic rules of evidence is essential to the paralegal investigator. In this chapter we will look at a number of reasons why this is true. Also in this chapter you will learn a number of the fundamental concepts that investigators need to know about evidence including:

- The difference between testimonial, real, documentary, and demonstrative evidence.
- The distinction between first-hand and second-hand knowledge and between direct and circumstantial evidence.
- The importance of being able to lay a proper foundation for certain kinds of evidence.
- The role of the burden of proof and the degree of proof required in civil and criminal cases.
- The various kinds of privileged information that cannot always be discovered, including trial preparation materials (the work product doctrine), the marital privilege, the spousal testimony privilege, the physician-patient privilege and the privilege against self-incrimination.

A. Introduction to the Rules of Evidence

1. What the rules of evidence do

The **rules of evidence** govern the information that may be heard and considered by the judge or jury in the course of a trial. These rules control in both civil and criminal trials. In our adversarial system, not just any fact, item of information, opinion, or exhibit can be offered as evidence at the whim of a party. The rules of evidence closely control what can be offered and received in evidence and thus what can be

SL EUTH ON THE LOOSE

Locate the text of the Federal Rules of Evidence discussed in this chapter online at *www.law.cornell.edu/ rules/fre/overview/ html.*

considered by the judge or jury in reaching a decision in a case. One fundamental rule in our system is that the **finder of fact** must decide contested issues based only on the evidence presented at trial. Consequently, most **objections** made at trial are evidentiary in nature—one party trying to limit or keep out some evidence tendered by the other side.

Seeing a judge apply the rules of evidence to allow some evidence in and disallow other evidence is often puzzling to the untrained observer. The ruling may appear illogical and arbitrary and the evidence disallowed may appear imminently relevant to the issue. And it may well be! But the various rules of evidence have been developed over a long period of time and, for the most part, are intended to ensure some level of genuineness and reliability before the proffered testimony or exhibit will be received.

2. The burden of proof

a. In a civil case

In a civil case the **burden of proof** is initially on the plaintiff to prove all the elements of the cause of action. If the defendant **counterclaims** against the plaintiff, crossclaims against another defendant, or files a **third-party claim** against a new defendant (see Chapters 3 and 4), the defendant, as counter plaintiff, cross plaintiff, or third-party plaintiff, will have the burden of proof on all the elements of those claims. And if the defendant raises any **affirmative defenses** to the claims of the plaintiff against him, the defendant will have the burden of proof on all the elements of those defenses.

EXAMPLE

> In a civil lawsuit in which the plaintiff is suing the defendant in negligence to recover for personal injuries, the plaintiff will have the burden of proving all the elements constituting his cause of action in negligence. If the plaintiff fails to carry that burden, his lawsuit will be dismissed by the judge, or the jury will find in favor of the defendant on that basis.
>
> If the defendant in that civil suit raises affirmative defenses of contributory fault by the plaintiff or assumption of the risk by plaintiff, then the defendant will have the burden of proving all elements of those affirmative defenses. If the defendant in that civil suit counterclaims against the plaintiff alleging negligence, then the defendant, as counter plaintiff, has the burden of proof on those allegations.

b. In a criminal prosecution

In a criminal case the government, as plaintiff, will have the burden of proving all elements of the crime alleged to have been committed by the defendant. If it fails to do so, the charges will be dismissed against the defendant, or the jury will find the defendant not guilty on that basis. If the criminal defendant raises an affirmative defense such as insanity, entrapment, self-defense, or alibi, then the burden will shift to the criminal defendant to prove the necessary elements to establish those defenses (see LBD 6-1).

3. The standard or degree of proof

a. In a civil case

The **degree of proof** required in civil cases is typically by a **preponderance of the evidence,** which means the plaintiff must convince the trier of fact that it is *more likely than not* that the allegations regarding the elements of the action are true. If the defendant in a civil action asserts an affirmative defense, the defendant will have the burden of proving all the elements of that defense and, again, the degree of proof required is typically by a preponderance.

In some civil actions the degree of proof required may be slightly higher than the preponderance. For example, in some states, civil fraud must be proven by **clear and convincing evidence,** not by a mere preponderance. (See LBD 6-2.)

b. In a criminal prosecution

In criminal cases the prosecution must prove the necessary elements of the crime alleged **beyond a reasonable doubt.** If the criminal defendant alleges affirmative defenses such as insanity, entrapment, or alibi, then in many states the burden of proof will rest on that defendant to prove all the elements of those defenses, usually by a preponderance. (See LBD 6-1.)

To do a thorough job of factual investigation, the paralegal must know and understand which party to the lawsuit has the burden of proof as to which issues and the standard or degree of proof to which each party will be held on each issue.

4. Means of proof

In both civil and criminal cases proof of facts relevant to the issues is controlled by the rules of evidence. Evidence may be presented to the court in several different ways:

- *Testimonial evidence* is evidence received from the sworn testimony of witnesses.
- *Documentary evidence* is evidence received from properly admitted documents.
- *Real or physical evidence* is evidence in the form of properly admitted objects (e.g., the weapon in a murder case).
- *Demonstrative evidence* is evidence in the form of properly admitted charts, graphs, diagrams, computer simulations, etc., that illustrate or demonstrate something for the court.

5. First-hand and second-hand knowledge

Information that is obtained from witnesses may be first-hand or second-hand. **First-hand knowledge** is something known to a person because they perceived it through one of the senses. It is something the person saw, heard, smelled, tasted, or felt. **Second-hand knowledge** is something known to a person only because someone else told them about it or they read it somewhere.

As common sense might suggest, first-hand knowledge is more reliable and thus more valuable to attorneys than second-hand knowledge. Although relevant first-hand knowledge is not always admissible as evidence, it usually is, whereas relevant second-hand knowledge often is excluded from evidence due to the hearsay rule (see discussion of the hearsay rule in Chapter 7).

EXAMPLE

One witness to a murder says she saw the defendant point a gun at the victim, shoot the victim, and run. That is first-hand knowledge and almost certainly admissible as evidence at trial. A second witness says she saw and heard nothing but did hear the first witness say that she saw the defendant shoot the victim. That is second-hand knowledge and, if offered as evidence by the prosecution at trial, will likely be excluded as hearsay.

Those involved in investigating work must be able to distinguish between first-hand and second-hand knowledge. Attorneys always prefer first-hand knowledge of relevant facts.

6. Direct and circumstantial evidence

Evidence is frequently categorized as being either direct or circumstantial. **Direct evidence** is evidence that, if believed, establishes a relevant fact without the need for any inference.

EXAMPLE

A witness testifies that she saw the defendant point a gun at the victim, shoot the victim, and run. If believed, that is direct evidence that the defendant shot the victim.

Circumstantial evidence is indirect evidence that requires an inference or conclusion to prove a relevant fact.

EXAMPLE

A second witness testifies that she heard a gun shot and turned to see the victim on the ground and the defendant running away with a gun in his hand. That would be circumstantial evidence that the defendant shot the victim, but not direct evidence of it.

Note that the circumstantial evidence offered by the second witness is first-hand knowledge. The second witness is testifying to what she saw and heard herself. But because she didn't actually see the defendant fire the gun at the victim, the jury will have to infer that he did from what the witness did see and hear.

Circumstantial evidence, if relevant to the issues, is usually admissible as evidence. But it isn't as reliable or convincing as direct evidence. Its **probative value** may not be as great as direct evidence. Or, as lawyers and judges sometimes say, it doesn't carry the "**weight**" of direct evidence. Judges will leave it to the jury to determine the weight of the relevant circumstantial evidence but will typically allow it to be heard.

Those involved in investigating work must be able to distinguish between direct and circumstantial evidence.

7. Laying the foundation

Many kinds of evidence are not admissible until a proper foundation has been established for them.

EXAMPLE

An expert witness cannot offer opinions as an expert until his credentials as an expert have been established by testimony or stipulation of the parties and the trial judge finds he is indeed qualified as an expert in the field in which he will offer his opinions. A document cannot be received in evidence until it has first been properly authenticated, that is, established by some proof to genuinely be what it appears to be. In a murder trial, the murder weapon will not be allowed in evidence until an adequate **chain of custody** has first been established showing that it is in fact the weapon found at the crime scene. That chain of custody will include proof as to how the weapon has been stored and preserved and in whose custody it has been every moment since its discovery by the police.

We call the establishment of this basis for the admissibility of evidence **laying the foundation.** As you study the various specific rules of evidence in Chapter 7, watch for references to the need to establish the foundation before evidence can be admitted. Laying a proper foundation for evidence is every bit as critical as the evidence itself, since without a proper foundation the evidence either will not be admitted by the trial judge or, if admitted under a cloud of doubt, will lose some or all of its probative value. Laying a proper foundation can sometimes take as much or more time than offering the testimony itself.

8. Rulings on admissibility and offers of proof

Under FRE 104, it is the presiding trial judge who makes the determination as to the admissibility of any offered evidence. It is the role of the jury to hear the factual evidence allowed in by the judge and to decide the factual issues before it based on that evidence. That is why the jury is called **the finder of fact.** But evidentiary questions are issues of law to be decided by the judge, not the jury.

When an objection is made to offered evidence, the judge will either **sustain** the objection, which means the objection is valid and the evidence will be disallowed, or the judge will **overrule** the objection, which means the objection is not valid and the evidence is allowed in.

However, it is within the province of the jury to decide what weight or **credibility** (believability) to give to evidence that is allowed in by the judge. See FRE 104(e). Just because the judge allows the jury to hear particular testimony does not mean the jury must believe it or give it any credence. Those decisions are up to the jury in its deliberations.

Frequently, when it is a close legal decision as to whether evidence ought to be admitted or not, the judge will choose to allow it in, saying it is up to the jury to accept it or not. And in a **bench trial** (a trial conducted without a jury) where the trial judge is the finder of fact, most judges are more lenient in allowing disputed evidence to be heard than they would be in a jury trial. Most trial judges reason that in a bench trial they, with their experience in the adversarial process, will not be confused or misled as a jury might be and can reliably give the disputed testimony its proper weight.

A party dissatisfied with the ruling of the trial judge on admitting evidence can preserve the ruling as an issue of alleged **error** for **appeal.** The attorneys must be careful at trial, however, to preserve the right to appeal the judge's evidentiary ruling. Under FRE 103(a)(1), a party cannot appeal the judge's ruling allowing evidence in as error unless that party makes a timely objection to its admission at trial.

Under FRE 103(a)(2), a party cannot appeal a judge's ruling excluding tendered evidence unless the substance of what the evidence would have been is evident from the excluded question or the party makes an **offer of proof** at trial. An offer of proof is conducted out of the jury's hearing for the purpose of preserving it for the record. It may consist of the witness testifying out of the hearing of the jury or of the lawyer summarizing what the witness would have said if allowed to testify.

B. The Role of the Rules of Evidence in Interviewing and Investigating

Knowledge of the basic rules of evidence helps the paralegal investigator in:

1. Planning and carrying out effective informal investigations

Having some idea of what kinds of facts and information will or will not be admissible in court enables the paralegal to prioritize the investigation, to seek usable information, and to avoid wasting time pursuing dead ends.

HYPOTHETICAL 6-1

Assume that the attorney you work for is representing Teed Off in a civil suit pending in the U.S. District Court (where the FRE apply) against Snap Hook, a professional golfer who plays on the PGA tour. Teed Off alleges that he was the full-time caddie for Snap Hook last year and that at the beginning of the year Snap Hook verbally promised to pay Teed Off ten percent of all his tournament winnings during the year plus a $200,000 cash bonus if Snap Hook won any one of the four major tournaments—the Masters, the U.S. Open, the British Open, or the PGA Tournament.

Snap Hook did win the PGA Tournament but has refused to pay Teed Off the bonus and denies that any such promise was made. Your lawyer has told Teed Off that the case looks like a swearing match and the jury will just have to decide who to believe. Teed Off is, well, teed off!

In the course of your assigned investigation, you discover at the court house in the county where Snap Hook lives that he has a twenty-year-old misdemeanor conviction for smoking marijuana (during a round of golf no less) and a three-year-old misdemeanor conviction for shoplifting (golf balls at a Wal-Mart). Both convictions were based on guilty pleas and the sentences in both cases were satisfied by community service hours.

Which lead is more useful to Teed Off in his case against Snap Hook? Which lead deserves more of your attention in follow-up investigation? Read FRE 609(a) and 609(b) and articulate a response to those two questions.

Assume that Snap Hook has given a deposition in this case and has denied under oath that he has any criminal convictions in his past. Does that alter your conclusion about the usefulness of both of these convictions? Read FRE 613 and articulate a response to that question.

2. Putting discovered information in admissible form

A number of evidentiary rules go not just to the content of the information but to its form. Unless the evidence is offered in proper form or unless a proper foundation is laid, it will be inadmissible, regardless of how relevant or persuasive it is.

HYPOTHETICAL 6-2

Assume that you make the discovery of the prior convictions of Snap Hook mentioned in Hypothetical 6-1 the day before trial is set to begin and in a county more than five hundred miles away from where the case is to be tried. You place a long-distance call to ask your supervising attorney how to proceed but he is not available to talk with you. As you hang up the phone, you look at the clock and realize that the clerk's office where you have found these records closes in ten minutes. You remember that Snap Hook denied in his deposition that he had any criminal convictions and that the case may be decided on the credibility of the two parties. A growing feeling of panic closes around your throat.

What can you do to make the information you have discovered admissible in court tomorrow? What form does it have to be in?

Fighting back the panic, you have the clerk of the court make you copies of the court records of the two convictions then head for your car to return home. But something keeps nagging at you, so you finally pull out your copy of the rules of evidence.

There it is, right there in FRE 901. How could you have forgotten? The records of these convictions, like all documents and things offered in evidence, must be properly authenticated (i.e., shown to be genuine) before they will be admitted in evidence. "I just need to arrange for an authenticating witness is all," you shout to yourself, delirious with relief. You bound back up the steps to the courthouse and slip your foot in the door of the clerk's office just as they are closing for the day. Putting on your best *you gotta love me* smile, you explain your dilemma to the clerk and ask if she will mind traveling out of town over night to appear in court five hundred miles away tomorrow in order to authenticate these records.

You can tell from the look on her face that she's not going to agree. She asks if you have a subpoena for her and you admit that you do not. She silently takes your copy of the rules of evidence from your trembling hand, turns to FRE 902(4) and points at it.

Sheepishly, you read that a copy of a public record (like the court records of Snap Hook's criminal convictions) may be self-authenticating (no live witness is needed to authenticate) if it is certified by the custodian or other authorized person. All you ever had to do was get copies of the records of the convictions certified by the clerk of the court where they are of record. The clerk graciously agrees to certify the records for you even though it is now after hours. A few minutes later you are stuck in rush-hour traffic on your way home but feeling no pain.

Just then, out of the blue, panic strikes again. What about the hearsay rule? One knowledgeable of the rules of evidence knows that these copies of the convictions are hearsay—out-of-court statements offered to prove the truth of them. Will that keep them out of evidence tomorrow? Your whole poor, pathetic life passes before your eyes. You swerve over to the shoulder of the road and grab your copy of the rules of evidence again. Finally, FRE 803(8) jumps out at you and you breathe easy. The sky is blue and the birds are singing. Why? Because FRE 803(8) says that public records are not excluded by the hearsay rule.

You head home now, at peace, visualizing the well deserved pat on the back your supervising attorney will give you. Maybe Teed Off will even give you some tips on getting rid of that nasty slice!

3. Drafting formal discovery requests and responses

As we saw in Chapter 4, the scope of permissible formal discovery under FRCP 26(b) is broader than the scope of what is admissible at trial under the rules of evidence. Still, under FRCP 26(b), information sought in formal discovery must be relevant to these issues, not privileged, and at least calculated to lead to the discovery of admissible evidence. Consequently, those involved in planning and drafting formal discovery requests must be familiar with what is—and isn't—admissible evidence.

HYPOTHETICAL 6-3

Assume that in the lawsuit between Teed Off and Snap Hook you locate a witness, Sand Trap, who was in the gallery at the PGA Tournament when Snap Hook made his winning putt on the last hole. Sand Trap tells you in an interview that he heard Snap Hook say something to himself as he stood over that last putt but couldn't understand what it was. He asked the man standing next to him what Snap Hook said and the man replied, "I think he said, 'This is a million for me and two hundred grand for my caddie.'"

Your supervising lawyer schedules the formal deposition of Sand Trap and asks him during the deposition what the man standing next to him told him that Snap Hook said. The attorney for Snap Hook objects to the question on the grounds that it calls for a hearsay response. Your supervising attorneys says, "That might be a good objection at trial but not here in this deposition."

> Assuming that the attorney for Snap Hook is correct that the question calls for a hearsay response (see Chapter 7), articulate a reason why your supervising attorney's response to the objection is correct under FRCP 26(b).
>
> Assuming that Sand Trap is able to answer your supervising attorney's question about what the man standing next to him in the gallery heard Snap Hook say, what will the next question to Sand Trap probably be?

For the same reasons, the rules of evidence may provide a basis to object to requested discovery if the asking party cannot demonstrate that the information sought is calculated to lead to the discovery of admissible evidence under FRCP 26.

HYPOTHETICAL 6-4

> Assume that the attorney for Snap Hook serves your office with interrogatories to be answered by Teed Off in the suit over the promised $200,000 bonus. Assume further that one of the interrogatories asks about Teed Off's medical history.
>
> Review the section of Chapter 7 dealing with relevant evidence and articulate a recommendation to your supervising attorney as to whether this question should be objected to and why.
>
> Based on what you know so far of the suit between Snap Hook and Teed Off, what, if any, argument might the attorney for Snap Hook make in defense of the propriety of his interrogatory to Teed Off?

4. Drafting affidavits or declarations for use in pretrial motions

Frequently when motions are made to the court prior to trial, particularly FRCP 56 motions for summary judgment, the motions will be supported or opposed by written statements of testimony called **affidavits** in some jurisdictions and **declarations** in others. These written statements are made under oath just like trial testimony and must comply with the rules of evidence. (See Illustrations 6-1 and 6-2.)

HYPOTHETICAL 6-5

> Assume that in the course of your investigation for Teed Off in his suit against Snap Hook you discover a letter written by Snap Hook to his mentor and coach, Double Eagle, prior to Snap Hook's winning the PGA Tournament. In the letter to Double Eagle, Snap Hook acknowledges the agreement to pay Teed Off the $200,000 bonus. Based on that letter, your supervising attorney may decide to file a Rule 56 motion for summary judgment on behalf of Teed Off on the grounds that there are no genuine issues of material fact and that Teed Off is entitled to judgment as a matter of law. The motion and supporting affidavit of Teed Off might look like Illustrations 6-1 and 6-2, respectively.
>
> If you assist in the preparation of the affidavit of Teed Off, you will have to be careful to ensure that all factual testimony given in the affidavit complies with the rules of evidence.
>
> Review the material in Chapter 7 on the authentication of documents and articulate an opinion as to whether paragraphs 5 and 6 of the Teed

Off affidavit set out in Illustration 6-2 lay a sufficient foundation for the introduction of the letter of Snap Hook addressed to Double Eagle into evidence. What more, if anything, would you suggest to your supervising attorney might be needed to ensure the admission of that letter into evidence? To add to its credibility or weight?

5. Planning the evidence to be offered at trial

For every witness your supervising attorney expects to call to testify at trial, his pretrial preparation will include a review of the projected testimony to anticipate and prepare for possible objections from the other side. For every document or object your supervising attorney intends to

Illustration 6-1   MOTION FOR SUMMARY JUDGMENT

IN THE UNITED STATES DISTRICT COURT
FOR THE EASTERN DISTRICT OF YOURSTATE
NORTHERN DIVISION

TEED OFF,
      Plaintiff

     v.

SNAP HOOK,
      Defendant

)
)
)   DOCKET NO. 04-00002
)
)

PLAINTIFF'S MOTION FOR SUMMARY JUDGMENT

Plaintiff, Teed Off, pursuant to Rule 56 of the Federal Rules of Civil Procedure, moves the court for an order entering summary judgment in his favor as to all allegations contained in the complaint. Plaintiff alleges that there are no genuine issues as to any material fact in this case and that plaintiff is entitled to judgment as a matter of law.

In support of this motion, plaintiff relies on the following, all of which are submitted with this motion:

    1. plaintiff's memorandum of law and fact;

    2. excerpts from the pleadings;

    3. excerpts from the depositions of plaintiff and defendant; and

    4. the affidavit of plaintiff, Teed Off.

Wherefore, plaintiff asks the court to enter an order awarding judgment in his favor against defendant in the amount of $200,000 plus prejudgment interest on that amount as prayed for in the complaint.

——————————————————
Mellow Fellow
Attorney for plaintiff Teed Off
(Address)

(Certificate of service omitted)

Illustration 6-2   AFFIDAVIT IN SUPPORT OF MOTION FOR SUMMARY JUDGMENT

IN THE UNITED STATES DISTRICT
COURT FOR THE EASTERN DISTRICT OF YOURSTATE
NORTHERN DIVISION

TEED OFF, 　　　Plaintiff 　　v. SNAP HOOK, 　　　Defendant	)))　　　DOCKET NO. 04-00002)))

AFFIDAVIT OF PLAINTIFF TEED OFF

STATE OF YOURSTATE)
COUNTY OF HARMONY)

Affiant, Teed Off, after first being duly sworn according to law, deposes and states as follows:

1. I am the plaintiff in this case.

2. I have personal knowledge of the matters contained in this affidavit. This affidavit is submitted in support of my motion for summary judgment.

3. I have been a caddie for professional golfers on the Professional Golfers Association (PGA) tour for approximately ten years. On or about December 20, 2002 I was contacted by phone by the defendant Snap Hook, a professional golfer. In that conversation Snap Hook offered me the full-time position as his caddie for the upcoming 2003 golfing season. In consideration for my agreement to be his full-time caddie during the 2003 season, Snap Hook promised to pay me ten percent of all his tournament winnings plus a cash bonus of $200,000 if he won any of the four major tournaments (including the Masters, the U.S. Open, the British Open, and the PGA Tournament) during the 2003 season.

4. I did caddie for Snap Hook during the entire 2003 golfing season as I had agreed to do. Snap Hook did pay me ten percent of all of his tournament winnings for the 2003 golfing season. However, on August 20, 2003, Snap Hook won the PGA tournament but he has failed and refused to pay me the $200,000 bonus.

5. Attached as Exhibit 1 to this affidavit is a copy of a handwritten letter dated May 5, 2003 and addressed to Double Eagle. Double Eagle is known to me to be the mentor and golfing coach for Snap Hook.

6. I am familiar with the handwriting of Snap Hook. I saw him sign many autographs for fans during the 2003 season. In those autographs he would sign his name and often write some personal message. Based on my knowledge of and familiarity with the handwriting of Snap Hook, I can state that the letter attached as Exhibit 1 to this affidavit was written by Snap Hook and that the signature on the letter is his.

FURTHER AFFIANT SAYETH NOT.

_____
　　　　　　　　　　　　　　　　TEED OFF

SWORN TO AND SUBSCRIBED BEFORE ME,
THE UNDERSIGNED NOTARY PUBLIC, THIS
　　　DAY OF MAY, 2004

_____
　　　　　　Notary Public

My commission expires on _____.

offer in evidence at trial he must anticipate and prepare for possible objections based on relevance, authentication, chain of custody, hearsay, or some other basis. The legal assistant may be asked to assist the attorney in anticipating objections and preparing to overcome them.

And, of course, for every witness the opposing party plans to call and every document or object the opposing party intends to offer in evidence, your supervising attorney pretrial preparation will include a determination of whether a valid objection can be raised to the testimony or document.

6. Assisting the lawyer at trial

No matter how thorough the pretrial preparation, the unexpected always happens at trial. The opposing party offers evidence that was not anticipated. Or the opposing party makes an unexpected objection to your side's evidence. Evidentiary objections must be made or responded to immediately or it is too late.

One of the most important qualities of a good trial lawyer is to be able to think quickly in such situations. If the paralegal is assisting at trial (or back at the office waiting for an emergency phone call from the courthouse), he needs to be qualified to render quick, competent assistance in such situations.

C. ▶ The Doctrine of Privileges

Closely related to evidentiary matters is the doctrine of privileges. The various privileges were developed through the **common law** (decisions of courts). Over the years, the courts determined that, due to various public policy concerns, certain information should not be subject to disclosure in informal investigation, formal discovery, or even in sworn testimony at trial. Consequently, if information can be fitted into one of the recognized privileges, it is excepted from discovery and need not be disclosed to anyone for any purpose. The one having the privilege is deemed immune from having to testify concerning the privileged information or otherwise disclose it. Accordingly, this area of the law is sometimes referred to as **privileges** and **immunities**.

In most states the recognized privileges have now been made **statutory** (i.e., enacted into law by the legislature of that state). Some, however, are still of common law authority only and you will need to check not only the statutes but the case law of your state to determine the exact privileges recognized in your jurisdiction. (See LBD 6-3 and 6–4.)

Not all states recognize the same privileges or apply them in the same way. Most states do recognize the **attorney-client privilege**, the **physician-patient privilege**, and a **spousal privilege** (sometimes called the **marital privilege**).

Furthermore, some privileges are **absolute** (meaning they apply in all circumstances), some are **qualified** (meaning that under certain circumstances the privilege may not apply) and any privilege may be waived. The following is a summary of the most widely recognized privileges other than the attorney-client privilege, which was discussed in detail in Chapter 2.

1. Trial preparation materials

Sometimes called the **work product rule,** this privilege has its origin in the seminal Supreme Court case of *Hickman v. Taylor,* 329 U.S. 495 (1947), and is now firmly embodied in federal law as Rule 26(b)(3) of the Federal Rules of Civil Procedure (see the text of the rules in Appendix B). Most states have substantially the same language in their state court rules of procedure but the paralegal should check the rules of the jurisdiction in which she practices.

This rule recognizes an **absolute privilege** for any material containing the "mental impressions, conclusions, opinions, or legal theories of an attorney or other representative of a party concerning the litigation." Such material is sometimes referred to as attorney work product.

In many law offices there is a policy to stamp any notes, memoranda, or correspondence containing such material with the designation *work product* or *attorney work product.* Such a procedure will not guarantee that the court will protect such material from disclosure if it is challenged, but the designation, if used in good faith, is a helpful indication of intent.

FRCP 26(b)(3) recognizes a qualified privilege for documents and things prepared in anticipation of litigation or for trial by or for the party or by or for the party's representative. The opposing side in a lawsuit can compel the disclosure of those materials in formal discovery only upon a showing of *substantial need* in preparation of its case and the inability to obtain the substantial equivalent of the materials by other means.

2. The physician-patient privilege

This privilege applies to confidential information disclosed to a treating physician by or on behalf of a patient and related to treatment or diagnosis of the patient. The privilege belongs to the patient and only the patient can waive the privilege and permit disclosure, or assert the privilege and prevent disclosure.

HYPOTHETICAL 6-6

Assume that as part of your pre-filing investigation in connection with the suit of Teed Off against Snap Hook you interview Double Eagle and take extensive notes during the interview. Your notes not only indicate your questions and his answers, they also contain your impressions of Double Eagle as a credible witness. Shortly after your interview with Double Eagle, he dies in an accident.

Later, your supervising attorney files suit on behalf of Teed Off. The attorneys for Snap Hook serve a document request on the attorney for Teed Off asking to see and copy the notes from your interview with Double Eagle.

1. Do these facts support an argument of "substantial need" under FRCP 26(b)(3)?

> 2. Will the attorneys for Snap Hook be able to obtain all your notes from the interview or only those portions containing the questions and answers? Why?
> 3. If Double Eagle were still alive and available to the attorneys for Snap Hook, what would be the appropriate response to this document request?

The most common example of waiver is seen when the patient puts her medical condition at issue, as by filing a personal injury lawsuit. The plaintiff's entire relevant medical history will then be discoverable.

3. The psychotherapist-patient privilege

Recognized by most states, the psychotherapist-patient privilege protects confidential communications related to the diagnosis or treatment of a mental or psychological condition. This privilege too is not absolute and is waived if the patient puts his mental or psychological condition at issue in a proceeding.

4. The marital (spousal) privilege

This privilege applies to confidential communications of all kinds between married persons. The privilege belongs to both spouses and either of them may refuse to disclose the communication and prohibit the other spouse or any third person from disclosing it. Most states provide that the privilege survives divorce so long as the confidential communication was made while the marriage was still valid.

Exceptions to the marital privilege are recognized in an action by one spouse against the other. And many states today are enacting statutes denying the privilege in criminal actions involving child or spousal abuse. (See LBD 6-3.)

5. The spousal testimony privilege

A related privilege recognized in many states is the privilege against spousal testimony, which provides that a spouse cannot be compelled to give any testimony against the other spouse regardless of whether the testimony would involve the disclosure of confidential marital communications.

6. The privilege against self-incrimination

The Fifth Amendment to the United States Constitution provides that no person "shall be compelled in any criminal case to be a witness against himself." As interpreted by the courts, this means that persons cannot be compelled to disclose any information that would tend to incriminate them. And the privilege can be asserted in a civil proceeding as well as a criminal one, because compelled disclosure of criminal conduct in a civil proceeding could lead to a criminal charge.

The privilege against self-incrimination is not absolute. The witness can be compelled to testify if the prosecution grants **transactional immunity,** which is full immunity from prosecution on all charges related to the witness's testimony. A witness granted transactional immunity cannot be prosecuted on any charge related to the witness's testimony even if the government obtains evidence of the crime independently of the testimony.

Or, the government may grant the witness **derivative use immunity,** commonly referred to only as **use immunity.** The granting of use immunity to a witness prohibits the government from using the witness's testimony or any evidence derived from it to prosecute the witness. However, any evidence the government obtains against the witness independent of the witness's testimony and not derived from it can still be used to prosecute the witness.

7. Miscellaneous privileges

There are a number of other types of privileges recognized by various states including **priest-penitent** and **accountant-client privileges.**

Whenever your case involves a state or federal statute, you should research the statute carefully to determine if it provides for any special privileges from disclosure in any lawsuit or administrative proceeding brought under the statute.

8. Procedural matters relating to privileges

A procedural question that often arises concerning cases pending in federal court is whether the privileges recognized by the law of the state in which the federal court sits will apply in the federal court proceeding. This is not always an easy question to answer, but primary guidance comes from FRE 501. That rule provides in essence that suits in federal court based on diversity jurisdiction (such suits are almost always controlled by state law) will be governed by state immunity law. Cases in federal court on some other jurisdictional basis (usually federal question cases) will be governed by the privilege rules as developed by the federal courts.

Again, care should be taken to inform yourself regarding the various privileges recognized in the jurisdiction in which you practice, the recognized exceptions to them, and the interpretation of them by the state courts. (See LBD 6-3 and 6-4.)

KEY WORDS AND PHRASES TO REMEMBER

absolute privilege
accountant-client privilege
affidavit
affirmative defense
attorney-client privilege
bench trial

beyond a reasonable doubt
burden of proof
by a preponderance
chain of custody
circumstantial evidence
clear and convincing evidence

common law
counterclaim
cross-claim
declaration
demonstrative evidence
direct evidence
documentary evidence
error
finder of fact
first-hand knowledge
laying the foundation
marital privilege
objection overruled
objection sustained
offer of proof
physician-patient privilege

priest-penitent privilege
probative value
psychotherapist-patient privilege
public policy
qualified privilege
real evidence
self-incrimination
second-hand knowledge
spousal testimony privilege
standard of proof
statutory law
testimonial evidence
third-party claim
transactional immunity
use immunity
weight of the evidence

LEARN BY DOING

LBD 6-1. Determine which party (the prosecution or criminal defendant) has the respective burden(s) of proof to prove or refute on the issue of insanity in your jurisdiction when the defendant raises the insanity defense. Also determine what standard or degree of proof (preponderance, clear and convincing, beyond a reasonable doubt) is required for the party having the burden to prove/refute. Put your findings in the form of a research memorandum.

LBD 6-2. Determine what standard or degree of proof is required of a plaintiff to prevail in a case of civil fraud in your jurisdiction. How do the statutes or court decisions of your state distinguish between the "preponderance" standard and the "clear and convincing" standard? Put your findings in the form of a research memorandum.

LBD 6-3. List and summarize the various statutory and common law privileges currently recognized in your state.

LBD 6-4. Research and prepare a memorandum regarding the history, development, and current status of the marital privilege in your state.

LBD 6-5. Interview a government prosecutor and/or a criminal defense lawyer concerning their agreement or disagreement with the marital privilege, the spousal testimony privilege, and the Fifth Amendment privilege against self-incrimination. Prepare a memorandum comparing the two viewpoints expressed as well as your own opinions on those privileges.

Chapter 7

Rules of Evidence for the Investigator—Part 2

CHAPTER OBJECTIVES

In this chapter you will learn the basic rules of evidence and how they apply in a practical way to interviewing and investigating work by the paralegal. We will consider the rules regarding:

- Relevant evidence
- Lay and expert witnesses
- Hearsay and its various exceptions
- Admissions by party opponent
- Character evidence
- Bias and interest
- Prior inconsistent statements
- Authentication of documents and things
- The best evidence rule
- The admissibility of evidence for alternative reasons

A. The Basic Rules of Evidence

This section is not intended to provide a comprehensive study of the rules of evidence. Rather, it is a brief summary of the most commonly used rules. The Federal Rules of Evidence are used here (see selected rules in Appendix D), but it should be kept in mind that in state court proceedings, the rules of evidence for that state will control. State court rules of evidence may differ significantly from the federal rules and will vary from state to state.

1. Relevance

To be admissible, evidence must be **relevant** to the issues in the lawsuit. See FRE 402. FRE 401 defines relevant evidence as "evidence having any tendency to make the existence of any fact that is of consequence to the determination of the action more probable or less probable than it would be without the evidence." There are two parts to this definition. Evidence must tend to prove something. And what it tends to prove must bear on the issues to be decided in the lawsuit. Evidence may be true, interesting, even shocking, but that doesn't mean it is relevant to the issues to be decided.

HYPOTHETICAL 7-1

Assume that you are assisting your supervising attorney with a civil lawsuit involving an alleged trespass to land. The defendant is alleged to have poured a concrete driveway that lies, in part, on the property of his neighbor, the plaintiff. Your supervising attorney has explained to you that this is a type of strict liability tort. That is, it doesn't matter whether the defendant knew that he was pouring concrete over the property line, only whether he in fact did so without the consent of the plaintiff.

With the issue framed like that, which of the following facts do you think would be deemed relevant under FRE 401 and 402 and why?

1. That the defendant was born with two heads and had one removed?
2. That at the defendant's last residence he poured a concrete driveway that encroached on his neighbor's property?
3. That while the defendant was having the driveway poured the plaintiff watched but said nothing.
4. That defendant poured the concrete at night?
5. That defendant had a survey of the property line done before he poured the concrete?
6. That defendant is a member of a fringe religious group that worships concrete and believes that all the earth should be placed under at least three inches of concrete. (You guessed it, he's a real estate developer!)
7. That defendant had previously planted a hedge along the property line that encroached on the plaintiff's property and the plaintiff had cut it down.
8. That plaintiff does not actually own the property encroached upon but rents it from the owner, the defendant.
9. That plaintiff wrote his initials and the date in the concrete after it was poured.
10. That the morning after the concrete appeared, the defendant and plaintiff were leaving their houses at the same time and the defendant pointed at the concrete and said, "Well, who did that?"

Now assume that your supervising attorney tells you that this is not a strict liability tort and that in order to recover the plaintiff must show that the defendant intentionally encroached on the property line. How does that change your decision regarding the relevance of the facts listed above?

Under FRE 403, even relevant evidence may be excluded if "its probative value is substantially outweighed by the danger of unfair prejudice, confusion of the issues, or misleading the jury, or by considerations of undue delay, waste of time, or needless presentation or cumulative evidence." Can you think of examples where this rule might come into play?

2. Lay witnesses

Witnesses must be competent (FRE 601). The non-expert witness, called a **lay witness** (as distinguished from the **expert witness**) must generally limit his testimony to matters of which he has personal knowledge (FRE 602). However, even the lay witness can offer a conclusion or inference from perceived facts if it is within the range of common experience (FRE 701).

EXAMPLE

> A lay witness might be able to testify that a reddish substance looked to her like blood. Or that the car appeared to be speeding. Or that the noise sounded like a gunshot. Or that someone's breath smelled of alcohol.

3. Expert witnesses

Witnesses qualified as **experts** (one qualified "by knowledge, skill, experience, training or education") can testify by opinion in the field of their expertise (FRE 702). It is up to the judge, not the jury, to decide if a witness is in fact qualified to testify as an expert. FRE 104(a). In two recent and significant cases regarding the role of the trial judge in determining the admissibility of expert testimony, the U.S. Supreme Court described the role of the trial judge as that of a *gatekeeper* and gave the trial judge broad discretion to allow or disallow expert testimony by testing its relevance and reliability based on a number of factors. See *Kumho Tire Co. v. Carmichael*, 526 U.S. 137 (1999); and *Daubert v. Merrell Dow Pharmaceuticals, Inc.*, 509 U.S. 579 (1993). (See LBD 7-2.)

Expert testimony is commonly used in all kinds of litigation today and it is critical for the paralegal to know how to locate, interview, do background checks on, communicate with, and otherwise work effectively with expert witnesses (see Chapter 15).

Under FRE 702, expert testimony may be used anytime such knowledge "will assist the trier of fact to understand the evidence or to determine a fact in issue."

What kind of experts do you think might be called to testify in the suit between Teed Off and Snap Hook described in Hypotheticals 6-1 through 6-5? In the suit between the parties in Hypothetical 7-1?

Experts may even testify to the **ultimate** (i.e., determinative) **issue** in the case (FRE 704).

EXAMPLE

> In a case in which the plaintiff is alleging that the defendant was negligent for failing to stop his car in time to avoid rear-ending the plaintiff's car, the plaintiff may call an accident reconstruction expert to testify. The following question may be permissible even though it goes to the ultimate question that the jury has to decide as fact finders: "Professor Brown, do you have an opinion as to whether defendant Smith was negligent in failing to brake sooner?"

Under FRE 703, experts may base their opinions and inferences on facts or data made known to them at trial or before trial (which could include hearsay) and even on facts or data not admissible in court if they are of a type reasonably relied on by the expert in forming opinions on the subject.

The state evidentiary rules regarding expert witnesses may differ significantly from the federal rules and special care should be taken by the paralegal to note any differences. (See LBD 7-1.)

4. Examination of witnesses

Both lay and expert witnesses testify by answering questions put to them by the attorneys (or by the judge). Questioning of a witness by the attorney who called the witness to testify is called **direct examination.** Following direct examination, every witness called to testify is subject to **cross-examination** by counsel for all other parties (FRE 614(a)). Generally, **leading questions** (questions calling for a yes or no response; see Chapter 10) cannot be asked of a witness on direct examination but only on cross-examination (FRE 611(c)).

The scope of cross-examination is limited to matters raised in the direct examination and to credibility of the witness (FRE 611(b)) (see discussion of credibility below). At the request of any party, witnesses who are not parties themselves or the designated representative of a business entity party (a corporation, partnership, etc.) will be sequestered (excluded from the courtroom) during the testimony of other witnesses (FRE 615).

5. The hearsay rule

Hearsay is defined by FRE 801(c) as "a statement, other than the one made by the declarant [the one making the statement] while testifying at the trial or hearing [i.e., an out-of-court statement] offered in evidence to prove the truth of the matter asserted."

Hearsay statements are *not admissible in evidence.* FRE 803. To determine whether offered testimony might run afoul of the hearsay rule, you must ask:

a. Is it a statement?

FRE 801(a) defines a statement for hearsay purposes as an oral or written assertion or conduct intended as an assertion. Not every sound a person makes would be hearsay if repeated in court, because it may not be intended as a statement or assertion of anything. For example, testimony that a person was heard humming to themselves or was seen doodling cartoon faces on a sheet of paper would probably not be hearsay. Gestures or bodily motions can be statements too. For example, the head shake or nod, the thumbs-up sign, or rolling the eyes.

b. Is it a statement made out of court?

Note that a witness may be asked in court to repeat a statement that she made herself out of court. That will trigger the hearsay rule just as if the witness was asked to repeat in court a statement made by someone else.

c. Is it a statement offered to prove the truth of the matter asserted?

Frequently, statements are offered in testimony not to prove the truth of what was said but for some independent purpose, usually to prove that something was in fact said whether true or not.

HYPOTHETICAL 7-2

Assume that you are assisting your supervising attorney at the trial of a civil fraud case. Your client is the plaintiff, Gulli Bull, who is alleging that the defendant, Smooth Talker, a used car salesman, sold him a car showing only 120,000 miles on the speedometer but which actually had more than 300,000 miles on it. Gulli Bull alleges that Smooth Talker knew that the mileage shown was incorrect but failed to disclose this information to him. Gulli Bull is suing for rescission of the contract to get his money back, for emotional distress, and for punitive damages.

You learned during your investigation that while Smooth Talker was trying to sell the car to Gulli Bull, another salesman, Honest John, whispered to Smooth Talker, boss, that car has at least 300,000 miles on it. According to Honest John, Smooth Talker just shrugged when he told him that and said nothing to Gulli Bull about the mileage.

Now, at trial, your supervising attorney has called Honest John to testify as a witness for the plaintiff. The attorney asks Honest John to tell the judge what he said to Smooth Talker that day. The attorney for Smooth Talker objects to the question on the basis of hearsay.

1. Is what Honest John is being asked to say a statement or declaration within the meaning of FRE 801(a)?
2. Is what Honest John is being asked to say a statement made out of court? Does it matter that Honest John is being asked to repeat in court his own statement made out of court to Smooth Talker?
3. Assume the trial judge finds that what Honest John is being asked to say is a statement within FRE 801(a) and that it is an out-of-court statement. She then asks your supervising attorney for what purpose he is asking Honest John this question. If the attorney says he is asking Honest John this question to prove that there were actually more than 300,000 miles on the car, how should the trial judge rule on the objection and why? If the attorney says he is asking Honest John this question only to prove that Smooth Talker had actual notice prior to the sale that the car had more than 120,000 miles on it, how should the trial judge rule on the objection and why?
4. If your supervising attorney responds to the judge's question by saying that he is asking the question only to show that Smooth Talker had actual notice prior to the sale that the car had more than 120,000 miles on it, is that fact *relevant* to this lawsuit?

Assume the trial judge allows Honest John to answer the question about what he said to Smooth Talker concerning the mileage on the car. Your supervising attorney then asks Honest John how Smooth Talker responded to his statement. Before Honest John can answer that Smooth Talker just shrugged, the attorney for Smooth Talker again objects saying that this question also asks for a hearsay response.

1. Was the shrug of Smooth Talker conduct intended as an assertion under FRE 801(a)?
2. If so, what was Smooth Talker arguably asserting by his shrug?

3. If so, was the shrug of Smooth Talker an out-of-court assertion?
4. Assuming the trial judge finds that the shrug of Smooth Talker was intended as an assertion, what purpose could your supervising attorney have in asking that question other than to prove that assertion?
5. How do you think the trial judge should rule on the hearsay objection to this question to Honest John? (Hint: You may want to review the discussion of FRE 801(d)(2) below before you answer that question too definitely.)

d. Is there a recognized exception for the statement?

Over the years, because of the harsh results of the strict application of the hearsay rule, the courts have developed numerous exceptions to it. When it is determined that testimony to be offered is or might be considered inadmissible hearsay, the next step is to look at the numerous exceptions to find one or more that may apply to allow the statement to be received in evidence.

The numerous recognized exceptions to the hearsay rule are set out in FRE 803 and 804. The difference between the two rules is that the exceptions recognized under FRE 803 apply without regard to whether the declarant (the person whose statement is being repeated in court) is available as a witness at trial. But the exceptions under FRE 804 apply only when the declarant is *not* available as a witness at trial.

6. Exceptions to the hearsay rule

The most commonly used exceptions to the hearsay rule are:

a. Present sense impression (FRE 803(1))

EXAMPLE

I smell smoke.
I'm not feeling so well.
This is exciting.
I'm sure having fun.
I really love this class.

b. Excited utterance (FRE 803(2))

EXAMPLE

Oh, _____, he just ran that light.
You scared me to death.
I think he might be dead.
I just can't get enough of this evidence stuff.

c. State of mind (FRE 803(3))

I think I might just drive all night so I can be in Miami by daybreak. I've decided to quit my job.

Note that the state of mind exception is very similar to the idea of a statement offered for a purpose other than to prove its truth illustrated in Hypothetical 7-2.

d. Statements made for purposes of medical diagnosis or treatment (FRE 803(4))

In any case where medical diagnosis or treatment is relevant to the issues, as it would be in a personal injury suit, statements made by the patient or by third persons, to obtain a diagnosis or treatment for the patient, will be admissible over a hearsay objection.

Assume that as part of his claim of emotional distress against Smooth Talker, Gulli Bull testifies that he has been unable to sleep since he learned of the fraud and has had to see a doctor and rely on medication to rest. The doctor's records discovered by the attorney for Smooth Talker show that on the first visit of Gulli Bull to the doctor, Gulli Bull's wife accompanied him and told the nurse that her husband was having trouble sleeping because his business was struggling.

At trial, will the attorney for Smooth Talker be able to have the doctor testify as to this statement by Mrs. Bull under FRE 803(4) notwithstanding a hearsay objection? What if Mrs. Bull had made the statement to a neighbor as she and her husband were leaving the house to go to the doctor's office?

e. Recorded recollection (FRE 803(5))

What happens if a witness forgets something that happened in the past? If there is some written record (a letter, diary entry, memorandum, computer file, or e-mail message, etc.) of the event, it may be possible to read it into evidence over a hearsay objection under this rule. A strict foundation must be laid, however, before the writing can be read in lieu of the testimony of the witness. It must be shown:

- that the writing was made or adopted by the forgetful witness;
- that the writing was made or adopted when the matter was fresh on the mind of the witness;
- that the writing reflects the witness's former knowledge of the matter accurately; and
- that the witness once had knowledge of the matter but now has insufficient recollection to testify.

The recorded recollection exception of FRE 803(5) should be distinguished from the use of a **writing to refresh a witness's recollection** allowed under FRE 612. Under that rule, the writing itself cannot be offered as an exhibit or read into evidence. Instead, the witness who indicates a lapse of memory is allowed to read it silently before or during her testimony and, if the writing refreshes her recollection, she then proceeds to testify without reference to the writing. Of course, the opposing party may use and refer to the writing on cross-examination to test the refreshed recollection of the witness.

EXAMPLE

Assume that prior to trial Honest John gave the attorney for Gulli Bull a written statement in which he described in detail his conversation with Smooth Talker on the day Gulli Bull bought the car, as related in Hypotheticals 7-1 and 7-2. At trial, however, Honest John freezes up and cannot even remember what day the sale occurred. The quick-thinking attorney may show Honest John his statement and ask questions that go like this:

ATTY: Mr. John, let me show you a document and ask you to look at it and then tell us if you recognize the signature at the bottom?

HJ: Uh, yes, sir. That's my signature.

ATTY: And tell us whether or not that is a written statement that you made to a paralegal from my office concerning the facts in this case?

HJ: It is, yes, sir.

ATTY: And when you gave my paralegal that written statement, were the things you talk about in there fresh on your mind?

HJ (smiling and blushing): Yes sir, I could remember everything then but I wasn't looking at a jury like I am now.

ATTY (laughing slightly): Well, sir, take a moment more and tell us if that statement you are holding refreshes your recollection of those events described.

HJ: Yes, it does, sir. It certainly does.

ATTY: Well, let me have the statement back then and let's proceed with our questions.

f. Business records (FRE 803(6) and (7))

The business records exceptions are very broadly construed by the courts to allow into evidence just about any type of relevant business record over a hearsay objection if the foundation is properly laid. To have documents or a data compilation containing what would otherwise be hearsay admitted in evidence, it must first be shown through the testimony of a custodian of the document or other qualified witness that:

- the document or compilation was created at or near the time of the events or transactions referenced in it;
- the document or compilation was created by a person with knowledge of the events or transactions referenced in it or from information transmitted by such a person;
- the document or compilation was kept in the course of a regularly conducted business activity; and
- it was the regular practice with regard to that business activity to make the document or compilation.

HYPOTHETICAL 7-4

Assume that as part of the pretrial investigation into the claim of Gulli Bull against Smooth Talker you are interviewing Honest John who is now a former employee of Smooth Talker. Honest John tells you about his conversation with Smooth Talker and you ask him how he knew the car had more than 300,000 miles on it. He responds that he had seen it in "the book." You ask him what book and he says:

Well, there's this book we sorta kept around there where when we took a car in on a trade we wrote down whatever the owner told us about it. And I remember seeing something in there on that car that said, "Mileage reads 120k but closer to 350k." Or something like that.

Recognizing the potential importance of this information and with the business records exception to the hearsay rule in mind, what additional questions will you now ask Honest John during the interview?

g. Public records (FRE 803(8) and (10))

(See Hypothetical 6-4.)

h. Former testimony (FRE 804(b)(1))

Note that this exception applies only if the declarant is unavailable for trial and only to former sworn testimony where the opposing party had the opportunity to examine the witness.

HYPOTHETICAL 7-5

If you interview Honest John as in Hypothetical 7-4 but he dies in an accident before trial:

1. Could your supervising attorney tender your notes of the interview as testimony under this exception?
2. If Honest John had given you a signed statement following your interview and then dies in an accident, could your attorney tender his statement as testimony at trial?
3. If Honest John was deposed in Gulli Bull's lawsuit against Smooth Talker under FRCP 30 and then dies in an accident, could your attorney tender the deposition transcript at trial?

i. Statements against interest (FRE 804(b)(3))

A statement made against the speaker's pecuniary (money), proprietary (ownership), or culpability (civil or criminal) interests is admissible pursuant to FRE 804(b)(3).

HYPOTHETICAL 7-6

Assume that you interview Honest John as in Hypothetical 7-4 and he tells you about his conversation with Smooth Talker regarding the actual mileage on the car purchased by Gulli Bull and about the book too. To save costs your supervising attorney does not bother to depose Honest John before trial. You subpoena Honest John to appear and give testimony at trial but he calls you the day before trial and says he won't repeat at trial what he told you in the interview because he is afraid of Smooth Talker. He will just say he can't remember. The attorney says that if Honest John does that then you will be called as a witness to testify to what Honest John told you in the interview! You say, "Won't that be inadmissible hearsay?" The supervising attorney says, "I think I can get it in under FRE 804(b)(3)."

List the arguments your lawyer should make under FRE 804(b)(3) to get your testimony in over a hearsay objection.

What are the ethical considerations in your being called as a witness in this situation?

If Honest John testified at trial and simply denied having the conversation with Smooth Talker that he told you about in the interview and denied the existence of the book, could your supervising attorney then have you testify to his interview statements under FRE 804(b)(3)?

j. Discretionary exceptions (FRE 803(24) and 804(b)(5))

These fairly recent additions to the FRE arguably reflect growing dissatisfaction with the antiquated hearsay rule and the increased willingness to give trial judges the discretion to admit testimony that, though technically hearsay, appears trustworthy and should, in all fairness, be considered. These exceptions allow in evidence hearsay statements that do not fit into any of the recognized exceptions but which the trial judge finds have "equivalent circumstantial guarantees of trustworthiness." (See LBD 7-4.)

7. Admission by party opponent

Under FRE 801(d)(2), any statement made by or on behalf of a party to the suit, or which has been adopted by the party as true, is admissible if offered against that party. Such statements are declared to be *not hearsay*.

This is one of the broadest categories of admissible evidence. The practical effect of this rule is to allow in evidence just about all statements made by a party or the party's authorized representatives so long as the statements are offered by an opposing party, are relevant to the issues in the suit, and are not privileged.

HYPOTHETICAL 7-7

Remember Smooth Talker's shrug after Honest John told him the car had at least 300,000 miles on it, in Hypothetical 7-2? That shrug was quite likely an out-of-court, declarative statement and testimony of it was probably offered to prove what it communicated to Honest John—Smooth Talker was in effect saying, "I don't care if the car has more than 300,000 miles on it." Classic hearsay. But admissible as non-hearsay under FRE 801(d)(2) if offered as evidence by Gulli Bull. Why would testimony of the shrug be inadmissible hearsay if offered by Smooth Talker?

Illustration 7-1 summarizes the hearsay rule and its exceptions and exclusions.

8. Character evidence

Under FRE 404(a), evidence of a person's character (truthful, reliable, etc.) or evidence of crimes, wrongs, or acts of a person that illustrate his

Illustration 7-1   THE HEARSAY RULE: ITS EXCEPTIONS AND EXCLUSIONS

THE RULE: Hearsay is a statement, other than one made by the declarant while testifying at trial, offered in evidence to prove the truth of the matter asserted. Hearsay evidence is inadmissible at trial.

THE EXCEPTIONS:

1. Present sense impression

2. Excited utterance

3. Statements made for the purpose of medical diagnosis or treatment

4. Recorded recollection

5. Statements used to refresh memory

6. Business records

7. Public records

8. Former testimony

9. Statement against interest

10. Discretionary exceptions

THE EXCLUSIONS:

1. Statement offered for non-hearsay purpose—not to prove the truth of the statement

2. Admission by party opponent

---

character, is generally not admissible for the purpose of proving that the person acted in conformity with that character trait on a particular occasion. Note that such evidence could arguably be quite relevant. And, in contrast, under FRE 406, evidence of a person's habit or routine practice is generally admissible in evidence to prove that the person acted in conformity with it on a particular occasion.

There are a number of exceptions to the general ban on character evidence.

a. Where character is an essential element

Character evidence is admissible when the character trait is an essential element of the claim or defense in the lawsuit.

EXAMPLE

> If plaintiff sues defendant for libel because defendant said plaintiff was a dishonest person, evidence of the character of plaintiff is admissible by either party to prove that he is, or isn't, a dishonest person. After all, that is the essential issue raised in the lawsuit.

b. The criminal accused

A criminal accused may put a pertinent trait of his or the victim's character in evidence. The prosecution may then offer character evidence to rebut it. See FRE 404(a)(1) and (2).

EXAMPLE

A criminal defendant being tried for aggravated assault may call witnesses to testify that he is not a violent person. The prosecution may then call *rebuttal witnesses* to testify that the defendant is in fact a violent person. The prosecution would not be allowed to do that if the defendant had not *opened the door* by first calling his character witnesses.

c. *Other crimes, wrongs, or acts*

For limited purposes, evidence of other crimes, wrongs, or acts of a person may be admissible, not to show that the person acted in conformity with them on a particular occasion, but for other purposes, such as to show motive, opportunity, etc. See FRE 404(b).

HYPOTHETICAL 7-8

Assume that Smooth Talker is arrested for breaking into the offices of the attorney for Gulli Bull the night before the civil trial is to begin and stealing the book containing the notation of Honest John regarding the true mileage on the car purchased by Gulli Bull. At the criminal trial, the prosecution wishes to present evidence of the civil fraud claim of Gulli Bull against Smooth Talker in order to prove that Smooth Talker is a dishonest person who again acted dishonestly when he broke into the attorney's office.

1. Under FRE 404(a), can the prosecution offer this evidence for this purpose?
2. Could this same evidence be admissible if offered under FRE 404(b)?

d. *Reputation for truthfulness*

Under FRE 608(a), the credibility of a witness may be attacked (or supported after attack) by evidence in the form of an opinion or known reputation as to the witness's character for truthfulness or untruthfulness. Specific instances of conduct offered to attack or support the witness's character may not be proved by **extrinsic evidence** (testimony of witnesses or exhibits other than the witness being attacked or supported) but the witness himself may be asked about them. See FRE 608(b).

HYPOTHETICAL 7-9

Assume that Gulli Bull wins his civil fraud suit against Smooth Talker and is awarded rescission of the contract, return of the purchase price of the car plus interest and $100,000 in punitive damages. Five years later Honest John is arrested and charged with forging the signature of another in order to cash a check and keep the proceeds. At the trial of Honest John on the forgery charge, his defense attorney calls Smooth Talker as a witness for Honest John.

1. On cross-examination of Smooth Talker, can the prosecution ask him specific questions about the judgment taken against him in the civil fraud matter five years before?
2. If, after Smooth Talker testifies, can the prosecution call Gulli Bull as a witness to talk about the judgment he obtained against Smooth Talker five years before? What if Smooth Talker denied any knowledge of the civil fraud judgment on cross-examination?

3. After Smooth Talker testifies, can the prosecution call Gulli Bull as a witness to testify to Smooth Talker's reputation for honesty?
4. After Smooth Talker testifies, can the prosecution call Gulli Bull as a witness to testify to Honest John's reputation for honesty?

e. Conviction of a felony or other crime involving dishonesty

Under FRE 609, the credibility of a witness may be attacked by showing that he was *convicted* (not just accused or arrested or tried unsuccessfully) of a felony or any crime involving dishonesty or false statement. However, if it has been more than ten years since the conviction or since the release of the witness from punishment imposed for the crime (whichever is later), such evidence is generally not admissible. See FRE 609(b). A pardon or annulment of the conviction may render it unusable (see FRE 609(c)), and a juvenile conviction is generally unusable. See FRE 609(d). (See Hypothetical 6-3.)

9. Bias and interest

The credibility of a witness may always be attacked under FRE 607. We call this **impeaching a witness**. And, under the federal rules, a witness can even be impeached by the attorney who called that witness to testify. Under some state evidentiary rules, however, the party calling a witness may not impeach him.

In contrast to the limited right to impeach a witness by showing character for truthfulness or untruthfulness under FRE 608 or prior conviction of certain crimes under FRE 609, a witness may *always* be impeached by showing **bias**. Bias constitutes any reason the witness might have to favor or disfavor one side or another in the dispute.

EXAMPLE

The witness is a relative or friend of the one for whom he testifies; or the witness bears a grudge against the party against whom he testifies.

A witness can also be impeached by showing **interest**. Interest is any self-serving reason the witness might have to not be objective in her testimony.

EXAMPLE

An employee testifies favorably for her employer—is she just trying to keep her superiors happy? A man testifies unfavorably against the former husband of his girlfriend—is he just trying to eliminate a potential rival?

In criminal proceedings the prosecution frequently allows one criminal to receive immunity from prosecution, plead to a lesser offense, or receive a reduced sentence in exchange for testifying for the prosecution against another criminal defendant. Counsel for the criminal defendant against whom such a witness testifies can always put the "deal" received by the witness in evidence, cross examine the witness on the terms of the deal, and use it to suggest that the witness has a self-serving motive to testify however the prosecution wishes. Most experienced criminal defense attorneys will tell you that they relish cross examining such government witnesses because of the ease of suggesting interest and because juries tend to be highly skeptical of the veracity of such witnesses.

Bias and interest can arise from innumerable relationships and factual contexts. Together, they can present a rich and important area for investigation by the paralegal. Nothing can be more important to the outcome of a lawsuit than to be able to discredit the critical witnesses of the other side by showing bias or interest.

HYPOTHETICAL 7-10

Assume that you are a paralegal working for the attorney defending Smooth Talker in the civil fraud case brought against him by Gulli Bull. The attorney learns of the devastating testimony that Honest John is going to give against Smooth Talker at trial and asks you to review the discovery done to date and to investigate Honest John to see if something can be found to discredit him. In the course of your investigation you come up with the facts listed below.

After reviewing the information below: (a) state whether each fact should be categorized as bias or interest or both or neither; (b) state whether you would recommend to your supervising attorney that each of these be offered in evidence to impeach Honest John and why or why not; (c) consider how and where you might have located each item of information; and (d) in connection with each fact give thought to additional information you might want to seek to make the impeachment of Honest John more effective.

1. Smooth Talker and Honest John are actually half-brothers, having the same mother. The mother had Smooth Talker first and raised him but gave Honest John up for adoption when he was born two years after Smooth Talker.
2. Honest John twice tried to buy the used car business from Smooth Talker but did not succeed.
3. Honest John has told several people over the past year that he intends to set up his own used car business in town.
4. Smooth Talker is active in the Republican Party. Honest John is a committed Democrat.
5. Last year Smooth Talker was the coach of the little league baseball team on which Honest John's son plays. The boy got very little playing time leading to several chin-to-chin confrontations between coach and father.
6. Several years ago Smooth Talker and Honest John were partners in a kangaroo meat taco venture that failed badly. Honest John had put up most of the money in the deal. Smooth Talker had contributed only a little cash but a lot of "expertise."
7. Last year Honest John went through a nasty divorce. His wife's attorney called Smooth Talker as a witness to testify to Honest John's compensation from the used car business. Smooth Talker agreed to testify without a subpoena and gave completely candid testimony, which cost Honest John a bundle.
8. Honest John has been Smooth Talker's best salesman for the last five years but has never received a raise or a bonus during that time, while other lower-producing salesmen have.
9. Smooth Talker's wife is divorcing him, though the divorce is not yet final. She and Honest John have been dating.

> 10. Honest John and Gulli Bull have recently formed a partnership in which they plan to revive the kangaroo meat taco idea. They are currently trying to raise capital.

10. Prior inconsistent statements

A witness may be impeached by a prior statement inconsistent with what the witness is now saying in his testimony. See FRE 613. The statement does not have to be shown (if in writing) or its contents disclosed to the witness when the witness is being questioned about it. But if the prior inconsistent statement is going to be proved by extrinsic evidence, the witness must first be given the opportunity to explain the statement or deny making it. FRE 613(b).

The most frequent prior inconsistent statement used is the pretrial deposition testimony of the witness. FRCP 32(a)(1) specifically permits prior deposition testimony of a witness to be used for impeachment in this manner and FRE 801(d)(1) specifically provides that such prior statements are not hearsay. Note that prior *consistent* statements of a witness can be offered to rebut a charge of recent fabrication. See FRE 801(d)(1).

A hearsay problem can arise when a prior inconsistent but *unsworn* statement of a witness is offered in evidence. See Hypothetical 7-11.

HYPOTHETICAL 7-11

Assume that you obtain a written statement from Honest John in which he discloses his conversation with Smooth Talker about the mileage on the car purchased by Gulli Bull. At trial, however, Honest John testifies that he did *not* have that conversation with Smooth Talker.

1. Can the unsworn statement of Honest John be offered in evidence as a prior inconsistent statement in order to prove that the version of events stated in it is true?
2. Can it be offered to prove that the witness previously made a different statement than the one being made at trial and thus is discredited?

Hypothetical 7-11 illustrates an important point about evidentiary rules that should always be borne in mind by the investigating paralegal. Whether or not something is admissible in evidence may depend on the reason for which it is offered and against whom it is offered. Note that if we were talking about the unsworn statement of defendant Smooth Talker in Hypothetical 7-11, it would be admissible over a hearsay objection as an admission by party opponent under FRE 801(d)(2).

11. Authentication of documents and things

Any document or demonstrative item (e.g., photograph, video, diagram, model, map, or computer simulation) or any physical object (e.g., the weapon in a criminal case or the defective machine in a civil product liability case) must be properly **authenticated** before it is received in evidence. That means there must be adequate proof that the document or thing is in fact what the offering party claims it is. See FRE 901(a). Presenting that adequate proof as a condition precedent to the introduction of the item into evidence is called **laying the foundation,** discussed in Chapter 6.

a. Authenticating physical objects

The authentication of objects typically is done by means of one or more testifying witnesses who can establish: (a) that the item is in fact the actual object claimed; and (b) that it is in substantially the same condition now as it was at the time of the incident. This second element is sometimes referred to as the **chain of custody.** To eliminate the possibility that an object has been switched or altered in a way that would mislead the finder of fact, witnesses must show who has had custody of the object and how they took care of it at all times it was in their possession.

Paralegals will frequently find themselves in custody and control of objects that will be offered as exhibits at trial and it is critical that they know the importance of preserving and protecting physical evidence (see Chapter 9). Establishing the chain of custody of physical exhibits prior to their admission in evidence is also part of laying the foundation.

b. Authenticating demonstrative evidence

Demonstrative evidence such as pictures, video tapes, diagrams, or computer simulations is typically authenticated by means of one or more testifying witnesses who can establish (a) that the exhibit is a genuine representation of the item pictured or event demonstrated; and (b) that the exhibit is a reasonably accurate depiction of the item shown or event demonstrated.

c. Authenticating documents

Authenticating a document (other than one that is self-authenticating as discussed below) is typically done by means of one or more testifying witnesses who can establish (a) what the document is and (b) who wrote or signed it. This latter matter frequently involves authenticating the signature, handwriting, or other origin of a document. Authenticating a signature or handwriting can involve calling a witness who is familiar with the signature or handwriting of the author of the document. Or it can involve the testimony of an expert who arrives at a professional opinion based on a comparison of patterns or distinctive characteristics of a person's other writings. See FRE 901(2) through (4).

HYPOTHETICAL 7-12

Assume that in your interview with Honest John as related in Hypothetical 7-4 he told you he was the one who made the entry in the book regarding the actual mileage of the car purchased by Gulli Bull. You are able to locate the book and have possession of it at trial. However, assume that Honest John was never deposed prior to trial and is deceased at the time of trial. List all the ways you can think of that the other attorney might be able to prove that the entry in the book is in the handwriting of Honest John.

FRE 902 simplifies the authentication process for a host of documents by declaring many categories of documents to be **self-authenticating.** Of particular importance are the following:

- Certified copies of public records. FRE 902(4) (See Hypothetical 6–4.)
- Books, pamphlets, and other publications purporting to be published by a public authority. FRE 902(5)
- Newspapers and periodicals. FRE 902(6)
- Acknowledged documents (i.e., sworn to and signed in the presence of a notary public). FRE 902(8)
- Commercial paper (promissory notes, drafts, etc.). FRE 902(9)

d. Authenticating voices

Voices that are identified in testimony must also be authenticated. Typically this is done by the testimony of the speaker himself or, if that is not possible, by another witness who is familiar with the speaker's voice and recognizes it.

EXAMPLE

> The plaintiff wants to offer in evidence a tape recorded threat from the defendant, Mr. Jones, that she found on her answering machine. Jones denies that it is his voice speaking. Plaintiff herself, if she is familiar with the defendant's voice from past dealings with him, may testify that it is the defendant's voice on the tape, but her identification of his voice may be challenged by defense counsel as not credible. What would be the basis of the defense lawyer's challenge to the plaintiff's authentication of defendant's voice? The plaintiff may prefer to call a non-party, disinterested witness who is familiar with defendant's voice to make the authentication. (See FRE 901(5).) Why?

Voice authentication can be difficult when a party or witness wants to testify to a telephone conversation with someone whose voice she has never heard before or since, and no one can be found to authenticate the voice. In those situations, FRE 901(6) raises some presumptions that help authenticate those discussions.

EXAMPLE

> If the witness or party offering the recorded message testifies that she called the number assigned in the phone book to Mr. Jones and spoke with someone who identified himself as Mr. Jones, that will sufficiently authenticate the voice with whom she spoke as that of Mr. Jones.

12. Best evidence rule

The original of a document, photo, or recording should be offered as the actual exhibit if it is available. However, the FRE are liberal in allowing copies to be offered so long as there is no issue regarding fairness or the authenticity of the original. See FRE 1002 and 1003. The best rule to follow is better safe than sorry—if you have the original, offer it as the exhibit unless the opposing side stipulates to the acceptability of a copy.

13. Generally prohibited matters

There are a number of rules generally barring the admissibility of certain types of evidence with which investigating paralegals should be familiar. There are **public policy** reasons behind the various rules prohibiting the admissibility of some kinds of evidence—we don't want to discourage these practices so we won't allow evidence of them to be offered at trial.

a. Subsequent remedial measures

Evidence of subsequent remedial measures taken after an event that is the subject of the lawsuit and that might have prevented it cannot be shown in evidence to prove liability. FRE 407.

EXAMPLE

> A person falls down a flight of stairs because the handrail was loose and the owner of the stairs fixes the loose handrail the next day. It cannot be shown at trial that the owner had the handrail fixed the day after the accident if that proof is offered to show that the handrail was in fact loose.

Do you see the public policy reasoning at work in this example? If we allow the plaintiff in her suit against the owner of the handrail to offer evidence of his repairing it, he may be less motivated to repair it, and we want him to repair it. Do you agree with that rationale?

Under FRE 407, evidence of the subsequent remedial measure may be offered as evidence if it is offered for a reason other than to prove liability.

EXAMPLE

> If the owner of the stairs denies at trial that he is responsible for them, evidence of his having repaired them may be offered to prove that he does in fact act as if he is responsible for them.

b. Settlement discussions and offers

In almost every civil case there are settlement discussions and even settlement offers made that are not accepted. These negotiations and offers cannot be made known to the finder of fact because we want to encourage settlement negotiations. FRE 408.

c. Paying or offering to pay expenses

Paying or offering to pay expenses related to an injury (such as medical costs) cannot be offered in evidence in order to prove liability. FRE 409. Again, public policy dictates this rule—we don't want to discourage persons from making these offers. Do you agree that such evidence should not be admissible on liability?

d. Plea bargain discussions or a guilty plea later withdrawn

In almost every criminal case there are plea bargain negotiations and offers to plea bargain that are not accepted. And sometimes a criminal defendant will enter a guilty plea then later withdraw it. None of this may be offered as evidence in court in any civil or criminal proceeding involving the defendant. FRE 410.

e. Liability insurance

That a defendant in a civil suit had or did not have liability insurance cannot be shown for the purpose of proving culpability. FRE 411. Remember that under FRCP 26(a)(1)(D), the existence and terms of liability policies must be disclosed in discovery but this does not make them admissible in evidence. Why do you think the federal rules allow the discovery of liability insurance but not its admissibility at trial?

f. Sexual history

In sex offense cases there are detailed rules governing whether and when the sexual history of the victim and the accused can be made known to the finder of fact. FRE 412 through 415.

g. Religious beliefs

A witness's religious beliefs or opinions (no matter how wacky or mainstream) cannot be used to impair or enhance the witness's character. FRE 610. Of course, they may be shown if otherwise relevant to the case.

EXAMPLE

> In a dispute among church members over who owns the church property, a witness could certainly testify that he was a member of that church.

B. Final Considerations Regarding Evidence

1. Admissibility for alternative reasons

As we have seen repeatedly in this review, evidence may be inadmissible for one reason but admissible for another. (Recall the discussions on hearsay, character evidence, prior inconsistent statements, and generally prohibited matters such as subsequent remedial measures.) FRE 105 expressly contemplates this possibility.

Experienced trial lawyers know that there are very few times when a reasonable, good-faith argument cannot be made for the introduction of evidence if it relates in some way to the case. But fashioning those arguments takes a solid knowledge of the rules of evidence and a willingness to plan the arguments for the admissibility (or inadmissibility) before the trial itself. (See LBD 7-3.) And flexible, creative thinking is essential to work in this important area.

2. Clearing all the hurdles

With many types of proof there are several evidentiary hurdles to be cleared before the proof will be received in evidence.

EXAMPLE

If there is a document your supervising attorney wants to have admitted in evidence, she must be able to show that it is relevant to an issue in the case and she must be prepared to overcome an objection to the document based on hearsay as well. She must also be sure she can properly authenticate the document. And she might have to be concerned about the best evidence rule if she doesn't have the original. Failing to successfully clear any one of those hurdles may result in the document not being allowed in evidence.

Conversely, if the other side has a document it wants in evidence and your side would like to keep it out, you may help your supervising attorney plan how best to oppose its admissibility. That may mean planning an attack at each hurdle.

Much of the pretrial preparation in which a lawyer and staff engage has to do with evidentiary matters; planning how to get desirable testimony into evidence over anticipated objections and how to successfully object to evidence the other side is expected to offer.

KEY WORDS AND PHRASES TO REMEMBER

admission by party opponent
authentication
best evidence rule
bias
business records
chain of evidence
character evidence
cross-examination
direct examination
discretionary exceptions
exceptions to the hearsay rule
excited utterance
expert witness
extrinsic evidence
former testimony exception
hearsay

impeaching a witness
inference
interest
leading questions
lay witness
present sense impression
prior inconsistent statement
probative value
public records exception
recorded recollection
relevant evidence
self-authenticating
state of mind
statement against interest
subsequent remedial measure
writing used to refresh recollection

LEARN BY DOING

LBD 7-1. Review FRE 701 through 704 regarding the use of expert testimony. Then research the rules regarding use of expert testimony in state court proceedings in your state. Prepare a memorandum comparing the differences between the federal rules and state rules.

LBD 7-2. Read the cases of *Kumho Tire Co. v. Carmichael*, 526 U.S. 137 (1999) and *Daubert v. Merrell Dow Pharmaceuticals, Inc.*, 509 U.S. 579 (1993). Prepare a memorandum summarizing the procedure and factors to be considered by a trial judge in deciding whether to admit expert testimony. Research the case law in your state or federal circuit since *Daubert* to see how those courts are applying these rulings of the Supreme Court. Include a summary of those findings in your memorandum.

LBD 7-3. Interview a trial attorney who utilizes paralegals or a litigation paralegal concerning the importance of the paralegal knowing the rules of evidence to effectively assist the attorney in pretrial investigation, formal discovery, trial preparation, and trial.

LBD 7-4. Research case decisions in your federal circuit or state courts or both regarding the discretionary hearsay exceptions found in FRE 803(24) and 804(b)(5). Prepare a memorandum summarizing your research. Discuss the kinds of evidence the appellate courts have allowed or disallowed under these exceptions. Do the courts seem to favor these exceptions by construing them broadly or disfavor them by construing them narrowly?

Use the Case Studies in Appendix A to complete the following:

LBD 7-5. Review Case Study No. 1 (The Rowdy Outlaw Case).

a. Assume the prosecution asks the police officer who interviewed Mrs. Outlaw to testify as to what Mrs. Outlaw told him that evening. List all objections that the defense should make to the admissibility of that testimony and all arguments the prosecution might make to have that testimony admitted.

b. Assume the prosecution asks the officer who interviewed Rowdy Outlaw to testify as to Outlaw's change of story regarding where he was the night of the murder. List all objections that the defense should make to the admissibility of that testimony and all arguments the prosecution might make to have that testimony admitted.

c. Assume the prosecution asks Connie Cornelius what her husband said in the car as they passed the Palace Towers on the morning of the murder. List all objections that the defense should make to the admissibility of that testimony and all arguments the prosecution might make to have that testimony admitted.

d. Assume the prosecution wants to offer the pick, turkey feather, and guitar string found at the murder scene into evidence at the trial. List every part of the evidentiary foundation the prosecution will have to lay in order to have these items admitted.

LBD 7-6. Review Case Study No. 2 (The Red Dog Saloon Case).

a. Assume Tanya Trucker cannot be located before trial. Assume further that counsel for Soupspoon Wise wants to have him testify as to her comments to him regarding the tag on the Ford Bronco and the comments of the driver of the Bronco and its passenger that she overheard. List all objections the defense is likely to make to the admissibility of such testimony and all arguments Soupspoon's counsel might make for their admissibility.

b. Assume that Tanya Trucker is located but at the trial in which the driver of the Bronco is a defendant she denies that she saw the license plate on the Bronco or that she heard the driver or occupant of that vehicle say anything. You learn in the course of your investigation that (1) the driver of the Bronco was the owner of a major Nashville recording studio and that subsequent to the accident Tanya signed with his studio; (2) that the driver of the Bronco has a two-year-old conviction for petty theft in a neighboring state (an offense that was a misdemeanor in that state but would be a felony in your state); (3) that the driver of the Bronco has a three-year-old civil judgment against him in your state for plagiarizing a song writer's work; and (4) that Tanya Trucker has 15 arrests and three convictions for prostitution in the last five years.

(1) Will counsel for Soupspoon be able to ask Tanya Trucker on cross-examination about her statements to Soupspoon regarding the tag and the comments of the Bronco driver and occupant and, if so, on what basis?

(2) After Tanya Trucker testifies, will counsel for Soupspoon be able to have Soupspoon testify regarding her comments to him on the tag and the statements of the Bronco driver and occupant and, if so, on what basis?

(3) If counsel for Soupspoon attempts to offer in evidence the matters you discovered in the course of your investigation, what objections will the defense likely make to each and what arguments will Soupspoon's counsel make for their admission?

(4) Assume the judge rules that the two-year-old conviction of the Bronco driver is admissible but the driver denies such conviction in his testimony. What will you need to do in order to get proof of that conviction in evidence?

c. Assume that both the driver and the occupant of the Bronco are located and identified and that the driver is a defendant in the lawsuit and the occupant is not. Assume further that counsel for Soupspoon wants to have the occupant testify as to his (the occupant's) comments to the driver and the driver's responses. List all objections the defense is likely to make to the admissibility of such testimony and all arguments Soupspoon's counsel might make for their admissibility.

d. Assume the owner of the Red Dog Saloon, as well as Turtle Shoop, the individual who operates the Saloon and leases the premises from the owner, are sued by Soupspoon for failure to adequately maintain the parking lot in a safe condition. Both defendants deny any negligence and both deny any responsibility for maintaining the parking lot, alleging that any such responsibility belongs to the other defendant. You learn in your investigation that the week after the accident, Turtle Shoop had lights installed in the parking lot of the saloon and that the written lease between Shoop and the owner of the premises requires the owner to maintain liability insurance covering the premises including the parking lot. Counsel for Soupspoon wants to offer in evidence proof of the lights being installed, the lease, and the liability insurance policy. List all objections the defendants are likely to make to these three items of proof and all arguments Soupspoon's counsel might make for their admissibility.

LBD 7-7. Read Case Study No. 3 (The Vidalia Unyon Case).

   a. Assume that in formal discovery you obtain all financial records of Mr. Unyon's veterinary practice, including some records of his accountant who is not a party to the divorce suit. How will Vidalia's counsel get the accountant's records into evidence over a hearsay objection?

   b. Will Mrs. Unyon be allowed to testify regarding her belief as to the identity of the voice that called her and told her of her husband's affair and, if so, what foundation must be laid for that evidence?

   c. What evidentiary foundation must be laid for the admissibility of Mr. Unyon's little black book?

   d. If Mrs. Unyon wants to testify to her husband's initial silence in response to her accusations of unfaithfulness, what objections might counsel for Mr. Unyon make to that offered testimony and what arguments would Mrs. Unyon's counsel make for its admission?

   e. Assume that when the divorce suit goes to trial, the paternity suit against Mr. Unyon by Georgia Peach is still pending. Assume further that Mr. Unyon has denied in the pleadings filed in the paternity suit that he is the father of Ms. Peach's baby. If counsel for Mrs. Unyon wants to offer testimony regarding the paternity suit pending against Mr. Unyon to prove his likely infidelity:

     (1) How will counsel offer that proof other than through the testimony of Mr. Unyon or Ms. Peach?

     (2) What objections will counsel for Mr. Unyon likely make to that offered proof and what arguments will counsel for Mrs. Unyon offer for its admissibility?

Chapter 8

Communication Skills for the Investigator

CHAPTER OUTLINE

A. The Importance of Communication in the Work of Attorneys and Paralegals
B. Verbal Communication—Going Beyond the Words
C. Nonverbal Communication—Body Language
D. Written Communication
E. Putting Communication Skills to Work in Interviewing and Investigating

CHAPTER OBJECTIVES

Communication skills are critical to successful interviewing and investigating. In this chapter you will learn:

- The three ways that all people communicate: verbally, nonverbally, and in writing.
- The role that verbal, nonverbal, and written communications play in the work of the attorney and the paralegal.
- How to use active listening skills to recognize the messages and signals others send us by body language.
- Practical guidelines for written communications in the law office.

By permission of Johnny Hart and Creators Syndicate, Inc.

175

A. The Importance of Communication in the Work of Attorneys and Paralegals

1. How we all communicate

In general, there are three ways in which we all communicate with each other:

a. Written communication

Written communication is communication in which we put our thoughts on paper or screen for electronic communication (e-mail).

b. Verbal communication

Verbal communication is the process of speaking to another either directly or through a mechanical device such as the telephone, dictating machine, tape recorder, video recorder, television, or computer.

c. Nonverbal communication

Nonverbal communication is the impression we convey to others by **body language,** which can include posture, gestures, facial expressions, eye contact, and even our clothes or our environment—the things with which we choose to surround ourselves.

2. The importance of written and verbal communication

Both written and verbal communication involve *words.* It is no exaggeration to say that words are the tools of the lawyer's trade. Like the hammer to the carpenter, like the brush to the painter, so words are to the lawyer. Lawyers are trained professionals not only in the law and in legal reasoning, but in the use of words as well.

Everything the lawyer does involves the spoken or written word. Consider the tasks that an attorney might perform on a typical day. She will engage in telephone or face-to-face conversations with clients, witnesses, office staff, other attorneys, court personnel, and others. If she goes to court, she will speak as an advocate to the court on behalf of her client. She will dictate correspondence of all kinds, draft contracts, and prepare pleadings, motions, or briefs for court filing. She may do legal research, draft memoranda, and spend time in continuing legal education by reading current developments in the law. The thing all these tasks have in common is words.

And, of course, other than going to court or giving legal advice to a client, the tasks enumerated above are what paralegals are called upon to do regularly under the supervision of the attorney. It is essential for the legal assistant to:

- appreciate the importance of words to her responsibilities;
- be competent in utilizing both the spoken and written word; and
- be constantly working to improve her verbal and writing skills.

Go to the Web site for the Harvard University Dialect Survey at *www.hcs.harvard.edu/ ~golder/dialect/* and review the research done to date on the various dialects used in our country. See if you can figure out why people may look at you strangely if you pronounce "aunt" as "ahnt" anywhere outside New England; or "pajamas" to rhyme with "jam" outside the Upper Midwest; or if you ask for a "soda" in the South.

In verbal communication this means the legal assistant must be concerned with **vocabulary, pronunciation, enunciation,** and **grammar.** In written communication this means the legal assistant must be concerned with **vocabulary, grammar, spelling, punctuation, sentence** and **paragraph structure,** and **writing style.**

It is beyond the scope of this text to provide detailed instruction in grammar, vocabulary, and spelling. But later in this chapter we will consider some suggestions for effective writing as it relates to the investigating task. And, included in Appendix E, Resources for the Investigator, is a comprehensive list of written and online resources to assist the paralegal in increasing competence in grammar, vocabulary, spelling, and related areas. (See LBD 8-2.)

3. The importance of nonverbal communication

We are all constantly sending important messages to others with our body language. And we are constantly receiving those messages from others. If you are not aware of the nonverbal messages you are sending others and not attune to the messages being sent by others, you cannot perform interviewing and investigating work effectively.

In this chapter we will consider all three means of communication as they relate to interviewing and investigating.

B. Verbal Communication—Going Beyond the Words

We all know from our common experience of interacting with others that verbal communication consists of more than just the words used. It's not just *what* people say, but *how* they say it. It's not just what they *say*, it's what they *mean*. What makes the Wizard Of Id cartoon at the beginning of this chapter humorous is that while the peasant understood what the King said, he misunderstood what the King meant! In interviewing and investigating we have to not only listen to what people say, but also **actively listen** for what they mean.

HYPOTHETICAL 8-1

> Scenario A: Assume that Honey Dew sees her boyfriend, Honey Don't, watching TV on the couch. She comes up behind him and begins tickling him. He grabs his sides and says, "Stop it." Honey Dew doesn't stop tickling him and soon they both fall on the floor laughing.
>
> Scenario B: Assume that Honey Dew sees her boyfriend, Honey Don't, watching TV on the couch. She comes up behind him and begins tickling him. He grabs his sides and says, "Stop it." Honey Dew doesn't stop tickling him and he slaps her hands away. They wind up angry at each other.
>
> 1. How do you think Honey Don't said, "Stop it" in Scenario A?
> 2. How do you think Honey Don't said, "Stop it" in Scenario B?

To understand both what a person says and what they mean in verbal communication, the investigator has to be sensitive to the speaker's:

1. Tone of voice

In Hypothetical 8-1, the tone of voice use by Honey Don't probably made all the difference in whether the outcome of the tickle attack was Scenario A or B.

2. Volume

A raised voice in most circumstances might indicate excitement, anger, or stress. A low voice might indicate insecurity or a desire to not be overheard. Of course, a voice might be raised because the room is noisy or lowered because a baby is asleep nearby.

3. Rate of speaking

Some people just talk rapidly. It's normal for them. But for others speaking rapidly indicates some excitement, concern, or rush. Others speak slowly. It may be normal for them, but for others it may be an indication of nervousness or impairment.

4. Voice inflection

The words a speaker emphasizes in a sentence can make a significant difference in meaning.

HYPOTHETICAL 8-2

Assume you are interviewing a witness about a case in which a boy has allegedly been injured by an animal. An eyewitness makes the following statement to you: "The big red dog jumped over the fence and bit the boy."

Try saying this sentence several different times. Each time you repeat the sentence place the greatest emphasis on one of the following words: big, red, dog, jumped, fence, and bit.

1. If the word "big" is emphasized, doesn't that suggest to you that there might be two or more red dogs suspected in the attack?
2. If the word "red" is emphasized, doesn't that suggest to you that there might be dogs of different colors suspected in the attack?
3. If the word "dog" is emphasized, doesn't that suggest to you that the kind of animal that attacked the boy is at issue?
4. If the word "jumped" is emphasized, doesn't that suggest to you that how the dog got out of the fenced-in area may be in question?
5. If the word "fence" is emphasized, doesn't that suggest to you that the direction the dog came from may be in question?
6. If the word "bit" is emphasized, doesn't that suggest to you that the kind of injury inflicted on the boy might be in question?

Another aspect of voice inflection is its absence—the *monotone*. Some people speak in a monotone naturally. Interviewing such people at length can pose a special challenge for the interviewer—to stay focused (or maybe even to stay awake!). But if a person who normally does not speak in a monotone does so on a particular occasion, what might that tell you? Are they fatigued? Bored? On medication?

Or if a person speaks with more than normal inflection—they emphasize odd words or all their words—what does that suggest to you about them?

5. Enunciation

A person who enunciates well speaks clearly. And it matters. If you are interviewing a client who runs sentences together or slurs his speech, making it hard to understand, what might that tell you about how effective a witness he will be at trial?

Or if a person who normally speaks clearly speaks with a distinct slur on a particular occasion, what might that tell you? Has he been drinking? Is he ill? Fatigued?

6. Vocabulary

Vocabulary is closely tied to education and training. It has been estimated that the average high school graduate in the United States uses only about seven hundred different words in the course of normal conversation. That number rises to twelve hundred for the college graduate.

In communicating with others during the course of an interviewing assignment, it is important that the paralegal take note of the vocabulary of others and adjust his own to communicate effectively with them.

EXAMPLE

> If you are interviewing an adult, fifth-grade dropout you probably don't want to ask him, "Can you articulate a plausible explanation for the scenario just described?" Instead, you want to try something like, "Do you have any idea why that happened?" Notice the difference in the length and complexity of the words in the two sentences.

7. Grammar

Nothing is more immediately striking about a person's speech than the use of improper grammar. Some grammatical mistakes are minor and cause us to do little more than note the goof.

EXAMPLE

> Recently at an awards show on television, a group of five persons accepted the award for best costuming. The spokesman for the group said, "This is a great honor for my team and I." Of course, he should have said, "my team and me," but minor slips like that are common and we don't make much of it.
>
> On the other hand, if the spokesman had said, "We'uns is right proud of this here honor. We know'd we done good but we never seen this acomin'," the audience would probably have gone into shock. What would be your impression of a person who spoke that way. Uneducated? Ignorant? Embarrassing himself and others? Fair or not, those are the opinions people form when they hear blatantly improper grammar used.

For the paralegal investigator, there are several lessons to be learned about the impact of using improper grammar. The first and most important is the one stressed in the first section of this chapter—don't use improper grammar yourself!

But there are other important lessons. Take note of the grammar of clients and witnesses you interview and consider the impression it will make on others—particularly on a judge or jury if the person will be a witness at trial. Be sure to report your observations and impressions to the supervising attorney. Don't react in any noticeable way when a client or witness uses improper grammar in your presence. They may notice your reaction and feel insulted or resentful at what they see as your arrogance.

8. Slang, colloquialisms, and accents

a. Slang

Slang is words or phrases used to mean something other than their standard definition. Some slang is generally referred to today as **street talk.**

EXAMPLE

duh	*you go girl*
out of sight	*no problem*
radical	*chill out*
space cadet	*shake a leg*
cool it	*googled*
go for it	

Slang varies among age groups, ethnic groups, trades and professions (e.g., *weasel words, rainmaker,* and *silk stocking firm* in legal slang) and also by region of the country.

b. Colloquialisms

Colloquialisms are words or phrases that are used incorrectly but that have gained widespread use in informal conversation.

EXAMPLE

"He is *about* eight years old" rather than, "He is approximately eight years old."

"We couldn't *help but notice* the change" rather than, "We couldn't help noticing the change."

"You *sure are* tall" rather than, "You are surely tall."

c. Accents

Although there has been a leavening of accents in our country due to national communications through television and radio, regional accents are still with us. How hard is it, after all, to pick out a New York City (*New Yawk*) or a Boston (*Haavud* is a school?) or a deep South (try saying *you* or *hi* with two syllables, *y'all*) accent?

In interviewing and investigating work, the paralegal should be careful to note and report witnesses who use noticeable slang, colloquialisms, or street talk to communicate, or who have a noticeable accent.

EXAMPLE

> If a paralegal working for an attorney with a case pending in a court in Birmingham, Alabama interviews an important witness with a distinct New York accent or who uses, like, you know, like California Valley Girl slang, she had best report it to the supervising attorney. It is something the attorney will take into account in determining the impact, pro or con, of that witness on the judge and jury. And, of course, the same would be true if the case was pending in New York or Los Angeles and the witness was from Birmingham (or, as the witness might say, "Buminham").

To the extent possible, the investigating paralegal should also try to be familiar with slang or colloquialisms used in the area where she works in order to be able to communicate effectively with witnesses.

C. ▶ Nonverbal Communication—Body Language

We all know from our common experience of interacting with others that nonverbal communication or **body language** can convey messages just as clearly—and sometimes more clearly—as any words.

HYPOTHETICAL 8-3

> Assume, following Scenario B in Hypothetical 8-1, that Honey Dew and Honey Don't not only argue, they break up and Honey Don't sues Honey Dew for the tort of battery. When she receives the suit papers, Honey Dew calls the attorney for whom you work asking him to represent her in defending the case. Your supervising attorney asks you to meet with Honey Dew and interview her regarding the facts of the case.
>
> Honey Dew comes to the office and meets with you in a small conference room where she sits immediately across the table from you. While you ask Honey Dew questions designed to obtain biographical and background information on herself, she seems relaxed and friendly. She sits forward in her chair with her hands clasped comfortably on the table in front of her. She smiles, laughs easily, and looks directly at you. She speaks at a normal pace, without any hesitation, and seems to express herself well.
>
> Then you begin asking her questions about the day of the alleged battery. You notice a frown appear on her forehead and she sits back in her chair. She folds her arms across her chest. You ask her directly if she did in fact tickle Honey Don't without warning or consent as he has alleged. Her eyes look away from yours and begin to scan the ceiling. You hear her clear her throat. Finally she speaks, but slowly, softly, and hesitantly. She seems to stumble over her words. What she says is, "Well . . . not . . . I mean . . . no . . . I just . . . He . . . No I didn't. He only . . . It's . . .
>
> It's . . . He's making this up just to. . . Because he wanted to . . . wants to break it off."
>
> 1. What did the nonverbal communication or body language of Honey Dew tell you before you got to questions about the day of the alleged battery?

2. List each way that the body language of Honey Dew changed during the interview?
3. What does each noted change in her body language communicate to you?
4. What changes did you note in Honey Dew's verbal communication style and what do those changes communicate to you?

Body language speaks volumes, doesn't it? In order to understand not only what a person says with words, but what they communicate with body language, the investigator has to be sensitive to the speaker's:

1. Body position

Body position includes both a person's posture and proximity. In Hypothetical 8-3, what did it communicate to you that at the beginning of the interview Honey Dew sat forward in her chair with her hands clasped comfortably in front of her on the table? That she was comfortable? Confident? Friendly? Candid? What did it mean when she later sat back in her chair and folded her arms across her chest? Defensive? Threatened? Uncertain?

Take a look at the picture of President Lyndon Johnson speaking to Supreme Court Justice Abe Fortas in Illustration 8-1. What does the body position of these two men suggest to you about their personalities? About their respective positions of authority? About their respect for other person's privacy? About their confidence?

As investigators we must be diligent students and observers of body language—our own and others.

2. Facial expressions

Try the experiment set out in Hypothetical 8-4.

HYPOTHETICAL 8-4

What kind of a mood are you in right now as you read this? No matter what mood it is, go to the nearest mirror and look at yourself. Does your face reflect your mood? Almost certainly it does. While you are in front of the mirror think of different moods than the one you are in now (happy, sad, amused, angry, confused, frightened, shocked, disapproving, disbelieving, frustrated, tired—oops, that's the one you were already in, right?). Try to adjust your face to reflect the different moods. Note two things when you do this: (1) your face *will* change with the different moods; and (2) it may be difficult to *make* your face change to reflect a mood you are not in presently.

If someone else is there with you, try to observe them for a moment without being noticed. What kind of mood do you think that person is in based on his or her facial expression? Once you decide, and if you dare, ask them what mood they are in. How close did you come to being right?

The lessons to be learned from the experiment in Hypothetical 8-4 are that people's facial expressions communicate a lot about them, and most people are not good enough actors to conceal those messages.

In Hypothetical 8-3, what did it communicate to you at the beginning of the interview that Honey Dew smiled and laughed easily? That she was relaxed? Friendly? Straightforward? What did it communicate later in the interview that her face clouded with a frown? Worried? Anxious? Just a headache coming on?

Frowns, smiles, winks, excessive blinking, pursing the lips, licking the lips, biting the lips, raised eyebrows, nose squinched—all these facial expressions tell us something about the person and the circumstances, if we are *listening.*

3. Eye contact

Have you ever had the experience of speaking face to face with a person who sort of looks past you to something behind you? How did that make you feel? Ignored? Insulted? Unimportant?

On the other hand, have you ever had the experience of speaking face to face with a person whose eyes seem to bore a hole in you and never seem to blink? How did that make you feel? Uncomfortable? Threatened? Intimidated?

People communicate volumes of information to each other by eye

Illustration 8-1
PHOTOGRAPH OF
PRESIDENT
JOHNSON
SPEAKING TO
ABE FORTAS

Abe Fortas gets 'the Johnson Treatment'

*Yoichi R. Okamoto — LBJ Library Collection

contact or the lack of it. Normally, close, steady eye contact (but not the hole-boring kind) is a sign of interest in what the other person is saying and respect for the person. Refusal to make steady eye contact can mean shyness, insecurity, or lack of truthfulness. (And now you know why your mother, when she doubted your story about how her favorite glass dish got broken, said, "Look me in the eye and tell me that.")

When people who have been making eye contact with us suddenly break it, that sends a message as well. In Hypothetical 8-3, what did it communicate to you when Honey Dew broke eye contact with you and started searching the ceiling as you asked her about tickling Honey Don't?

4. Nervous signals

The body tends to give us away when we are nervous or feeling pressure. Think about yourself. What signals do you give when you are anxious? It may be that line of sweat over the upper lip, on the forehead, or under the arms. Or that frog in the throat. It may be the inability to sit still. It may be a slight tremor in the hands or the knees or the voice. It may be an elevation of the voice, by volume or pitch, or an accelerated rate of speaking. It may be a wringing of the hands, a yawn when you aren't sleepy, a giggle when nothing's funny, or a rubbing of the brow.

Of course there may be more than one explanation for any body language. A person may begin to perspire because the room is overheated or he is dressed too warmly. A frog in the throat can mean a voice that has been overexerted. A tremor in the hands can be a sign of aging or illness. Some people "talk with their hands," using many gestures as they speak. It is not necessarily a sign of nervousness unless the person normally doesn't use those gestures or unless they are excessive even for that person. We have to use our common sense and instincts in interpreting body language.

5. The sounds of silence

You've undoubtedly heard the phrase, "The silence was deafening." We understand that saying because we know that in certain situations a person's silence can be telling us something significant.

In Hypothetical 8-3, what did it communicate to you when Honey Dew paused before answering your question about whether she did in fact tickle Honey Don't? That's called the *pregnant pause* or the *tell-tale hesitation*. A pause can, of course, mean that the person simply didn't hear the question or that their mind was on something else. Again, we have to use our common sense and instincts to interpret body language.

6. Clothes and environment

Clothes do make a statement—and surroundings do too. We communicate messages to others by our choices regarding clothing and personal grooming styles, and by the way we maintain the space around us.

HYPOTHETICAL 8-5

Assume you are conducting the interview of Honey Dew as assigned in Hypothetical 8-3. You conduct the interview in the conference room of the law office where you work. Before she says a word, what would your initial impressions of Honey Dew be if she arrives for the interview:

1. Dressed in short shorts, a halter top, and sandals?
2. Dressed in a conservative navy blue suit with matching shoes and purse?
3. Dressed in a nurse's uniform?
4. Dressed in black leather pants, motorcycle jacket, and boots, with "Kiss This" written on the back side of her pants?
5. With her hair pulled back in a pony tail and tied with a pink bow that matches her dress?
6. With her hair spiked and colored half green and half orange?
7. Nicely dressed, but with her hair dirty and unkempt?

What might her impression of you be if you arrived at that interview dressed and groomed as mentioned above?

Assume you conduct the interview of Honey Dew at her office where she manages a temporary employment agency. You are escorted into her office, seated, and told she will be with you shortly. As you wait for Honey Dew, you look around her office. Having not yet spoken to or seen her, what would your initial impressions of her be if, as you look around the office, you notice:

1. An 18 x 24 portrait of Honey Dew immediately behind her chair?
2. A wall full of awards and pictures of Honey Dew with local and state politicians?
3. A mounted deer head on the wall?
4. Nothing on the walls?
5. Several pictures of Honey Dew with a man and two small children?
6. Several pictures of Honey Dew with different men?
7. A neat, orderly desk and light rock music playing softly in the background? (What if it was hard rock? Country? Rap? Big band? Blues? Golden oldies from the '50s and '60s?)
8. A messy, disorganized desk, files on the floor, and half of an obviously stale hamburger closer to your chair than you would like?
9. Childrens' crayon drawings taped to the side of her computer monitor?
10. An open bottle of Pepto Bismol on the desk beside several rolls of antacid tablets?

Assume an unexpected guest comes to your home at this moment. What impression would they probably form of you from the condition of. . .oh, okay, we won't pursue this one!

We Are All Experts

When it comes to interpreting the unspoken messages contained in verbal and nonverbal communication, we are all experts. Why? Because we are experienced social creatures. From the moment of birth we have been constantly interacting with others and honing these skills. Grammar, spelling, and punctuation are learned arts. Writing skills must be developed. But picking up on the nuances of verbal communication and interpreting body language comes naturally to us all because we have been doing it all of our lives. In interviewing and investigating work we have to consciously and conscientiously exercise those skills to be effective.

D. Written Communication

Illustration 8-2 sets forth a list of the kinds of written communications paralegal investigators routinely produce.

In other chapters we consider each of these kinds of written communication in more detail. But here are some general suggestions applicable to all written communications.

SLEUTH ON THE LOOSE

Identify a major news story from the past week and read articles written on that story in several different national newspapers including *USA Today* (*www.usatoday.com*); the *New York Times* (*www.nytimes.com*); the *Washington Post* (*www.washingtonpost.com*); the *Wall Street Journal* (*www.wsj.com*); and the *Los Angeles Times* (*www.latimes.com*). Note differences in the stories from each paper including different slants or more or less detail.

1. Be aware of grammar

Grammar matters—and spelling, punctuation, vocabulary, and sentence and paragraph structure do too.

2. Use tools for effective writing

Keep the necessary tools for effective writing close at hand. These include a good dictionary, legal dictionary, thesaurus, and grammar and style text. (See Appendix E, Resources for the Investigator, for suggestions regarding helpful grammar and style texts.)

3. Avoid slang and colloquialisms

Be familiar with slang and colloquialisms in order to communicate effectively when speaking with clients and witnesses. But unless you are quoting someone else or summarizing what another person said, never use them yourself in written communications.

4. Be precise

Say exactly what you mean. That may mean reworking phrases and sentences until you get them right. With experience you will do less rewriting. Be sure you know the meaning of every word you use. If you're not sure about meaning, spelling, punctuation, capitalization, etc., don't guess—look it up.

5. Be thorough but concise

Cover everything you need to in the document you write, but say it as briefly as possible. No one wants to read more than necessary and learning to use words economically will prove a blessing to your reader.

Illustration 8-2   TYPES OF WRITTEN COMMUNICATION THAT PARALEGAL INVESTIGATORS ROUTINELY PRODUCE

1. correspondence to clients
2. correspondence to other law offices
3. correspondence to witnesses and non-witness information sources
4. correspondence to courts
5. internal case-file memoranda
6. internal legal research memoranda
7. internal investigation reports
8. draft pleadings
9. draft discovery documents (interrogatories, document requests, deposition notices, requests to admit)
10. draft motions
11. subpoenas and subpoenas *duces tecum*
12. proposed court orders
13. fee agreements
14. witness statements
15. records authorizations

6. Avoid repetition

Say it as well as you can the first time. And don't say it again!

7. Be consistent

Make sure your document is internally consistent. Nothing is more confusing than receiving a memo, letter, or other document that starts out saying one thing then seems to say another.

8. Use shorter, simpler, non-technical words

Sometimes we must use technical words. If, in a letter you are drafting to a client, you need to tell him that the theory of *res ipsa loquitur* may be available in his case, you will use that Latin phrase, although you will have to explain what it means. But when technical words are not required, avoid them.

Always try to select shorter, simpler words and phrases over longer, more complex ones. The well known acronym *KISS* stands for *Keep It Simple Stupid*—a good rule to remember in legal writing. Set out in Illustration 8-3 is a list of phrases commonly seen in legal writing. The use of these phrases almost always represents poor writing. Beside each phrase is a single word that could better express the same thought. Those phrases in the list with no word beside them could be deleted completely with no loss of meaning.

Illustration 8-3

COMMONLY USED
PHRASES THAT
COULD BE
ELIMINATED

1. for the reasons stated	therefore
2. by virtue of the fact that	because
3. in the event that	if
4. due to the fact that	because
5. by means of	by
6. for the purposes of	for
7. comes the plaintiff (defendant)	plaintiff (defendant)
8. in order to	to
9. there can be no doubt that	doubtless
10. notwithstanding the fact that	regardless or although
11. at this time (or as of this moment)	presently
12. for all intents and purposes	
13. all things considered	
14. as far as we are concerned	
15. the fact is that	

9. Use paragraphs

Paragraphs are the way we address different topics in a written document. Organize them logically. Each should begin with a topic sentence and when the topic changes a new paragraph should begin. In general, when in doubt, begin a new paragraph. Shorter paragraphs are generally to be preferred over longer ones.

10. Use drafts and proof your work

You should make it a personal goal *never* to turn in a written document to your supervising attorney that contains a typographical error. In law offices, there is no margin for error in what we write because it is so critical to clients. Part of performing at a professional level is insisting on error-free documents—from yourself and others.

The only way to guarantee this level of writing is to *draft* documents before putting them in final form. If time allows, your documents may go through several drafts. Every draft should be thoroughly proofed, not only for errors, but to improve word choice, sentence and paragraph structure, and writing style. If practical, have someone else in the office proof your work. We can look at our own documents so many times that we don't catch the mistakes. A person looking at your document for the first time will be more likely to catch them.

11. Protect confidentiality and privilege

It is always critical in drafting, finalizing, and distributing documents to protect client confidentiality and all applicable privileges. Documents you are working on in the office should be put away safely when you are not present—even for a short while. Work taken home should be carefully shielded from other eyes. Copies distributed in the office should be handdelivered or sent in routing envelopes to prevent accidental reading by unauthorized persons.

Documents mailed should be carefully and properly addressed only to the person(s) authorized to receive them and care should be taken not to copy anyone with confidential correspondence who is not also privileged. Take care in addressing envelopes as well. Because we do not have control over who will actually handle the envelope at the receiving end (a child or spouse at home; a secretary or receptionist at the office), envelopes containing confidential or privileged material should be conspicuously marked *CONFIDENTIAL* or *PERSONAL* or both. See Illustration 8-4.

12. Practice makes perfect—and reading helps too

Writing does not come easy to most people and no one is naturally perfect at it. Writing well is a learned art, so don't be discouraged if you have a long way to go. The more you write, and the more different things you write, the better you will become at it.

It also helps to read good writing by others. Read well-written books and articles of all kinds. Note the word choice, sentence, and paragraph structure in what you read.

E. ▶ Putting Communication Skills to Work in Interviewing and Investigating

1. What are you communicating to others?

In interviewing and investigating work, we must be constantly aware of what we are communicating to others verbally and nonverbally. Illus-

Illustration 8-4   ENVELOPE CONTAINING CONFIDENTIAL OR PRIVILEGED MATERIAL

Smith, Jones & Greely
Attorneys at Law
114 Main Street
Harmony City, Yourstate 11212

       Mr. Frank Childs
       Childs Industries
       911 Madison Street
       Harmony City, Yourstate 11212

PERSONAL AND CONFIDENTIAL

Illustration 8-5

CONTEXTS IN
WHICH THE
PARALEGAL'S
COMMUNICATION
SKILLS ARE
CRITICAL

- working with your supervising attorney(s)
- working with other attorneys and staff in your office
- working with attorneys and staff in other law offices
- working with clients
- working with witnesses
- working with non-witness information sources
- working with court personnel

tration 8-5 lists the contexts in which the paralegal's own communication skills are critical to success.

In any business or profession, successful people are the ones with superior communication skills.

HYPOTHETICAL 8-6

Assume that Dis Tracted is a paralegal working for attorney Good Guy. Over the weekend, with Christmas only a few days away, Dis Tracted broke up with her boyfriend and on Monday morning she is, shall we say, not in the best of moods. Nonetheless, she gets to work on time at 8:30 A.M. only to find a note on her desk telling her Good Guy needs her to cover an interview for him. Dis Tracted groans because she already has too much to do. But she takes her pen and legal pad and heads for Good Guy's office. On the way she passes the office runner, Eager One, in the hall. Eager One smiles and says hello pleasantly but Dis Tracted doesn't notice; she's wondering if the store will take back that sweater she bought for her ex-boyfriend. She doesn't see Eager One give her a puzzled look and then a frown after she passes by him.

Dis Tracted knocks on Good Guy's door and he tells her to come in. He greets her with a quick smile as he shuffles through a small mountain of papers on his desk, motions her to a chair in front of his desk, and without looking up at her says, "Hope you had a good weekend because we've got a lot to do."

Dis Tracted lays the legal pad and pen aside and says, "Thanks for asking. In fact I had a terrible weekend. I've been dating this guy Jack for six months and I thought everything was going okay. Then Saturday night we had this big fight and I hoped he would call me Sunday to apologize so I hung around the apartment. . . ."

Good Guy interrupts by clearing his throat and says, "Do you think we could talk about this later? We've got Sad Shape, that divorce client I took on last week, in the conference room and somebody needs to talk to her. I've got to leave for court right now so you'll need to cover it. Apparently her husband pulled some dumb stunt over the weekend and we may need to seek a restraining order against him. Go meet with her and find out what's going on and we'll talk when I get back from court, okay?" Without saying more, Good Guy grabs his coat and briefcase and is out the door.

Dis Tracted makes a few notes on her legal pad then walks back to her office. Her secretary, Teaor Coffee, is sitting at her desk outside Dis Tracted's office taking some aspirin with water. Dis Tracted says, "Teaor, get me the Sad Shape file from the file room," then goes into her office. After throwing her legal pad on the desk and muttering under her breath, Dis Tracted glances out the door to see Teaor Coffee putting the aspirin away in a desk drawer. Angrily, Dis Tracted says, "Teaor, I need that file, now," and watches as the secretary scurries away to get the file.

A few moments later, Dis Tracted enters the conference room and sees Sad Shape sitting at the long table, sobbing. Dis Tracted puts on the best smile she can manage and cheerily says, "Good morning, Mrs. Shape. Do you remember me? I'm Dis Tracted, the paralegal assisting Mr. Guy with your case." As Sad Shape tries unsuccessfully to control her tears, Dis Tracted takes a seat at the head of the conference room table, sighs audibly, looks at her watch, and asks, "What can we help you with today?"

Thirty minutes later the interview is over. Dis Tracted has the vague suspicion it didn't go as well as it could have but she attributes that feeling to it being Monday. She is surprised later in the week to learn that she is getting no year-end bonus and no raise for the new year. At home she tells her boyfriend (with whom she made up Tuesday night), "You know, Jack, no matter how hard you try, you just can't please some people."

1. How did Dis Tracted fail to communicate effectively with Eager One? What should she have done differently?
2. How did Dis Tracted fail to communicate effectively with Good Guy? What should she have done differently?
3. How did Dis Tracted fail to communicate effectively with Teaor Coffee? What should she have done differently?
4. How did Dis Tracted fail to communicate effectively with Sad Shape? What should she have done differently?

2. What are others communicating to you?

Communication is a two-way street. Just as it is critical to be aware of what we are communicating to others verbally and nonverbally, it is just as critical to be aware of what others are communicating to us.

Many of the mistakes Dis Tracted made in Hypothetical 8-6 were attributable to her failure to notice what others were communicating to her. If you didn't do so already in connection with Hypothetical 8-6, make a list of every verbal and nonverbal signal Dis Tracted missed in her communications with Eager One, Good Guy, Teaor Coffee, and Sad Shape.

3. Suggestions for phone communications

Legal investigators spend a lot of time on the telephone—many investigations are accomplished primarily or completely over the phone. Here are some suggestions for communicating effectively over the phone.

a. Your voice is critical

Use a pleasant tone. Remember that in a phone conversation your voice is all the other person has to go by to determine if they like you and if they want to help you. If you are speaking to a stranger, that person will form an immediate first impression of you from your voice.

In investigating work, we make phone calls hoping that the people to whom we speak will assist us in some way. Make sure your voice works for you to accomplish that purpose.

b. Identify yourself properly

Paralegals are required, ethically and professionally, to properly identify themselves in phone conversations. (E.g., "Hello, this is Martha King. I am a paralegal in the office of attorney Marvin Jones.") Avoid the temptation to play act or otherwise mislead the other person to obtain their assistance.

c. Return calls promptly

This is true of all calls, but especially calls from clients. You will recall that part of the ethical duty owed to clients is a duty to keep them reasonably informed regarding the matter of the representation (see Chapter 2). One of the most frequent ethical complaints made against attorneys is their (or their assistant's) failure to return calls. Don't just return calls—return them promptly.

d. Sound interested—even if you're not

e. Take notes while you talk

Never assume that you will recall all the details of even a brief phone conversation. Making contemporaneous notes of your conversation will help you recall it later, and the notes can be placed in the file for others working on the case to see and to support later billing.

f. Phone ego—"Please hold for Mr. Big"

Ever been on the receiving end of one of these calls? A secretary interrupts you with a call and then makes you wait while the caller moseys to the phone? First, don't do this to others. Second, if others do it to you, don't lose your cool. If it's a client, a supervising attorney, or someone else you cannot afford to offend, tolerate it. Third, if it's a client who does this to you, bill him for the waiting time!

g. Phone conversations with information sources

Here are six suggestions to follow when you place a call seeking information or cooperation. Call them the six Bs:

- Be ready. Know exactly what you are going to ask before you get on the phone.
- Be brief. Remember that everybody's time is important.
- Be friendly. The sweet draws the flies, not the sour.
- Be patient. It is usually rewarded.
- Be polite. Using "please" and "thank you" will make people like you.
- Be grateful. And say so; you may need this person again!

4. The investigator as a LOvER!

Simply stated, the paralegal cannot be successful at interviewing and investigating work unless she is constantly aware of what others, particularly clients and witnesses, are communicating to her both verbally and nonverbally. We can understand intellectually what communication involves, and we can acknowledge that we are all experts at comprehending the unspoken signals in verbal communication and in interpreting body language, but unless we consciously turn those systems on when we engage in interviewing and investigating tasks we are going to miss critical information. How do we turn those systems on? By being a LOvER! This means the investigator has to be:

- A Listener
- An Observer
- An Evaluator
- A Reporter

a. A Listener

We will not pick up on nuances and subtle signals sent to us in verbal communication unless we actively listen to others. Hearing and listening are not the same thing. In the Wizard Of Id cartoon, the peasant *heard* the King clearly enough but he wasn't really *listening* so he didn't *understand*! **Active listening** is an activity of the mind as well as the ears; it is concentration on what is being said and how it is being said.

b. An Observer

We will not catch the important messages that body language and physical surroundings may be sending to us if we do not consciously observe what is going on with and around others. As listening is more than hearing, so observing is more than seeing; it is a concentrated mental activity.

c. An Evaluator

As was stressed in the discussion on aspects of verbal and nonverbal communication, the investigator must use instinct, experience, and common sense to interpret what is seen and heard. Remember Honey Dew from Hypothetical 8-3? When the frown crossed her face and she sat back in her chair and crossed her arms, was it because she felt threatened and defensive? Or could it have been a headache? Was she uncomfortable in the chair? Was it too cold in the room? We have to evaluate, reasonably and systematically, the verbal and nonverbal data we perceive in order to draw reliable conclusions.

d. A Reporter

In all interviewing and investigating work the paralegal is under the attorney's supervision. It is critical to report back to the supervising attorney in an effective way all that was heard and observed and an evaluation of that data given. The attorney can then make his own analysis of the information and decide how best to use it for the benefit of the client.

KEY WORDS AND PHRASES TO REMEMBER

accent

active listening

body language

clarity

colloquialisms

enunciation

eye contact

facial expressions

grammar

KISS

LOvER

nervous signals

nonverbal communication

paragraph structure

phone etiquette

pregnant pause

pronunciation

punctuation

rate of speaking

sentence structure

slang

spelling

street talk

tone of voice

verbal communication

vocabulary

voice inflection

volume

writing style

LEARN BY DOING

LBD 8-1. Over the course of a week, maintain a journal documenting your observations of three different people with whom you come in regular contact. Note and record your impressions of their voices, body language, and facial expressions. Keep a running record of dates and times of observation, physical surroundings, and a description of your observations. Choose both people you know well and people you don't know well. Don't tell them what you are doing and make every effort to not be obvious or unduly obtrusive. Following each observation, interpret it—write down what you think you have observed tells you about that person. What were they consciously or unconsciously communicating to you at the time?

LBD 8-2. If you have access to *The CLA Review Manual* by Virginia Koerselman (West Publishing, 2d ed. 1998), study Chapter 2 on Communications and then complete the self-test at the conclusion of the chapter. Repeat the test until you score at least a 90 percent on it.

LBD 8-3. Review the list of books pertaining to verbal and nonverbal communication skills in Appendix E, Resources for the Investigator. Select one of the books and prepare a book report briefly summarizing the main points of each chapter.

LBD 8-4. Arrange and conduct the interview of an experienced trial lawyer. In the interview focus on the lawyer's experience at using the verbal and nonverbal communication skills discussed in this chapter to evaluate clients, witnesses, juries, judges, and opposing counsel. Let the interviewee know in advance that you will be focusing on this particular skill.

FORMULATING AND EXECUTING A
PLAN OF INVESTIGATION

PART OUTLINE

Chapter 9

Formulating a Plan of Investigation

CHAPTER OBJECTIVES

In this chapter we consider what a plan of investigation is and how to formulate an effective and successful plan. You will learn:

- That an effective investigator has a number of distinguishing traits including persistence, creativity, flexibility, and skepticism.
- That having a carefully thought-out plan of investigation is essential to a successful investigation.
- That formulating a plan of investigation begins with what we know, is defined and guided by the law of the case, and is organized in steps to help us locate all information relevant to the client's case.
- That every plan of investigation has limits imposed by a number of factors including client resources, client authorization, and the value of the case.
- That every plan of investigation must be modified as it is executed.
- That the paralegal investigator is frequently the custodian of documents and physical evidence located in an investigation and must know how to label, secure, and document such items of evidence to comply with the rules of evidence.

A. Introduction

Simply put, factual investigation in a law office is the process of locating, gathering, and verifying factual information related to the representation of a client. Historically, attorneys have received no real training in how to conduct factual investigations themselves and have had to learn the hard way—on the job. Because of their lack of training in this critical area and because of other factors (including their chronic lack of time!), attorneys have relied on private investigators to conduct anything other than the simplest investigations.

Today that is changing rapidly. Well-trained paralegals are able to conduct effective, competent factual investigations for their supervising attorneys. It is one of the skills that makes them so valuable—and so marketable.

B. ▶ Traits of the Effective Investigator

Before considering the specifics of how to plan an effective investigation, it may be helpful to consider a number of traits that the effective investigator should have. The adjectives in Illustration 9-1 describe some of these traits. Consider what you would add to that list.

1. The effective investigator is *knowledgeable*

SLEUTH ON THE LOOSE

Identify a small community in another part of your state and assume you are sent there on an investigation assignment. Access *www.mapquest.com* to get a detailed map showing how to get there from where you are.

- of the substantive law controlling the case (see Chapter 1);
- of the adversarial system and procedural law (see Chapters 3 through 5);
- of the rules of evidence (see Chapters 6 and 7); and
- of ethical rules and professional standards (see Chapter 2).

2. The effective investigator is *skilled*

- at factual analysis (see Chapter 1);
- at communicating with others (see Chapter 8);
- at interviewing clients and witnesses (see Chapters 10 through 13);
- at identifying potential witnesses, locating missing witnesses, and working with experts (see Chapters 14 and 15); and
- at locating information from public and private sources (see Chapters 16 through 18).

3. The effective investigator is *persistent*

Information does not always come easy in this line of work. Where to find what you need is not always obvious. Witnesses are missing,

Illustration 9-1
TRAITS OF THE
EFFECTIVE
INVESTIGATOR

The effective investigator must be:

Knowledgeable	Perceptive
Skilled	Skeptical
Persistent	Flexible
Creative	

uncooperative, or even hostile. Documents are not where they should be and clients prove unhelpful. The investigator must learn to expect all this and resolve to keep digging.

Those who have done legal investigation for years know that persistence always pays. Persistent factual investigation always yields *something* of value—and frequently of great value—to the client's case.

HYPOTHETICAL 9-1

Assume that Never Quit is a paralegal working for the attorney representing Speed Freak. Speed Freak has been sued by Granny Puttalong, a 70-year-old grandmother who was involved in an automobile accident with Speed Freak. Puttalong alleges in her complaint that she was putting along the road under the speed limit (as always) when Speed Freak came up behind her and proceeded to honk and ride her bumper. She panicked, lost control of her car, and hit a telephone pole. Speed Freak denies he was tailgaiting Puttalong. He contends he kept a safe distance from her but she stopped without warning. That's when he honked. He says she seemed to panic when he honked and swerved into the telephone pole.

Puttalong has sued Speed Freak for negligence and alleges permanent injury to her back. In her deposition, Granny Puttalong denied any prior problems with her back. In interrogatories served on Puttalong, the attorney for Speed Freak asked Puttalong to list all her doctors or other health care providers for the ten years preceding the accident. Those interrogatory answers have been received and the medical records from the identified physicians have been obtained and reviewed by Never Quit.

Assume Never Quit can find no reference in the medical records of Puttalong to any complaints of or treatment for back problems prior to the accident with Speed Freak. However, there are references in the medicals to three other doctors seen by Puttalong years before who were not identified in the interrogatory answers. All three of those doctors practice in a neighboring state. They are apparently doctors seen by Puttalong more than ten years preceding the accident. Should Never Quit do any more investigation into Puttalong's medical history or should Never Quit quit? Why?

Well, Never Quit never quits! Instead she uses the medical authorization obtained from Puttalong to obtain the medicals from the three newly discovered doctors. Medicals come to Never Quit from two of those doctors but are not helpful. The medical authorization from the third doctor, whose name is Nohome Visit, is returned to Never Quit with the handwritten message on it, "Doctor Visit is deceased." Should Never Quit do any more investigation into Puttalong's medical history or should she quit? Why?

Well, Never Quit never quits! Instead she locates and places a call to the agency that licenses medical doctors in the state where Nohome Visit practiced and makes inquiries regarding when Dr. Visit passed away. She is advised that Dr. Visit has been deceased for eight years. What else do you think Never Quit might want to ask? That's right! She asks about other physicians with whom Dr. Visit may have practiced or who may have taken over his practice following his death.

She learns that Dr. Visit's practice was taken over by his partner, Dr. Bedside Manner. Unfortunately, she learns that Dr. Manner is himself deceased as of three years ago and no other physician took over that practice. Should Never Quit do any more investigation into Puttalong's medical history or should she quit? Why?

Well, as you now know, Never Quit never quits! Instead she determines that Dr. Manner has a surviving widow who still lives in the same small community in which her husband and Dr. Visit practiced. Never Quit places a phone call to Mrs. Manner and learns that, yes, she does still have all of her late husband's old medical records and, yes, those records would probably include the old files of Dr. Visit. They're in her dusty old attic and Never Quit can come look for what she wants anytime.

1. How justifiable would it have been for Never Quit to quit earlier than this?
2. We still don't know if Dr. Visit's file on Granny Puttalong is in Mrs. Manner's attic or what it might contain. Who will have to decide whether to spend the extra time and money to make that search?
3. If it is decided to make that search, what are the different ways we might arrange to do it?
4. What does this Hypothetical say about the importance of an investigation plan being flexible?
5. Under the substantive law of negligence and damages in your state, what might be the legal significance of a factual determination that Granny Puttalong was in fact treated by Dr. Visit for chronic back problems 12 years before the accident? Does this help you understand why Never Quit would be so persistent in pursuing this information?

4. The effective investigator is *creative*

The imagery may be appropriately out of fashion these days, but the truth behind the old saying "there's more than one way to skin a cat" is still valid. Some investigative tasks are straightforward and routine (e.g., "Go over to the courthouse and get a copy of the divorce decree."). However, many assignments require the exercise of discretion and judgment. Decisions have to be made about how to go about the assignment economically and effectively. The investigator will hit roadblocks to finding what is needed and will have to think of other ways to get what is wanted. In investigation, there is no substitute for creative thinking.

HYPOTHETICAL 9-2

Assume that Never Quit is authorized to travel to the neighboring state where Mrs. Manner, the widow of Dr. Bedside Manner, resides to look through the records of Granny Puttalong. Never Quit travels to Mrs. Manner's house along with Better Idea, a paralegal from a local in-state law office who is assisting with this part of the investigation.

Unfortunately, when Never Quit and Better Idea arrive, Mrs. Manner gets nervous and balks at letting the two investigators look through her husband's records to locate Puttalong's old medical file. She says she knows it wouldn't be violating any laws or anything but it just makes her nervous. She says she should have thrown those old files out long ago and is going to do so soon.

Never Quit tries to think what to do. She can:

   a. strong-arm her way past the frail widow and take the file by force;

   b. wait until Mrs. Manner is out, then break in and steal the file; or

   c. come back later disguised as a state investigator who needs to see the files for official purposes.

Fortunately, Never Quit quickly eliminates these possibilities and tells Better Idea they have no option but to recommend that the attorney for Speed Freak have Mrs. Manner subpoenaed to a deposition and require her to bring the file with her. They agree that would involve added time and expense when they don't even know if the file will prove helpful.

Then, Better Idea says, "Wait a minute, I have a better idea." Better Idea tells Never Quit to wait in the car then goes back to the front door of Mrs. Manner's house and rings the doorbell. When Mrs. Manner answers, Never Quit hears Better Idea begin to ask her about the roses growing next to her porch. Mrs. Manner comes out on the porch to answer the questions and a long conversation follows.

Before long, Never Quit sees Mrs. Manner go back inside the house then return with a quilt. She and Better Idea sit down together in the porch swing and continue talking, apparently about the quilt. After a while Never Quit begins to nod off. The last thing she sees is Better Idea going inside the house with Mrs. Manner.

Sometime later Never Quit is awakened by Better Idea shouting good-byes to Mrs. Manner and opening the car door. As Never Quit sits up, Better Idea hands her a cut rose, a plate full of fresh-baked cookies (I believe they were chocolate chip), and the file of Granny Puttalong, which Better Idea has permission to copy and return to Mrs. Manner. As Better Idea gets in the car he says, "You know, it occurred to me that Mrs. Manner was uptight because she really didn't know us. I thought if I visited with her a little and got to know her she might relax. And what do you know, it worked!"

1. How much time, trouble, and expense have been saved by Better Idea's creative thinking?
2. How important are communication skills (people skills) in investigating?
3. How does this Hypothetical illustrate the importance of a plan of investigation being flexible?
4. Why was Never Quit wise to eliminate her first ideas on how to obtain the Granny Puttalong file?

5. The effective investigator is *perceptive*

Factual investigation is analogous to driving an automobile. We all learn early on that when driving a car you must stay constantly alert. Even when driving routes you take every day, you've got to stay alert.

The same type of awareness is required to be an effective investigator. You have to be perceptive, that is, alert and observant. Even if you are tired. Even if you are in a hurry. Even if you have done this a hundred times before. Why? Because if you are not, you are going to miss information you should have noticed. And that information could be critically important to the client's case (not to mention your future).

Another aspect of perceptiveness in investigating is **intuition.** Experienced investigators learn to trust their hunches, that is, their feelings or intuitive instincts. They know that the investigator has to be aware—watching, listening, and sensitive to impressions at all times. Such subjective vibes can be just as valuable to the investigator as any learned skill. But you have to consciously flip that invisible switch in your mind to activate those intuitive sensors or you won't be on the receiving end of some important signals.

Assume that Eye Seenit has been identified by Granny Puttalong as an eye witness to the accident between her and Speed Freak. Assume also that Over Worked, another paralegal in the office of the attorney representing Speed Freak, is assigned to interview Seenit. Over Worked contacts Eye Seenit, prepares his questions, arrives at the interview on time, and gets through all his questions in under 15 minutes notwithstanding the witness's irritating habit of leaving the room every few moments.

Following the interview, Over Worked reports back to the supervising attorney that Eye Seenit confirms Granny Puttalong's version of the accident (see Hypothetical 9-1). Disappointed, the attorney concludes that Speed Freak is likely to lose the case on liability and considers settling.

Now assume that instead of Over Worked handling the interview of Eye Seenit that task is assigned to Under Paid (a good paralegal who is, alas, underpaid). Under Paid contacts Eye Seenit, arranges the interview, prepares her questions, shows up on time, and begins asking her questions.

Maintaining close eye contact with Eye Seenit, she notices that he looks at her directly until she begins to ask about the details of the accident. Then he looks away from her. About five minutes into the interview, Eye Seenit drains the cup he is drinking from at his desk and excuses himself, leaving the room with the cup.

While Eye Seenit is gone from the room, Under Paid looks around and notices a pair of eyeglasses laying on the desk under a pile of papers. Soon Eye Seenit returns with his cup refilled and the interview resumes. Under Paid asks about the glasses and learns that Eye Seenit is nearsighted and was not wearing his glasses or contacts the day he saw the accident. He is pretty sure he saw what happened, though.

Under Paid notices that Eye Seenit sips from the cup frequently and smacks his lips each time. He also wipes his mouth with his hands after each swallow. Soon the cup is empty and again Eye Seenit leaves the room with it. While he is gone Under Paid continues looking around the room. She notices what appears to be a family photo on the wall—a family reunion maybe?

When Eye Seenit returns (with refilled cup in hand), Under Paid asks about the picture and particularly about a little old gray-haired lady in the back. Turns out the little old lady is none other than Granny Puttalong, who is married to Eye Seenit's uncle who is also his business partner.

As Eye Seenit continues to sip from his cup and answer questions, Under Paid notices that his speech is becoming slurred, his voice raised, and his answers slower. He is also a lot more relaxed and friendly than when the interview began. She finds an excuse to lean over Eye Seenit's desk to point at something and gets her nose within a few inches of his cup. Want to bet on what she smelled?

Having finished all other questions, Under Paid finally asks Eye Seenit about the contents of the cup and he admits, albeit somewhat defensively, that he needs a little sip to get him through the day and, yes, he would have been sipping the day of the accident because one day is just like another.

When Under Paid reports back to the supervising attorney, he compliments her, says there is no way they will settle the case now, and adds, "You know, Under Paid, I'm glad we hired you. You're worth every cent of that big salary we pay you!"

1. List everything you can think of that Over Worked failed to do or failed to do well.
2. How would you summarize the differences in how Under Paid and Over Worked handled this interview?
3. Was Under Paid wise to confront Eye Seenit with her suspicions of his drinking? Could that have backfired? What do you think of her decision to wait until all other questions have been asked before addressing that issue?
4. If Eye Seenit had denied that the liquid in the cup was alcohol or that he was a drinker, what other investigation might Under Paid have recommended to pursue this lead?

6. The effective investigator is *skeptical*

By skeptical we don't mean cynical. We do mean that the investigator should remember the first and second commandments of legal investigating: **assume nothing** and **verify everything**. It does not matter what the source of our information is—the client, a witness, a document, a government record—we always seek to verify the information given to us. If a lawyer is going to depend on certain facts to advise a client or to take an adversarial position on behalf of the client in civil or criminal litigation, the facts must first be tested in the crucible of investigation.

Specifically, that means that good investigators:

a. Evaluate the source of information

We always evaluate the *source* of information that comes to us to determine its reliability. Is the source reliable? Does this person seem believable? Does he seem competent? Does he have any motive to misstate facts or to leave out facts or to exaggerate? Is there any reason to believe he could have been mistaken in what he saw or heard? Or, is the document genuine? Is it complete? Is it the original?

b. Test information for internal consistency

We always *test* information given to us to see if it seems consistent, logical, and believable on its own. Does this information seem reliable? Will it hold up as true and credible if an opposing party examines it?

c. Look for gaps in information

We always look for *holes* or *gaps* in the information given to us— incomplete time lines, incomplete explanations, or implausible stories—

and then determine how we can fill in those gaps with reliable information.

d. Compare new information to information already gathered

We always test information given to us by **comparing** it to other information we have to see if there are **contradictions** or **inconsistencies.** If there are, we work diligently to determine why. Why is this witness's story different from that witness's? Why is this document not consistent with what others have told me? Why does the public record say this when my client told me something else? Which one is correct?

e. Seek corroborating information

We always seek **corroborating** (confirming or supporting) information in the form of other witnesses or documents that can back up or confirm the information.

f. Seek explanations and details

We always need to know **who, why, where, what, when,** and **how.** If we come across a thread of new information in an interview or investigation we follow it until the whole ball is unraveled! We stay curious.

g. Seek leads to more information

We always seek **leads** to other sources of information and then follow those leads with the same energy and curiosity.

7. The effective investigator is *flexible*

In this chapter you will learn how to plan an effective investigation. But you will also learn to expect that plan to change, sometimes considerably, as you execute it. That is the nature of factual investigation.

As you will learn in the chapters on interviewing (see Chapters 10 through 13), an interviewer should never make a list of questions and follow it mindlessly in an interview. The investigator must be ready to follow up on answers given or observations made during the interview by asking other or different questions. Similarly, in all investigative activity, we set out with a plan but what we actually find—or don't find—will require us to modify it along the way. That flexibility is essential to effective investigating. See Hypotheticals 9-1, 9-2, and 9-4.

HYPOTHETICAL 9-4

Assume that the medical records of Granny Puttalong obtained from Mrs. Manner's attic showed that Dr. Visit had treated Puttalong for chronic back problems for a number of years; that she had undergone surgery on her back twice; and that she had become addicted to the pain medication prescribed for her. She stopped going to Dr. Nohome Visit when he refused to write her additional prescriptions for pain medication. His records indicate the permanent nature of the disability, the addiction, his recommendation of treatment for the addiction, and his warning that she not operate a motor vehicle because of her nervous condition.

1. In light of these discoveries, what new or additional direction(s) would you recommend for this investigation on behalf of Speed Freak?

2. Under the rules of evidence for your state courts, how will the attorney for Speed Freak get the discovered medical records of Dr. Visit for Granny Puttalong admitted in evidence and how might that affect the investigation Never Quit is doing now?

C. The Importance of Having a Plan of Investigation

No investigation should be undertaken until a written plan has been formulated. Initiating an investigation without a plan is like leaving on a trip without a planned route; you may get there but you probably will be late! And the odds of getting lost will be much greater. Practically speaking, a planned investigation will be:

- more efficient in use of time;
- more efficient economically;
- more likely to be thorough;
- less stressful; and
- more likely to be done effectively.

There will be times when it is tempting to jump into an investigation without doing the planning recommended in this chapter. Time deadlines, busy schedules, the complacency that comes from having done similar tasks many times before, or just pure old laziness may all combine to tempt you. But experienced investigators know that it is always a mistake to shortcut the planning process. For even the briefest or most routine interview or investigation assignment, make a plan before you act, and put it in writing.

D. Formulating a Plan of Investigation

1. Start with what you already know

If I am planning to travel from Nashville, Tennessee (where I have been trying unsuccessfully to break into the country music business as the long-lost love child of Patsy Cline and Buddy Holly) to Los Angeles, California (where I now plan to succeed in the movie business as Cleft Chin, the next great leading man), I would be smart to plan my route starting from Nashville. It would be foolish to plan my trip from Chicago or Baltimore. This sounds obvious but, in reality, many investigations go awry because the investigator fails to carefully take account of the factual and legal basis from which the investigation begins. They fail to consider what they already know before they launch an effort to learn more.

So the first step in planning an investigation is to prepare a summary of all facts that you already have at your disposal. For each fact included in your summary, it is a good idea to note the *source* of that information (i.e., client, witness, document) and an indication of whether the information is deemed *reliable* or *questionable*.

Now go over the summary, looking for information that needs to be verified. Look for gaps or inconsistencies in the information. Make a note regarding how you intend to fill in those gaps.

Illustration 9-2 gives you an idea of how this first step might look in an investigation plan prepared by a paralegal doing pre-filing investigation on behalf of Granny Puttalong in connection with her potential claim against Speed Freak.

2. Identify the specific goals of your investigation

In other words, determine as precisely as you can where it is you want to go with your investigation—what is it exactly that you want to accomplish? In planning my big career move from Nashville to Los Angeles, I would be unwise to pack up and pull out in traffic before I have specifically identified the location of L.A. on the map. Instead, I'm going to identify *where* I am going and then plan *how* to get there *before* I leave.

It's like that in a factual investigation. Having established what you already know—where you are—now determine what exactly you want to accomplish—where you want to go. Only after these first two steps are completed can we plan the particulars of the investigation—how you're going to get there.

a. Consider the law of the case

Recall the discussion of the relationship between fact and law in Chapter 1. We undertake factual investigation only because the client

Illustration 9-2 FIRST STEP IN FORMULATING THE PLAN OF INVESTIGATION: SUMMARIZE INFORMATION ALREADY KNOWN

INVESTIGATION PLAN

CLIENT: Granny Puttalong
FILE NO.: 2004-0001
ADVERSE PARTY: Speed Freak
DATE: March 1, 2004

I. SUMMARY OF FACTS KNOWN TO DATE	SOURCE	RELIABLE (Y-N)	STILL TO DO
1. Client is a 70-year-old retired school teacher living with her 2nd husband. . . .	Client	Y	Is age correct? (See accident report.)
6. On October 10, 2003 client struck a telephone pole head-on while driving her 2002 Saturn automobile.	Client/Accident report	Y	
7. Saturn purchased in March '02 for $16,500. Car totaled in crash. . . .	Client/Invoice/ Accident report	Y	Who owns car?
12. Client has 2 fused discs and surgery upcoming; broken fibula. . . .	City Hospital ER records/Dr. Helen Smith reports	Y	
15. Driver behind client, Speed Freak, tailgating, honking; caused client to panic and lose control. . . .	Client/Accident report inconclusive	N	Need to locate & interview witnesses

---

has a legal problem of some kind and we must locate factual information related to that legal problem. The law defines the context for the investigation. It will point us in the direction we need to go.

In the Granny Puttalong case, we are representing her with a view toward suing any and all parties responsible for the automobile accident in which she was injured. The most obvious legal theory for this contemplated personal injury action is negligence. The most likely target is the other driver, Speed Freak. If Puttalong is going to be able to recover from Speed Freak for negligence she will have to prove that:

- Speed Freak owed her a duty of care in operating his vehicle;
- he breached that duty of care in some way;
- his breach of duty of care was the actual and proximate (foreseeable) cause of injuries sustained by Puttalong; and
- the injuries and other damage Puttalong did in fact sustain due to the breach of duty by Speed Freak.

That is the law of the case. It will provide the context in which we undertake factual investigation in the Granny Puttalong case. Of course, we know from our study of tort law (and our discussions with the supervising attorney) that in negligence actions there are legal defenses that may be raised—comparative fault, assumption of the risk, third-party intervening causation, and so forth. Sometimes defendants in negligence actions also counterclaim against a plaintiff, alleging that it was the plaintiff who violated a duty of care owed to the defendant and caused damages sustained by defendant. We also know that counterclaims occur with great frequency in automobile accidents where both drivers typically sustain damage to their personal property (the vehicles) and often to their persons. So in our factual investigation for Granny Puttalong we will have to look for facts that might give rise to such defenses or counterclaims on behalf of Speed Freak or other potential defendants. All of these legal considerations define the factual investigation we are planning.

b. Write down the ultimate goals of the investigation

Now that you have summarized what you already know and have considered the legal context of the case, give thought to what else you need to learn. What are the specific goals of your remaining investigation? Write down your goals as you identify them. Putting your plan into words will help you organize it and get it clear in your mind. Illustration 9-3 gives you an idea how this second step might look in the investigation plan prepared by a paralegal doing pre-filing investigation on behalf of Granny Puttalong in connection with her potential claim against Speed Freak.

Illustration 9-3 is by no means an exhaustive list. Each case will raise its own unique questions that must be answered by investigation. See Hypothetical 9-5.

HYPOTHETICAL 9-5

Assume you are a paralegal working for the attorney defending Speed Freak in the anticipated claim to be made by Granny Puttalong. What might the stated goals of your pre-filing investigation plan look like?

Illustration 9-3 SECOND STEP IN FORMULATING THE PLAN OF INVESTIGATION: IDENTIFY THE GOALS OF THE INVESTIGATION

INVESTIGATION PLAN

CLIENT: Granny Puttalong
FILE NO.: 2004-0001
ADVERSE PARTY: Speed Freak
DATE: March 1, 2004

II. Goals of this investigation

1. Identify all possible plaintiffs.
   • Can the client's husband make a loss of consortium claim?
   • Is he a co-owner of the damaged car?

2. Determine the nature and extent of damages.
   • Value of the damaged car
   • Obtain current medical records on client
   • Ask treating physician for disability rating/future medicals

3. Identifying each possible defendant.
   • Was Speed Freak the owner of the car?
   • Was Speed Freak acting as an agent for another (vicarious liability)?
   • Did Speed Freak have a passenger or was he talking on car phone?
   • Did client's car—brakes, air bag, steering—malfunction in any way?

4. Identify and evaluate all possible legal theories against each potential defendant based on the available facts (e.g., simple negligence, strict liability, breach of warranty, breach of contract, fraud, infliction of emotional distress, etc.).

5. Identify possible defenses (including affirmative defenses) which could defeat client's claim(s) or mitigate damages.
   • Statutes of limitation or repose
   • Comparative fault
   • Assumption of risk
   • Lack of causation
   • Prior existing medical condition(s)
   • Intervening third-party act

6. Identify and evaluate possible personal jurisdiction problems with regard to each possible defendant.

7. Determine the relative financial position of each possible defendant (including the existence of liability insurance and its limits) to evaluate whether pursuing them to judgment will be worthwhile.

8. Determine the options regarding subject matter jurisdiction. Can we file this in federal as well as state court? If we have a choice which would we prefer?

9. Preserve existing evidence.
   • Photo and video scene
   • Photo and video autos
   • Photo and video client injuries
   • Client diary

10. Identify and interview witnesses.
    Eye Seenit

11. Identify and retain accident reconstruction expert.

3. Brainstorm for specifics

Let's see, now. I'm going from Nashville to L.A., so I want to leave Nashville on I-40 West and stay on it through Memphis. Maybe I can get there about noon and try some of those barbeque ribs the city is famous for. And maybe I'll have time to take in Graceland; if Elvis is alive, isn't that where he would be? I'll stay on I-40 all the way to Little Rock. There I'll pick up I-30 and go on to Dallas. H'm, if I travel on a weekend I wonder if I could catch the Cowboys at home. And from Dallas. . .

Once the traveler knows where he is leaving from and where he is going to he can then plan the specifics of the trip. Similarly, once the investigator has determined what he knows so far and what he still needs to accomplish, then—and only then—is he ready to plan the specifics of the investigation.

A good way to begin identifying the specific things to be done to accomplish the identified goals of the investigation is to **brainstorm.** Make a list of all the things you need to do to answer every question or achieve every purpose on the list you compiled in step two of the plan. At this stage, don't bother to put the things you think of down in a particular order, just get them out of your head and on paper (or computer file). Here are some tips for the brainstorming step:

- Use the supervising attorney, the client, notes and memoranda in the file, documents gathered to date, and anyone else in the office working on the case as sources for ideas.
- Utilize the old tried and true: who, what, where, why, when, and how.
- Don't confine yourself to the obvious—wonder about things.

There will always be basic things you need to do in an investigation and those will typically come to your mind first (e.g., get the accident report, get the medicals, interview the witnesses, etc.). Be sure to list those. But at that point you have only begun to plan. Let your mind wonder. (Not *wander* off the subject, but *wonder*!) With regard to each thing you know about the case, let yourself wonder about what you don't know. Did Speed Freak tailgate Granny Puttalong and honk at her for going slow? I wonder why he did that. Could he have had an emergency? Was he late to work? Is he just a road rage jerk? Does he do this all the time? I wonder where he had been immediately before this accident or earlier in the day. I wonder why he was in such a hurry. I wonder who might have seen him before he came up on Granny's car. Was anything wrong with his car? I wonder what was on his mind to preoccupy him. I wonder if he could have been angry or upset and why. Was he on a business errand at the time and, if so, for whom?

I wonder, I wonder, I wonder. If you take the time to do this, the creative juices will begin to flow and you might be amazed at what you think of to look into. Of such creative thinking winning cases are made.

Illustration 9-4 shows you how this third brainstorming step might look as applied to stated goal number 2, "Determine the nature and extent of damages" from Illustration 9-3.

Illustration 9-4 THIRD STEP IN FORMULATING THE PLAN OF INVESTIGATION: BRAINSTORM FOR SPECIFICS

INVESTIGATION PLAN

CLIENT: Granny Puttalong
FILE NO.: 2004-0001
ADVERSE PARTY: Speed Freak
DATE: March 1, 2004

III. BRAINSTORMING FOR SPECIFICS. . .

2. Determine the nature and extent of damages.
   • Get all hospital records for client admission, surgery, discharge.
   • Get updated medicals from Dr. H. Smith and ask when disability determination will be made. Will she give us a preliminary determination in writing for possible settlement effort?
   • Get final bills from hospital, ambulance service, towing service, storage facility. Will city charge client for damage to telephone pole? (Should we call city about that or wait and see—don't want to give them the idea—or do we? Ask attorney.)
   • Get updated bill from Dr. Smith. Ask about future medicals. (Can she go ahead and estimate for settlement effort? In writing?)
   • Get value of car from NADA book. Was there any personalty lost in car?
   • Interview Granny's husband re loss of consortium theory.
   • Any photos or videos of injuries, scene or vehicles? Suggest they take photo/video of injuries, disabilities.
   • Suggest client start daily diary to supplement pain and suffering, loss of enjoyment of life claims.
   • Insurance policies? Locate. Notification yet? Verify. Coverage questions?
   • Disability insurance on Granny? Social Security claim?
   • Verify she's not working—workers' comp?
   • Ask about pre-existing condition on back stuff. Other doctors seen? Chiropractors? Get old medicals on her—how far? Ask attorney.
   • Any plans to go back to work in the future? Possible now?
   • Other medical problems that will be worsened by accident? Arthritis exacerbated? Ask Dr. Smith.
   • Who to use for accident reconstruction if needed?
   • Who to use to calculate present value numbers—economist, banker?

---

4. Identify all possible sources of information

As you create your brainstorming list, or after you have done so, identify and write down all sources from which you will attempt to obtain each item of information. Be specific. What person, government office, private business, document, or other source will be likely to provide you with what you need? In general, all information comes from one of eight sources:

- the client
- the opposing party
- eyewitnesses
- non–eyewitness information sources
- the scene, site, or thing involved in the incident
- public documents
- private documents
- consulting experts

5. Organize your plan into a logical format and chart it

There is no single format for a final plan of investigation. In this section we will discuss four different formats for final plans of investigation: (1) a **chronological to-do list format**; (2) a **topical format**; (3) a **sources format**; and (4) a **litigation or cause of action format.**

These formats are suggestive only. As the paralegal gains experience in investigation she will develop her own customized format for a plan of investigation. However, it will always be important for the paralegal investigator to go through steps 1 to 4 before formatting the final plan of investigation. And it will also be important, no matter what format you use, to chart your plan of investigation. That is, put it in some form of writing that makes it easy to read and review, to locate needed information quickly, and to update as you proceed with the investigation. Samples of charted investigation plans are presented with each of the formats discussed in this chapter. (See Illustrations 9-5, 9-6, 9-7, and 9-8.)

If possible, the investigator should keep the charted investigation plan on computer. That generally makes the plan easier to access than a hard (paper) copy sitting in the file folder. (Now where is that darn file? I thought I left it right here on the desk.) It also makes it easier to change and to update the status of the investigation. If you need a hard copy of the investigation plan chart, you can always print it out.

a. The chronological to-do list format

Useful primarily for shorter, less complicated investigations, the to-do list format is simply a list of things to do placed in chronological order. For that reason it is sometimes referred to as a **time line** format. Beside each item on the list a place should be provided to indicate (1) the date when work on that item was initiated, (2) the status of the work on that item at any given time, and (3) the date work on that item is completed.

If the paralegal assisting the attorney representing Granny Puttalong is instructed by the attorney to obtain the client's medicals for the past ten years; get the accident report; and interview the investigating officer, Puttalong's husband, and Eye Seenit, a chronological to-do list format for the investigation plan might look like Illustration 9-5.

b. The topical format

Using this format, the plan of investigation is organized by topic or subject matter. If, for example, the paralegal assisting the attorney representing Granny Puttalong is instructed by the attorney to obtain information on the client's injuries and expenses, a topical format for the plan of investigation might look something like Illustration 9-6.

c. The sources format

This format organizes the final plan of investigation around the various sources from which information will be sought. Sources in any given case might include the parties, fact witnesses, expert witnesses, and documentary proof. Illustration 9-7 shows how the sources format for

Illustration 9-5   PLAN OF INVESTIGATION USING A TO-DO LIST FORMAT

INVESTIGATION PLAN

CLIENT: Granny Puttalong
FILE NO.: 2004-0001
ADVERSE PARTY: Speed Freak
DATE: March 1, 2004

V. INVESTIGATION TO BE DONE

ASSIGNMENT	DATE INITIATED	STATUS	DATE COMPLETED
1. Contact police dept. for accident rept. records			
2. Photo/video scene			
3. Photo/video car at Moore's Garage			
4. Prepare medical records authorization for client			
5. Interview client re medical providers last 10 years			
6. Have client sign med. auth.			
7. Interview husband			
8. Interview investigating officer			
9. Interview Eye Seenit			

a plan of investigation prepared by a paralegal assisting the attorney representing Granny Puttalong might look.

d. The cause of action format

The litigation or cause of action format organizes a final plan of investigation around the specific elements of each cause of action or defense to be pled in the case. Each such element is charted allowing the paralegal investigator to identify (1) information needed; (2) sources for that information; (3) the informal investigation you plan to do to gather that information; (4) the formal investigation you recommend be done to gather that information; and (5) a time frame for accomplishing each part of the plan. A litigation chart in a negligence case might look something like Illustration 9-8.

Again, it should be kept in mind that the four formats for plans of investigation discussed here are suggestions only. The style of the individual investigator as well as the nature of a particular case may require a customized format.

E. ▶ Limitations on a Plan of Investigation

We cannot always do all the investigation we want or need to do on a particular case. A number of factors determine and limit the scope of the investigation you will be authorized to do. Those factors include:

Illustration 9-6   PLAN OF INVESTIGATION USING A TOPICAL FORMAT

INVESTIGATION PLAN

CLIENT: Granny Puttalong
FILE NO.: 2004-0001
ADVERSE PARTY: Speed Freak
DATE: March 1, 2004

V. INVESTIGATION TO BE DONE

ASSIGNMENT	DATE INITIATED	STATUS	DATE COMPLETED
1. INJURIES			
a. Prepare medical records auth. and have client sign	_____	_____	_____
b. Obtain hospital records including ER records	_____	_____	_____
c. Obtain med. records of Dr. Helen Smith	_____	_____	_____
d. Interview Dr. Smith re injuries/prognosis/disability	_____	_____	_____
e. Interview client re injuries/diary	_____	_____	_____
f. Interview husband re injuries/disabilities	_____	_____	_____
2. EXPENSES			
a. Obtain hospital bills from City Hospital	_____	_____	_____
b. Obtain ambulance bill from Emergency Service, Inc.	_____	_____	_____
c. Obtain towing/storage bill from Cedar Bluff Towing	_____	_____	_____
d. Determine book value of car	_____	_____	_____
e. Obtain invoice on car from client/husband or dealer (Dodge Dart Cars in city)	_____	_____	_____
f. Interview client/husband re car value and personal property loss	_____	_____	_____
g. Interview client re plans for work or other lost income	_____	_____	_____

---

1. The amount of work actually required

Engaging in investigation can sometimes require the same type of judgment call that doctors have to make in deciding whether to run more tests on a patient. When is enough enough? At what point have we done all we really need to do and any more would just be running up the bill? It is up to the supervising attorney to decide that question in the exercise of her professional judgment on behalf of the client.

2. The cost of the work to be done

Investigative work can be expensive. In addition to the time of the investigator, there are out-of-pocket expenses frequently incurred, such as long-distance phone calls, postage, copying, mileage and other traveling

Illustration 9-7   PLAN OF INVESTIGATION USING A SOURCES FORMAT

INVESTIGATION PLAN

CLIENT: Granny Puttalong
FILE NO.: 2004-0001
ADVERSE PARTY: Speed Freak
DATE: March 1, 2004

V. INVESTIGATION TO BE DONE

A. FACT WITNESSES

Name	Address/ Phone	Areas of Knowledge	Intervw'd/ Date & By	Follow-up Needed (Y-N)	Documents Provided
1. G. Puttalong					
2. H. Puttalong					
3. S. Freak					
4. E. Seenit					
5. Officer D. Lewis					

B. EXPERT WITNESSES

Name	Address/ Phone	Areas of Knowledge	Intervw'd/ Date & By	Follow-up Needed (Y-N)	Documents Provided
1. Dr. F. Scalion					
2. Officer D. Lewis					

C. DOCUMENTARY EVIDENCE

Description	Source	Location- Originals	Copies in file? (Y-N)	Custodian/ Witness
1. Hospital bills				
2. Doctor bills				
3. Photos (8) of accident scene				

expenses. Anytime an investigative task is going to require an unexpected or significant expense the paralegal should consult with the supervising attorney to obtain advance authority.

3. The value of the case

Small cases do not justify the outlay of significant time or expenses for investigation. It is up to the supervising attorney and the client to decide how much investigation is warranted on a particular case.

4. The resources of the client

The ability of the client to pay for the time and expenses incurred in an investigation must also be considered. Even in a case handled by the

Illustration 9-8   PLAN OF INVESTIGATION USING A CAUSE OF ACTION FORMAT

INVESTIGATION PLAN

CLIENT: Granny Puttalong
FILE NO.: 2004-0001
ADVERSE PARTY: Speed Freak
DATE: March 1, 2004

V. INVESTIGATION TO BE DONE

A. NEGLIGENCE THEORY

Element	Information Needed	Sources for Information	Informal Investigation	Formal Discovery	Date\ Deadline
1. Duty					
2. Breach					
3. Cause in fact					
4. Proximate cause					
5. Damages					

B. DEFENSES TO NEGLIGENCE

Element	Information Needed	Sources for Information	Informal Investigation	Formal Discovery	Date\ Deadline
1. Plaintiff's fault					
2. Assumption of risk					
3. Intervening cause					
4. Statute of repose					

law firm on a contingency basis, the client is responsible for the out-of-pocket expenses.

5. The resources of the law office

The resources of the law office may be limited by staffing shortages or by busy schedules, limitations that the supervising attorney should consider in deciding whether to take a case at all. And before taking the case, the attorney should advise the client of the limited resources of the office so the client can make an informed choice.

There are ethical consequences to these decisions and actions. The ethical and professional obligation that the attorney owes the client to represent the client competently and vigorously might be violated by accepting a case that the office does not have the resources to handle. Your responsibility as a paralegal is to always let the supervising attorney know of any limitations on your time to undertake necessary investigation on a matter.

6. Client authorization

The law office cannot undertake investigative work without the approval of the client. This authorization may come at the beginning of the representation and be valid for the duration of the case. Or it may be necessary to obtain authorization for each new investigative task as it arises. The investigating paralegal should always check with the supervising attorney to be sure that the client has expressly or impliedly authorized a task before performing it.

Remember that any plan of investigation must be pre-approved by the supervising attorney before it is undertaken. It is up to the supervising attorney to obtain the client's approval. Likewise, you should keep the attorney advised on suggested changes in the investigation as it progresses and let the attorney know if such changes are going to make a significant difference in costs or time.

F. Flexibility of a Plan of Investigation

The plan of investigation will be constantly under review and revision. That is as it should be. As you accomplish one investigative task, it may lead to another task that you did not originally anticipate. Always update your investigation plan so you do not forget anything. Check it regularly to be sure you are getting things done on time. And do not forget to keep the supervising lawyer advised on a regular basis of the status of your investigation.

G. The Handling of Documents and Physical Evidence During an Investigation

During the course of the investigation the paralegal may come into the possession of a variety of documentary and physical evidence. Before discussing the proper handling of such material, it will be helpful to define what we mean by *documentary evidence* and *physical evidence*.

1. Distinguishing between documentary and physical evidence

By **documentary evidence** we mean any type of data compilation, in paper or other form and of public, private, or business origin. This is a very broad definition and encompasses all writings, correspondence, memoranda, reports, records, books, publications, sketches, drawings, diagrams, charts, maps, blueprints, photographs, video recordings, movies, slides, audio recordings, microfiche, microfilm, x-ray, MRI or laser imagery, CD-ROM disks, computer disk files (including e-mail), and any similar materials however denominated.

By **physical evidence** we mean any physical or material object that is not documentary in nature, such as machinery, equipment, tools, vehicles, works of art, and all types of consumer and commercial products (food, clothing, cleaning products, etc.).

It is not the purpose of this section to deal with identifying and obtaining documentary and physical evidence. Those subjects are addressed in Chapters 16 through 18. In this section we deal only with the proper handling, storage, and recording of documents and things that come into the possession of the investigator.

2. Creating demonstrative evidence

Although much documentary and physical evidence is collected or gathered by the investigator from various public and private sources, sometimes the law office will itself create or hire a professional to create such evidence.

EXAMPLE

The paralegal may be asked by the supervising attorney to take photographs, video tape, or make sketches of the scene of an accident, the vehicle, or other object involved in the case or to arrange for a professional photographer or commercial artist to do so. Charts or diagrams designed to present financial or other statistical information in a more understandable or striking way may be prepared at the request of the attorney. Computerized simulations may be created by a consulting expert so the jury can more realistically visualize an incident that occurred in the past.

The paralegal may create such documentary or physical evidence herself if it is within the range of her competence. Taking photographs, making a video recording, or generating a simple graph are good examples of tasks frequently assigned to paralegals.

Or the paralegal may be asked to locate, contact, and make arrangements with an expert (see Chapter 15) to generate the items requested. Sketches, drawings, complex graphs and charts, as well as computerized simulations are all examples of more specialized tasks normally requested of experts. Even when work is turned over to an expert, the paralegal will frequently be the primary contact between the expert and the law office and will be responsible for forwarding needed information to the expert.

3. The role of the rules of evidence in handling documents and things

Whether the documents and things that come into the possession of the paralegal are gathered from witnesses or generated by law office personnel or a retained expert, the paralegal who is responsible for handling and storing those items must be always mindful of relevant rules of evidence. Mishandling evidence could have a severe negative impact on a client's case and may amount to malpractice as well as an ethical violation (remember the duty of competence?).

The most significant evidentiary rules that come into play in the handling and storage of documentary and physical evidence are the rules regarding authentication, chain of custody, privilege, attorney work product, and the best evidence rule. Consequently, the investigating paralegal who comes into custody of documentary or physical evidence should:

- Determine and keep a record of who has the original document or thing.
- Determine and keep a record of who the authenticating witness(es) will be for the document or thing.
- Carefully handle and store documentary or physical evidence, and document its whereabouts at all times.
- Locate the original document or thing and, in the absence of the original, have an authentic copy available and be able to explain why the original is not available.
- Maintain all documents and things in such a way that client confidentiality is not compromised.
- If the document or thing qualifies as work product, label it as such and maintain it in such a way that the privilege is not compromised.

HYPOTHETICAL 9-6

Assume you are a paralegal working for the attorney representing the plaintiff in a products liability case. The plaintiff alleges that a toaster she bought was unreasonably defective because the first time she used it, the toast shot up out of the toaster with such force that it struck her in the left eye even though her face was at least two feet above the toaster at the time. The rocketing toast caused plaintiff severe swelling and permanent partial loss of vision in that eye.

Your supervising attorney has instructed you to take possession of the toaster and the receipt showing the plaintiff's purchase of the toaster and to take some pictures of the plaintiff's swollen eye. You visit the plaintiff's house and are surprised to see that the plaintiff is using the toaster to make toast for her family. She asks if you mind if she makes just one more piece of toast before you take the toaster away and you agree. You watch with amazement as the toast, when it is done, shoots out of the toaster at great speed and rises at least five feet in the air. Finally you take the pictures requested and leave with the pictures, toaster, and receipt.

As you leave the plaintiff's house you toss the toaster in the back seat. Since you were on your way home anyway, you take the toaster in, show it to your family, and demonstrate the flying toast. Your family is so entertained that they invite the neighbors over and the toast party goes on all night. Everyone enjoys the pictures of the injured client as well; they are amazed that a simple piece of toast could cause such swelling. Your little sister asks if she can take the toaster and pictures to school the next day for show and tell. Since you dote on her and can't tell her no, you say okay so long as she brings them back home right after school.

Fortunately, your supervising attorney is out of the office the next day so no questions are asked about the toaster and pictures. The receipt you toss in your work file.

The next day you bring the toaster and pictures to work with you. You store the pictures in the work file containing the receipt. Since the toaster is such a conversation piece, you keep it in your office and demonstrate the flying toast to clients, friends, and others in the office.

A month later your supervising attorney comes in your office with an expert he has retained to help in the toaster case. He wants the expert to take a look at the toaster and formulate an opinion regarding the defect. The expert leaves with the toaster. Your supervising attorney says he will meet with you and the expert tomorrow to review the case. He tells you to be sure to bring the receipt and pictures to the meeting.

The next day, moments before the meeting, you look in the work file but can't find that darn receipt anywhere. You sit down and type up a receipt that looks as much like the original as you can remember. The pictures are in the file but they were placed facing each other and became stuck together. They rip apart as you separate them, making your client look a lot like the phantom of the opera.

Sheepishly, you go into the conference room for the meeting. Your supervising attorney and the expert are studying the toaster, which the expert reports is working just fine.

1. As a result of your work on this file you can consider yourself:
   a. a superstar
   b. promoted
   c. toast
2. Review Chapters 6 and 7 on the rules of evidence and list every evidentiary problem you have created if the toaster, receipt, and pictures are ever offered as evidence at trial.
3. What ethical violations have you committed on this case?

4. Procedures for handling documents and things in your custody

When the paralegal is given custody of documentary or physical evidence, certain procedures should be followed:

a. Label the evidence

The evidence should be labeled or tagged with some identifying number or description. For physical evidence, this may be an adhesive label that can be removed without damaging or defacing the object. If attaching an adhesive is not feasible, then consider tying a tag to the item or placing the item in another larger container and labeling that container. For documentary evidence, labels or tags may be used or the documents may be placed in a labeled folder.

Whenever evidence is labeled or tagged, the label or tag should never be placed over any legible part of the evidence.

b. Secure the evidence

The evidence should be placed in a secure place where no unauthorized person can obtain entry. For documentary evidence and small physical objects, this may mean locking the item away in a fire-proof file cabinet or safe. Larger or more numerous items may require a locked evidence room or a secure storage facility outside the office.

c. Keep an evidence log

Information concerning the evidence should be entered in an **evidence log** or chart. The evidence log should contain certain basic information including:

- a description of the evidence;
- the date it was received in custody;
- the source from whom it was obtained;
- whether the item is the original;
- identity of the custodian or other authenticating witness;
- a record of who has checked the item out and when; and
- when the checked-out item was returned.

An evidence log used in the Granny Puttalong case might follow the form set out in Illustration 9-9.

As with the final plan of investigation, it is advisable to place the evidence log on computer if possible for ease of access and update.

5. Procedures for documents and things not in your custody

Many times it is not possible to take literal possession of evidence. It may be the property of the adverse party or a non-party. It may be something the client needs for his business. In those situations, it is important to obtain exact copies of documents or comprehensive pictures or video recordings of the items as soon as possible. We cannot assume that documents will be preserved or left unchanged, or that things will not be discarded, lost, destroyed, or materially changed.

If, for example, in the toaster case from Hypothetical 9-6, the plaintiff had sold the toaster to another person who would not allow us to take custody of it, we would then try to obtain permission to photograph it, video tape it in use, and have our consulting expert examine it. If by the time of trial it is gone or changed, we will still have admissible proof regarding the defect.

Of course, if the person to whom the plaintiff sold the toaster will not allow us access to it for any purpose, our only recourse will be to subpoena the custodian to produce the item for inspection. Locating and obtaining various kinds of information is discussed in more detail in Chapters 16 through 18.

Illustration 9-9   EVIDENCE LOG

Document/ Item	Date Rec'd	Source	Original/ Copy	Custodian/ Auth. Wit.	Checked Out By	C/O Date	Ret. Date
1.							
2.							
3.							
4.							

CLIENT: Granny Puttalong
FILE NO.: 2004-0001
ADVERSE PARTY: Speed Freak

H. The Importance of Diligence and Thoroughness in Executing a Plan of Investigation

1. Diligence

SLEUTH ON THE LOOSE

Identify a major news story from the past week then access *www.liszt.com* or *www.newsville.com/ news/groups* to locate articles written on that story in domestic and foreign papers.

Time is always of the essence in performing a factual investigation. The investigator should always remember that witnesses forget (what were you doing two months ago today?), they lose their initial interest in helping, they move, become ill, and they die. Documents and physical objects get destroyed, discarded, changed, or lost. Accident sites change with the weather and the seasons or with construction.

When a new case is assigned to you for investigation, locate and take possession of all the documentary and physical evidence that you can or to obtain genuine copies, photos, or video as quickly as possible. Identify, locate, and interview all relevant witnesses as soon as possible. The old saying, "the early bird gets the worm" doesn't refer only to early risers.

2. Thoroughness

When you are assigned to inspect an accident site, physical object, or any other item of evidence, be sure you do it thoroughly. Take pictures from every conceivable angle. Remember some may not turn out well.

Be sure to keep the negatives of pictures taken. You may want to make more copies later and negatives produce new originals far superior in quality to photographed originals. Your supervising attorney may want to have certain pictures to be used at trial enlarged. Having the negatives will guarantee a better quality enlargement.

Remember that photographs, videos, sketches, drawings, and diagrams must present a reasonably accurate depiction of the thing shown in order to be admissible at trial. Thus you must be concerned about lighting, angle, and scale when doing such work.

EXAMPLE

> Assume you are photographing skid marks on a highway that are about 15 feet in length. If you are using a 35mm camera with an ordinary lens you will have to get several feet away from the skid marks to get them all in one picture. When the picture is developed you probably won't be able to tell if the marks are 15 feet or 15 inches in length! Why? Because your picture is not to scale. Try placing a ruler or yardstick in the picture to help bring it into scale.
>
> Similarly, if you are photographing or video taping an object the height of which cannot be determined from the picture, try placing a person in the picture to bring it into scale. Wide angle and zoom lenses can help produce more accurate pictures.

When you are photographing or video taping the scene of an accident, do so, to the extent possible, at the same time of day and in the same season and weather as the accident.

If you are not proficient with cameras, recommend hiring a professional photographer. And always consider who will be the authenticating witness for the photographs, video tapes, sketches, drawings, and diagrams that you make. For ethical and other reasons, you will generally not want to be the authenticating witness yourself. So be sure you have another person who can authenticate the exhibits you produce or consider taking another person with you who can observe and later testify.

If you are copying documents, do it carefully to be sure all the documents are copied and all the copies are good.

If you are inspecting documents or records, do it thoroughly no matter how lengthy the task or how boring the material. Many leads may be waiting for you in those documents that you will miss if you use too little care.

KEY WORDS AND PHRASES TO REMEMBER

assume nothing
brainstorm
client authorization
compare information
corroborating evidence
creative
documentary evidence
evaluate information
evidence log
flexible
intuition
investigation chart
investigation plan
knowledgeable
leads
litigation chart

litigation or cause of action
perceptive
persistent
physical evidence
plan of investigation
skeptical
skilled
sources of information
sources of investigation plan
test information
to-do list investigation plan
topical investigation plan
value of the case
verify everything
who, why, what, when, where, and
    how

LEARN BY DOING

LBD 9-1. Use the Case Studies in Appendix A for the following:

a. Review Case Study No. 1 in Appendix A (The Rowdy Outlaw Case). Assume that Rowdy Outlaw has been charged with first degree murder under the governing statute(s) of your state. Assume further that your law office has been retained to defend Outlaw on that charge. Prepare an initial plan of investigation for the defense of Mr. Outlaw. If your instructor directs, be prepared to present your plan of investigation to the class for discussion and critique.

b. Review Case Study No. 2 in Appendix A (The Red Dog Saloon Case). Assume that your law office is retained to represent Soupspoon Wise in connection with a civil suit to recover his damages in the Red Dog Saloon incident. Prepare an initial plan of investigation for the claims of Mr. Wise. If your instructor directs, be prepared to present your plan of investigation to the class for discussion and critique.

c. Review Case Study No. 3 in Appendix A (The Vidalia Unyon Case). Assume that your law office is retained to represent Mrs. Unyon in her divorce action against Mr. Unyon. Prepare an initial plan of investigation for the representation of Mrs. Unyon. If your instructor directs, be prepared to present your plan of investigation to the class for discussion and critique.

d. Review Case Study No. 4 in Appendix A (The Rocky Road Project). Assume that your law office is retained to assist Rocky Road, Inc., with the legal aspects of its business plans. Prepare an initial plan of investigation for the representation of Rocky Road, Inc. If your instructor directs, be prepared to present your plan of investigation to the class for discussion and critique.

Chapter 10

Preparing for a Client Interview

CHAPTER OBJECTIVES

Arranging and conducting the interview of a client or witness is a basic paralegal skill. In this first of four chapters, which focus on interviewing, you will learn:

- The various kinds of interviews that paralegals are expected to conduct.
- The goals to be accomplished in the initial client interview.
- How to communicate with a potential client to schedule an interview.
- The steps that interviewers go through to prepare for an effective interview.
- The kinds of questions that interviewers use for different purposes.
- The importance of skillfully phrasing questions.
- The importance of seating arrangements in an interview.

A. Introduction to Interviewing

1. Persons to interview

The ability to arrange, plan, and conduct an effective interview is a basic paralegal skill and an essential component of investigating. The people that the paralegal may be expected to interview generally fall into three categories:

- clients;
- fact witnesses; or
- other information sources.

a. Clients

By **clients** we mean not only persons whom the supervising attorney has agreed to represent, but any person who contacts the law office seeking legal advice, regardless of whether the attorney takes the case. In this chapter we will consider scheduling and preparing for the client interview. In Chapter 11 we will consider how to conduct the client interview.

b. Fact witnesses

By **fact witness** we mean persons who have or who might have knowledge of facts directly relevant to the matter being handled for the client. In Chapter 12 we will consider arranging and preparing for a witness interview, and in Chapter 13 we will consider how to conduct the interview of a fact witness.

c. Other information sources

SLEUTH ON THE LOOSE

To learn more about how to obtain information on the nation's military and individual veterans, access *www.searchmil.com* and review the information and links available there.

By **other information sources** we mean persons who, though not fact witnesses, can provide us with information we need. An example would be the assistant court clerk who helps us locate a recorded document. Contacts with these people are typically brief and less formal than the interview of a client or fact witness. Frequently such contacts are made by phone. But they are important nonetheless. If approached correctly, these people can save us a considerable amount of time. They are also often people that we go back to more than once for help. Remembering the six B's from Chapter 8 will help you in dealing with these types of information sources.

- Be ready. Know what you are going to ask before you call or see this person.
- Be brief. Remember everybody's time is important.
- Be friendly. The sweet draws the flies, not the sour.
- Be patient. It is almost always rewarded.
- Be polite. Using "please" and "thank you" will make people like you.
- Be grateful. And show it—you may need this person again.

2. Different methods and locations for interviews

Interviews may be conducted by phone or in person. They may be conducted in the paralegal's office or outside the office (sometimes referred to as a **field interview**), including a client or witness's home, workplace, automobile, or in a hospital or nursing home. Some interviews are not recorded, some are tape recorded by the interviewer, some are conducted in the presence of a court reporter who records and transcribes it, and some are video taped. Sometimes we obtain a written statement from a witness who is interviewed. On some occasions the supervising attorney will conduct the interview with the paralegal present to assist and sometimes the attorney will ask the paralegal to conduct the interview by himself. As we consider client and witness interviews in this and the next three chapters, we will refer to these differences and how they impact on the planning and execution of client and witness interviews.

B. ► **Reasons for Conducting Client Interviews**

During the course of representation, there will typically be several occasions on which the client is interviewed by the attorney or paralegal. Client interviews can generally be categorized according to the various reasons for conducting them.

1. The initial client interview

This is the first meeting that occurs after the client contacts the law office seeking legal advice. It is a critical meeting and in this chapter we will consider in detail scheduling and preparing for the initial client interview.

2. Subsequent information-gathering interviews

Once the attorney has agreed to undertake representation of the client, there frequently will be one or more subsequent interviews to gather additional information from the client. Depending on the nature of the case, these information-gathering interviews may continue throughout the representation.

3. The update or status report interview

As we have noted while studying the ethical and professional duties lawyers owe to clients (see Chapter 2), it is critical that the client be kept informed concerning the status of his case. And this is true even if nothing is currently going on in his case. Accordingly, the paralegal may be asked to contact the client regularly for what is usually a brief, informal update regarding the matter being handled.

C. ► **Goals of the Intitial Client Interview**

The initial client interview is, in many ways, the most important of all the interviews and contacts you will have with the client. That is because it is in this interview that the foundation for the relationship between the client and the law office is established. In addition, a number of fundamental tasks are usually accomplished during or as an immediate result of the initial interview. Illustration 10-1 sets forth a list of the various goals to be accomplished in the initial client interview.

D. ► **Scheduling the Initial Client Interview**

When you are asked by the supervising attorney to contact a potential new client to schedule the initial interview, keep in mind the goals and purposes of this interview as set forth in Illustration 10-1. You will begin

Illustration 10-1   GOALS TO BE ACCOMPLISHED IN THE INITIAL CLIENT INTERVIEW

1. Establish a relationship of trust and confidence with the client.
2. Open solid communication channels with the client.
3. Check for potential conflicts of interest.
4. Obtain all relevant information regarding the client's problem.
5. Determine the specific nature of the representation—what is it exactly that the client wants the attorney to do.
6. Establish the fee arrangement and explain billing rates, expenses, and billing procedures.
7. Obtain all needed authorizations from the client.
8. Explain the role of each person involved.
9. Determine a plan of action regarding the agreed-upon representation.
10. Evaluate the client's demeanor, credibility, and reliability.

accomplishing those goals with this very first contact, and we all know how important first impressions can be.

Interviews are typically scheduled by a phone call to the person to be interviewed. Therefore, when making that phone call, use your communication skills and the phone etiquette we considered in Chapter 8. Here are some guidelines for scheduling the initial client interview.

1. Check all participants' schedules before you call

Before you call the client, check the schedules of any other persons who may be participating in the conference.

2. Have several dates and times in mind before you call

Select several possible dates and times for the interview before you call since the client may have a scheduling conflict with one or more of your suggested times.

3. Allow for plenty of time

Pick a date and time that will allow plenty of time for the interview. Don't try to cram it in before, after, or between other scheduled events.

4. Make sure the interview room is available

If the interview is going to be conducted in a conference room at your office, be sure the room is available for that date and time.

5. Consider what the client needs to bring

Give thought to what you want the client to bring with him to the interview. There are almost always documents that need to be located and brought in for review as soon as possible—court papers that have been served on the client, accident reports, medical records or bills, insurance policies, car titles, contracts, etc. Do not assume that the client will know what to bring, even if it should be obvious. And make your list before you call so you don't leave out anything.

6. Identify yourself as a paralegal when you call

When you call the client always identify yourself promptly as a paralegal. As we have learned, this is an ethical requirement and for good reason. Lay persons receiving a call from a law office may assume they are speaking to an attorney.

7. Cover all necessary details in the scheduling call

In the conversation cover all the necessary details including:

- the date and time of the interview;
- directions to the place of the interview; and
- what the client needs to bring to the interview.

8. Take comprehensive notes during the scheduling call

9. Things to do following the scheduling call

- Confirm the reservation of the conference room for the scheduled date and time
- Notify all participants of the scheduled date and time
- Enter the date and time of the scheduled conference in the docket control system
- Run a conflict of interest check
- Prepare a confirmation letter to the client
- Prepare a work file for your own use

HYPOTHETICAL 10-1

Assume that Paul Perfect works as a legal assistant for Betty Busy, an attorney in your city. Today Betty Busy drops by Paul's office and hands him a phone call slip. She tells Paul that she received a call from a potential new client, Harrison Bored, who has just been sued by his next-door neighbor, Jessica Slang. The attorney isn't sure of the details but apparently Harrison Bored gave a neighborhood party at his house about a month ago and some food or beverage was spilled on a hardwood floor. Jessica Slang apparently slipped in it and fell on the floor, injuring herself. She apparently wasn't so badly injured that she couldn't sock Harrison Bored in the nose, fracturing it. Now Jessica Slang has sued Harrison Bored for negligence. Busy instructs Paul Perfect to contact Harrison Bored and set up an initial conference sometime next week. The attorney explains that she will try to conduct the interview herself but will want Paul there to assist. However, it is possible she may be unable to attend (because she is so *busy*) so he should be prepared to handle the interview himself.

Paul Perfect has been taking notes as the supervising attorney explains this assignment. He now staples the phone call slip to his notes. As he does so, he asks Betty Busy if she has her calendar with her or if he should check with her secretary. She tells him to check with her secretary. He then asks how much time they should schedule for the conference and she replies an hour to an hour and a half should be sufficient.

After the supervising attorney leaves, Paul Perfect checks his own schedule for available times then calls the attorney's secretary to compare. Having found three convenient dates and times that suit both their calendars, he calls the receptionist to check on the availability of the conference room for each date and time.

He enters the name of Jessica Slang into the firm's computerized conflict of interest system as a potential adverse party and finds no conflict.

Paul Perfect then makes notes on what he should ask Harrison Bored to bring with him to the interview. The list includes:

- the suit papers;
- any correspondence that Harrison Bored may have received from Jessica Slang or her attorney before suit was filed;
- Harrison Bored's homeowner's or lessee's insurance policy, if any, or any umbrella policy he may carry;
- any pictures that might have been taken of the spill or of Jessica Slang;
- any medical records he has concerning treatment for his broken nose; and
- medical bills he has incurred from having his nose treated.

Can you think of anything Paul Perfect should add to that list?

Now Paul Perfect places his call to Harrison Bored. Let's listen in to the first part of that conversation:

HB: Hello?

PP: Hello, is this Mr. Harrison Bored?

HB: Yes, it is.

PP: Mr. Bored, my name is Paul Perfect. I am a paralegal in the office of attorney Betty Busy. Ms. Busy asked me to call you and set up a time for you to come in and meet with us about the suit filed by Jessica Slang.

HB: Sure. I was expecting someone to call. When did you want me to come in?

Paul Perfect finds a good time for Harrison Bored to come in, asks him to bring the documents with him, and gives him directions to the office. He also learns that Bored did have to see a doctor to have his broken nose set. He will have to wear a brace-type device on his face for a month and he missed three days of work because of the injury. He is a salesman who depends on commissions and he feels that having to wear the facial device will result in his losing sales and income. He is seeing Dr. Samuel L. Jaxon for his nose and has paid $250 so far on medical bills. He has medical insurance but the co-pay is $500. Now let's listen in again to the end of the conversation.

> **PP:** Okay, I think that's all we need to cover today. We'll see you next Tuesday at 2:00 in the afternoon here at our offices. Did you have any other questions?
> **HB:** No, I don't think so. I guess I'll see you next week then.
> **PP:** Yes, sir. Take care and we will see you then.
>
> Immediately after hanging up with Bored, Paul Perfect calls the receptionist and reserves the conference room for the agreed-upon time. He then calls Betty Busy's secretary and asks her to note the conference on the attorney's calendar. Next he enters the date and time of the conference in his own calendar and the firm's tickler system. Now he dictates a memorandum to Betty Busy (see Illustration 10-2) and a confirmation letter to Harrison Bored (see Illustration 10-3). Before signing and sending the letter, he leaves it with Betty Busy's secretary and asks her to have the attorney look it over and tell him if it is okay to send. The next morning, Betty Busy calls Paul Perfect and says, "Paul, the letter looks perfect to me. Go ahead and send it out."

E. ▶ Preparing for the Initial Client Interview

Once the client interview is scheduled there are a number of things the paralegal will need to do to get ready.

1. Prepare forms

Prepare any forms that the client may need to sign during the initial interview in the event that the attorney agrees to take the case. We will consider two types of forms clients are regularly asked to sign in the initial conference—records authorizations and fee agreements.

a. Records authorizations

Depending on the kind of case and the particular facts, the client may need to sign a medical records authorization (see Illustration 10-4), or an employment records authorization (see Illustration 10-5), or an educational records authorization (see Illustration 10-6) to enable the attorney to inspect and copy those records.

b. Fee agreements

In addition, the client may need to sign the fee agreement at the initial client conference if the attorney agrees at that time to undertake the representation. Remember that because of the prohibition on the paralegal engaging in the unlicensed practice of law, only the attorney can make the decision to undertake representation of the client. Accordingly, the attorney should typically be present when the client signs the fee agreement. The role of the paralegal will be to prepare the type of fee agreement the supervising attorney authorizes in a particular case. If the attorney is not present at the initial client interview, the paralegal may

Illustration 10-2   MEMORANDUM SUMMARIZING CLIENT CONTACT

MEMORANDUM

TO: Betty Busy, Attorney
FROM: Paul Perfect,
            Paralegal
DATE: September 27, 2003
RE: Harrison Bored
            File Number: 03-335-L

At your instruction I called and spoke by phone with Mr. Harrison Bored today. Mr. Bored was very personable and cooperative in the conversation. My initial impression of him is that he is friendly and forthright. He gave me no reason to doubt his veracity.

Mr. Bored confirmed that he received the suit papers filed on behalf of Jessica Slang two days ago. The incident itself occurred on August 28 of this year. Mr. Bored also stated that Jessica Slang hit him in the nose as he was trying to help her up after the fall in the kitchen of Mr. Bored's home on Humphrey Bogart Lane here in the city.

Mr. Bored has been seeing Dr. Samuel L. Jaxon whose offices are next to City Hospital. He has paid $250 so far in medical expenses. He has a medical insurance policy (a group policy through his employer) but the co-pay is $500.

Mr. Bored has to wear a device he refers to as a nose brace for the next month. He says it is very uncomfortable and interferes with sleeping and eating. In addition, Mr. Bored advised me that he is a district salesman with Hollywood Sports Equipment and depends on commissions for his income. He missed three days of work because of his broken nose and fears he will lose sales and commissions during the coming month because of the nose brace.

Mr. Bored is coming in next Tuesday, October 5, at 2 P.M. This time was available on both my calendar and yours. I have scheduled the conference room from 2 P.M. until 3:30 P.M. that day. I have drafted a confirmation letter to Mr. Bored for your review and approval. As the letter indicates, Mr. Bored is bringing the suit papers, his homeowner's policy, pictures he took of the spill right after the incident, and his medical bills to date.

It is my understanding that you plan to handle the interview with Mr. Bored and would like me to be present to assist. I will draft a medical records authorization and an employment records authorization to have available at the conference. Please let me know if you would like me to prepare a legal services agreement to have available at the conference and, if so, what terms we should draft.

I have also run a preliminary conflicts check based on the name of Jessica Slang as a potential adverse party and nothing turned up.

Please let me know if there is anything further I need to do at this time.

---

later send the fee agreement to the client to sign and return, but only after the attorney has decided to take the case and authorized the paralegal to send the fee agreement to the client.

In general, there are three kinds of fee agreements used by attorneys: (1) an **hourly rate plus expenses agreement;** (2) a **flat fee agreement;** or (3) a **contingency fee agreement.** There are innumerable variations to these agreements and every attorney will develop his own customized form for each kind of agreement. In addition, the legal and ethical requirements for fee agreements vary from state to state, so no one form is going to be suitable for all attorneys in all situations.

Sometimes fee agreements are referred to as **retainer agreements,**

Illustration 10-3   CONFIRMATION LETTER TO CLIENT

Date

Mr. Harrison Bored
(Address)

Re: *Conference on Jessica Slang lawsuit*

Dear Mr. Bored:

It was a pleasure to speak with you earlier this week. This will confirm the meeting we have scheduled for next Tuesday, October 5, at 2 P.M. here in our offices. Please remember to bring the following with you to the conference:

1. The suit papers served on you.
2. Your homeowner's insurance policy.
3. The pictures you took of the spill the night of the accident with negatives.
4. The medical bills you have incurred to date for treatment of your nose.

We look forward to seeing you next Tuesday. Please feel free to call if you have any questions.

Sincerely yours,
Paul B. Perfect
Paralegal

cc: Betty Busy, attorney
    PBP/ck

Illustration 10-4   MEDICAL RECORDS AUTHORIZATION

To: Doctor's Name and Address

You are hereby authorized to permit my attorney, _____ of the law firm _____, or his designated agent, to inspect and obtain copies of my complete medical records including, without limitation, all patient information sheets, correspondence, notes, memoranda, laboratory reports, and fee statements. This authorization is effective as of the date below and will continue in effect until revoked by me in writing but for no longer than one year from the date below.

My attorney, _____, of the law firm _____, has assured me that he/she will comply with all requirements of the privacy rules promulgated by the U.S. Department of Health and Human Services pursuant to the Health Insurance Portability and Accountability Act of 1996 and found at 45 CFR 160 and 164.

Date: _____

_____
John J. Patient
Soc. Sec. No. XXXXXX
DOB 10-1-63

---

meaning that it is the agreement pursuant to which the client **retains** or employs the attorney. But the phrase retainer agreement can be confusing since the word **retainer** is also used by attorneys to refer to an advance payment that is required no matter what type of fee agreement is entered into. For example, in Hypothetical 10-1, Betty Busy may require Harrison

Illustration 10-5   EMPLOYMENT RECORDS AUTHORIZATION

Name of Employer: _____

Address: _____

Name of Employee: _____

Employee ID or Soc. Sec. No. _____

To: Records Custodian or Director of Human Resources:

I hereby authorize and request that you permit attorney _____ of the law firm _____,
or his designated agent, to inspect and copy my employment file(s) and provide him or his designated agent
with any and all other information that he may request concerning my employment with you.

This authorization shall remain in effect until the _____ day of _____, 2005 or until revoked in
writing by me.

Date: _____   (Signature) _____

                                                             (Name of employee)

Illustration 10-6   EDUCATIONAL RECORDS AUTHORIZATION

Name of School or Institution: _____

Address: _____

Name of student: _____

Maiden or former name (if applicable): _____

Student ID or Soc. Sec. No. _____

Date(s) of enrollment _____

Date of graduation (if applicable) _____

To: Student Records Custodian:

I hereby authorize and request that you permit attorney of the law firm, or his designated agent, to inspect and
copy any and all records or information of any kind whatsoever, academic or otherwise, related to my having
been a student at and to provide him or his designated agent with any and all other information that he may
request concerning my having been a student there.

This authorization shall remain in effect until the _____day of _____, 2005 or until revoked
in writing by me.

Date: _____   (Signature) _____

                                                       (Name of student)

Bored to pay a $5,000 *retainer* before representation will be undertaken.
Better phrases to use for these agreements are **legal services agreement**
or **fee agreement.**

    1. The hourly rate fee agreement.   In many cases attorneys will
charge the client an agreed-upon hourly rate for their services. If more
than one attorney or a paralegal is to be involved in the case, the hourly
rates for each may vary. The hourly rate fee agreement may or may not
require payment of a retainer. Typically, out-of-pocket expenses incurred
by the attorney are billed to the client in addition to the hourly rate
charges. See Illustration 10-7.

Illustration 10-7   HOURLY RATE LEGAL SERVICES AGREEMENT

LEGAL SERVICES AGREEMENT

This Legal Services Agreement (the "Agreement") is entered into between _____ ("Client") and _____ ("Attorney"), this _____ day of _____, 20_____.

1. SCOPE OF REPRESENTATION. Client hereby employs Attorney to represent Client in connection with _____ (the "Matter").

2. ATTORNEY'S DUTIES. Attorney shall provide the legal services that, in her independent legal judgment, are reasonably required to effectively represent Client in this Matter and shall make reasonable effort to keep Client informed of the status of the Matter.

3. CLIENT'S DUTIES. Client shall cooperate fully with Attorney in connection with the Matter; keep Attorney advised of Client's current address and telephone number and of all developments concerning the Matter; pay all bills received from Attorney on time; and otherwise perform all of Client's obligations under this Agreement in good faith.

4. LEGAL FEES. Client shall pay Attorney for the legal services to be provided by Attorney in connection with this Matter on an hourly basis as follows:

Partners at $200 per hour
Associates at $125 per hour
Paralegals at $90 per hour
Law Clerks and other personnel at $50 per hour

5. RETAINER. Client shall pay the sum of $5,000 to Attorney immediately as an advance against future billings of time and expenses by Attorney. Attorney will deposit the retainer amount in a trust account and it will be used to pay both Attorney fees as agreed to in *Paragraph 4* of this Agreement and expenses as agreed to in *Paragraph 6* of this Agreement. Client hereby authorizes Attorney to withdraw funds from the retainer amount in the trust account to pay bills for time and expenses at the time those bills are mailed to Client. Any unused balance of the retainer amount remaining after payment of the final bill for time and expenses shall be refunded promptly by Attorney to Client.

6. OUT-OF-POCKET EXPENSES. Client also agrees to reimburse Attorney for out-of-pocket expenses incurred by Attorney in connection with the representation including, but not limited to, charges for long-distance phone calls at a minimum rate of $2.00 per call; copy costs at $.15 per page; travel costs including car travel at $.315 per mile; outgoing facsimile charges at $1.00 per page; postage; court filing fees; service of process fees; consultants; experts; court reporters; and similar related expenses.

7. STATEMENTS FOR TIME AND EXPENSES. Attorney will provide Client an itemized statement of time and expenses on a regular basis, usually monthly, and such statement will be payable by the Client within thirty (30) days of receipt.

8. ATTORNEY'S LIEN. Client hereby grants Attorney a lien on any and all claims or causes of action related to the Matter which lien will be for any and all sums due from Client to Attorney at the conclusion of Attorney's representation of Client in the Matter. This lien shall attach to any recovery obtained by Client by judgment, settlement, arbitration, or otherwise.

_____
Attorney

_____
Client

Illustration 10-8   FLAT FEE LEGAL SERVICES AGREEMENT

LEGAL SERVICES AGREEMENT

This Legal Services Agreement (the "Agreement") is entered into between _____ ("Client") and _____ ("Attorney"), this _____ day of _____, 20_____.

1. Attorney hereby agrees to prepare and file the necessary documents for the incorporation of an entity to be known as Super Sucker, Inc., under the laws of the state of _____. Specifically, Attorney agrees to prepare the charter, bylaws, and organizational minutes for said corporation and to cause the charter to be properly filed with the Secretary of State of the state of _____.

2. Client agrees to pay Attorney the sum of one thousand dollars ($1,000) in advance as the full and final fee for the legal services described in *Paragraph 1* of this Agreement.

3. Attorney agrees to pay all out-of-pocket expenses incurred in performing the legal services described in *Paragraph 1* of this Agreement, including copy costs, long-distance phone calls, mailing costs, filing fees, and the cost of one (1) minute book out of the advance payment received from Client as described in *Paragraph 2* of this Agreement.

_____

Attorney

_____

Client

---

2. The flat fee agreement.   Sometimes attorneys charge the client a flat fee for the service to be rendered. This way the client knows what the total bill is going to be regardless of the time the attorney spends. The flat fee agreed to may include expenses or the agreement may specify that out-of-pocket expenses are to be paid in addition to the flat fee. Flat fee agreements are generally used for more routine legal services where attorneys, from experience, know almost exactly how much time it will take them to perform the work. Examples include no-fault divorces, simple wills, setting up corporations, and individual bankruptcies. See Illustration 10-8.

3. The contingency fee agreement.   In cases where a monetary recovery is sought for a client, and particularly in cases where the client cannot afford an hourly fee arrangement, the contingency fee agreement will be used. In a contingency arrangement, the attorney receives as her fee an-agreed upon percentage, usually one-third of any recovery made. If no recovery is made, the attorney receives no fee. Out-of-pocket expenses are due whether a recovery is made or not. See Illustration 10-9.

HYPOTHETICAL 10-2

Assume that Betty Busy calls Paul Perfect the day before the scheduled interview with Harrison Bored and tells Paul that he will have to conduct the interview because she is too *busy.* Paul swings into action.

He has already drafted a medical records authorization for Harrison Bored to sign, as well as an employment records authorization in the event Harrison Bored has missed work because of the fractured nose. Paul Perfect has also drafted a legal services agreement providing that

Betty Busy would represent Bored on an hourly fee basis in defending the suit by Jessica Slang (subject to Bored's homeowner's policy providing coverage) and on a contingency basis in connection with the anticipated counterclaim Bored will probably file against her for tortious battery. However, since Betty Busy will not be present during the interview and Paul Perfect knows that only the attorney can decide to accept the case, that decision and finalizing the legal services agreement will have to wait until after the interview.

1. Why did Paul Perfect prepare a medical records authorization for Harrison Bored to sign?
2. Why did Paul Perfect prepare an employment records authorization for Harrison Bored to sign?
3. Why did Paul Perfect prepare two different kinds of fee agreements in this case?

2. Prepare your questions

If the paralegal is assigned by the supervising attorney to conduct the interview himself, preparing questions for the interview is the next important step. Even if the paralegal utilizes an intake sheet or standardized checklist (discussed in the next section), specific questions still should be planned for the initial client interview. Here is a suggested method for preparing your questions for the interview.

a. Review your notes

Review your notes from the assignment conference (or assignment memo from the supervising attorney) closely. Be sure you understand exactly what the supervising attorney has told you concerning the potential client you will be interviewing and what is known about the legal problem that will be presented. The more you know about the potential new client and the legal matter the more thorough preparation you can make. If there are any documents already in possession of the supervising attorney, or any other notes in the file, review those carefully. If you have any questions about the assignment, go back to the supervising attorney for clarification.

b. Consider what you know so far of the legal question involved

In interviewing, always remember that the factual questioning we do is determined by the legal context—what is the legal issue or problem we are dealing with? You may want to review the discussion of factual analysis in Chapter 1 at this time. There we learned that unless the investigator has a basic understanding of the law that is at issue in a client's case, he will be unable to do effective investigation. He won't know what factual information to look for or even recognize relevant information if he stumbles over it. So, as the interviewer plans his questions, thought must be given to what is known so far of the legal problem the client will present.

Illustration 10-9   CONTINGENCY FEE LEGAL SERVICES AGREEMENT

LEGAL SERVICES AGREEMENT

This Legal Services Agreement (the "Agreement") is entered into between _____ ("Client") and _____ ("Attorney"), this _____ day of _____, 20_____.

1. Client hereby employs Attorney to represent Client in connection with any and all civil legal claims for compensation or other damages against _____ and any other person or entity acting with or on the behalf of such person or who may be responsible for the actions of such person in connection with the automobile accident in which Client was involved on January 6, 2000, in Capital City, Yourstate.

2. Client agrees to pay Attorney, as attorney fees for this representation, a contingency rate of thirty-three percent (33%) of all revenues collected from any source whatsoever in whole or partial satisfaction of any or all of the civil claims that are the subject of this representation, regardless of whether such revenues are collected by compromise, accord, settlement, judgment following suit, collection, or otherwise. In the event a final judgment is entered in a court of law on any or all of the civil claims that are the subject of this representation and in the further event that an appeal shall be instituted from such judgment by either the plaintiff or the defendant(s) in such suit, Client agrees that the contingency rate for attorney fees in this representation shall then be forty percent (40%) of all revenues collected.

3. In addition to the obligation for attorney fees as set forth in Paragraph 2 of this Agreement, Client also agrees to reimburse Attorney for out-of-pocket expenses incurred by Attorney in connection with the representation including, but not limited to, charges for long-distance phone calls at a minimum rate of $2.00 per call; copy costs at $.15 per page; travel costs including car travel at $.315 per mile; outgoing facsimile charges at $1.00 per page; postage; court filing fees; service of process fees; consultants; experts; court reporters; and similar related expenses. Attorney will provide Client an itemized statement for these out-of-pocket expenses on a regular basis, usually monthly, and such statement will be payable by the Client within thirty (30) days of receipt.

4. Client agrees to cooperate fully with Attorney in connection with this representation.

5. Attorney agrees to apply his independent legal judgment in pursuit of the resolution of the claims that are the subject of this representation and in acting on behalf of the Client. Settlement of any and all claims shall require the express consent of the Client.

6. Attorney may terminate this Agreement and withdraw from representing Client in this matter if (a) Attorney determines, in his sole professional judgment, that the claims which are the subject matter of this representation have no merit; (b) a conflict of interest arises; (c) Client fails or refuses to cooperate with Attorney in connection with this representation; (d) Client provides incorrect, incomplete, or deceptive information to Attorney or another person in connection with this representation; (e) Client fails to pay the statements for out-of-pocket expenses in a timely manner; (f) Client otherwise fails to comply with his/her/its obligations under this Agreement; or (g) if the Code of Professional Reponsibility or any succeeding code of ethics governing Attorney's representation permits or requires withdrawal of representation.

7. Client may terminate this Agreement upon ten (10) days written notice to Attorney. In the event Client terminates this Agreement, Client agrees to compensate Attorney out of the gross proceeds of any ultimate recovery for the claims that are the subject matter of this representation as follows: as attorney fees, a percentage of the gross proceeds otherwise payable to Attorney as a contingency fee under this Agreement equal to the ratio determined by comparing the number of hours measured in tenths of an hour that Attorney expended on this representation prior to termination with the total number of hours measured in tenths of an hour expended on the matter by Attorney and successive counsel.

8. This Agreement becomes effective when signed by Client and returned to Attorney. By signing this Agreement, Client acknowledges that he/she/it has read and understands all of its terms and agrees to it in full.

9. All amendments or alterations to this Agreement must be in writing and be signed by the parties.

_____
Client

_____
Attorney

EXAMPLE

If the paralegal is instructed by the supervising attorney to meet with a potential new divorce client, the planned questions will relate to residency requirements, grounds for a divorce, possible defenses, property ownership and division, income and debts, child custody and support, spousal support, the need for a domestic protective order, etc.

If the paralegal is instructed by the supervising attorney to meet with a potential new client regarding a business contract dispute, the planned questions will relate to the business, the contract, the nature of the dispute, the elements of an enforceable contract, possible defenses or counterclaims, damages including mitigation efforts, etc.

If the paralegal is instructed by the supervising attorney to meet with a potential new client on defending a criminal charge, the planned questions will relate to the nature of the charges, status of the criminal proceeding (how far along is it), details of the arrest and police interrogation, if any, knowledge of the events surrounding the alleged crime (though not necessarily whether the accused committed the crime—the attorney is more concerned with whether the state can prove the accused committed the crime), possible defenses to the specific crime alleged including alibis, mistake, self- or third-person defense, etc.

If the paralegal is instructed by the supervising attorney to meet with a potential new client regarding a personal injury claim related to a defective product, the planned questions will relate to the details of the event in which the person was injured, including time and place, the nature and extent of the injuries, the purchase and prior use of the product, the maker and distributor(s) of the product, the whereabouts and condition of the product, and possible defenses such as misuse, changed condition, appreciation of the risk, etc.

If the paralegal is instructed by the supervising attorney to meet with a potential new client on a workers' compensation injury, the planned questions will relate to the details of the injury, including nature of the injury, the time and place of the injury, how the injury is work-related, notification of the employer, medical care to date, possible third-party responsibility, etc.

The known legal context controls the questions to be asked.

c. Consider special needs of the client

If you will be interviewing a child, an adult with little education, or anyone whose English is poor, you will want to plan your questions using simple, non-complex words. And you will want to make your questions shorter. With a teenager you may want to deliberately use some recognizable slang or street talk if it will aid communication. Conversely, with an older person you will probably avoid current slang or street talk.

d. Brainstorm a list of topics to be covered

Once you have reviewed the assignment notes and given careful thought to what you know of the legal issues this interview will raise, brainstorm and make a comprehensive list of all topics that need to be covered. Don't worry about organization yet. Just get everything that needs to be covered down on paper in any order that it comes to mind.

e. Organize the topics in a logical fashion

Now organize the topics into the order in which they should be addressed. There is no one right way to organize topics for an interview. Different interviewers have different preferences. With experience in different kinds of cases, you will learn what is effective for you. Some interviewers prefer to address topics chronologically. Some prefer to address them as they relate to the elements of the legal cause of action or defense involved (e.g., in a negligence case by duty, breach, causation, damages, defenses, etc.). And others prefer to approach them by subject matter in some other logical way.

HYPOTHETICAL 10-3

Paul Perfect is preparing his questions for the interview of Harrison Bored. He reviews the file, which consists of his notes from speaking to Betty Busy about the case initially, the notes of his telephone conversation with Harrison Bored, and copies of his memo to Betty Busy (Illustration 10-2) and his letter to Harrison Bored (Illustration 10-3).

Now Paul gives consideration to what he knows of the law involved in the case. He knows from experience and from his discussion with Betty Busy that this is a premises liability case based in negligence. He reviews the law in his jurisdiction regarding the elements of a negligence action in general and defenses to it. Because he knows that this case will involve specific questions about the duty of care that a homeowner owes to his social guests, he researches some case law on that. He finds that the rulings of the state supreme court establish that a homeowner owes a duty of reasonable care to social guests to keep the premises in a reasonably safe condition. That duty of reasonable care has been construed to mean that a homeowner must either remove or warn of hazards that the homeowner knows of (actual knowledge) or should reasonably have discovered (constructive knowledge). However, the state supreme court has distinguished the duty owed by a homeowner to social guests (social invitees) from the duty that the operator of a public business owes to business invitees. Whereas the operator of a public business has a duty to inspect the premises on a regular basis to locate potential hazards, the homeowner owes no such duty to his social guests—only the duty to remove or warn of hazards of which he has actual or constructive knowledge. Among the defenses to premises liability slip-and-fall cases that Paul reads about are assumption of the risk (the plaintiff knew of the hazard herself and still voluntarily encountered it) and comparative fault (the plaintiff failed to exercise reasonable care herself to observe and avoid the hazard). He also reads up on third-party liability as minimizing the defendant's share of the fault or possibly giving rise to an indemnity claim by the defendant.

Betty Busy has advised that there might be a counterclaim by Harrison Bored against Jessica Slang. Paul Perfect also reviews the law regarding the torts of assault and battery. He notes that they are intentional torts, but the state courts have held that the intent required to prove the causes of action is not an intent to cause the harm inflicted, only an intent to do the act that caused the harm.

Having reviewed everything in the file carefully, and given thought to what he knows of the law of the case, Paul now brainstorms on the various topics he needs to cover with the client. His list looks like this:

Explain Betty Busy's absence; paralegal limitations

Biographical and background for file, work, and health history—use intake sheet

Previous history as neighbor of Jessica Slang; what he knows about her, troublemaker? Other suits?

Details of party

Details of food(?) on floor—how, what, who responsible for it

Did HB know it was there before fall?

How long had it been there?

Location of HB and JS between time (likely time?) of spill and fall

Possible JS saw or should have seen spill?

How large spill area, color, texture?

Details of fall—witnesses—who saw, how JS injured, what said, what happened later, who helped her up

Detail of punch in the nose—how it happened, witnesses, hit anybody else?

Was JS conscious/awake at the time of punch? Say anything to anybody about it then or later?

Punch intentional for HB or just anybody? Could it have been reflex? How hard the blow?

Detail of treatment for JS after fall, ambulance? Witnesses? Anyone go home with her? Ambulatory? Talking?

Detail of treatment for HB. ER? Witnesses?

Get authorizations signed

Prognosis from doctor; next appointment; other treatment possible? Surgery?

Details on income—last three years; how impacted since injury? How to calculate expected loss?

Pain and suffering and loss of enjoyment of life?

Family life? Wife? Loss of consortium?

Indemnity claim v. whoever responsible for causing spill?

Check homeowner's policy—copy

Review pictures taken—get negatives if available

Copy suit papers

Copy medical bills

1. Is there anything you would add to this list?
2. What topics can you identify from the list that clearly relate to the legal issue of the homeowner's duty of care that Paul Perfect researched?
3. What topics can you identify from the list that clearly relate to the legal issue of intent in the torts of assault and battery?

f. Prepare specific questions within each topic

Now you are ready to prepare the specific questions to be asked within each topic. As you do so, keep in mind that there are different kinds of questions, effective for different purposes. There are:

- open-ended questions
- closed-ended questions
- leading questions
- pressure questions
- hypothetical questions
- multiple-choice questions

- opinion questions
- explanatory questions
- silence as a question

Let's consider examples of each type of question and their usefulness in interviewing.

1. Open-ended questions.   These questions encourage the client to provide a narrative of events or a detailed explanation or to otherwise give extended information in the answer. They are overview or summary-type questions used to obtain a broad outline of an event or situation:

What had you been doing during the hours before the accident occurred?
Now tell me what happened as you entered the intersection?

Open-ended questions are often used at the beginning of the interview in order to get the person talking:

What can we do for you today?

They are also used to obtain an initial comprehensive understanding of the facts or an outline of the events before delving into details with more specific questions. Sometimes it might be appropriate to begin the substantive portion of the interview by stating clearly that you intend to ask broad questions first and then to narrow the focus.

EXAMPLE

> **INTERVIEWER:** Mrs. Brown, let me begin by asking you some general questions so I can get an overview of what happened. Then we will come back to the details. Is that all right?
> **MRS. BROWN:** Sure. That will be fine.
> **INTERVIEWER:** Why don't you begin by telling me what happened that day as you remember it?

Think of open-ended questions as asking the person to tell you a story. That is really what you want them to do. Use these questions to get the story told completely and thoroughly—the entire narrative from beginning to end—so you can then go back and examine it more closely for details.

Open-ended questions can also be used to keep a client talking:

What happened next?

or to fill in blanks left by the answer:

What happened when you told him that?

Open-ended questions also provide an excellent opportunity for the interviewer to observe the client and evaluate how well she expresses herself and organizes her thoughts.

2. Closed-ended questions.   Questions that call for a specific, narrow answer requiring few words and little or no explanation are closed-ended:

What color was the car that entered the intersection from your right?
What was the man that you saw wearing?

These questions are used to confirm detail in a story:

Did you agree to do as he asked?

or to get the sequence of events straight:

So, it was after the gun came out that you ducked under the counter?

or to pin the person down to a particular version:

What you're saying then is that the blue car came to a complete stop before it started into the intersection?

Closed-ended questions are most often used after the interviewer has asked a series of open-ended questions to obtain the necessary overview of the events or situation.

3. Leading questions. A specific type of closed-ended question is the **leading question**, which suggests its own answer by calling for a yes or no response:

The first car that you saw enter the intersection was red, is that correct?

Like all forms of closed-ended questions, leading questions are used to confirm detail or pin down a client to a particular version of events. However, it is the unique phrasing of the leading question that distinguishes it from other types of closed-ended questions. In the last example, it is the phrase, "is that correct" that makes it a leading question. That phrase almost demands a yes or no response and that is its purpose.

Leading questions should be used infrequently in interviewing because we want the person to tell us what they know in their own words. (Of course the attorney will use leading questions in cross-examination of witnesses at trial—see Chapter 6.) However, leading questions are legitimately used in an interview to jog the memory of one who is forgetful:

I think the speed limit was 50 miles per hour there, wasn't it?

or one who is being deliberately difficult or vague, or if the interviewer is having a difficult time pinning down details. Leading questions may also be used to lead a wandering client back onto the path of relevant inquiry:

Well, that's all quite interesting, Mrs. Brown. But you told me a moment ago that you took a single Valium tablet about 30 minutes before the collision, isn't that right?

4. Pressure questions. These questions challenge the interviewee directly or indirectly and compel a response involving emotion or feeling as well as fact:

As you sat there watching the train approach, you didn't honk your horn or try to do anything to warn the children playing on the track?

Pressure questions may be used to get a wishy-washy or forgetful person to commit to a particular version of events:

If you're not sure if the light was on in the kitchen, how can you be so sure it was Mr. Burnes you saw going out the window?

or simply to see how a person will likely handle challenging or accusative questions at trial or deposition:

> *If you signed the release and accepted the severance pay on the day they terminated you, why do you say now that they tricked you?*

Pressure questions can be effective but must be used carefully and with forethought. Because they do involve a challenging element, they can offend or anger the person being questioned. To lessen that risk, you probably want to lower your voice and ask such a question softly and with little inflection rather than raising your voice and adopting an accusatory tone.

5. Hypothetical questions. Here the client is asked to assume some set of facts on which to premise an answer:

> *Assume that the blue car was doing no more than 30 miles per hour. Do you think the accident would still have happened?*

Lawyers frequently pose hypothetical questions to expert witnesses to elicit their opinions at trial or deposition. For the interviewer's purposes, hypothetical questions may be used to get some idea how the interviewee's knowledge coincides with other information, or to see how the person will handle a challenge to his testimony from the opposing side, or to jog the witness's memory.

EXAMPLE

> **INTERVIEWER:** Mr. Crebbs, do you recall how fast the blue car was going?
> **MR. CREBBS:** No, I really couldn't say.
> **INTERVIEWER:** You wouldn't hazard a guess as to the speed of that car?
> **MR. CREBBS:** Not really.
> **INTERVIEWER:** Well, let me ask you this. Assume that blue car was going no more than, say, 30 miles an hour. Do you think the accident would still have happened?
> **MR. CREBBS:** Probably. But I'm sure that car was doing more than 30.

6. Multiple-choice questions. Closely related to hypothetical questions, multiple-choice questions invite the person to choose among two or more options offered by the interviewer:

> *Did the sound you heard seem to come from directly behind you or above you or off to one side?*

Multiple-choice questions can be useful to clarify previous answers that were imprecise:

EXAMPLE

> **INTERVIEWER:** You say you heard a sound just before the gun fired?
> **CLIENT:** That's right, I did.
> **INTERVIEWER:** Where did the sound come from in relation to where you were standing at the time?

> **CLIENT:** Well, it seemed to come from back behind me somewhere.
> **INTERVIEWER:** Did the sound you heard seem to come from directly behind you or above you or off to one side?

7. Opinion questions. With these questions, the person is simply asked to express an opinion about something or even to speculate:

Why do you think he did that?
What do you believe caused him to say that?
What could have been on his mind to make him go there?

Remember that at trial attorneys generally cannot ask lay witnesses to speculate or offer their opinions about matters. But in interviewing we have no such limitations. Asking a person to speculate or offer an opinion can frequently lead to new and unexpected information or additional lines of inquiry.

EXAMPLE

> **INTERVIEWER:** When Jesse left the house, did he say where he was going?
> **CLIENT:** As I recollect, he said he was going by the bank and then was headed to Lisa's house.
> **INTERVIEWER:** He said he was going by the bank first?
> **CLIENT:** Yep. That's what I recall.
> **INTERVIEWER:** What could have been on his mind to make him go there before he went to his girlfriend's house?
> **CLIENT:** Well, I'd say it was to cash that last paycheck since he got laid off earlier that morning.
> **INTERVIEWER:** So Jesse got laid off from work the morning before he and Lisa disappeared?

8. Explanatory questions. Closely related to the opinion question, the explanatory question asks the person to explain an answer or expound further on it:

What do you mean by that?
Why do you roll your eyes when you say his name?
How did that come about?

9. Silence as a question. We have all heard phrases such as *the sounds of silence* and *the silence was deafening* and *the pregnant pause.* Silence—the meaningful pause—can be used by the interviewer as an effective question in some situations by pausing after an answer is given as if expecting the person to say more. The silent pause certainly should not be overused. But it may prove useful when the interviewer thinks the client has more to say but is reluctant. The interviewer's pause may be an encouragement to speak. Or when the interviewer believes the answer given to a question is obviously false, the pause may be a signal that the interviewer recognizes the falsehood and is giving the person an opportunity to correct the answer.

g. Consider the phrasing of questions

Questions can be phrased to accomplish different purposes or adjust to different kinds of witnesses.

1. Questions phrased as direct questions

Who else was there?
Why did you do that?
What did you see?
When did you first meet him?
Where did you go after that?
How did you get the door open?

2. Questions phrased as an order or directive

Tell me who else was there.
Explain why you did that.

3. Questions phrased as conclusions

And you're sure no one else was there?
So you're telling me you did that just to get him hired?
What you're saying then is that you came to a complete stop before you entered the intersection?
So, in other words, there wasn't time to honk or shout?
If I understand what you're saying, the police officer never actually told you to stay there?

4. Questions phrased to challenge

But if you were looking to your left at the truck how do you know when the boy to your right stepped into the street?
What about the fact that you forgot your glasses that morning?
How do you know he went out the back door?

5. Questions phrased to sound skeptical

Are you sure you came to a complete stop?
If the gun was locked up as you say, how did the boys get hold of it?

6. Questions phrased as a request for assistance

Can you tell me when you first met Gary?
What I'm trying to figure out is, how could you be in two places at once?
I'm wondering how many times you had seen him swing on the chain before the time it broke?
What we need to know is, did you actually see him fire the gun or did you just hear the shot?
What I need you to show me is about where you were standing at the time in relation to the red car?

As you can tell from these sample questions, we are trying to accomplish something different with each of them. Some people respond better to questions phrased as a request for help. People like to help and many of us are trained to automatically respond to a request for assistance. (Have you ever worked somewhere where they told you that customer

Illustration 10-10   PAGE OF INTERVIEWER'S QUESTIONS AND NOTES

QUESTIONS	NOTES

service is the most important thing?) Other people respond better to questions phrased as directives or orders—they just need to be lead.

Deciding what kinds of questions to use in an interview and how to phrase questions is a true skill. It is in many ways the heart of the interviewing task. The ability to do it well starts with what we are doing here, learning about kinds of questions and phrasing. But in addition to education, you must have experience in preparing questions and asking them in a real-life interview. (See LBD 10-1.)

h. Put questions in a format consistent with any checklist or intake sheet being used

(See discussion of checklists below.)

i. Put questions in a format conducive to taking good notes during the interview

Some interviewers like to use a legal pad with planned questions written on one-half to two-thirds of the left side of the page and leaving the right side of the page blank for notes or spontaneous questions to be written in during the interview. Illustration 10-10 shows how such a page might look.

j. Be flexible—always expect to ask other questions in the interview

No matter how carefully the interviewer plans, many questions will have to be spontaneously formulated during the interview. No interview goes according to a script. For example, going into an initial client interview, the interviewer may have incomplete or inaccurate information about the specific legal problem the new client will present. That potential divorce client may turn out to be a woman already divorced who needs assistance in enforcing a child support decree entered in another state. That business contract dispute may turn out to be a potential trade name infringement matter. That personal injury product liability client may turn out to be an unhappy (but perfectly healthy) consumer with a potential fraud claim. That workers' compensation claim may turn out to be a possible Americans with Disabilities Act claim. The interviewer has to be flexible and able to adjust his questions from one legal context to another with little or no notice.

In addition, something will always require that the interviewer ask unplanned questions—the answers given, the demeanor or personality of the client, or the environment in which the interview is conducted. Expect this—it's a normal part of interviewing. And remember that the careful crafting of well-worded questions comes with hard work and experience. The more you do it, the better you will be at it.

k. Have the supervising attorney review questions and forms

HYPOTHETICAL 10-4

Paul Perfect now puts his brainstorm list in chronological order and drafts specific questions for each topic. These are his questions on the topic of what he finally calls, "Client's prior knowledge of Plaintiff."

5. Client's prior knowledge of plaintiff (JS)
  • Where does JS live in relation to your house?
  • How long has she lived there?
  • Is she married or living with anyone?
  • Do you know if she has children?
  • Where does she work?
  • What does she do there?
  • Do you know how long she has worked there?
  • How long have you known her?
  • How did you two meet?
  • Would you say you know her well?
  • Do you consider her a good friend?
  • How did she come to be invited to the party?
  • Did she come with anyone else?
  • Is she close friends with anyone else who was at the party?
  • Have you ever had any problems of any kind with her before?
  • Do you have any reason to believe she doesn't like you?
  • Did anything unpleasant or negative occur between the two of you at the party before the fall?
  • Do you have any reason to believe she would stage the fall?
  • Do you have any reason to believe she would exaggerate her injuries?

Would you add any questions to the list under this topic?
Having prepared his questions, Paul Perfect makes a copy of everything he plans to use in the interview and gives it to Betty Busy's secretary with a note asking the attorney to look it over and let him know if it looks okay to use.

3. Using a checklist or intake sheet

Many law offices have developed written **checklists** or use a new client form called an **intake sheet** to conduct initial client interviews.

Personal injury, divorce, medical malpractice, workers' compensation, bankruptcy, and estate planning are examples of areas of the law lending themselves to such checklists or intake sheets. Illustration 10-11 presents a sample checklist that might be used in the personal injury area.

Checklists can be very useful to the interviewing paralegal. They will help you identify the topics you must cover with the client. They can serve as a literal checklist to check off topics as you cover them, and

Illustration 10-11   CHECKLIST FOR PERSONAL INJURY CASE

1. CLIENT BACKGROUND INFORMATION
   Full name
   Nickname/former names
   Current address
   Addresses last ten years
   Phone no. (home/work/mobile)
   FAX no.
   E-mail no.
   Soc. Sec. no.
   DOB
   Marital status (S/M/D)
   Spouse's name
   Children & D's OB
   Current employer name
   Current employer address
   Current employer phone no.
   Employment duties/title
   Supervisor(s)
   Salary
   Other annual earnings/income
   Former employment last ten years

2. INCIDENT INFORMATION
   Date
   Place
   Summary of incident
   Known witnesses
   Other parties involved in incident
   Third parties who may be responsible
   Incident job related (Y/N)
   Investigating authority
   Investigating officer
   Accident report (Copy Y/N)
   Other physical evidence (photos, etc.)

3. PROPERTY DAMAGE
   Property damaged
   Description of damage (total/partial)
   Owner(s)
   Value and source of estimate

4. PERSONAL INJURY
   Persons injured
   Description of injuries
   Prognosis

Future disabilities/treatment
Prior medical history
Health/medical condition prior to incident
Medications taking at time of accident
Treating hospital
Dates of treatment
Treating physician
Dates of visits
Other physicians
Description of medical treatment to date
Medications prescribed
Physical therapy (Y/N)
Physical therapy provider
Medical bills to date (copies Y/N)

5. OTHER DAMAGES
   Lost time from work
   Lost income/how calculated
   Pain and suffering (description)
   Witnesses to pain and suffering
   Loss of consortium claim
   Other loss or damage

6. INSURANCE INFORMATION
   Client's auto insurance carrier/policy no.
   Client's medical insurance carrier/policy no.
   Client's other insurance/policy no.
   Other party's auto insurance carrier
   Other party's other insurance

7. STATUTES OF LIMITATION/REPOSE
   Relevant statutes
   Relevant dates
   Dates entered into docket control (Y/N)

8. OTHER RELEVANT INFORMATION

9. INTERVIEW CONDUCTED BY

10. DATE OF INTERVIEW

11. CONFLICT OF INTEREST CHECK COMPLETED (Y/N)
    Date completed
    Performed by

12. REPRESENTATION UNDERTAKEN (Y/N)
    Date representation undertaken
    File no.

they help ensure you have covered everything and gotten all documents signed before you let the client leave.

Use caution with checklists, however. No matter how comprehensive, no pre-existing list of questions can anticipate all that needs to be asked in a particular interview. Every case is unique in some way. Every client is certainly unique. Therefore, it is important to plan specific questions separately from the checklist. Never become a slave to a checklist. It may stifle creativity and prevent you from following up on leads given in answers.

4. Prepare the physical environment where the interview is to take place

Whether the interview is conducted in an office or a conference room, there are basic things you want to do.

- Be sure the area is clean and neat
- Put away materials related to other clients
- Be sure enough chairs are available and arranged properly
- Be sure the incidental things are available like note pads, pens, paper clips, etc., and a tape recorder or video camera with extra tapes and batteries

5. Give thought to any special needs of the client

Clients with disabilities affecting *sight, speech, vision,* or *mental comprehension* may require special preparation. If the client is deaf or extremely hard of hearing, consider having a sign interpreter present for the interview. The visually impaired may require a Braille expert.

If you are interviewing a child, remember that the permission and usually the presence of a parent or guardian is required.

Is the client bringing one or more children with her because she has no one to keep them? If possible, arrange for someone else in the office to entertain them while you conduct the interview. Or find some suitable toys or distractions (quiet ones!) for the children.

Is anyone accompanying the client? Any companions will probably need to be excluded from the interview to preserve the attorney-client privilege, so be sure to have a place where they can sit and something for them to read.

6. Plan the seating arrangement

When the paralegal sets up the room where the interview takes place, careful thought should be given to seating arrangements. Where the client is seated in the interview room can make a difference:

- in how comfortable they feel;
- in their attention level; and
- in the formal or informal tone of the session.

We will consider seating arrangements in an office with a desk and seating arrangements in an office or conference room around a rectangular or round conference table. Keep in mind that there is no one right seating arrangement. There are alternatives to be considered depending on the physical location of the interview, the person you are interviewing, and the nature of the interview. Each alternative has its advantages and disadvantages.

a. In an office with a desk

In an office there is typically a desk and two or more chairs placed somewhere in front of the desk. In a larger office, you might also have a small, usually round, conference table or couch. In an office with the desk and chairs in front, the interviewer (I) may choose to sit behind the desk with the client (C) in one of the chairs in front of the desk. (See Illustration 10-12(a).) Be aware that this creates a more formal tone for the interview—the position behind the desk is an authoritative one, which may make the client less comfortable.

If the interviewer chooses to come out from behind the desk and sit in one of the chairs across from the client, the tone set is more informal. Since the interviewer has abandoned the authoritative position, the two people are on more of an equal basis and the client may feel more comfortable. (See Illustration 10-12(b).) One disadvantage of this arrangement is that it may make it more difficult for the interviewer to take good notes or to handle necessary documents. A solution may be to seat the person on one side of the desk, diagonally across from the interviewer. (See Illustration 10-12(c).) The desk can still be used for note taking and handling documents but the arrangement is not so authoritative since both people are at the desk.

b. At a rectangular conference table

If the interview is to be conducted at a rectangular conference table, keep in mind that the table will have a recognizable head seat or seat of authority. That is usually the seat at one of the short ends of the table. A guest entering a room with a rectangular table will almost never voluntarily take the head seat. Instead, they will be naturally drawn to one of the seats on a long side of the table. If the interviewer chooses to position herself at the head seat of a rectangular table, a formal tone is set and obvious authority is being asserted. (See Illustration 10-13(a).)

The interviewer may choose to avoid the head seat and select a seat on the side of the rectangular table directly across from the person being interviewed. (See Illustration 10-13(b).) No particular authority is being asserted in this position but some people may feel that sitting directly across from another lends a confrontational tone to the meeting.

Another alternative is for the interviewer to select a seat next to the person on the same side of the table. (See Illustration 10-13(c).) This is non-authoritative and very informal. But it may feel too informal, particularly in a first meeting. Also, any time the interviewer uses this arrangement, she must be careful not to sit too close to the client, which can be perceived as threatening or intrusive. This arrangement also has the disadvantage of making it more difficult to shield notes being taken.

Illustration 10-12   SEATING ARRANGEMENTS IN AN OFFICE

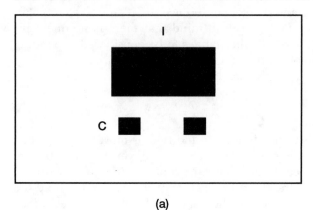

Creates a formal tone.
The interviewer
sits in a position
of authority.

(a)

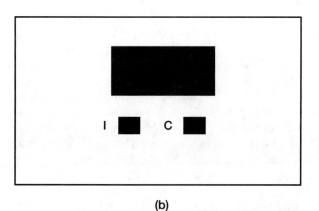

Less formal. Taking
notes and handling
documents may
be more difficult.

(b)

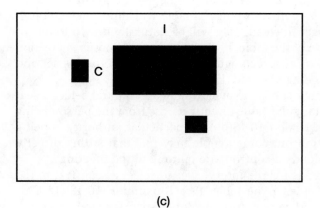

Still informal. Taking
notes and handling
documents easier.

(c)

Illustration 10-13   SEATING ARRANGEMENTS AT A RECTANGULAR CONFERENCE TABLE

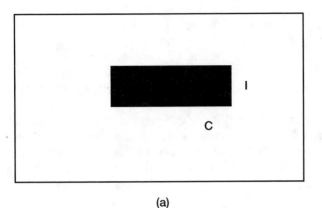

Interviewer is in the
seat of authority.
Formal tone.

(a)

Less authoritative, more
informal tone.

(b)

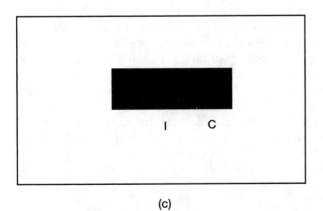

Very informal, but don't
sit too close.

(c)

c. At a rounded conference table

The advantage of a rounded conference table is that it has no head seat. That is why many attorneys and paralegals prefer rounded (circular or oval) conference tables for their offices and conference rooms. It is still possible for the interviewer to sit directly across from the person being interviewed at a rounded table and in some situations that may be viewed as confrontational. Or it may create too great a feeling of distance. (See Illustration 10-14(a).)

Alternatives are to sit diagonally to the person (see Illustration 10–14(b)), or immediately next to them at the table (see Illustration 10–14(c)). The confrontational element is removed from these arrangements, but the closer the interviewer moves to the person being interviewed, the more difficult it is to properly shield notes being taken.

d. Other considerations in seating

No matter what physical arrangement is available for the interview or what seating arrangement is selected, there are several miscellaneous matters to keep in mind:

1. Never sit too close.   We all like our space. When another person gets too close to us without our permission it is very uncomfortable and even threatening.

2. Be conscious of the location of doors.   In general, you do not want to seat a client with his back to the door leading into the room. It can have the *Wild Bill Hickock effect* on some people, making them uncomfortable in that position. (See Illustration 10-15(a).)

3. Be conscious of the location of windows.   Avoid seating a person so that he is looking past the interviewer and out a window, or looking out a window to their side. The view may prove distracting. The interviewer wants the person being interviewed to concentrate on the questions and answers. So, instead, place the person with his back to the window. (See Illustration 10-15(b).)

4. Keep your notes shielded from view.   Sit where you can keep your notes shielded from the wandering eyes of the client. Your notes may, and should, contain your impressions of the client and his answers. Only you and the supervising attorney should ever see those notes.

5. No one seating arrangement is always right.   Use different seating arrangements in different situations. For example, in some interview situations, the interviewer may want to seat herself in a position of authority relative to the client or witness. Maybe you have been assigned to interview a potential client who is a successful business man. Over the phone he sounded very full of himself and condescending toward you as a paralegal. In that initial interview, you may want to stake out a formal authoritative position for yourself. He may respect that more than a less formal arrangement. If you are interviewing a hostile witness (see Chapter 12), you may deliberately choose a formal or even confrontational arrangement.

7. Avoid interruptions during the interview

If the interview is to take place in your office, switch the phone out so it doesn't ring in your office. Tell the receptionist not to transfer calls

Illustration 10-14   SEATING ARRANGEMENTS AT A ROUNDED CONFERENCE TABLE

(a)

(b)

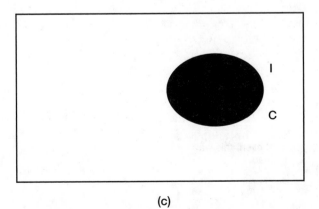

(c)

Illustration 10-15   DOORS AND WINDOWS IN SEATING ARRANGEMENTS

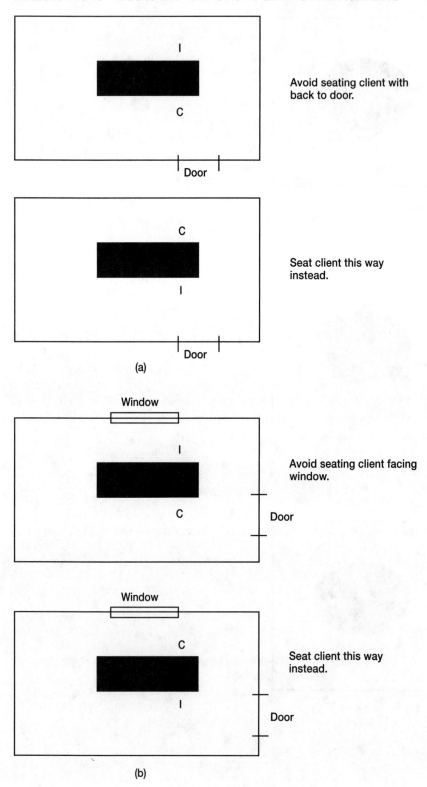

Avoid seating client with back to door.

Seat client this way instead.

(a)

Avoid seating client facing window.

Seat client this way instead.

(b)

while you are in the interview. Tell your secretary that you are not to be disturbed (unless the building is on fire!).

8. Be physically and mentally prepared for the interview

It is also important for the interviewer to prepare himself physically and mentally for interviewing. The act of conducting an interview is taxing. We will do better if we prepare ourselves. That means:

a. Get enough rest the night before the interview

You won't do the job that you should if you're tired.

b. Leave your personal life outside the interview room

Not your *personality,* your personal life. Put aside whatever you are anxious about on a given day and focus 100 percent on this interview. While you worry about cooking for those guests tonight or whatever else is on your mind, you are going to miss a word, a phrasing, a look, or a gesture by the witness that you should have caught.

HYPOTHETICAL 10-5

The evening before the interview with Harrison Bored, Paul Perfect looks over his notes one more time, then prepares for bed at 10 P.M. As he is brushing his teeth, the phone rings. It's his best friend from paralegal school whom he hasn't seen in years. The friend is in town to assist his supervising attorney with a deposition tomorrow morning. He suggests that Paul come down to his hotel and have a drink with him since he has to leave right after the deposition tomorrow. Paul is tempted, but then remembers his interview with Harrison Bored tomorrow afternoon and takes a rain check. He knows that if he stays out late tonight he will be dragging by tomorrow afternoon.

On the way to work in the morning Paul has a flat tire—on the interstate, in the rain, during rush hour. And the tires on his car are almost new! Paul begins thinking about the spleen-venting phone call he is going to make later to the dealer who sold him the tires. He vows to do it as soon as he gets to the office. He rehearses biting and sarcastic remarks to the dealer—was there a typo in that warranty? Was the 60,000 miles supposed to be only 600? He imagines the dealer apologizing and coming down to the office personally to deliver a new tire and offering him a year of free oil changes to make it up to him.

As he enters his office, still soggy, Paul Perfect sees the materials he left for Betty Busy on his desk with a note from her saying she has looked them over and they are fine. He makes his phone call to the tire dealer who (rats!) is out for the week and can't be reached regarding Paul's complaint (probably on a sailboat in the Caribbean, Paul thinks, vacation paid for by yours truly). The person answering the phone does promise to have the assistant manager call as soon as he comes in that morning.

The assistant manager apparently *doesn't* come in that morning because he doesn't call. Before he leaves for lunch at noon, Paul calls the dealership again only to be told that the assistant manager is out to lunch. Paul starts to comment on how true that obviously is but bites his tongue. He asks that the assistant manager call him as soon as he returns and is promised that he will. When Paul returns from lunch there is no message from the assistant manager. Paul groans and starts to dial the dealership number again. Then he looks at the clock and sees that there's barely an hour before his interview with Harrison Bored. He puts the phone down and tells himself to get his act together for the interview.

A little after 1 P.M. Paul checks the conference room where the interview will be held and picks up some papers left over from a previous conference. He politely asks the receptionist to please clean off the top of the table, which has a few cup rings showing from the last use.

Paul looks over the rectangular table with a seat at each end and six chairs on each side. He recalls how friendly and informal Harrison Bored sounded on the phone. He decides that he will sit in one of the chairs on the side of the table—the one facing out the window—and put Bored directly across from him, looking toward the closed door.

About thirty minutes before Harrison Bored is expected to arrive, Paul calls the receptionist and reminds her that Bored is coming and to call Paul as soon as he arrives. He tells her where he wants the client to be seated in the conference room. He also reminds her to not put any calls through to the conference room while he is in there. He reminds his secretary of the same thing. Then he reviews the file one last time to be sure everything is ready. Just as he finishes, his phone rings and the receptionist tells him that Mr. Harrison Bored is here to see him.

KEY WORDS AND PHRASES TO REMEMBER

closed-ended questions
confirmation letter
contingency fee agreement
educational records authorization
employment records authorization
fact witness
field interview
flat fee agreement
hypothetical question
information source
initial client interview
intake sheet
interview checklist

leading questions
legal services agreement
medical records authorization
multiple-choice questions
open-ended questions
opinion questions
phrasing of questions
pressure questions
retainer
retainer agreement
seating arrangement
work file

LEARN BY DOING

LBD 10-1. Schedule and prepare for the client interview in one of the following cases as assigned to you by the instructor. Contact the person who will be playing the role of the client. Schedule the interview then prepare: (1) a memo to the instructor summarizing your contact with the client; (2) a confirming letter to the client; and (3) any forms you might need for the interview. Prepare your questions for the interview.

a. Case Study No. 1 (The Rowdy Outlaw Case) Rowdy Outlaw
b. Case Study No. 2 (The Soupspoon Wise Case) Soupspoon Wise
c. Case Study No. 3 (The Vidalia Unyon Case) Vidalia Unyon
d. Case Study No. 4 (The Rocky Road Project) Rocky Road

LBD 10-2. Using one of the four Case Studies included in Appendix A as directed by your instructor, and the information outlined below, draft a fee agreement for the client and a letter to the client (1) transmitting the fee agreement; (2) briefly describing the initial investigation your office has agreed to undertake on behalf of the client; and (3) estimating the cost and time for completing that investigation.

a. Case Study No. 1 (The Rowdy Outlaw Case): The supervising attorney has agreed that Outlaw will pay a $50,000 retainer up front. Monthly billings will show the charges for time and expenses made against the retainer and the remaining balance. The retainer amount will be replenished at the same level ($50,000) within ten days of the receipt by the client of a monthly statement showing the balance of the original retainer to be below $15,000, or two weeks before trial, whichever occurs first. Hourly rates to be charged are $200 per hour for partner attorneys, $125 per hour for associate attorneys, and $80 per hour for paralegals.

b. Case Study No. 2 (The Soupspoon Wise Case): The supervising attorney has agreed that Wise will pay a $10,000 retainer up front to be applied against expenses only, not legal fees. Expenses are to include all out-of-pocket costs incurred by the law office in connection with the representation including, but not limited to, long-distance phone calls, mailing, printing and copy costs, travel expenses (including mileage, food, and lodging), filing fees, court reporter costs, expert fees and expenses, and charges for online research or communications. The legal fee will be a contingency fee of one-third of the gross amount of any recovery by settlement, arbitration, judgment, or otherwise from whatever source and will increase to 40 percent in the event of an appeal by any party. If out-of-pocket expenses exceed the $10,000 retainer amount during the representation, all expenses in excess of $10,000 will be payable out of the balance of the gross recovery after the deduction of the legal fee. If there is no recovery, expenses in excess of the retainer amount will be paid within six months of the dismissal of the case or the termination of the representation, whichever occurs first.

c. Case Study No. 3 (The Vidalia Unyon Case): The supervising attorney has agreed that a motion for temporary support will be filed promptly after the divorce action is commenced, asking that Mr. Unyon be ordered to pay Mrs. Unyon's fees and expenses in connection with the representation or to designate funds in an identifiable account with sufficient balance for that purpose for her discretionary use. In the event that motion is not granted or the court does not order Mr. Unyon to pay or make sufficient funds available to pay the legal fees and expenses of Mrs. Unyon, Mrs. Unyon will pay monthly bills for all excess amounts within ten days of receipt of the statement. Hourly rates will be charged at $125 per hour for the supervising attorney and $90 per hour for paralegals.

d. Case Study No. 4 (The Rocky Road Project): The supervising attorney has agreed that RRI will make no advance payment. There will be monthly billings showing time and expense charges, but only the expenses will be payable, within 30 days of receipt. Accrued attorney fees will be shown on each statement but will not be payable until closing on the optioned ten acres or until the current option expires, whichever occurs sooner. Attorney fees accrued after the closing on the optioned ten acres will be payable as owed at the closing on the additional parcels to be purchased by RRI for the shopping center project or six months from the date of the final bill, whichever occurs sooner. Rocky Road, president of RRI, will sign a personal guaranty securing payment of all corporate fees and expenses owed to the firm now and in the future. Hourly rates will be charged at $225 per hour for partner attorneys, $175 per hour for associate attorneys, and $100 per hour for paralegals.

Chapter 11

Conducting a Client Interview

CHAPTER OBJECTIVES

In Chapter 10 we considered scheduling and preparing for the initial client interview. In this chapter we consider conducting the client interview. You will learn:

- How to greet and make the client feel comfortable and welcome.
- The important things to keep in mind throughout the client interview.
- How to begin a client interview, move to the substantive areas, and conclude the interview.
- How to use active listening skills in a client interview.
- How to evaluate, test, and seek verification of information obtained in a client interview.
- How to work successfully with difficult clients.
- How to prepare an interview summary for the supervising attorney.
- How to prepare follow-up communications to a client.
- The role of the paralegal when the attorney conducts the interview.
- Guidelines for handling subsequent client interviews and contacts.

A. Introduction

This chapter continues our study of preparing for and conducting an initial client interview. When we left Paul Perfect at the end of Chapter 10, the receptionist had just called and told him that the potential new client, Harrison Bored, was here to see him. Now let's learn how to actually conduct an effective new client interview.

B. ► Ten Things to Remember Throughout the Client Interview

1. Be friendly but professional

Don't use the client's first name unless you already know him or he invites you to do so. If appropriate, express empathy for the client's condition or circumstances but never appear *condescending, patronizing,* or *pandering*. Avoid being *judgmental* or appearing *shocked*—you're going to hear it all in this job. Be obvious about *paying close attention* by maintaining *good eye contact*. Never appear *bored* (even if you are bored to tears) or let the client know that this is *routine* (even if it is). Never appear *rushed* or indicate to the client how *busy* or *overworked* you are.

Avoid expressing *personal opinions* in an interview—about the case, the opposing party, or the opposing party's attorney. Don't create *expectations* in the client's mind about the merits of the case one way or another; it is the attorney's responsibility to evaluate the case.

2. Avoid legal or technical jargon except as necessary

Remember that the client is not familiar with legal terms or concepts. He has come with a problem, and may be intimidated just by being in a law office. If the interviewer starts throwing around legal terms and concepts—*res judicata* or *res ipsa loquitur*—it may only increase the client's anxiety, hindering communication rather than advancing it. Some paralegals mistakenly think that using important-sounding legal terms will make them appear more professional in the eyes of a client. Usually it has the opposite effect, making the paralegal appear pompous and self-important. Of course there are times when we must and should use legal terms. With Harrison Bored, Paul Perfect may have to explain that he is asking questions about the punch that Jessica Slang threw because Harrison Bored may have (depending on the analysis of the facts by the supervising attorney) a potential counterclaim against her. He will explain as simply as he can what a counterclaim is.

3. Be cognizant of the dangers of the unauthorized practice of law

Even though you will have explained to the client at the beginning of the interview that you cannot give legal advice (see discussion below), it will be easy for the client to forget that. The questions raised by the client during the course of the interview about legal rights or remedies may be questions to which you know the answer and it would expedite the interview to give an answer and move on. But unless you have been specifically authorized by the supervising attorney to communicate that information in response to a specific question, don't do it, for all the reasons we considered when we talked about UPL in Chapter 2.

4. Take good notes

Good notes are accurate and comprehensive notes. There is an art to good note taking (as most people learn in high school and college). And it is a real challenge to be able to take good notes while you are also observing and actively listening to the witness. But it must be done. We cannot trust ourselves to accurately remember statements made and impressions perceived for longer than a few moments.

Many interviewers develop their own shorthand to make note taking more efficient. Just don't forget your own abbreviations. If the interview is being recorded (see discussion in Chapter 13), the need for notes is lessened, but you will still want to record impressions that the tape recorder will not pick up.

5. Engage in *active listening*

Recall the discussion of **active listening** in Chapter 8. In interviewing, we listen not just to hear words, but to catch *meanings* as well. And watch for that *body language* (facial expressions, eye contact, body position and gestures, nervous signs) that tells us so much about a person.

6. Evaluate the demeanor and behavior of the client

Note traits or characteristics of the client that the supervising attorney will need to know about—relaxed or nervous demeanor, neat or unkempt appearance, appropriate or inappropriate dress, correct or incorrect grammar, normal or abnormal behavior. Evaluate the client's credibility, intelligence, and personality. Make a special note of anything about the client that seems odd or troubles you. For example, is the client egotistical, temperamental, easily manipulated, a political or religious zealot, profane, sexist? Get the idea? Make careful notes of your impressions.

7. The client will not know what to tell you— you have to ask

Because clients are not trained in the law or at factual analysis they do not appreciate, as the interviewer does, the relationship between the law and relevant facts (see Chapter 1). They will typically have no idea which facts are relevant to their problem and which are not. Do not assume that what the client tells you is the problem is everything you need to know. We have to know what to ask. It is up to the interviewer, not the client, to get out all the relevant information.

SLEUTH ON THE LOOSE

Identify a world famous business leader then access *www.sookoo .com* and see if you can locate the text of interviews with that person or information on corporate strategies for that person's company.

8. Remember the commandments

Recall the two great commandments of interviewing and investigating:

a. *Assume nothing*

b. *Verify everything*

And that is why in every interview, we:

- evaluate the source of the information
- test the information for internal consistency

- look for holes or gaps in the information
- compare new information to information already gathered
- seek corroborating information
- seek explanations
- seek details
- seek leads to other information

9. Keep an emotional distance between yourself and the client

It is easy to connect emotionally with clients who have suffered tragedy or who are going through an ordeal of some kind, particularly those who are innocent victims of another's cruelty. We do—and should—feel normal human compassion, express sympathy, and show empathy in those situations.

But there is a danger here for the unwary. None of us can carry all the burdens of the world on our shoulders. We all have the normal load of emotional involvement and resulting stress that comes from our own lives. If you allow yourself to become too personally involved in the problems of the client, you run the risk of losing your objectivity (how objective are you about perceived attacks on family or friends?). Or, you run the risk of emotional burnout from simply taking too much on yourself. We have to develop the ability to feel for clients but at the same time to keep an emotional distance from them in order to protect ourselves and do our jobs. The ability to do that starts with recognizing the danger.

10. Overcome *internal* obstacles to effective interviewing

In any interview we may encounter internal barriers—those of our own making—that can interfere with doing an effective job. Four of the greatest internal obstacles that interviewers face are:

a. *Concentrating too intently on your next question*
A common error of new interviewers is to be so engrossed in wording the next question just right that they miss something in the answer to the last one.

b. *Concentrating too hard on taking good notes*
It is important to take good notes in an interview. But there is a real art to being able to do that *and* make consistent eye contact with a witness. The ability to do this well comes with experience.

c. *Being a slave to the prepared list of questions*
Another common error of the beginner is to so slavishly follow the carefully prepared questions that they fail to follow up on leads to new information. Remember, the interviewer must be *flexible*—ready to change directions during the interview at any time based on what you hear. Be ready to test information that seems questionable and ready to

follow new leads. If you concentrate solely on that list of questions, you will always miss something important.

d. Letting your own biases affect you

We all have biases, and we're are not always conscious of having them. We can identify them, however, because they usually express themselves as either positive or negative feelings toward people. The interviewer has to catch himself when he becomes aware of those negative or positive feelings creeping into the interview to keep them from interfering with his objectivity, his duties to the client, or his commitment to legal ethics and professionalism.

In interviewing, we have to remain objective. We have to recognize and overcome our own prejudices and do the job for the client. How would *you* handle each of the situations described in the examples?

EXAMPLE

> You are interviewing a criminal defendant client who, you discover, has been convicted of child abuse in the past. You have intense feelings of disgust and dislike for the client and think it wouldn't be so bad to see him convicted on the current charge and put away permanently.
>
> You are interviewing a divorce client who admits to having beaten his wife but says it was okay because she beat on him too. He is 6'4" and 250 pounds and the wife is 5'2" and 100 pounds. You realize that you despise this guy.
>
> You are interviewing the wife of the 6'4" 250-pound spouse abuser. She describes in detail the repeated beatings she has suffered and says she would like to kill him. You so closely identify with her that you feel the urge to offer your help!

In interviewing, we have to remain objective. We have to recognize and overcome our own prejudices and do the job for the client. How would *you* handle each of the situations described in the examples?

C. ▸ The Order and Manner of Conducting a Client Interview

1. Greeting the client

Once the potential client arrives for the interview, recall that one of the most important goals we have in connection with the initial client interview is to establish a relationship of trust, confidence, and cooperation. That goal is furthered by greeting the client, making him feel welcomed, and seating him comfortably where the interview is to take place.

In some offices the paralegal may leave it to the receptionist to take care of these tasks, but be sure your receptionist knows how to do this effectively. (See Hypothetical 11-1.)

HYPOTHETICAL 11-1

> Assume Paul Perfect tells the receptionist to "go ahead and put Mr. Bored in the conference room and tell him I'll be right with him." Here is

the dialog that might take place between the receptionist (R) and Harrison Bored (HB):

R (putting the phone down and smiling): Mr. Bored, Mr. Perfect will be right with you. He asked me to go ahead and show you to the conference room. If you'll just follow me down the hall this way.

HB: Sure, that will be fine.

R (while guiding HB down the hall): I hope you didn't have any trouble finding our office. (Or, did you find a parking place okay? Or, how were the roads with all that ice and snow? Or, isn't this wonderful weather we're having?)

HB: No, none at all. Mr. Perfect gave me *perfect* directions. (HB laughs at his joke.)

R (laughing politely with HB at the joke although she has heard a million puns made on Paul Perfect's name): Well, good (motioning into conference room). Here we are. Just have a seat by the window there and Mr. Perfect will be right with you.

HB: Fine. Thank you very much.

R: May I get you a cup of coffee or a soft drink?

HB: Coffee sounds good, please.

R: Would you like it black or with cream or sugar?

HB: Just black, please.

R: Fine. Make yourself comfortable and I'll be right back with that.

Some interviewers prefer to come out to the reception area and greet the potential client themselves, direct them to the conference room, and ask if they would like a refreshment.

HYPOTHETICAL 11-2

If Paul Perfect was to greet Harrison Bored and guide him to the conference room, the dialog might sound something like this:

R (putting the phone down and smiling): Mr. Bored, Mr. Perfect will be right with you.

HB: Okay, that will be fine.

PP (entering reception area and approaching HB with hand extended to shake): Hello, Mr. Bored? I'm Paul Perfect. It's a pleasure to meet you.

HB (shaking hands with PP): Hi, I'm pleased to meet you as well. Except for this contraption on my nose (motioning to the nose brace and laughing nervously).

PP: Don't worry about that at all. If it was on my nose people would say it's an improvement. (Everybody laughs, including receptionist.) Let me show you to the conference room. Right this way.

HB: Fine, thanks.

PP (while guiding HB down the hall): I hope you didn't have any trouble finding our office. (Or, did you find a parking place okay? Or, how were the roads with all that ice and snow? Or, isn't this wonderful weather we're having?)

HB: No, none at all. You gave me *perfect* directions. (HB laughs at his joke.)

PP (laughing politely with HB at the joke although he has heard endless puns made on his name): Well, good (motioning into conference room). Here we are. Just have a seat by the window there.

HB: Fine. Thank you very much.

PP: Would you like a cup of coffee or a soft drink before we begin?

HB: Coffee sounds good, please.

PP (picking up phone and dialing receptionist): Would you like it black or with cream or sugar?

HB: Just black, please.

PP: Fine (to receptionist) Janice? Will you bring Mr. Bored a cup of coffee, black, in the conference room, please? Thanks. No, nothing for me. Thanks again. (To HB) She'll be right here with that.

Is there anything you would have done differently from Paul Perfect in this situation?

Each scenario will be different, but the goal is to make the potential client feel welcomed and comfortable. A good initial impression has been made and now a solid basis exists to create confidence and trust.

2. Beginning the interview

In addition to the greeting, there are a number of steps to beginning the interview of a client. You will rarely if ever jump right into your questions.

a. If appropriate, express empathy toward the client

Empathy is the capacity to identify with another's feelings. If the client is still ill at ease or upset following the greeting, take additional time to make her feel secure and comfortable. Additional small talk about weather, parking, directions, refreshment choices, etc., may help. For the client who is visibly upset, tell her to take as much time as needed to collect herself, offer tissues for tears, offer to leave them alone for a while, or in the extreme case, to reschedule the interview.

b. Explain the absence of the attorney

c. Explain your role as a paralegal

Be sure the client understands that you are a paralegal and not an attorney. Make it clear that you cannot answer questions involving legal advice or decide, for example, whether to accept the case or what legal strategies to pursue. Explain that you are there to collect necessary information for the attorney to evaluate and that you or the attorney will then contact her concerning decisons the attorney has made. Ask the client if she understands what you are saying and if she has any questions.

d. Explain the attorney-client privilege

The client needs to understand that everything he tells you in the interview is confidential, whether or not the attorney decides to undertake the representation.

e. Briefly review the goals to be accomplished in the interview

An estimation of the time that will be spent might be a good idea, too.

f. Explain that you will be taking notes during the interview

Let the client know that note taking is standard procedure in an interview.

g. Ask if the client has any questions

Give the client this opportunity before you begin the substantive portion of the interview. This may prevent questions later that disrupt the flow of the interview.

h. Obtain biographical information for the file

Before getting to your substantive questions—those related to the reason for the client's visit—obtain the biographical data you will need to set up the file on this client if the supervising attorney decides to take the case. This data typically includes full name, nicknames, address, employer's name and address, phone numbers (home, work, and emergency), e-mail addresses, and source of reference to the attorney.

Sometimes the office will have an **intake sheet** (see discussion in Chapter 10) that the new client is asked to fill out while she is waiting to meet with the interviewer. In that case, look over the form as the interview begins to be sure it is complete. Ask any additional questions needed to complete the form.

| HYPOTHETICAL 11-3 |

Assume that Paul Perfect is beginning his interview with Harrison Bored. Let's listen in:

PP (returning to the table after asking the receptionist to bring HB coffee and seating himself directly across from HB at the rectangular conference table): Mr. Bored, we appreciate your coming in so promptly. Ms. Busy had hoped to be here today, but she had another commitment she couldn't avoid.

HB: No problem. I know how that happens.

PP: Before we begin, I need to explain to you that I am not an attorney. I am a paralegal, or legal assistant. I work under Ms. Busy's supervision and help her with certain tasks like meeting with you today and getting the information she will need in order to decide whether to take your case and exactly how we should proceed legally. Because I'm not an attorney, I can't make the decision whether to take your case or give you any legal advice at all. Do you understand what I'm saying?

HB: Yes, I believe I do. But when will I know whether she will agree to take my case?

PP: Well, what will happen is, as soon as we are finished here, I will prepare a written report for her, summarizing all the information I get from you today. She will look it over as soon as she can and either she or I will call you and let you know. I don't know her schedule over the next few days, but I know she is aware of how important this is to you and will make it a priority. And I will too. I'll remind her that you're anxious to hear back. Is that okay?

HB: Sure, I understand. That sounds fine.

PP: Now. . .(pausing for the knock at the door). Come in. (The receptionist comes in, smiles, and places the cup of coffee and a coaster in front of HB.)

HB: Thank you very much.

PP (To the receptionist leaving the room): Thank you, Janice. (To HB) Now, I also want you to understand that everything you tell me today is confidential. You've probably heard of attorney-client confidentiality. (HB nods his head.) Even though Ms. Busy is not here, that same confidentiality attaches because I'm here as her assistant. And that means no one can compel us to disclose what you tell me today without your consent. And that's true by the way whether or not Ms. Busy agrees to take your case. Do you understand that?

HB: Yes, I do. And I'm glad you mentioned it because I was wondering.

PP: Well, good. (Placing his notes in front of him) Okay, what we're going to do today is go over this entire situation with Jessica Slang pretty thoroughly. I'll be asking you a lot of questions about yourself and about her and the party and the fall and the injuries you both have sustained and just the whole ball of wax. Okay?

HB: Sure. That's what I expected.

PP: And I'll be taking notes as we go along, which is sort of standard operating procedure in these situations, so don't let that distract you. I may pause sometimes between questions if I'm still writing, but just bear with me. I really scribble pretty fast. Of course, no one can read it but me (smiling).

HB: (smiling back) Gotcha. I'm ready if you are.

PP: Great. First, let me get some biographical information on you for the file.

3. Conducting the substantive portion of the interview

a. Briefly review any documents the client brought

Take a moment to look over these documents. Doing this at the beginning of the substantive portion of the interview will help you focus more quickly on the facts and give you a better idea of the areas you need to address in your questions.

b. Obtain a broad overview of the client's story

In most interviews it is logical and effective to begin consideration of the substantive portion of the interview by obtaining a **narrative summary** of the problem from the client. It provides the interviewer with an overview of the entire situation and an extended opportunity to observe and evaluate the client. Open-ended questions are ideal for this.

Now, tell me, what we can do for you?

Why don't you tell me how the accident happened first, and then we'll go over the details?

To begin with, tell me how this whole thing happened.

In general, *let the client talk.* Interrupt as little as possible. Make copious notes. Remember you will have plenty of time later to ask follow-up questions. Try to get the entire story or sequence of events out at this stage. If the client seems to pause or hesitate before getting everything out, encourage them with positive statements such as:

Please go on.
What happened then?
That must have been quite a shock to you.

c. Fill in gaps in the information given

It is critical for the interviewer to get a complete picture of the event or circumstances being described by the client. As the client goes through the narrative explanation, the interviewer should be watching for gaps or incomplete explanations. Now go back and fill those in. Closed-ended, explanatory, and opinion questions are ideal for this purpose.

> *Now, what happened between the time the light turned green and you began your turn?*
> *Tell me more about what Mr. Brown said when you told him you were quitting.*
> *How many times did you try to call him before you went over there?*
> *What did you mean a few moments ago when you described your neighbor as "nosey"?*
> *Why do you think he refused to talk to you when you called?*

d. Ask for definitions of unfamiliar words and phrases

There is no virtue in pretending to know something you don't. Our goal in the interview is to obtain information that we can understand, evaluate, and apply to the client's legal problem. So if the client uses technical, foreign, slang, or other unfamiliar words, ask for a definition.

e. Ask for details

Interviewers have to get the complete factual picture. Clients not only don't always know what we need to know, they don't understand that we need to know *everything*. Never assume the client has told you all she knows until you've made sure of that by asking for details. We need details of *times, places, distances, colors, sounds, smells, events, transactions, people, documents,* and *sequences.* Think *who, why, what, when, where,* and *how.*

> *Tell me as exactly as you can what time it was when you left home that day.*
> *Try to remember each and every person you saw standing around the wreck area after you came to.*
> *Estimate for me in feet how far away the gunman was from you.*
> *Why did you go back in there when they warned you not to?*
> *Would there be any written record of that agreement and, if so, who would have it?*

Be **thorough** in your questioning. Think of interviewing a client as analogous to wringing out a wet rag. Get all the water you can out of it! Squeeze hard. Squeeze repeatedly. Squeeze one way and then another. You haven't done the job until you are satisfied that you know everything relevant to the matter.

If you need to, be **persistent.** If you think the client or witness is withholding information for any reason, don't drop it. Move on to something else then come back to the subject again. Consider confronting them with your suspicions:

> *If you don't mind, let's go back over the reasons you had for wanting this divorce.*
> *Mrs. Brown, I may be mistaken here, but I get the impression you are reluctant to talk about the reasons for your divorce from your ex-husband. Am I right?*

Try to get the client **committed** to as much detail as possible. Obviously, if a person doesn't really know something, then that is the honest answer. We never want to influence people to say something they don't know or believe. But be sure that you find all that they do know, down to the last detail. Use **repetition** and proper phrasing of questions to get the client to commit on details.

> *And you're sure that he said. . .*
> *So what you're telling me is. . .*
> *Now if I understand you correctly, she. . .*

f. Ask for leads to witnesses and documents

Listen closely during the interview for the mention of other persons with knowledge of relevant facts or of documents. If the client doesn't mention it, ask if there are such persons or documents. If the client does mention it, ask if there are others. We are always interested in leads to more helpful information.

g. If helpful, have the client draw a sketch or diagram

Let the client illustrate what happened or what she saw if it will help your understanding of the events. In interviewing we are not limited to words. There is no reason that a client cannot be asked to draw something for us. That drawing or sketch can be helpful to refresh their recollection later and even become an important part of their testimony.

Most people will initially balk at being asked to draw or illustrate something, urging lack of talent for it. The interviewer needs to expect that, explain that talent doesn't matter, and encourage the client to give it a try. (See Hypothetical 11-4.)

The interviewer should ask the client to initial or sign the diagram or sketch to confirm that she did in fact draw it, and to date it. Witnesses may be providing a sketch of the same scene later and that will avoid confusion. In addition, the signature or initials placed on the client's or witness's sketches may help authenticate those sketches later for evidentiary purposes. (See Illustration 11-1.)

Any relevant distances shown on the sketch but not drawn to scale (and they almost never are) should be identified by estimated miles, yards, feet, inches, etc., as appropriate.

HYPOTHETICAL 11-4

Assume that Paul Perfect asks Harrison Bored to draw a sketch of the layout of the kitchen in Harrison Bored's house showing where Jessica Slang was found after the fall in relation to the refrigerator and island.

> **PP:** Mr. Bored, would you mind taking this sheet of paper and just sort of sketching the layout of the kitchen and where you first saw Ms. Slang on the floor after the fall?
> **HB:** Whoa, I don't know about that. I'm no artist.
> **PP** (laughing politely): I understand. I'm not either. But it really doesn't matter how well you can draw. It will help us sort of visualize how things looked so we can all get a better handle on it. (Extending sheet of paper and pen to HB.) Do you mind giving it a try?
> **HB:** Well, all right. Just don't enter this into any contest, okay?
> **PP** (laughing politely again): You got it.

The sketch that Harrison Bored draws for Paul Perfect can be seen in Illustration 11-1.

h. Establish an accurate chronology of events

The easiest way to understand and evaluate a situation is usually to establish the chronology of events. In most interviews this should be a specific goal of the interviewer. Ask specific detailed questions to get the sequence of events as clearly as the client can recall them. Leading questions can be helpful for this purpose (see Hypothetical 11-5).

Illustration 11-1   DIAGRAM OR SKETCH DRAWN IN INTERVIEW

It might even be helpful to have the client draw a **time line** for you. A time line that the interviewer might ask the client to draw in Hypothetical 11-5 might look like Illustration 11-2.

HYPOTHETICAL 11-5

Assume a paralegal (I) is interviewing a client (C) about his work history:

I: Now, let's see if I have this straight. You went to work at Marlin Enterprises on January 5, 2003, right?

C: That's right.

I: And you gave notice there the last day of March, 2003, is that correct?

C: No, it was the last day of May.

I: Okay, so it was the last day of May, 2003, when you gave notice to Marlin Enterprises, is that it?

C: Right, that's it.

I: And it was the last day of March, 2003, that you interviewed for the job at Weaver Company, is that right?

C: That's right. Now you've got it.

I: And you actually started working for Weaver on May 17, 2003, before you gave notice to Marlin Enterprises, is that correct?

C: Yes.

I: And then you were terminated by Weaver on February 3, 2004, is that right?

C: That's right.

It might even be helpful to have the client draw a **time line** for you. A time line that the interviewer might ask the client to draw in Hypothetical 11-5 might look like Illustration 11-2.

i. Clarify errors, inconsistencies, or vagueness in the client's story

Remember the first commandment of interviewing: *assume nothing.* Never simply assume that any person you interview, including the client, is giving you correct, complete, accurate, or even truthful information about everything. It may be helpful to review the realities we considered about people in connection with factual analysis in Chapter 1:

Illustration 11-2   TIME LINE DRAWN BY CLIENT

- Sometimes people lie.
- Sometimes people tell half-truths.
- Sometimes people are mistaken in what they thought they heard or saw.
- Sometimes people guess but don't tell you they're guessing.
- Sometimes people forget or misremember what they heard or saw in the past.
- Sometimes people make unwarranted assumptions and pass those assumptions off as fact.
- Sometimes people speak in conclusions that are not supported by fact.
- Sometimes people allow their prejudices to color what they "know."
- Sometimes people have only second- or third-hand information rather than first-hand information but leave it to the interviewer to figure that out.
- Sometimes people confuse their opinions with facts.
- Sometimes people are reluctant to tell what they know.
- sometimes two honest people can hear or see the same event and each describe it differently from the other.
- Sometimes the same types of inaccuracies and falsehoods get included in documents.

So we watch and listen for **inconsistencies** or **contradictions** and try to clear them up. Closed-ended, leading, or sometimes pressure questions are useful for this purpose.

Tell me again where you were at 3 P.M. that afternoon?
But you said that at 3 P.M. you were still at your house, isn't that right?
If you were still at your house at three that afternoon, how could you have seen her leave the office downtown a few moments after three?

j. Verify all information given as best you can

Remember the second commandment: *verify everything.* That means we:

- Attempt to determine if the *source* of the information is *competent, honest, reliable,* and *objective.*
- Try to filter out *opinions, guesses, assumptions,* and *statements of prejudice* to get to real provable fact.
- Distinguish between *first-hand information* and *second-* or even *third-hand information.*

SLEUTH ON THE LOOSE

Choose someone who is in the news right now, then access *www.newsville.com/ news/groups* and see what current articles you can find concerning that person.

We know from our study of the rules of evidence (see Chapters 6 and 7) about the importance of a witness who testifies at court speaking from personal knowledge. When a client tells you something, always determine the source of their knowledge—how do they know that? Is it something known to someone else that has been passed on to the client or is it even their guess or opinion?

And remember that people don't always express themselves clearly. A person may say they know something, or even that they "know it for a fact" when they don't know it at all in a factual, legal sense. They've heard it or believe it or assume it. It is the interviewer's job to sort out all the hyperbole and exaggeration.

k. Seek corroborating information

Closely related to the verification task is the need to seek *corroborating information*—information that confirms or supports what the client tells us. Ask about witnesses to the events that the client described. Ask about others who might know if there were other witnesses. Ask who else does or might have knowledge of things the client tells you. Ask about records, correspondence, or other documents that might confirm what the client is saying.

HYPOTHETICAL 11-6

Assume a paralegal (I) is interviewing a client (C) about the job history of a witness. Let's listen in:

C: Well, I can tell you he's never been able to hold down a job in his life.
I: Oh, really?
C: Absolutely.
I: Why do you say that?
C: Well, because I know it for a fact, that's why.
I: What jobs do you know of that he's had and then lost?
C: Why, that job over at the chemical plant for one. He didn't work there more than three months and they let him go.
I: You mean the Vestal Chemical Company plant here in Capital City?
C: That's the one.
I: And when did he work there?
C: Oh, I'm not sure of that. Probably two, three years ago.
I: And do you know for sure how long he worked for Vestal Chemical?
C: No, but I'd say it was no more than three or four months.
I: You're not sure, though.
C: No, I'm not positive on that.
I: And you say Vestal let him go?
C: That's what I heard.
I: Who did you hear that from?
C: Oh, you know, just talk around town.
I: So you can't remember the name of anyone in particular who told you that Vestal let him go?
C: No, not in particular.
I: Did he ever tell you that himself?
C: Him? No, he never told me that himself.
I: Could he have just been laid off in a slow period at the plant or in a reduction in force?
C: Well, I guess it could have been. I know he didn't work there long.
I: Is it possible he quit Vestal himself to go to work somewhere else?
C: I suppose it is.
I: What other jobs do you know of, other than the one at Vestal, that he's had and then lost?
C: Well, none I can call to mind, but I know there have been others.
I: How do you know there have been others?
C: I don't know, it just stands to reason there would have been. And I see him around town all the time and he ain't working.
I: So it's because you see him around town a lot that you think he must not be working?

SLEUTH ON THE LOOSE

Identify a large corporation then try to access information on the corporation at *www.switchboard .com*. While you are at that site, try searching for information about the company by type of industry and state. Then try the same with a smaller corporation.

C: That's right.

I: Or that he gets a job but can't keep it?

C: That's right, exactly.

I: But you don't know of any specific jobs—other than the one at Vestal Chemical—that he had and lost, is that right?

C: That's right, I guess.

I: And you don't know for sure whether he was fired from Vestal or just laid off with others, or quit, is that correct?

C: That's correct, uh-huh.

1. Compare the conviction of this client at the beginning of the interview to the admissions at the conclusion of it.
2. Do you think the client was being dishonest or deliberately misleading at the beginning of the interview or just overstating his knowledge without thinking?
3. If the interviewer had not attempted to pin down the sources of the client's professed knowledge, what misimpression could these statements have created in the mind of the supervising attorney?
4. What, factually, does this client really know about the job history of the person in question?
5. If the interviewer had delved into the motives of the client toward the person in question, what do you think he might have found? How would you ask such questions of this client?

l. Get the particulars on persons and documents mentioned

When the client mentions the names of others during the interview who might have information, it is not enough simply to get their names. You will need to know as much about them as possible to find them and interview them. Find out their full names, what names they go by, where they live, where they work, their phone numbers, the last time the client saw them, if they are still in town, if they've moved, who would know how to reach them, etc.

It is not enough to be told there might be other documents related to the client's matter. You need to know what documents, how they are titled, who has them now, can the client get them for you, if not who can, who has the originals, etc.

m. Review documents closely and copy or arrange to keep them

You will have briefly reviewed documents brought by the client at the beginning of the interview. But before it is over, take a break and look them over thoroughly. Determine if the documents the client has brought are originals and, if not, who has the originals. Make copies or make arrangements to keep the original documents. Be sure you understand all the information in the documents. If the documents are signed but not acknowledged, see if the client can identify (authenticate) the signatures or handwriting.

n. Determine what the client wants

One of the things that should come out of the initial client interview is a clear understanding of exactly what the client wants the attorney to do. From this will come the scope of the representation. Determining this may not be as easy as it sounds. Clients rarely come to the lawyer's office with a clear understanding of the law or their legal rights. Instead they come with a factual problem and maybe a poorly articulated request for some type of help—maybe not the kind of help that the lawyer can provide.

In addition, some clients relate facts about a number of different legal problems, but they may really only be seeking help with one of them. Or the attorney may only do work in one area in which they need help.

Of course, it is up to the supervising attorney to decide whether to undertake the representation and the scope of it. The job of the paralegal investigator is to get all the facts. But if what the client wants the lawyer to do is not made evident, ask the potential client that specifically and communicate the answer(s) to the attorney as best you can.

o. Check off the topics on your question list as you go
This helps ensure that you have covered everything you need.

4. Dealing with special problem clients

a. The reluctant client
People can be reluctant to tell us everything they know for any number of reasons. The interviewer has to recognize the reluctance and find a way to convince the client to open up. There are a number of approaches to consider in getting the reluctant witness to open up, depending on the cause of the reluctance.

1. A simple case of nerves. If the interviewer senses that it is a simple case of nervousness, the best approach may be to take a little more time to visit with the client. Be open, friendly, patient, and reassuring. Lean slightly closer to the client and maintain close eye contact. Let the client see that smile through your eyes. Try to identify with the client—talk candidly about how nerve-wracking you know it is to come to a lawyer's office.

2. Feelings of guilt, shame, or embarrassment. Sometimes people feel guilt over admitting some wrongdoing. They can also feel shame or embarrassment at having to disclose intimate facts about their circumstances. If the interviewer senses that the client is feeling guilt, shame, or embarrassment, the best approach may be to remind him of the attorney-client privilege. Nothing that is said is going to be repeated outside the office without the client's permission. A lower, quieter voice may be appropriate. Remember that the client would not have come to the lawyer's office if he didn't feel the need for help. Play on that by reminding the client, gently, that the attorney cannot help without full information.

3. Fear of providing harmful information. If the interviewer senses that the client is holding back bad news for fear of hurting his own case or exaggerating the information that might be favorable to the case, the best approach may be to stop and explain to the client that the attorney will need *all* information, good and bad, to be able to help him. Again, appeal to the fact that the client would not have come if he did not feel the need for help.

b. The highly emotional client

Clients can be highly emotional during the initial interview for any number of reasons. They may be deeply saddened by some personal loss, they may be frightened by an uncertain future, or they may be angry at some perceived injustice.

One general rule for dealing with the highly emotional client is to let him vent his emotions. The parents who have just lost a child—let them weep. The wife who has just been deserted by her no-good husband leaving her with three children and no money—let her cry and curse him. The businessman who believes he has just been cheated—let him call the wrongdoer colorful names. If the interviewer shows discomfort or disapproval of these displays of emotion, it alienates the client—the opposite of what we want. It also causes the client to internalize the emotions at a time when he needs to vent them so he can begin to think rationally. Give the client the opportunity to vent.

Empathize with the emotional client without getting too personally involved and without offering personal opinions about the matter. Acknowledge the right to be sad, afraid, or angry. After a while, take a break to give the client time to compose himself. Offer some refreshment.

If it becomes clear after a while that the client simply can't get past the emotion to think rationally, it may be appropriate to suggest rescheduling the conference.

c. The self-important or condescending client

Self-important or condescending clients may let you know in one way or another that it is beneath them to have to deal with a *mere* paralegal (or maybe even with a *mere* lawyer). They may presume that they know more about your business than you do and they—not you—will decide what you need to know about the case. These clients are a real headache, but don't reach for the aspirin just yet. There are ways to handle them.

Don't be intimidated by this client. That is the single biggest mistake you can make. If you are intimidated into not asking the questions you should, the attorney will be disadvantaged in trying to help the client. And you have reinforced the problem for future contacts.

Don't confront or offend this client, tempting though it may be. He is, after all, the *client,* the one the attorney bills and collects from in order to pay, among others, *you.* We can't just insult him and run him off. He may even be a good friend or business associate of the supervising attorney; insulting him could cost you your job.

Unfortunately, we have to stroke the ego of the self-important client—without patronizing—and ignore the condescension. The investigator may want to apologize for having to take the client's time to ask a few more questions. And patiently explain to the client that the attorney may need to know the information the client is objecting to providing in order to advise the client properly.

If none of those approaches work, then go to the supervising attorney, explain the situation to her, and suggest that it might be more appropriate for her to handle this interview.

d. The obviously lying client

As you have learned, we never assume the truth or accuracy of any information we receive, but always test it in various ways in order to verify it. Any time the interviewer senses that the client has told an untruth, first use your closed-ended, leading, or pressure questions to test the apparent misstatement and seek clarification.

But sometimes the interviewer comes across a client who lies and does not care about contradictions or inconsistencies being exposed. That's his story and he's sticking to it. In that situation, *non-hostile confrontation* is generally the next step. Tell the client in a soft but clear voice, with steady eye contact, that the client's case could be severely damaged by the attorney relying on incorrect information. If it is a litigation matter, remind the client that the opposing party at some point will probably be asking the same questions under oath in a deposition or in court and giving incorrect information in those circumstances could have serious consequences.

If non-hostile confrontation does not work, the paralegal should advise the supervising attorney at the earliest opportunity of her belief that the client is lying and let the attorney decide how to precede.

5. Concluding the client interview

- Be sure you have covered everything
- Be sure the client signs all authorizations
- Be sure that a plan of action has been discussed
- Give the client an opportunity to ask any other questions
- Advise the client not to discuss the case with others
- Give the client a business card
- Be cordial while walking the client out

HYPOTHETICAL 11-7

Assume that Paul Perfect is concluding his interview with Harrison Bored. Let's listen in one more time.

PP: Well, Mr. Bored, I believe we are about done. If you will, give me just a moment to look over my notes here.

HB (yawning and stretching): Sure.

PP (after looking over notes carefully): Okay, please sign this medical authorization I mentioned earlier so we can get your medical records from Tee Totaler. (Hands medical authorization to HB.) And this employment records authorization in the event we need to get those records. (Hands HB the employment record authorization and waits for him to sign.) Okay, great. Now, as I've mentioned, I will report promptly to Ms. Busy about what we've discussed here today. She will make the decision on taking your case and then either she or I will be in touch with you. We'll see where we are and go from there. Is that going to be okay?

HB: Sure, that's fine. I look forward to hearing from you.

PP: Remember not to discuss the case with anyone who may contact you about it. If you are contacted by an insurance company or an attorney for Jessica Slang, give them our name and number and tell them to contact us. Okay?

HB: Sounds good to me.

PP: Do you have any questions about anything?

HB: No, I can't think of anything.

PP: Well, if you do, don't hesitate to call me or Ms. Busy. (Rises and extends hand to HB.)

HB (rising and shaking hands with PP): I'll do that.

PP: And let me give you one of my business cards so the number will be handy. (Hands business card to HB.)

HB (taking card): Thanks.

PP (walking to the door with HB): Do you remember the way back to the reception area?

HB: I think so. Just to the right and down the hall, right?

PP: That's it. Take care and we'll be in touch shortly.

HB: I'll wait to hear. Thanks for everything.

6. The role of the paralegal when the supervising attorney conducts the interview

When the supervising attorney conducts the client interview the paralegal's role is to assist as requested. You may still be asked to schedule the interview and assist in preparing for it by arranging for the conference room, preparing forms to be signed, and even making suggestions regarding questions.

If you are asked to attend the interview with the attorney, be sure to take good notes. Suggest additional questions to the attorney as appropriate. Point out to the attorney discreetly—usually by written note handed to her—observations you make regarding the client or witness and areas you think might be explored further.

Also assist your supervising attorney by making sure all forms do get signed by the client at the conclusion of the conference and that everyone understands the next steps to be taken.

7. Following the interview

No matter who conducted the interview, the paralegal will typically have a number of responsibilities following the initial client interview.

a. If needed, do another conflict of interest check

During the interview the client may have provided you with additional names of persons whose involvement could give rise to a conflict.

b. Prepare an interview summary

An **interview summary** ought to be clear, organized, and thorough. If an intake sheet or checklist was used, the interview summary may be organized around its headings. In any event, the interview summary ought to contain, at a minimum, the following:

- a heading indicating the name of the client interviewed, the date of the interview, the file name and number;
- background information on the client;
- factual information gathered from the client in a logical order. As with the interview, the order may be chronological or topical, whichever is more appropriate for the particular case;
- the interviewer's observations and evaluation of the client in terms of demeanor, credibility, and reliability. Anything unusual or special that the interviewer noted, whether positive or negative, should be pointed out in the interview summary;
- a statement of the next steps agreed to at the conclusion of the interview;
- a listing of all authorizations and other documents signed during the interview and a statement of where the originals are;
- a listing of all documents provided by the client and an indication of where they are;
- the interviewer's conclusions and recommendations regarding what should be done next.

Illustration 11-3 contains some portions of the interview summary prepared by Paul Perfect following the interview of Harrison Bored.

c. Prepare a follow-up letter to the client

The **follow-up letter** should be signed by either the paralegal or the supervising attorney and will summarize the decisions made at or following the interview and enclose any additional documents that need to be signed. As with all correspondence signed by the paralegal, the supervising attorney should review and approve the letter before it is sent. A follow-up letter that Paul Perfect might draft for Betty Busy to send to Harrison Bored following the interview and the decision to take the case is shown in Illustration 11-4.

D. ▶ Subsequent Client Interviews and Contacts

You may have numerous opportunities to work with a client after the initial interview. Many of these contacts will be by phone call and letter. In all verbal and written communication with the client, remember to be polite but professional. (See Illustrations 10-2 and 11-4.)

Remember too the importance of maintaining a good working relationship with the client throughout the representation. The matter may continue for weeks, months, or for years. Always assume that a relationship you establish with a client will be long term. Not only does a good working relationship with a client enhance the likelihood of good results in the current representation, it also improves the chances for future representation in other matters. Repeat business from clients brings joy to an attorney's heart. And it is good news for the paralegal who makes it happen, too. The attorney will be more likely to remember you fondly at bonus time and good work tends to increase job security.

As we have noted, paralegals often have as much or more direct

Illustration 11-3   MEMORANDUM SUMMARIZING INITIAL CLIENT CONFERENCE

MEMORANDUM

TO: Betty Busy, Attorney
FROM: Paul Perfect, Paralegal
DATE: October 6, 2003
RE: Interview summary for potential client: Harrison Bored
              Client/File Number: 03-335-L

1. CLIENT BACKGROUND INFORMATION:

Harrison Bored (HB) was interviewed in our offices on October 5, 2003. HB is a 38-year-old Caucasian male, DOB 8-1-65. He lives at 111 Humphrey Bogart Lane, Capital City, Yourstate 44444 and has resided there for the past 12 years. He lives by himself since a divorce three years ago. He has no children. HB works as a district salesman for Hollywood Sports Equipment on Harvest Drive in the city. He has worked for Hollywood for almost ten years and before that worked two years for Oscar's Imports, also as a salesman. Oscar's went bankrupt in 1989. He is a 1987 graduate of State University, majoring in Business, and did a four-year tour of duty in the U.S. Army before going to work for Oscar's. Other background data includes:

Home phone: (111) 667-1234
Work phone: (111) 668-4321
Cellular phone: (111) 668-9876

2. FACTS:

A. History leading up to the party on August 28, 2003. The neighborhood in which HB lives is upper middle class and he advises that the neighbors are unusually friendly with each other. He says that block parties are organized several times a year and when anyone in the neighborhood has a party, everyone is invited. Jessica Slang (JS) lives only three houses down the street from HB at 117 Humphrey Bogart Lane. She is a divorcee who moved there with her two young children (a boy about 10 and a girl about 5) a little over two years ago. She has been active in neighborhood events as has HB so he has considered her a friend for some time. He denies any prior trouble with JS although he says he has noticed that she is somewhat of a heavy drinker at these neighborhood gatherings. He has heard her joke more than once at such parties that someone needs to drive her home even though she is within walking distance of her house and does walk, not drive, there.

HB says that JS is a realtor but is unsure of which realty company she is with. He believes her company specializes in commercial property. He describes her as intelligent, fairly attractive, and having a good personality. He thinks she is in her early 40s. He repeatedly stated during the interview that he was surprised when JS hit him in the nose and thinks she only did it because she had too much to drink that night. . . .

B. The August 28, 2003 party. HB says he planned the party as an end-of-summer fling. Everyone in the neighborhood was invited as usual. About 60 people were there and the party was held in the house and the backyard where he has a nice barbeque grill. The party started at 6 P.M. He doesn't recall exactly when JS arrived and has no idea if she came with anyone. She usually came to neighborhood events by herself he thinks. Pretty much everybody was drinking—beer and wine mostly—but there was some hard liquor there too. He has no idea what or how much JS drank before the fall and assault but she always drank and he believes she would have that night. He cannot recall smelling liquor on her when he tried to pick her up after the fall but says since everyone was drinking—including himself—the smell would have been in the air.

HB says that JS fell in the kitchen of his house. He has an island in the middle of the kitchen and the beer, wine, and liquor bottles were set out there. The fall occurred at around 9:30 P.M. He was not in the kitchen at the time and did not see it. He was out in the backyard tending the barbeque grill when another neighbor, Denzel Washingtub, told him that JS had fallen and was hurt and he had better come check on her. When he got to the kitchen several people were standing over JS who was laying on her back at the corner of the island nearest the refrigerator. A diagram that HB drew showing the layout of the kitchen and exactly where he saw JS is attached to this memo.

HB really doesn't recall everyone who was standing around JS. He sheepishly admits he had a few too many beers during the evening. He knows that Washingtub, a golfing buddy of HB, came to get him. And he remembers another man, Tom Shanks, bending over JS and asking her where it hurt. He also recalls hearing the shrill

Illustration 11-3 MEMORANDUM SUMMARIZING INITIAL CLIENT CONFERENCE *(continued)*

voice of a woman neighbor, Julia Sloberts, telling someone to call 911. He thought she would never shut up. HB located the phone numbers of these three witnesses for me in the phone book. They are:

Denzel Washingtub: Home—667-4356; Work—669-7777
Tom Shanks: Work—669-3680
Julia Sloberts: Home—668-0098

HB said that when he got to the kitchen and saw JS on the floor he immediately bent down and took her hand and asked her how she was. He didn't think to look at the floor to see what might have caused her to slip. There were 6 to 8 other people immediately around him and the rest of the kitchen was full of people, too.

It was while he was kneeling down beside JS that she threw the punch that caught him flush in the nose. He was on her left side holding her left hand and had just asked her how she was. He remembers that her eyes were closed when he first knelt beside her. When he spoke to her, her eyes opened and her right hand came out of nowhere to hit him. He knew his nose was broken immediately because he heard the crack. He recalls that it didn't hurt at first and his only impression was surprise that someone so little (JS is 5'2" and 110 lbs.) could throw such a punch from a prone position. He recalls too that as soon as JS hit him she closed her eyes again and smiled. The room went dead except for the ever noisy Julia Sloberts, who gasped and said, "Did you see that?". . .

D. Injuries and treatment for HB. HB has been seeing Dr. Samuel L. Jaxon whose offices are on Silver Screen Avenue next to City Hospital. HB did not seek treatment for his nose until the next morning (8-29) when he went to the City Hospital emergency room. His friend Denzel Washingtub, who lives on the next block from HB, drove him there. By that morning he says the nose was three times its normal size and a bright purple color. The nose was x-rayed in the ER and the break confirmed. Dr. Jaxon was called in by the ER staff physician whose name HB does not recall. Dr. Jaxon set the nose there in the ER and the brace he is currently wearing was placed on the nose. Dr. Jaxon told HB he will have to wear the brace for 30 days. He has been told that depending on how the break heals he may or may not need surgery later. HB has seen Jaxon twice since the brace was put on his nose. He has received bills for $250 so far from the ER and Jaxon and paid them. He brought the original bills and they have been placed in the file. He has a group medical insurance policy at Hollywood Sports but the deductible is $500. After he has met that, his share of the co-pay is 20%.

HB says the pain and discomfort have been terrific. He cannot breathe through his nose at all. Eating is painful and swallowing difficult. He has to take pain medication regularly (Percodan). Historically a good sleeper, he now has trouble going to sleep and wakes up several times a night.

HB's biggest concern is his livelihood. At Hollywood Sports he receives a base salary/draw of $2,000 each month and depends on commissions for other income. For the past three years his total income from Hollywood has been $79,000 ('02), $82,000 ('01), and $72,000 ('00). He has made $52,000 through August 2003. He missed three days of work following the assault, which will translate into lost commissions for September. Lower commissions don't reduce his monthly salary/draw unless they drop below the total draw amount for the year ($24,000), in which case he would have to repay the company for the difference. He is in no danger of that since he has had a good year so far, but believes his commissions will be reduced for the rest of the year due to missing time, not feeling well and, frankly, the ridiculous looking brace on his nose which turns customers off. . . . .

3. OBSERVATIONS AND EVALUATION:

HB is of medium height, about 200 pounds, bald-headed with a full beard going gray. He was dressed in a nice-looking sport coat and tie for the interview. He speaks with a distinct nasal sound due undoubtedly to the injury to his nose and the brace. I took several pictures of HB by Polaroid and those are in the file.

HB expresses himself well. He smiles easily and has a good sense of humor. He appears very much at ease. His years as a salesman seem to have helped him acquire good skills with people. He is polite and likeable and makes a good impression. He will make a good witness for himself.

HB also seemed forthright and credible. The only time in the interview when I sensed a lack of forthrightness was when I questioned him about the witnesses to the fall. When I asked him for detail about Julia Sloberts whom he had described as "shrill" and "near hysterical," his mood seemed to shift from pleasant to dark. A

Illustration 11-3   MEMORANDUM SUMMARIZING INITIAL CLIENT CONFERENCE *(continued)*

small frown creased his forehead, his eye contact diminished, and he became fidgety with his fingers. His answers to my questions about how well he knows Julia Sloberts were short and clipped. As summarized above, he denies knowing her well but I wonder if there is some history we need to explore further. . . .

4. DOCUMENTATION:

Currently in the file we have:

Suit papers filed by JS v. HB in State Superior Court on 9-20-03 and served on HB on 9-23-03
Signed medical authorization
Signed employment records medical authorization
Original statements for medical bills to date
Unsigned legal services contract already reviewed and approved
Copy of HB's homeowner's policy with Extra Safe Insurance Co.
35-mm pictures (3) of the floor where JS fell, taken after she had left and the party was over together with negatives
Polaroid pictures (5) taken by PP of HB with nose brace

If we undertake representation, HB is to provide us with:

Canceled checks for the medical bills paid to date
His employment contract with Hollywood Sports

5. RECOMMENDATIONS:

I believe the assault case of HB v. JS is a viable one. There are several witnesses to JS striking HB whom we should interview. At this time the only valid defense I can see that JS might raise to a claim of tortious battery is lack of intent if she was unconscious or semiconscious when she acted due to the fall or due to being intoxicated. But the force of her blow to HB and the smile on her face afterwards should cause her difficulty on such a defense. She appears to be a person of some means against whom a judgment could be collected. We know nothing of insurance for her as yet.

Regarding defense of the negligence suit of JS v. HB, the homeowner's policy does seem to provide coverage for that defense and the claim made in the suit papers ($100,000) is within the policy coverage limits of $250,000. We should contact, or have HB contact, the company regarding the claim promptly.

If our firm is retained to defend HB by the carrier, there are some unknowns. We don't know exactly what the substance on the floor was although there was something there on the floor according to HB. HB had not been in his kitchen in over an hour before the fall, so arguably did not create the hazard, whatever it was. The question may be whether he was negligent for NOT checking the kitchen area more frequently. But JS may have difficulty herself proving just what the hazard was which caused her to fall and how long it had been there for HB to find. Third-party negligence appears to be a valid defense on these facts—some other partygoer probably created the hazard. And comparative fault seems valid here since, at the least, JS was almost certainly somewhat incapacitated by drink herself (and voluntarily so) at the time of the fall.

The amount of damages incurred by HB is still open. We will need to wait and see what the prognosis is from Dr. Samuel L. Jaxon on the nose. And we will need to see how HB's commission income holds up during the remainder of the year. If you decide to take the case or look at it further, I recommend we proceed to:

interview the three witnesses we know of;
obtain the medical records to date on HB; and
obtain the additional documents requested from HB.

Please let me know how you would like to proceed.

Illustration 11-4   FOLLOW-UP LETTER TO CLIENT

Date

Mr. Harrison Bored
(Address)

Re: *Jessica Slang lawsuit*

Dear Mr. Bored:

As I indicated to you in our phone conversation earlier today, we will be pleased to represent you in connection with your claim against Jessica Slang. I am enclosing a legal services agreement in connection with your contemplated claim against Jessica Slang. Please review this agreement and call me with any questions you may have about it. If the agreement looks acceptable, please sign and date it where indicated and return it to us in the enclosed self-addressed stamped envelope. As soon as we receive the signed agreement back from you, we will undertake further investigation in your case.

Regarding the defense of the suit filed by Jessica Slang against you, and as you authorized in the telephone conversation this morning, we are sending a letter of notification to Extra Safe Insurance Co. formally notifying that company of the suit and of your request for defense. A copy of that letter is enclosed for your records. The company has the right, under the policy, to choose counsel to represent you in defending the suit. We have advised them in the letter that we will be representing you in your counterclaim against Jessica Slang and of your desire that we receive the defense assignment as well. We will advise you of their response. If you should hear from the company yourself please let us know right away.

Keep in mind, as we discussed today, that because the suit papers of Jessica Slang were served on you on September 23, 2003, you have only until October 23, 2003, to file an answer or other response with the court. If you fail to do that, a default judgment could be taken against you on her claim. Accordingly, we want to expedite the company's decision regarding your defense.

Please send us copies of your employment contract with Hollywood Sports and the canceled checks for medical bills paid to date.

We look forward to working with you on this matter. If you have any questions, please do not hesitate to call me or Mr. Perfect.

Sincerely,

Betty B. Busy
Attorney at Law

BBB/db

---

contact with clients than the attorney over the course of a case. That is both a responsibility for you and an opportunity.

Before you make a follow-up contact with a client by phone or letter, remember that it is just as important to prepare for and plan that contact, however brief, as it was to prepare for the initial contact. Before picking up the phone and calling the client, think carefully about what you want to accomplish in that phone call and how you want to handle that particular client. Make notes for yourself to use in the phone call so you don't forget anything. It is a waste of the client's time and unprofessional to have to make a second call and say, "Oh, there's something else I forgot to ask you."

Do the same planning before you write a letter to a client. What is it you want to say or accomplish with this letter and how can you best communicate with this particular client? And have you covered everything you need to before the letter goes to the supervising attorney for review and out to the client?

Keep in mind the ethical and professional responsibility we have to keep the client reasonably informed regarding the status of the representation. The client is entitled to be advised promptly about every development in the case. Even if nothing is going on in a client's case at the time, it is a good idea to periodically touch base with them by phone or letter to let them know their matter is not being neglected. One of the most frequent ethical complaints made against attorneys is that they do not keep the client adequately informed about the matter. Conversely, one of the nicest things a client can experience is to be contacted by the attorney's office with an update on the case even when he wasn't requesting an update or expecting the contact. When paralegals do things like that for a client, the client doesn't forget. And that's when the client says good things to the attorney about the paralegal.

Finally, always return a client's call promptly—the same day if at all possible. And remember the importance of meeting deadlines for getting documents organized and drafted or locating information. Meet your deadlines, and work patiently but firmly to help clients meet theirs.

KEY WORDS AND PHRASES TO REMEMBER

active listening
body language
condescending client
corroborating information
emotional client
empathy
flexible
follow-up letter
initial client interview
intake sheet

internal barriers
interview checklist
interview summary
lying client
narrative summary
non-hostile confrontation
reluctant client
repetition
self-important client
time line

LEARN BY DOING

LBD 11-1. Conduct the interview of the client in one of the following cases from Appendix A assigned to you by the instructor. Then prepare a memorandum to your instructor containing an interview summary and a follow-up letter to the client.

    a. Case Study No. 1 (The Rowdy Outlaw Case) Rowdy Outlaw
    b. Case Study No. 2 (The Soupspoon Wise Case) Soupspoon Wise
    c. Case Study No. 3 (The Vidalia Unyon Case) Vidalia Unyon
    d. Case Study No. 4 (The Rocky Road Project) Rocky Road

Chapter 12

Preparing for a
Witness Interview

CHAPTER OBJECTIVES

In this third chapter on interviewing we turn our attention to the fact witness. In this chapter we will learn how to prepare for the fact witness interview. You will learn:

- The goals to be accomplished in the witness interview.
- The different kinds of witnesses the paralegal is called upon to interview.
- How to communicate with the witness to schedule an interview.
- The steps that interviewers go through to prepare for an effective witness interview.
- The special considerations that go into preparing for a field interview.
- The importance of using active listening skills and observing the witness's environment.

A. ► Introduction

As discussed in Chapter 10, a fact witness, as distinguished from a client or a non-witness information source, is a person who has or who might have knowledge of facts directly relevant to the matter being handled for the client. In this chapter we will consider why the investigating paralegal conducts interviews with fact witnesses, the different kinds of witnesses encountered in interviewing, and procedures for scheduling and preparing for the interview of a fact witness.

B. ► Goals of the Witness Interview

There are a number of goals to be achieved in the interview of a fact witness and several or all of them may need to be achieved in a single interview. Illustration 12-1 summarizes these goals.

C.   Kinds of Witnesses

Witnesses can be categorized in different ways depending on their personalities and their attitudes toward being interviewed. We will consider here a number of different types of witnesses. Different kinds of witnesses call for different approaches and interviewing techniques.

However, categorizing witnesses has its dangers too. Any given witness may fall into more than one of these categories (e.g., they may be friendly but nosey). Also, witnesses may initially impress you as being of one type, but as the interview progresses you realize they are of another (e.g., they start out skeptical but become too helpful). Never be too quick to categorize a person as one type or another. With those caveats in mind, consider the various witness types.

1. The friendly witness

Friendly witnesses are those who, for whatever reasons, look favorably on your client or on you. They will cooperate in scheduling the interview and will be as helpful as they can during it. The friendly witness is therefore the easiest to interview in many ways. But be careful. Don't let his cooperative attitude keep you from asking the tough questions you may need to ask.

And be aware that whatever makes them friendly toward you or your client (e.g., they are friends or relatives of the client) may be used by the opposing side to show bias or interest (e.g., that friendly witness is an employee of the client—and wants to keep his job!). In interviewing the friendly witness try to anticipate a suggestion of bias by the opposing party and give the witness an opportunity to reject that bias as a motive for what they are saying. (See Hypothetical 12-1.)

2. The hostile witness

This is the witness who, for whatever reasons, does not look favorably on your client or you. This witness will not want to cooperate in granting an interview or to say anything helpful if they are prevailed upon to grant one.

Illustration 12-1   GOALS TO BE ACHIEVED IN A FACT WITNESS INTERVIEW

1. Find out in detail everything the witness knows about the subject we are interested in.
2. Discover all documents and things the witness may have access to that relate to the subject we are interested in.
3. Discover leads to other witnesses or other documents and things to which the witness may be able to direct us.
4. Observe the witness for purpose of evaluating his strengths and weaknesses, credibility, effectiveness as a witness, cooperativeness, etc.
5. Get the witness committed to a particular version or recollection of the incident.
6. If the witness can damage our client's position, look for information the supervising attorney may use to discredit or impeach that witness including inconsistencies, bias, interest, or unreliability.

How do we convince a hostile witness to even grant us an interview? Here are several suggestions:

a. Be friendly and patient with the witness

The hostile witness may frustrate you by promising to call you back and then not doing so or promising to show and then canceling. But most people feel guilty about acting so rudely, and a little polite persistence may pay off.

b. Try to get the witness to like you

If it is your client whom the witness does not like, try to get the witness to like you. In your conversations with him, not only bowl him over with politeness, but try to find common ground. Use his name frequently to personalize the conversation. He may eventually agree to cooperate because he likes you, even if he still detests your client.

c. Use the witness's natural instinct to help

People have a natural urge to help others; it is ingrained in us. Most people want to help others because it's polite or the right thing to do. Almost everyone today has worked in a service industry where helping the customer was a priority. Use this knowledge to your advantage in working with hostile witnesses. Let them know you need their help and that no one else can provide the information they have. Join that approach with appreciation for the sacrifice of time they are making to do this and an assurance that you will not waste their time.

d. Use subpoena power as a motivator—if you must

As a *last resort*, consider reminding the hostile witness that the supervising attorney can utilize the subpoena to compel his attendance at a formal deposition, which may be set at a much less convenient time and place and involve more time and lawyers, etc.

If the hostility of the witness becomes apparent only during the interview, sometimes the suggestions above can be used then to engender a little cooperation. But sometimes you just have to do the best you can in a difficult situation. Don't be intimidated by the hostile witness into forgoing questions you really need to ask.

HYPOTHETICAL 12-1

Assume that paralegal Dee Termined works for an attorney representing N. Big Trouble, a business owner whose business has been sued. The issues in the suit go back to a time when N. Big Trouble owned the business with another man, Dis Gruntled. N. Big Trouble bought out Dis Gruntled's interest in the business last year. The attorney for N. Big Trouble needs information from Dis Gruntled. Unfortunately, N. Big Trouble and Dis Gruntled did not part on good terms. Dee Termined places a call to Dis Gruntled to see if she can schedule a conference with him.

DG (answering phone): Hello?
DT: Is this Dis Gruntled?
DG: Yes it is.

DT: Mr. Gruntled, my name is Dee Termined. I am a paralegal in the office of attorney Smart Thinkin. We represent N. Big Trouble, a former business partner of yours. I'm calling to see if I could arrange to speak with you briefly about the business you and Trouble owned.

DG: N. Big Trouble? No way I'll help. That guy's a thief as far as I'm concerned. He ran our business into the ground and then forced me to sell out to him for next to nothing.

DT: Yes, sir, Mr. Gruntled. I understand that you and Mr. Trouble had your differences when he bought out your interest.

DT (raising his voice): Differences! That's an understatement. Ma'am, I'm sorry, but I can't help you. N. Big Trouble in my opinion is a no-good cheat and a lousy businessman.

DT: I understand how you feel, Mr. Gruntled. Anyone would have a right to be upset if they felt they weren't treated right. And I certainly am not trying to change your mind about. . .

DG (laughing derisively): Well, that's a good thing, let me tell you, because you couldn't change my mind about that skunk in a million years.

DT (laughing politely as if DG has said something amusing and without malice): Mr. Gruntled, you sound as hard-headed as me. My daddy always told me that a hard head and thick skin were the two greatest assets you could have in business.

DG (laughing politely himself and without derision this time): Well, your daddy was a wise man, I'd say.

DT: Well, I always thought so and I appreciate you saying that. Mr. Gruntled, I truly do understand your feelings and I am simply trying to get some information I need about the business while you were still there. If you could accommodate me with just a few moments of your time, I'll promise to be brief and then get out of your hair.

DG (laughing easily now): Oh, I didn't mean to take all that out on you. Sure, I'll give you a few moments—just don't bring the bum with you!

1. What techniques did Dee Termined use to convince Dis Gruntled to grant her an interview?
2. Identify each point in this conversation when Dee Termined could have given up.
3. Identify the place in this conversation when it first appeared that Dee Termined was going to win over Dis Gruntled.

If the hostile witness has given you information that hurts your client, you will want to bring out the reasons for the hostility. It may be best to do this at the end of the interview. Your supervising attorney may be able to use this information to show bias or interest and thus discredit the witness.

3. The neutral or disinterested witness

This is the witness who doesn't feel strongly one way or the other about the matter you are interested in. If the neutral witness will cooperate in giving the interview, he tends to make a credible, reliable witness who will not fabricate or exaggerate.

Assume that Dee Termined is also assigned to interview Reluc Tant, a supplier who has done business with the company owned by N. Big Trouble. The problem is that Reluc Tant is also a customer of the company that is suing N. Big Trouble's company and doesn't want either side to get upset with him. He is, shall we say, reluctant to get involved!

RT (after listening to DT explain why she is calling): Oh, boy. I was afraid someone would call about that mess. Listen, isn't there someone else you can talk to about this?

DT: Well, Mr. Tant, we are talking to everyone who might know something but, unfortunately, that's just it, we have to talk to everybody.

RT (sighing): Well, I know what's between the rock and the hard place now. I just don't think I can afford to get involved in this. I don't have a dog in the fight but. . .(lets his voice trail off)

DT: Mr. Tant, I know what a pain it is to get drawn into this. And I understand that you do business with both of these parties. But keep in mind that all we want you to do is tell us what you know and what you recall. I think both sides would want you to do that.

RT: Maybe so, but you just never know who's going to get mad at you and that's grief I don't need, let me tell you.

DT: I understand what you're saying. But I hope you understand that Mr. Trouble really needs your help here. A lot of people know a few things. But frankly, Mr. Tant, no one knows what you do. And what you know could be critical to a full understanding of what went on last year. If that doesn't come out, then Mr. Trouble stands to lose his entire business and could be facing bankruptcy. I know you don't want that to happen to him, or anybody.

RT: I know, I know. It's just. . . (lets voice trail off again)

DT: And I promise not to take any more of your time than is absolutely necessary. I know how busy you are. The sooner all of us can get this behind us the better.

RT: That's for doggone sure. All right, when do you want to do this?

1. What techniques did Dee Termined use to convince Reluc Tant to grant her an interview?
2. Identify each point in this conversation when Dee Termined could have given up.
3. Identify the place in this conversation when it first appeared that Dee Termined might win over Reluc Tant.

4. The skeptical witness

This is the disinterested witness who just doesn't want to get involved. This person may be suspicious of you or your motives or just reluctant to go to the trouble. Consider using the friendly, common-ground, and urge-to-help approaches discussed in connection with the hostile witness. For example, if your supervising attorney is representing a person injured in an accident, consider telling the skeptical witness a little about the person's injuries and his or her need for the witness's cooperation (though, of course, nothing confidential or privileged). In other words, play on the witness's sympathies. Shameless maybe, but effective.

5. The nosey witness

Beware of the witness who asks a lot of questions about the case. Some people are intrigued to be involved in a live case. They get excited and want to know details. You may feel pressure to satisfy their desire for details in hopes of obtaining the cooperation. Certainly you want to be friendly toward any cooperating witness, but resist the urge to share details you shouldn't. It's part of being professional.

6. The busy witness

Many witnesses are reluctant to submit to an interview at all because they are busy ("I would like to help but I really don't have time"). Or they grant you an interview but hurry you through it directly ("Are we about done?") or indirectly (looking at their watch every ten seconds). Some witnesses really *are* busy and it really *is* a favor for them to grant us an interview. Many public officials fall into this category. Others just *think* they are that busy. Whichever it may be, we generally gain nothing by suggesting to this witness that they really *do* have time for us.

Instead, treat the busy witness much like you would the skeptical witness. To get the busy witness to cooperate, be outspokenly considerate of his time and grateful for his willingness to give you even a little piece of it. You may want to use the urge-to-help/play-on-their-sympathies approach if needed. See Hypothetical 12-2.

When a busy witness does grant you an interview, be respectful of his wish to expedite the matter. Don't engage in more than brief greetings at the beginning, and avoid extended chitchat. Express your appreciation for his cooperation, assure him you will be as brief as you can, and honor that. But always be sure to do a thorough job. Don't let the busy witness hurry you so much that you skip questions that should be asked or neglect to follow up on answers or observations.

7. The too-helpful witness

Every interviewer loves the helpful, cooperative witness. But some witnesses can be too helpful. They try to guess what we want them to say and then they say it. They agree with everything we say. They accept every characterization we make. They make few or no suggestions themselves that would contradict anything they think favors our client. Something may be wrong here.

Frequently, the too-helpful witness is a relative or close friend of the client. Instead of being candid and truthful, they are just saying what they think will help the most. It is dangerous to rely on such information or for the attorney to put someone like that forward as a testifying witness.

If you sense during an interview that a witness is being too helpful, don't accuse him of it directly. Instead, politely remind him of your need to obtain candid information about the case or matter, whether it is helpful or hurtful to the client.

8. The show-off witness

These are witnesses who feel the need to impress you. They may be name-droppers. Or they may boast of other cases in which they have testified (and probably won the case singlehandedly). Or they may tell you that they have been urged for years to go to law school or run for president and are just flipping burgers until they decide. What a pain, right?

Tolerance but persistence are the keys to handling show-off witnesses. If you don't tolerate them, you will offend them and lose their cooperation. On the other hand, if you encourage them you will never get to what you need to know from them. So, tolerate their boasting with a smile and an occasional "Oh, really" or "Uh-huh," but don't ask follow-up questions about the boasting. Lead them back to the subject you need them to talk about.

9. The big-ego witness

Closely related to the show-off witness is the witness with the big ego. The difference between these two types is that the show-off witness is usually a *wannabe,* whereas the big-ego witness has made it at something, and everyone—including you—simply *must* acknowledge it!

What has the big-ego witness made it at? It can be anything—business, politics, sports, a profession (some lawyers and doctors are among the worst offenders). But whatever it is, they will either expect you to know or will let you know quickly. Some will let you know directly ("Hello, I'm Big Shot. That's the Shot in Shot, Snooty, and Proud, you know.") or indirectly (look at all those pictures of famous people on this guy's wall!). Certainly not every successful person has an out-sized ego, but when it happens it must be dealt with.

Unfortunately, with the big-ego witness, you're usually going to have to do a little stroking if you want cooperation. So stifle the urge to pop his balloon. Let him feel important and give you the tour of the trophy case. Laugh at his jokes and compliment his achievements. Eventually he will reward you with his attention. At the same time, avoid obvious pandering to this kind of witness. If he catches you doing that, it will turn him off and you will lose his cooperation.

10. The condescending witness

Closely related to the big-ego witness is the condescending witness. This is the person who, for whatever reason, looks down on you. It may be a big ego, but more frequently it is something this person perceives or assumes about you that triggers the condescension. It may be that you're young and he assumes you cannot possibly know what you are doing. It may be that you are not a lawyer and he is offended the lawyer isn't there but instead sent the "hired help." The racial- or gender-biased witness you will occasionally encounter falls into this category as well. And often, with this type of witness, the condescension expresses itself with a hostile or too-busy attitude that we have already considered.

The condescending witness is generally best treated by ignoring the condescension and doing your job. If you do that, with many of these people, you will win their respect—and respectful treatment—before you are done. It may be difficult, but remember the number one priority is to get the job done for the client, not to seek redress for your own wounded feelings.

11. Special problem witnesses

a. Language barriers

What about the witness who speaks little or no English? If communication in English is possible but difficult, consider speaking slower than usual in the interview. Also use simple words and short sentences. If communication in English really isn't feasible, then locate a reliable interpreter. Today many courts maintain a list of interpreters for use in formal proceedings and your court clerk may be able to help you locate one. High schools and colleges, churches, the local bar organization, as well as social organizations are also good sources to locate interpreters.

b. Physical barriers

What about the witness who is hearing-impaired or deaf? If appropriate, arrange to sit closer to the hearing-impaired witness, speak a little louder, try to speak so that the witness can see your face (many hearing-impaired persons are lip and expression readers), speak slower, and consider using simpler words and shorter sentences. Offer to repeat yourself, and be willing to do so patiently. Watch for tell-tale signs of hearing impairment—a hearing apparatus in or near the ear, a person turning one ear toward you when you speak, a pattern of asking you to repeat a question, or answers that reflect that the witness does not understand.

For the truly deaf witness, inquire without embarrassment about their ability to lip-read. Or a qualified signer may be engaged to assist. The courts, schools, and churches are good sources to locate persons qualified to sign and interpret for the hearing-impaired.

c. Mental barriers

What about the witness who is slow of mind? If the problem appears to be a serious one, there may be a question of minimal competence to understand a question and provide a rational answer. The interviewer must simply do the best she can and report back to the supervising attorney her observations and impressions of the witness. Use simple words and short sentences, speak slowly, and be ready and willing to repeat a question or ask it in a simpler way. Also be sure not to appear condescending or impatient with such a witness.

d. The Romeo (or Juliet!)

Who needs it, right? But it happens. How do you handle the witness who appears interested in, shall we say, more than just your questions? The rule here is to be professional. Be friendly but firm about focusing on the interview. Don't flirt back or lead the witness on in order to secure his cooperation. You will have a bigger problem later and a far less cooperative witness when he realizes what you've done.

But what if you like him too? Remember that the job comes first. Not only are you there to conduct an interview on behalf of a client but personal relationships with witnesses can produce conflict of interest problems for you and your supervising attorney. Better to wait until the case is over, or at least the witness's role in it, before you show an interest in, shall we say, more than just his answers!

Of course, if you have a more serious problem, a groper for example, or someone who is just too aggressive to feel comfortable around, use your sound judgment and protect yourself. If you have reason before the interview to believe the witness will be this way, take someone with you. Or if it happens unexpectedly in your office, ask someone else to come in. But if you're on the witness's turf—home or office—get out of there. Report the situation to the supervising attorney. No interview is worth endangering yourself or tolerating outrageous behavior.

e. The witness for sale

This does not happen often, but it is always a serious matter. You arrive for an interview and the witness either directly or indirectly suggests that some compensation could make a difference in his memory. Do not ever respond to such a suggestion in any way that could be considered positive. Don't go along with him just to see what he has in mind. Tell the person in a friendly way, but very clearly, that you cannot even consider that suggestion for both legal and ethical reasons. Tell him that you certainly want him to tell the complete truth and you are sure that's what he wants to do as well.

Report this event to your supervising attorney immediately and document in the file what was said and done. Do not ever leave yourself open to a later charge that you initiated such an offer, or considered it, or did anything other than reject it.

HYPOTHETICAL 12-3

Assume that attorney Betty Busy has assigned her paralegal, Paul Perfect, to conduct witness interviews with Tom Shanks, Denzel Washingtub, and Julia Sloberts in the Harrison Bored case. (Review Hypotheticals 10-1 and 10-2 and the sample interview summary in Illustration 11-3.) Paul Perfect has learned from the client that Denzel Washingtub is an insurance agent, and a close friend and regular golfing buddy of the client as well. When Paul contacted Denzel Washingtub by phone to arrange the interview, Washingtub told him he would do whatever he could for Bored and would rearrange his schedule to accommodate Paul Perfect as soon as possible.

1. In which witness category(s) would you suggest that Paul Perfect place Denzel Washingtub as he prepares for this interview?
2. In what ways might the interview with Washingtub be easy for Paul Perfect?
3. In what ways might the interview with Washingtub be difficult for Paul Perfect?
4. What recommendations would you make to Paul Perfect as he prepares for this interview?

Paul Perfect has learned from the client that Tom Shanks is president and sole owner of Shanks Motors, which operates new and used car dealerships all over the state. Harrison Bored told Perfect he doesn't know Shanks well and only met him at the party. Shanks doesn't live in Harrison Bored's neighborhood and was attending the party with a girlfriend who does, Sandra Tullock. Bored has told Paul Perfect that Shanks is a self-made multimillionaire who has powerful local, state, and national political connections and possible political aspirations himself. When Perfect called his office for an appointment, he could not get through to Tom Shanks himself. Instead, he was transferred to several different people. Finally someone identifying herself as Shank's appointments secretary told him Tom Shanks could see him for 15 minutes a week from Friday at 7 A.M. in Shank's office.

1. In which witness category(s) would you suggest that Paul Perfect place Tom Shanks as he prepares for this interview?
2. In what ways might the interview with Tom Shanks be easy for Paul Perfect?
3. In what ways might the interview with Tom Shanks be difficult for Paul Perfect?
4. What recommendations would you make to Paul Perfect as he prepares for this interview?

Paul Perfect has learned from the client that Julia Sloberts is an accountant with a local accounting firm, Debit & Credit. When Perfect called Sloberts at the accounting firm to schedule the interview, she hesitated a long time before agreeing to the interview. Even after agreeing to do it, she protested that she really didn't know anything that could help Harrison Bored, that this was her busiest season at work, that the interview would have to be somewhere other than her office, and that Paul Perfect would have to make it a quick interview.

1. In which category(s) would you suggest that Paul Perfect place Julia Sloberts as he prepares for this interview?
2. In what ways might the interview with Julia Sloberts be easy for Paul Perfect?
3. In what ways might the interview with Julia Sloberts be difficult for Paul Perfect?
4. What recommendations would you make to Paul Perfect as he prepares for this interview?

D.   Scheduling and Preparing for the Witness Interview

The student should review the material regarding scheduling and preparing for the initial client interview covered in Chapter 10. That material is largely applicable here.

1. Scheduling the witness interview

Witness interviews are scheduled much as initial client interviews are, usually by phone call. Let's briefly review those procedures here and then we will look at some special considerations for scheduling the witness interview.

Before calling the witness to schedule the interview, the paralegal should:

- Check all participants' schedules
- Have several dates and times in mind
- Plan for plenty of time to conduct the interview
- If the interview is to be conducted in the paralegal's office, make sure the interview room is available
- Make a list of what the witness needs to bring

When the paralegal calls the witness to schedule the interview, the paralegal should:

- Identify himself as a paralegal
- Cover all the necessary details including time and place of the interview, what to bring, and directions if the witness is traveling to the interview, or directions you need to reach the witness
- Take comprehensive notes

After concluding the scheduling call, the paralegal should:

- Confirm the reservation of the conference room
- Notify other participants of the date and time
- Enter the date and time in the docket control system
- Send a confirmation letter to the witness
- Prepare a memorandum summarizing the call
- Place all notes in the client file

2. Preparing for the witness interview

Preparation for a witness interview is much the same as preparing for a client interview, but because the goals of the witness interview differ from those of the client interview (compare Illustration 10-1 and Illustration 12-1), that will affect preparation. In preparation for a witness interview, the paralegal will:

- Prepare needed authorizations
- Prepare questions by
  - reviewing the file;
  - considering the legal issues presented in the case;
  - considering any known special needs of the witness;
  - brainstorming a list of topics to be covered;
  - organizing the topics in a chronological or topical fashion;
  - preparing specific questions;
  - putting questions in a format consistent with any checklist being used;
  - putting questions in a format conducive to taking good notes; and
  - being flexible—expect to ask more or different questions during the interview

- Have the supervising attorney review all questions and forms
- Prepare the interview room
- Consider any special needs of the witness
- Plan the seating arrangement
- Make arrangements to avoid interruptions
- Prepare yourself physically and mentally for the interview

3. Special considerations in scheduling and preparing for a witness interview

There are some special considerations that apply to scheduling and preparing for the interview of a fact witness as opposed to a client.

a. Contacting a witness represented by counsel

The paralegal should never contact a witness without the permission of the supervising attorney. And remember that it is unethical and unprofessional to make direct contact with someone who we know is represented by counsel. We are to deal with that person's attorney.

If you are already speaking to a witness when he advises you that he has an attorney, immediately ask for the name and phone number of the attorney. Explain that you did not know he had counsel and that you are obligated to speak to the attorney first. You cannot continue to speak with the person directly *even if he tells you it's okay!*

End the phone call without discussing the substantive matter any further. Then advise your supervising attorney of this development and, if he authorizes, contact the other attorney. Disclose to the other attorney that you did speak to his client but did not know of the representation and that as soon as you learned of it you terminated the conversation. (Your supervising attorney may want to make this explanation to the other attorney.)

b. Preserving client confidences and secrets

In dealing with witnesses, we must be careful to avoid disclosing any confidential or secret information or any information related to the attorney's case strategy. This can be a challenge when confronted with a friendly but inquisitive witness, a relative or friend of the client, or the reluctant witness who demands to know exactly why she should cooperate.

The problem can arise when the interview is being scheduled and the witness is asking questions. It can also arise during the interview if the witness asks to see information in the possession of the interviewer or is able to see it because of the seating arrangements.

c. Don't use tricks

Never use deceit or make false promises to a witness to gain his cooperation.

I'll take no more than ten minutes of your time, I promise.
If we can talk with you now, you won't be bothered with this matter any more.

These tactics do far more harm than good in the long run. When the interview begins, the witness will quickly realize he has been duped. He may become uncooperative or even hostile—then you can forget about getting his help later in the case.

d. The location of the witness interview—the field interview

One significant difference between client and witness interviews is where the interview occurs. The witness interview usually will occur in a place selected by the witness. That may be the office or home of the witness. Or we may have to go to the hospital where the witness is a patient or the nursing home where they are a resident. Certainly clients are sometimes interviewed outside the law office. Sometimes cooperative witnesses will come to our offices. But most witness interviews are **field interviews**—those conducted outside the office of the interviewer.

That means the interviewer has little or no control over the location or environment of the interview. It may be noisy, dirty, busy, cold, hot, crowded, and so on. The significance of this for our preparation is that we must generally be prepared for anything and surprised by nothing! We have to adapt to the circumstances we find and still do our jobs.

The interviewer's lack of control over the environment of field interviews also presents an important opportunity. The interviewer gets to see the witness in his own environment. If we are the careful observers we have been trained to be (see Chapter 8), that can provide us an abundance of helpful information about the witness.

HYPOTHETICAL 12-4

Assume that Paul Perfect is scheduled to interview Tom Shanks this afternoon at 3 P.M. At noon he gets a call from the secretary for Shanks who tells him that Shanks has a business emergency that will require him to leave for Europe immediately. He won't be back for a month so if Paul wants to interview him before that he should come to Shank's office right away. Fortunately, our man Paul Perfect is ready for this interview, so he grabs his coat and races over to Shank's office.

When Paul Perfect arrives in the reception area he sees a small crowd of people walking toward him, surrounding a well-dressed middle-aged man whom he takes to be Tom Shanks. As this group of chattering people passes by Paul, a man reaches out and grabs his arm. He says, "Are you the one from the lawyer's office?" Paul says he is, and he is then pulled into the little group going out the office door, down the elevator, and into a waiting limousine.

In the back of the limousine Paul finds himself facing Tom Shanks, who is on the phone. Beside Paul sits a woman looking at papers and dictating into a hand-held Dictaphone. Beside Shanks sits a younger man who looks at his watch, and tells Paul they will be at the airport in ten minutes and he can ask Shanks questions on the way.

When Shanks gets off the phone, Paul starts to introduce himself but Shanks pays no attention to him and instead gives some orders to the young man next to him who then gets on the phone. Finally, Shanks looks at Paul and says, "Did you need to ask me something?"

1. How would you be feeling in Paul Perfect's position? Confident? Ready for that interview?

2. Should Paul Perfect make some light conversation at this point to break the ice?
3. What should Paul Perfect do and say at this point?
4. What should Paul Perfect's demeanor be at this point?

Paul Perfect finds Tom Shanks responsive to his questions and quite helpful about the events at the party involving Jessica Slang. However, he has to sit with his knees drawn up nearly to his chin to ensure that the woman sitting next to him cannot observe his notes or other documents in the file. Moreover, the limousine arrives at the airport in what seems like two minutes instead of ten. As the limo pulls to a stop in front of the terminal and the doors fly open, Paul has time to say, "I have a few more questions if I may." Shanks and the young man whisper to each other and the young man says to Paul, "You can walk with him into the terminal. We don't have time to wait here."

Paul Perfect finds himself trotting through the airport terminal beside a briskly moving Shanks. He is trying to ask questions, take notes, and watch where he is going all at the same time. Shanks answers his questions while giving orders to his two associates about luggage and tickets and business matters. Shanks dashes into the men's room and tells Paul to stand at the door and keep asking his questions. Paul does so but gets a number of funny looks from other men coming in and out of the restroom.

The group finally makes its way to a long line of people waiting to pass through the metal detector. In front of them a mother holds a crying baby. A screaming toddler pulls at her skirt. Behind them two men are arguing in a language Paul does not recognize. Shanks doesn't seem fazed. The young man who is Shank's assistant looks at his watch again and says, "It's going to be close." Just then the toddler in front of Paul Perfect deposits his last meal (which happened to be strawberry ice cream) on Paul's new loafers.

1. How would you be doing in Paul's position now? Are we having fun? Glad you decided to become a paralegal?
2. Why was Paul so concerned about the young woman next to him in the limousine being able to see his notes and other materials? Was he overreacting?
3. Should Paul ask the mother to try and keep her children quiet or to clean up his shoes? Should he ask the men behind him to take their argument outside?
4. Should Paul suggest that Tom Shanks sit down with him for a few moments to finish the interview?
5. Should Paul give up and tell Tom Shanks he will call when Shanks returns to the country?
6. What should Paul do at this point?

Having passed through the metal detector, Shanks and his two associates are now sprinting toward the departure gate. Paul Perfect is struggling to keep up and wishing he was in better shape. (He's also thinking that they didn't cover this in any paralegal course he ever took!) Paul has never heard himself talk while sprinting; he sounds funny to himself.

As they arrive at the departure gate, a flight attendant opens the door leading out to the jet and the noise of the jet engines fills the concourse, along with the smell of jet fuel and a blast of hot air. Now Paul has to shout to be heard. Shanks shouts his answers back as he waits in line to board. By the time they reach the ticket agent collecting the tickets of the boarding passengers, they are absorbed in the questions and answers. Shanks hands the agent his ticket and moves toward the plane. Paul Perfect feels a hand on his chest and an anxious voice asks, "Do you have a ticket, sir?" Paul realizes he is about to commit a federal offense and stops. He looks up in time to see Shanks wave at him as he boards the plane.

Later that evening, back at the office, Betty Busy sticks her head in Paul's office. "How did the interview with Tom Shanks go?" she asks.

Paul thinks a moment about how to answer and then says, "Perfect. Just perfect."

e. Telephone interviews and recording or video taping interviews

Witness interviews are frequently conducted by telephone and frequently recorded or video taped than are client interviews. We will consider recording/video taping interviews and the telephone interview in detail in Chapter 13.

f. Planning multiple witness interviews

The investigating paralegal will frequently be assigned to interview more than one witness in a given case. In that event, consideration should be given to the logical order in which the witnesses should be interviewed. It may be chronological—who was involved first, second, etc. It may be topical—if you need to talk to witness A at length about a particular matter and witness B knows a little about that matter but nothing about anything else, wouldn't it make sense to interview B before A?

If you don't make the effort to plan a logical progression among witnesses, you may have to go back to the first witness you interviewed to ask additional questions. You may find that first witness less than pleased that you are bothering him again or even refusing to talk with you a second time. And you may find yourself in big trouble with the supervising attorney!

HYPOTHETICAL 12-5

Assume that Paul Perfect has been assigned to interview Tom Shanks, Julia Sloberts, Sandra Tullock, and Denzel Washingtub in the Harrison Bored case.

1. Based on what you know so far, in what order would you recommend he conduct those interviews?
2. Why?

KEY WORDS AND PHRASES TO REMEMBER

big-ego witness
busy witness
condescending witness

disinterested witness
field interview
friendly witness

hostile witness
in-office interview
language barriers
mental barriers
multiple witness interviews
nosey witness

physical barriers
recorded interview
show-off witness
skeptical witness
too-helpful witness
video taped interview

LEARN BY DOING

LBD 12-1. Schedule and prepare for the interview of one of the witnesses in one of the following cases as assigned to you by the instructor. Contact the person whose name you are given who will be playing the role of this witness. Schedule the interview and then prepare: (1) a memo to the instructor summarizing your contact with the witness; (2) a confirming letter to the witness; and (3) any forms you might need for the interview. Also prepare your questions for the interview.

a. Case Study No. 1 (The Rowdy Outlaw Case)

Candy Carmichael	Detective Willie Parker	Ima Jean Grouse
Outlaw	Dr. Michael Melody	Jack Gates
Connie Cornelius	Georgette B. Good	Kato

b. Case Study No. 2 (The Soupspoon Wise Case)

Korn Pone	Tanya Trucker	Turtle Shoop

c. Case Study No. 3 (The Vidalia Unyon Case)

Georgia Peach	Hobo Booth	Nosey Nelly

d. Case Study No. 4 (The Rocky Road Project)

Grace Slickspot	Real E. Smart

Chapter 13

Conducting a Witness Interview

CHAPTER OUTLINE

A. Introduction
B. Things to Remember Throughout the Witness Interview
C. The Order and Manner of Conducting a Witness Interview
D. Recording or Taping the Interview
E. The Telephone Interview
F. The Written Witness Statement

CHAPTER OBJECTIVES

In this final chapter on interviewing skills you will learn:

- The important things to keep in mind throughout the witness interview.
- How to begin a witness interview, move to the substantive areas, and conclude the interview.
- How to use active listening and observation skills in a witness interview.
- How to evaluate, test, and seek verification of information obtained in a witness interview.
- How to seek information to impeach the credibility of an unhelpful witness.
- How to prepare a witness interview summary for the supervising attorney.
- How to properly record or video tape an interview.
- How to prepare for and conduct a telephone interview.
- How to prepare a written witness statement.

A. Introduction

This chapter continues our study of preparing for and conducting a fact witness interview. Paul Perfect has pretty much recovered from that wild ride with Tom Shanks. But Betty Busy has several more assignments for him in connection with witnesses in the Harrison Bored case. Let's see what Paul Perfect can teach us about actually conducting an effective witness interview.

B. ► Things to Remember Throughout the Witness Interview

As discussed in detail in Chapter 11 in connection with a client interview, the interviewer should remember these points throughout the witness interview.

- Be friendly but professional.
- Be cognizant of the dangers of UPL.
- Avoid using legal or technical jargon except when necessary.
- Take good notes.
- Engage in active listening.
- Evaluate the demeanor and behavior of the witness.
- Remember the witness does not know what you want or need to know—you have to ask.
- Keep an emotional distance between yourself and the witness.
- Overcome internal obstacles to effective listening and observing:
  - thinking about the next question so intently you don't catch the last answer
  - concentrating so hard on taking notes that you miss something you should see or hear
  - being a slave to a prepared list of questions
  - being affected by your own biases.

There are some special things the interviewer should remember for the witness interview.

1. Observe and evaluate the witness's environment

One of the opportunities presented to the interviewer in going to the witness for the interview is that we get to see the witness's environment and *listen* to what it tells us. Don't forgo this opportunity. Before, during, and after the interview, while you are in the witness's home or office or conference room:

- Observe the witness's space carefully.
- Evaluate what you see.
- Make note of it.
- Make use of it in the interview.

The observations and evaluations you make of the witness and his space can be used to good advantage before the interview by the careful observer.

EXAMPLE

Use your observations as **ice breakers.** Is there a putter sitting in the corner? Ask about his golf game. Is there a picture of the witness with Ronald Reagan on the wall? Ask where he met the former president. Is there a crayon drawing taped to the side of the desk? Ask about it. Is the latest best-seller sitting on the desk? Ask how they like the book or author.

Observations of the witness's space can also be used to advantage *during* the interview.

EXAMPLE

Is the witness reluctant to say much about what she saw at the accident site and you sense she is reluctant to get involved with lawyers and all that hassle? You see a family picture on the bookcase showing the witness with her husband and two small kids. Try mentioning to the witness that your client has children whose lives are going to be made more difficult because of this injury to their parent and see if that doesn't help.

HYPOTHETICAL 13-1

Assume that Paul Perfect arrives at the office of Denzel Washingtub to conduct that interview in the Harrison Bored case. Paul identifies himself to the receptionist and tells her he has an appointment to see Washingtub. The receptionist tells Paul to have a seat in the reception area and he does. Instead of looking over his notes (which he did thoroughly before leaving the office), he spends his time looking around the reception room. Here are some of the things he notes:

• The magazines on the coffee table in the reception area are all sports related: *Sport, Sports Illustrated, Field and Stream,* etc. He also notes some NRA (National Rifle Association) literature on the table. The address labels of all the magazines and literature have Washingtub's name on them.
• The furniture in the reception area is modern in style and fairly new. What appears to be a quite nice Oriental rug covers the floor.
• A large Impressionist oil painting (an original—Paul knows because he got up and walked over to it) hangs over the couch in the reception area. On two other walls are smaller framed prints that complement the oil painting.
• The fourth wall in the reception area is covered with framed photographs and prints of the State University football team in action. An old team jersey (with No. 12 on it) is also framed and hanging there.
• Paul notes that the receptionist is a well-dressed, middle-aged woman. The phone rings almost constantly while he sits there. He notes that she answers the phone quietly. Although he is no more than 15 feet away from her he can hear her voice but not the words. She smiles as she speaks and seems very efficient. Her desk is neat and orderly. A small picture of a young woman sits in one corner of her desk.

Paul has not yet met Washingtub. But merely from sitting in the reception room for five minutes Paul believes he knows a few things about Washingtub.

1. What do you think are Paul's initial impressions concerning:
   a. the success of Washingtub's insurance business?
   b. Washingtub's efficiency as a business person?
   c. Washingtub's education?
   d. Washingtub's hobbies and interests?
   e. Washingtub's political leanings?
2. Based on what Paul Perfect has observed so far, should he jump to conclusions with regard to any of these matters?

3. What other initial impressions would you suggest to Paul Perfect about Denzel Washingtub based on what you have seen?
4. What ice-breaking comments or questions might Paul use when he first is introduced to Washingtub?

2. Overcome *external* obstacles to active listening and observing

We have considered the need to overcome *internal* obstacles in interviewing. But the witness interview is usually conducted away from the interviewer's office. The interview may occur in the home or office of the witness, on a factory floor, in an open field, in a hospital room or, as we saw in Hypothetical 12-4, in a speeding car, an airport terminal, in a long noisy line, or even a restroom!

Any time the interview occurs outside the interviewer's office, she doesn't control the space or environment of the interview. She may not find it as physically convenient or comfortable to conduct the interview in the place chosen by the witness. More distractions and interruptions may occur that she can't do anything about. Phones may ring and be answered by the witness, people may come in and out, the witness may be called away, there may be distracting noises outside, the room may be too hot or too cool.

It is easy to allow these **external obstacles** to interfere with our interview. They can cause us to lose concentration, fail to listen actively, fail to observe things we should, or to get frustrated and let it show. Our job is to overcome these barriers, keep our cool, and do a thorough professional job despite them. A good rule of thumb to keep in mind during any interview is no matter what happens, don't be surprised. Tell yourself, "I thought something like this might happen today and I'm ready for it." Didn't it seem that Paul Perfect did this in Hypothetical 12-4?

3. Avoid disclosing confidential or privileged information

In interviewing a witness, remember that this is not the client. Even if the witness is friendly and helpful or a relative of the client, he is not the client and we must avoid the disclosure of confidential information. It is a breach of our ethical and professional obligation. You should even avoid giving a witness your *opinion* about anything related to the case. Remember you are there to obtain information, not provide it.

Beware the nosey or inquisitive witness who asks questions about the case. Avoid the temptation to tell the reluctant witness more than you should in order to obtain their cooperation.

C. ► The Order and Manner of Conducting a Witness Interview

Many of the considerations for conducting the witness interview are similar to those for conducting a client interview, considered in Chapter 11. That is especially true when the interview of the fact witness is conducted in the interviewer's office or conference room. When interviewing the fact witness, the paralegal will want to consider the following points.

1. Beginning the interview

a. *Greet the witness*

If the interview is conducted in the paralegal's office, make the witness feel welcome (see Hypothetical 11-1). If the interview is conducted in the office or home of the witness or at some neutral location, be friendly and patient with everyone who assists you. Try to make a good impression.

No matter where the witness interview occurs, some greeting and exchange of pleasantries is appropriate. The nature and extent of the greeting will vary with the witness, however. Some people expect to visit for a while before getting down to business and others do not.

There are *geographical* or *regional* distinctions to be made here. Although it is possible to overgeneralize, if you are conducting interviews in a rural area or very small town you might increase your likelihood of success if you slow down and take a little more time to smile and visit with folks before getting down to work. But if you are conducting those interviews in an urban setting you might not gain anything by this except a puzzled look.

The nature and extent of the greeting will vary with the *circumstances* as well.

EXAMPLE

> If you enter an office for an interview and find people sitting around taking it easy, a little visiting may be in order. But if you enter the same office and phones are ringing, and people are typing or running to and fro, it would be inappropriate to do anything but offer a quick greeting and get to the point of your visit.
>
> If you are visiting an elderly person in a nursing home, you might want to take a while to visit before asking your questions. But if you are interviewing that same elderly person when she is very ill in the hospital, your greeting would be brief (so as not to tire the patient) and quiet.
>
> If you are interviewing a couple in their front yard on a Saturday morning while they water the flowers, you will take some time to visit (and admire those flowers, of course). On the other hand, if you are interviewing a police officer getting ready to go on duty (which is when you usually can catch them, by the way), the officer will likely be all business and in no mood for extended visiting.

b. Express appreciation for the witness's cooperation

If the paralegal is conducting a witness interview, that means the witness is cooperating in the informal discovery to some extent. (If she wasn't cooperating, she would be subpoenaed to a deposition to be handled by the attorney.) Always express genuine thanks to the witness for that cooperation. You may need that witness again!

If it is appropriate, empathize with the witness as you would a client.

c. Disclose your status as a paralegal

The witness may assume that you are an attorney even if you explained your status to them in the scheduling phone call. Better safe than sorry— tell them again.

d. Briefly state the purpose of your interview

In a client interview, we may go into detail concerning what the interview is intended to accomplish to assist the client. Not so in a witness interview. Again the paralegal must remember that the witness—even the helpful, friendly witness, and even a relative of the client—is not the client. So the interviewer will just briefly state the purpose of the interview:

> Mrs. Brown, I appreciate you seeing me today. As I told you on the phone, I want to ask you some questions about the car accident last week in which you were a passenger in your neighbor's car.

e. Obtain background information on the witness

While this is covered in depth in initial client interviews, generally you won't need the life story of the witness. But having some background information on any witness is helpful for a number of reasons:

SLEUTH ON THE LOOSE

Identify three companies you would like to know more about then locate their Web site addresses at *www.companylink.com.*

- It helps us know the witness better and understand what she tells us.
- It helps us know better what to ask during the interview.
- It helps us investigate the witness further if we need to do that later.
- It helps us locate her later if she moves.

Therefore, try to obtain some biographical and other background data on the witness: full name, home address and phone, work address and phone, marital status and name of spouse (especially important when the witness is a married woman because phone and other listings may be in the husband's name), employment of spouse, length of time at residence and job, length of time in the community, and familiarity with the client or subject of the interview.

2. Conducting the substantive portion of the witness interview

Again, there are certain similarities between conducting the substantive portion of a witness interview and that of the client interview considered in detail in Chapter 11. But there are some special considerations here too for the witness interview. In handling the substantive portion of the witness interview, the interviewer should:

a. Briefly review any documents the witness has made available

b. Obtain a narrative summary of what the witness knows

As we have learned, open-ended questions are ideal for this purpose. And, as with clients, it is generally a good idea to *let the witness talk.* The more the witness talks, the more the interviewer learns about the witness and the incident. It's also an opportunity to observe and evaluate the witness. There is a limit to anything, of course, and if the witness is a runaway talker we eventually have to interrupt (politely) and get back to the subject:

> *That's interesting, Mrs. Brown. But did I hear you say a little while ago that you knew where John had been the night before the robbery?*

But let the witness talk, and act interested even if you are not.

c. Fill in any gaps in the story

Use closed-ended, explanatory, and opinion questions for this purpose:

> *So you had never met Bill Simmons until he went to work at the company?*
> *Tell me why you decided to go home early that day.*
> *Do you think he would have quit if the supervisor hadn't said that to him?*

d. Ask the witness to define unfamiliar terms

e. Ask for details

Use those who, what, where, when, why, and how questions. Be *thorough* and *persistent.* And lock in helpful statements. When a witness provides us with statements helpful to our client's position (or that minimize any hurtful information), it is good to lock those statements in by having them repeated. Use repetition and proper phrasing of questions to do this:

> *And you're sure that he said. . .*
> *So what you're telling me is. . .*
> *Now if I understand you correctly, she. . .*

f. Seek leads to other witnesses and documents

g. If helpful, have the witness draw a sketch or diagram

See Hypothetical 11-4 and Illustration 11-1.

h. Establish the chronology of events known to the witness

If appropriate, have the witness draw a time line. (See Hypothetical 11-2 and Illustration 11-5.)

i. Clarify errors, inconsistencies, or vague points

Remember that we assume nothing in interviewing. So listen for inconsistencies and contradictions and try to clear them up. Closed-ended, leading, or sometimes pressure questions are useful for this purpose:

> Tell me again what you saw just before the explosion.
> But you said earlier that you didn't meet Jack until after the graduation, isn't that right?
> If you were in Vietnam until March 1973, how could you have attended Nixon's second inauguration in January of that year?

j. Attempt to verify information provided by the witness

Treat information from witnesses as you would information from a client for this purpose (see Hypothetical 11-6):

- Attempt to determine if the *source* of the information is *competent, honest, reliable,* and *objective.*
- Try to filter out *opinions, guesses, assumptions,* and *statements of prejudice* to get to real provable fact.
- Distinguish between *first-hand information* and *second-* or even *third-hand information.*

k. Ask about corroborating sources

Who else would know? Who else might have seen or heard? Does the witness know who else might know? What documents might there be? Who else might know about documents?

l. Get the particulars on all persons and documents mentioned

What is the person's full name? Nickname? Married name? Maiden name? Where do they live? Where do they work? What do they do? Who has that document? Who had it last? Who keeps the records for the company?

m. Make copies of documents produced or arrange to keep them

Before the interview is over, closely review all documents produced during the interview and get permission to take custody of them or make copies.

n. Ask the witness to tell you anything else they remember

Before concluding the interview, always give a witness the opportunity to relate anything else he can remember about the incident or matter that hasn't been mentioned:

> Okay, I think that's all I had to ask you. Is there anything else you can recall about that night that I haven't asked?
> Is there anything else you wanted to tell me?
> Is there anything I've left out or skipped?

Tell him to call you if he thinks of anything after you have left.

o. Ask about other interviews

Remember you may not be the only person who has contacted this witness or who will do so in the future. In a litigation matter, it is quite likely that the office representing the opposing party will contact this witness. Ask about prior interviews. If they have been interviewed, find out by whom and when.

If the witness gave a written statement to the other interviewer, see if there is a copy of the statement and if you can obtain it. Ask the witness to let you know if someone contacts them in the future for an interview and to allow you to have a copy of any written statement given in that interview.

p. Make sure you have covered everything

Check off topics as you cover them in the interview and review your notes before you conclude to be sure you have covered everything.

3. Impeaching a witness

In this section we will consider a matter of special concern in the witness interview: consciously seeking a basis to impeach or discredit the witness.

In interviewing we need to know the facts—the truth as the witness knows or believes it. We need to know those facts whether they are helpful or hurtful to the legal position of our client. However, when a witness says something that is hurtful to the legal position of our client, the paralegal should remember that the supervising attorney will be interested in anything that might discredit either the facts related by the witness or the credibility of the witness himself.

When a witness says something helpful to the interests of our client the paralegal must remember that the opposing party will at some point seek to impeach or discredit what that helpful witness has said. So the supervising attorney needs you to test it for reliability—see if the witness or the information is impeachable.

In either situation, probe for:

a. Inconsistencies or contradictions in the statement

We have already learned to automatically do this in every client or witness interview. However, when a witness makes statements harmful to the client, you want to focus particularly on those harmful statements. Use repetition—come back to the subject again. See if the statement comes out the same way each time and if it is told consistently. Consider the story of the witness as a whole to see if there are any holes in it. Seek details.

b. Unreliability of the witness's information

1. The witness who saw something.   as the witness told you she *saw* something? To test it, focus your questions on the witness's *capacity* and *opportunity* to see. Regarding the capacity to see, does she wear glasses or contact lenses? Was the witness wearing them at the time she saw what she claims to have seen? Were the glasses or contacts old or new?

Was the witness taking any medications or had she consumed any alcohol prior to observing?

Regarding opportunity, how clear was the witness's line of vision at the time? What was the distance and the angle of the witness from what was seen? Any obstacles? Any weather or lighting problems that might make the testimony unreliable?

2. The witness who heard something. as the witness told you she *heard* something? Again, focus on the capacity and opportunity to hear. Regarding capacity, how well does she hear? Does she use any hearing aids? When, if ever, has she had her hearing tested? Any hearing problems in the family?

Regarding opportunity, what was her distance from the sound or voice she heard? What were the acoustics? Were there any competing noises?

3. The witness who said something. Has the witness told you she *said* something? If so, was it recorded? Was it committed to writing? Is she sure of *exactly* what she said? How long ago was it said? Could she be guessing or paraphrasing after the passage of time? Were there any witnesses to it and if so who?

c. Bias of the witness

A witness with harmful testimony may be **biased** for the opposing party or against our client or both. A helpful witness may be biased against the opposing party or for our client or both. The interviewer should determine if this witness might have any reason to favor one party over the other. So we ask, is the witness a relative, friend, neighbor, or co-worker of the party who is helped by his testimony? Does he have common interests or circumstances with that party—religion, politics, age, occupation, etc.? Does the witness have any reason to dislike or disfavor the party who is harmed by his testimony—any past history of problems, business or personal disputes, dislike?

How these questions are asked may vary depending on whether the witness has given helpful or damaging information for our client's case. For the friendly witness, we would never want to sound insulting, accusatory, or disbelieving in the way we phrased a question regarding bias. A question on bias to a helpful witness might be phrased like:

> *If you don't mind me asking, have you ever had any run-ins or problems with Sam Jones?*
>
> *I remember you told me earlier that you had never liked Sam Jones. Is there any possibility that could have unconsciously influenced what you remember that he said?*

Although we certainly do not try to be deliberately rude to a witness because they have given damaging information regarding our client, the interviewer will try to lock in statements from which bias might be implied. The same questions we ask of the helpful witness might be phrased a little more pointedly to the unhelpful witness:

> *Have you ever had any run-ins with Sam Jones? Any problems with him? You have never liked Sam Jones, isn't that what you told me? Couldn't that have an influence on what you remember that he said?*

d. Interest of the witness in the outcome of the case

Interest, or more specifically, *self-interest,* can arise in many contexts. If a witness testifies at trial favorably to his employer, the attorney who offers the employee's testimony will suggest that the employee/witness is being truthful. The attorney for the other party will suggest that the employee just wants to keep his job. Interest in the outcome of a case can impact on the credibility of the witness.

Monetary interest is what we usually look for to discredit a witness, but it can be anything that arguably will advance the personal circumstances of the witness.

It could be the prospect of **advancement** at work:

If Mr. Casey's discharge is upheld, could you be promoted to his position?

Or a possible **inheritance:**

If this will is set aside as invalid, you will inherit the entire estate, won't you?

Or a perceived **romantic advantage:**

Is it true you have been dating Mrs. Jones since she separated from her husband?

Or a perceived **advantage to another:**

The ejection of this player from the team could make your boyfriend the starting quarterback, couldn't it?

As with questions on bias, questions regarding possible self-interest will be worded and phrased differently depending on whether the witness has said something damaging or helpful to our client.

Your tone of voice might be different as well. Using the sample questions above, ask them out loud as you would to a helpful witness and then again to an unhelpful witness. The tone of voice makes a lot of difference, doesn't it? Would you rephrase any of those questions to make them better suited for a helpful or unhelpful witness?

e. History of the witness affecting credibility

The history can include:

1. **Prior bad acts probative of truthfulness.** (See FRE 608(b).)

   When you were in college, didn't you write research papers for other students to earn extra money?

2. **Reputation for truthfulness.** (See FRE 608(a).)

   These questions are generally asked of a witness about another witness.

   Does Jerry Smith have a reputation for not telling the truth?

3. **Prior inconsistent statements.** (See FRE 613 and 801(d)(1)(A).)

   You say that the first car that entered the intersection was the blue car, but didn't you tell the investigating officer that the red car started first?

4. **Prior convictions.** (See FRE 609.)

Unless you already have knowledge of a prior conviction, or unless the witness brings it up, it may be offensive to the witness to have this question asked directly. Be sure to obtain the approval of your supervising attorney before doing so. This is something that can usually be located in public records (see Chapters 16 and 17).

4. Concluding the witness interview

At the conclusion of the interview, express gratitude to the witness for agreeing to talk with you. Remember you, or your supervising attorney, may need this witness again—for further information or to testify in the case. Leave the witness with a positive impression of you so that door is open to future contact. If appropriate, leave a business card with the witness, particularly if you have asked him to call you if he thinks of anything else.

5. The interview summary

Following the interview, prepare an **interview summary.** (Or, if the interview was recorded, prepare a transcript. See discussion below.) The interview summary for a witness interview should follow the same basic format of the summary of a client interview (see Illustration 11-3). The witness interview summary ought to be clear, organized, and thorough. It should contain, at a minimum, the following:

- a heading indicating the name of the witness interviewed, the date of the interview, and the file name and number
- background information/personal data on the witness
- factual information gathered from witness and placed in a logical order, usually chronological or topical
- the interviewer's observations and evaluation of the witness's demeanor, credibility, and reliability. Anything unusual or special that the interviewer noted, whether positive or negative, should be pointed out in the interview summary.
- a statement of the next steps agreed to at the conclusion of the interview, if any
- a listing of all authorizations and other documents signed during the interview and a statement of where the originals are
- a listing of all documents provided by the witness and an indication of where they are
- the interviewer's conclusions and recommendations regarding what should be done next

Illustration 13-1 shows portions of the interview summary prepared by Paul Perfect following the interview of Tom Shanks.

D. ▶ Recording or Taping the Interview

It is common to tape record a witness interview. Sometimes they are video taped as well. There are some special considerations to keep in mind when recording a witness interview.

Illustration 13-1   MEMORANDUM SUMMARIZING WITNESS INTERVIEW

MEMORANDUM

TO: Betty Busy, Attorney
FROM: Paul Perfect, Paralegal
DATE: October 11, 2003
CLIENT: Harrison Bored (File Number: 03-335-L)
RE: Interview with Tom Shanks

1. BACKGROUND INFORMATION:

Tom Shanks (TS) was interviewed beginning at the offices of Shanks Motors on East Broadway in Capital City on October 11, 2003. The interview moved with the departing TS into his limousine and then into the airport terminal. TS is a 59-year-old Caucasian male, DOB 5-3-44. He lives at 9101 Estate Circle, Capital City, Yourstate 44445, and has resided there for the past 23 years. He is a widower, his wife of 30 years, Barbara, having passed away two years ago from cancer. The couple had three children, all of whom are grown.

TS is the sole owner and president of Shanks Motors, Inc., a Yourstate corporation that owns and operates approximately 25 car dealerships around the state. The car business is the only business TS has ever worked in. He is a high school graduate who went to work washing cars at his uncle's used car lot, took it over when his uncle retired, and has built his company from those roots.

Home phone: (111) 669-5432
Work phone: (111) 668-0087

2. FACTS:

TS did not know Harrison Bored (HB) before the party on August 28, 2003. He was invited to the party by Meg Bryan, a woman in her early 30s who previously worked for Shanks Motors. (Home phone: 669-7654) TS has been dating Ms. Bryan for a couple of months, though he describes her as "just a friend." Meg Bryan lives in HB's neighborhood at 123 Gardener Street.

TS and Meg Bryan arrived at the party a little late, around 8 P.M. as the witness recalls. They did not stay together after the first few moments. There were a number of people that TS knew at the party and he and Meg Bryan sort of went their own ways. He does recall meeting Jessica Slang (JS) at the party before the fall. Meg Bryan introduced them shortly after they arrived. He did not know her before meeting her at the party.

TS did not see JS fall. He was in the kitchen around 9 P.M. refreshing his drink. He had been in the kitchen about five minutes and was talking with a woman he did already know, Julia Sloberts (JS) when the accident happened. He never saw HB come into the kitchen prior to the fall. He recalls JS coming into the kitchen and saying they needed more ice in the backyard. A man (he doesn't know who but knows it was a man's voice) told her to check the refrigerator freezer compartment and she walked behind TS toward the refrigerator. He says the male voice added loudly, "Be careful over there, it's slippery." Almost at the same time he heard that statement he also heard a gasp behind him and the sound of something hitting the floor. He then remembers that Julia Slobert's hand flew up to her mouth and she. . .

TS says that while he was bent over JS lying there on the floor of the kitchen, he definitely noticed a pool of water or some liquid under her legs and feet. He didn't pay a lot of attention to it but did assume it was what had caused her to slip. He said it could have been water from the ice maker in the refrigerator or liquor that had been spilled. The island containing the liquor bottles was only about two feet away from the refrigerator where JS fell. I have attached to this memo a rough sketch TS prepared (standing in a line and drawing on the back of his assistant's attache case) showing the layout of the kitchen, where JS was after she fell, and where the puddle was that he spotted. . . .

Illustration 13-1   MEMORANDUM SUMMARIZING WITNESS INTERVIEW *(continued)*

TS did not know anyone else in the kitchen at the time of the fall other than Julia Sloberts and JS. He does recall that 2 or 3 others were there but he did not know them. He says he does not know Denzel Washingtub and does not recall meeting him at the party. . . .

TS does recall JS striking HB with her right fist. He laughed as he recalled it and shook his head, saying he had never seen a woman throw a punch like that. He said that HB came into the kitchen about 2 or 3 minutes after the fall. Someone apparently had called him though TS doesn't know who. He also has no idea where HB was at the time of the fall. HB entered the kitchen and bent down over JS on her left side as she lay on the floor. As HB knelt, TS says he stood up. HB said something to JS that TS couldn't make out and JS, without even opening her eyes, swung her right hand and caught HB flush in the nose. TS said you could distinctly hear the sound of bone. . . .

3. OBSERVATIONS AND EVALUATION:

TS is a short, slim gentleman with silver hair that appears to be colored. He probably has gone gray. He carries himself with confidence, walks and talks quickly and with authority. He does not hesitate to tell you what he knows or doesn't know. He is a no-nonsense type of person. You can tell he is used to giving orders.

Our interview was conducted in a rushed non-private environment. When I arrived at the Shanks Motors offices. . .

Though TS emanates authority and success, I found him very polite (which I frankly had not expected) and considerate. He answered all my questions for as long as he could before boarding the plane and did so candidly and considerately. I found him entirely candid and credible. He did seem a little uncomfortable when speaking of his relationship with Meg Bryan. He quickly (a little too quickly maybe) volunteered that they are "just friends." She is considerably younger than he and it is probably understandable he should be a little sensitive to disclosing that. On the other hand, he did not hesitate to offer her name or phone number if we wish to contact her.

4. DOCUMENTATION:
TS had no documents relevant to the case other than the attached sketch I had him draw.

5. RECOMMENDATIONS:
I believe we should interview Meg Bryan just to confirm TS's story to the extent possible. TS will be an important and helpful witness for us and we need to ensure that his credibility is unassailable.

1. Obtain the prior consent of the supervising attorney

Before you record or tape any interview, be sure the supervising attorney consents. In general, if a witness is going to provide information hurtful to the legal position of our client, we will not record or tape that interview. Depending on the scope of the work product privilege in your state, a tape recording or video of the witness interview may be discovered by the opposing party. So we usually make no physical record of the interview with the unhelpful witness. There are exceptions to that rule, however, and it is always the supervising attorney's call to make.

2. Consider using a court reporter

You may want to use a court reporter to tape record or video tape the witness interview. She will do a professional job of recording the witness accurately and, if you request it, will prepare a written transcript of the questions and answers given in the interview. If you plan to use a court reporter to record or tape the interview, make the arrangements well in advance.

Sometimes it is not feasible to utilize a court reporter due to the expense involved, or the attorney may feel the witness may be intimidated by the increased formality of having a court reporter present for the interview, or it may just be impracticable to take a court reporter along. In that event, it is entirely appropriate for the interviewer to record or tape the interview herself.

3. Obtain the witness's consent *before* recording or taping

Consent is needed whether the interview is to be done by phone (discussed below) or in person. Recording or taping a witness without the prior consent of the witness is unethical and even illegal in some jurisdictions.

4. Repeat and record the statement of consent

After you obtain the consent of the witness to record the interview, repeat the statement of consent and record it as you begin the interview.

HYPOTHETICAL 13-2

Assume that Paul Perfect is going to interview Meg Bryan and wants to record the interview. He asks her before he turns on the tape recorder if she minds him recording it, and she says she doesn't mind at all.

PP (turns on recording machine): Okay, we are now recording. It is October 29, 2003, at 10 A.M. Ms. Bryan, as you know, my name is Paul Perfect and I am a paralegal for attorney Betty Busy. I have your permission to record this interview regarding a lawsuit filed by Jessica Slang against our client, Harrison Bored, involving a slip and fall at the house of Harrison Bored in August of this year, is that correct?

MB: Yes, that is correct.

5. Identify yourself and your position in the recording

You are ethically obligated to make that disclosure and doing so in the recording should negate any later claim by the witness that you deceived her regarding your identity or the purposes of the interview. (See Hypothetical 13-2 above.)

6. State the date and time the interview begins

See Hypothetical 13-2 above.

7. Identify all persons present

Add a statement establishing the connection with the subject matter of each identified person.

HYPOTHETICAL 13-3

Assume that Paul Perfect is interviewing Meg Bryan at her home where she is babysitting her nieces.

PP: We are here at the home of Meg Bryan located at 123 Gardener Street in Capital City. Present for this interview are Ms. Bryan and myself and Ms. Bryan's two nieces whom she is babysitting this morning. We have, is it Peg Bryan?

MB: Yes, Peg Bryan, who is three.

PP: Okay, Peg Bryan aged three. And her sister, Bett, aged. . .

MB: Bett is four and a half.

PP: Bett, aged four and a half. And I think it is safe to say that Peg and Bett know absolutely nothing about this incident and are here only to be babysat, is that correct, Ms. Bryan?

MB: That is correct.

8. Handling interruptions in the interview

If the recording of the interview is interrupted, always state on the recording that there is going to be a break in the recording, the time the recording device is being turned off, and the time it is resumed.

HYPOTHETICAL 13-4

Assume that Paul Perfect is 20 minutes into his interview with Meg Bryan when:

PP: Ms. Bryan, where were you at the time you first learned that someone had fallen or been hurt at the party?

MB: Well, I was in the sun room talking with. . .

PB (loud and demanding): Aunt Meg, I'm hungry!

MB: Okay, Peg, it's probably snack time for you guys, isn't it?

PB and BB (together): Yea!

MB: I'm sorry, Mr. Perfect, but I'd better stop and get them something or we'll never have any peace.

PP: No problem. Take all the time you need. Let me just make a note here for the record. It is now 10:35 A.M. on October 29, 2003. We are going to take a break and stop recording at this time so Ms. Bryan can get her nieces a snack. We will hopefully resume shortly. (Turns off recording machine.)

When the interview resumes after the interruption, record the time of resumption. Try to pick up at the same place you were at in the questioning before the break. We want to avoid any allegation later by the witness or anyone else that part of the interview was erased or edited. Even with interruptions, it should flow smoothly and be a consistent whole.

HYPOTHETICAL 13-5

PP (turns recorder back on): It is now 10:52 A.M. on October 29, 2003, and we are resuming the interview with Meg Bryan. (Smiling) Are your two charges content for a while, you think?

> **MB:** For as long as the cookies hold out.
> **PP:** Okay. Let's see, I believe I had asked you where you were when you first heard that someone had fallen or gotten hurt at the party.
> **MB:** That's right. As I recall I was in the sun room. . .

9. Avoid "talking over"

Don't "talk over" the witness and encourage the witness to not talk over you. By *talking over,* we mean that someone begins to speak while another person is already speaking. Some people do this without realizing it and certainly without realizing how it sounds on a voice recording. Two or more people talking at the same time will produce an unintelligible recording. If a witness is repeatedly talking over the interviewer, the interviewer should politely point it out.

10. How to conclude the taped interview

At the conclusion of the interview, give the witness an opportunity to add anything she wishes, or to change or supplement answers given.

HYPOTHETICAL 13-6

> **PP:** All right, Ms. Bryan, I believe that's all the questions I have. Is there anything that you would like to add to what you've told me today?
> **MB** (shaking her head): No, I don't think so.
> **PP:** Is there anything you recall about the night of the incident that I haven't asked or you haven't mentioned?
> **MB:** No, I think we covered it all.

State the time the interview is concluding, and have the witness reconfirm that the interview has been taped in its entirety with her permission and that she has given her answers voluntarily and freely.

HYPOTHETICAL 13-7

> **PP:** Again, Ms. Bryan, let me thank you for taking the time to talk with me. It is now (looking at watch) 11:15 A.M. on October 29, 2003, and we are concluding this interview with Meg Bryan. Ms. Bryan, is it correct that this interview has been taped with your knowledge and consent?
> **MB:** Yes, it has.
> **PP:** And the answers you have given me today have been given voluntarily and freely?
> **MB:** Yes.
> **PP:** And the answers you have given me today have been truthful and complete?
> **MB:** Absolutely.

11. Transcribe the tape or prepare a summary

Ask the supervising attorney if she wishes you to transcribe the tape for the file or to summarize the interview in a memorandum. (See Illustration 13-1.)

12. If appropriate, provide the witness a transcript

Some states require by law or ethical rule that the witness receive a transcript of the interview. Some attorneys do this as a matter of courtesy. The paralegal should be familiar with the laws and ethical rules of her state regarding this procedure and should be aware of the preferences of the supervising attorney. (See LBD 13-2.)

13. Preserve the tape of the interview

Preserve the tape unless the supervising attorney directs otherwise. Mark it and treat it as attorney work product to shield it from discovery by opposing parties, if that is feasible under the laws of your state. (See discussion of privileges in Chapter 6, and LBD 13-2.)

E. The Telephone Interview

When the interviewer has a choice between conducting an interview in person or by phone, the in-person interview is to be preferred. This permits the interviewer the opportunity to observe the conduct and demeanor of the witness, which, as we have learned, can tell us so much. But in the real world, it is not always possible to conduct every interview in person. Considerations of distance and expense often dictate that witnesses be interviewed by phone.

1. Speak and listen carefully

The rules for conducting a telephone interview are basically similar to conducting any interview. However, since the interviewer cannot observe the conduct and manner of the witness, more emphasis must be placed on listening carefully to the voice of the witness to catch meanings. More care must be taken to speak slowly and carefully so that the witness can understand the questions. This is especially true when a speaker phone (or conference phone) is used. Sometimes the quality of voice transmission is not as high with such equipment. Also, it is easier in a phone interview for the participants to talk over each other, and that must be avoided.

2. Ensure privacy and preserve confidentiality

Since the interviewer is unable to see the witness during a phone interview, the interviewer cannot be 100 percent sure that the witness is alone even if the witness says that she is. Again, use of a speaker or conference phone increases the risk that others on the witness's end of the line can overhear questions and answers. The interviewer should do her best to make sure the witness is alone and listen for sounds of others in the background.

3. Video conferencing

New technology is now available that minimizes some of the vision-related problems of the long-distance interview. Video conferencing using satellite downlink systems allows the participants to see as well as speak to each other. If such facilities are available to both the interviewer and the witness, this means of conducting the interview is preferred over the traditional telephone interview.

4. Using documents in a telephone interview

A special problem for the interviewer in telephone interviews is how to show documents to the witness in order to ask questions about them. This problem requires forethought and planning. The interviewer must decide in advance what documents she wants to show the witness and mail or fax the documents to the witness beforehand. Or, if it is the witness that is bringing the documents to the interview, arrangements must be made to obtain copies of the documents as far in advance of the interview as possible. The interviewer will want time to review them and prepare questions about them before the interview begins.

Even when both the interviewer and the witness have the same documents, confusion can arise in a telephone interview as the two parties to the conversation try to figure out which document the other is referring to. To prevent a guessing game, it is a good idea to number or label the documents in advance so both parties can identify each document quickly. For example, if ten different documents will be referred to during the interview, a list of the documents can be prepared and each one numbered one to ten. The list would then be provided to the witness along with copies of the documents. Now the interviewer can ask the witness to take a look at "the third paragraph of document number three" or "page five of document number ten" and in seconds both parties are, literally, on the same page.

5. Recording the telephone interview

Telephone interviews, like live interviews, are frequently recorded. To record an interview, the paralegal must have reliable equipment. In offices where interviews are regularly conducted by phone and recorded, the phone systems are equipped with a recording capacity.

The rules for recording a telephone interview are substantially the same for recording an in-person interview. Again, consent to record should be obtained *before* the recording begins and then that consent should be repeated and recorded as the taping starts. One difference in the recorded phone interview is that the opening statement made by the interviewer should state clearly that the interview is being conducted by phone.

HYPOTHETICAL 13-8

If Paul Perfect is conducting the interview of Meg Bryan by phone, it might begin like this:

> **PP:** This is Paul Perfect, a paralegal working for attorney Betty Busy, and I am recording a telephone interview with Ms. Meg Bryan beginning at 10:00 A.M. on October 29, 2003. Ms. Bryan is speaking to me from her home at 123 Gardener Street in Capital City, Yourstate. Is that correct, Ms. Bryan?
>
> **MB:** Yes, that's correct.
>
> **PP:** I'm going to be asking Ms. Bryan some questions regarding a lawsuit filed by Jessica Slang against our client, Harrison Bored, involving a slip and fall at the house of Harrison Bored in August of this year. And Ms. Bryan, I am recording this telephone interview with your knowledge and consent, is that correct?
>
> **MB:** Yes, that is correct.
>
> **PP:** Fine. Ms. Bryan, would you tell me your full name and spell your last name for me?

F. The Written Witness Statement

It is very common in interviewing to have the witness sign a written statement containing a verbatim account or a summary of the information they have supplied. The decision to have the witness sign a statement is to be made by the supervising attorney, not the paralegal. Depending on the status of the work product privilege in your state (see LBD 13-2), the statement may be discoverable by the opposing party. So always check first with the supervising attorney before having a witness sign a statement.

The witness statement may take a number of different forms. The essential things are that (1) the statement be signed by the witness in a manner that clearly adopts the statement as the witness's own; and (2) that the signature of the witness and the statement as a whole be provable (capable of authentication) at trial.

1. The format of a witness statement

The different formats that may be utilized for a witness statement include:

- a copy of the transcript of a recorded interview signed by the witness
- a typed summary signed by the witness
- a handwritten summary signed by the witness
- a questionnaire completed and signed by the witness
- a letter written by the interviewer summarizing the interview and signed by the witness

2. How attorneys use witness statements

To better understand the importance of the witness statement to the supervising attorney, it is helpful to remember the various evidentiary and other uses attorneys can make of properly prepared witness statements.

(Review the rules of evidence in Chapters 6 and 7.) Such statements may be used:

- To refresh the witness's memory before testifying
- As part of a settlement effort
- To evaluate the case for the client
- At trial to refresh a witness's recollection (See FRE 612.)
- At trial as a prior inconsistent (or consistent) statement (See FRE 613.)
- At trial as an admission if the witness is an opposing party (See FRE 801(d)(2).)
- At trial for any reason coming within a hearsay exception (See FRE 803 or 804.)

3. Preparing the written witness statement

To be useable by attorneys for the various purposes mentioned, the witness statement should comply with the following guidelines.

a. It should identify the witness by name and state the date of the interview

Other identifying information, such as age, address, and social security number, is not essential but may be included.

b. It should be written in the witness's own words

If the witness writes or types up the statement herself, or if the interview is recorded and then transcribed, this is no problem. But it can become a problem when the interviewer prepares the statement based on the interview with the witness.

To the extent possible, the interviewer should use the witness's own words and phrasing when drafting a statement for the witness to sign. Touchy situations can arise, however, concerning the witness's use of poor grammar, incomplete sentences, slang, profanity, and so forth. Do we incorporate those verbatim into the statement? Judgment has to be exercised to achieve the goal of getting an accurate statement without offending the witness. And many people would be offended to see their poor grammar or unconscious use of profanity reduced to paper. If you are in doubt in these situations, go to the supervising attorney for guidance. If you are drafting the witness statement in the field and don't have the time or opportunity to check with the supervising attorney, use your best judgment in the situation.

c. It should state the total number of pages it contains

For example:

I have read this statement consisting of __4__ pages given this __5th__ day of __Jan.__, 2004.

If the statement is only a single page in length, that statement should be drafted as follows:

I have read this statement consisting of __1__ page given this __5th__ day of __Jan.__, 2004.

d. The pages of the statement should be numbered

Each page of a written statement more than one page in length should be numbered consecutively, usually at the bottom, and each page should refer to the total number of pages in the entire statement as in:

Page 1 of 3 pages

This will help avoid a situation in which a witness might later allege that pages were added or deleted to her original statement after she signed it.

e. Every page should be signed or initialed by the witness

If the statement is more than one page long, the witness should be asked to sign her name or initial each page separately in her own hand, usually in a corner of the page. This will help avoid a situation in which the witness later alleges that a page of the original statement has been substituted. If the statement is only one page long, this is not necessary since that one page will be signed by the witness. (See Illustration 13-2.)

f. It should be read and corrected by the witness before it is signed

Before having the witness sign the statement, always give her an opportunity to read and make corrections in the statement. It is, after all, the witness's statement. Each change made by the witness should be initialed by the witness in her own hand. (See Illustration 13-3.)

g. It should be signed by the witness

The statement should be signed by the witness at the end and the signature should appear immediately beneath a sentence giving the date of the statement, affirming that the witness has read the statement, noting the number of pages in the statement, and verifying that the statement is true and correct to the best of the witness's knowledge and belief:

I have read this statement consisting of __4__ pages given this __5th__ day of __Jan.__, 2004, and the information contained in this statement is true and correct to the best of my knowledge and belief.

Fan Miller
Fact Witness's signature

h. The witness's signature should be witnessed by another

And you may want to have the witness to the signature sign the statement as such:

Illustration 13-2   HANDWRITTEN WITNESS STATEMENT

I, Meg Bryan, am a 30 year old female. I reside at 123 Gardener Street in Capital City, Yourstate. On August 28, 2003, I attended a party at the home of a neighbor, Harrison Bored, at 111 Humphrey Bogart Lane. I brought a friend, Tom Shanks, to the party with me. Mr. Shanks and I arrived at the party about 8 p.m. We stayed together for only a few moments and then separated.

I did not see Mr. Shanks from about 8:20 p.m. until a little after 9 p.m. At that time, people began to say that a woman had slipped and fallen in the kitchen of Harrison Bored's house. I did not go to the kitchen. When Mr. Shanks came out of the kitchen, he was laughing a little. He said the woman who had slipped and fallen had punched Harrison Bored in the nose as he bent down and tried to help her. He had been on the other side of the woman at the time and she hit Bored without even opening her eyes. He said that if she had been up to throwing a combination, she would have hit him too.

Mr. Shanks and I left the party shortly after.

I have read this statement consisting of one page given this 29th day of October, 2003, and the information contained in this statement is true and correct to the best of my knowledge and belief.

Meg Bryan
October 29, 2003

Illustration 13-3   TYPED WITNESS STATEMENT

My name is Denzel Washingtub. I reside at 456 Humphrey Bogart Lane in Capital City, Yourstate. I am 42 years old. My social security number is 999-23-1234. I own and operate Washingtub Insurance Agency in Capital City.

On August 30, 2003 [28 DW] I was a guest at a party in the home of a neighbor, Harrison Bored, at 111 Humphrey Bogart Lane in Capital City. A little before 9 p.m. the evening of the party I entered the kitchen of Mr. Bored's home hoping to speak with Mr. Tom Shanks, a local businessman. I had not met Mr. Shanks but knew of him and was hoping to make his acquaintance and possibly be able to obtain some of his personal or company insurance work.

As I entered the kitchen I saw Mr. Shanks speaking with Julia Sloberts, another neighbor. There were five or six other people in the kitchen at the time. While waiting for Mr. Shanks to finish his conversation with Ms. Sloberts, I went to the island in the kitchen where the drinks were set out. Stepping around the island I noticed that right in front of the refrigerator there was a puddle of water or other clear liquid on the hardwood floor. The puddle was a rough circle about ten [12 DW] inches in diameter. It was fairly visible against the brown oak wood of the floor.

After pouring myself a drink I moved around the kitchen to locate a dishrag to clean up the spill. A few seconds later, another neighbor, Jessica Slang, entered the kitchen and said, "We need more ice out in the backyard." I responded to her by saying, "Check the freezer over the refrigerator." Just as I said that I remembered the puddle there in front of the refrigerator and said, in a loud voice, "But watch out for the water over there."

Page 1 of 2 pages   DW

Jessica Slang didn't respond to what I said and seconds later she slipped and fell in front of the refrigerator. I don't know if she heard me or not but I spoke loudly enough that I thought she could hear me over the conversations in the room.

A couple of people went to the assistance of Jessica Slang on the floor. I left the room to go find Harrison Bored and tell him about the fall. I located him in the backyard at the barbeque grill. He immediately rushed away toward the kitchen.

I did not go back in the kitchen after that because so many people were crowding in there. I learned later from others that Jessica Slang punched Harrison Bored in the nose but I did not see that myself.

I have read this statement consisting of two pages given this 20th day of October, 2003, and the information contained in this statement is true and correct to the best of my knowledge and belief.

Denzel Washingtub
Denzel Washingtub

Clint Yeastwood
Clint Yeastwood, witness

Page 2 of 2 pages

*I have read this statement consisting of __4__ pages given this __5th__
day of __Jan.__, 2004, and the information contained in this statement
is true and correct to the best of my knowledge and belief.*

_____
Fact Witness's signature

_____
Witness

Having the signature of the fact witness witnessed by another is done
for authentication purposes. If the fact witness ever repudiates the statement by alleging the signature is not hers, the one who witnessed her
signature can testify that it is in fact the signature of the fact witness. If
the witness is willing, you may also have the statement signed in the
presence of a notary public who can then certify the signature. Under
the FRE and most state rules of evidence a properly notarized signature
is self-authenticating.

Illustration 13-2 shows how the handwritten statement of Meg Bryan
might look. Illustration 13-3 shows how the typed statement of Denzel
Washingtub might look.

KEY WORDS AND PHRASES TO REMEMBER

bias
external obstacles
ice-breaker
impeachment of a witness
interest
internal obstacles
monetary interest

prior bad acts
recorded interview
reputation for truthfulness
telephone interview
video conderencing
video taped interview
witness statement

LEARN BY DOING

LBD 13-1. Conduct the interview of one of the witnesses (as assigned
by your instructor) in one of the following Case Studies from Appendix
A. Then prepare a draft witness statement for the witness to sign. Do
not actually have the person playing the role of the witness sign the
statement; instead turn it in to your instructor for review as you would
to a supervising attorney.

a. Case Study No. 1 (The Rowdy Outlaw Case)

Candy Carmichael	Detective Willie Parker	Ima Jean Grouse
Outlaw	Dr. Michael Melody	Jack Gates
Connie Cornelius	Georgette B. Good	Kato

b. Case Study No. 2 (The Soupspoon Wise Case)

Korn Pone	Tanya Trucker	Turtle Shoop

c. Case Study No. 3 (The Vidalia Unyon Case)

Georgia Peach	Hobo Booth	Nosey Nelly

d. Case Study No. 4 (The Rocky Road Project)

Grace Slickspot	Real E. Smart

LBD 13-2. Determine if any statute, court ruling, or ethical rule or guideline in your state requires or encourages attorneys to provide witnesses a transcript of a recorded interview or a copy of any written statement made by the witness. If there is some requirement to provide the witness with a transcript or copy of their statement, determine if the requirement is conditioned on a verbal or written request from the witness. Prepare a memorandum summarizing your findings. In that memorandum, state whether you agree with the policy of your state on this matter and if not, how you would recommend it be changed.

Chapter 14

Identifying and Locating Fact Witnesses

CHAPTER OBJECTIVES

The paralegal investigator must know how to identify potential witnesses in client cases and how to locate the missing witness. In this chapter you will learn:

- A number of techniques for identifying and locating fact witnesses
- About a variety of people sources and documentary sources
- How to use resources that are available to assist the investigator, including the Internet, data base vendors, and tracing companies

A. Introduction

Nothing is more basic to the investigation process than identifying fact witnesses—persons who have or who might have knowledge of facts directly relevant to the matter being handled for the client—and locating missing fact witness. Be sure to distinguish between the two concepts.

In the first section of this chapter we will focus on *identifying* fact witnesses, that is, learning the identity of persons who might have information regarding our client's case. In the second section of this chapter we will take up the other concept, *locating* the witness we know about but cannot find. Both sections of this chapter should be read in conjunction with Appendix E, Resources for the Investigator, which contains an abundance of specific sources for use in identifying and locating witnesses.

B. Identifying Fact Witnesses

The need to identify fact witnesses can arise in any type of civil or criminal litigation.

EXAMPLE

In a car accident case, depending on the specific facts, we may need to determine who might have witnessed the accident, or the course of the vehicles before or after the accident, or the words and behavior of the parties before, during, or after the accident.

In a civil fraud case, depending on the specific facts of the case, we may need to determine who might have witnessed the alleged fraudulent transaction, who might have knowledge of the truth of the matter, or who might have had a similar experience with the alleged perpetrator of the fraud.

In a products liability case, depending on the specific facts, we may need to determine who might have witnessed the injury that occurred due to the alleged defective product; who might have knowledge of the product's alleged defective design, manufacture, or packaging; and who might have knowledge of the plaintiff's awareness of the danger or misuse of the product at the time of the accident.

In an employment dispute case, depending on the specific facts, we may need to determine who might have witnessed the hiring event, heard discussions involving alleged promises made, heard threats made, witnessed the discriminatory events, or been present at the discharge event.

In an armed robbery case, depending on the specific facts, we may need to determine who might have witnessed the crime, or the behavior of the alleged criminal before, during, or after the crime, or who else might have had a motive to commit the crime.

1. People sources

In any given matter, there typically will be a number of people who can help you identify witnesses. Who those people are will depend on the nature and facts of the matter. The following list is only suggestive.

a. The client

Your client is almost always the basic source of information about the matter, including the identity of likely witnesses. Beginning with the initial client interview (see Chapters 10 and 11), you should use this source liberally. Keep in mind that your client may not know how much he knows. In other words, the client will not necessarily appreciate the kinds of information that you need in order to represent his interests and thus will not know what to volunteer to you. You must know to ask and not assume that the client has told you all that he knows.

b. Other witnesses

Witnesses lead to witnesses. When you have located one witness, he may lead you to others. One question that should always be asked of a witness is, "Who else knows or may possibly know something about. . .?"

c. The investigating officer(s)

In an automobile accident case where a formal investigation was made, the officer who investigated is one of the first people you should interview and is an important source for witnesses. Keep in mind that sometimes, not all witnesses to an accident get reported on the official accident report prepared by the officer. We have to ask if there were others. Also, although only one officer may be listed on the accident report as the investigating officer, other officers may have been present at the accident site and may have unreported knowledge of potential witnesses.

d. Ambulance, rescue squad, and emergency room personnel

In an accident case, consider who may have come to the scene for any reason. Someone had to treat the injured person at the scene, transport him to the hospital, and treat him there. The various documents generated in the case may contain all the names of the persons involved in those tasks.

EXAMPLE

> If you find that the county rescue squad arrived at an accident site you are investigating and retrieved an injured passenger from a mangled car, some report was probably generated by that rescue squad regarding the incident, but it may mention or be signed by only one member of the team. You will need to ask who else participated in the rescue effort and interview all members of the team to be sure you locate all leads. When a person is transported to an emergency room with an injury, make a list of all the different people they are likely to encounter before they are released or admitted to the hospital, then work your way through the list.

e. The scene or neighborhood canvass

Often it is a good idea to simply **canvass** the scene or neighborhood where the incident occurred to determine who might have seen something relevant. Police officers are well acquainted with this investigative procedure when they look for possible witnesses to a crime.

Plan the canvass carefully. How will you present yourself to strangers at their doors or in their shops? At someone's door where you are a stranger, don't stand too close to the door or try to peer inside, as this may be seen as suspicious or threatening. Dress well and have that smile and friendly greeting ready when the door is opened. Remember that you may be being scrutinized through a peep hole or a crack in the curtain before the door is opened.

Exactly what questions will you ask and how will you ask them? Look over the area to be canvassed very carefully to be sure you include all locations where someone could possibly have seen something. If practicable, go at the same time of day that the incident occurred. Be prepared to go back several times if need be to make contact with everyone possible.

f. The neighborhood regulars

Closely related to the neighborhood canvass is the effort to discover persons who regularly pass through a given area where the incident occurred and who may have seen something. The list of possibilities is limited only by your own imagination—delivery people, people on their way to work or school, postal workers, utility workers, etc.

g. The media

If an accident or incident was covered by TV, radio, newspaper, or periodical, consider making contact and identifying the investigating reporter, photographer, and crew. Many media people are fairly cooperative in granting interviews and sharing notes, photos, and video. (Here again, your communication skills become critical—see Chapter 8.)

Remember that sometimes the media does investigate an event but an editorial decision is made not to use the story. So even though an accident or crime was not reported in the media, some reporter may still have information you can use. And remember that if a story carried in the media uses a single photo there may be many more they didn't use. If they used a five-second video clip there may be several more minutes of video that you can obtain if you get to it before it is reused. Or if they showed a ten-second interview there may be many more minutes of recorded interview. You may be seeing or hearing only the tip of a considerable iceberg of information.

h. Advertisements

Sometimes it is appropriate to run an advertisement in the area media asking witnesses to an event to come forward and identify themselves. This may be done where you have good reason to believe that there were witnesses to a matter but other means have failed to identify them. Ads in local newspapers are cost efficient, although other media (the Internet, TV, radio, billboard, or periodicals) may be justifiable depending on the nature of the matter. Newspaper ads can be run in the classifieds or, for additional cost, as a freestanding ad in the paper. The ad should be creative and eye-catching to attract as much attention as possible.

Illustration 14-1 suggests a creative ad that might be used in the Getta Life case from Hypothetical 14-1.

HYPOTHETICAL 14-1

Assume that you work as a paralegal for the attorney representing Getta Life who has been accused of murdering his ex-girlfriend, Turnme Loose. The state alleges that Getta Life was angry and distraught after Turnme Loose broke up with him following a six-month romance. Supposedly, Turnme Loose told friends at work on Monday morning that she broke up with Getta Life the preceding Saturday when he picked her up at her home and told her they were going to see *Gone with the Wind* at the local arts theater. She complained that Getta Life had a fetish about *Gone with the Wind*, that they had been to see it together more than a dozen times while they were dating, and that she demanded they go see something else. When he refused, she broke it off. She also told friends at work on that Monday morning that all day Sunday following the breakup she had seen Getta Life driving slowly by her house.

At 5 P.M. on Monday, Turnme Loose was hit by a car and killed as she was crossing the street in front of her office building on her way to the parking lot on the other side of the street. According to the police accident report prepared by Officer Keepda Peace, a co-worker of Turnme Loose, Omi Gosh, had walked outside with her and witnessed the collision. Omi Gosh told Keepda Peace that a dark-colored car that looked new came around the corner to their left just as she and Turnme Loose came out of their building. The car stopped in the street about 100 feet away.

Omi Gosh noticed the car briefly and just thought it was going to let someone out. It had tinted windows so she could not see the occupants. As soon as Turnme Loose stepped into the street the car suddenly accelerated, hit Turnme Loose with the fender of the car on the passenger side, and kept going without ever slowing.

Getta Life has been arrested and charged with first degree murder. According to a story on the incident that appeared in the local paper under the byline of a reporter named Scoop This, the family of Turnme Loose has already retained an attorney to file a civil wrongful death action against Getta Life.

Getta Life confirms that he and Turnme Loose broke up the Saturday preceding her death but vigorously denies that he was upset by the breakup or that he was anywhere near her house on Sunday or that he ran her over on Monday. He admits that he has a thing for *Gone with the Wind*. In fact, he says that at the time of the death on Monday he was at the arts theater watching *Gone with the Wind* for his 1,000th time. On Sunday he was alone in his apartment all day watching a video tape of GWTW, although he prefers to see it on the big screen. He also spent some time on the Internet sending e-mail messages to other GWTW fans—apparently there is a club. He does own a new dark blue Saturn automobile but only drove it once on Sunday; he returned the video tape to the store at about 8:30 P.M.

1. What questions will you ask Getta Life in order to identify potential witnesses helpful to his defense?
2. What witnesses do we know of so far who could lead us to others and what will we ask them?
3. What questions do we want to ask Officer Keepda Peace beyond what appears on the accident report in order to identify other potential witnesses?
4. What scenes or neighborhoods might we want to canvass in this case and for what purposes?
5. If the reporter Scoop This will speak with us, what questions would we like to ask him?
6. See Illustration 14-1 for a newspaper ad that might be utilized in the Getta Life case. Can you think of a different one?

2. Documentary sources

In almost every kind of legal matter there will be documents or other records (e.g., computer files and e-mail messages) that may lead the investigator to potential witnesses. These documents and records should be identified, obtained, and carefully reviewed for potential witnesses. The following list is illustrative rather than comprehensive. The student should consider this section in conjunction with Chapters 16 through 18 in which identifying and obtaining information from all kinds from public and private sources is discussed in greater detail.

a. Medical records

Consider the medical records generated by the hit and run involving Turnme Loose in Hypothetical 14-1. An ambulance crew was called,

Illustration 14-1   NEWSPAPER ADVERTISEMENT SEEKING WITNESSES

to call me if you saw or have any information regarding the hit and run accident that occurred on 5th St. in front of the Culpepper Building on Monday, 10-4-04 at approximately 5 P.M. Please call Patty Paralegal COLLECT at 999-111-2222.

examined Turnme Loose at the scene, began treatment, moved her to the ambulance, and transported her to the hospital emergency room. In the emergency room (ER) a team of nurses and physicians administered trauma care until she underwent surgery. After an hour of surgery she was declared dead. Everyone involved in the treatment of Turnme Loose will generate records that may be a valuable resource for identifying witnesses. The ambulance crew will make detailed records of the call, her condition upon their arrival, the examination, the treatment, the transfer, and her condition upon arrival at the hospital. There will be admissions records at the ER, nurses' notes, physicians' records, lab reports, and pharmacy records. There will be surgical records generated by everyone involved in the procedure including the physician(s), the nurses, and the anesthesiologist.

Assume there is a question in the civil wrongful death suit filed by the survivors of Turnme Loose regarding whether she regained consciousness following the accident. This factual question will go to the legal issue of whether the plaintiffs can recover for her pain and suffering. Both sides will be looking for witnesses who can testify one way or another on that factual question. The medical records will be an invaluable source to locate those witnesses.

Or what if the movie Getta Life says he was attending at the time of the accident got out at 4:40 P.M. and we have witnesses who saw Getta Life leaving the theater at that moment? Did he have time to leave the theater, drive to the scene of the hit and run, and commit it? The exact moment of the hit and run might be critical on those facts and the medical records could be critical to determining who arrived at the scene, when, and how they documented the time. Documents help us identify important witnesses.

b. Employment records

What kinds of records did the employer of Turnme Loose maintain on her? If someone deliberately struck Turnme Loose with a car and it wasn't Getta Life, who was it? The attorney defending Getta Life in both the criminal and civil actions will certainly want to find out. Who else would know where Turnme Loose worked and when she got off work and where she parked? Was she having trouble with a co-worker that she might have reported to another co-worker or superior? If so, it might be documented in her employment records.

In the civil case, on the issue of damages, what was Turnme Loose making at her job? Was she in line for promotions or about to be fired? The employment records may lead us to people who know.

c. Educational records

Was Turnme Loose currently a student at the local college? What about looking at those records for indications of a stalker or hostile fellow student or problems with a professor?

In the wrongful death case, what kind of a student was she? Who were her professors whom we might ask?

d. Personal correspondence and journals

Everybody has some of this kind of information and many have a lot of it—for example, correspondence, e-mail messages, journals, diaries, etc. If defense counsel is looking for someone else with a motive to kill Turnme Loose, think of the valuable resource her letters, diary, and other personal writings might be in locating suspects or others who might lead us to suspects.

e. Business records

Every business activity generates some records and correspondence.

EXAMPLE

SLEUTH ON THE LOOSE

Identify a company that makes a widely distributed product then access the Web site of the Consumer Product Safety Commission at *www.cpsc.gov* to see if that company has had a product recalled.

> Consider a single memo generated by the sales force supervisor of a small company involved in selling aluminum siding. Perhaps the memo suggests a change in the pricing structure for some of the company's products. That memo probably didn't happen in a vacuum. There may have been preceding memos or correspondence leading up to it or at least verbal communications among the memo's author and other people inside or outside the company. To whom was the memo sent and who is shown on the memo as receiving copies or who may have received copies that isn't shown on the memo? Even the simplest, most routine business record may be a rich source of potential witnesses to be interviewed.

In the Getta Life case, remember he says he spent some time on the Internet that Sunday afternoon e-mailing members of the GWTW club? Did you think to ask the client for the identity of those he e-mailed in order to confirm the times? Does this club have any records? Maybe the records from Getta Life's own computer or his Internet service provider can confirm the times of his e-mail messages as well as their content. After all, a man supposedly freaking out over his girlfriend's dumping him arguably wouldn't get too wrapped up in an esoteric debate over whether GWTW, the book, should be required reading in all English literature courses. On the other hand, if Getta Life's Sunday afternoon e-mail messages argued that Rhett Butler should have run Scarlet down with a buggy the first time she rejected him, the defense may have a problem!

f. Personal credit, utility, and financial records

Has Getta Life had any repair work done on his car since the accident? How would the prosecution determine that? His checking account records or credit card charges might help. Did Getta Life make any phone calls to Turnme Loose following the breakup? His phone records and hers might be checked to see. His phone records might also confirm whether or not his computer modem was being accessed Sunday afternoon as he says.

And identifying others with a motive to kill Turnme Loose? Her credit and financial records might reveal disputes with persons to whom she owed money or who owed money to her. Or perhaps there are persons she had been paying regularly whose payments stopped without explanation.

g. Public records—local, state, and federal

It is essential for the legal assistant engaged in investigating work to be familiar with the various local, state, and federal governmental offices and agencies and the various records available to the public through such

SLEUTH ON THE LOOSE

Identify a company that makes a widely distributed product then access the Web site of the Occupational Safety and Health Administration at *www.osha.gov* to see if that company's product has been reported to the government as having caused injury or damage.

offices and agencies. (See Chapters 16 through 18 for a detailed discussion of accessing such records.) Had Turnme Loose been involved in any litigation (like a debt dispute, divorce, custody, or domestic violence problem) with another person recently? The court records will tell us. Did anyone catch all or a part of the license plate number on the car that struck Turnme Loose? The state department of motor vehicles can possibly identify the car and owner or we can at least determine whether it matches the number on Getta Life's car. Had Turnme Loose asserted an involuntary lien against anyone's property recently, been the grantee of a voluntary lien by anyone who owed her money, purchased or sold real property, paid her property taxes, set up a business venture with others, inherited property, filed bankruptcy, made a creditor's claim in a bankruptcy proceeding, etc.? Public records will tell us these things and lead us to people who may know something relevant to her death.

C. ▶ Locating Missing Witnesses

Once we know the identity of witnesses we then have to locate them. If we have a name and a current home and/or work address and phone number, this is easy. But sometimes we know the identity of a witness but not enough information to locate him easily. We may have a physical description without a name ("it was a big guy with a tattoo of an eagle on his right arm") or some vocational information but no name ("a guy driving a Yellow Cab") or just some general description without a name ("an older lady walking an apricot poodle"). Even if we have a name and other information, locating the witness may be difficult. After all, people do move, change jobs, or change names.

How do we find the missing witness? Again, the exercise of common sense and creative thinking are important.

1. Let's play *This Is Your Life*

The key to locating the missing witness is to start with what you already know and then plan what sources to check for more information. We will say more about specific sources to check shortly but first consider a creative technique that can be used to help you identify specific sources to check in a given case. We will call it *This Is Your Life.*

The premise of this game is that all of us have a history. More specifically, all of us have a personal, social, family, religious, educational, vocational, financial, recreational, medical, and community history. To a large extent our lives can be defined around these areas. If you want to find a person (or just find out as much as you can about a person), give thought to the individuals you might contact and to the public and private sources of documentary information you might check to obtain information in each of the listed categories concerning that person. (See Hypothetical 14-2.) And keep in mind that non-natural persons such as corporations, partnerships, limited liability companies, trusts, and unincorporated associations also have histories that can be outlined and inquired into.

It is not going too far to say that you ought to be able to take one solid piece of information about a person and think of several possible trails to follow to locate them. Everyone has past and present relatives, friends, neighbors, co-workers, supervisors, teachers, fellow students, acquaintances, and business contacts that can tell us something about them. It is in neighborhoods and communities that people are born, go to schools, shop, bank, travel, get jobs, change jobs, go on unemployment, see doctors, choose churches, get married, have children, divorce, buy and sell property, pay taxes, apply for loans, sue each other, vote, get arrested, subscribe to newspapers and magazines, order merchandise by mail, join clubs, have hobbies, join professional associations, belong to unions, get business licenses, file bankruptcy, join the military, drive cars with license plates, rent movies, subscribe to utilities, leave forwarding addresses, write wills, get sick and die and a lot of other stuff in between! All of these activities leave trails—people trails and paper trails—that can be followed by the enterprising investigator.

HYPOTHETICAL 14-2

Assume that in the Getta Life case you have interviewed Omi Gosh, the co-worker of Turnme Loose who saw her get hit by the car. You have also interviewed Keepda Peace, the investigating officer. You have learned from Omi Gosh that there was another woman on the street at the time of the hit and run who may have gotten a better look at the license plate on the car that hit Turnme Loose. Omi Gosh told you she had never seen this woman before, but that she was a well-dressed older woman (late 60s with short white hair) walking an apricot poodle on a leash and carrying a sack of groceries.

1. How would you go about locating this woman? Before you go driving madly around the streets looking for someone fitting this description, take a moment to play *This Is Your Life*. Start with what you already know about this witness:

a woman	at about 5 P.M.
in her late 60s	on Fifth Street in front of the
short white hair	Culpepper Building
well dressed	carrying a sack of groceries
walking an apricot poodle	

   If she was walking a poodle doesn't that suggest she lives near where the accident happened? And doesn't the grocery bag also tend to confirm that likelihood? Some door knocking at apartments in the immediate vicinity might be in order. And where did she buy those groceries? Probably nearby—she was walking. Let's check grocers in the immediate vicinity and ask the managers and clerks. Even if they don't recognize her, maybe they will let us post a notice that this lady will see next time she's in.

   And what about that poodle? Those dogs usually are groomed pretty regularly at dog parlors. Maybe a check with parlors in the vicinity of the scene might yield some results. And what about veterinarians?

   Failing all that, we might do a surveillance of the scene and neighborhood at the same time of day as the accident. After all, dog owners usually walk their pets on a pretty routine basis.

   Can you come up with other ideas to help locate this witness?

> 2 Assume further that Omi Gosh told you there was a yellow cab parked just down the street from where the hit and run occurred and she remembers the cab pulling out sort of fast right after the collision almost like it was going after the hit and run car. How would you go about locating the cabbie?
>
> 3. Assume further that Omi Gosh told you that a big guy wearing jeans and a tank top who had a tattoo of an eagle on his right arm took pictures of the hit and run car driving away. He had a pretty nice-looking camera strapped over his neck and just started clicking away. How would you go about locating this photographer?
>
> 4. Assume further that Keepda Peace told you that while he was at the scene, a Hispanic man approached him and told Keepda Peace he saw the whole thing. Keepda Peace told him to wait around but the man didn't. All Keepda Peace can recall is that the man wore a blue work shirt with the name Julio's Plumbing sewn onto a white oval attached to the shirt pocket. How would you go about locating this witness?

2. Sources of information for locating the missing witness

The sources we use to locate the missing witness can be logically divided into people sources, organizational sources, and documentary sources.

a. People sources

As already mentioned, everyone has past and present relatives, friends, neighbors, co-workers, supervisors, teachers, fellow students, former landlords, mail carriers, local merchants, acquaintances, and business contacts that can tell us something about them. When we start with what we know and then play the *This Is Your Life* game, we begin to think of other people who might lead us to the person we need to find. We did this with the older lady walking the apricot poodle in Hypothetical 14-2. We considered who might live near where she lives, who might have sold her groceries, who might groom her pet, and what veterinarian might treat her pet. What people sources did you plan to contact to locate the other missing witnesses in Hypothetical 14-2?

b. Organizational sources

At some time during our lives, we are all members of different public and private organizations. As a student at the school where you are studying this material, you are part of an organization and will leave a trail of people and records behind you. If you work, you are part of the employer's organization and will leave a people and records trail behind. Just think of all the organizations that people might be part of and that can become sources by which to locate them: schools, employers, clubs, religious organizations, unions, professional and trade associations, sports teams, political parties, the military, homeowners or neighborhood associations, service organizations, charitable groups, etc. Can you add to the list? What organizations did you think to check to locate the witnesses in Hypothetical 14-2?

Many organizations will provide membership information. Many have written membership directories going back years that can be accessed. Today many of them (e.g., school alumni directories) maintain Web sites with membership information on them. (See Appendix E, Resources for the Investigator, for a list of resources available to help identify the numerous clubs and professional associations to which people might belong.)

c. Documentary sources

People not only leave people trails, they leave paper trails or records trails. There are a number of public and private records and private documentary sources that can help us locate people when we have the person's name. The student should consider this section in conjunction with Chapters 16 through 18 in which various sources of information from public (local, state, and federal governments) and private sources as well as procedures for accessing that information are discussed in much greater detail. For that reason the following list is a representative sampling only of the many documentary sources that may be available for locating missing persons.

1. The telephone book.   Not only the current book but out-of-date books as well can be useful sources for locating people. The local library will typically have current books for surrounding communities (and maybe many more) but it is a good idea for the law office to keep out-of-date books for later use.

2. City/county directories.   Many counties and municipalities publish directories that provide information about individuals and businesses cross-referenced to phone numbers, addresses, and employment information. As with telephone books, it is a good idea for the investigator to keep out-of-date directories. They may be useful to pick up the trail of someone who was once present in the community but has been gone for some time or who has moved or changed jobs within the community. Sometimes, a city/county directory will contain residential phone numbers that are unlisted.

3. Court records.   Not only can the court clerks tell us who has sued who in the past or who has been charged with a crime, but the court files themselves often prove a treasure trove of information about people. Consider the kind of information that gets put in a court file during a lawsuit—pleadings containing much factual information, sworn answers to interrogatories, transcripts of sworn deposition testimony, briefs and motions containing factual allegations and the affidavits of witnesses, not to mention judgment and lien dockets. (See Chapters 3 through 5.)

4. Property and tax records.   Local and state government offices maintain detailed records regarding the purchase and sale of real property, the pledging of real and personal property as security for loans, and the payment of real and personal property taxes. All this information is recorded or filed with detailed information about the owners, their addresses, etc.

Thanks to the computerization of records, in many communities today just punching in a name or property address can disclose information regarding land transactions or taxes paid that used to take hours to locate by searching through mountains of dusty books.

5. Voter registration records. These records, usually maintained at the city or county level, may contain basic biographical information such as full name, date of birth, current (and possibly former) residence, etc., and are generally accessible to the investigator.

6. Car registration and driver's license information. If automobiles have to be registered with the local government there may be a searchable record in the office that maintains those records. If the information is kept by the state government only, check your state rules regarding access to such information. Driver's license and driving record information is usually maintained at the state level and accessibility is determined by state rules (see extended discussion of such records in Chapter 17 on accessing state and local records).

7. Marriage licenses and birth certificates. In most states, marriage licenses are on file with the county court and are searchable by the public. Birth certificates may be maintained locally and with the state department of vital statistics.

8. The post office. Forwarding addresses are kept for six months to a year by the post office as standard procedure. For privacy reasons, the post office no longer provides forwarding address information on request as to individuals or families who have moved, except to process servers or pursuant to court order. It will provide such information for businesses or private institutions in response to a written request directed to the appropriate postmaster and payment of a nominal fee, currently $3.

However, during the time that the mail forwarding order is in effect, the investigator may send a letter to the missing person at the old address and allow the post office to forward it. Or, the investigator can send a letter to the old address with instructions on the envelope: "DO NOT FORWARD. ADDRESS CORRECTION REQUESTED," and the postmaster will provide the forwarding address for a nominal fee.

Post office personnel may also be a helpful source of information about people and neighborhoods. Think what your mail tells the person who delivers it about you! (See LBD 14-4.)

Any investigation into post office rules and procedures should begin with a review of the U.S. Postal Service's home page at www.usps.gov.

9. The Social Security Administration (SSA). The SSA will not disclose the social security number of an individual. Nor will it disclose personal information on another person whose social security number you may have. However, the SSA will forward a letter to the missing person on behalf of the person seeking him if all three of the following conditions are satisfied:

- The missing person would want to know about the contents of the letter.
- The SSA could reasonably be expected to have a valid mailing address.
- All other means of contacting the person have failed.

Of course, the letter is sent without disclosing the address to the sender.

Having the social security number of the person you are seeking can be a valuable tool. Many public and private records that are accessible to the investigator (see Chapters 16 through 18) are keyed to the social security number.

Moreover, when a person really does "disappear," they frequently go back to the state where they were born or where they grew up—which often can be determined by their social security number. The first three digits in everyone's social security number designate the state in which the card was issued. Most persons currently over 20 years of age probably obtained their social security number in the state where they were living when they first went to work, around 14 to 18 years of age. A few years ago, however, the federal tax laws were changed to require that children be assigned a social security number if they are to be claimed as a dependent (and a deduction) on the tax return of a parent or guardian. So most people probably had a social security number assigned to them in the state where they were living as a child.

EXAMPLE

> If you are searching for a missing person whom you know to be 45 years old and who has a social security number beginning with the numbers 301, you know that the person was living in the state of Ohio when that number was issued because that is one of the numbers (268-302) assigned to Ohio. You can also consider that the number was probably assigned to him when he was a teenager or young adult going to work for the first time. All of this information can provide you valuable leads to locating the missing person who may have returned to Ohio or left a trail of records there, which can be picked up and traced.

Appendix E, Resources for the Investigator, sets out the three-digit prefix numbers assigned to each state and the District of Columbia by the SSA.

10. Utility company records.   People living in a community will need water, electricity, a phone, and, of course, cable TV! Subscribing to these services produces records—a paper trail that can be searched by the investigator.

11. Business license records.   It is typically the local government (as opposed to state or federal government) that issues business permits or licenses. These records are generally available for inspection to the public and can reveal a great deal more than biographical data about a person. Sometimes work history, financial data, and even credit information may be available here.

12. State licensing agencies.   In every state there are numerous trades and professions that can be practiced only with a license issued by the state. Licensing information is generally available for inspection by the public and must be kept current by the licensed person.

13. The board of education.   Records of who was enrolled at a particular school at a particular time, as well as who was employed to teach may be available here.

14. Newspaper indexes. Most newspapers will make back issues available for inspection to the public. Check obituary pages, birth announcements, local sports reports, local interest stories, community activities, organizational news, or employment announcements for the period the person was present in the community. Many public libraries and local colleges also keep back issues of area newspapers.

d. Miscellaneous sources for locating the missing witness

There are a number of other resources available to the paralegal investigator to assist in locating the missing witness. These resources are discussed in detail in Chapter 18 and so are mentioned only briefly here.

1. The Internet. It is now possible to perform sophisticated people searches on the Internet (see Note on the Internet at the beginning of Chapter 16). Most popular search engines such as Yahoo, Lycos, Excite, and WebCrawler provide this service. The Internet also provides telephone and address directories, reverse directories, and even map and directional services once an address has been located. (See Appendix E for a comprehensive listing of Internet resources available for performing people searches including numerous search engines and details on how to access them.)

2. Database vendors. There are various commercial **database vendors** that make people search libraries available for subscribers. Westlaw and Lexis are two of the better known and widely used vendors. These vendors compile information from numerous sources, public and private, and make it available to subscribers for searches. For example, the People Finder library on Westlaw allows you to search a network of public information and records containing 146 million names, 92 million households, 71 million telephone records, 40 million death certificates, and 160 million social security numbers. People Finder obtains this information from the U.S. Census Bureau, change of address records of the Postal Service, voter registration records, telephone directories, publishers mailing lists, county and city tax rolls, credit bureau information, etc. (See Appendix E for a comprehensive listing of database vendors and information on how to contact them.)

3. Tracing companies. There is always the option of utilizing a tracing company to locate the missing witness. These are private businesses, sometimes called **skip-tracing companies,** that will help locate people for a fee. Typically, the company is provided with all the information you have available about the person sought and it then uses its resources, including online computer resources that cater to these companies, to locate the person. A few of the better-known tracing companies are Infoquest, Old Friends Information Service, and USSearch. (Information on how to contact these companies is provided in Appendix E.)

4. Genealogical services. When locating a relative of the missing person would help or when trying to confirm whether the missing person is still living, a good genealogical service can be of assistance. The National Archives and Records Administration (online at www.archives.gov) maintains genealogical records in Washington and at the eleven National Archives branches around the country (see Appendix E for the location of NARA branch offices).

SLEUTH ON THE LOOSE

Think of an Internet domain name then go to *www.networksolutions .com* to see who owns that domain name. At the top left of the screen click on "WHOIS."

In addition, the Church of Jesus Christ of Latter Day Saints (LDS) has gathered what is probably the best genealogical database in the world through its Family History Library in Salt Lake City, Utah. This data is now being made available by the LDS on the Internet for no charge at www.familysearch.com. LDS also operates over 2,000 computerized Family History Centers around the country, which can provide you assistance in accessing these records. (See Appendix E for information on locating and contacting the LDS Family History Library and the Family History Center nearest you.)

5. Books.   Finally, there are a number of good books devoted to assisting the investigator in locating missing witnesses. Information on several of these is also set forth in Appendix E.

KEY WORDS AND PHRASES TO REMEMBER

accident report
business records
city/county directory
database vendors
documentary sources
educational records
employment records
investigating officer

medical records
neighborhood canvass
organizational sources
people sources
skip-tracing
This Is Your Life
Westlaw

LEARN BY DOING

LBD 14-1. Using one of the four Case Studies included in Appendix A and the information outlined below, outline a detailed plan to identify currently unknown witnesses in each case. In your plan, designate each people source and each documentary source you intend to check.

a. Case Study No. 1 (The Rowdy Outlaw Case). We need to identify any witnesses who saw Rowdy Outlaw the night of the murder.

b. Case Study No. 2 (The Soupspoon Wise Case). We need to identify all witnesses who may have been present at the Red Dog Saloon at the time of the accident.

c. Case Study No. 3 (The Vidalia Unyon Case). We need to identify all of Greene Unyon's golf partners during the last year.

d. Case Study No. 4 (The Rocky Road Project). We need to identify all owners and operators of the gas station that sits on one of the parcels our client is interested in.

LBD 14-2. Prepare an advertisement to run in the local paper seeking the witnesses described in LBD 14-1 and asking them to contact you.

LBD 14-3. We have been unable to locate the following witnesses and would like to interview them. Based on what we currently know, prepare a memorandum summarizing how you would suggest we go about locating these persons.

a. Georgette B. Good in the Rowdy Outlaw Case (Case Study No. 1).
b. Tanya Trucker in the Red Dog Saloon Case (Case Study No. 2).
c. The anonymous caller in the Vidalia Unyon Case (Case Study No. 3).
d. The heirs of farmer Edward Dig Deep in the Rocky Road Project (Case Study No. 4).

LBD 14-4. How might someone in another part of the country go about finding you if they had only your name and the name of the community you lived in fifteen years ago? Play *This Is Your Life* for yourself. Make a list of all the sources—people sources, organizational sources, and documentary or records sources—that might be utilized by an investigator to locate you.

LBD 14-5. Think of someone you haven't seen since childhood but would enjoy visiting with again. Using the people locating resources set out in Appendix E, see if you can locate that person. Keep a record of what resources you use to accomplish this task.

Chapter 15

Working with Expert Witnesses

CHAPTER OBJECTIVES

In this chapter we will consider in detail the expert witness. You will learn:

- Why attorneys use expert witnesses.
- Where to locate qualified experts.
- How to evaluate the resume of an expert
- How to assist your supervising attorney in preparing to cross examine an opposing expert witness.
- How to work effectively with an expert.

A. Who Experts Are and Why Attorneys Use Them

1. The definition of an expert

The generally accepted definition of an expert is that contained in Rule 702 of the Federal Rules of Evidence:

> If scientific, technical or other specialized knowledge will assist the trier of fact to understand the evidence or to determine a fact in issue, a witness qualified as an expert by knowledge, skill, experience, training or education, may testify thereto in the form of an opinion or otherwise.

2. Distinguishing consulting experts from testifying experts

As we have seen in Chapter 4, for purposes of formal discovery, Rule 26(b)(4) of the Federal Rules of Civil Procedure distinguishes between experts who merely consult with attorneys without testifying at trial (the **consulting expert**), and experts who not only consult but who testify as expert witnesses at trial (the **testifying expert**).

Generally, in a civil case, a party may discover the identity of experts the opposing party intends to offer as witnesses at trial as well as the substance of the facts and opinions to which they are expected to testify.

But if an expert is retained by a party only to consult with the attorney and not to testify, the opposing party may not discover either the identity of the consulting expert or the facts known or opinions held by such expert except upon a showing that the party seeking the discovery cannot obtain the facts and opinions on the same subject by other means (FRCP 26(b)(4)). Once a testifying expert has been disclosed, the opposing party may take the pretrial deposition of that expert.

In a criminal case (see Chapter 5), discovery of expert testimony is limited to receiving a written summary of the expected testimony of the testifying witness as well as reports or studies the expert may have conducted in the case (FRCrP 16(a)(1)(D) and (E) and (b)(1)(B) and (C)). There is no provision in the FRCrP for the routine pretrial deposition of the opposing party's experts.

3. How attorneys use experts

The distinction between consulting and testifying experts is important for more reasons than the different discovery rules that relate to them. Often, experts will do both consulting and testifying work. But sometimes an expert will do consulting work only. The expert may be outstanding in their field and able to assist the attorney in understanding the technical subject matter involved in the lawsuit. But that same expert may do poorly at explaining things in lay terms to a jury or may do poorly at holding up under aggressive cross-examination. So that expert, who has rendered a valuable service to the attorney as a consultant, will not testify. Another expert, more experienced and with trial-related skills, will do so instead.

Today, attorneys make regular and frequent use of experts for both consulting and testifying in all kinds of matters. For example, in the Rowdy Outlaw case (Case Study No. 1 in Appendix A), the prosecution may anticipate using:

- an expert in guitars to testify that the guitar string found at the scene of the crime was a string that had been on a guitar owned by Rowdy Outlaw;
- a pathologist to testify as to the cause of death;
- a forensic scientist to testify that the defendant's fingerprints were found on items at the scene of the murder; and
- a jury consultant to develop a juror profile and make recommendations regarding jury selection.

In the Soupspoon Wise case (Case Study No. 2 in Appendix A), the plaintiff may anticipate using:

- an accident reconstruction specialist to testify as to how the accident likely occurred;
- the treating physician to testify regarding the injuries (including causation), treatment, disability, and prognosis for Wise;
- a vocational specialist to testify regarding the available job market for Wise in his permanently disabled state and anticipated income levels;

- an economist or other qualified expert to testify regarding the present value of future medical expenses and lost income to be incurred by Wise; and
- a car salesman to testify regarding the value of the totaled vehicle.

In the Vidalia Unyon case (Case Study No. 3 in Appendix A), the attorney for Mrs. Unyon may anticipate using:

- a DNA expert to prove that Greene Unyon is the biological father of the child born to Georgia Peach;
- an accountant, banker, or financial specialist to trace the bank accounts and financial transactions of Greene Unyon; and
- a real estate appraiser to testify regarding the value of the real property at issue.

In the Rocky Road project (Case Study No. 4 in Appendix A), the attorneys for Rocky Road, Inc., may anticipate using:

- a real estate appraiser to offer an opinion regarding the value of the parcels;
- a surveyor to survey one or more of the parcels to determine their actual size; and
- a water or soil engineer to test the water and soil for contamination.

In many types of civil cases, the use of experts at trial is not just optional, it is necessary in order for the party to establish all the elements of its case.

EXAMPLE

In a personal injury case based on a negligence theory the plaintiff must present proof to establish all four elements of a negligence claim:

(1) The defendant owed plaintiff a duty of care.
(2) The defendant breached that duty of care by failing to act as a reasonable person would under the circumstances.
(3) The breach of duty by defendant was the actual and proximate (foreseeable) cause of the injuries sustained by plaintiff.
(4) The plaintiff has sustained such injuries.

In many negligence cases it is necessary to have expert proof to establish the third and fourth elements of the cause of action. Assume the case involves an automobile collision in which the plaintiff suffered permanent loss of use of the right leg. The plaintiff herself can testify about the accident and the problems she has with her leg, but she is not a qualified expert to testify concerning the medical treatment she will need in the future, or that her leg will never get better, or the extent to which she has lost the use of that leg (50 percent or 20 percent, etc.). And that's true even though it's her leg! Her attorney will have to call a qualified expert— probably the treating physician—to testify concerning his professional opinion on these matters to make out the fourth element of the cause of action. And it will probably be that same expert who will offer the necessary opinion that the injuries sustained by the plaintiff were in fact caused (the third element of the cause of action) by the automobile collision.

B. ▶ Locating Qualified Expert Witnesses

SLEUTH ON
THE LOOSE

To learn more about the resources available from Service Corps of Retired Executives including the availability of such retired workers to serve as consulting experts access the Small Business Administration Web site at *www.sba.gov.*

The paralegal may be called on by the supervising attorney to help locate an expert to assist the attorney in consulting and/or testifying on a case. We need to know where to go to locate qualified experts. Fortunately, there are a number of sources for the paralegal. Consult Appendix E, Resources for the Investigator, which contains comprehensive sources of information for locating experts.

1. The supervising attorney or other paralegals

Attorneys usually keep files on experts they have used successfully in the past or who have been recommended to them by others. Experienced paralegals also maintain files on experts they have worked with under the attorney's supervision. So the first source to turn to may be other people in your office.

2. Other attorneys or paralegals in the area

Consider who you know in your community that you might call for a reference to a good expert: other attorneys in town who have worked on the kind of case your attorney is handling now or other paralegals with more experience. Be sure to get your supervising attorney's okay before you make those calls.

3. Attorneys or paralegals in other parts of the country

If you learn of a case from any part of the country similar to the one you are working on (as you may do in your legal research) in which a favorable outcome was obtained, contact the attorney who worked on that case or a paralegal in that office and ask for the name of the expert they used, and for a recommendation regarding the expert.

4. Lawyer organizations

Many lawyers' groups maintain lists of experts available for consulting and/or testifying work. Two examples of nationwide groups that do so are the Association of Trial Lawyers of America (ATLA), an organization for plaintiffs' attorneys, and the Defense Research Institute (DRI), an organization for defense counsel. Both ATLA and DRI maintain expert witness data banks that may be searched by their members, as well as brief banks, articles, members' forums, and links to state and local organizations that may be utilized to locate potential experts. Many state and local bar associations maintain expert witness lists as well. (See Appendix E for information on how to contact ATLA and DRI and other national organizations maintaining expert witness databases.)

5. Referral companies

There are private businesses that connect attorneys with needed experts. One of the best known is Technical Advisory Service for Attorneys (TASA). TASA maintains extensive lists of experts who agree to allow TASA to recommend them to inquiring attorneys. If the attorney retains the expert, the fee for the expert is paid to TASA, which takes its contractual percentage as a fee and passes along the balance to the expert. A leading service for locating medical experts is Technical Assistance Bureau (TAB) in Washington, D.C. (See Appendix E for details on how to contact TASA and TAB.)

6. Directories

SL EUTH ON THE LOOSE

Identify a physician you want to learn more about then access the American Medical Association's Physician Select Web site at *www.ama-assn.org.* Type in the physician's name and see what information you can obtain concerning that physician.

There are numerous directories of experts in different fields. A good example is *Lawyers Desk Reference,* which lists experts by category. The *American Jurisprudence Desk Book* is a helpful source for experts. Martindale-Hubbell maintains a state-by-state consultant service as well. A leading source book for experts used by news media and talk shows is the *Yearbook of Experts, Authorities & Spokespersons.*(See Appendix E for more information on these directories.)

7. Professional, technical, and trade organizations

These organizations frequently provide the service of recommending their members who wish to work as experts to inquiring attorneys. For example, if you have a construction lawsuit and are looking for an expert with experience in commercial construction, contact your local builders' association; if you need a realtor for that lawsuit, contact your local or state realtor's association; if you need an experienced educator, contact the local school board or the National Education Association; or if you need an expert plumber, contact the union that plumbers belong to in your area.

8. Private businesses

Many private companies and firms (accountants, engineers, etc.) have employees who will serve as experts for attorneys. Typically the company or firm receives all or a portion of the fee.

9. Colleges and universities

Colleges and universities are excellent sources for experts. Contact the head of the relevant department within the college or university and ask about faculty (or retired faculty) who serve or who might be interested in serving as an expert. For example, if you are looking for an economist, contact the economics department; if you are looking for an accountant, contact the accounting or business department; or if you are looking for an engineer, contact the school of engineering. A quick look at the current catalog for the college or university will advise you of how the school is organized into various departments. Also, many colleges and universities now maintain Web sites, which provide online faculty biographies.

10. Government agencies

Government agencies or departments, whether federal or state, can sometimes refer you to retired employees who perform consulting/testifying services for attorneys.

11. Literature in the field of expertise

Don't forget to check the current literature in the field of expertise you need. Get the names of authors of notable books or recent articles in the field and contact them. If they do not wish to help you, they likely can refer you to someone who does.

12. Other experts

Other experts can refer us to new experts. If the expert your supervising attorney has been using retires, ask him to refer you to someone. Or if you contact one expert who does not wish to help, ask that expert for references.

Be sure to start and maintain your own file for experts with whom you have worked as a paralegal. Some experts may be used regularly by the supervising attorney but others may be used only on rare occasions. It is efficient and helpful to be able to check your own file and come up with the name of that expert who did so well for a client five or ten years ago.

13. The Internet

There are numerous resources available on the Internet for locating experts in many fields. See Appendix E for a comprehensive listing of Web sites useful for this purpose.

C. ▶ Evaluating the Expert

SLEUTH ON THE LOOSE

Identify a physician you want to learn more about then go to the Web site of the Federation of State Medical Boards at *www.fsmb .org* to see what you can learn concerning the status of the physician's medical license and whether he or she has ever been professionally disciplined.

An expert may look good on paper—the resume—but that doesn't mean he can be effective or successful. Unfortunately, you cannot always trust the information set out in the resume to be completely reliable.

1. Why we evaluate experts

There are two situations in which we evaluate experts:

- When we are considering using an expert for the first time
- When an expert will testify for the opposing party

2. The expert's resume

The basic tool we use to evaluate an expert is the expert's **resume,** sometimes referred to as a **biography** (or "bio" for short) or as a **curriculum vitae** (or "C.V." for short). An example of an expert's resume is set out in Illustration 15-1.

777777

7777

77777

Illustration 15-1 EXPERT'S RESUME

RUSS T. NAIL
112 Dunwoody Lane
Atlanta, Georgia 66332
(919) 444-1290 (H)
(919) 444-1356 (W)
(919) 444-9876 (FAX)
e-mail: rtnail@waxnet.com

EDUCATION:
Ph.D. (Industrial Engineering) Yourstate Institute of Technology, 1973
M.S. (Electrical Engineering) Capital City University, 1970
B.S. (Mechanical Engineering) Capital City University, 1965

EXPERIENCE:
1989-present Professor, Industrial Engineering, State University
(Head of the Department of Industrial Engineering since 1991)
1985-1989 Associate Professor, Industrial and Mechanical Engineering, Western University
1978-1985 Hammer, Saw & Nail, Consulting Engineers, Capital City, Yourstate
1973-1978 Proctor & Proctor Corporation, Assistant Planning Engineer
1965-1968 U.S. Army, Corps of Engineers

REGISTRATIONS:
Registered Professional Engineer in Yourstate since 1973 (License No. 234156)
Licensed Master Electrician

PROFESSIONAL MEMBERSHIPS:
American Society of Safety Engineers (ASSE)
Institute of Industrial Engineers (IIE)
Human Factors Society
American Society of Engineering Education
American Society of Testing and Materials
(Member, Committee E-32 on Housing Testing Evaluation)
(Member, Committee E-06 on Construction Materials)
Institute of Electrical and Electronic Engineers (IEEE)

CONSULTING:
Human Factors Analysis of U.S. Soldier Under Stress in Conflict Involving Chemical Weapons, for U.S. Army, 1982-1983
Safety Analysis of Lightweight Plastic Furniture, for American Association of Furniture Manufacturers, 1986
Product Strength Analysis, for Proctor & Proctor, 1988 and 1989
Have worked as case consultant for attorneys in more than 50 cases in 13 different states
Have testified as expert in more than 20 cases

PUBLICATIONS:
Why Geese Fly But Turkeys Can't, Doctoral Dissertation, Yourstate Institute of Technology, May 1973
Stress Experienced by Males in War and Shopping: A Statistical Analysis, International Symposium on Male Problems, Ontario, Canada, September 1981
Fatigue as a Factor in Industrial Accidents, Journal of American Industrial Engineering, Vol. XIII, No. 2, July 1991
The Role of the Computer in Electrical Engineering: A Glimpse into the Future, The Electrical Engineer, Vol. III, No. 1, September 1997
The Basics of Mechanical Engineering, College Technical Publishing, Inc., 2002 (co-authored with Heavy Hammer)

SLEUTH ON THE LOOSE

Pick a medical specialty then access *www.guideline.gov/ index.asp* to check for practice guidelines for practitioners in that specialty.

3. How to evaluate an expert

There are a number of things we can do to evaluate an expert.

a. *Look for education, training, and work experience*

Review the resume carefully to determine if the expert has the requisite expertise based on education, training, work experience, and other objective indicators. Although no one factor is ever determinative to a decision about an expert, in general, the more education the expert has the better qualified they are. The same is true with longer and more varied work experience. We also look for other positives such as professional licenses, certifications and affiliations, teaching experience, consulting experience, and authorship—the publication of books and articles in the field.

b. *Look at the specific area of expertise*

Review the resume carefully to determine if the expert has the requisite expertise in the specific field needed.

EXAMPLE

> A physician may be a highly qualified pediatrician, but if the case involves alleged malpractice in heart surgery performed on a baby, we are really looking for a well-qualified pediatric cardiopulmonary surgeon.

c. *Verify information on the resume*

1. Why it is important to verify information on the resume.   We check the educational history, work experience, and publications references on the resume to ensure that they are accurate and complete. Of course, people do sometimes make honest mistakes on their resume. But it is a sad commentary on our society that some people, even some highly qualified people, fudge their resumes by putting inaccurate, exaggerated, or incomplete information on them. (In doing your own resume, always resist that urge!)

Sometimes the inaccuracy is blatant. There was an actual case where an expert testified at a trial and claimed under oath to have a Ph.D. from a school that it turned out had never had him registered as a student. But usually the errors are minor—the person identifies himself as the sole author of an article that was actually co-written with another. Or the person misstates his job title at a prior place of employment. These may appear to be small errors, but they can be devastating to the credibility of the expert if discovered and exposed by opposing counsel.

Trial attorneys know that one way they can destroy the credibility of the opposing party's expert at trial is to demonstrate that there is some inaccuracy in the resume. Whether honest mistake or dishonesty, it is crushing. So we have to be careful to check the data given on the resume of our own experts the first time we use them. And your supervising attorney may have you check on the expert named by the opposing party.

2. How to verify an expert's credentials.   If you are checking on a person's educational background, a phone call or letter to the registrar or other student records custodian of the schools listed is appropriate.

Most schools will disclose basic registration and degree information on former students (see Chapter 18). If you are checking on a person's work background, a phone call or letter to the former employer is appropriate, asking only that the dates of employment and job titles be confirmed.

If the expert is licensed to practice his trade or profession, check with the state licensing board or agency (see Chapter 17) to confirm the dates of licensure and to learn of any disciplinary actions. Learn of any malpractice suits filed against the expert by searching the defendant's index in the clerk's offices of the various courts in the expert's state (see Chapters 16 and 17).

Listed publications can be checked by asking the expert to provide a hard copy of the book or article or by locating the publication yourself. Your public library may have a comprehensive catalog of publications. If not, try the library of the nearest college or university. Papers written to fulfill the requirements for masters or doctorate degrees (referred to usually as a thesis or dissertation) are kept on file by the college or university that granted the degree. You can check with the campus librarian or the head of the department of the expert's field.

d. Check the expert's Web site

Many experts have their own Web sites or the company they work for has one. Compare information provided about the expert there with the information on his resume. Clarify any contradictions.

e. Review the expert's publications

Review publications of the expert for consistency of opinion. Many experts list publications on their resume. Others will volunteer a list. For some others, we have to run the publications down through author/publications indexes available in the reference section of the library.

Another trap an expert can fall into is to formulate an opinion for an attorney in a pending case and then have the attorney for the opposing party confront the expert with something contradictory he wrote years earlier in a book or article. For that reason we have to be careful to either check earlier writings of the expert to be sure there is no potential conflict or to have the expert review his own prior writings.

Of course, checking the prior publications of an expert for the opposing party is a standard procedure performed by attorneys who hope to find just such a contradiction. Your supervising attorney may have you check the publications of an expert for the opposing party for that purpose, or may ask his own consulting expert to do so.

This is a time-consuming task, but remember that many technical and scientific publications are available online now. See the Appendix E materials on experts and media sources for resources available to help locate online professional publications.

f. Review publications on which the expert bases his opinions

Any book or article or other publication on which the expert claims to base all or part of his opinion should be reviewed carefully. We want to make sure the publication says what the expert says it does and to determine whether the publication is (or isn't) consistent with the opinion the expert is now expressing. This would include publications by persons other than the expert himself. Experts frequently rely on other experts for their opinions. The attorneys who will be examining the expert on either direct or cross-examination will want to be familiar with those publications.

g. Locate and review prior testimony by the expert

If the expert has testified previously either by deposition, at trial, or by affidavit, locate a copy or transcript of that testimony if possible and review it for consistency with the positions now being taken by the expert. You may locate these in the court file of the prior cases, obtain them from one of the attorneys involved in the prior cases, or ask the expert himself if he has copies or transcripts.

h. Ask for references

Ask the expert for references to other attorneys for whom the expert has consulted or testified and check them. Good experts do not mind giving these references and other attorneys do not mind being asked their opinion of an expert they have previously used. A phone call or a letter to the other attorney will almost always produce a cooperative response. Illustration 15-2 sets out typical questions to be asked of attorney references concerning an expert your supervising attorney is considering retaining.

i. Interview the expert

Interview the expert, in person if possible, but by phone if necessary. The supervising attorney will typically handle this interview, but may want the paralegal to help prepare for it or to participate. In the initial interview, discuss the case only generally without disclosing any details or privileged information. Using your communication skills (see Chapter 8), form an opinion regarding the expert's intelligence, competence, common sense (some highly educated people lack it), attitude for loyalty and

Illustration 15-2   QUESTIONS TO ASK ATTORNEY REFERENCES CONCERNING AN EXPERT WITNESS

1. Was the expert truly knowledgeable in her field?

2. Was the expert able to communicate effectively with laypersons, including the judge and jury, or did the expert confuse or turn off listeners with too much technical jargon?

3. Was the expert cooperative and easy to work with?

4. Did the expert get things done on time and meet promised deadlines?

5. How well did the expert do in testifying?

6. Did the expert communicate effectively with the jury?

7. Did the jury like/trust/believe the expert?

8. How well did the expert stand up under cross-examination?

9. What result did you obtain from the case and to what extent was the expert responsible for that result?

cooperation, and credibility. If you handle the expert interview, pass this information along to your supervising attorney.

HYPOTHETICAL 15-1

Assume that you are working as a paralegal for an attorney who has agreed to handle a products liability case involving an automobile that allegedly self-accelerated. In other words, it unexpectedly accelerated when the driver's foot was not on the gas pedal and crashed, causing the driver serious injuries. The attorney is searching for a mechanical engineer to assist in consulting with him on the case and possibly to testify as well. The resume of Russ T. Nail in Illustration 15-1 is one that you have obtained. Review that resume.

1. Looking at the educational credentials of Russ T. Nail, does he appear to be qualified to consult on this type of case? Are his degrees in the specific areas where expertise is required for this case?
2. Is Russ T. Nail's work experience varied, and do you see that as a strength or weakness?
3. Regarding the professional licenses and affiliations of Russ T. Nail, does he appear qualified to consult on this case?
4. Do the consulting history and publications of Russ T. Nail suggest he has expertise in the specific area involved in this case?
5. What questions might you want to ask Russ T. Nail to get a better idea of his expertise for this assignment?
6. If Russ T. Nail was identified to you as an expert expected to testify for the defendant in this case, what specific steps would you take to do a background check on him?

D. ▶ Working Successfully with Expert Witnesses

The paralegal may have several duties in connection with the expert's work on a client's case. Illustration 15-3 contains a list of typical duties undertaken by the paralegal in connection with expert witnesses.

In many cases the paralegal may become the expert's primary contact in the office and spend more time working with him than anyone else. It is therefore critical for the paralegal to know how to work successfully with experts.

1. Obtain the expert's fee schedule early

Experts typically charge for their services on an hourly basis. Some charge more for deposition or in-court time (e.g., $150 per hour for consulting and $200 per hour for testifying). If so, ask which rate they charge for preparing to testify. Some experts charge for their travel time as well as expenses. Often they will ask for a retainer to be paid in advance. You need to find out how much that will be. Some will bill monthly and expect prompt payment; others will bill at the end of the case. Ask what the expert charges for mileage by car and for copying costs; there is typically a flat rate (e.g., 35 cents a mile for travel by car and 20 cents a page for copying). You should collect all fee-related

Illustration 15-3   TYPICAL DUTIES OF THE PARALEGAL IN CONNECTION WITH EXPERT WITNESSES

1. The paralegal may assist the attorney in identifying a potential expert to work with the attorney on the case as a consulting and/or testifying expert.

2. The paralegal may assist the attorney in evaluating a potential expert by obtaining and reviewing the expert's resume, interviewing the expert, and by checking the background of experts identified by opposing parties.

3. The paralegal may serve as the contact person between the law office and the expert, obtaining and forwarding information for the expert's review.

4. The paralegal may assist the expert in viewing the scene or in conducting tests to support the expert's conclusions.

5. The paralegal may draft interrogatory answers involving the expert's opinions and the factual basis for the opinions.

6. The paralegal may draft interrogatory questions designed to elicit information regarding experts to be used by opposing parties.

7. The paralegal may assist in arranging the discovery deposition of the expert.

8. The paralegal may assist in preparing the expert for deposition or trial testimony.

9. The paralegal may summarize or index the deposition testimony of the expert.

10. The paralegal may assist the expert in preparing the required report under Rule 26(a)(2)(B) of the Federal Rules of Civil Procedure or in reviewing the Rule 26(a)(2)(B) report submitted by the expert for an opposing party.

information early and pass it on to the supervising attorney so an informed decision can be made.

Don't be shy about asking an expert about fees. It is just business and we do not want any misunderstandings or hard feelings to arise later that might interfere with the case.

2. Be sure the expert does not have a conflict of interest

In the initial conversation with the expert tell the expert enough about the case and the parties so you and the expert can determine that there are no conflicts of interest. For example, you want to make sure the expert has not already been contacted by a potential adverse party or isn't working on another matter for the adverse party.

3. Become familiar with technical terms and concepts in the expert's field

The paralegal (as well as the supervising attorney) must learn to speak the expert's language.

How do you acquire this knowledge and information? A trip to the library or bookstore may be in order to check out or purchase books or to review articles that will get you started. A few excursions onto the Internet may enable you to locate helpful information, too. Don't hesitate to ask the expert for help in learning the basics of terminology, concepts, and procedures in the field. But however you do it, it is important to be able to converse with the expert and understand the technical or trade terms the expert uses.

EXAMPLE

> If you are going to be working with an electrical engineer in an electrocution case you will need to become familiar with the terminology and concepts that the expert will be using to formulate his opinions—watts, volts, conductivity, arcing, grounding, etc. If you are going to be working with an economist, you will need to become familiar with inflation rates, prime interest rates, points, discounting, capitalization formulas, etc. If you are going to be working with an appraiser in a land dispute case, you will need to become familiar with comparative sales, income flow, distress sale, arms'-length transactions, etc. If you are going to be working with a medical expert in a malpractice case, you will need to become familiar with the medical terminology for the specialty involved, with the body parts and systems affected, with the medications involved, and with the relevant medical procedures involved.

4. Do not identify the expert in discovery until the decision has been made to use him for testimony

Experts are usually retained early on in a case to consult with the attorney. It may be expected that they will eventually testify as well but that decision is typically not finalized until later in the litigation. Interrogatories asking about the identity of experts who will be testifying may be served prior to that final decision being made.

Care must be taken to avoid identifying your expert(s) to the opposing party as anticipated witnesses until that decision has been made. Care must also be taken to supplement your interrogatory answers promptly to provide that information as soon as the decision has been made that the expert will testify. Illustration 15-4 sets forth a typical expert witness interrogatory and appropriate answer prior to the decision of whether a consulting expert will testify.

Illustration 15-4   SAMPLE EXPERT WITNESS INTERROGATORY AND ANSWER

Interrogatory: Identify each and every expert whom you anticipate will testify at trial in this cause and for each one identified state:

a. each and every opinion they will offer at trial;
b. the factual and circumstantial basis for each such opinion; and
c. all information that has been considered by the expert in formulating such opinion.

Answer: The plaintiff (defendant) has not yet made a final decision regarding experts who may be expected to testify at trial of this cause. When that decision has been made, the answer to this interrogatory will be supplemented.

---

5. Do not supply the expert with privileged materials

You should assume that during the course of discovery the opposing party is going to ask your testifying expert witness to produce all the information listed in Illustration 15-5.

If the paralegal has supplied the expert with materials or information subject to the attorney-client privilege or which otherwise constitute attorney work product, these privileges may be deemed waived and the opposing party allowed to see them. (See LBD 15-1.) Without the express consent of the supervising attorney, never send an expert any materials or communicate any information containing the attorney's mental impressions processes concerning the case and certainly don't communicate your own to the expert. Be sure the supervising attorney reviews *in advance* all of your correspondence to the expert as well as anything you enclose with that correspondence.

6. Always communicate a neutral picture of the case to the expert

It is critical to the credibility of the expert that the opinions expressed to the trier of fact by the expert appear and, in fact, be objective. Next to having his credentials impeached, the worst thing that can happen to an expert (and the client on whose behalf he has been called to testify) is to have the judge or jury conclude that the expert is biased or that his opinions are for sale.

Remember that anything the paralegal sends to the expert in writing or by recorded (video or sound recording) or electronic communication (e-mail) may be discovered and reviewed by the opposing party using the discovery requests set out in Illustration 15-5. Once that information is discovered, the attorney for the opposing party is then going to question your expert in a discovery deposition about all such conversations and materials, hunting for a way to suggest to the jury at trial that your expert is not objective in his opinions, has been led to those opinions by your supervising attorney (or maybe by you!), and is only selling his opinions for a fat fee.

Consequently, all of your communications to the expert should adopt

Illustration 15-5 INFORMATION TYPICALLY SOUGHT BY ATTORNEYS IN DISCOVERY CONCERNING THE OPPOSING PARTY'S EXPERT WITNESSES

The opposing attorney will use interrogatories and document requests to ask the other party to:

- produce for inspection everything that has been supplied to the expert from the law office including correspondence
- produce for inspection everything else the expert has looked at or considered in formulating his opinions
- produce for inspection everything the expert has written or recorded regarding the case, including notes, preliminary reports, drafts, correspondence, and final reports
- relate the substance and detail of all verbal communications the expert has had with anyone, including the attorney who retained him, the attorney's assistants and staff, and the attorney's client, concerning the case

a neutral tone. We cannot be seen to be urging the expert to formulate a particular helpful opinion. We must be seen as providing the expert with raw data and allowing the expert to formulate his opinions in a fair and objective fashion based on the data. It is usually permissible to indicate to the expert potential theories of the case, but this is better done verbally rather than in writing and is never done in such a way as to influence the expert. (See Hypothetical 15-2.)

HYPOTHETICAL 15-2

Assume that Dr. Russ T. Nail, whose resume we considered in Illustration 15-1, has been retained as an expert to consult with and testify for the plaintiff in the self-acceleration lawsuit described in Hypothetical 15-1. Assume further that counsel for plaintiff writes Dr. Nail the following letter.

Dear Dr. Nail:

We are pleased you will be working with us on this case. You have been a great asset to this office in obtaining several favorable settlements and judgments over the past years and we look forward to another mutually successful venture in this case.

Once you have examined the automobile in question, we hope to be able to use your expert opinion to support one or both of the following theories:

1. that the car self-accelerated due to a malfunction in or improper design of the regulator of the fuel injection system; or
2. that the car self-accelerated due to improper installation at the factory of the tension rod under the foot pad of the gas pedal. . . .

a. How many problems do you see in the wording and tone of this letter?
b. What kinds of arguments could the opposing attorney make concerning the objectivity of any opinion Russ T. Nail offers in this case based on this letter?
c. Reword this letter to correct the problems you see with it.

7. Provide materials requested by the expert promptly

You do not want to be responsible for any delays in furthering the expert's work. Often experts need considerable time, even after receiving materials concerning the case, to do the necessary review and formulate their opinions. Help them out by getting information to them promptly.

8. Keep a record of all materials sent to or received from the expert

At any given time during a case, you should be able to trace exactly what an expert has received from your office and what has been received from the expert. In addition, if original documents or other physical evidence is sent to an expert, document that in your evidence log for chain-of-custody purposes. (See Chapter 9 and Illustration 9-8.)

9. Do not allow the expert to put preliminary opinions in writing

In fact, the opinions of the expert should not be reduced to writing at all until they have been communicated to and discussed with the attorney. Why? Again, because anything produced in writing by the expert may be requested by the opposing party during discovery. If the expert has put preliminary opinions or potential problems or just musings in writing, those writings may be discovered (see Illustration 15-5 above) and used on cross-examination to challenge the validity or credibility of his final opinions.

EXAMPLE

> *Dr. Smith, when you wrote this letter containing your preliminary report to Attorney Davis six months ago, you weren't so certain of the conclusions you've expressed to the jury today, were you?*
>
> or
>
> *Well, Dr. Smith, sometime during the six months since you wrote that preliminary report, Attorney Davis got you to change your opinions to help his client's case a little, didn't he?*

10. Be familiar with all rules of evidence and procedure that apply to the expert

The paralegal must not only be familiar with the discovery rules affecting experts (see Chapters 4 and 5), but with the rules of evidence as they relate to expert testimony (see Chapters 6 and 7), and with local rules of court as they may impact on the discovery or required disclosure of expert testimony.

KEY WORDS AND PHRASES TO REMEMBER

American Jurisprudence Desk Book	fact witness
ATLA	*Lawyers Desk Reference*
background check	resume
biography	TAB
consulting expert	TASA
curriculum vitae	testifying expert
dissertation	thesis
expert witness	

LEARN BY DOING

LBD 15-1. Read and brief the case of *Bogosian v. Gulf Oil Corp.*, 738 F.2d 587 (3d Cir. 1984). Also research the law of your state courts to see if there is a ruling on the waiver of attorney work product or other privilege by providing an expert with privileged materials. Do a memorandum summarizing your conclusions.

LBD 15-2. Using the information on locating experts provided in Appendix E, locate one or more expert witnesses in your area whom you would recommend that your supervising attorney consider retaining for consulting and/or testifying purposes in the following cases. If possible, obtain a current resume or CV from each expert. If your instructor consents, it is permissible to contact these experts directly but be sure to explain to them that you are engaged in a learning exercise and not an actual case from which they could expect a fee.

    a. Case Study No. 1 (The Rowdy Outlaw Case): a fingerprint expert
    b. Case Study No. 2 (The Soupspoon Wise Case): a vocational expert
    c. Case Study No. 3 (The Vidalia Unyon Case): a DNA expert
    d. Case Study No. 4 (The Rocky Road Project): a soil contamination and reclamation expert

LBD 15-3. Arrange and conduct an interview with someone in your area who has worked as a consulting and testifying expert for attorneys. Your questions should focus on the kinds of cases on which she has worked as an expert, what credentials she believes are most impressive to a judge or jury, what methods or techniques she utilizes to be most effective (believable) with a judge or jury, the importance of appearing objective to a judge or jury, and how she prepares for cross-examination. Ask how well she thinks attorneys do at cross-examination of experts, and what are the positive and the negative aspects of working with attorneys. Prepare a memorandum summarizing your interview for your instructor.

LBD 15-4. Read the cases of *Kumho Tire Co. v. Carmichael,* 526 U.S. 137 (1999) and *Daubert v. Merrell Dow Pharmaceuticals,* 509 U.S. 579 (1993). Prepare a memorandum summarizing the procedure and factors to be considered by a trial judge in deciding whether to admit expert testimony. Research the case law in your state or federal circuit since *Daubert* to see how those courts are applying these rulings of the Supreme Court. Include a summary of those findings in your memorandum. (Note: Do not use this LBD if LBD 7-2 was used.)

Chapter 16

Public Sources of Information—Federal

CHAPTER OBJECTIVES

In this chapter you will come to appreciate the vast amount of information that is available to the investigator from the various agencies and departments in the federal government. You will learn:

- What we mean by public records as they are maintained by different government sources.
- How the U.S. government is structured around the three branches.
- Sources, including Internet sources, that enable the investigator to determine what records and information a particular federal agency or department maintains.
- Practical procedures for obtaining information from federal agencies and departments, including the Freedom of Information Act and the Privacy Act.

A. Introduction

Simply put, locating information is at the heart of the investigative task. In addition to interviewing clients and witnesses, locating missing witnesses, and working with experts, the paralegal investigator must be skilled at locating pertinent, helpful information in a proper useable form.

This chapter will deal with accessing public information from federal government sources. Chapter 17 will deal with accessing public information from state and local government sources, and Chapter 18 will deal with locating information from private (non-governmental) sources.

By **public records** or **public sources** we mean information compiled and maintained by government agencies and offices at the **federal, state,** and **local** (i.e., city and county) levels. By **private sources** we mean information in the custody of private individuals, businesses, educational institutions, or any other non-governmental custodian.

There are two distinct skills to be learned in connection with accessing public and private information as part of your investigation: (1) being able to identify the various sources of public and private information; and (2) knowing how to obtain the information from that source. In other words, knowing *where* to go for information and *how* to obtain it when you get there. And, as always in fact investigating, there are no substitutes for creative thinking and vigorous pursuit of information.

In Chapters 16 through 18 we will be making frequent references to sources of public and private information available on the Internet. Be sure to review the Note on the Internet below. As you read these chapters, consult the supplemental materials in Appendix E, Resources for the Investigator, for details on contacting and accessing information from federal, state, and local government sources.

B. Public Records in General

The amount of information gathered and maintained by government at its various levels (federal, state, and local) is truly staggering. But for the investigator, public records can present a veritable gold mine of relevant information. Not all of it is accessible in every case or by just anyone, but much of it is truly public—accessible at any time by anyone. Also, much information maintained by the government that is not truly public can be obtained in particular ways or by particular persons.

C. The Importance of Knowing How Government Works

The more the investigating paralegal knows about how government works at its various levels and the many offices and agencies maintained by the federal, state, and local governments, the more effective and efficient she will be at this investigating task. Here are some specific suggestions for those who wish to be highly skilled at locating public information:

- You should have a basic knowledge of how the federal government and your state and local governments are organized and operate.
- You should familiarize yourself with the various governmental agencies at both the federal and state level and understand what each of them does.
- If you have not had a course in administrative law in your formal course of study, go to your school, public library, or to a bookstore and obtain a current administrative law text and educate yourself.
- You should keep within arm's reach a source that gives you the addresses and phone numbers of the central, regional, and/or local governmental offices and agencies.

NOTE ON THE INTERNET

"Few technologies have spread as quickly, or become so widely used, as computers and the Internet. These information technologies are rapidly becoming common fixtures of modern social and economic life, opening opportunities and new avenues for many Americans. Not only are many more Americans using the Internet and computers at home, they also are using them at work, school, and other locations for an expanding variety of purposes." From: *A Nation Online: How Americans Are Expanding Their Use of the Internet*, a study produced by the National Telecommunications Information Administration and the Economics and Statistics Administration and released in February 2002. This study shows that Internet growth in the United States alone is phenomenal—more than half the nation (54%) was online at the time of the study and there are an estimated 2 million new Internet users per month. Forty-five percent of the American population now uses e-mail,

up from 35% in 2000. As the study concludes, "We are truly a nation online."

Indeed, we are now a world online. More than 30% of the growth in the U.S. economy since 1995 is attributable to Internet technology industries. The Department of Commerce estimates that worldwide Internet commerce—both business-to-business and business-to-consumer—will reach almost $7 trillion by 2004. By 2005, 1 billion people will be connected to the Internet and more than 75% will be outside the United States (from remarks by Secretary of Commerce Donald L. Evans before the Global Internet Summit in Reston, Virginia on March 7, 2001). More than 8 billion e-mail communications are sent within the United States each day and more than 2 billion e-mail communications are sent across international borders each day.

The Internet is now a fixture in our lives, both as consumers and professionals. Every day, more and more

information is being made available there. In today's world, one cannot be a successful investigator without having regular access to the Internet and knowing how to use it. Knowing how to use the Internet involves knowing what sites to go to in order to obtain needed information. For that reason, this work includes a large number of Internet addresses and directories. All Internet addresses and directories mentioned in this work delete the prefix *http://* to avoid repetition.

In November 2000, the Global Name Registry, which holds the rights to administer the suffix authorizations for Internet Web sites created seven new suffixes to join the original six. The authorized domain names today are:

.info—for informational sites
.name—for individuals
.aero—for the aviation industry
.pro—for professionals
.edu—for educational institutions

.org—for non-profit organizations or foundations
.mil—For military entities
.biz—for businesses only
.museum—for museums
.coop—for business cooperatives
.com—for commercial entities
.gov—for governmental bodies
.net—for a network operation

Be aware that Web sites are still of varying quality and notoriously fickle—here today, gone tomorrow. The investigating paralegal should maintain a computerized or hard-copy file of relevant Internet addresses used in investigating work and keep that list current. Periodicals for attorneys and paralegals are good sources for new and updated Web addresses. It is standard practice now to make Internet information available at seminars. Don't hesitate to ask others in the business for helpful Web sites and to share your list with others. Networking benefits us all.

• You should also keep written notes on the names and disposition of individuals you deal with by phone or in person in government offices and cultivate those contacts for future use. (See Chapter 8 on Communication Skills.)

D. Structure of the Federal Government

The starting point to knowing what records are available from the various branches, departments, and agencies of the federal government is understanding how the government is organized, becoming familiar with the various departments and agencies in each branch of the federal government, and knowing generally what each does. Illustration 16-1 sets forth in diagram form the basic structure of the federal government.

Note that although we are using the terms **departments** and **agencies,** a number of federal entities are denominated as **boards, commissions, bureaus, services, authorities,** or **offices.** A comprehensive listing of all such federal entities is not feasible here but Illustrations 16-2 and 16-5 list a few of the numerous federal agencies with which attorneys and paralegals have frequent contact.

E. ▶ Determining What a Federal Agency or Department Does and the Records It Maintains

The names of the departments and agencies in Illustrations 16-1, 16-2, and 16-5 must become more than just names on a page to the investigating paralegal. You should have a general understanding of what each federal department or agency is responsible for doing. That will provide you with knowledge, or at least an educated guess, as to the kinds of information or records the department or agency is likely to compile and maintain.

You should also know the location of the national, regional, and/or local offices of the federal agencies with which you most frequently work. Keep handy an up-to-date source from which you can quickly locate the address and phone number for these government agencies and offices.

There are a number of sources the paralegal can utilize to obtain information on federal departments and agencies:

1. Experienced people in the office

The supervising attorney or more experienced paralegals in your office will be primary sources to help you determine which federal agencies might be a source for what kinds of records or at least to direct you to someone who should know. As the paralegal gains experience in working with different federal departments and agencies, she will become the office expert on what is available where. However, the supervising attorney cannot always provide complete direction and the inexperienced paralegal must rely on her own knowledge, initiative, and common sense to track down and obtain available information from government sources. Fortunately, there are a number of helpful sources of information available to you.

2. Government publications

The government prints several helpful publications available in the reference section of many schools or public libraries or from the United States Government Printing Office (GPO). These include the *United States Government Manual* (accessible online through **GPO Access** at www

Illustration 16-1   STRUCTURE OF THE FEDERAL GOVERNMENT

THE GOVERNMENT OF THE UNITED STATES

THE CONSTITUTION

LEGISLATIVE BRANCH

THE CONGRESS
Senate   House

Architect of the Capitol
United States Botanic Garden
General Accounting Office
Government Printing Office
Library of Congress
Congressional Budget Office

EXECUTIVE BRANCH

THE PRESIDENT
THE VICE PRESIDENT

Executive Office of the President

White House Office   Office of Management and Budget
Office of the Vice President   Office of National Drug Control Policy
Council of Economic Advisers   Office of Policy Development
Council on Environmental Quality   Office of Science and Technology Policy
National Security Council   Office of the U.S. Trade Representative
Office of Administration

JUDICIAL BRANCH

The Supreme Court of the United States

United States Courts of Appeals
United States District Courts
Territorial Courts
United States Court of International Trade
United States Court of Federal Claims
United States Court of Appeals for the
  Armed Forces
United States Tax Court
United States Court of Veterans Appeals
Administrative Office of the
  United States Courts
Federal Judicial Center
United States Sentencing Commission

DEPARTMENT OF AGRICULTURE

DEPARTMENT OF COMMERCE

DEPARTMENT OF DEFENSE

DEPARTMENT OF EDUCATION

DEPARTMENT OF ENERGY

DEPARTMENT OF HEALTH AND HUMAN SERVICES

DEPARTMENT OF HOUSING AND URBAN DEVELOPMENT

DEPARTMENT OF THE INTERIOR

DEPARTMENT OF JUSTICE

DEPARTMENT OF LABOR

DEPARTMENT OF STATE

DEPARTMENT OF TRANSPORTATION

DEPARTMENT OF THE TREASURY

DEPARTMENT OF VETERANS AFFAIRS

INDEPENDENT ESTABLISHMENTS AND GOVERNMENT CORPORATIONS

African Development Foundation
Central Intelligence Agency
Commodity Futures Trading Commission
Consumer Product Safety Commission
Corporation for National and Community Service
Defense Nuclear Facilities Safety Board
Environmental Protection Agency
Equal Employment Opportunity Commission
Export-Import Bank of the U.S.
Farm Credit Administration
Federal Communications Commission
Federal Deposit Insurance Corporation
Federal Election Commission
Federal Emergency Management Agency
Federal Housing Finance Board

Federal Labor Relations Authority
Federal Maritime Commission
Federal Mediation and Conciliation Service
Federal Mine Safety and Health Review Commission
Federal Reserve System
Federal Retirement Thrift Investment Board
Federal Trade Commission
General Services Administration
Inter-American Foundation
Merit Systems Protection Board
National Aeronautics and Space Administration
National Archives and Records Administration
National Capital Planning Commission
National Credit Union Administration
National Foundation on the Arts and the Humanities

National Labor Relations Board
National Mediation Board
National Railroad Passenger Corporation (Amtrak)
National Science Foundation
National Transportation Safety Board
Nuclear Regulatory Commission
Occupational Safety and Health Review Commission
Office of Government Ethics
Office of Personnel Management
Office of Special Counsel
Panama Canal Commission
Peace Corps
Pension Benefit Guaranty Corporation
Postal Rate Commission
Railroad Retirement Board

Securities and Exchange Commission
Selective Service System
Small Business Administration
Social Security Administration
Tennessee Valley Authority
Thrift Depositor Protection Oversight Board
Trade and Development Agency
U.S. Arms Control and Disarmament Agency
U.S. Commission on Civil Rights
U.S. Information Agency
U.S. International Development Cooperation Agency
U.S. International Trade Commission
U.S. Postal Service

Source: The United States Government Manual.

.access.gpo.gov/nara/browse_gm.html) and the *Congressional Directory* (accessible online at www.access.gpo.gov/su_docs). These publications not only provide information on the scope of responsibilities of the various federal departments and agencies with addresses, phone, fax, and e-mail numbers for Washington and regional and/or local offices, they also contain current Web site addresses for the agencies.

There are numerous other more specific publications that can be obtained from the GPO. A few examples include:

- *Where to Write for Vital Records: Births, Deaths, Marriages and Divorces*
- *Fire Investigation Handbook*
- *Crime Scene Search and Physical Evidence Handbook*
- *Forensics: When Science Bears Witness*

A catalog of U.S. government publications can be obtained without cost from the Superintendent of Documents, U.S. Government Printing Office, Washington, DC 20402 or viewed and ordered at GPO Access (www.access.gpo.gov.).

A number of federal agencies also publish their own brochures summarizing the various publications available through that agency. A phone call to the agency will be sufficient to obtain the guide, usually at no cost.

There are also 1,400 federal depository libraries across the country, which contain comprehensive collections of substantially all publications of the federal government. To locate the depository library nearest you, visit www.access.gpo.gov/su_docs/dpos/adpos/adpos003.html. See Appendix E for a comprehensive listing of resources for locating and contacting the various federal departments and agencies.

3. Agency Web sites

Most federal departments and agencies have now created their own Web sites accessible on the Internet, which can provide a wealth of information on the activities of the agency, information available from it, and, frequently, instructions on how to access that information. (See Hypothetical 16-1.) Illustration 16-2 lists the Web site addresses for a number of frequently contacted federal agencies.

Illustration 16-2

WEB SITE ADDRESSES FOR FREQUENTLY CONTACTED FEDERAL AGENCIES

Social Security Administration	www.ssa.gov
Securities Exchange Commission	www.sec.gov
Federal Election Commission	www.fed.gov
Internal Revenue Service	www.irs.ustreas.gov
Consumer Product Safety Commission	www.cpsc.gov
Small Business Administration	www.sba.gov
Government Printing Office	www.access.gpo.gov
Postal Service	www.usps.gov
Environmental Protection Agency	www.epa.gov
Federal Trade Commission	www.ftc.gov

Comprehensive listings of Web site addresses for all federal agencies are available in the government publications mentioned above and from numerous online sources including:

(1) www.firstgov.gov   The best single-source site to access federal government information
(2) www.fedworld.gov   Known as FedWorld, this site is an indispensable gateway to all things federal. Operated by the U.S. Department of Commerce.
(3) www.whitehouse.gov   The White House Web site includes numerous links to practically all federal departments and agencies.
(4) //law.house.gov   The U.S. House of Representatives Internet Law Library.

Appendix E contains a comprehensive listing of online and other resources for locating and contacting federal agencies and departments.

4. State and local bar directories and handbooks

Many state and local bar associations publish directories or handbooks containing information on the various federal agencies, including how to contact regional and local offices. (See LBD 16-2.)

5. The phone book

In many locations the phone book has a separate section for government offices. Sometimes referred to as the "blue (or red, green, etc.) pages," for their distinctive color coding, this section of the phone book is a quick source for addresses and phone numbers of regional or local offices of federal agencies.

6. Commercial sources

There are numerous commercial sources available in many school and public libraries containing lists of the various federal departments and agencies, descriptions of their responsibilities and functions, as well as information on how to contact them. These resources include:

- *American Jurisprudence* 2d Desk Book
- West's *The Guide to American Law*
- Philo's *Lawyer's Desk Reference*

The leading commercial source for information on the federal government is probably CQ Press, a division of Congressional Quarterly, Inc. (online at books.cq.com), which publishes more than three hundred titles related to government activity, including the comprehensive *Washington Information Directory,* the *Federal Staff Directory,* the *Federal Regulatory Directory,* and *How to Access the Federal Government on the Internet.* (See Appendix E for details on these and other commercial resources.)

7. Treatises

There are also a number of affordable treatises devoted to this subject including:

- *Confidential Information Sources: Public and Private,* by John M. Carroll
- *Introduction to United States Government Information Sources,* by Joe Morehead, et al.
- *How to Access the Federal Government on the Internet,* by Bruce Maxwell

(See Appendix E for details on these and other treatises.)

8. Enabling statutes and regulations

To get a better understanding of the responsibilities of a particular government department or agency and the kinds of records it maintains, it is frequently helpful to review its **enabling legislation,** that is, the federal statute that created the particular agency or department. The particular federal regulations governing that agency or department should be reviewed as well. The **Code of Federal Regulations** (CFR) (searchable online at law.house.gov/cfr.htm) contains the current federal regulations for each federal agency and department. The **Federal Register** (www .access.gpo.gov/nara/#fr), published daily by the U.S. government, provides information regarding the status of proposed new or amended regulations.

HYPOTHETICAL 16-1

Assume that you work as a paralegal for the attorney representing Rocky Road Developers, Inc. (see Case Study No. 4 in Appendix A). Your supervising attorney is concerned that the two acres lying alongside the creek on which a gas station was located for years may cause his client some environmental pollution problems if it is purchased. He specifically mentions the Clean Water Act, 33 U.S.C. §1251, et seq. He wants you to determine whether the federal agency responsible for enforcing the Clean Water Act has ever inspected this property or acted on it in any way. Do the following:

a. Determine which federal agency is responsible for administering the Clean Water Act.
b. Locate the enabling legislation and current federal regulations for that agency.
c. Locate the address, phone number, e-mail address, and Web site address, if any, for the Washington, D.C. and local offices of that agency.

Mastering the organization of the many federal agencies is challenging not only because of their number but because the control of many agencies with related functions is hardly centralized. For example, there are numerous federal law enforcement agencies but their administration is spread among several different departments. The Department of Justice has administrative control over the Federal Bureau of Investigation, the Drug Enforcement Administration, and the U.S. Marshall's Service. But

SLEUTH ON
THE LOOSE

To see what changes have been made in the structure of the various agencies of the executive branch of the federal government due to passage of the Homeland Security Act in 2002 access the U.S. Government Manual at *www.access.gpo.gov/ nara/browse-gm.html.* Compare the information you locate there to the chart in Illustration 16-1.

the Treasury Department controls the Bureau of Alcohol, Tobacco, and Firearms, the Internal Revenue Service, and the Customs Service while the Department of the Interior oversees the National Park Service and the Fish and Wildlife Service. The Transportation Department administers the U.S. Coast Guard while the Defense Department directs the Army, Navy, and Air Force.

Moreover, nearly identical responsibilities often are spread among more than one federal agency. In early 2002, for example, there was publicity over the fact that, in the area of food safety, the Food and Drug Administration (FDA) is responsible for the safety of cheese pizza while the Department of Agriculture (AG) is responsible for pepperoni pizza! AG is responsible for the safety of open-faced sandwiches, the FDA for closed-face sandwiches!

And, of course, Congress occasionally exercises its power to create new agencies or merge existing ones. As the second edition of this work is being readied, the Homeland Security Act of 2002 has been signed into law (Public Law 107-296, November 25, 2002, 116 Stat. 2135) creating a major new federal agency and mandating the most significant realignment of federal agencies in a generation. The new Department of Homeland Security will merge 170,000 federal employees from 22 existing agencies and will incorporate a portion of the responsibilities of 8 other cabinet departments. (See LBD 16-6.)

The more you know about the organization of the federal government, the more efficient you will be at knowing where to go to obtain what you need.

F. ▶ How to Access Information from the Federal Government

Pursuant to the U.S. Constitution, the federal government is divided into three branches—the judicial, the executive, and the legislative. In light of the different kinds of information obtainable from each branch and the different methods of obtaining such information, we will address how to access information from each branch separately.

1. The judicial branch—court records

a. Kinds of information available in federal court records

SLEUTH ON
THE LOOSE

To learn more about government sources of information available on the Internet subscribe to the Government Sources listserv by sending an e-mail to *listserv@psuvm .psu.edu* and in the message write, "Subscribe GovDoc-L" along with your name.

A brief review of the adversarial process and, in particular, the rules of pleading and discovery covered in Chapters 3 through 5 should help the student appreciate the wealth of information that may be available in federal court records. Sworn answers to interrogatories; deposition transcripts; affidavits; positions taken in prior litigation; detail concerning an individual's personal, financial, and business affairs; or a company's history, finances, and activities may be among these public records available for a copying fee to the investigator who knows where and how to look.

b. How to conduct searches in federal court records

Records of proceedings in the federal courts, unless placed under seal by order of the court, are public records accessible by anyone. The standard way to obtain copies of court files is to visit the office of the clerk of the court in which the case was heard, ask for the file by assigned docket number, and pay the going rate for any copies made (usually 50 cents to a dollar per page). Requests for copies of files can also be accomplished by phone call or letter to the clerk's office, though there may be a delay in processing such requests and some court clerks may request payment in advance for copy and mailing costs.

After a federal court file has been closed, it will eventually be sent to a regional branch of the National Archives and Records Administration (NARA) (online at www.access.gpo.gov/nara). To locate a file there, you must obtain the case locator number for the file, which is available from the clerk of the originating court. Details on this process are available in *The Sourcebook of Federal Courts*. (See Appendix E for the addresses of the branch offices of NARA.)

Though case files in the clerk's offices will be maintained there by assigned docket number, the investigator who does not have a docket number can still locate files in which a particular person was a litigant. That is because federal court clerks maintain detailed party indexes of all civil and criminal cases that come before the court, regardless of their disposition. Increasingly, those index systems have been computerized and the investigator will be expected to conduct the search at a computer terminal. If you are unfamiliar with the computerized index system used in the clerk's office, just ask for help.

In other clerk's offices, the party index system may consist of bound computer printout sheets, or be kept on microfilm or microfiche, or even be recorded in a card file or ledger book. Needless to say, if the index system is nonelectronic, searches can be tedious and time consuming.

However they are kept, the indexes are maintained alphabetically by the names of the litigants. In criminal cases, this means cases are indexed by the defendant's name. In addition to the name, the criminal index will typically state the charge, the disposition, and the docket number. In civil cases, the cases are indexed by the names of the parties, either plaintiffs or defendants. In bankruptcy and U.S. Tax Court proceedings, the cases are indexed by the name of the petitioner(s). The civil index will typically provide the name of the case, the disposition, and the docket number.

In some clerk's offices, separate indexes are maintained for corporations that are litigants. Some index systems may contain separate plaintiff and defendant indexes though, increasingly, most systems merge both into a "party index." In older index systems, multi-party cases may be indexed only under the first-listed plaintiff and/or the first-listed defendant. But in modern systems, cases are cross-indexed under the names of all the parties.

c. Computerized resources for searching federal court records

1. Computerized database vendors. A number of resources exist to enable the investigator to search federal court files and dockets by computer modem. The two leading computerized database vendors, Westlaw, owned by West Group, and Lexis, owned by Reed Elsevier, are available by paid subscription only. Both provide docket search libraries that enable the investigator to perform online searches covering cases decided in all the federal appellate courts, increasing numbers of U.S. district courts, the U.S. bankruptcy courts, U.S. tax courts, and other specialized federal courts. Access to both Westlaw and Lexis is now available to subscribers through the Internet, eliminating the need for specialized software and phone numbers. Easy-to-use graphic and point-and-click tools have replaced search queries. The new Lexis Xchange can be previewed at www.Lexis.com. And Westlaw's Internet access can be previewed at www.westlaw.com.

2. PACER. The court indexes and dockets of most civil, criminal, bankruptcy, and appellate cases filed in the federal courts throughout the country are now searchable using the Public Access to Court Electronic Records (PACER) system. Created and administered by the Administrative Office of the U.S. Courts, this service allows any subscriber to dial in by modem to a particular federal district or bankruptcy court clerk's office and quickly retrieve case information and dockets. The charge is currently $.60 per minute and information can be downloaded and copied by the user. The U.S. Party/Case Index feature of PACER allows subscribers to search regionally or nationwide by name or social security number in the bankruptcy index, by name and nature of suit in the civil case index, by defendant in the criminal index, and by party name in the appellate court index. (See Appendix E for details on subscribing to PACER.)

3. The Internet. Increasing amounts of information on the judicial branch of the federal government are available on the Internet. A comprehensive list of such sources is available in Appendix E, but a few noteworthy sites are as follows:

- www.supremecourtus.gov This is the official site of the U.S. Supreme Court. It offers access to court slip opinions, term orders, argument calendar, court rules, etc.
- www.uscourts.gov This is the Federal Judiciary home page. It offers information on the structure of the judiciary, statistics on case loads, judicial vacancies, answers to FAQs, lists of publications and links to other Web sites.
- www.law.indiana.edu/law This is the site for Indiana University's Virtual Library.
- www.law.cornell/edu This is the site for Cornell University's comprehensive collection of law-related resources.
- www.kentlaw.edu/legal_resources This is the site for Chicago Kent's Guide to Legal Resources.

LawCrawler (www.lawcrawler.com) is a powerful tool for locating law-related sites on the Internet. See Appendix E for a comprehensive listing of such sites.

HYPOTHETICAL 16-2

Assume that the attorney for whom you work has asked you to do some research on a corporation that does business in your area. (For purposes of this Hypothetical, choose an actual corporation doing business in your area—a large retailer, for example.) Specifically, your attorney has asked you to find information on every federal lawsuit this corporation has been a party to in the last five years. That would include being a plaintiff or defendant in a civil suit or a defendant in a federal criminal action.

Write out a plan of investigation covering the sources you intend to search to access this information for your supervising attorney. In your plan, list the sources in the order you plan to access them. (To perform further work using this Hypothetical, see LBD 16-1.)

2. The legislative branch—Congress

SLEUTH ON
THE LOOSE

Identify some piece of federal legislation currently being considered by Congress then go to //thomas.loc.gov and see if you can locate the text of committee debate on the legislation or other information regarding its status.

Congressional records are, for the most part, readily available to the public. Sessions of Congress are normally open to the public and televised. Most congressional committee hearings are likewise open to the public. The *Congressional Record* (accessible online at law.house.gov and available through Westlaw and Lexis) is the official record of Congress and contains floor debate as well as the text of proposed bills and amendments. All committee reports (except those containing classified information) and most committee hearings are published by the government. The *United States Code Congressional and Administrative News* is a valuable source for selected committee reports as well.

In addition, copies of the numerous publications authorized by Congress are available at federal depository libraries throughout the country or through the GPO. (See discussion above and Appendix E.) Furthermore, all members of Congress retain staff members who are typically responsive to requests for information regarding the status of legislation, congressional investigations, or other official matters—at least to their constituents.

a. Congress on the Internet

Information from and about Congress is increasingly available on the Internet. The Web site of the GPO has already been mentioned, and a comprehensive listing of Web sites for congressional information is provided in Appendix E. Here are the Internet addresses for a few significant Web sites that may prove important to the legal investigator:

- www.access.gpo.gov/su_docs   GPO Access provides access to the CFR, Federal Register, U.S. Code, Congressional Directory, U.S. Government Manual, Government Administrative Office (GAO) reports, and the monthly catalog of U.S. government publications.
- thomas.loc.gov   A government operated site, Thomas provides information on congressional procedures, legislation pending in Congress, and select committee reports.
- www.senate.gov   This is the home page of the U.S. Senate.
- www.house.gov   This is the home page of the U.S. House of Representatives.

- lcweb.loc.gov/homepage/lchp.htm   This is the home page of the Library of Congress.

b. Accessing Congress through database vendors

Westlaw and Lexis both provide online legislative research capabilities. Both access the Congressional Record. Westlaw's Congressional Quarterly's Washington Alert (CQ-ALERT) database provides access to all congressional actions beginning with the 98th Congress. Its BILLS database provides the full text of all bills pending in Congress and BILLTRK provides data for tracking pending congressional legislation. Within the GENFED library of Lexis, one can select BILLS to obtain the full text of pending legislation, BLTRCK to trace legislation as it moves through Congress, or CMTRPT to obtain committee reports.

Other computerized database vendors provide congressional information as well. The Electronic Legislative Search Service (ELISS) prepared by Commerce Clearing House (www.cch.com) will, for a fee, provide copies of bills, committee reports, and congressional testimony. Dialog (online at www.dialog.com), "the world's largest card catalog," provides a congressional research service. Congressional Information Services (CIS, online at www.cispubs.com and available through Lexis and Dialog) provides detailed legislative histories of public laws. (See Appendix E for a comprehensive listing of database vendors.) (See LBD 16-2.)

3. The executive branch

a. Executive orders

According to the National Archives and Records Administration, President Kennedy signed 214 executive orders between 1961 and 1963; Johnson, 324 (1963 to 1969); Nixon, 346 (1969 to 1974); Ford, 169 (1974 to 1977); Carter, 320 (1977 to 1981); Reagan, 381 (1981 to 1989); Bush, 166 (1989 to 1993); and Clinton, 363 (1993 to 2001). Executive order tables can be viewed online at www.nara.gov/fedreg/eo.html.

b. Obtaining information from the White House

The home page of the White House is www.whitehouse.gov. The GPO's **Federal Bulletin Board** also provides access to numerous White House documents at fedbbs.access.gpo.gov.

SL EUTH ON THE LOOSE

To learn more about making a Freedom of Information Act request to a federal agency, including forms and information on the FOIA officers for a particular agency, access a site operated by the American Civil Liberties Union at *www.aclu.org/library/foia.html.*

c. Obtaining information from executive agencies

As Illustration 16-1 suggests, most federal agencies and departments are under the authority of the executive branch. The executive branch of the federal government includes the cabinet departments, the branches of the military, various regulatory agencies such as the Environmental Protection Agency, the Food and Drug Administration, and the Securities Exchange Commission, government corporations, and various law enforcement agencies.

1. The Freedom of Information Act. The primary means of accessing information from agencies and departments of the executive branch of government is the Freedom of Information Act, 5 U.S.C. §552 (FOIA). The FOIA was enacted by Congress in 1966 and establishes a presumption that records in the possession of agencies and departments of the executive branch of the federal government are accessible by the public. The scope of the FOIA is broad. It includes the agencies, offices, and departments of the executive branch of the federal government such as the Department of Defense, the Office of Management and Budget, and the National Security Council. It also includes independent federal regulatory agencies such as the Federal Trade Commission, the Environmental Protection Agency, the Securities Exchange Commission, and the Federal Communications Commission. Included too are federal government-controlled corporations such as the Post Office, the Tennessee Valley Authority, the Smithsonian Institution, and Amtrak.

The FOIA does not apply to Congress, the federal courts or the Executive Office staff such as the White House Chief of Staff or others whose function is to advise and assist the president. It also does not cover state and local government agencies (although, as we will see in Chapter 17, every state has laws guaranteeing citizens access to some records of state agencies), private businesses, private organizations, schools, or individuals.

In general, the kind of information that can be obtained from federal agencies under the FOIA is information concerning how the agency operates, what actions it has been taking, how it has spent money, and what statistics or information it has collected in the course of its operation. All agency records are accessible through the FOIA except those falling into one of nine designated **exemption** categories as follows:

- matters related to foreign policy or national security;
- information related to the internal personnel rules and practices of the agency;
- information declared exempt under other federal laws—known as the "catch-all" exception;
- trade secret and other confidential business information;
- internal agency correspondence and policy memoranda;
- documents that would constitute an unwarranted invasion of an individual's privacy, such as medical or personnel information (this exemption only applies to living natural persons);
- information that would interfere with law enforcement activities;
- information related to federal regulation of banks; and
- certain geological information regarding oil and gas wells.

The burden is on the agency receiving the request to demonstrate that information requested falls into one of the exempt categories; otherwise it must be produced. If part of a record falls within an exemption and part does not, the part that does not must be produced. Moreover, other than the "catch-all" exemption, the government agency can exercise its discretion to release records that might fall within one of the other exemptions if the requester can convince the agency it is "in the public interest" to do so.

There is no central government office which handles FOIA requests. Each agency is required to designate an officer to handle requests submitted to that agency. The statute requires that an agency respond to a citizen's request for records within ten working days, though the agency may request an extension. The agency may also charge a nominal fee for locating, reviewing, and copying documents. It is prudent to request the fee schedule from an agency before making the request. Some agencies may require prepayment of fees. Sometimes agencies will waive the fee.

The current name, address, and phone number of the FOIA officer designated by a particular agency can be located in the regulations for that agency. Regulations for the various federal agencies are collected in the **Code of Federal Regulations** (CFR) (searchable online at law.house.gov/cfr.htm). Or the paralegal can simply call or write the particular federal agency to obtain that information. The Congressional Directory, the U.S. Government Manual (searchable online at www.access.gpo.gov/su_docs), and other written resources contain comprehensive lists of FOIA officers. The Office of Information and Privacy (OIP) within the Department of Justice (www.usdoj.gov) is the principal contact point within the executive branch for advice and policy guidance on matters pertaining to the FOIA. The OIP maintains a FOIA Counselor Service that may be reached at (202) 514-3642 (514-FOIA). The OIP also maintains an excellent Web site with updated lists of FOIA officers for the various federal agencies at www.usdoj.gov/foia/att_a.htm and a site with a collection of links to agency FOIA sites at www.usdoj.gov/foia/other_age.htm.

Two excellent guides that are available to assist you in successfully completing a FOIA request are *How to Use the Federal FOI Act* and *A Citizen's Guide on How to Use the Freedom of Information Act and The Privacy Act Requesting Government Documents.* The American Civil Liberties Union also has a comprehensive publication on the FOIA called *Using the Freedom of Information Act: A Step-by-Step Guide,* which can be ordered from the ACLU or downloaded from its Web site at www. aclu.org/library/foia .html#addresses. (See Appendix E for comprehensive information on available FOIA resources.)

FOIA requests must be made in writing, directed to the specific agency from which the records are sought, and must specify the records sought. Illustration 16-3 shows a typical FOIA request letter.

2. The Privacy Act. Another federal statute that is available for accessing records from executive agencies and departments of the federal government is the Privacy Act, 5 U.S.C. §552a. Passed in 1974 as an amendment to the FOIA, the Privacy Act allows an individual to access personal information held by an agency about him- or herself and to seek the amendment of incorrect information. The executive departments and agencies subject to the FOIA are also subject to the Privacy Act.

Generally speaking, an individual may succeed in accessing more information about himself under the Privacy Act than he could about another person under the FOIA. However, the Privacy Act also recognizes exemptions that an agency may rely on to withhold information. Those exemptions include:

- information classified in the interests of national defense or foreign policy;
- information related to law enforcement activities;

SLEUTH ON THE LOOSE

Visit the Web site of the Center for Democracy and Technology at *www.cdt.org* and see what privacy issues are currently being discussed there.

Illustration 16-3   FOIA LETTER

Date

FOIA Officer (or Agency Head)
Name of Federal Agency
City, State and Zip Code

Re: Freedom of Information Act Request

Dear _____:

Pursuant to the provisions of the Freedom of Information Act, 5 U.S.C. §552, I request a copy of the following documents: (list and describe in detail the specific records sought).

In order to determine my status as to fees, you should be aware that I am (insert an appropriate requester description from the five that follow):

• a representative of the news media and this request is for news gathering and not for commercial use
• a representative of a public interest organization and this request is for news gathering and not for commercial use
• affiliated with an educational or non-commercial scientific institution and this request is made for scholarly or scientific purpose and not for commercial use
• an individual seeking information for personal use and not for commercial use
• affiliated with a private corporation and seeking information for use in the company's business

I will reimburse you for fees up to the amount of $_____. If you determine that the costs will exceed that amount, please advise me of the anticipated total cost before making the copies.

(or)

I am requesting a waiver or reduction in fees for complying with this request because the requested release of information is primarily benefiting the public and not for commercial use.

Thank you for your consideration of this request.

Sincerely,

Name
Address
Phone No.

• information developed in connection with Secret Service protection;
• information related to the identity of confidential sources in connection with making decisions regarding federal employment, military service, federal contracts or classification; and
• information related to testing or examination for promotion in federal service or the armed services.

Illustration 16-4 shows a typical Privacy Act request.

Since the Privacy Act is limited to an individual's right to request information about himself, its usefulness to the investigator is primarily in assisting a client or cooperative witness to make such a request to obtain relevant information the government may have.

Illustration 16-5 lists several of the agencies mentioned in Illustrations

Illustration 16-4 PRIVACY ACT LETTER

> Date
>
> Privacy Act Officer (or System of Records Manager)
> Name of Federal Agency
> City, State and Zip Code
>
> Re: Privacy Act Request
>
> Dear _____:
>
> Pursuant to the provisions of the Privacy Act of 1974, 5 U.S.C. §522a, I request a copy of (or access to) any and all records (or list and describe in detail specific records sought) concerning me maintained by your agency. This request is also made under the Freedom of Information Act, 5 U.S.C. §552.
>
> I will reimburse you for copying costs up to the amount of $_____. If you determine that the costs will exceed that amount, please advise me of the anticipated total cost before making the copies.
>
> Enclosed is a notarized signature page (or other identifying document) that will verify my identity.
>
> Thank you for your cooperation.
>
> Sincerely,
>
> Name
> Address
> Phone No.

Illustration 16-5 SELECTED FEDERAL AGENCIES AND THEIR RECORDS

> 1. Social Security Administration (SSA) (www.ssa.gov). The SSA maintains extensive records of employment and earnings for virtually all Americans living or dead as well as millions of foreigners who work or once worked in this country. In addition, the SSA maintains records concerning income, indebtedness, marital status, medical history, and household arrangements for anyone who has ever applied for Social Security benefits including SSI, Medicare, Medicaid, or AFDC. SSA records are confidential and generally not available for public or even law enforcement review. However, any individual can access their own SSA records. (See, e.g., the Request for Earnings and Benefit Statement in Illustration 16-6.) In addition, the SSA will consider forwarding requested mail contact "for humanitarian purposes" to a person on whom it maintains records. (See Chapter 18.) Also, the social security number of a person itself, although not obtainable directly from the SSA, can provide the investigator with valuable clues regarding the person's whereabouts and can be used to access other information about the individual in the private domain (see Chapter 14 and the Social Security Index of Assigned Numbers in Appendix E).
>
> 2. Bureau of the Census (www.cb.gov). The Census Bureau collects and maintains substantial data on U.S. residents every ten years, including names, ages, addresses, gender, race, ethnic origin, employment, income, and marital status. The records of the bureau are confidential but can be accessed by the individual concerned, the parent or guardian of a minor, or the surviving spouse or executor of a deceased person.
>
> 3. Bureau of Labor Statistics (BLS) (www.bls.gov). The BLS gathers and processes a substantial amount of statistics related to the American work force. Its annual *Area Wage Survey* and monthly *Employment and Earnings Report* are recognized as authoritative guides in this area. But in addition to its publications, the BLS, through its Public Affairs Office, can make available other and more specific statistical breakdowns.
>
> 4. Securities and Exchange Commission (SEC) (www.sec.gov). The SEC gathers and maintains records on over 1,100 corporations whose stock is publicly traded, over 1,200 broker-dealers, and over 5,000 investment companies. A company seeking permission to make a public stock offering must file a registration statement

Illustration 16-5   SELECTED FEDERAL AGENCIES AND THEIR RECORDS *(continued)*

(Form S-1), including a prospectus, with the SEC. Those documents, along with the required annual reports (Form 10-K), quarterly reports (Form 10-Q), and proxy statements, are open to public inspection and contain enormous amounts of data not only on the company itself but on the affairs of its officers, directors, insider owners, and beneficial owners of five percent or more of its shares. Whether a regulated company or any of its principals is the target of an investigation by the SEC is determinable by consulting the *Securities Violations Bulletin,* issued quarterly by the SEC. Further, if a civil suit or criminal prosecution has been brought against a company or any of its principals, that litigation file will be open to public inspection in the forum court.

The SEC can provide a wealth of information to the investigator on any company it regulates. This information is easily accessible. All documents on file for regulated corporations may be located, searched, and downloaded from a Web site maintained by the SEC called EDGAR (Electronic Data Gathering Analysis and Retrieval System) at www.sec.gov/edgarhp.htm. There is no charge and exhibits are included. The search may be made by company name, type of record sought (e.g., 10-K, proxy statement, etc.), or date of filing. Records are generally accessible on EDGAR within one business day of their filing. SEC filings can also be obtained on Westlaw or Lexis, both of which maintain a "SEC-Online" database. Or the investigator can utilize a public records search company such as CCH Washington Service Bureau (see Appendix E).

Other federal agencies that require periodic filings of companies within the scope of their regulatory activities and that are accessible to the public include the Interstate Commerce Commission, the Federal Communications Commission, the Environmental Protection Agency, the Food and Drug Administration, and the Bureau of Alcohol, Tobacco and Firearms.

5. Federal Housing Authority (FHA) (www.fha.gov). The FHA maintains records on all persons who have applied for federal housing assistance. Most of those records are accessible by means of a proper FOIA request.

6. Internal Revenue Service (IRS) (www.irs.ustreas.gov). The IRS administers the federal tax laws and maintains records on the age, gender, and marital status of taxpayers and their dependents as well as all sources of income. The records of the IRS are confidential, but a taxpayer or his authorized representative can request copies of his tax returns or audit report forms. (See Request for Copy or Transcript of Tax Form set out in Illustration 16-7.) Moreover, the annual reports of charities and tax-exempt corporations and foundations (Form 990) are accessible. These may contain information about the officers of the organization. If the IRS has settled a dispute with a taxpayer for less than the amount originally owed, an IRS Form 7249-M will be filed at the regional IRS office for one year and thereafter in Washington. Furthermore, if the dispute between a taxpayer and the IRS has made its way into the U.S. Tax Court or the U.S. District Court, those case files will be open to public inspection.

7. Federal Election Commission (FEC) (www.fec.gov). The FEC requires candidates for federal public office to file campaign finance reports containing information on donors, consultants, and vendors used by the candidate. These reports are accessible.

8. General Services Administration (GSA) (www.gsa.gov). The GSA maintains records on a wide range of government activity, including its real and personal property, operating costs, construction projects, and personnel. For example, the Civilian Personnel Records Correspondence Section of the GSA is a primary source for information on non-active military personnel, as well as job title, grade, salary, and duty station of all former federal employees. The Office of Personnel Management (www.opm.gov) also maintains records on retired military and civilian employees. Information on a veteran's military record can be obtained from National Personnel Records Center, Military Personnel Records, 9700 Page Blvd., St. Louis, MO 63132-5100. Use Standard Form 180, Request Pertaining to Military Records (available online at www.nara.gov/regional/mprsf180.html) or from a regional office of the Department of Veteran's Affairs.

To obtain available information on current federal employees, contact the employing agency directly or contact the Civil Service Commission (www.csc.gov). For information on current military personnel, contact the particular branch of the military in which they serve. Each branch operates a locator service, the address of which is available in the U.S. Government Manual (reviewable online at www.access.gpo.gov/nara/browse-gm.html).

9. The National Archives and Records Administration (NARA) (www.nara.gov or www.archives.gov). The NARA makes available a wealth of information on individuals. It provides access to family histories and allows a genealogy search; it maintains veteran's records; and from its Web site it provides access to numbers of government documents including the U.S. Constitution, the CFR, the Federal Register, and the U.S. Government Manual.

Illustration 16-6   REQUEST FOR EARNINGS AND BENEFITS STATEMENT

Form Approved
OMB No. 0960-0466

SP ☐

Request for Earnings and Benefit Estimate Statement

☐ Please check this box if you want to get your statement in Spanish instead of English.

Please print or type your answers. When you have completed the form, fold it and mail it to us. (If you prefer to send your request using the Internet, contact us at http://www.ssa.gov)

1. Name shown on your Social Security card:

_____   _____
First Name   Middle Initial

_____
Last Name Only

2. Your Social Security number as shown on your card:

☐☐☐ – ☐☐ – ☐☐☐☐

3. Your date of birth (Mo.-Day-Yr.)

☐☐ – ☐☐ – ☐☐☐☐

4. Other Social Security numbers you have used:

☐☐☐ – ☐☐ – ☐☐☐☐

☐☐☐ – ☐☐ – ☐☐☐☐

5. Your Sex: ☐ Male   ☐ Female

Form **SSA-7004-SM** (6-98) Destroy Prior Editions

For items 6 and 8 show only earnings covered by Social Security. Do NOT include wages from State, local or Federal Government employment that are NOT covered for Social Security or that are covered ONLY by Medicare.

6. Show your actual earnings (wages and/or net self-employment income) for last year and your estimated earnings for this year.

   A. Last year's actual earnings: *(Dollars Only)*

   $ ☐☐☐ , ☐☐☐ . 0 0

   B. This year's estimated earnings: *(Dollars Only)*

   $ ☐☐☐ , ☐☐☐ . 0 0

7. Show the age at which you plan to stop working.

   ☐☐ *(Show only one age)*

8. Below, show the average yearly amount (not your total future lifetime earnings) that you think you will earn between now and when you plan to stop working. Include performance or scheduled pay increases or bonuses, but not cost-of-living increases.

   If you expect to earn significantly more or less in the future due to promotions, job changes, part-time work, or an absence from the work force, enter the amount that most closely reflects your future average yearly earnings.

   If you don't expect any significant changes, show the same amount you are earning now (the amount in 6B).

   Future average yearly earnings: *(Dollars Only)*

   $ ☐☐☐ , ☐☐☐ . 0 0

⊛ Printed on recycled paper

9. Do you want us to send the statement:
   • To you? Enter your name and mailing address.
   • To someone else (your accountant, pension plan, etc.)? Enter your name with "c/o" and the name and address of that person or organization.

Name
_____

Street Address (Include Apt. No., P.O. Box, or Rural Route)
_____

_____
City   State   Zip Code

NOTICE:
I am asking for information about my own Social Security record or the record of a person I am authorized to represent. I understand that if I deliberately request information under false pretenses, I may be guilty of a Federal crime and could be fined and/or imprisoned. I authorize you to use a contractor to send the statement of earnings and benefit estimates to the person named in item 9.

▲

Please sign your name (Do Not Print)

_____

Date _____   _____
              (Area Code) Daytime Telephone No.

Illustration 16-7   REQUEST FOR COPY OR TRANSCRIPT OF TAX FORM

Form **4506**
(Rev. May 1997)

Department of the Treasury
Internal Revenue Service

Request for Copy or Transcript of Tax Form

▶ Read instructions before completing this form.

▶ Type or print clearly. Request may be rejected if the form is incomplete or illegible.

OMB No. 1545-0429

Note: *Do not* use this form to get *tax account information.* Instead, see instructions below.

1a Name shown on tax form. If a joint return, enter the name shown first.	1b First social security number on tax form or employer identification number (see instructions)
2a If a joint return, spouse's name shown on tax form	2b Second social security number on tax form

3   Current name, address (including apt., room, or suite no.), city, state, and ZIP code

4   Address, (including apt., room, or suite no.), city, state, and ZIP code shown on the last return filed if different from line 3

5   If copy of form or a tax return transcript is to be mailed to someone else, enter the third party's name and address

6   If we cannot find a record of your tax form and you want the payment refunded to the third party, check here . . . . . . ▶ ☐

7   If name in third party's records differs from line 1a above, enter that name here (see instructions) ▶

8   Check only one box to show what you want. There is **no charge** for items 8a, b, and c:

a   ☐ Tax return transcript of Form 1040 series filed during the **current calendar year** and the **3 prior calendar years** (see instructions).

b   ☐ Verification of nonfiling.

c   ☐ Form(s) W-2 information (see instructions).

d   ☐ Copy of tax form and all attachments (including Form(s) W-2, schedules, or other forms). **The charge is $23 for each period requested.**
   Note: *If these copies must be certified for court or administrative proceedings, see instructions and check here* . . . . . ▶ ☐

9   If this request is to meet a requirement of one of the following, check all boxes that apply.
   ☐ Small Business Administration   ☐ Department of Education   ☐ Department of Veterans Affairs   ☐ Financial institution

10 **Tax form number** (Form 1040, 1040A, 941, etc.)	12 Complete only if **line 8d** is checked. Amount due:	
	a Cost for each period	$ 23.00
11 **Tax period(s)** (year or period ended date). If more than four, see instructions.	b Number of tax periods requested on line 11	
	c Total cost. Multiply line 12a by line 12b. .	$
	Full payment must accompany your request. Make check or money order payable to "Internal Revenue Service."	

Caution: *Before signing, make sure all items are complete and the form is dated.*

I declare that I am either the taxpayer whose name is shown on line 1a or 2a, or a person authorized to obtain the tax information requested. I am aware that based upon this form, the IRS will release the tax information requested to any party shown on line 5. The IRS has no control over what that party does with the information.

Please Sign Here ▶

Signature. See instructions. If other than taxpayer, attach authorization document.   Date

Title (if line 1a above is a corporation, partnership, estate, or trust)

Spouse's signature   Date

Telephone number of requester
(   )

Best time to call

TRY A TAX RETURN TRANSCRIPT (see line 8a instructions)

Instructions

Section references are to the Internal Revenue Code.

TIP: If you had your tax form filled in by a paid preparer, check first to see if you can get a copy from the preparer. This may save you both time and money.

Purpose of Form.—Use Form 4506 to get a tax return transcript, verification that you did not file a Federal tax return, Form W-2 information, or a copy of a tax form. Allow 6 weeks after you file a tax form before you request a copy of it or a transcript. For W-2

information, wait 13 months after the end of the year in which the wages were earned. For example, wait until Feb. 1999 to request W-2 information for wages earned in 1997.

   Do not use this form to request Forms 1099 or tax account information. See this page for details on how to get these items.

Note: *Form 4506 must be received by the IRS within 60 calendar days after the date you signed and dated the request.*

How Long Will It Take?—You can get a tax return transcript or verification of nonfiling within 7 to 10 workdays after the IRS receives your request. It can take up to 60 calendar

days to get a copy of a tax form or W-2 information. To avoid any delay, be sure to furnish all the information asked for on Form 4506.

Forms 1099.—If you need a copy of a Form 1099, contact the payer. If the payer cannot help you, call or visit the IRS to get Form 1099 information.

Tax Account Information.—If you need a statement of your tax account showing any later changes that you or the IRS made to the original return, request tax account information. Tax account information lists

(Continued on back)

For Privacy Act and Paperwork Reduction Act Notice, see back of form.   Cat. No. 41721E   Form **4506** (Rev. 5-97)

16-1 and 16-2 together with a brief summary of the kinds of records they maintain and that you will find that you can—or can't—access.

The examples given in Illustration 16-5 are just a drop in the bucket compared to all of the information accessible from federal agencies. The investigating paralegal should be constantly expanding her knowledge of what the different agencies do, the records they maintain, what records are accessible and how.

3. Agency Web sites. The various federal agencies are placing increasing amounts of information on their Web sites. Take note of the numerous agency Web site addresses set out in Illustrations 16-2 and 16-5 and the resources provided for locating all such sites in Section E.3 of this chapter and in Appendix E. The paralegal should maintain her own updated list of such sites and when performing an investigation try assessing the information on those sites before undertaking a FOIA request.

HYPOTHETICAL 16-3

Assume that the attorney you work for is defending Rowdy Outlaw on charges he murdered Bobbette Bouvier (see Case Study No. 1 in Appendix A). Your supervising attorney says that she wants you to obtain Rowdy Outlaw's military service records and those of Jack Gates. She is particularly interested in accessing information regarding the circumstances of Gates's discharge from the military.

a. What government sources will you contact to obtain this information and how will you make contact with them?
b. If you think it advisable or necessary to prepare one or more FOIA or Privacy Act requests, draft those for your instructor's review in as final a form as possible.
c. What additional information would it be helpful to have to complete this assignment?

4. Online database vendors. Much information concerning the actions taken by executive federal agencies is now accessible through online database vendors. For example, Westlaw provides access to both the Code of Federal Regulations (CFR), the Federal Register, and the ability to track the history of proposed federal regulations through its USREGTRK database. Its Federal Filings database provides securities filing data on thousands of companies. The GENFED database in Lexis provides access to the CFR and Federal Register and the ability to locate cases interpreting a particular provision of CFR. Lexis also maintains a DOCKET database within which there is a Sanction file that provides information on sanctions and other oversight actions taken by a myriad of federal agencies including the Securities Exchange Commission, Food and Drug Administration, and the Department of Justice fraud task force, to name just a few.

There are also search companies that, for a fee, will perform electronic searches for public record information available from federal agencies. See Appendix E for a comprehensive list of search companies.

KEY WORDS AND PHRASES TO REMEMBER

administrative agency	GPO
administrative law	home page
blue pages	Internet
browser	ISP
case/party index	judicial branch
CFR	legislative branch
clerk's office	Lexis
database vendor	local government
Dialog	PACER
ELISS	Privacy Act
enabling legislation	private records
executive branch	public records
federal government	search engine
Federal Bulletin Board	state government
Federal Register	URL
federal regulation	Web
FOIA	Westlaw

LEARN BY DOING

LBD 16-1. For the actual corporation you selected for Hypothetical 16–2, use the federal judiciary information sources set out in Appendix E to determine every federal lawsuit to which this corporation has been a party in the last five years. That includes being a plaintiff or defendant in a civil suit or a defendant in a federal criminal action. Prepare a memorandum summarizing each case you locate by name, court, docket number, date of filing, and a brief summary of the disposition of the case. Also summarize the different resources you utilized to locate this information.

LBD 16-2. Determine whether your state or local bar associations have a handbook or other material listing the national, regional, and/or local offices of federal departments and agencies. Determine who publishes the source you locate, its cost, and how frequently it is updated. Also visit your local library and determine what resources are there to assist you in learning about the various federal departments and agencies, what they do, and how to contact them. As part of your visit, see which of the printed federal government resources listed in Appendix E are available in your local library.

LBD 16-3. Arrange a visit to the local or regional office of a federal agency to tour the office, learn what the agency does, and its procedures, especially its procedures for handling requests for information. Your instructor may want to arrange a group visit for the entire class. Prepare questions to ask while you are there.

LBD 16-4. Select a federal agency and prepare and submit an actual Privacy Act request for yourself. Think of records or information that may be maintained by a federal agency that you would like to see and prepare an actual FOIA request to the appropriate agency.

LBD 16-5. Review today's or a recent newspaper to locate an article discussing legislation currently moving through Congress. Then use the online congressional information sources set out in Appendix E to locate all the information you can on that legislation, including congressional committee reports in both houses.

LBD 16-6. Locate the Homeland Security Act of 2002, 6 U.S.C. §101, et. seq. Prepare a research memorandum discussing (1) the areas of responsibility the Department of Homeland Security has been given by Congress; (2) the various previously existing federal agencies that were transferred into this new department; (3) whether, as of the date of your research, the Department has promulgated any rules or regulations; (4) the accessibility of Department information through a FOIA request; and (5) in general, the extent to which the Department has been successfully implemented as of the date of your research.

LBD 16-7. Prepare a memorandum discussing the extent to which the terrorist attack on the United States on September 11, 2001 has resulted in (1) federal agencies or state agencies in your state choosing to post less information on their Web sites; (2) the federal government or your state government imposing greater restrictions on information that can be legally accessed through the FOIA, the PA, or your state's open records act.

LBD 16-8. Review the E-Government Act of 2002, 44 U.S.C. §3601, et. seq. (Public Law 107-347). Prepare a memorandum summarizing how the new statute is intended to make more government information available by Internet access. At the time this statute became law, some public interest groups were warning that some White House policies could undermine the law by making it harder and more costly for citizens to use the Internet to find government documents or take advantage of essential federal services. At issue was the White House's policy to allow private companies to bid for printing jobs, a move aimed at weakening the Government Printing Office's (GPO) long-standing near-monopoly on printing government documents. The possibility that the White House policy could hobble the GPO's role in coordinating the archiving of government documents had librarians and e-government advocates most alarmed. Visit the Web site for the Center for Democracy and Technology at *www.cdt.org* and conduct a search on this controversy. See if you can form an opinion as to whether the E-Government Act of 2002 is accomplishing its intended purposes or is being thwarted by the privatization of access to government information. Include your research on this issue in your memo.

Chapter 17

Public Sources of Information—State and Local

CHAPTER OBJECTIVES

In this chapter you will learn how to access information from state and local government sources. We will consider:

- The way that state and local governments are organized
- The kinds of records they maintain
- Various resources for accessing those records, including state open records acts and various Internet resources

A. The Structure of State and Local Governments

All 50 states pattern their governments on the federal model. That is, they each have a legislative, executive, and judicial branch. However, within that broad three-branch model, the specific organization of state governments varies greatly, as do the rules for accessing their records.

In addition, though state government offices and records are centralized to a large extent in the state capital, all states have political subdivisions—counties and cities—(local governments), which collect and maintain their own records. And, some "state" records are primarily or even exclusively accessible at offices on the local level (e.g., civil and criminal case files of the *state* courts accessible in the *county* courthouses). Consequently, it is best to learn about the kinds of state and local records that exist and how to access them by dividing the topic into state and local sources rather than focusing on the three branches of government as we did in considering federal records.

The more familiar the investigating paralegal is with the organization of the state and local governments, the more effective they will be at accessing the available records. Most state and many local governments publish handbooks or manuals containing names, addresses, and phone numbers, e-mail addresses, and, increasingly, Internet addresses, for the various government departments and agencies. In addition, many state and local bar organizations publish guides containing this information. The investigating paralegal should have ready access to these and keep them current. Also, most phone books will contain separate listings for county and city government offices and the local offices of state agencies. (See LBD 17-3.)

B. ► State Open Records Acts and Other Governing Statutes

SLEUTH ON THE LOOSE

Go to *www.govspot .com* and see what information you can access there concerning your state government or the local government of your state capital or the local government of a nearby large city.

Pursuant to its fundamental responsibility to provide for the health, safety, and welfare of its citizens, each state regulates a wide range of personal and business activities. Many state and local records are open for public inspection and copying upon demand (e.g., unsealed state court files and county records of property transfers). However, the records of some state agencies are not so easily accessible. A good example is adoption records. All states strictly regulate who may gain access to the birth certificate information of an adoptee (many states deny access even to the adult adoptee) or to family placement information (many states deny access to an inquiring biological parent).

Anytime you are seeking to access state or local records and it is not clear that they are available to the public, you should check two sources:

1. State open records acts

Similar to the FOIA for accessing records held by federal executive agencies, state legislatures have enacted what are usually referred to as **open records acts** to govern accessibility of records maintained by state government agencies. Most states have adopted the relevant exemptions from disclosure contained in the FOIA (see Chapter 16). All states prohibit or restrict access to personal records such as medical records and income tax returns; to sensitive business information qualifying as trade secrets; and to public safety information such as police investigation records. Otherwise, there is wide diversity among the states regarding what information held by state agencies is accessible.

EXAMPLE

In some states you can find out how much money special interest lobbyists have spent courting state legislators and in some you can't. In some states you can find out what funeral homes have been cited for using bait and switch practices to convince families of a deceased to purchase a higher-priced coffin and in some you can't. In some states you can find out which slaughterhouses have been warned about processing contaminated meat and in some you can't.

In most states, the attorney general's office is designated as the office responsible for receiving and processing requests under the open records act. Three states, however (Washington, Connecticut, and New York), have a separate department or commission designated to handle requests for state records.

The investigating paralegal should have a working familiarity with the open records statute of her state (see LBD 17-1). A listing of citations to the open records acts for all 50 states and the District of Columbia is available in Appendix E.

2. Other governing state statutes and regulations

As is frequently true with adoption records, many states have enacted legislation separate and apart from their open records statute governing accessibility of specific kinds of records. For example, records regarding state investigation into child sexual abuse allegations. The investigating paralegal must be able to track down those specific statutes (or regulations promulgated under them) to determine the rules of access. (See LBD 17-2.)

C. ▶ How to Access Records from State and Local Governments

1. By personal visit or written request

If the state or local government office that has the records you are seeking is nearby, a personal visit may expedite obtaining it. Phone requests for accessible records usually will be honored but there may be substantial delay. If a personal visit is not feasible, then a phone call to be sure that the record is there and will be provided should be made. Some government offices may require payment of copy costs in advance and this should be determined when you call. Some government offices may require written requests for their records or may even have a standard form to fill out. Written requests can be expedited by using fax or e-mail correspondence if the government office permits.

2. Internet sources of state and local records

States and large municipalities are creating their own Web sites where public information can be accessed for no charge. Today, every state has an Internet home page through which you can access increasing amounts of records. (See LBD 17-8.) A number of academic and scientific Web sites are now on the Internet containing public records information at no charge. The Yahoo search engine at www.yahoo.com/Regional/U_S_States is an excellent tool to locate Web sites containing state and local records, as is the LawCrawler search engine at www.findlaw.com/11stategov/index.html. A comprehensive listing of Internet resources for locating state and local records is provided in Appendix E.

3. Online database vendors

The leading online commercial vendors for accessing state and local records are **Westlaw** and **Lexis/Nexis** (www.lexis-nexis.com), the news and business information service of Lexis. (See Appendix E for details on how to contact these vendors.) Both provide their subscribers with online libraries accessing numerous state and local public records sources. Illustrations 17-1 and 17-2 give a representative sampling of the kinds of public records information available from these two vendors.

4. Public records search companies

There are a number of document search companies that, for a fee, will conduct the search of state and local (as well as federal) records for you. Some of these search companies are only statewide or regional and you should look to your local advertising services (e.g., the yellow pages or state and local bar publications) to locate them. Others are national. Some of the leading national document search companies are:

- Information America (owned by Westlaw) (www.infoam.com)
- CorpAmerica (www.LawService.com)
- Washington Document Service (www.wdsdocs.com)
- CT Corporation System (www.cch-lis.com)
- Dow Jones News/Retrieval Service (www.djnr.com)
- Parasec (www.parasec.com)
- CDBInfotek (www.cdb.com/public)
- Ameri-Search (www.amerisearch.com)
- Corporation Service Company (www.incspot.com)

(See Appendix E for a comprehensive listing of search companies and details on how to contact them.) For a fee, these companies will do research nationwide on real and personal property assets, licensing in-

Illustration 17-1   SUMMARY OF STATE AND LOCAL RECORDS ACCESSIBLE THROUGH WESTLAW

1. Asset Locator (ASSET): Searches state and local public records to identify real and personal property holdings of businesses and individuals.
2. County Records (COU): Provides abstracts of UCC filings, deeds, liens, judgments, and execution dockets.
3. Corporate and Limited Partnership Records (ALLCORP): Provides abstracts of corporate, limited partnership, and limited liability company filings in 45 states.
4. Executive Affiliation (EA): Provides information on more than 30 million executives gathered from corporate and limited partnership records.
5. Lawsuits (LS): Provides abstracts of civil suits in selected state and county courts.
6. SLEUTH: An investigative service that will search state and local records to identify business relationships between individuals and businesses.
7. Bankruptcy Records (BKR): Provides abstracts of business bankruptcy filings in all 50 states and personal filings in most states. (Though the U.S. Bankruptcy Court is a federal court, the information is made available on a state-by-state basis.)
8. BILLTRK: Provides data for tracking pending state legislation.
9. BILLS: Provides full text of bills from selected state legislatures.
10. LEGIS-ALL: Provides state legislative information from all 50 states.

Illustration 17-2   SUMMARY OF STATE AND LOCAL RECORDS ACCESSIBLE THROUGH LEXIS

1. LEX-DOC: Searches and retrieves UCC filings in all 50 states.
2. DOCKET: Searches court indexes and dockets in selected state and municipal courts.
3. INCORP: Provides information on incorporation, corporate status, corporate offices, and registered agents in all states.
4. LIENS: Searches the judgment dockets of most states for judgment and tax liens.
5. DBA: Locates "doing business as" records from state and local filings.
6. ASSETS: Accesses real estate and personal property records for individuals and businesses.
7. ALLVER: Provides information on verdicts and settlements in state litigation.
8. INSOLV: Provides information on business and personal bankruptcy filings on a state-by-state basis.

dexes, tax lien filings, court dockets and judgments, judgment liens, UCC filings, motor vehicle records, and much more.) A good source to learn about all public records search companies is *The Sourcebook of Public Records Providers* (see Appendix E for details).

5. CD-ROM resources

There are also a number of CD-ROM databases that can be purchased, containing various kinds of state and local records. Examples include The County Locator (LOCUS) and the Public Record Research System by BRB Publications (see Appendix E for a comprehensive listing of CD-ROM products and information on how to contact the vendors). CD-ROM products are typically updated every quarter.

D. ▶ Records Maintained by State Government

Listed below are categories of records typically maintained by the state and frequently sought by investigators. A couple of caveats, though. First, this list is intended to be representative not comprehensive. There will be many more kinds of records maintained by your state. You should be as familiar as possible with the departments and agencies of your state government and the records they maintain. (See LBD 17-3.) You also must think creatively to locate the right agency—sometimes under a lot of pressure (see Hypothetical 17-1).

HYPOTHETICAL 17-1

Assume you are working as a paralegal for Bragg, Boast & Bluster, the silkiest of the silk stocking firms in town. One afternoon you are working quietly at your desk, waiting for 5:00 to roll around, when the phone rings. You answer it and hear the voice of the firm's senior partner, Justa Boorish Bragg, on the line. (He prefers to go by J.B. I wonder why?) This is the first time Mr. Bragg has ever spoken to you. You didn't even know he knew your name. (And, truthfully, you kind of liked it that way!) Without thinking, you stand up, striking your knee on the corner of the desk and knocking over the chocolate milkshake you shouldn't have had at your desk anyway. Grimacing with pain, and trying to mop up the mess with your free hand, you listen to your next assignment.

It seems that Mr. Bragg is, at this moment, in conference with one of the firm's most important clients. This client owns residential property adjoining the largest river flowing through your state. (You don't have to look that up, do you?) The client is upset because the commercial barge traffic using the river has increased lately and the barges seem to be coming closer to her property than ever before. She has told Mr. Bragg that the barges sometimes come so close that the workers on the barges can be heard whistling and shouting unseemly things at persons using the swimming pool in her backyard.

Mr. Bragg tells you that he is going to call the responsible agency himself to complain on behalf of the client. (Of course, this enables the firm to bill Mr. Bragg's $300 per hour for this work rather than your piddling $75 per hour. But, we digress.) Mr. Bragg laughingly confesses, however, that he does not know which state agency is responsible for supervising barge traffic on the river. He would like for you to check on it and let him know something—WITHIN 15 MINUTES! You start to say that you will get right on it, but realize that he has already hung up.

Think through how you would go about locating this information for Mr. Bragg:

1. What written or electronic sources could you use to determine this?
2. What people sources around you might be helpful?
3. If you need to call someone for assistance, how would you decide who to call first?
4. If you are going to depend on helpful government employees to assist you with this, how important will your phone communication skills be? (See Chapter 8 on Communication Skills.)

Your instructor may want you to actually locate the agency in your state that would be responsible for the barge traffic on navigable rivers. (See LBD 17-4.)

A second caveat: some of the state records listed below may be maintained at the local government level rather than the state. Or they may be available at both levels. For example, vital statistics records are often available at both the state and county levels. UCC-1 financing statements are sometimes filed at both the state and county levels. Records that are maintained solely at the state level are usually accessible through departments and agencies located in the capital city of the state.

1. Vital statistics

Vital records statistics include information and certificates for births, deaths, marriages, and divorces. Every state has a centralized vital records bureau of some kind. The U.S. Department of Health and Human Services has issued a pamphlet obtainable through the GPO (online at www.access .gpo.gov) entitled *Where to Write for Vital Records: Births, Deaths, Marriages and Divorces,* which provides the address of each state vital records office and tells how far back the state records go. Such records are usually accessible by written request or personal visit. An online site helpful for locating information on vital records is Vital Records Resource at www.vitalcheck.com. (See Appendix E for a comprehensive listing of resources for locating vital statistics information.)

Marriage and divorce records originate at the county level, as do birth and death certificates in many states, and may be accessible there as well as through the state vital records bureau. Even if the issuance of birth and death certificates is now handled exclusively by the state, counties or even city health departments may have older records on file, as may your local public library, especially if it maintains a genealogy section.

2. Motor vehicle and driving records

Every state has an agency or bureau responsible for maintaining records regarding vehicle registration, driver's licenses, driving record, and accident reports. Accessibility of those records varies from state to state, but has been made more uniform in recent years by provisions of the Driver's Privacy Protection Act (DPPA), 18 U.S.C. §2721, effective September 1997, which prohibits state departments of motor vehicles from releasing or anyone from using certain personal information provided to the departments in connection with a motor vehicle record. There are a number of exceptions to the prohibition on releasing information under the DPPA, including information disclosed to a legitimate business for use in a court or administrative proceeding, or an investigation in anticipation of litigation. Some states have revised their statutes in recent years to make them even more restrictive than required by the DPPA because of increasing public concern over stalking incidents.

In states where driver's license information can be obtained, the state will furnish an abstract telling you the subject's date of birth, license number, social security number, gender, basic physical characteristics (height, weight, and eye and hair color) and driving restrictions, if any. Some state departments will also perform searches of license plate numbers or vehicle identification numbers (VIN). A few states require the subject's permission to perform a search of these records and at least two states, Massachusetts and Washington, will not supply driver's license information.

3. Corporate and other business records

As you learn when you study business organizations, corporations and other business entities such as limited partnerships and limited liability companies are created under state laws. Every state has a department, usually called the Secretary of State or something similar, responsible for collecting and maintaining public filings made by these entities. Organizational documents such as corporate charters, amended charters, certificates of limited partnership, notices of dissolution, etc., are filed there and, in most states, are accessible to the public upon request. Tremendous amounts of information may be disclosed in these business filings. Access to tax returns and other financial filings may be more strictly limited. (See discussion of state departments of revenue below.)

The Secretary of State's office usually also handles UCC filings relating to the creation and release of security interests in personal property.

Most state offices will perform searches of their UCC records (some for a fee, some for free) and provide an abstract of all recorded filings for your subject. Usually a UCC-3: Request for Information or Copies must accompany the request. As discussed above, there are a number of records search companies who will search these and other accessible state records in a timely fashion for a fee. (See Appendix E for a comprehensive listing of public records search companies.)

4. Licensing agencies

States license a great many professions, occupations, trades, and crafts. Illustration 17-3 contains a representative sampling.

A quick review of your state code will probably reveal many more occupations that are regulated by your state and require some licensing process. In some states, there will be one centralized department to handle licenses. In other states, there may be multiple departments or agencies. Since these occupations hold themselves out to the public, most states make license information readily available. There may be some limitations on accessing information regarding complaints or license suspensions, but the investigator should check the state statute and any governing regulations. Many states are members of **CLEAR** (Clearinghouse on Licensure, Enforcement, and Regulation, homepage at www.clearhq.org), a national clearinghouse in Lexington, Kentucky for the reporting of disciplinary actions taken against licensed persons in all professions and trades. (See LBD 17-6.)

5. Regulatory commissions

States typically have entire departments or commissions dedicated to the regulation of certain industrial, business, or consumer activities. Examples include departments responsible for regulating hospitals and nursing homes; home health care services; funeral homes; cemeteries;

Illustration 17-3   TYPICAL PROFESSIONS AND OCCUPATIONS LICENSED BY STATES

accountants	contractors	physician assistants
actuaries	dental hygienists	physicians
acupuncturists	dentists	private investigators
aircraft mechanics	dieticians	psychologists
aircraft pilots	electricians	realtors
appraisers	embalmers	securities brokers
arbitrators	financial management consultant	security guards
architects	nurse consultants	surveyors
attorneys	nurses	teachers
auctioneers	nurse's aides	therapists
bankers	pawnbrokers	travel agents
barbers	pest controllers	veterinarians
brokers	pet groomers	vocational experts
carpenters	pharmacists	
chiropractors	pharmacist's aides	

insurance companies; banks, credit unions, and other financial services companies; oil and gas producers and distributors; public utilities; fish and game activities; gambling and gaming activities; and alcohol and beverage control. States differ widely on the accessibility of information from these regulatory commissions and the investigator should become familiar with the governing statutes and regulations for them.

SLEUTH ON THE LOOSE

See if you can find the location of the office in your state that maintains corporate records by accessing *www.internet-prospector.org/company.htm.*

6. Department of taxation and revenue

Every state has one or more departments responsible for collecting taxes—personal and corporate income taxes, property taxes, sales taxes, use taxes, etc. Some real and personal property assessment values for tax purposes may be accessible but, in general, access to tax returns for individuals and businesses is strictly limited. However, if an individual or business is involved in litigation with the state over a tax levy or in other civil litigation involving the company's finances or if an individual is involved in a divorce action, tax records may be accessible as discovery information located in the court file or as an exhibit at trial.

7. Securities filings

As a counterpoint to the Securities Exchange Commission, states have their own "blue sky" laws requiring certain corporations active in trading securities within the state to make regular filings with a designated state securities agency. Access to these filings varies with the states and the investigator must check governing statutes and regulations of the agency.

8. Social services agencies

Every state has one or more agencies responsible for overseeing matters related to family support services, child welfare, health care, and unemployment. Many of these agencies work in conjunction with federal agencies, and the accessibility of their records is frequently governed by federal as well as state rules and regulations.

9. Workers' compensation commission

Every state has a department or agency charged with overseeing the state's workers' compensation statutes. Accessibility of these records will vary among the states, but is usually restricted. However, in many states, a particular workers' compensation suit or settlement may be processed through the state courts or a special administrative board, the records of which are public and accessible.

10. State police and highway patrol

Like the federal government, states typically have various levels of law enforcement: a state police or bureau of investigation to provide security for government officials and to investigate state crimes, and the highway patrol, responsible for highway traffic and accidents. Most such records are kept at the state capital and are subject to various restrictions on access. Though records related to ongoing investigations will almost always be inaccessible, some states will allow a criminal background check. Most states allow access to car accident reports, though some restrict this access to the parties involved and their insurance companies.

HYPOTHETICAL 17-2

Assume you work as a paralegal for the attorney defending Rowdy Outlaw in connection with the murder charges pending against him in your state (see Case Study No. 1 in Appendix A), the attorney representing Soupspoon Wise in his potential personal injury action (see Case Study No. 2), the attorney representing Vidalia Unyon in her divorce action against Greene Unyon (see Case Study No. 3), and the attorney representing Rocky Road Developers, Inc. (see Case Study No. 4). Your supervising attorneys have assigned you the task of locating the information outlined below on those cases. For each item of information:

1. Determine which state agency(s) you would contact to obtain the information.
2. Describe the procedure you would follow to obtain the information.
3. Identify any items of information that you think will not be accessible.
4. For each case, are there other kinds of information you would recommend seeking from state public sources?

Note: Because the Case Studies present fictitious cases, you will not be contacting any state office to actually obtain information on the case. You will be determining which state offices you would contact for each type of information and the procedure you would follow to do so.

A. The Rowdy Outlaw case

1. Determine if Jack Gates is in fact a licensed insurance agent and the status of that license. Do the same for Candy Carmichael's hairdresser license and Perry Peter's security guard license.
2. Determine if Dr. Michael Melody is an employee of the state in any capacity including, possibly, a faculty member of a state educational institution.

B. The Red Dog Saloon case

1. Determine whether the Red Dog Saloon or its manager, Turtle Shoop, have a valid liquor license and, if so, the status of that license.
2. Locate a copy of the accident report.
3. Determine whether the Red Dog Saloon is incorporated or some other registered business entity and, if so, who owns it and the name and address of its registered agent for service of process.
4. Determine the status of Tanya Trucker's masseuse license.

C. The Vidalia Unyon case

1. Check the status of Greene Unyon's veterinarian's license, including how long he has been licensed, whether his license is currently in good standing, whether his license has ever been suspended or revoked, and whether any ethical or other complaints have been filed against him with the licensing agency.
2. Find out how the three vehicles are titled and whether any liens exist against them.

3. Determine whether Mr. Unyon's veterinary practice is set up as a professional corporation, professional limited liability company, or other entity and, if so, the status of that entity with the state.

D. *The Rocky Road Project*

1. Locate records of any environmental reports or investigations by the state on the old gas station property or the stream next to it.
2. Determine if Rocky Road, Inc., is in good standing with the state as a corporation. Obtain a copy of its charter and any amendments.

E. ▶ Records Maintained by Local Government

By local records we mean records maintained at the county and city level. Illustration 17-4 provides a summary of the kinds of records typically accessible at the county courthouse, town hall, city municipal building, public utilities offices, sheriff's office, police station, election commission, draft board, school board office, and other local offices.

Following is a summary of frequently contacted **sources of local records.** Every investigating paralegal needs to know her way around the local court house, town hall, and other public places where records are kept. She also needs to be familiar with the kinds of records maintained in each of those offices.

1. Court clerk's offices

The clerks of the civil and criminal state courts as well as county and municipal courts will maintain indexes of pending and closed files that may be searched and copied unless sealed by court order. The civil indexes will be keyed to the names of the parties and will disclose the names of the parties, the nature of the suit, its disposition if closed, and the docket number assigned to the case with which you can obtain the file itself. The criminal case index is keyed to the name of the defendant and will disclose the charge, the disposition, and the docket number.

In addition, the **judgment docket** (sometimes called the abstract

Illustration 17-4
EXAMPLES OF
LOCAL
GOVERNMENT
RECORDS

birth and death certificates	liens and releases
building permits	marriage records
business licenses and permits	mortgages
civil cases pending	pet licenses
civil judgments	probate records
contracts	property appraisals
criminal cases pending	property tax records
criminal convictions	school records
deeds of conveyance	tax liens
divorce records	UCC filings
easements—public and private	voter registration records
library records	zoning regulations

of judgment index) along with the wage assignment, garnishment, or execution index maintained by the civil court clerk will disclose judgments taken against named defendants, the amount of the judgment, whether it has been satisfied, and possibly how.

As discussed earlier in connection with records of federal judicial proceedings, case files can be rich sources of information on parties and witnesses because they contain pleadings that set out the parties' formal allegations, discovery, and motion material. As in the federal system, these local records are increasingly computerized.

2. Office(s) of permits and licenses

Local governments **license** or **permit** just about every public activity that occurs in their jurisdictions: vehicle permits, animal licenses, vendor licenses, building projects, parades and marches, signs, fictitious businesses name registration, etc. Individuals and business acquiring these licenses and permits are required to disclose substantial amounts of information and it is usually accessible.

3. Register/recorder of deeds office

In most counties, land transaction records are centralized in one office. Warranty deeds, quitclaim deeds, easements, mortgages, option contracts, rights of first refusal, leases, releases, judgment liens, tax liens, liens *lis pendens*—all that stuff you learned about in your real property course is here, and it is freely accessible.

Somewhere in your county court house (frequently maintained in the register's office along with land transaction records) are records of local UCC filings—UCC-1 financing statements and releases of personal property liens—also available for public inspection.

4. Tax assessor's office

Assessments of the value of real and personal property for tax purposes are available here, together with records of tax payments and delinquencies.

5. Probate court

Wills offered for probate are accessible by the public, as is information in the probate file regarding the collection and distribution of the estate. If a will is contested, the litigation file will typically be open to public inspection. The probate file may also contain information on guardianships, conservatorships, and trusts.

6. Vital statistics

As discussed in connection with state records, local offices may also maintain current or older records on births and deaths. The county coroner's office may be the place to go for death certificate information.

Marriage licenses are issued by the local county clerk, legal separations and divorces are granted by local courts, and all those records are accessible.

7. Election commission

Information that may be obtainable from the election commission includes name, current and prior addresses, occupation, political party, place and date of birth, and possibly social security number.

8. Public utilities

Gas, electric, water, sewer, and phone records can disclose much information about a person. In most states, this locally maintained information is accessible.

9. Police and sheriff's departments

Local law enforcement records are usually restricted in certain ways and the investigator must check applicable statutes, regulations, and rules. However, in many localities, traffic accident reports and some arrest and jail records are accessible.

10. Public school records

Access to records of public schools is generally limited to the student or, if the student is a minor, his parents or legal guardian. The school district office may, however, be helpful in providing information about the school system and in locating a current or former teacher or student.

SL EUTH ON THE LOOSE

Access the Web site for the New York Public Library at *www.nypl.org* and see what holdings of the library are accessible online. (Or try the Internet Public Library at *www.ipl.com*; the Carnegie Library at *www.clphg.org*; or the Library of Congress at *www.lcweb.loc.gov.*)

11. The public library

The local library can be a rich source of information about people and businesses in the community and about the community itself. Genealogy records, current and out-of-date phone books, current and out-of-date city and county directories, current city and county ordinances, census information, and information on local business and industry are just some examples of the kinds of information available in the local library. Another asset valuable to the investigator is the reference librarian, who is typically knowledgeable and helpful not only about the library resources, but about people in the community as well. Often the library staff can refer you to someone likely to have the information you are seeking. The library's ability to obtain information from other libraries by interlibrary loan may be helpful also.

HYPOTHETICAL 17-3

Assume you work as a paralegal for the attorney defending Rowdy Outlaw in connection with the murder charges pending against him in your state (see Case Study No. 1 in Appendix A), the attorney representing Soupspoon Wise in his potential personal injury action (see Case Study

No. 2), the attorney representing Vidalia Unyon in her divorce action against Greene Unyon (see Case Study No. 3) and the attorney representing Rocky Road Developers, Inc. (see Case Study No. 4). Your supervising attorneys have assigned you the task of locating the information outlined below on those cases. For each item of information:

1. Determine which local government office(s) you would contact to obtain the information.
2. Describe the procedure you would follow to obtain the information.
3. Identify any items of information that you think will not be accessible.
4. For each case, are there other kinds of information you would recommend seeking from local government sources?

Note: Because the Case Studies present fictitious cases, you will not be contacting any local government office to actually obtain information on the case. You will be determining which local government offices you would contact for each type of information and the procedure you would follow to do so.

A. The Rowdy Outlaw case

1. Confirm Bobbette Bouvier's ownership of the Palace Towers condominium and any outstanding indebtedness on it.
2. Determine if Bobbette Bouvier, Candy Outlaw, or Rowdy Outlaw has been a party to any civil litigation in the past three years.
3. Determine if Rowdy Outlaw has any prior arrests or criminal convictions.
4. Check on any existing probate proceeding for Bobbette Bouvier.
5. Locate the marriage license for Rowdy Outlaw and Candy Outlaw. If it shows any prior marriages for either, locate the divorce/annulment records.
6. Obtain a copy of the death certificate for Bobbette Bouvier.

B. The Red Dog Saloon case

1. Obtain a copy of all business permits, liquor license, etc., for the Red Dog Saloon.
2. Obtain a copy of the accident report.
3. See if the Red Dog Saloon or its owner has been a defendant in any civil suits in the last ten years.

C. The Vidalia Unyon case

1. Locate the mortgage in favor of First City Bank on the residence of the parties. Determine the date it was executed, the amount of indebtedness secured and the payment terms. Check for any release or renewal of that mortgage and for other recorded indebtedness on the house.
2. Determine the current assessed value of the residence for tax purposes, the date of the most current assessment, and whether the taxes are paid up.
3. Determine if Mr. Unyon has owned or conveyed any realty in the last ten years other than the residence or whether he has pledged any personal property as collateral for any indebtedness during that time.

4. Locate all civil suits in which Mr. Unyon or his veterinary practice has been named as a party, summarize the claims made in each such suit, the disposition of each if not still pending and, if any judgments were rendered, whether they have been satisfied.

D. The Rocky Road Project

1. Make sure the option agreement on the ten acres is properly recorded.
2. Determine if a probate proceeding has been filed for Edward Dig Deep and, if so, locate any existing will.
3. Determine the titled owner of the old gas station property; confirm that Edward Dig Deep was the sole owner of the five-acre tract and that the city has clear title to the three-acre tract. Check for outstanding or potential liens on any of the parcels (including liens *lis pendens*), and check the status of property taxes on each.

KEY WORDS AND PHRASES TO REMEMBER

abstract of judgment
birth certificate
blue sky laws
business license
clear
death certificate
execution index
judgment docket
Lexis/Nexis
lien *lis pendens*
local government
open records acts

political subdivision
probate
probate court
professional license
register/recorder of deeds
Secretary of State
state government
tax assessor
VIN
vital records
Westlaw

LEARN BY DOING

LBD 17-1. Locate the open records act for your state (see Appendix E). Prepare a memorandum summarizing the scope and procedure set forth in the statute for obtaining records.

LBD 17-2. Locate the adoption records statute or regulations for your state. Prepare a memorandum summarizing the scope and procedure set forth in the statute for accessing the birth and placement records of an adoptee.

LBD 17-3. Determine whether your state or local bar association(s) have a handbook or other material listing central and local offices of state departments and agencies. Determine who publishes the sources you locate, its cost, and how frequently it is updated. Also visit your local library and determine what resources are there to assist you in learning about the various state departments and agencies, what they do, and how to contact them. As part of your visit, see which of the resources listed in Appendix E are available in your local library.

LBD 17-4. Review Hypothetical 17-1. Determine the state agency in your state responsible for supervising commercial barge traffic on your state's navigable rivers. Keep a record of all sources you consult to determine this and in what order, the names of any and all persons you spoke with by phone or in person, and how long it took you to find this information. Here are some suggestions for other state agency questions you may want to use for this exercise; you may think of others as well:

- the agency responsible for regulating billboards on the state highways;
- the agency responsible for air traffic over government buildings;
- the agency responsible for trash/litter pick-up along state roads;
- the agency responsible for regulating the raising of wild animals on private property;
- the agency responsible for regulating the size of trailer trucks;
- the agency responsible for monitoring the size and explosive force of firecrackers sold in the state; and
- the agency responsible for changing burned-out lightbulbs in public buildings.

LBD 17-5. Through your instructor, plan and conduct a visit to the central or local office of a state agency to tour the office, get an idea of what the agency does, and its procedures, especially its procedures for handling requests for information. Your instructor may want to arrange a group visit for the entire class. Prepare questions to ask while you are there.

LBD 17-6. Select one or more occupations from the list in Illustration 17-3 and determine whether a license is required by your state to engage in that occupation. Also determine whether information regarding complaints, license suspensions, or revocations is available to the public and, if so, the procedure for obtaining that information.

LBD 17-7. Through your instructor, plan and conduct a visit to the county courthouse and/or city hall or municipal building in your area. Visit each different local office or department located in the facilities you visit. Ask the personnel on duty to describe their areas of responsibility, the kinds of records maintained by the office or department, and whether such records are available to the public. Your instructor may want to arrange a group visit for the entire class. Prepare questions to ask while you are there.

LBD 17-8. Utilizing the online resources for state and local governments set out in Appendix E, locate the Internet home page for your state, county, and/or city. Beginning with those sites, compile a directory of Internet addresses for as much online government information as you can find for your state, county, or city.

Chapter 18

Private Sources of Information

CHAPTER OBJECTIVES

In this chapter you will learn how to access many different types of information from private sources (as opposed to public or governmental sources) including:

- Medical, employment, and educational records.
- Telephone numbers and phone call records.
- Credit records on individuals and credit information on businesses.
- Financial information on individuals and businesses.

You will also learn about Internet resources for locating information, online database vendors, and search companies. And finally you will learn how to locate and work successfully with a reliable private investigator.

A. An Overview of Private Sources of Information

By **private sources of information** we mean information of any kind that is in the possession of private individuals, businesses, educational institutions, or any other non-governmental custodian. Frequently, information that is maintained by one or more governmental agencies is simultaneously in the possession of a private source. For the investigator, this means that there may be more than one means of accessing this information.

HYPOTHETICAL 18-1

Assume that Soupspoon Wise (see Case Study No. 2 in Appendix A) makes a social security disability claim based on the injuries he received in the car accident in the parking lot of the Red Dog Saloon. As part of that claim he has his medical records submitted to the SSA. Now his medical records are part of a file maintained by a government agency, but they are simultaneously maintained by his private physicians. The medical records are the same in either place, but attempting to access them through the SSA would constitute seeking a public record, whereas attempting to access them through his physicians would constitute seeking a private record—information held by Soupspoon's private physicians and the hospitals where he received treatment.

We will learn how to access information from private sources in this chapter. But, for now, assume you work for the attorney representing the Red Dog Saloon and your supervising attorney is anticipating that Soupspoon might file a civil suit for personal injury against her client in the future. She learns of his social security filing and would like to access that file to see his medicals. Based on what you learned in Chapter 16, are you going to be able to get that information for her at this time?

If Soupspoon is denied social security benefits and loses his appeal of this decision through the administrative process, he may initiate a civil action in the U.S. District Court to establish his right to the benefits. His medical records will likely be exhibits to his pleadings or to motions made in the civil case or be produced in response to formal discovery requests made in the case. How accessible will those records be now?

SLEUTH ON THE LOOSE

To more fully appreciate the growing problem of identity theft and invasion of privacy in the information age access the Federal Trade Commission site on identity theft at *www.consumer.gov/idtheft.*

This chapter will summarize various private sources for accessing information commonly sought by paralegals assisting attorneys. However, it does not purport to be a complete listing of such sources; no list could be. The fact is that the means of accessing privately held information in a legal and ethical fashion (see Ethical Note below) are limited only by the imagination and creativity of the investigator. In an investigation we always ask, "Who might have this information?" and "How might I get it?" And never, ever underestimate the effectiveness of simply **asking** for what you want.

HYPOTHETICAL 18-2

Assume that you work for the attorney representing Vidalia Unyon in a possible divorce action against her husband, Greene Unyon (see Case Study No. 3 in Appendix A). In the initial conference with you and your supervising attorney, Mrs. Unyon shows you two ticket stubs to the Sly Dog concert that took place in your city last month and a book of matches bearing the logo of the Ooh La La Motel in your city. She tells you that she found these in her husband's coat pocket and she suspects he took a girlfriend to the concert because he certainly didn't take her. She also says she has never been to the Ooh La La Motel and can only assume her husband has rented a room there at some time with a lover. Your supervising attorney slides the ticket stubs and book of matches over to you and tells you, "Check it out."

You sit in your office for an hour trying to decide how you can determine whether Greene Unyon purchased two tickets to the Sly Dog concert or rented a room at the Ooh La La Motel. Finally, in frustration, you go back to your supervising attorney and tell him you need some guidance. He peers at you quizzically over his reading glasses for a moment, then clears his throat and says, "Why don't you just call 'em up and ask?"

After slinking out of his office and back into yours, you call the clerk at the Ooh La La Motel, introduce yourself, and ask her if she could tell you whether a Greene Unyon has rented a room there in the last three months or so. She puts you on hold (a Sly Dog tune is playing—what a coincidence!) then gets back on the line and tells you that, yes, a Greene Unyon has rented a room there every Monday for the past two and a half months, which is as far back as the current ledger goes. Now before you hang up the phone and start dancing on your desktop:

1. What else do you want to ask this helpful information source?
2. What documents might you want to ask her to let you see and copy?
3. How quickly should you get down to the motel office and why?

Later you call the ticket office of the arena where the Sly Dog concert was held. In the middle of your first question, the surly voice on the other end says, "We don't give out that kind of information," and slams the phone down. Oh, well, one out of two isn't bad. But what other sources might you check to determine if Greene Unyon in fact purchased tickets to the Sly Dog concert and attended it?

ETHICAL NOTE

Hypotheticals 18-1 and 18-2 demonstrate the importance of making sure you follow the law and comply with ethical and professional standards in investigating. For example, in some states there may be statutes or regulations restricting access to private records such as motel registration information. If so, you need to be aware of such laws. Or there may be court decisions holding that it is a tortious invasion of an individual's privacy for such information to be disclosed. These are matters you need to be familiar with and cover with your supervising attorney before seeking to access privately held records.

Similarly, ethical and professional standards always come into play in seeking information. For example, what consequences might there be if you had called the Ooh La La Motel, represented yourself as Greene Unyon's executive secretary, and said that you needed the requested information for his tax records?

Or what if your supervising attorney in the Red Dog Saloon case told you to go ahead and contact the local SSA office handling Soupspoon Wise's disability claim and ask to see his file even though it would violate SSA regulations? "After all," he tells you, "weren't you taught that it never hurts to ask?" It hurts in that situation, doesn't it?

Or what if you told a licensed private investigator helping you on the Red Dog Saloon case about your difficulties in accessing Soupspoon Wise's social security file and he says, "Don't worry, I know how to get hold of stuff like that. I'll do it for $200, just don't ever ask me how." Can you agree to let him do this?

This last example of the private investigator illustrates an important point to remember in investigating. The vast majority of licensed private investigators and information brokers (discussed in more detail later in this chapter) are scrupulously honest and ethical. However, there are some who are willing and quite able to skirt or bend the rules to access information for a paying client. No matter how tempting it might be in a particular case to use someone like this to obtain otherwise inaccessible information, RESIST THAT URGE. Ethical attorneys and paralegals do not engage in that kind of activity, do not request others to do it, do not encourage others to do it even passively, and do not knowingly use information obtained in that way. Not only is it unethical and unprofessional (and possibly illegal), it is morally wrong. If we don't all obey the rules, the rules become meaningless and the system fails.

B. ▶ Accessing Private Sources of Information

1. Medical records

Medical records constitute one of the most frequently sought-after kinds of information in the legal field. Lawyers regularly need to obtain the medical records of their own clients, of opposing parties in lawsuits, or of non-party witnesses.

Medical records will always be deemed confidential either by state mandate (see LBD 18-1) or by the private rule of the medical practitioner or facility. Thus those records are accessible from the practitioner or facility only upon the written **authorization** of the patient, by **court order,** or by **subpoena.**

a. Obtaining medical records by written patient authorization

To obtain the medical records of his own client, the attorney will have you prepare and have the client sign an appropriate authorization to obtain medical records. Illustration 10-4 shows a typical **medical records authorization** directed to a physician. Illustration 18-1 shows a typical medical records authorization directed to a hospital.

b. Drafting the medical records authorization

The medical records authorization should provide the full name of the patient, the patient's social security number and date of birth, and the name of the doctor, hospital, or other health care provider to whom it is directed. It should be dated, state how long it is effective, and name the persons to whom the medical office or hospital are authorized to permit inspection and copying of the records.

The authorization should state in a comprehensive fashion and with specificity what records are to be made available. Doctor's offices and hospitals typically will not provide the investigator with any more documentation than he specifically asks for. The inexperienced paralegal may have no idea of the number and kinds of different medical records that may be found in a doctor's or hospital's patient file.

The authorization should contain language assuring the provider of compliance with the privacy rules found at 45 CFR Parts 160 and 164 that govern access to medical information. The authorization should also be signed by the patient or, in the event the patient is a minor or incompetent, by the parent or guardian of the patient. A person who has executed a valid power of attorney for health care has probably authorized the holder of the power of attorney to obtain or authorize another to obtain the patient's records.

Illustration 18-1   MEDICAL RECORDS AUTHORIZATION (HOSPITAL)

To: Hospital's Name and Address

You are hereby authorized to permit my attorney, _____, of the law firm _____, or his designated agent, to inspect and obtain copies of my complete medical records including, without limitation, all patient information sheets, fact sheets, admission summaries, emergency room records, out-patient records, patient consents, patient history and physical data, physician orders and progress notes, consultation reports, nurses' notes, operative reports, anesthesia records, radiology records, medications, pharmacy records, physical therapy records, discharge records [or, if appropriate, death certificate or autopsy records], correspondence, notes, memoranda, laboratory reports, and fee statements. This authorization is effective as of the date below and will continue in effect until revoked by me in writing but for no longer than one year from the date below.

My attorney, _____, of the law firm _____, has assured me that he/she will comply with all requirements of the privacy rules promulgated by the U.S. Department of Health and Human Services pursuant to the Health Insurance Portability and Accountability Act of 1996 and found at 45 CFR 160 and 164.

_____   Date_____
John J. Patient
Soc. Sec. No. XXXXXX
DOB 10-1-63

c. Using the medical records authorization

The medical authorization is usually mailed to the doctor's office or the hospital's **records custodian** with a cover letter. Illustration 18-2 shows a cover letter forwarding an authorization to a doctor's office. Illustration 18-3 shows a cover letter forwarding an authorization to a hospital. You can determine the name and address of the records custodian with a quick phone call. The letter to the hospital should indicate the dates the patient is believed to have been a patient. This will expedite the location and production of the records needed. The letter to an attending physician from the patient's attorney may also request an update on the patient's prognosis if not previously determined.

Many doctors' offices and hospitals will not automatically make copies of everything in the patient's file—even if you request it. Therefore, the authorization should be comprehensive and specific and, whenever possible, you should physically take the authorization to the medical office and review the file yourself before having copies made. While you

Illustration 18-2   COVER LETTER TO DOCTOR'S OFFICE

Date

Name of Physician
Address

Re: John J. Patient
Patient No. (if known) or Soc. Sec. No.
DOB

Dear Dr. _____:

   This office represents Mr. Patient with regard to personal injuries he sustained in an automobile accident on September 1, 2003. Please provide us with a copy of Mr. Patient's entire medical file per his signed authorization, a copy of which is enclosed.

   If there is a charge for the copies made, please enclose your invoice with the copies and it will be paid promptly.

   Also, please provide us with your diagnosis and treatment of Mr. Patient's injuries resulting from the September 1 accident and your prognosis of future medical disabilities and treatment.

   The records made available to us will be used only for the resolution, by negotiation or litigation, of the personal injury claim made or to be made on behalf of Mr. Patient arising out of the automobile accident of September 1, 2003 against those deemed to be legally responsible. The records made available to us and all copies thereof made for the stated purpose will be returned to you or destroyed at the end of that process. And we will otherwise comply with all requirements of the privacy rules promulgated by the U.S. Department of Health and Human Services pursuant to the Health Insurance Portability and Accountability Act of 1996 and found at 45 CFR 160 and 164.

   Thank you for your assistance. If you have any questions, please do not hesitate to call.

Sincerely,

(Signature)
Legal Assistant

Illustration 18-3 COVER LETTER TO HOSPITAL RECORDS CUSTODIAN

Date

Name of Hospital
Address

Re: John J. Patient
Patient No. (if known) or Soc. Sec. No.
DOB

Dear Records Custodian:

This office represents Mr. Patient with regard to personal injuries he sustained in an automobile accident on September 1, 2003. Please provide us with a copy of Mr. Patient's entire medical file per his signed authorization, a copy of which is enclosed.

If there is a charge for the copies made, please enclose your invoice with the copies and it will be paid promptly.

Our information is that Mr. Patient was a patient at _____ Hospital from September 1 to September 15, 2003.

The records made available to us will be used only for the resolution, by negotiation or litigation, of the personal injury claim made or to be made on behalf of Mr. Patient arising out of the automobile accident of September 1, 2003 against those deemed to be legally responsible. The records made available to us and all copies thereof made for the stated purpose will be returned to you or destroyed at the end of that process. And we will otherwise comply with all requirements of the privacy rules promulgated by the U.S. Department of Health and Human Services pursuant to the Health Insurance Portability and Accountability Act of 1996 and found at 45 CFR 160 and 164.

Thank you for your assistance. If you have any questions, please do not hesitate to call.

Sincerely,

(Signature)
Legal Assistant

---

are doing so, ask the file custodian if everything is in the file as it is presented to you. Be sure that no patient records are maintained in a separate file and that no patient records are still being processed. Remember that, with regard to hospital records in particular, the number and volume of records generated is substantial and may be quite expensive to copy.

d. Special medical records authorizations

Psychiatrists, psychologists, and institutions treating mental disorders typically have their own pre-printed authorization form that the patient must sign.

The written medical authorization may also be used to obtain the medical records of an opposing party in a pending suit when it is undisputed that the records are relevant and the attorney for the opposing party has no objection to his client signing the authorization.

e. Obtaining medical records by court order

When seeking the medical records of an opposing party in pending litigation, it is customary in some jurisdictions to utilize an agreed court order rather than a written authorization. Illustration 18-4 shows an agreed court order allowing one party access to the medical records of the opposing party.

The agreed order should be as specific about the medical records to be reviewed and copied as the authorization.

f. Obtaining medical records by Rule 45 subpoena

When a civil suit is pending and the attorney needs to obtain the medical records of a non-party witness who refuses to give a written

Illustration 18-4   AGREED ORDER ALLOWING INSPECTION OF MEDICAL RECORDS

IN THE UNITED STATES DISTRICT COURT
FOR THE EASTERN DISTRICT OF YOURSTATE
NORTHERN DIVISION

SOUPSPOON WISE,   )
          Plaintiff   )
     v.   )   DOCKET NO. 04-00005
THE RED DOG SALOON, INC.   )
          Defendant   )

AGREED ORDER ALLOWING INSPECTION AND COPYING OF MEDICAL RECORDS

On motion of defendant, The Red Dog Saloon, and plaintiff having no objection, it is hereby,

ORDERED, that defendant Red Dog Saloon, by and through its attorneys, Dip, Duck & Dodge, is hereby authorized to inspect and copy at its own expense any and all medical records of plaintiff Soupspoon Wise including, without limitation. . . . And it is further,

ORDERED, that defendant shall provide plaintiff's attorneys with copies of all such records copied by or on behalf of defendant within five (5) business days of defendant's copying of such records.

ENTER.

_____
U.S. District Judge

APPROVED FOR ENTRY:

_____
Mellow Fellow
Attorney for plaintiff Soupspoon Wise
(Address)

_____
Hard Case, Esq.
Attorney for defendant The Red Dog Saloon, Inc.
(Address)

authorization or from an uncooperative opposing party, it may be necessary to use a Rule 45 **subpoena duces tecum.** The subpoena will be served on each custodian of such records and will, in the case of a trial subpoena, direct the custodian(s) to appear with the records at the time and place of trial. In the case of a deposition subpoena, it will direct the custodian(s) to appear at the time and place of the Rule 30 deposition. See FRCP 34(c) and 45(a)(2). Illustration 18-5 shows a deposition subpoena duces tecum seeking the production of medical records.

Whenever a subpoena is served seeking the medical records of a party or non-party who doesn't want them produced, there may be a motion to quash the subpoena filed with the court that issued it. The issue in such a motion will typically turn on the relevance of the records sought. As previously indicated, your state may have special rules and procedures for accessing medical records by subpoena with which you should become familiar. (See LBD 18-1.)

2. Employment records

Like medical records, **employment records** will always be deemed confidential either by state mandate (see LBD 18-1) or by the private

Illustration 18-5   DEPOSITION SUBPOENA DUCES TECUM SEEKING PRODUCTION OF MEDICAL RECORDS

IN THE UNITED STATES DISTRICT COURT
FOR THE EASTERN DISTRICT OF YOURSTATE
NORTHERN DIVISION

SOUPSPOON WISE,	)	
Plaintiff	)	
v.	)	DOCKET NO. 04-00005
THE RED DOG SALOON, INC.	)	
Defendant	)	

SUBPOENA DUCES TECUM

To: Records Custodian
Capital City Hospital
(Address)

YOU ARE HEREBY COMMANDED to appear and give testimony under oath at the law office of Mellow Fellow, Shake, Rattle & Roll, 100 South Main St., Capital City, Yourstate on the _____ day of _____, 2004 at 1:30 P.M. You are also commanded to bring the following:

All medical records of Soupspoon Wise, Soc. Sec. No. XXX-XX-XXXX including, without limitation, all patient information sheets, fact sheets, admission summaries, emergency room records, out-patient records, patient consents, patient history and physical data, physician orders and progress notes, consultation reports, nurses' notes, operative reports, anesthesia records, radiology records, medications, pharmacy records, physical therapy records, discharge records, correspondence, notes, memoranda, laboratory reports, and fee statements.

DATED: _____

_____
Clerk, U.S. District Court

policy of the employer. In recent years, many state legislatures have passed laws giving added protection to employment records and courts have expanded the concept of protected privacy rights to include such records. Thus the investigator should use caution in attempting to access these records without the consent of the employee.

When accessing the employment records of a current or former government employee, the employing agency may have its own special regulations and procedures with which the investigator should be careful to comply. In the case of a state or local government employee, reference should be made to the state's open records act.

As with medical records, employment records are typically accessible from the employer only upon the written authorization of the employee, by court order, or by subpoena. Illustration 10-5 shows a written authorization to be signed by the employee allowing an attorney access to his employment records.

3. Educational records

Access to **educational records** from a public school or college may be controlled by a state's open records act or by separate statute. (See LBD 18-1.) Private institutions may be regulated by state rules as well or may have their own internal rules regarding accessibility of records.

Most schools will confirm whether a person ever attended and what degree, if any, was granted and when. Otherwise, the student herself or, in the case of a minor, her parents or legal guardian, have the right to access academic records from either a public or private institution. As with medical and employment records, anyone else seeking to access such records must do so by written authorization, court order, or subpoena. Also as with medical and employment records, if access cannot be agreed upon, a showing of relevance will have to be made to the court which is asked to order access or uphold the validity of a subpoena.

Illustration 10-6 shows an authorization permitting access to educational records.

4. Other sources of academic information

Though access to academic records is limited without the student's consent, investigators should not overlook other sources of information available concerning a student's academic career. Student directories, high school and college yearbooks, faculty directories, campus newspapers and periodicals, master's theses and doctoral dissertations are generally available to anyone from the school library or other school offices.

5. Telephone records

a. Finding telephone numbers

Locating a person's telephone number is usually as simple as checking the phone book. It's a good idea for the investigator to keep out-of-date phone books to pick up the trail of a missing person, or make sure your local library has them. Most large public libraries also keep telephone directories for a number of other cities around the state and country as well.

1. **City/county directories.** Many cities and counties have **criss-cross** or **reverse directories.** A reverse directory will list residences and businesses first by street name and number. It then lists telephone numbers numerically. Thus you can find an address even if all you have is a phone number and a phone number when all you have is an address. Many such directories also provide the names of all persons living in the household and places of employment. The city/county directories may be purchased from the phone company or found in the local library. Keeping old issues of the city/county directory is a good idea for the investigator.

2. **CD-ROM products.** There are CD-ROM products that can be purchased containing phone and address directories and criss-cross directories. Cole's Directory is a popular criss-cross directory and is available in CD-ROM format. CD-ROM products are typically updated on a quarterly basis and thus are more current than paper directories, which appear annually. (See Appendix E for details on Cole's Directory and other CD-ROM products.)

3. **The Internet.** A number of Internet resources now offer access to data banks providing reverse directory phone number and address data for individuals and businesses on a nationwide scale. Appendix E contains a comprehensive list of such sites.

b. Accessing unlisted phone numbers

A person can request that the phone company not list their phone number, in which case the number will not appear in the phone book or city/county directory and should not appear in any of the Internet or CD-ROM services—though it might slip in. There is no legal or ethical way for the paralegal investigator to obtain unlisted numbers from the phone company without consent or court order and she shouldn't allow a private investigator to do so either. (See Ethical Note above.)

However, people frequently give out their phone numbers, even when unlisted, to friends, employers, creditors, credit card companies, advertisers, merchants, service providers, and phone solicitors. If the investigator locates the number through one of those sources, no law is broken and no ethical violation occurs. Phone numbers, listed and unlisted, are the kind of header information that compilers of marketing mailing lists obtain from these sources, place in their data banks, and sell or make available for a fee to online database vendors and search companies. (See extended discussion below.)

c. Phone call records and wiretapping

The phone company will not voluntarily release a customer's phone call records. Of course, the subscriber may consent to the release of that information. If a civil or criminal lawsuit is pending and the information in the phone records is relevant, it may be obtainable in formal discovery, by court order, or by subpoena.

The federal wiretapping law, 18 U.S.C. §2510, prohibits the nonconsensual monitoring or recording of electronic communications to which you are not a party subject to certain exceptions. States also have their own wiretapping laws, which may be more restrictive than the federal law, and with which the legal investigator should be familiar. (See LBD 18-2.)

6. Credit records on individuals

There are three major **credit reporting agencies**—companies that collect and disseminate information for a fee on the credit history and creditworthiness of individuals. They are Equifax, Trans Union, and Experian. (See Appendix E for details on how to contact these companies.) In addition, there are some 1,300 regional and local credit reporting agencies around the country.

The files of these agencies will contain data on a person's loan repayment history, including car payments, credit card payments, lines of credit, and other secured and unsecured debt. They will also contain much public record information (that you can access in other ways, as you now know), including tax lien information, judgments, and bankruptcy filings. Residence information, employment information, and arrest records are sometimes included in the data. The files credit reporting agencies will reflect not only the consumer's payment history, but a record of credit inquiries (who has asked about the consumer's creditworthiness) and a credit scoring record as well (how creditworthy the agency deems the consumer based on the data collected). Thus, these records can be a gold mine of information about the financial affairs of an individual.

Credit reporting agencies obtain their data not only from public records but also from subscribing lenders, individual creditors, and businesses that extend credit to consumers. These subscribers will both provide data to the credit reporting agency and purchase a credit report on a consumer from the agency when that consumer applies for credit.

However, not just anyone can legally access the records of a credit reporting agency. These agencies, and access to the very sensitive information they maintain, are governed by the Fair Credit Reporting Act, 15 U.S.C. §§1681 et seq. (FCRA). Some states have their own laws in this area. For example, in Vermont, permission of the consumer is required to access information and in Rhode Island, the consumer must be notified when information is requested.

Under the FCRA, an individual can request to see most information in her own file, including the substance of information maintained there, the sources of the information, and the names of those to whom information has been supplied within the past six months or ten months if the information was supplied for employment purposes. There is also a procedure in place for correcting errors.

Access to credit reports by persons other than the consumer herself is limited by the FCRA to persons seeking the information:

- for decisions regarding extension of credit;
- for underwriting insurance;
- for employment evaluation;

- pursuant to court order;
- for granting a government license;
- pursuant to a written authorization by the consumer; or
- for other legitimate business purposes.

It is this last ground for accessing information, the **legitimate business purpose**, that is the most controversial. Banks, department stores, insurance companies, credit card issuers, employers, and landlords can show a legitimate business interest and typically obtain a written consent anyway. But it is well known (and controversial) that some credit reporting agencies are less than diligent in confirming the purported "business purpose" of someone seeking information. And some licensed private investigators seem able to obtain a credit report on request. (See Ethical Note above.) (See LBD 18-3.)

For the paralegal investigator who is not a licensed private investigator and who does not have the consent of the individual being investigated, the only other way to access this information is to locate an existing credit report in the files of an obliging creditor that has previously obtained the report. In general, once a creditor has obtained a report from a credit reporting agency, the creditor is not expressly restricted from showing it to others. Every circumstance is different, however, and care should be taken to ensure that it is legal and ethical for the source to provide the report to the investigator under the existing circumstances.

HYPOTHETICAL 18-3

Assume that in the course of investigating Greene Unyon (see Case Study No. 3 in Appendix A), you learn that until six months ago he leased the offices of his veterinary practice from a man named Leaky Faucet. You know from searching the court house records that Leaky Faucet sued Greene Unyon for unpaid rent, claiming that Greene Unyon abandoned the leased premises before the lease term expired. You interview Leaky Faucet and, being no fan of Greene Unyon, he tells you that he obtained a credit report on Greene Unyon a year ago when Unyon first leased the premises and you can see it if you want.

1. Is this credit report on Greene Unyon information you would like to see? How could it help your supervising attorney in representing Vidalia Unyon?
2. Under the FCRA (or any applicable state law) can you legally accept this credit report from Leaky Faucet?
3. Can you ethically accept this credit report from Leaky Faucet?

7. Credit information on businesses

There are a number of business credit reporting agencies that collect credit information on corporations and other businesses. Dun & Bradstreet, Experian, Standard & Poors, and Moody's are examples of companies that collect information on businesses and make it available to subscribers.

Most of the credit information compiled by these companies is now accessible over the Internet to direct subscribers or to subscribers of various online database vendors (see full discussion of such vendors below). For example, credit reports compiled by Dun & Bradstreet on more than 9.5 million businesses and by Experian on more than 12 million businesses are accessible to subscribers of Westlaw and Lexis-Nexis. A number of the printed business credit report publications produced by these companies, such as *Dun & Bradstreet Ratings,* are available at public libraries and freely accessible there.

8. Bank account, credit card, and general financial information on individuals

In general, bank account, credit card, and other loan information held by a bank or lender is not accessible by anyone other than the customer himself. Of course, when accounts are jointly held by spouses or business partners, either spouse or any partner can access that information—important to remember in domestic cases or disputes between business partners.

The customer may also provide a written consent for a third person to access this information. If the information is relevant to issues in a pending civil or criminal lawsuit, it may be obtained by formal discovery request, court order, or subpoena.

Keep in mind, though, that financial information on individuals is frequently included in public records (see Chapters 16 and 17) by being included in required filings or in testimony in a civil or criminal lawsuit. This information is also included in publicly recorded land transactions, mortgages or personal property lien-filings, bankruptcy proceedings, or federal or state corporate filings.

Keep in mind that general financial information, while not accessible directly from the bank or lender, is often included in other private records that are accessible.

HYPOTHETICAL 18-4

Assume that you are still sitting in the office of Leaky Faucet trying to decide what to do with the credit report on Greene Unyon when Leaky hands you something else. "You might be able to use this, too," he says. He has handed you a rental application form filled out by Greene Unyon which lists his personal and business bank accounts by bank and account number, his outstanding debts by lender name, balance due and monthly payments, and all his sources of income. Best of all, attached to the back of the form is a dated and signed personal balance sheet in which Greene Unyon has listed all of his assets and liabilities and a separate balance sheet for his veterinary practice.

1. How will this information be useful to your supervising attorney in representing Vidalia Unyon?
2. Is there any legal or ethical reason you cannot accept this information from Leaky Faucet?
3. What other private sources might have obtained financial information on Greene Unyon?

Other non-governmental places to look for general financial information on individuals are the newspaper or other local publications, the local library, professional associations, and community organizations. In addition, if the individual you are researching is nationally or regionally prominent or just involved in a particular trade or profession, you might check various directories available in many public libraries and, increasingly, online. The best known of these is probably the *Who's Who In America* series, which includes numerous directories based on criteria such as an individual's wealth, corporate affiliations, profession, or hobby. For example, if you were investigating a person you know to be an art collector you might take a look in *Who's Who In American Art*.

If the individual is involved in a corporation, you might check *Standard & Poor's Register of Corporations, Directors and Executives* or Gale's *Owners and Officers of Private Companies*. If the individual is an attorney, check the *Martindale-Hubbell Law Directory*. If the individual is a physician, check your state's medical directory. The legal investigator should become familiar with the various directories available. (See LBD 18-4.) A good source to check to get an idea of all these directories is *Directories In Print*. (See Appendix E for a comprehensive listing of business-related directories.)

The best place to locate printed directories is the library. But remember that more and more directories are available online, which can speed up your search and give you access to more sources than your local library may provide.

SLEUTH ON THE LOOSE

Identify a well-known company then access *www.hoovers.com* for a brief company profile. While you are there, try looking up information on other companies of various sizes.

9. Financial and general business data on corporations and other businesses

As we saw in Chapters 16 and 17, corporations—especially publicly traded corporations—and other business entities are closely regulated by the federal and state governments, which often means public filings are made disclosing financial and general business information. Corporations and other businesses also leave a significant paper trail through other accessible public records such as civil suit filings, land and personal property transactions, etc., that disclose much financial information.

Not only is such information concerning corporations and other business entities available in various public records, much of it is collected by attorney organizations and made available to organization members. For example, the Association of Trial Lawyers of America (ATLA) and the Defense Research Institute (DRI), discussed in Chapter 15 (see Appendix E for information on how to contact ATLA and DRI), maintain and operate brief banks, articles, members' forums, and links to state and local organizations that may be contacted to locate information on businesses with whom other organization members have had prior dealings.

There are many other private sources of financial and business data available on businesses and the individuals involved with them as owners, officers, or directors.

EXAMPLE

Many companies, large and small, publish sales brochures, annual reports, and other materials, which are available for the asking from their public affairs offices or stockholders, or which may be available in libraries. Such companies may run advertisements in phone yellow pages, local newspapers, and regional or national publications. They issue press releases from time to time. Many companies have established their own Internet Web sites accessible to anyone surfing the Net.

SLEUTH ON THE LOOSE

Identify a small publicly held corporation and see if you can locate information on it at //business.lycos.com/ companysearch/ crtop.asp.

Other good sources of information on businesses include the local Chamber of Commerce and the Better Business Bureau; business periodicals; professional or trade publications; and pamphlets or other information frequently generated by local or statewide business development groups to attract new business, tourists, or residents.

In addition, there are numerous directories that collect financial and other data on corporations and other businesses. Dun & Bradstreet, Moody's, Standard & Poors and other publishers produce literally scores of different business directories. Illustration 18-6 contains a small sampling of such directories.

A good source for the paralegal to learn about the numerous business periodicals available is the *Business Periodical Index*, available in most libraries. Also, most business directories and many business periodicals are now available on the Internet.

10. Online database vendors

There are a number of commercial companies that make available online and by subscription vast amounts of information in library or

Illustration 18-6 EXAMPLES OF BUSINESS DIRECTORIES

1. *S&P's Register of Corporations, Directors and Executives.* A directory of over 55,000 public and private companies along with biographical sketches of executives and directors.
2. *S&P's Corporation Records.* In-depth sketches of over 11,000 publicly held corporations along with general news and financial information (annual reports and interim earnings reports).
3. *D&B's Ratings.* Data on thousands of businesses including credit information, organizational charts, stockbrokers, and wholesale and retail dealers.
4. *MacRae's Blue Book.* Contains information on all manufacturers of industrial equipment, products, and materials. Lists manufacturers alphabetically by company name, product classification, and trade name.
5. *Directory of Corporate Affiliations.* Information on 100,000 companies showing parent/subsidiary relationships and summary business information on each company.
6. *Thomas Register of American Manufacturers.* Directory of over 180,000 companies and 53,000 classes of products and services.
7. *D&B Million Dollar Directory.* Current business information on over 161,000 companies with a net worth of $500,000 or more.
8. *Ward's Business Directory.* Financial and marketing information on more than 150,000 American companies; includes up to ten recent news items on each company gathered from more than 3,000 newspapers and periodicals.
9. *S&P's Stock Reports.* Contains profiles on publicly traded companies.
10. *Moody's Industry Review.* Contains financial and statistical data for several thousand public and private companies.

database form. Typically, these companies will charge a base subscription fee plus an additional charge per search.

Westlaw (www.westlaw.com), owned by West Group (www.westpub .com), and Lexis/Nexis (www.lexis-nexis.com), the news and business information service of Lexis owned by Reed Elsevier, are the leading commercial vendors of this kind of information. Both make available libraries or databases containing all kinds of business and financial information; hundreds of daily newspapers, magazines, and newsletters from around the world; business, scientific, and professional journals and periodicals; information summaries; business and financial analyses; national reverse phone/address directories; people finder services; whole treatises on every academic and scientific subject imaginable as well as theses and dissertations; encyclopedias; transcripts of speeches; and much more.

Because these vendors have managed to get legal access to some information sources usually inaccessible to the public (e.g., credit bureaus) and because they have the means to locate and compile vast amounts of data from so many sources (from public records nationwide to direct mail marketers' mailing lists), the subscriber is able to access information she could not practically locate otherwise. Illustration 18-7 provides a sampling of the various business and general information databases available to subscribers of Westlaw.

Illustration 18-8 provides a sampling of the various business and general information databases available to subscribers of Lexis/Nexis.

Another large database vendor is Dialog (www.dialog.com). Dialog may be accessed through Westlaw or subscribed to separately. Illustration 18-9 provides a sampling of the various business and general information databases available to subscribers through the information services division of Dialog.

There are many online database vendors in business today. Some cater primarily to licensed private investigators, but most are available

Illustration 18-7   EXAMPLES OF GENERAL BUSINESS INFORMATION AVAILABLE ON WESTLAW

1. News and Business: Interfacing with Dow Jones News/Retrieval and Dialog, this provides information in the fields of business, medicine, technology, science, social policy, and consumer affairs drawn from thousands of publications and other information sources. It also supplies profiles on companies with more than 20 employees including affiliate information, access to SEC filings, and credit history for companies.
2. Dun & Bradstreet Credit Services: Provides detailed financial information on millions of public and private companies.
3. WestClip: Accesses all the major wire services, hundreds of local and national newspapers, trade journals, and other sources to enable the investigator to track and monitor people, businesses, industries, and topics.
4. The World Reporter: Provides international news from hundreds of sources world-wide.
5. People Finder: Compiles information from the Census Bureau, U.S. Postal Service, voter registration files, telephone directories, professional and trade associations, credit bureau information, city/county tax rolls, publishers mailing lists, vital statistics sources to provide information on more than 146 million individuals, 92 million households, 71 million telephone numbers, 40 million death certificates, and 160 million social security numbers.
6. Public Records: Provides access to more than one billion state and local public records which may contain an abundance of information on businesses and individuals.
7. Federal Filings: Provides securities filing data on companies and their officers and directors.

Illustration 18-8   EXAMPLES OF GENERAL BUSINESS INFORMATION AVAILABLE ON LEXIS/NEXIS

1. NEWS: This database (formerly called NEXIS) permits a topical search of nearly 700 news, business, and financial periodicals and newspapers and provides access to the full text of articles found.
2. Electronic Clipping Service (ECLIPSE): Accesses all the major wire services, hundreds of local and national newspapers, trade journals and other sources to enable the investigator to track and monitor people, businesses, industries, and topics.
3. Financial Information Service: Provides access to SEC filings, corporate information on thousands of companies, as well as national and international economic news.
4. FINDER: A people and business search tool.
5. National Automated Accounting Research System (NAARS): Provides access to financial and business information on thousands of publicly traded companies and their affiliates.
6. MEDIS: Provides access to comprehensive medical sources including medical journals and texts.
7. ALLVER: Provides access to information on verdicts and settlements in cases across the country as well as jury polls and background information on expert witnesses.

Illustration 18-9   EXAMPLES OF GENERAL BUSINESS INFORMATION AVAILABLE ON DIALOG

1. Business & News: Provides news and research on a company's finances, product lines, and demographics.
2. Government: Provides detailed legislative and regulatory data.
3. Intellectual Property: Provides detailed information on patent, trademark, and copyright activity.
4. Search: A people and business search tool.
5. Science & Technology: Provides access to the latest news and developments in science, medicine, the environment, computer technology, chemistry, aerospace, and virtually every engineering discipline.

to subscribers. An increasing number of these vendors are headquartered in Europe and specialize in business, scientific, and technical information from around the world. Appendix E contains a comprehensive listing of online database vendors and information on how to contact them. (See LBD 18-5.)

11. Search companies

Mention has already been made of the various public records search companies, which, for a fee, will search federal, state, and local records. A number of those companies will also conduct searches in non-governmental databases and prepare detailed reports, including general business and background information on your subject. An example is History Associates, Incorporated of Rockville, Maryland (online at www.history-associates.com). This firm conducts business and industry research from the National Archives in Washington, Federal Records Centers, presidential libraries, the Library of Congress, state and local governments, private corporations, universities, and professional associations.

Another example is Experian (online at www.experian.com/ small-business), which provides current business information on over 10 million businesses around the United States. It also provides new homeowner information; consumer lists totaling nearly 100 million records selectable by income, gender, and dozens of other variables; new movers information; new parents information; and "behavior bank" data on over 25 million consumer households broken down into over three hundred data categories. Stock brokerage firms may also be of help in obtaining financial information about companies and their principals. (See Appendix E for a comprehensive listing of search companies and information on how to contact them.)

12. Private investigative firms

A number of private investigative firms specialize in background screenings of potential employees and **due diligence** probes on behalf of corporate clients involved in buyouts, mergers, acquisitions, and divestitures. Other private investigative firms do more routine P.I. work: domestic disputes, including surveillance; criminal defense; and people locating, sometimes called **skip-tracing** (as in so-and-so skipped town and we need to trace his whereabouts). These investigative firms have access to the public records sources and online database vendors we have mentioned—including those that cater to private investigators—and also to their own ever-growing databases.

Most people have little awareness of how much personal information about themselves, including information they thought was private, has been located, compiled, and is sold every day to essentially anyone who wants it. As we have seen, most information on an individual collected by various government agencies is accessible, from vital statistics to marital history, business and professional licenses, property ownership, debt information, charitable contributions, travel reservations, voter registration information, motor vehicle records, civil and criminal court proceedings, and on and on we go.

But, in addition, any time an individual allows their name, address, and phone number to appear in a phone book, applies for credit with a lender or department store, fills out a credit card application, orders merchandise by mail, sends in a product registration or warranty card, makes a charitable contribution, subscribes to a magazine, answers a consumer questionnaire, places their name on a free mailing list, joins a book club, participates in a polling survey, signs a guest registration book at a tourist attraction, or registers to win a free prize, they have given out free information about themselves, which can be and regularly is sold to information brokers. Also, many banks and other businesses, and even state and local governments, have been found to be selling information about their customers and constituents to information brokers without the knowledge or permission of the persons involved (see LBD 18-7).

In the information brokerage trade, all of this private, personal information from consumers is called **header information,** and it is collected and organized in various ways to make it more useable, for example, by geographic region, age, gender, education level, income level, trade, or profession. Merchandising companies seek this information to use for various mailing lists or phone solicitations, trying to sell the consumer something else. But this information is also sold to and used by all kinds of people in the information business, such as the database vendors and search companies already mentioned. It is also acquired and used by private investigative firms or by information warehouses that assemble huge databases and then make them accessible to private investigators for a fee.

With the advent of the Internet, online information brokers have blossomed. For approximately $1,000 these brokers, many of whom are private investigative firms, promise to provide a *profile* of personal and financial information on individuals and businesses. In many cases, they cater to attorneys seeking information on the assets of a potential defendant or seeking assets to seize to enforce a judgment already rendered. This can be a valuable service. But the profiling business is controversial for two reasons. First, many of these information brokers historically have used deceptive and fraudulent methods to obtain financial information on the target. For example, they call a bank with the customer's social security number and pretend to be the customer in order to learn the balances on account, a method known as **pretext calling.** Second, whether ethical procedures are utilized or not, the perceived invasion of privacy involved is troublesome. As a result, the federal government and some state governments recently have enacted legislation that prohibits *pretexting* methods and regulates the providing of customer information to information brokers or other financial institutions (see LBD 18-7).

So long as the private investigative firm is not engaged in illegal or unethical conduct, it is perfectly permissible for the law office to utilize these resources for information searches that, for reasons of time or limited resources, cannot be done by that office. (See Ethical Note above.)

a. Locating a reliable private investigator

There are many private investigators (P.I.'s) around to choose from and they are easy to locate. The yellow pages of the phone book is handy. Many state and local bar organizations publish directories or handbooks listing P.I.'s. State volumes of Martindale-Hubbell carry private investigator listings. Some P.I.'s will advertise their areas of expertise in the yellow pages or in directory listings. The Internet contains a number of sites with directories of P.I.'s. (See Appendix E for a comprehensive listing of resources for locating a private investigator and other related information.)

Regardless of how you locate a P.I., you want to be sure to find someone who is both competent and ethical. Not only because your own standards are high, but because you owe a duty to your client whose work the P.I. will be doing. Seek recommendations from attorneys or other paralegals in your area whose judgment and ethics you trust. When you make contact with a P.I., don't hesitate to interview him. Ask about any client complaints to the state licensing agency, any license suspensions or revocations, or lawsuits filed against him. Ask them for references from attorneys or paralegals he has worked with previously and follow up on those.

Depending on what you want the P.I. to do, it may not be necessary or wise to retain someone local. If you want a P.I. to perform a national search for a person or documents, you may want to contact a regional or national P.I. firm. They probably subscribe to all the computer service companies that cater to private investigators. On the other hand, if you only need some surveillance done locally, a local P.I. will be more logical.

b. Working effectively with a private investigator

When you have located a private investigator that seems dependable and qualified, you want to establish a good, responsible working relationship with him. We owe it to our clients to do so. Here are some suggestions.

1. **Fees and expenses.** Always ask in advance about the P.I.'s fee schedule and expenses, and find out about his billing schedule and any required advances. Communicate this information to the client and get the client's approval before formally retaining the P.I.

2. **Scope of the assignment.** Always communicate clearly to the P.I. exactly what the assignment is and any time deadlines you expect him to meet. If there is no time deadline, find out in advance the time frame in which he expects to be able to perform the work and let him know you expect to hear from him within that time frame. Be sure he knows to contact the supervising attorney or you (so *you* can contact the supervising attorney) before undertaking any activities or incurring any expenses outside the scope of the assignment.

3. **P.I. reports.** Let the P.I. know whether you want written reports on his work or verbal reports only. Most P.I.'s will do written reports in memorandum or letter form if you do not specify. Ask the supervising attorney which she prefers and advise the P.I.

4. **Work product.** Mark all your correspondence to the P.I. as work product and ask him to mark his correspondence or written reports to you the same way. It is better if the P.I. directs his written correspondence or reports to the supervising attorney. In states that recognize the work product privilege for P.I. material produced on behalf of an attorney, this will strengthen the argument that the material is not subject to discovery by an opposing party.

5. **Disclosure of status and avoidance of UPL.** Make sure the P.I. knows and understands that you are not a licensed attorney. Working with a P.I. is like any other task the paralegal undertakes—it is done under the supervision and authority of an attorney. So be careful not to exercise independent judgment in directing the activities of the P.I. Always run your recommendations by the supervising attorney and communicate her directions.

6. **Confidentiality.** Make sure the P.I. you use understands the importance of attorney-client confidentiality. The P.I. retained by the attorney works as an agent of the attorney and a sub-agent of the client. The P.I. will almost certainly learn confidences and secrets of the client and will need to know to avoid disclosing those. Most P.I.'s are not trained formally in legal ethics and only pick up bits and pieces on the job. Don't let him learn at the expense of your client.

7. **No illegal or unethical conduct.** Make it clear to the P.I. that you do not expect or wish for him to engage in any illegal or unethical conduct in the work he performs on your client's case. Assuming that pretexting methods of compiling personal and financial profiles (or the use of information obtained by those methods) have not yet been

prohibited legally (see discussion above and LBD 18-7), the supervising attorney will need to make a decision regarding whether it is ethical to utilize an investigative firm known to use such methods.

8. **Frequent contact.** If the P.I. you use does not stay in regular, frequent contact, you must initiate the contact. Stay in touch with him so that if the supervising attorney should ask you at any time about the status of the P.I.'s work you can give her a fresh report.

9. **Pay your bills.** Try to make sure that the P.I.'s statements for services are paid on time. It's the way we all want to be treated. Taking care of his bills will keep him happy and committed to the client's case.

13. Resources on the Internet

SLEUTH ON THE LOOSE

To learn how to better use the Internet for legal investigation, subscribe to the Net-Lawyer listserv by sending an e-mail to *net-lawyers-request @webcom.com* and in the message write, "Subscribe Net-Lawyers" along with your name.

Just as more public records are accessible directly on the Internet today (see Chapters 16 and 17 and especially the Note on the Internet in Chapter 16), so too is more business and individual information and scholarly research data as well. As just one example, the Survey Research Center of Princeton University (www.princeton.edu/~abelson/index/html) provides a comprehensive index of polling and survey information on social issues, consumer research, and policy analysis. A number of colleges and universities have established Web sites allowing access to their library holdings and many industries have Web sites where you can access general information about the industry.

Numerous businesses today operate individual Web sites where they will post business summaries, officer and director biographies, shareholder reports, and general financial information. To locate an Internet site operated by a school, industry, or company utilize a good search engine (see Appendix E for a comprehensive listing of search engines) and type in the name to be searched. Or direct your browser to www.[insert the name to be searched or its abbreviation]. (See LBD 18-4 and 18-6.)

Numerous newspapers from around the world are accessible on the Internet. For example, thousands of newspapers and periodicals are organized and sorted by region of the world, country, and state, at News Index and Total News (www.niu.edu/newsplace/). All the major television networks have sites where information is available, as do increasing numbers of local television and radio stations.

Hundreds of periodicals are on the Internet too. For example, the Time/Warner family of publications (including Time, Fortune, Life, People, and Money magazines) is available at www.pathfinder.com.

As previously suggested in the Note on the Internet in Chapter 16, because of the mass of information available on the Internet and the ever-growing number and changing locations of Web sites, the paralegal investigator needs to keep her own notebook of current sites useable to access different kinds of information. Watch for articles in professional publications advising you of new and updated sites and take note of information made available at seminars. There are also a steady stream of books publishing Web site addresses for all kinds of information but if you're going to invest in one, make sure it is current. Finally, remember that, in general, information located on an Internet Web site may not be as comprehensive or reliable as information accessed through an online commercial vendor or search company.

KEY WORDS AND PHRASES TO REMEMBER

agreed order

authorization

business directory

city/county directory

credit reporting agency

criss-cross directory

Dialog

due diligence

Fair Credit Reporting Act

header information

information broker

information wholesaler

Internet

Lexis/Nexis

people finder

pretext calling

records custodian

reverse directory

search company

search engine

skip tracing

subpoena duces tecum

Web site

Westlaw

wiretapping

LEARN BY DOING

LBD 18-1. Familiarize yourself with the privacy rules for medical records promulgated by the U.S. Department of Health and Human Services (DHHS) pursuant to the Health Insurance Portability and Accountability Act of 1996 (HIPAA) which became effective on April 15, 2003 and which are located at 45 CFR 160 and 164. Check the comprehensive answer guide for the new privacy rules put together by the DHHS Office of Civil Rights at *www.hhs.gov/ocr/hipaa*. Then prepare a memorandum answering the following questions:

(a) Who is a "covered entity" under the HIPAA rules?

(b) What patient information is considered "protected health information" under the HIPAA rules?

(c) How does an attorney go about obtaining health information for a client or other party under the rules?

(d) What are the potential civil and criminal penalties for violating the HIPAA rules?

(e) Does the state in which you work have any statute or regulation governing the accessibility of medical records that contain requirements additional to those set out in the HIPAA rules?

LBD 18-2. Utilizing the current and earlier city/county directories for your city or county, see if you can determine everyone who has lived at your (or any other) current address during the past five, ten, fifteen, or twenty years. Determine whether any of those former residents are still in the area and, if so, where.

LBD 18-3. Research the meaning of "legitimate business purpose" under the Federal Credit Reporting Act, 15 U.S.C. §1681, or any analogous state law, and prepare a memorandum summarizing your research as it pertains to the following questions:

a. How have the courts (particularly your state's courts and the federal courts sitting in your state) interpreted that phrase?
b. Do licensed private investigators always have a legitimate business purpose allowing them to access another person's credit records?
c. Do attorneys or those assisting them have a legitimate business purpose allowing them to access another person's credit records simply because they are investigating a matter for a client?
d. What penalties/liability have been imposed on persons or businesses violating the FCRA?

LBD 18-4. Choose a large local corporation and perform a background investigation of it using the sources of corporate and business information set out in Appendix E. See if you can locate the following information on the company you select and, while doing so, keep a written summary of the information you locate and the research tools you used to locate each item of information.

a. Locate the exact name and all business address(es) of the company.
b. Obtain a detailed description of the business of the company, including its leading products, services, or primary customers.
c. Obtain the names of the officers of the company for the past three years, as well as the name(s) of the chairman of the board of directors and new directors of the company during that time.
d. Determine the profit (or loss) enjoyed (or sustained) by the company for each of the past three years and the average share price at year-end for each of the past three years.
e. Obtain a copy of shareholder reports, advertisements, and press releases issued by the company during the past three years.
f. If the company has a Web page, locate it, then download and print the home page information.

LBD 18-5. If you have access to a commercial information vendor such as Westlaw, Lexis/Nexis, or Dialog, use one or more of these services to locate financial, business, and other information on the company you selected in LBD 18-4. Then use one or more of those services to perform the searches itemized in LBD 18-6.

LBD 18-6. If you have access to the Internet, determine who your Internet access provider is and all search engines available to you through that access provider. Using one or all of the search engines available to you, perform a word or phrase search to:

a. locate a friend you haven't seen in years
b. determine the current wholesale and retail value of your car
c. locate an attorney in your area specializing in estate planning
d. locate a surgeon in your area specializing in pediatric cardiology
e. locate current financial information on the company you chose to research in LBD 16-1 and Hypothetical 16-2
f. determine last Friday's closing stock exchange averages in Hong Kong
g. locate the front page lead headline in last Sunday's London Times

> h. locate the home page of the state university of your state
> i. locate the home page of a major industry in your state
> j. locate the home page of a corporation or other business that is a major employer in your state

LBD 18-7. Review the Federal Financial Modernization Act (commonly known as the Gramm-Leach-Bliley Act) (GLB) at 15 U.S.C. §§6801 et. seq. which was signed into law on November 12, 1999 and which went into full effect on July 1, 2001. Also review the regulations promulgated to enforce GLB at 16 CFR 313.1 et. seq. Prepare a memorandum addressing the following questions:

> a. What is included in the concept of "non-public information" that is protected from disclosure in GLB? Is it financial information only? Review the decision in *Individual Reference Services Group v. FTC*, 145 F. Supp. 2d 6 (D. D.C. 2001) in connection with your answer.
>
> b. How does the statute work? What entities are governed by the mandates of GLB? Under what circumstances can a financial institution disclose non-public information on a consumer? What rights are consumers given to prohibit that disclosure?
>
> c. Does GLB prohibit pretexting? If so, does it punish the party requesting the information or the party providing the information or both? Does it punish the use of information gathered in this manner? What is the penalty?
>
> d. Does GLB prohibit states from providing consumers with greater protection from disclosure of their personal information?
>
> e. Has your state, by statute, regulation, or case decision, provided more protection than GLB for consumers from disclosure of their personal information?

Appendix A
Case Studies

CASE STUDY NO. 1

THE ROWDY OUTLAW CASE

The law office where you work as a paralegal has been retained by country music star Rowdy Outlaw to defend him on first degree murder charges brought against him by your state (Yourstate). Mr. Outlaw is accused of murdering Bobbette Bouvier, his back-up singer, on September 1. The trial has been scheduled for three months from today. Below you will find a summary of the new client memorandum prepared by your supervising attorney from the initial interview with Mr. Outlaw and the police report.

Summary of new client memorandum and police report:

Rowdy Outlaw (real name Herman F. Fripp, DOB 10-1-52) hit the country music big-time two years ago with his record-breaking song, *There's Room in My Saddle for Two.* He and his band, the Holdups, struggled for more than five years before breaking through with the hit song.

During those lean years, Rowdy had an ongoing relationship with his female back-up singer, Bobbette Bouvier. But after finding success some two years ago, he surprised everyone by marrying Candy Carmichael, a sometime hair stylist and groupie who had followed the band around the country for years. Outlaw says that, as far as he knows, Bobbette took his marriage to Candy Carmichael in stride. And he heard from one of the members of the band approximately six months ago that she was seeing someone else but he doesn't know who.

Bobbette Bouvier owned a condominium in Palace Towers, a high-rise condo just outside of Capital City, Yourstate, where the band is based. None of the other band members live in Palace Towers.

In the early morning hours of September 1 (2:10 A.M. per the police report), a next-door neighbor to Bouvier heard a scream and sounds of scuffling. She called the police and they arrived around 2:30 A.M. Entering Bouvier's apartment, the police found her body on the floor of her bedroom, in a nightgown, strangled to death with a guitar wire, which was still wrapped around her neck. The lock on the door to her condo had been jimmied and the bedroom showed signs of a struggle, with lamps and tables knocked over. On the floor near the body, police found a black guitar pick with the initials *RO* on it in red. In the living room leading to the bedroom, they found a single turkey feather on the floor. Mr. Outlaw is widely known for using only black guitar picks and has all his picks monogrammed in red with his initials. He also wears a black cowboy hat with turkey feathers protruding from the hat band. Police have the guitar pick, string, and turkey feather in their possession.

The neighbor who called the police also told them that after she called it became quiet next door and she peeked out her door in time to see the back of someone leaving the Bouvier apartment. The person leaving had on a long western style coat, red and black cowboy boots, and a black cowboy hat with turkey feathers sticking out of the band, all of which is the standard stage costume of Mr. Outlaw. According to the police report, the neighbor's name is Georgette B. Good, a part-time legal secretary (working through a temp service) and aspiring country singer whose career hasn't gone anywhere yet. The police report says she has positively identified the man she saw leaving the Bouvier apartment as Rowdy Outlaw.

Acting on the information provided by Good, police obtained a warrant to search Outlaw's house in Capital City. The search was conducted at 6:30 A.M. on September 1. Mrs. Outlaw, the former Candy Carmichael, was at home and awakened by the police. Under questioning, she said her husband had not been home all evening and she had no idea where he was. In fact, she said he had not been home in weeks and she didn't care whether he ever came home again.

Attached to Outlaw's house is a private recording studio. In the course of searching that studio, the police discovered one of Rowdy's guitars with a string missing. They have taken the guitar into their custody.

Mrs. Outlaw also told the police about Rowdy's prior affair with Bobbette and stated that she "wouldn't be surprised if they were back at it again, 'cause there ain't been nothin' going on around here in a long long time."

The police obtained a warrant for Rowdy's arrest later that morning and put out an all-points bulletin for his arrest. That afternoon Rowdy turned himself in and the arrest report describes him as looking disheveled, bleary-eyed, and barely coherent. He waived his right to counsel (this was before he called us) and initially told the police he had been home all night. Confronted with the statements of his wife, Rowdy changed his story and told the police he had been out drinking all night with Kato, the drummer for the Holdups.

Police apparently haven't located Kato yet. He doesn't have a permanent residence but, according to Outlaw, just sleeps over at a variety of friends' houses, moving every few weeks when he wears out his welcome.

Outlaw was arrested and processed and that's when he called us. He is still in custody and his preliminary hearing is coming up soon.

Since we were retained, two other witnesses have come to our attention. Jack Gates is an old friend of Outlaw's. They went to high school together in Capital City, joined the Army together following high school graduation, and even did a tour in Viet Nam together in 1970–1971. Outlaw says that he's not sure of the details but knows that Gates got in some trouble in the Army and was dishonorably discharged. Rumor had it that the discharge had something to do with drugs. Gates changed after that, Rowdy says. He is now an insurance agent, and handles Outlaw's insurance and most of his financial dealings.

According to newspaper reports, Gates called the police following Outlaw's arrest and volunteered that Rowdy was supposed to have dinner with him the evening before the murder occurred but did not show. They had been scheduled to meet at 8 P.M. at Farley's Fish Shack and then go to Gates' office to review Outlaw's insurance portfolio. Gates supposedly told the police that he arrived at Farley's, waited there until it closed at 11 P.M. and then left. He tried to call Outlaw several times while he waited but could not reach him. One call he made was to Outlaw's house. He talked with Mrs. Outlaw and was told the same thing she told the police—Outlaw wasn't there, hadn't been there in weeks, and wouldn't be welcomed if he came back.

According to the newspaper account, the police were also contacted sometime after the story of the arrest appeared in the media by a Connie Cornelius. Cornelius, according to the media, told the police that she was on her way to work at the Capital City Daily News (she operates a press) and passed in front of Palace Towers at about 2:15 A.M. the morning of the murder. She said she saw Rowdy Outlaw coming out the front doors of Palace Towers, running as if in a hurry. She said she didn't recognize him at first, but her husband, Fred Cornelius, who was driving her to work, recognized him and said, "Hey, look, that's that famous singer, what's-his-name. I wonder if we could get his autograph."

Yesterday we received a call from a man named Perry Peters, who said he had heard about the arrest from the newspaper accounts and had something we might want to know. He says he was working as the parking lot security guard at Palace Towers the night of the murder. He said he was in the parking lot of the building from 10 P.M. until 5 A.M. and never saw any sign of Rowdy Outlaw. He told us he did see someone leave the building between 2 and 2:30 A.M. but it was definitely not Rowdy Outlaw. He said it was someone a lot taller and thinner than Outlaw (who is about 5'9" and stocky) and, as he thought about it, the person looked a lot like Mick Jagger.

We have also received a call from a lady who identifies herself as Ima Jean Grouse. She told us she can provide an alibi for Rowdy Outlaw the night of the murder. Rowdy says he does not know this lady, but was drinking heavily with Kato all that night and that anything is possible.

The arresting officer with the Capital City P.D. was Detective Willie Parker. Strangely, according to the police report, Parker says Rowdy Outlaw admitted committing the crime to him, though he does not have it tape recorded and Outlaw vehemently denies to us that he did so.

We are told by the District Attorney's office that they have an expert, Michael Melody, who will testify that the guitar string found around Bobbette's neck is the same size as the missing string on Rowdy's guitar and will offer the opinion that, at one time, the string in question had in fact been strung on Rowdy's guitar.

CASE STUDY No. 2

THE RED DOG SALOON CASE

The law office where you work as a paralegal has been retained to represent Soupspoon Wise in connection with potential personal injury and property loss claims arising out of an incident at the Red Dog Saloon. Below you will find a summary of the new client memorandum prepared by your supervising attorney based on her interview with Mr. Wise.

Summary of new client memorandum:

Our client is Soupspoon Wise, a well-known blues artist reputed to be the best saxophone player living today. He has played concerts all over the world and cut several albums.

One month ago today, Soupspoon was leaving the Red Dog Saloon just outside the city limits with his new girlfriend, Tanya Trucker, a licensed masseuse. Soupspoon and Tanya had just gotten into his one-year-old black Porsche, which was parked in the Red Dog parking lot, and put on their seat belts when a white Ford Bronco came racing from behind the Red Dog building and swerved right at them. The Bronco driver hit the brakes but it was too late and it slammed head-on into Soupspoon's Porsche.

The air bag on the passenger side of the Porsche deployed on impact and Tanya T. was not hurt. However, Soupspoon says the air bag on his side did not deploy and, even though he was wearing his seat belt, his head was thrown forward and struck the steering wheel.

Soupspoon was knocked unconscious and doesn't remember anything else about the accident. He says that Tanya has told him that the Ford Bronco sped away from the scene. It hasn't been seen since and the occupants are unknown at this time. However, Tanya told the investigating officer that the Bronco had California plates, though she couldn't make out any particular number.

She also told the officer that there were two men in the Bronco, one driving and the other in the back seat. The windows were down in the Bronco and she told the officer that following the collision, she heard the driver curse and say, "Where did that car come from? I can't see a thing in this dark parking lot. Why don't they have any lights here?" She heard the figure in the back say, "Let's just get out of here. This is your second accident this week and you're going to lose your license and your insurance." That's when the Bronco drove off.

Soupspoon does recall that other Red Dog patrons were coming out into the parking lot while he and Tanya were leaving, but he didn't know any of them or what they saw. For some reason, he does remember a pickup truck being parked near his car that had KP's Plumbing Service printed by hand on the side of the driver's door.

Tanya T. has broken up with Soupspoon since the accident, gone to Nashville to pursue a singing career, and assumed a stage name he can't remember. The manager of the Red Dog Saloon is a man named Turtle Shoop.

Soupspoon bought his Porsche used three months before the accident at Goosie Hoots Hot Cars and the owner, Goosie Hoots, is the salesman that sold him the car.

Damages:

The Porsche was totaled. Soupspoon spent three weeks in Capital City Hospital with several broken facial bones, including his jaw, as well as a severe concussion. He says his doctor tells him it will take at least six months for the jaw to heal and there is real concern about whether the injury will affect his ability to play the sax. He has had to cancel four appearances scheduled during the last month and fifteen dates he had scheduled over the next six months. Beyond that, we don't know yet.

CASE STUDY NO. 3

THE VIDALIA UNYON CASE

The law office where you work as a paralegal has been retained to represent Mrs. Vidalia Unyon in a possible divorce action. Below you will find a summary of the new client memorandum prepared by your supervising attorney based on her interview with Mrs. Unyon.

Summary of new client memorandum:

Vidalia Unyon is a 45-year-old housewife. She was referred to us by Bill Richards, a local accountant, who is married to Yellow Unyon Richards, the oldest daughter of Vidalia and Greene Unyon.

Mr. and Mrs. Unyon have been married for 27 years. They were married right out of high school and their first child, Yellow, was born a year later. Mrs. Unyon has never worked outside the home and never continued her education after marrying Greene Unyon. Mr. Unyon, however, went on to college at Yourstate University, taking his undergraduate degree and then continuing at Yourstate University School of Veterinary Medicine. He has been a licensed and practicing veterinarian in this state for 20 years and has what is believed to be a thriving practice here in Capital City, Yourstate.

Mrs. Unyon has never been active in the business and has no financial data on her husband's practice. The couple have two children who are still at home, Greene, Jr., who is sixteen and a daughter, Sweet, who is ten.

Property:

(a) Assets: The couple own their residence in the city, which they built ten years ago. There is a mortgage on the house, the balance of which Mrs. Unyon believes is about $75,000 (held by First City Bank), though she says Mr. Unyon keeps all the financial records for the family as well as his business. She does not have a good estimate of the value of the house, but can recall her husband saying recently he thought they could get half a million for it in a good market. There are some certificates of deposit, savings accounts, and checking accounts but, again, her husband keeps up with all that. She does know that they have a joint checking account at First City Bank that she uses but there may be others, she just doesn't know.

She knows her husband uses the Morgan Stanley, Dean Witter brokerage firm, but has no idea what investments her husband may have or whether they are in his name only or joint. She also thinks he has a 401K plan through his veterinary practice but she doesn't know the details.

The couple own three cars, a 1999 BMW 325e, a 2000 Cadillac Seville, and a 1998 Jeep Grand Cherokee, which the 16-year-old son drives. She has no idea how the vehicles are titled.

The couple have collected antiques for the last 15 years or so. That is Mrs. Unyon's area of specialty, and she says they have some valuable Federal period furniture and French porcelain pieces. Their collection has never been appraised so she cannot put a dollar value on it, but would like to keep it all in the divorce.

Mr. Unyon is an avid gun collector. She knows nothing about guns but says he has a room full, including some that her husband has said are illegal to purchase now. He can have them as far as she is concerned.

(b) Debts: In addition to the mortgage on the house, Mrs. Unyon knows of only a Visa bill and an American Express bill that are owed. She doesn't know the balances but thinks it's a few hundred dollars each. She says that every month lots of mail comes in that looks like bills but her husband always takes care of it.

Property settlement:

Mrs. Unyon wants to keep all the antiques. She wants to be able to live in the house as long as the two minor children are at home. She has no idea of the size of Mr. Unyon's estate or the value of his business since he has always taken care of that, but feels she has raised his family and kept his home and should get a fair portion of it. She wants to keep the BMW and the Jeep. Mr. Unyon can keep the Cadillac.

Grounds:

Mrs. Unyon said that her relationship with her husband has not been good for several years. They have grown apart in their interests and attitudes toward life in general. She has always been more family-oriented than he, although he is very close to the son. She is a very religious person, and although Mr. Unyon used to go to church with her while the son was young, a few years ago he stopped going and would not let her make the son go anymore.

As he has become more successful in his practice she feels Mr. Unyon has stopped loving her. He plays golf all weekend with the son or with his buddies at the Capital City Country Club where they are members and, when he is home, watches sports on TV. His regular caddy at the country club is someone named Hobo Booth.

The couple's sex life has been nonexistent for longer than she can remember and they no longer even have many mutual friends. She also believes he may be having an affair. An anonymous female called her a couple of months ago and told her that Mr. Unyon was having an affair with someone at the office. She isn't sure who the caller was, but thought the voice might be that of a woman who worked as Mr. Unyon's receptionist until a few months ago. She never knew this woman's name, but her husband always called her Nosey Nelly.

About two weeks ago, she found a little black book in her husband's suit coat pocket that had nothing in it but the names of women with phone numbers alongside, all in his handwriting. She confronted her husband with her suspicions at that time, accusing him directly of sleeping with someone else. He didn't deny it, but wouldn't talk about it either. When she kept on badgering him about it he finally said, "Well, what if I am?"

The last straw came yesterday when her husband was served at home with suit papers from a neighboring state. It seems that a woman named

Georgia Peach has filed a paternity suit against him alleging that he is the father of her newborn child and demanding support.

Custody:

Mrs. Unyon wants to have sole custody of both the minor children. She doesn't expect that to be a problem with the ten-year-old daughter but fears her husband will contest custody of the sixteen-year-old son and that the son, if allowed to choose, will go with his father. She is concerned about the influence that environment may have on her son, who is going through a rebellious stage anyway.

Support:

Mrs. Unyon wants to go back to school. She is interested in the new paralegal program at Yourstate University and feels that if she does well in it, she may even go on to law school. However, she doesn't work, hasn't ever worked, and has no marketable skills. She will need her husband to support her while she is in school. She will also want child support for the children through college. The oldest daughter graduated from Yourstate University, being put through college by her parents.

Miscellaneous:

Mrs. Unyon says her husband does not know she is seeing a lawyer. She has not mentioned divorce to him but is fed up with her marriage and wants out. She says they had a big fight about a week ago and he threatened to have her killed if she ever left him. She thinks he means it. He knows how to use all the guns in his collection. He's just not the man she married 27 years ago.

CASE STUDY NO. 4

THE ROCKY ROAD PROJECT

The law office where you work as a paralegal has been retained to represent Rocky Road Developers, Inc. (RRD), in a real estate development project. Below you will find a summary of the new client memorandum prepared by your supervising attorney based on his interview with Mr. Rocky Road, president of RRD.

Summary of new client memorandum:

RRD is a domestic corporation owned solely by Mr. Rocky Road, the president and sole director of the corporation. RRD has done a few real estate development projects in Yourstate and neighboring states and is now working on a deal here in Capital City.

RRD has a one-year option to buy ten acres of farmland east of Capital City. The option expires three months from today. RRD has hopes of acquiring a total of 20 acres in that location and building a strip mall with two anchor tenants and eight to ten smaller tenants. Rocky Road advised that he thinks the other ten acres may now be available.

Five acres adjoining the ten he has optioned were owned by a farmer by the name of Edward Dig Deep, who Road has learned passed away two weeks ago. Road has no information regarding whether Farmer Deep left a will or not.

Three additional adjoining acres are owned by Capital City and the mayor's office has advised Road that the city has decided not to utilize those acres and may be willing to sell them.

Two other adjoining acres are the site of an old gas station (with a small office and separate garage) that recently closed and has a for sale sign on the window. A shallow stream flows just behind the old gas station site and Rocky Road says it looks like a lot of junk has been thrown in there recently. He wonders if it might be polluted.

He stopped by there several months ago to ask if it might be for sale and talked to a woman named Grace Slickspot, who seemed to be running the place. When Rocky Road asked Grace Slickspot if she was the owner, she answered him, "You're close enough." She didn't express any interest in selling then and Rocky Road left Ms. Slickspot his business card and asked her to call if she changed her mind. Two days ago Rocky Road had a message in his voice mail from Grace Slickspot telling him in a near whisper that the property was now available if he would hurry.

Rocky Road would like us to advise and assist him in obtaining title to the ten acres he does not yet have optioned and concerning the legal requirements he needs to satisfy to get his project approved.

Regarding tenants, Road advised that he spoke with a Mr. Real E. Smart, a vice president in the real estate department of World Mart, Inc., the world's largest retail discounter, about six months ago concerning its interest in locating a new store on the site. Smart expressed great interest on behalf of World Mart in this project, though neither World

Mart nor any other tenant has signed a lease commitment with RRD. Rocky Road also hopes he can land Super Foods as the other anchor tenant and would like us to help with the negotiations with those two companies.

Appendix B

Federal Rules
of Civil Procedure
(Selected Rules)

FEDERAL RULES OF CIVIL PROCEDURE (SELECTED RULES)

RULE 11. SIGNING OF PLEADINGS, MOTIONS, AND OTHER PAPERS; REPRESENTATIONS TO COURT; SANCTIONS

(b) Representations to Court. By presenting to the court (whether by signing, filing, submitting, or later advocating) a pleading, written motion, or other paper, an attorney or unrepresented party is certifying that to the best of the person's knowledge, information, and belief, formed after an inquiry reasonable under the circumstances,—

(1) it is not being presented for any improper purpose, such as to harass or to cause unnecessary delay or needless increase in the cost of litigation;

(2) the claims, defenses, and other legal contentions therein are warranted by existing law or by a nonfrivolous argument for the extension, modification, or reversal of existing law or the establishment of new law;

(3) the allegations and other factual contentions have evidentiary support or, if specifically so identified, are likely to have evidentiary support after a reasonable opportunity for further investigation or discovery; and

(4) the denials of factual contentions are warranted on the evidence or, if specifically so identified, are reasonably based on a lack of information or belief.

(c) Sanctions. If, after notice and a reasonable opportunity to respond, the court determines that subdivision (b) has been violated, the court may, subject to the conditions stated below, impose an appropriate sanction upon the attorneys, law firms, or parties that have violated subdivision (b) or are responsible for the violation. . . .

(2) Nature of Sanction; Limitations. A sanction imposed for violation of this rule shall be limited to what is sufficient to deter repetition of such conduct or comparable conduct by others similarly situated. Subject to the limitations in subparagraphs (A) and (B), the sanction may consist of, or include, directives of a nonmonetary nature, an order to pay a penalty into court, or, if imposed on motion and warranted for effective deterrence, an order directing payment to the movant of some or all of the reasonable attorneys' fees and other expenses incurred as a direct result of the violation.

(A) Monetary sanctions may not be awarded against a represented party for a violation of subdivision (b)(2).

(B) Monetary sanctions may not be awarded on the court's initiative unless the court issues its order to show cause before a voluntary dismissal or settlement of the claims made by or against the party which is, or whose attorneys are, to be sanctioned.

RULE 12. DEFENSES AND OBJECTIONS—WHEN AND HOW PRESENTED—BY PLEADING OR MOTION—MOTION FOR JUDGMENT ON THE PLEADINGS

(b) **How Presented.** Every defense, in law or fact, to a claim for relief in any pleading, whether a claim, counterclaim, cross-claim, or third-party claim, shall be asserted in the responsive pleading thereto if one is required, except that the following defenses may at the option of the pleader be made by motion: (1) lack of jurisdiction over the subject matter, (2) lack of jurisdiction over the person, (3) improper venue, (4) insufficiency of process, (5) insufficiency of service of process, (6) failure to state a claim upon which relief can be granted, (7) failure to join a party under Rule 19. A motion making any of these defenses shall be made before pleading if a further pleading is permitted. No defense or objection is waived by being joined with one or more other defenses or objections in a responsive pleading or motion. If a pleading sets forth a claim for relief to which the adverse party is not required to serve a responsive pleading, the adverse party may assert at the trial any defense in law or fact to that claim for relief. If, on a motion asserting the defense numbered (6) to dismiss for failure of the pleading to a state a claim upon which relief can be granted, matters outside the pleading are presented to and not excluded by the court, the motion shall be treated as one for summary judgment and disposed of as provided in Rule 56, and all parties shall be given reasonable opportunity to present all material made pertinent to such a motion by Rule 56.

RULE 13. COUNTERCLAIM AND CROSS-CLAIM

(a) **Compulsory Counterclaims.** A pleading shall state as a counterclaim any claim which at the time of serving the pleading the pleader has against any opposing party, if it arises out of the transaction or occurrence that is the subject matter of the opposing party's claim and does not require for its adjudication the presence of third parties of whom the court cannot acquire jurisdiction.

(b) **Permissive Counterclaims.** A pleading may state as a counterclaim any claim against an opposing party not arising out of the transaction or occurrence that is the subject matter of the opposing party's claim. . . .

(g) **Cross-Claim Against Co-Party.** A pleading may state as a cross-claim any claim by one party against a co-party arising out of the transaction or occurrence that is the subject matter either of the original action or of a counterclaim therein or relating to any property that is the subject matter of the original action. Such cross-claim may include a claim that the party against whom it is asserted is or may be liable to the cross-claimant for all or part of a claim asserted in the action against the cross-claimant. . . .

RULE 14. THIRD-PARTY PRACTICE

(a) When Defendant May Bring in Third Party. At any time after commencement of the action a defending party, as a third-party plaintiff, may cause a summons and compliant to be served upon a person not a party to the action who is or may be liable to the third-party plaintiff for all or part of the plaintiff's claim against the third-party plaintiff. The third-party plaintiff need not obtain leave to make the service if the third-party plaintiff files the third-party complaint not later than 10 days after serving the original answer. Otherwise the third-party plaintiff must obtain leave on motion upon notice to all parties to the action. . . .

RULE 15. AMENDED AND SUPPLEMENTAL PLEADINGS

(a) Amendments. A party may amend the party's pleading once as a matter of course at any time before a responsive pleading is served or, if the pleading is one to which no responsive pleading is permitted and the action has not been placed upon the trial calendar, the party may so amend it at any time within 20 days after it is served. Otherwise a party may amend the party's pleading only by leave of court or by written consent of the adverse party; and leave shall be freely given when justice so requires. A party shall plead in response to an amended pleading within the time remaining for response to the original pleading or within 10 days after service of the amended pleading, whichever period may be the longer, unless the court otherwise orders. . . .

(c) Relation Back of Amendments. An amendment of a pleading relates back to the date of the original pleading when. . .

(2) the claim or defense asserted in the amended pleading arose out of the conduct, transaction, or occurrence set forth or attempted to be set forth in the original pleading. . . .

RULE 16. PRETRIAL CONFERENCES; SCHEDULING; MANAGEMENT

(a) Pretrial Conferences; Objectives. In any action, the court may in its discretion direct the attorneys for the parties and any unrepresented parties to appear before it for a conference or conferences before trial for such purposes as

(1) expediting the disposition of the action;

(2) establishing early and continuing control so that the case will not be protracted because of lack of management;

(3) discouraging wasteful pretrial activities;

(4) improving the quality of the trial through more thorough preparation, and;

(5) facilitating the settlement of the case.

RULE 26. GENERAL PROVISIONS GOVERNING DISCOVERY; DUTY OF DISCLOSURE

(a) Required Disclosures; Methods to Discover Additional Matter.

(1) Initial Disclosures. Except in categories of proceedings specified in Rule 26(a)(1)(E), or to the extent otherwise stipulated or directed by order, a party must, without awaiting a discovery request, provide to other parties:

(A) the name and, if known, the address and telephone number of each individual likely to have discoverable information that the disclosing party may use to support its claims or defenses, unless solely for impeachment, identifying the subjects of the information;

(B) a copy of, or a description by category and location of, all documents, data compilations, and tangible things that are in the possession, custody, or control of the party and that the disclosing party may use to support its claims or defenses, unless solely for impeachment;

(C) a computation of any category of damages claimed by the disclosing party, making available for inspection and copying as under Rule 34 the documents or other evidentiary material, not privileged or protected from disclosure, on which such computation is based, including materials bearing on the nature and extent of injuries suffered; and

(D) for inspection and copying as under Rule 34 any insurance agreement under which any person carrying on an insurance business may be liable to satisfy part or all of a judgment which may be entered in the action or to indemnify or reimburse for payments made to satisfy the judgment. . . .

(2) Disclosure of Expert Testimony.

(A) In addition to the disclosures required by paragraph (1), a party shall disclose to other parties the identity of any person who may be used at trial to present evidence under Rules 702, 703, or 705 of the Federal Rules of Evidence.

(B) Except as otherwise stipulated or directed by the court, this disclosure shall, with respect to a witness who is retained or specially employed to provide expert testimony in the case or whose duties as an employee of the party regularly involve giving expert testimony, be accompanied by a written report prepared and signed by the witness. The report shall contain a complete statement of all opinions to be expressed and the basis and reasons therefor; the data or other information considered by the witness in forming the opinions; any exhibits to be used as a summary of or support for the opinions; the qualifications of the witness, including a list of all publications authored by the witness within the preceding ten years; the compensation to be paid for the study and testimony; and a listing of any other cases in which the witness has testified as an expert at trial or by deposition within the preceding four years. . . .

(b) Discovery Scope and Limits. Unless otherwise limited by order of the court in accordance with these rules, the scope of discovery is as follows:

(1) In General. Parties may obtain discovery regarding any matter, not privileged, that is relevant to the claim or defense of any party, including the existence, description, nature, custody, condition, and location of any books, documents, or other tangible things and the identity and location of persons having knowledge of any discoverable matter. For good cause, the court may order discovery of any matter relevant to the subject matter involved in the action. Relevant information need not be admissible at the trial if the discovery appears reasonably calculated to lead to the discovery of admissible evidence. . . .

(3) Trial Preparation: Materials. Subject to the provisions of subdivision (b)(4) of this rule, a party may obtain discovery of documents and tangible things otherwise discoverable under subdivision (b)(1) of this rule and prepared in anticipation of litigation or for trial by or for another party or by or for that other party's representative (including the other party's attorney, consultant, surety, indemnitor, insurer, or agent) only upon a showing that the party seeking discovery has substantial need of the materials in the preparation of the party's case and that the party is unable without undue hardship to obtain the substantial equivalent of the materials by other means. In ordering discovery of such materials when the required showing has been made, the court shall protect against disclosure of the mental impressions, conclusions, opinions, or legal theories of an attorney or other representative of a party concerning the litigation. . . .

(4) Trial Preparation: Experts.

(A) A party may depose any person who has been identified as an expert whose opinions may be presented at trial. If a report from the expert is required under subdivision (a)(2)(B), the deposition shall not be conducted until after the report is provided.

(B) A party may, through interrogatories or by deposition, discover facts known or opinions held by an expert who has been retained or specially employed by another party in anticipation of litigation or preparation for trial and who is not expected to be called as a witness at trial, only as provided in Rule 35(b) or upon a showing of exceptional circumstances under which it is impracticable for the party seeking discovery to obtain facts or opinions on the same subject by other means. . . .

(f) Conference of Parties; Planning for Discovery. Except in categories of proceedings exempted from initial disclosure under Rule 26(a)(1)(E) or when otherwise ordered, the parties must, as soon as practicable and in any event at least 21 days before a scheduling conference is held or a scheduling order is due under Rule 16(b), confer to consider the nature and basis of their claims and defenses and the possibilities for a prompt settlement or resolution of the case, to make or arrange for the disclosures required by Rule 26(a)(1), and to develop a proposed discovery plan. . . .

RULE 30. DEPOSITIONS UPON ORAL EXAMINATION

(a) When Depositions May Be Taken; When Leave Required.

(1) A party may take the testimony of any person, including a party, by deposition upon oral examination without leave of court except

as provided in paragraph (2). The attendance of witnesses may be compelled by subpoena as provided in Rule 45. . . .

(b) Notice of Examination: General Requirements; Method of Recording; Production of Documents and Things; Deposition of Organization; Deposition by Telephone.

(1) A party desiring to take the deposition of any person upon oral examination shall give reasonable notice in writing to every other party to the action. The notice shall state the time and place for taking the deposition and the name and address of each person to be examined, if known, and, if the name is not known, a general description sufficient to identify the person or the particular class or group to which the person belongs. If a subpoena duces tecum is to be served on the person to be examined, the designation of the materials to be produced as set forth in the subpoena shall be attached to, or included in, the notice.

(2) The party taking the deposition shall state in the notice the method by which the testimony shall be recorded. Unless the court orders otherwise, it may be recorded by sound, sound-and-visual, or stenographic means, and the party taking the deposition shall bear the cost of the recording. Any party may arrange for a transcription to be made from the recording of a deposition taken by nonstenographic means. . . .

(5) The notice to a party deponent may be accompanied by a request made in compliance with Rule 34 for the production of documents and tangible things at the taking of the deposition. The procedure of Rule 34 shall apply to the request.

(6) A party may in the party's notice and in a subpoena name as the deponent a public or private corporation or a partnership or association or governmental agency and describe with reasonable particularity the matters on which examination is requested. In that event the organization so named shall designate one or more officers, directors, or managing agents, or other persons who consent to testify on its behalf, and may set forth, for each person designated, the matters on which the person will testify. A subpoena shall advise a non-party organization of its duty to make such a designation. The persons so designated shall testify as to matters known or reasonably available to the organization. . . .

(7) The parties may stipulate in writing or the court may upon motion order that a deposition be taken by telephone or other remote electronic means. . . .

RULE 33. INTERROGATORIES TO PARTIES

(a) Availability. Without leave of court or written stipulation, any party may serve upon any other party written interrogatories, not exceeding 25 in number including all discrete subparts, to be answered by the party served or, if the party served is a public or private corporation or a partnership or association or governmental agency, by any officer or agent, who shall furnish such information as is available to the party. Leave to serve additional interrogatories shall be granted to the extent consistent with the principles of Rule 26(b)(2). Without leave of court or written stipulation, interrogatories may not be served before the time specified in Rule 26(d).

(b) Answers and Objections.

(1) Each interrogatory shall be answered separately and fully in writing under oath, unless it is objected to, in which event the objecting party shall state the reasons for objection and shall answer to the extent the interrogatory is not objectionable.

(2) The answers are to be signed by the person making them, and the objections signed by the attorney making them.

(3) The party upon whom the interrogatories have been served shall serve a copy of the answers, and objections if any, within 30 days after the service of the interrogatories. A shorter or longer time may be directed by the court or, in the absence of such an order, agreed to in writing by the parties subject to Rule 29.

(4) All grounds for an objection to an interrogatory shall be stated with specificity. Any ground not stated in a timely objection is waived unless the party's failure to object is excused by the court for good cause shown.

(5) The party submitting the interrogatories may move for an order under Rule 37(a) with respect to any objection to or other failure to answer an interrogatory. . . .

(d) Option to Produce Business Records. Where the answer to an interrogatory may be derived or ascertained from the business records of the party upon whom the interrogatory has been served or from an examination, audit or inspection of such business records, including a compilation, abstract or summary thereof, and the burden of deriving or ascertaining the answer is substantially the same for the party serving the interrogatory as for the party served, it is a sufficient answer to such interrogatory to specify the records from which the answer may be derived or ascertained and to afford to the party serving the interrogatory reasonable opportunity to examine, audit or inspect such records and to make copies, compilations, abstracts or summaries. . . .

RULE 34. PRODUCTION OF DOCUMENTS AND THINGS AND ENTRY UPON LAND FOR INSPECTION AND OTHER PURPOSES

(a) Scope. Any party may serve on any other party a request (1) to produce and permit the party making the request, or someone acting on the requestor's behalf, to inspect and copy, any designated documents (including writings, drawings, graphs, charts, photographs, phono-records, and other data compilations from which information can be obtained, translated, if necessary, by the respondent through detection devices into reasonably usable form), or to inspect and copy, test, or sample any tangible things which constitute or contain matters within the scope of Rule 26(b) and which are in the possession, custody or control of the party upon whom the request is served; or (2) to permit entry upon designated land or other property in the possession or control of the party upon whom the request is served for the purpose of inspection and measuring, surveying, photographing, testing, or sampling the property or any designated object or operation thereon, within the scope of Rule 26(b).

(b) Procedure. The request shall set forth, either by individual item or by category, the items to be inspected, and describe each with reasonable particularity. The request shall specify a reasonable time, place, and manner of making the inspection and performing the related acts. . . .

The party upon whom the request is served shall serve a written response within 30 days after the service of the request. . . .

(c) Persons not Parties. A person not a party to the action may be compelled to produce documents and things or to submit to an inspection as provided in Rule 45.

RULE 35. PHYSICAL AND MENTAL EXAMINATION OF PERSONS

(a) Order for Examination. When the mental or physical condition (including the blood group) of a party or of a person in the custody or under the legal control of a party, is in controversy, the court in which the action is pending may order the party to submit to a physical or mental examination by a suitably licensed or certified examiner or to produce for examination the person in the party's custody or legal control. The order may be made only on motion for good cause shown and upon notice to the person to be examined and to all parties and shall specify the time, place, manner, conditions, and scope of the examination and the person or persons by whom it is to be made. . . .

RULE 36. REQUESTS FOR ADMISSION

(a) Request for Admission. A party may serve upon any other party a written request for the admission, for purposes of the pending action only, of the truth of any matters within the scope of Rule 26(b)(1) set forth in the request that relate to statements or opinions of fact or of the application of law to fact, including the genuineness of any documents described in the request. Copies of documents shall be served with the request unless they have been or are otherwise furnished or made available for inspection and copying. Without leave of court or written stipulation, requests for admission may not be served before the time specified in Rule 26(d).

Each matter of which an admission is requested shall be separately set forth. The matter is admitted unless, within 30 days after service of the request. . .the party to whom the request is directed serves upon the party requesting the admission a written answer or objection addressed to the matter, signed by the party or by the party's attorney. If objection is made, the reasons therefor shall be stated. The answer shall specifically deny the matter or set forth in detail the reasons why the answering party cannot truthfully admit or deny the matter. A denial shall fairly meet the substance of the requested admission, and when good faith requires that a party qualify an answer or deny only a part of the matter of which an admission is requested, the party shall specify so much of it as is true and qualify or deny the remainder. An answering party may not give lack of information or knowledge as a reason for failure to admit or deny unless the party states that the party has made reasonable inquiry and that the information known or readily obtainable by the party is insufficient to enable the party to admit or deny. . . .

RULE 37. FAILURE TO MAKE OR COOPERATE IN DISCOVERY: SANCTIONS

(a) Motion for Order Compelling Disclosure or Discovery. A party, upon reasonable notice to other parties and all persons affected thereby, may apply for an order compelling disclosure or discovery as follows. . . .

(2) *Motion.*

(A) If a party fails to make a disclosure required by Rule 26(a), any other party may move to compel disclosure and for appropriate sanctions. The motion must include a certification that the movant has in good faith conferred or attempted to confer with the party not making the disclosure in an effort to secure the disclosure without court action.

(B) If a deponent fails to answer a question propounded or submitted under Rule 30(b)(6) or 31(a), or a party fails to answer an interrogatory submitted under Rule 33, or if a party, in response to a request for inspection submitted under Rule 34, fails to respond that inspection will be permitted as requested or fails to permit inspection as requested, the discovering party may move for an order compelling answer, or a designation, or an order compelling inspection in accordance with the request. The motion must include a certification that the movant has in good faith conferred or attempted to confer with the person or party failing to make the discovery in an effort to secure the information or material without court action.

RULE 45. SUBPOENA

(a) Form; Issuance.

(1) Every subpoena shall

(A) state the name of the court from which it is issued; and

(B) state the title of the action, the name of the court in which it is pending, and its civil action number; and

(C) command each person to whom it is directed to attend and give testimony or to produce and permit inspection and copying of designated books, documents, or tangible things in the possession, custody or control of that person, or to permit inspection of premises, at a time and place therein specified; and

(D) set forth the text of subdivisions (c) and (d) of this rule.

(b) Service.

(1) A subpoena may be served by any person who is not a party and is not less than 18 years of age. Service of a subpoena upon a person named therein shall be made by delivering a copy thereof to such person and, if the person's attendance is commanded, by tendering to that person the fees for one day's attendance and the mileage allowed by law.

RULE 56. SUMMARY JUDGMENT

(a) For Claimant. A party seeking to recover upon a claim, counterclaim, or cross-claim or to obtain a declaratory judgment may, at any time after the expiration of 20 days from the commencement of the action or after service of a motion for summary judgment by the adverse party, move with or without supporting affidavits for a summary judgment in the party's favor upon all or any part thereof.

(b) For Defending Party. A party against whom a claim, counterclaim, or cross-claim is asserted or a declaratory judgment is sought may, at any time, move with or without supporting affidavits for a summary judgment in the party's favor as to all or any part thereof. . . .

(e) Form of Affidavits; Further Testimony; Defense Required. Supporting and opposing affidavits shall be made on personal knowledge, shall set forth such facts as would be admissible in evidence, and shall show affirmatively that the affiant is competent to testify to the matters stated therein. Sworn or certified copies of all papers or parts thereof referred to in an affidavit shall be attached thereto or served therewith. The court may permit affidavits to be supplemented or opposed by depositions, answers to interrogatories, or further affidavits. When a motion for summary judgment is made and supported as provided in this rule, an adverse party may not rest upon the mere allegations or denials of the adverse party's pleading, but the adverse party's response, by affidavits or as otherwise provided in this rule, must set forth specific facts showing that there is a genuine issue for trial. If the adverse party does not so respond, summary judgment, if appropriate, shall be entered against the adverse party. . . .

Federal Rules of Criminal Procedure (Selected Rules)

FEDERAL RULES OF CRIMINAL PROCEDURE
(SELECTED RULES)

RULE 3. THE COMPLAINT

The complaint is a written statement of the essential facts constituting the offense charged. It shall be made upon oath before a magistrate judge.

RULE 4. ARREST WARRANT OR SUMMONS UPON COMPLAINT

(a) Issuance. If it appears from the complaint, or from an affidavit or affidavits filed with the complaint, that there is probable cause to believe that an offense has been committed and that the defendant has committed it, a warrant for the arrest of the defendant shall issue to any officer authorized by law to execute it. Upon the request of the attorney for the government a summons instead of a warrant shall issue. More than one warrant or summons may issue on the same complaint. If a defendant fails to appear in response to the summons, a warrant shall issue.

(b) Probable Cause. The finding of probable cause may be based upon hearsay evidence in whole or in part.

(c) Form.

(1) Warrant. The warrant shall be signed by the magistrate judge and shall contain the name of the defendant or, if the defendant's name is unknown, any name or description by which the defendant can be identified with reasonable certainty. It shall describe the offense charged in the complaint. It shall command that the defendant be arrested and brought before the nearest available magistrate judge.

(2) Summons. The summons shall be in the same form as the warrant except that it shall summon the defendant to appear before a magistrate at a stated time and place. . . .

RULE 5. INITIAL APPEARANCE BEFORE THE MAGISTRATE JUDGE

(a) In General. Except as otherwise provided in this rule, an officer making an arrest under a warrant issued upon a complaint or any person making an arrest without a warrant shall take the arrested person without unnecessary delay before the nearest available federal magistrate judge or, if a federal magistrate judge is not reasonably available, before a state or local judicial officer authorized by 18 U.S.C. §3041. If a person arrested without a warrant is brought before a magistrate judge, a complaint, satisfying the probable cause requirements of Rule 4(a), shall be promptly filed. . . .

RULE 5.1. PRELIMINARY EXAMINATION

(a) Probable Cause Finding. If from the evidence it appears that there is probable cause to believe that an offense has been committed and that the defendant committed it, the federal magistrate judge shall forthwith hold the defendant to answer in district court. The finding of probable cause may be based upon hearsay evidence in whole or in part. The defendant may cross-examine adverse witnesses and may introduce evidence. Objections to evidence on the ground that it was acquired by unlawful means are not properly made at the preliminary examination. . . .

RULE 6. THE GRAND JURY

(a) Summoning Grand Juries.

(1) Generally. The court shall order one or more grand juries to be summoned at such time as the public interest requires. The grand jury shall consist of not less than 16 nor more than 23 members. The court shall direct that a sufficient number of legally qualified persons be summoned to meet this requirement. . . .

(d) Who May Be Present. Attorneys for the government, the witness under examination, interpreters when needed and, for the purpose of taking the evidence, a stenographer or operator of a recording device may be present while the grand jury is in session, but no person other than the jurors may be present while the grand jury is deliberating or voting.

(e) Recording and Disclosure of Proceedings.

(1) Recording of Proceedings. All proceedings, except when the grand jury is deliberating or voting, shall be recorded stenographically or by an electronic recording device. . . .The recording or reporter's notes or any transcript prepared therefrom shall remain in the custody or control of the attorney for the government unless otherwise ordered by the court in a particular case.

(2) General Rule of Secrecy. A grand juror, an interpreter, a stenographer, an operator of a recording device, a typist who transcribes recorded testimony, an attorney for the government, or any person to whom disclosure is made under paragraph (3)(A)(ii) of this subdivision shall not disclose matters occurring before the grand jury, except as otherwise provided for in these rules. No obligation of secrecy may be imposed on any person except in accordance with this rule. A knowing violation of Rule 6 may be punished as a contempt of court. . . .

(f) Finding and Return of Indictment. An indictment may be found only upon the concurrence of 12 or more jurors. The indictment shall be returned by the grand jury to a federal magistrate judge in open court. If a complaint or information is pending against the defendant and 12 jurors do not concur in finding an indictment, the foreperson shall so report to a federal magistrate judge in writing forthwith. . . .

RULE 7. THE INDICTMENT AND THE INFORMATION

(a) Use of Indictment or Information. An offense which may be punished by death shall be prosecuted by indictment. An offense which may be punished by imprisonment for a term exceeding one year or at hard labor shall be prosecuted by indictment or, if indictment is waived, it may be prosecuted by information. Any other offense may be prosecuted by indictment or by information. An information may be filed without leave of court.

(b) Waiver of Indictment. An offense which may be punished by imprisonment for a term exceeding one year or at hard labor may be prosecuted by information if the defendant, after having been advised of the nature of the charge and of the rights of the defendant, waives in open court prosecution by indictment.

(c) Nature and Contents.

(1) In General. The indictment or the information shall be a plain, concise and definite written statement of the essential facts constituting the offense charged. It shall be signed by the attorney for the government. It need not contain a formal commencement, a formal conclusion or any other matter not necessary to such statement. Allegations made in one count may be incorporated by reference in another count. It may be alleged in a single count that the means by which the defendant committed the offense are unknown or that the defendant committed it by one or more specified means. The indictment or information shall state for each count the official or customary citation of the statute, rule, regulation or other provision of law which the defendant is alleged therein to have violated. . . .

(f) Bill of Particulars. The court may direct the filing of a bill of particulars. A motion for a bill of particulars may be made before arraignment or within ten days after arraignment or at such later time as the court may permit. A bill of particulars may be amended at any time subject to such conditions as justice requires.

RULE 9. WARRANT OR SUMMONS UPON INDICTMENT OR INFORMATION

(a) Issuance. Upon the request of the attorney for the government the court shall issue a warrant for each defendant named in an information supported by a showing of probable cause under oath as is required by Rule 4(a), or in an indictment. Upon the request of the attorney for the government a summons instead of a warrant shall issue. If no request is made, the court may issue either a warrant or a summons in its discretion. More than one warrant or summons may issue for the same defendant. The clerk shall deliver the warrant or summons to the marshal or other person authorized by law to execute or serve it. If a defendant fails to appear in response to the summons, a warrant shall issue. When a defendant arrested with a warrant or given a summons appears initially before a magistrate judge, the magistrate judge shall proceed in accordance with the applicable subdivisions of Rule 5. . . .

RULE 10. ARRAIGNMENT

Arraignment shall be conducted in open court and shall consist of reading the indictment or information to the defendant or stating to the defendant the substance of the charge and calling on the defendant to plead thereto. The defendant shall be given a copy of the indictment or information before being called upon to plead.

RULE 11. PLEAS

(a) Alternatives.

(1) In General. A defendant may plead not guilty, guilty, or nolo contendere. If a defendant refuses to plead or if a defendant corporation fails to appear, the court shall enter a plea of not guilty.

(2) Conditional Pleas. With the approval of the court and the consent of the government, a defendant may enter a conditional plea of guilty or nolo contendere, reserving in writing the right, on appeal from the judgment, to review of the adverse determination of any specified pretrial motion. A defendant who prevails on appeal shall be allowed to withdraw the plea.

(b) Nolo Contendere. A defendant may plead nolo contendere only with the consent of the court. Such a plea shall be accepted by the court only after due consideration of the views of the parties and the interest of the public in the effective administration of justice. . . .

RULE 12. PLEADINGS AND MOTIONS BEFORE TRIAL; DEFENSES AND OBJECTIONS

(a) Pleadings and Motions. Pleadings in criminal proceedings shall be the indictment and the information, and the pleas of not guilty, guilty and nolo contendere. All other pleas, and demurrers and motions to quash are abolished, and defenses and objections raised before trial which heretofore could have been raised by one or more of them shall be raised only by motion to dismiss or to grant appropriate relief, as provided in these rules.

(b) Pretrial Motions. Any defense, objection, or request which is capable of determination without the trial of the general issue may be raised before trial by motion. Motions may be written or oral at the discretion of the judge. The following must be raised prior to trial:

(1) Defenses and objections based on defects in the institution of the prosecution; or

(2) Defenses and objections based on defects in the indictment or information (other than that it fails to show jurisdiction in the court or to charge an offense which objections shall be noticed by the court at any time during the pendency of the proceedings); or

(3) Motions to suppress evidence; or

(4) Requests for discovery under Rule 16; or

(5) Requests for a severance of charges or defendants under Rule 14. . . .

(d) Notice by the Government of the Intention to Use Evidence.

(1) At the Discretion of the Government. At the arraignment or as soon thereafter as is practicable, the government may give notice to the defendant of its intention to use specified evidence at trial in order to afford the defendant an opportunity to raise objections to such evidence prior to trail under subdivision (b)(3) of this rule.

(2) At the Request of the Defendant. At the arraignment or as soon thereafter as is practicable the defendant may, in order to afford an opportunity to move to suppress evidence under subdivision (b)(3) of this rule, request notice of the government's intention to use (in its evidence in chief at trial) any evidence which the defendant may be entitled to discover under Rule 16 subject to any relevant limitations prescribed in Rule 16. . . .

(f) Effect of Failure to Raise Defenses or Objections. Failure by a party to raise defenses or objections or to make requests which must be made prior to trial, at the time set by the court pursuant to subdivision (c), or prior to any extension thereof made by the court, shall constitute waiver thereof, but the court for cause shown may grant relief from the waiver. . . .

(i) Production of Statements at Suppression Hearing. Rule 26.2 applies at a hearing on a motion to suppress evidence under subdivision (b)(3) of this rule. For purposes of this subdivision, a law enforcement officer is deemed a government witness.

RULE 12.1. NOTICE OF ALIBI

(a) Notice by Defendant. Upon written demand of the attorney for the government stating the time, date, and place at which the alleged offense was committed, the defendant shall serve within ten days, or at such different time as the court may direct, upon the attorney for the government a written notice of the defendant's intention to offer a defense of alibi. Such notice by the defendant shall state the specific place or places at which the defendant claims to have been at the time of the alleged offense and the names and addresses of the witnesses upon whom the defendant intends to rely to establish such alibi.

(b) Disclosure of Information and Witness. Within ten days thereafter, but in no event less than ten days before trial, unless the court otherwise directs, the attorney for the government shall serve upon the defendant or the defendant's attorney a written notice stating the names and addresses of the witnesses upon whom the government intends to rely to establish the defendant's presence at the scene of the alleged offense and any other witnesses to be relied on to rebut testimony of any of the defendant's alibi witnesses.

RULE 12.2. NOTICE OF INSANITY DEFENSE OR EXPERT TESTIMONY OF DEFENDANT'S MENTAL CONDITION

(a) Defense of Insanity. If a defendant intends to rely upon the defense of insanity at the time of the alleged offense, the defendant shall, within the time provided from the filing of pretrial motions or at such later time as the court may direct, notify the attorney for the government in writing of such intention and file a copy of such notice with the clerk. If there is a failure to comply with the requirements of this subdivision, insanity may not be raised as a defense. The court may for cause shown allow late filing of the notice or grant additional time to the parties to prepare for trial or make such other order as may be appropriate.

(b) Expert Testimony of Defendant's Mental Condition. If a defendant intends to introduce expert testimony relating to a mental disease or defect or any other mental condition of the defendant bearing upon the issue of guilt, the defendant shall, within the time provided for the filing of pretrial motions or at such later time as the court may direct, notify the attorney for the government in writing of such intention and file a copy of such notice with the clerk. The court may for cause shown allow late filing of the notice or grant additional time to the parties to prepare for trial or make such other order as may be appropriate.

(c) Mental Examination of Defendant. In an appropriate case the court may, upon motion of the attorney for the government, order the defendant to submit to an examination pursuant to 18 U.S.C. §4241 or 4242.

RULE 12.3. NOTICE OF DEFENSE BASED UPON PUBLIC AUTHORITY

(a) Notice by defendant; government response; disclosure of witnesses.

(1) Defendant's Notice and Government's Response. A defendant intending to claim a defense of actual or believed exercise of public authority on behalf of a law enforcement or Federal intelligence agency at the time of the alleged offense shall, within the time provided for the filing of pretrial motions or at such later time as the court may direct, serve upon the attorney for the Government a written notice of such intention and file a copy of such notice with the clerk. Such notice shall identify the law enforcement or Federal intelligence agency and any member of such agency on behalf of which and the period of time in which the defendant claims the actual or believed exercise of public authority occurred.

(2) Disclosure of Witnesses. At the time that the Government serves its response to the notice or thereafter, but in no event less than twenty days before the trial, the attorney for the Government may serve upon the defendant or the defendant's attorney a written demand for the names and addresses of the witnesses, if any, upon whom the defendant intends to rely in establishing the defense identified in the notice.

RULE 15. DEPOSITIONS

(a) When Taken. Whenever due to exceptional circumstances of the case it is in the interest of justice that the testimony of a prospective witness of a party be taken and preserved for use at trial, the court may upon motion of such party and notice to the parties order that testimony of such witness be taken by deposition and that any designated book, paper, document, record, recording, or other material not privileged, be produced at the same time and place. . . .

RULE 16. DISCOVERY AND INSPECTION

(a) Governmental Disclosure of Evidence.

(1) Information Subject to Disclosure.

(A) Statement of Defendant. Upon request of a defendant the government must disclose to the defendant and make available for inspection, copying, or photographing: any relevant written or recorded statements made by the defendant, or copies thereof, within the possession, custody, or control of the government, the existence of which is known, or by the exercise of due diligence may become known, to the attorney for the government; that portion of any written record containing the substance of any relevant oral statement made by the defendant whether before or after arrest in response to interrogation by any person then known to the defendant to be a government agent; and recorded testimony of the defendant before a grand jury which relates to the offense charged. The government must also disclose to the defendant the substance of any other relevant oral statement made by the defendant whether before or after arrest in response to interrogation by any person then known by the defendant to be a government agent if the government intends to use that statement at trial. . . .

(B) Defendant's Prior Record. Upon request of the defendant, the government shall furnish to the defendant such copy of the defendant's prior criminal record, if any, as is within the possession, custody, or control of the government, the existence of which is known, or by the exercise of due diligence may become known, to the attorney for the government.

(C) Documents and Tangible Objects. Upon request of the defendant the government shall permit the defendant to inspect and copy or photograph books, papers, documents, photographs, tangible objects, buildings or places, or copies or portions thereof, which are within the possession, custody or control of the government, and which are material to the preparation of the defendant's defense or are intended for use by the government as evidence in chief at the trial, or were obtained from or belong to the defendant.

(D) Reports of Examinations and Tests. Upon request of a defendant the government shall permit the defendant to inspect and copy or photograph any results or reports of physical or mental examinations, and of scientific tests or experiments, or copies thereof, which are within the possession, custody, or control of the government, the existence of which is known, or by the exercise of due diligence may become known, to the attorney for the government, and which are material to the preparation of the defense or are intended for use by the government as evidence in chief at the trial.

(E) Expert Witnesses. At the defendant's request, the government shall disclose to the defendant a written summary of testimony that the government intends to use under Rules 702, 703, or 705 of the Federal Rules of Evidence during its case-in-chief at trial. If the government requests discovery under subdivision (b)(1)(C)(ii) of this rule and the defendant complies, the government shall, at the defendant's request, disclose to the defendant a written summary of testimony the government intends to use under Rules 702, 703, or 705 as evidence at trial on the issue of the defendant's mental condition. The summary provided under this subdivision shall describe the witnesses' opinions, the bases and the reasons for those opinions, and the witnesses' qualifications.

(b) The Defendant's Disclosure of Evidence.

(1) Information Subject to Disclosure.

(A) Documents and Tangible Objects. If the defendant requests disclosure under subdivision (a)(1)(C) or (D) of this rule, upon compliance with such request by the government, the defendant, on request of the government, shall permit the government to inspect and copy or photograph books, papers, documents, photographs, tangible objects, or copies or portions thereof, which are within the possession, custody, or control of the defendant and which the defendant intends to introduce as evidence in chief at the trial.

(B) Reports of Examinations and Tests. If the defendant requests disclosure under subdivision (a)(1)(C) or (D) of this rule, upon compliance with such request by the government, the defendant, on request of the government, shall permit the government to inspect and copy or photograph any results or reports of physical or mental examinations and of scientific tests or experiments made in connection with the particular case, or copies thereof, within the possession or control of the defendant, which the defendant intends to introduce as evidence in chief at the trial or which were prepared by a witness whom the defendant intends to call at the trial when the results or reports relate to that witness' testimony.

(C) Expert Witnesses. Under the following circumstances, the defendant shall, at the government's request, disclose to the government a written summary of testimony that the defendant intends to use under Rules 702, 703, or 705 of the Federal Rules of Evidence as evidence at trial: (i) if the defendant requests disclosure under subdivision (a)(1)(E) of this rule and the government complies, or (ii) if the defendant has given notice under Rule 12.2(b) of an intent to present expert testimony on the defendant's mental condition. This summary shall describe the witnesses' opinions, the bases and reasons for those opinions, and the witnesses' qualifications.

RULE 17. SUBPOENA

(a) For Attendance of Witnesses; Form; Issuance. A subpoena shall be issued by the clerk under the seal of the court. It shall state the name of the court and the title, if any, of the proceeding, and shall command each person to whom it is directed to attend and give testimony at the time and place specified therein. The clerk shall issue a subpoena, signed and sealed but otherwise in blank to a party requesting it, who shall fill in the blanks before it is served. . . .

(c) For Production of Documentary Evidence and of Objects. A subpoena may also command the person to whom it is directed to produce the books, papers, documents or other objects designated therein. The court on motion made promptly may quash or modify the subpoena if compliance would be unreasonable or oppressive. The court may direct that books, papers, documents, or objects designated in the subpoena be produced before the court at a time prior to the trial or prior to the time when they are to be offered in evidence and may upon their production permit the books, papers, documents, or objects or portions thereof to be inspected by the parties and their attorneys. . . .

RULE 26.2. PRODUCTION OF WITNESS STATEMENTS

(a) Motion for Production. After a witness other than the defendant has testified on direct examination, the court, on motion of a party who did not call the witness, shall order the attorney for the government of the defendant and the defendant's attorney, as the case may be, to produce, for the examination and use of the moving party, any statement of the witness that is in their possession and that relates to the subject matter concerning which the witness has testified.

(b) Production of Entire Statement. If the entire contents of the statement relate to the subject matter concerning which the witness has testified, the court shall order that the statement be delivered to the moving party.

(c) Production of Excised Statement. If the other party claims that the statement contains privileged information or matter that does not relate to the subject matter concerning which the witness has testified, the court shall order that it be delivered to the court in camera. Upon inspection, the court shall excise the portions of the statement that are privileged or that do not relate to the subject matter concerning which the witness has testified, and shall order that the statement, with such material excised, be delivered to the moving party.

(f) Definition. As used in this rule, a "statement" of a witness means:

(1) a written statement made by the witness that is signed or otherwise adopted or approved by the witness;

(2) a substantially verbatim recital of an oral statement made by the witness that is recorded contemporaneously with the making of the oral statement and that is contained in a stenographic, mechanical, electrical, or other recording or a transcription thereof; or

(3) a statement, however taken or recorded, or a transcription thereof, made by the witness to a grand jury. . . .

Appendix D

Federal Rules of Evidence (Selected Rules)

FEDERAL RULES OF EVIDENCE
(SELECTED RULES)

RULE 201. JUDICIAL NOTICE OF ADJUDICATIVE FACTS

(b) Kinds of Facts. A judicially noticed fact must be one not subject to reasonable dispute in that it is either (1) generally known within the territorial jurisdiction of the trial court or (2) capable of accurate and ready determination by resort to sources whose accuracy cannot reasonably be questioned.

RULE 401. DEFINITION OF "RELEVANT EVIDENCE"

"Relevant evidence" means evidence having any tendency to make the existence of any fact that is of consequence to the determination of the action more probable or less probable than it would be without the evidence.

RULE 402. RELEVANT EVIDENCE GENERALLY ADMISSIBLE; IRRELEVANT EVIDENCE INADMISSIBLE

Evidence which is not relevant is not admissible. . . .

RULE 404. CHARACTER EVIDENCE NOT ADMISSIBLE TO PROVE CONDUCT; EXCEPTIONS; OTHER CRIMES

(a) Character Evidence Generally. Evidence of a person's character or a trait of character is not admissible for the purpose of proving action in conformity therewith on a particular occasion, except:

(1) *Character of Accused.* Evidence of a pertinent trait of character offered by an accused, or by the prosecution to rebut the same;

(2) *Character of Victim.* Evidence of a pertinent trait of character of the victim of the crime offered by an accused, or by the prosecution to rebut the same, or evidence of a character trait of peacefulness of the victim offered by the prosecution in a homicide case to rebut evidence that the victim was the first aggressor;

(3) *Character of Witness.* Evidence of the character of a witness, as provided in rules 607, 608, and 609.

(b) Other Crimes, Wrongs, or Acts. Evidence of other crimes, wrongs, or acts is not admissible to prove the character of a person in order to show action in conformity therewith. It may, however, be admissible for other purposes, such as proof of motive, opportunity, intent, preparation, plan, knowledge, identity, or absence of mistake or accident, provided that upon request by the accused, the prosecution in a criminal case shall provide reasonable notice in advance of trial, or during trial if the court excuses pretrial notice on good cause shown, of the general nature of any such evidence it intends to introduce at trial.

RULE 405. METHODS OF PROVING CHARACTER

(a) Reputation or Opinion. In all cases in which evidence of character or a trait of character of a person is admissible, proof may be made by testimony as to reputation or by testimony in the form of an opinion. On cross-examination, inquiry is allowable into relevant specific instances of conduct.

(b) Specific Instances of Conduct. In cases in which character or a trait of character of a person is an essential element of a charge, claim, or defense, proof may also be made of specific instances of that person's conduct.

RULE 407. SUBSEQUENT REMEDIAL MEASURES

When, after an injury or harm allegedly caused by an event, measures are taken that, if taken previously, would have made the inquiry or harm less likely to occur, evidence of the subsequent measures is not admissible to prove negligence, culpable conduct, a defect in a product, a defect in a product's design, or a need for a warning or instruction. This rule does not require the exclusion of evidence of subsequent measures when offered for another purpose, such as proving ownership, control, or feasibility of precautionary measures, if controverted, or impeachment.

RULE 408. COMPROMISE AND OFFERS TO COMPROMISE

Evidence of (1) furnishing or offering or promising to furnish, or (2) accepting or offering or promising to accept, a valuable consideration in compromising or attempting to compromise a claim which was disputed as to either validity or amount, is not admissible to prove liability for or invalidity of the claim or its amount. Evidence of conduct or statements made in compromise negotiations is likewise not admissible. . . .

RULE 409. PAYMENT OF MEDICAL AND SIMILAR EXPENSES

Evidence of furnishing or offering or promising to pay medical, hospital, or similar expenses occasioned by an injury is not admissible to prove liability for the injury.

RULE 410. INADMISSIBILITY OF PLEAS, PLEA DISCUSSIONS, AND RELATED STATEMENTS

Except as otherwise provided in this rule, evidence of the following is not, in any civil or criminal proceeding, admissible against the defendant who made the plea or was a participant in the plea discussions:

(1) a plea of guilty which was later withdrawn;

(2) a plea of nolo contendere;

RULE 411. LIABILITY INSURANCE

Evidence that a person was or was not insured against liability is not admissible upon the issue whether the person acted negligently or otherwise wrongfully. This rule does not require the exclusion of evidence of insurance against liability when offered for another purpose, such as proof of agency, ownership, or control, or bias or prejudice of a witness. . . .

RULE 608. EVIDENCE OF CHARACTER AND CONDUCT OF WITNESS

(a) Opinion and Reputation Evidence of Character. The credibility of a witness may be attacked or supported by evidence in the form of opinion or reputation, but subject to these limitations: (1) the evidence may refer only to character for truthfulness or untruthfulness, and (2) evidence of truthful character is admissible only after the character of the witness for truthfulness has been attacked by opinion or reputation evidence or otherwise.

(b) Specific Instances of Conduct. Specific instances of the conduct of a witness, for the purpose of attacking or supporting the witness' credibility, other than conviction of crime as provided in rule 609, may not be proved by extrinsic evidence. They may, however, in the discretion of the court, if probative of truthfulness or untruthfulness, be inquired into on cross-examination of the witness (1) concerning the witness' character for truthfulness or untruthfulness, or (2) concerning the character for truthfulness or untruthfulness of another witness as to which character the witness being cross-examined has testified.

RULE 609. IMPEACHMENT BY EVIDENCE OF CONVICTION OF CRIME

(a) General Rule. For the purpose of attacking the credibility of a witness,

(1) evidence that a witness other than an accused has been convicted of a crime shall be admitted, subject to Rule 403, if the crime was punishable by death or imprisonment in excess of one year under the law under which the witness was convicted, and evidence that an accused has been convicted of such a crime shall be admitted if the court determines that the probative value of admitting this evidence outweighs its prejudicial effect to the accused; and

(2) evidence that any witness has been convicted of a crime shall be admitted if it involved dishonesty or false statement, regardless of the punishment.

(b) Time Limit. Evidence of a conviction under this rule is not admissible if a period of more than ten years has elapsed since the date of the conviction or of the release of the witness from the confinement imposed for that conviction, whichever is the later date, unless the court determines, in the interests of justice, that the probative value of the conviction supported by specific facts and circumstances substantially outweighs its prejudicial effect.

RULE 610. RELIGIOUS BELIEFS OR OPINIONS

Evidence of the beliefs or opinions of a witness on matters of religion is not admissible for the purpose of showing that by reason of their nature the witness' credibility is impaired or enhanced.

RULE 701. OPINION TESTIMONY BY LAY WITNESSES

If the witness is not testifying as an expert, the witness' testimony in the form of opinions or inferences is limited to those opinions or inferences which are (a) rationally based on the perception of the witness and (b) helpful to a clear understanding of the witness' testimony or the determination of a fact in issue.

RULE 702. TESTIMONY BY EXPERTS

If scientific, technical, or other specialized knowledge will assist the trier of fact to understand the evidence or to determine a fact in issue, a witness qualified as an expert by knowledge, skill, experience, training, or education, may testify thereto in the form of an opinion or otherwise.

RULE 703. BASES OF OPINION TESTIMONY BY EXPERTS

The facts or data in the particular case upon which an expert bases an opinion or inference may be those perceived by or made known to the expert at or before the hearing. If of a type reasonably relied upon by experts in the particular field in forming opinions or inferences upon the subject, the facts or data need not be admissible in evidence.

RULE 704. OPINION ON ULTIMATE ISSUE

(a) Except as provided in subdivision (b), testimony in the form of an opinion or inference otherwise admissible is not objectionable because it embraces an ultimate issue to be decided by the trier of fact.

(b) No expert witness testifying with respect to the mental state or condition of a defendant in a criminal case may state an opinion or inference as to whether the defendant did or did not have the mental state or condition constituting an element of the crime charged or of a defense thereto. Such ultimate issues are matters for the trier of fact alone.

RULE 705. DISCLOSURE OF FACTS OR DATA UNDERLYING EXPERT OPINION

The expert may testify in terms of opinion or inference and give reasons therefor without first testifying to the underlying facts or data, unless the court requires otherwise. The expert may in any event be required to disclose the underlying facts or data on cross-examination. . . .

RULE 801. DEFINITIONS

The following definitions apply under this article:

(a) Statement. A "statement" is (1) an oral or written assertion or (2) nonverbal conduct of a person, if it is intended by the person as an assertion.

(b) Declarant. A "declarant" is a person who makes a statement.

(c) Hearsay. "Hearsay" is a statement, other than one made by the declarant while testifying at the trial or hearing, offered in evidence to prove the truth of the matter asserted.

(d) Statements Which Are Not Hearsay. A statement is not hearsay if—

(1) *Prior Statement by Witness.* The declarant testifies at the trial or hearing and is subject to cross-examination concerning the statement, and the statement is (A) inconsistent with the declarant's testimony, and was given under oath subject to the penalty of perjury at a trial, hearing, or other proceeding, or in a deposition, or (B) consistent with the declarant's testimony and is offered to rebut an express or implied charge against the declarant of a recent fabrication or improper influence or motive, or (C) one of identification of a person made after perceiving the person; or

(2) *Admission by Party-Opponent.* The statement is offered against a party and is (A) the party's own statement, in either an individual or a representative capacity or (B) a statement of which the party has manifested an adoption or belief in its truth, or (C) a statement by a person authorized by the party to make a statement concerning the subject, or (D) a statement by the party's agent or servant concerning a matter within the scope of the agency or employment, made during the existence of the relationship, or (E) a statement by a coconspirator of a party during the course and in furtherance of the conspiracy.

RULE 802. HEARSAY RULE

Hearsay is not admissible except as provided by these rules or by other rules prescribed by the Supreme Court pursuant to statutory authority or by Act of Congress.

RULE 803. HEARSAY EXCEPTIONS; AVAILABILITY OF DECLARANT IMMATERIAL

The following are not excluded by the hearsay rule, even though the declarant is available as a witness:

(1) Present Sense Impression. A statement describing or explaining an event or condition made while the declarant was perceiving the event or condition, or immediately thereafter.

(2) Excited Utterance. A statement relating to a startling event or condition made while the declarant was under the stress of excitement caused by the event or condition.

(3) Then Existing Mental, Emotional, or Physical Condition. A statement of the declarant's then existing state of mind, emotion, sensation, or physical condition (such as intent, plan, motive, design, mental feeling, pain, and bodily health), but not including a statement of memory or belief to prove the fact remembered or believed unless it relates to the execution, revocation, identification, or terms of declarant's will.

(4) Statements for Purposes of Medical Diagnosis or Treatment. Statements made for purposes of medical diagnosis or treatment and describing medical history, or past or present symptoms, pain, or sensations, or the inception or general character of the cause or external source thereof insofar as reasonably pertinent to diagnosis or treatment.

(5) Recorded Recollection. A memorandum or record concerning a matter about which a witness once had knowledge but now has insufficient recollection to enable the witness to testify fully and accurately, shown to have been made or adopted by the witness when the matter was fresh in the witness' memory and to reflect that knowledge correctly. If admitted, the memorandum or record may be read into evidence but may not itself be received as an exhibit unless offered by an adverse party.

(6) Records of Regularly Conducted Activity. A memorandum, report, record, or data compilation, in any form, of acts, events, conditions, opinions, or diagnoses, made at or near the time by, or from information transmitted by, a person with knowledge, if kept in the course of a regularly conducted business activity, and if it was the regular practice of that business activity to make the memorandum, report, record, or data compilation, all as shown by the testimony of the custodian or other qualified witness, unless the source of information or the method or circumstances of preparation indicate lack of trustworthiness. The term "business" as used in this paragraph includes business, institution, association, profession, occupation, and calling of every kind, whether or not conducted for profit.

(7) Absence of Entry in Records Kept in Accordance With the Provisions of Paragraph (6). Evidence that a matter is not included in the memoranda reports, records, or data compilations, in any form, kept in accordance with the provisions of paragraph (6), to prove the nonoccurrence or nonexistence of the matter, if the matter was of a kind of which a memorandum, report, record, or data compilation was regularly made and preserved, unless the sources of information or other circumstances indicate lack of trustworthiness.

(8) Public Records and Reports. Records, reports, statements, or data compilations, in any form, of public offices or agencies, setting forth (A) the activities of the office or agency, or (B) matters observed pursuant to duty imposed by law as to which matters there was a duty to report, excluding, however, in criminal cases matters observed by police officers and other law enforcement personnel, or (C) in civil actions and proceedings and against the Government in criminal cases, factual findings resulting from an investigation made pursuant to authority granted by law, unless the sources of information or other circumstances indicate lack of trustworthiness.

(9) Records of Vital Statistics. Records or data compilations, in any form, of births, fetal deaths, deaths, or marriages, if the report thereof was made to a public office pursuant to requirements of law.

(10) Absence of Public Record or Entry. To prove the absence of a record, report, statement, or data compilation, in any form, or the nonoccurrence or nonexistence of a matter of which a record, report, statement, or data compilation, in any form, was regularly made and preserved by a public office or agency, evidence in the form of a certification in accordance with rule 902, or testimony, that diligent search failed to disclose the record, report, statement, or data compilation, or entry.

(11) Records of Religious Organizations. Statements of births, marriages, divorces, deaths, legitimacy, ancestry, relationship by blood or marriage, or other similar facts of personal or family history, contained in a regularly kept record of a religious organization.

(12) Marriage, Baptismal, and Similar Certificates. Statements of fact contained in a certificate that the maker performed a marriage or other ceremony or administered a sacrament, made by a clergyman, public official, or other person authorized by the rules or practices of a religious organization or by law to perform the act certified, and purporting to have been issued at the time of the act or within a reasonable time thereafter.

(13) Family Records. Statements of fact concerning personal or family history contained in family Bibles, genealogies, charts, engravings on rings, inscriptions on family portraits, engravings on urns, crypts, or tombstones, or the like.

(14) Records of Documents Affecting an Interest in Property. The record of a document purporting to establish or affect an interest in property, as proof of the content of the original recorded document and its execution and delivery by each person by whom it purports to have been executed, if the record is a record of a public office and an applicable statute authorizes the recording of documents of that kind in that office.

(15) Statements in Documents Affecting an Interest in Property. A statement contained in a document purporting to establish or affect an interest in property if the matter stated was relevant to the purpose of the document, unless dealings with the property since the document was made have been inconsistent with the truth of the statement or the purport of the document.

(16) Statements in Ancient Documents. Statements in a document in existence twenty years or more the authenticity of which is established.

(17) Market Reports, Commercial Publications. Market quotations, tabulations, lists, directories, or other published compilations, generally used and relied upon by the public or by persons in particular occupations.

(18) Learned Treatises. To the extent called to the attention of an expert witness upon cross-examination or relied upon by the expert witness in direct examination, statements contained in published treatises, periodicals, or pamphlets on a subject of history, medicine, or other science or art, established as a reliable authority by the testimony or admission of the witness or by other expert testimony or by judicial notice. If admitted, the statements may be read into evidence but may not be received as exhibits.

(19) Reputation Concerning Personal or Family History. Reputation among members of a person's family by blood, adoption, or marriage, or among a person's associates, or in the community, concerning a person's birth, adoption, marriage, divorce, death, legitimacy, relationship by blood, adoption, or marriage, ancestry, or other similar fact of personal or family history.

(20) Reputation Concerning Boundaries or General History. Reputation in a community, arising before the controversy, as to boundaries of or customs affecting lands in the community, and reputation as to events of general history important to the community or State or nation in which located.

(21) Reputation as to Character. Reputation of a person's character among associates or in the community.

(22) Judgment of Previous Conviction. Evidence of a final judgment, entered after a trial or upon a plea of guilty (but not upon a plea of nolo contendere), adjudging a person guilty of a crime punishable by death or imprisonment in excess of one year, to prove any fact essential to sustain the judgment, but not including, when offered by the Government in a criminal prosecution for purposes other than impeachment, judgments against persons other than the accused. The pendency of an appeal may be shown but does not affect admissibility.

(23) Judgment as to Personal, Family, or General History, or Boundaries. Judgments as proof of matters of personal, family or general history, or boundaries, essential to the judgment, if the same would be provable by evidence of reputation. . . .

RULE 804. HEARSAY EXCEPTIONS; DECLARANT UNAVAILABLE

(a) Definition of Unavailability. "Unavailability as a witness" includes situations in which the declarant—

(1) is exempted by ruling of the court on the ground of privilege from testifying concerning the subject matter of the declarant's statement; or

(2) persists in refusing to testify concerning the subject matter of the declarant's statement despite an order of the court to do so; or

(3) testifies to a lack of memory of the subject matter of the declarant's statement; or

(4) is unable to be present or to testify at the hearing because of death or then existing physical or mental illness or infirmity; or

(5) is absent from the hearing and the proponent of a statement has been unable to procure the declarant's attendance (or in the case of a hearsay exception under subdivision (b)(2), (3), or (4), the declarant's attendance or testimony) by process or other reasonable means.

A declarant is not unavailable as a witness if exemption, refusal, claim of lack of memory, inability, or absence is due to the procurement or wrongdoing of the proponent of a statement for the purpose of preventing the witness from attending or testifying.

(b) Hearsay Exceptions. The following are not excluded by the hearsay rule if the declarant is unavailable as a witness:

(1) *Former Testimony.* Testimony given as a witness at another hearing of the same or a different proceeding, or in a deposition taken in compliance with law in the course of the same or another proceeding, if the party against whom the testimony is now offered, or, in a civil action or proceeding, a predecessor in interest, had an opportunity and similar motive to develop the testimony by direct, cross, or redirect examination.

(2) *Statement Under Belief of Impending Death.* In a prosecution for homicide or in a civil action or proceeding, a statement made by a declarant while believing that the declarant's death was imminent, concerning the cause or circumstances of what the declarant believed to be impending death.

(3) *Statement Against Interest.* A statement which was at the time of its making so far contrary to the declarant's pecuniary or proprietary interest, or so far tended to subject the declarant to civil or criminal liability, or to render invalid a claim by the declarant against another, that a reasonable person in the declarant's position would not have made the statement unless believing it to be true. A statement tending to expose the declarant to criminal liability and offered to exculpate the accused is not admissible unless corroborating circumstances clearly indicate the trustworthiness of the statement.

(4) *Statement of Personal or Family History.*

(A) A statement concerning the declarant's own birth, adoption, marriage, divorce, legitimacy, relationship by blood, adoption, or marriage, ancestry, or other similar fact of personal or family history, even though declarant had no means of acquiring personal knowledge of the matter stated; or

(B) a statement concerning the foregoing matters, and death also, of another person, if the declarant was related to the other by blood, adoption, or marriage or was so intimately associated with the other's family as to be likely to have accurate information concerning the matter declared. . . .

(6) *Forfeiture by Wrongdoing.* A statement offered against a party that has engaged or acquiesced in wrongdoing that was intended to, and did, procure the unavailability of the declarant as a witness.

RULE 901. REQUIREMENT OF AUTHENTICATION OR IDENTIFICATION

(a) General Provision. The requirement of authentication or identification as a condition precedent to admissibility is satisfied by evidence sufficient to support a finding that the matter in question is what its proponent claims.

(b) Illustrations. By way of illustration only, and not by way of limitation, the following are examples of authentication or identification conforming with the requirements of this rule:

(1) *Testimony of Witness With Knowledge.* Testimony that a matter is what it is claimed to be.

(2) *Nonexpert Opinion on Handwriting.* Nonexpert opinion as to the genuineness of handwriting, based upon familiarity not acquired for purposes of the litigation.

(3) *Comparison by Trier or Expert Witness.* Comparison by the trier of fact or by expert witnesses with specimens which have been authenticated.

(4) *Distinctive Characteristics and the Like.* Appearance, contents, substance, internal patterns, or other distinctive characteristics, taken in conjunction with circumstances.

(5) *Voice Identification.* Identification of a voice, whether heard firsthand or through mechanical or electronic transmission or recording, by opinion based upon hearing the voice at any time under circumstances connecting it with the alleged speaker.

(6) *Telephone Conversations.* Telephone conversations, by evidence that a call was made to the number assigned at the time by the telephone company to a particular person or business, if (A) in the case of a person, circumstances, including self-identification, show the person answering to be the one called, or (B) in the case of a business, the call was made to a place of business and the conversation related to business reasonably transacted over the telephone.

RULE 902. SELF-AUTHENTICATION

Extrinsic evidence of authenticity as a condition precedent to admissibility is not required with respect to the following:

(1) Domestic Public Documents Under Seal. A document bearing a seal purporting to be that of the United States, or of any State, district, Commonwealth, territory, or insular possession thereof, or the Panama Canal Zone, or the Trust Territory of the Pacific Islands, or of a political subdivision, department, officer, or agency thereof, and a signature purporting to be an attestation or execution.

(2) Domestic Public Documents Not Under Seal. A document purporting to bear the signature in the official capacity of an officer or employee of any entity included in paragraph (1) hereof, having no seal, if a public officer having a seal and having official duties in the district or political subdivision of the officer or employee certifies under seal that the signer has the official capacity and that the signature is genuine. . . .

(4) Certified Copies of Public Records. A copy of an official record or report or entry therein, or of a document authorized by law to be recorded or filed and actually recorded or filed in a public office, including data compilations in any form, certified as correct by the custodian or other person authorized to make the certification, by certificate complying with paragraph (1), (2), or (3) of this rule or complying with any Act of Congress or rule prescribed by the Supreme Court pursuant to statutory authority.

(5) Official Publications. Books, pamphlets, or other publications purporting to be issued by public authority.

(6) Newspapers and Periodicals. Printed materials purporting to be newspapers or periodicals.

(7) Trade Inscriptions and the Like. Inscriptions, signs, tags, or labels purporting to have been affixed in the course of business and indicating ownership, control, or origin.

(8) Acknowledged Documents. Documents accompanied by a certificate of acknowledgment executed in the manner provided by law by a notary public or other officer authorized by law to take acknowledgments.

(9) Commercial Paper and Related Documents. Commercial paper, signatures thereon, and documents relating thereto to the extent provided by general commercial law. . . .

Resources for the Investigator

TABLE OF CONTENTS TO APPENDIX E

1. SEARCH ENGINES AND ONLINE DIRECTORIES

A. GENERAL SEARCH ENGINES AND DIRECTORIES

All-In-One Search (www.albany.net)
Alta-Vista (www.altavista.net)
AlltheWeb (www.alltheweb.com)
Ask Jeeves (www.askjeeves.com)
Copernic (www.copernic.com)
DirectHit (www.directhit.com)
Dogpile (www.dogpile.com)
Euroseek (www.euroseek.net)
Excite (www.excite.com)
FastSearch (www.alltheweb.com)
Google (www.google.com)
GoTo (www.goto.com)
HotBot (www.hotbot.com)
Inference Find (www.infind.com)
Infoseek (www.infoseek.com)
Internet Sleuth (www.isleuth.com)
Locate (www.locate.com)
Lycos (www.lycos.com)
Mama (www.mama.com)
McKinley Internet Directory (www.mckinley.com)
MetaCrawler (www.metacrawler.com)
Northern Light (www.northernlight.com)
Open Text (www.index.opentext.net)
Profusion (www.profusion.com)
Search Engine Watch Newsletter (www.searchenginewatch.com)
Snaps (www.snaps.com)
Teoma (www.teoma.com)
Virisimo (www.virisimo.com)
WebCrawler (www.webcrawler.com)
Yahoo (www.yahoo.com)

B. LEGAL SEARCH ENGINES AND DIRECTORIES

Alllaw (www.alllaw.com)
CataLaw (www.catalaw.com)
Chicago-Kent Guide to Legal Resources (Kentlaw.edu/lawnet/
   lawlinks.html)
Cornell Law School's Legal Information Institute
   (www.law.cornell.edu)
CounselQuest (www.counselquest.com)
Emory Electronic Reference Desk (www.law.emory.edu/LAW/
   refdesk/doc.html)
FindLaw (www.findlaw.com)
HandiLinks Guide (www.ahandyguide.com)
Heiros Gamos (www.hg.org)
Indiana University School of Law's Virtual Law Library
   (www.law.indiana.edu)

Institute for Continuing Legal Education (www.icke.org)
Internet Sleuth (www.isleuth.com/legal.html)
Internets Law Databases (www.internets.com/slegal.htm)
LawCrawler (www.lawcrawler.com)
Law Guru (lawguru.com/lawlinks.html)
Law Lists (www.lib.uchicago.edu/cgi-bdn/law-lists)
The Law Office (www.thelawoffice.com)
Law Research (www.lawresearch.com)
Law Source (www.lawsources.com)
'Lectric Law Library (www.lectlaw.com)
Legal Ethics (www.legalethics.com)
Legal Pad (www.legal-pad.com)
LexisOne (www.LexisOne.com)
The Legal Resources Guide (www.ilrg.com)
Piper Resources (www.piperinfo.com/state/states/html)
Purdue University's Catalogue of Databases (thorplus.lib.purdue.edu)
Rominger Legal On-Line Research (www.romingerlegal.com/)
The Seamless Website (www.seamless.com)
Search-the-Law.com (www.search-the-law.com)
Special Search Engine (www.ntu.edu.sg/library/specialcat.htm)
Surf Searcher (www.melt.co.uk/surfsearcher/)
University of Arizona's International Law Society
    (aruba.ccit.arizona.edu/~rdespeld/ils.html)
University of Chicago (www.lib.uchicago.edu)
University of Michigan's Internet Public Library (ipl.sils.umich.edu)
Villanova Center for Information Law and Policy (www.vcilp.org)
Washburn University School of Law (www.wuacc.edu)
Yahoo Law (dir.yahoo.com/Law/)
Yale University Lawweb (www.yale.edu/lawweb)

2. LAWYER DIRECTORIES — ONLINE

Legal Industry Directory (www.lawinfo.com)
Martindale-Hubbell Law Directory (www.martindale.com)
USA Law Attorney Directory (www.usalaw.com/firmsrch.cfm)
West Lawyer Directory (www.wld.com)
Yahoo Directory of Lawyers (dir.yahoo.com/Business/Companies/
    Law/Firms/)

3. LEGAL ORGANIZATIONS

1. American Association for Paralegal Education (AAfPE), 2965 Flowers Road South, Suite 105, Atlanta, GA 30341, (770) 452-9877 (www .aafpe.org)
2. American Association of Legal Nurse Consultants, 4700 W. Lake Ave., Glenview, IL 60025, (877) 402-2562 (www.aalnc.org)
3. American Bankruptcy Institute (ABI) (www.abiworld.org)
4. American Bar Association (ABA), 750 No. Lake Shore Drive, Chicago, IL 60611, (312) 988-5000 (www.abanet.org)

5. American Civil Liberties Union, 125 Broad St., New York, NY 10004, (212) 549-2500 (www.aclu.org)
6. American Law Institute (ALI) (www.ali.org)
7. Association of Trial Lawyers of America (ATLA), 1050 31st St. NW, Washington, DC 20007, (800) 424-2725 (www.atlanet.org)
8. Defense Research Institute, 150 North Michigan Ave., Third Floor, Chicago, IL 60601, (312) 795-1101 (www.driorg/index.html)
9. Legal Assistant Management Association, 2965 Flowers Road South, Suite 105, Atlanta, GA 30341, (770) 457-7746 (www.lamanet.org)
10. National Association of Criminal Defense Lawyers, 1025 Connecticut Ave. NW, Washington, DC 20036, (202) 872-8600 (www.criminal justice.org)
11. National Association of Legal Assistants (NALA), 1516 S. Boston, Suite 200, Tulsa, OK 74119, (918) 587-6828 (www.nalanet.org)
12. National Federation of Paralegal Associations (NFPA), 32 West Bridlespur Terrace, P.O. Box 33108, Kansas City, MO 64114-0108, (816) 941-4000 (www.paralegals.org)

4 . EXPERTS

A. RESOURCES FOR LOCATING EXPERTS—ORGANIZATIONS

1. Association of Trial Lawyers of America (ATLA), 1050 31st St. NW, Washington, DC 20007, (800) 424-2725 (www.atlanet.org)
2. Defense Research Institute, 150 North Michigan Ave., Third Floor, Chicago, IL 60601, (312) 795-1101 (www.driorg/index.html)
3. National Association of Criminal Defense Lawyers, 1025 Connecticut Ave. NW, Washington, DC 20036, (202) 872-8600 (www.criminal justice.org)
4. SCORE—Service Corps of Retired Executives, c/o Small Business Administration, 1110 Vermont Ave. NW, Washington, DC 20005, (202) 606-4000 (www.sba.gov)
5. Technical Advisory Service for Attorneys (TASA), 1166 DeKalb Pike, Blue Bell, PA 19422-1853, (800) 523-2319 (www.tasanet.com)
6. Technical Assistance Bureau (TAB), 13017 Wisteria Drive, Suite 223, P.O. Box 1779, Germantown, MD 20874-1779, (800) 336-0190 (www.tabexperts.com)

B. RESOURCES FOR LOCATING EXPERTS—ONLINE

1. Legal Industry Directory (www.lawinfo.com)
2. Legal Research Network (www.witness.net)
3. Directory of Experts and Consultants (expertpages.com)
4. Consolidated Consultants Co. Expert Witness Referral (www.attorneyreferral.net/expert.htm)
5. NOCALL (www.nocall.org/experts.htm)
6. Legal Concierge (www.legalconcierge.com)
7. Consolidated Consultants Expert Witness Referral (www.attorney referral.net/expert.htm)

8. Yearbook (www.yearbooknews.com)
9. Medical Experts (www.evidence.com/HTML/experts.htm) (The online medical resources listed in this Appendix are also helpful for this purpose.)

C. RESOURCES FOR LOCATING EXPERTS—PUBLICATIONS

1. *American Jurisprudence 2d, Desk Book*. St. Paul, MN: West Group
2. *American Men and Women of Science* (3 vol.) and *Directory of American Technology*, 31st ed. New Providence, NJ: R.R. Bowker (800) 521-8110
3. *Annual Guide to Public Policy Experts*. Washington, DC: Heritage Foundation (800) 544-4848 (www.townhall.com)
4. *Dun & Bradstreet Consultants Directory*. Bethlehem, PA: Dun & Bradstreet Information Services, 1996. (800) 526-0651 (www.dbisna.com)
5. *Faculty Directory of Higher Education*: *Business, Education and Law, National Faculty Directory*, 99th ed., and *Research Centers Directory*, 23d ed. supplemented by *New Research Centers*, 22d ed. Detroit, MI: Gale Research, Inc. (800) 877-4253 (www.gale.com)
6. Lesko, Matthew, *Lesko's Info-Power II*. Kensington, MD: Information USA, 1993. (A good source to locate government experts.)
7. *Martindale-Hubbell Law Directory*. New Providence, NJ: Martindale-Hubbell. (www.martindale.com)
8. Philo, Harry M., *Lawyer's Desk Reference*, 9th ed. St. Paul, MN: West Group, 2001
9. *Register of Higher Education: The Who's Who of Higher Education*, 10th ed. Princeton, NJ: Petersons, 1997. (800) 338-3282 (www.petersons.com)
10. *The Yearbook of Experts, Authorities&Spokespersons:An Encyclopedia of Sources*, 17th ed. Washington, DC:Broadcast Interview Source, 1999. (800) 932-7266 (www.yearbook.com)

D. MISCELLANEOUS INFORMATION ON EXPERTS

1. Professional Standards (www.lib.waterloo.ca/society/standards.html.)
2. Business and Professional Codes (www.law.cornell.edu/statutes.html#state)
3. Technical, Scientific Information and Publications (www.ecola.com)
4. Internet Public Library (www.ipl.org)
5. World Wide Web Virtual Library (www.vlib.org)
6. Standards and Specifications (www.lib.uwater.ca/society/standards.html)
7. CLEAR (Clearinghouse on Licensure, Enforcement, and Regulation) (www.clearhq.org)

5. PRIVATE INVESTIGATORS

A. PUBLICATIONS—BOOKS

1. Dempsey, John S., *An Introduction to Public and Private Investigations*. St. Paul, MN: West Publishing Co., 1996

2. *Reporter's Handbook to Documents and Techniques: An Investigator's Guide,* 3d ed. New York: St. Martin's Press, 1995
3. *The Source Book of Public Records Providers: The National Guide to Companies That Furnish Automated Public Record Information, Search Services and Investigative Services,* 3d ed. The Public Record Research Library, Tempe, AZ: BRB Publications, 1995 (available on CD-ROM)

B. PUBLICATIONS—PERIODICALS

1. *The IRE Journal.* Investigative Reporters and Editors, Inc., 100 Neff Hall, University of Missouri, Columbia, MO 65211 (bimonthly)
2. *The Legal Investigator.* 3304 Crescent Drive, Des Moines, Iowa 50312
3. *P.I. Magazine.* 755 Bronx, Toledo, Ohio (quarterly)
4. *Searcher: The Magazine for Database Professionals.* 143 Old Marlton Pike, Medford, NJ 08055
5. *Special Libraries.* 1700 18th Street NW, Washington, DC 20009
6. *The Database Files,* 5622 Wood Lane, St. Louis Park, MN 55436
7. *Lesko's Info-Power Newsletter,* Information USA, P.O. Box E, Kensington, MD 20895
8. *Privacy Journal,* P.O. Box 28577, Providence, RI 02908
9. *Private Investigator's Connection,* National Association of Investigative Specialists, Inc., P.O. Box 33244, Austin, TX 78764
10. *Uplink,* National Institute for Computer-Assisted Reporting, 120 Neff Hall, University of Missouri, Columbia, MO 65211

C. ONLINE RESOURCES FOR LOCATING A PRIVATE INVESTIGATOR

1. Legal Industry Directory (www.lawinfo.com)
2. Private Investigators Mall (www.pimall.com/)

D. MISCELLANEOUS INFORMATION ON PRIVATE INVESTIGATORS

1. CCS International's Spyzone Site (www.spyzone.com/) All kinds of information about the P.I.'s work.
2. Investigative Reporters and Editors, Inc. (www.ire.org) Outstanding site maintained in connection with University of Missouri School of Journalism. Connects to investigator's resource center, a database library on government information, and a bookstore for current publications.
3. National Association of Investigative Specialists (www.pimall.com/nais/home.html) Maintained by Thomas Investigative Publications of Austin, Texas. Billed as "the world's largest investigative resource on the Internet." Links to investigative software; missing persons resources; civil, criminal, and domestic relations resources; and media guide for new publications and CD-ROM products.

6. ALTERNATIVE DISPUTE RESOLUTION (ADR)

A. ONLINE RESOURCES

1. American Arbitration Association (www.adr.org) Offers information on ADR including text of AAA rules, AAA forms, and articles on ADR.
2. American College of Civil Trial Mediators (www.acctm.org) This organization offers mediation services throughout North America. Provides assistance in locating a qualified mediator in numerous areas of specialty and links to helpful articles and publications in the field. ACCTM publishes a newsletter, *The Alternative.*
3. CPR Institute for Dispute Resolution (www.cpradr.org) An organization dedicated to promoting ADR in corporate and law firm practices. Provides training in ADR, assistance in locating qualified mediators, and many excellent publications in the field. The Institute also publishes a newsletter, *Alternatives.*
4. Federal Judicial Center (www.fjc.gov) Provides numerous articles relating to ADR.
5. Virtual Magistrate Arbitration Program (www.vmag.org) A pilot project for online dispute resolution sponsored by several organizations, including the American Arbitration Association, the Villanova Center for Information Law and Policy, and the Cyberspace Law Institute.
6. World Intellectual Property Organization Arbitration Center (www.wto.org).

B. BIBLIOGRAPHY ON ADR

1. Bennett, Mark D., and Michele S.G. Hermann, *The Art of Mediation.* Notre Dame, Indiana: National Institute for Trial Advocacy
2. Burton, John W., *Conflict Resolution: Its Languages and Processes.* Lanham, MD: The Scarecrow Press, Ltd., 1996
3. Bush, Robert A., and Joseph P. Folger, *The Promise of Mediation: Responding to Conflict Through Empowerment and Recognition.* San Francisco: Jossey-Bass Publishers, 1994
4. Carpenter, Susan L., and W.J.D. Kennedy, *Managing Public Disputes.* San Francisco: Jossey-Bass Publishers, 1991
5. Costello, Edward J., Jr., *Controlling Conflict: Dispute Resolution for Business.* Chicago: CCH, Inc., 1999
6. Davis, Barbara, and Sarah V. Corley, *Rockin' Role Plays: A Collection of the Finest for Mediation Trainers.* Asheville, NC: The Mediation Center, 1996
7. Frey, Martin A.: Alternative Methods of Dispute Resolution. Clifton Park, NY: Delmar Learning, 2003
8. Gleason, Sandra E., *Workplace Dispute Resolution.* East Lansing, MI: Michigan State University Press, 1997
9. Jandt, Fred E., *ADR for Paralegals.* Cincinnati: Anderson Publication Co., 1997
10. Kolb, Deborah M., *When Talk Works: Profiles on Mediators.* San Francisco: Jossey-Bass Publishers, 1994

11. Lechman, Barbara A.: Conflict and Resolution. NY: Aspen Publishers, 1997.

12. Leeson, Susan M., and Johnston, Bryan M., *Ending It:Dispute Resolution in America,* 2d ed. Cincinnati, OH:Anderson Publishing, 1998.

13. Lovenheim, Peter, *How to Mediate Your Dispute.* Berkeley, CA: Nolo Press, 1996

14. Manuel, Joe E., et al., *ADR Handbook.* Charlottesville, VA: Harrison Publishing Co., 1997

15. Mitchell, Christopher, and Michael Banks, *Handbook of Conflict Resolution: The Analytical Problem-Solving Approach.* New York: Pinter, 1996

16. Moore, Christopher W., *The Mediation Process.* San Francisco: Josey-Bass Publishers, 1996

17. Mosten, Forrest, *The Complete Guide to Mediation.* Chicago: The American Bar Association, 1997

18. Novak, John J., *How to Mediate: A Step-by Step Guide to the Art and Science of Mediation.* Crystal Clarity, 1991

19. Patterson, Susan, and Grant Seabolt, *Essentials of Alternative Dispute Resolution.* Dallas, TX: Pearson Publications Company, 1997

20. Pearce, W. Barnett, and Stephen W. Littlejohn, *Moral Conflict: When Social Worlds Collide.* Thousand Oaks, CA: SAGE Publishers, 1997

21. Riskin and Westbrook, *Dispute Resolution for Lawyers,* 2d ed. St. Paul, MN:The West Group, 1998

22. Schellenberg, James A., *Conflict Resolution: Theory, Research, and Practice.* New York: State University of New York Press, 1996

23. Singer, Linda R., *Settling Disputes: Conflict Resolution in Business, Families, and the Legal System.* Boulder, CO: Westview Press, 1994

7. COMMUNICATION SKILLS—VERBAL AND NONVERBAL

1. Briscoe, Jill, *Body Language.* New York: Victor Books, 1987

2. Fast, Julius, *Body Language.* New York: MJF Books, 1970

3. Fast, Julius, *Body Language in the Workplace.* New York: Penguin Books, 1994

4. Hayakawa, S.I., *Language in Thought and Action.* New York: Harcourt, Brace & Co., 1949

5. Malloy, John T., *Dress for Success.* New York: Warner Books, 1975

6. Nierenberg, Gerald I., and Henry H. Calero, *How to Read a Person Like a Book.* New York: E.P. Dutton, 1971

7. Sarnoff, Dorothy, *Speech Can Change Your Life.* New York: Doubleday, 1970

8. COMMUNICATION SKILLS—WRITING

1. Enquist, Anne and Laurel Currie Oats, *Just Writing: Grammar, Punctuation and Style for the Legal Writer.* NY: Aspen Publishers, 2001.

2. Fowler, H. Ramsey, and Jane E. Aaron, *The Little, Brown Handbook,* 7th ed. New York: Longman, 1998

3. Garner, Bryan A., *"Writing for Litigation," Scribes Journal of Legal Writing.* Dallas, TX: The American Society of Writers on Legal Subjects, 1990

4. Good, Edward C., *A Grammar Book for You and I . . . Oops, Me!: All the Grammar You Need to Succeed in Life.* Sterling, VA: Capital Books, Inc., 2002.

5. Koerselman, Virginia, and National Association of Legal Assistants, Inc., *CLA Review Manual,* 2d ed. (Chapter 2). St. Paul, MN: West Publishing Co., 1998

6. Robey, Cora L., et al., *New Handbook of Basic Writing Skills,* 4th ed. New York: Harcourt, Brace College Publishers, 1997

7. Strunk, William Jr., and E.B. White, *The Elements of Style,* 3d ed. New York: MacMillan Publishing Co., Inc., 1979 (online at www.cc .columbia.edu/acis/bartleby/strunk)

8. Venolia, Jan, *Write It Right! A Desk Drawer Digest of Punctuation, Grammar and Style.* Berkeley, CA: Ten Speed Press, 1988

9. Wydick, Richard, *Plain English for Lawyers,* 2d ed. Durham, NC: Carolina Academic Press, 1985

10. Online Help (www.english.penn.edu/ ~ jlynch/Grammar)
    (www.wordsmith.org)
    (www.educationindex.com)
    (www.edunet.com/english/grammar/index.html)
    (www.lawprose.com)
    (www.plainlanguage.com)
    (www.careertrack.com)

9. FREEDOM OF INFORMATION ACT/PRIVACY ACT

A. PUBLICATIONS

1. *Using the Freedom of Information Act: A Step-by-Step Guide,* prepared by The American Civil Liberties Union, 125 Broad St., New York, NY 10004 (212) 549-2500 (www.aclu.org)

2. *How to Use the Federal FOIA Act,* 7th ed., 1994, Rebecca Daughtery, ed., published by the Freedom of Information Service Center, 1735 I Street NW, Washington, DC 20006

3. *A Citizen's Guide on How to Use the Freedom of Information Act and the Privacy Act Requesting Government Documents,* prepared by the U.S. House of Representatives Committee on Government Operations. Contact: Superintendent of Documents, United States Printing Office, Washington, DC 20402 (www.access.gpo.gov)

B. OTHER RESOURCES

1. The FOIA Service Center, 1735 I Street NW, Washington, DC 20006. A joint project of the Reporter's Committee for Freedom of the Press and the Society of Professional Journalists.

2. The Center for National Security Studies (CNSS), 2130 H Street NW, Suite 701, Washington, DC 20037, (202) 994-7060 (www.fundforpeace .org/cnss.htm). Sponsored by the Fund for Peace.
3. Freedom of Information Clearinghouse, P.O. Box 19367, Washington, DC 20036. A project of Ralph Nader's Center for the Study of Responsive Law.
4. Fund for Open Information and Accountability, Inc., 239 Waverly Place, New York, NY 10012.

C. LOCATING THE FOIA/PA OFFICER FOR FEDERAL AGENCIES

1. American Civil Liberties Union (www.aclu.org/library/foia.html #addresses)
2. Code of Federal Regulations (searchable online at law.house.gov/ cfr.htm) as supplemented by the Federal Register (searchable online at www.access.gpo.gov/nara/#fr)
3. FOIA Counselor Service of the U.S. Department of Justice's (DOJ) Office of Information and Privacy (OIP) at (202) 514-FOIA (3642)
4. Government Printing Office (GPO) Federal Bulletin Board (www- .access.gpo.gpv)
5. U.S. DOJ Office of Information and Privacy Web sites: (www.usdoj .gov/foia/att_a.htm) or (www.usdoj.gov/foia/other_age. htm)
6. U.S. Government Manual (searchable online at www.access.gpo.gov/ nara/browse-gm.html)

10. LOCATING AND CONTACTING FEDERAL GOVERNMENT DEPARTMENTS

A. PUBLICATIONS

1. *American Jurisprudence 2d, Desk Book.* St. Paul, MN: West Group
2. Carroll, John M., *Confidential Information Sources: Public and Private,* 2d ed. Boston: Butterworth-Heinemann, 1991
3. *Congressional Directory.* The United States Government Printing Office (202) 512-1705 (www.access.gpo.gov)
4. Maxwell, Bruce, *How to Access the Federal Government on the Internet.* Washington, DC: Congressional Quarterly Books, 1995
5. Moorehead, Joe, and Mary Fetzer, *Introduction to United States Government Information Sources,* 4th ed. Englewood, CO: Libraries Unlimited, 1992
6. Philo, Harry M., *Lawyer's Desk Reference,* 9th ed., St. Paul, MN: West Group, 2001
7. *United States Government Manual.* Washington, DC: Office of the Federal Register, National Archives and Records Administration. Available from the GPO (202) 512-1705 (www.access.gpo.gov) or searchable online (www.access.gpo.gov/nara/browse-gm.html)
8. *U.S. Government Periodicals Index.* Bethesda, MD: Congressional Information Service, Inc. (a division of Lexis/Nexis) (800) 638-8380

9. *Washington Information Directory, Federal Regulatory Directory, Congressional Staff Directory, Federal Staff Directory,* and *How to Access the Federal Government on the Internet.* Alexandria, VA: CQ Press (800) 638-1710 (books.cq.com)
10. *West's Guide to American Law.* St. Paul, MN: West Publishing Co.

B. ONLINE SOURCES

1. First Gov (www.FirstGov.gov)
2. SearchGov (www.searchgov.com)
3. The Government Printing Office (GPO) Federal Bulletin Board (fedbbs.access.gpo.gov)
4. General Accounting Office Reports (www.access.gpo.gov/su_docs)
5. U.S. House of Representatives Home Page (www.house.gov) and Internet Law Library (law.house.gov/home.htm)
6. Library of Congress (www.loc.gov/)
7. The White House (www.whitehouse.gov)
8. FedWorld Information Network, operated by the U.S. Department of Commerce (www.fedworld.gov)
9. The National Archives and Records Administration (www.access .gpo.gov/nara)
10. Thomas (thomas.loc.gov). Provides numerous links to the White House, Congress, and all federal agencies
11. Federal Depository Libraries (www.access.gpo.gov/su_docs/dpos/ adpos/adpos003.html). Lists the location of all 1,400 federal depository libraries across the United States
12. Federal Statistics (www.fedstats.gov)
13. Northern Light One-Stop Government Locator (www.usgovsearch. com)
14. The Federal Web Locator (www.law.vill.edu/fed-agency/fedwebloc .html). Provides links to all federal agencies and departments in all three branches of the federal government
15. U.S. Federal Agency Directory (www.lib.lsu.edu/gov/fedgov.html)
16. Citizen's Guides to the U.S. Government (www.uncle-sam.com) or (www.capweb.net)
17. All Things military (www.searchmil.com)

11. NATIONAL ARCHIVES BRANCH LOCATIONS

1. Atlanta: 1557 St. Joseph St., East Point, GA 30344, (404) 246-7477
2. Chicago: 7358 South Pulaski Rd., Chicago, IL 60629, (312) 581-7816
3. Fort Worth: P.O. Box 6216, Fort Worth, TX 76115, (817) 334-5525
4. Los Angeles: 2400 Avila Rd., First Floor, Laguna Niguel, CA 92677, (714) 643-4241
5. Boston: 380 Trapelo Road, Waltham, MA 02154, (617) 647-8100
6. Denver: P.O. Box 25307, Denver, CO 80225, (303) 236-0817
7. Kansas City: 2312 East Bannister Rd., Kansas City, MO 64131, (816) 926-6934

8. New York: Building 22, Mil. Ocean Ter., Bayonne, NJ 07002, (201) 823-7252
9. Philadelphia: 9th & Market Sts., Room 1350, Philadelphia, PA 19107, (215) 597-3000
10. Seattle: 6125 Sand Point Way NE, Seattle, WA 98115, (206) 526-6507
11. San Francisco: 1000 Commodore Drive, San Bruno, CA 94066, (415) 876-9009

12. U.S. CONGRESS INFORMATION

1. Code of Federal Regulations (law.house.gov/cfr.htm)
2. Congressional Record (www.law.house.gov) or (thomas.loc.gov)
3. Federal Register (www.access.gpo.gov/nara/#fr)
4. Internet Law Library of the U.S. House of Representatives (law.house .gov/home.htm)
5. Thomas (thomas.loc.gov). Provides information on congressional procedures and full texts of all House and Senate bills, the Congressional Record, and many committee reports. Also provides numerous links to the White House, Congress, and all federal agencies.
6. United States Code Online (www.law.cornell.edu/uscode)
7. United States Code Congressional and Administrative News (law .house.gov/home.htm) or (thomas.loc.gov)

13. FEDERAL JUDICIARY INFORMATION

A. PUBLICATIONS

1. *Sourcebook for Federal Courts.* Available from GPO (www.access.gpo .gov)
2. *Judicial Staff Directory,* Alexandria, VA: CQ Press (800) 638-1710 (books .cq.com)

B. ONLINE RESOURCES

1. Cornell Law School's Legal Information Institute (www.law.cornell .edu). Federal Rules of Evidence, Federal Rules of Civil Procedure, and all decisions of the U.S. Supreme Court relating to constitutional issues are available at supct.law.cornell.edu/supct
2. Emory University Courts Finder (www.law.emory.edu). Provides links to the home pages of the U.S. Federal Circuit Courts
3. Emory University Federal Case Finder (www.law.emory.edu/ FEDCTS). Capable of searching for federal court decisions by party name, topic, or circuit
4. Supreme Court Web site (www.supremecourtus.gov)
5. National Archives and Records Administration (www.access.gpo .gov/nara). The field branches of the NARA (listed elsewhere in this Appendix) are the primary source for inactive federal court records.

6. OYEZ (oyez.nwu.edu/oyez.html). All decisions of the U.S. Supreme Court relating to constitutional issues are available here, as well as capacity to listen to oral arguments made before the court.
7. PACER—Public Access to Court Electronic Records. To subscribe, contact PACER Service Center in San Antonio, TX, (800) 676-6856. For more information, contact the Administrative Office of the Federal Courts (202) 273-1500 or (www.ao.dcn/publications/pubaccess .html).
8. Federal Judiciary Homepage (www.uscourts.gov). Provides information on the structure of the federal judiciary, case load statistics, judicial directory, judicial vacancies, employment opportunities, answers to frequently asked questions, lists of judiciary publications, and links to related Web sites
9. Washburn University Federal Case Finder (lawlib.wuacc.edu/ washlaw/search/html)

14. STATE AND LOCAL GOVERNMENT RESOURCES

A. PUBLICATIONS

1. *Monthly Checklist of State Publications.* Library of Congress (LOC) publication. (202) 707-5522 (online at www.loc.gov/)
2. Rhyne, Charles S., *The Law of Local Government Operations.* Kingsport, TN: The Kingsport Press, 1980
3. *The Sourcebook of Local Court and County Record Retrievers,* 2d ed., and *The Sourcebook of State Public Records,* 2d ed., The Public Record Research Library, Tempe, AZ: BRB Publications, 1995 (available on CD-ROM)
4. *State and Local Government 1999-2000, CQ's Desk Reference on the States,* and *CQ's State Fact Finder 1999,* Alexandria, VA: CQ Press (800) 638-1710) (books.cq.com)

B. ONLINE RESOURCES

1. SearchGov (www.searchgov.com)
2. GovSpot (www.govspot.com)
3. University of Michigan Library Document Center (www.lib.umich .edu/govdocs/index.html)
4. Governing (www.governing.com/govlinks/g\state.htm). An index to state government sites.
5. Legal Information Institute (www.fatty.law.cornell.edu/topics/ state_statutes.html). Provides links to state statutes and regulations, and a variety of state and local government sites.
6. LawCrawler Search Engine (www.findlaw.com)
7. LawInfo Legal Directory (www.lawinfo.com). Provides a legal directory for all states as well as links to Net resources for state information
8. Lexis Counsel Connect's LAWlinks (www.counsel.com). Provides links to numerous state laws
9. National Association of State Resource Executives (www.nascio.org)

10. National Center for State Courts (www.ncsonline.org)
11. Piper Resources (www.piperinfo.com/state/states/html)
12. P-LAW Legal Resource Locator (www.dorsai.org). Provides links to state research sites, statistical data, and specialized research on various topics
13. Rominger Legal On-Line Research (www.romingerlegal.com/)
14. Scruffy (www.prairienet.org/ ~ Scruffy/f.htm)
15. Yahoo State Search Engine (www.yahoo.com/Regional/U_S__States)
16. State business and professional codes (www.law.cornell.edu/statutes.html#state)

15. Citations to State Open Records Acts

Alabama	Ala. Code §36-12-40
Alaska	Alaska Stat. §09.25.110
Arkansas	Ark. Code Ann. §25-19-105
Arizona	Ariz. Rev. Stat. §39-121.01
California	Cal. Govt. Code §6253
Colorado	Col. Rev. Stat. §24-72-203
Connecticut	Conn. Gen. Stat. §1-210
Delaware	Del. Code Ann. tit. 29 §10003
Florida	Fla. Const. art. 1, §24
Georiga	Ga. Code Ann. §50-18-70
Hawaii	Haw. Rev. Stat. §92-4
Idaho	Idaho Code §9-337
Illinois	5 Ill. Comp. Stat. 160/4
Indiana	Ind. Code §5-14-3-3
Iowa	Iowa Code §22.2
Kansas	Kan. Stat. Ann. §45-215
Kentucky	Ky. Rev. Stat. Ann. §61.872
Louisiana	La. Rev. Stat. Ann. §44:31
Maine	Me. Rev. Stat. Ann. tit. 1 §408
Maryland	Md. Code Ann. §10-612
Massachusetts	Mass. Gen. Laws ch. 66, §10
Michigan	Mich. Comp. Laws §750.492
Minnesota	Minn. Stat. §13.03
Mississippi	Miss. Code Ann. §25-59-27
Missouri	Mo. Stat. Ann. §109.180
Montana	Mont. Code Ann. §2-6-102
Nebraska	Neb. Rev. Stat. §84-712
Nevada	Nev. Rev. Stat. §239.010
New Hampshire	N.H. Rev. Stat. Ann. §91-A:4
New Jersey	N.J. Stat. Ann. §47:1A-2
New Mexico	N.M. Stat. Ann. §14-2-1
New York	N.Y. Pub. Off. Law §88
North Carolina	N.C. Gen. Stat. §132-9
North Dakota	N.D. Cent. Code §44-04-18
Ohio	Ohio Rev. Code Ann. §149.43
Oklahoma	Okla. Stat. tit. 51, §24A

Oregon	Or. Rev. Stat. §192.420
Pennsylvania	65 Pa. Cons. Stat. §66.2
Rhode Island	R.I. Gen. Laws §45-43-7
South Carolina	S.C. Code Ann. §30-4-30
South Dakota	S.D. Codified Laws §1-27-1
Tennessee	Tenn. Code Ann. §10-7-503
Texas	Tex. Govt. Code Ann. §63-2-201
Utah	Utah Code Ann. §63-2-201
Vermont	Vt. Stat. Ann. tit. 1, §316
Virginia	Va. Code Ann. §2.1-342
Washington	Wash. Rev. Code §42.17.260
West Virginia	W. Va. Code §29B-1-3
Wisconsin	Wis. Stat. §19.35
Wyoming	Wyo. Stat. Ann. §16-4-202
Washington, DC	D.C. Code Ann §1-1504

16. CRIMINAL LAW—SOURCES OF INFORMATION

1. The Federal Bureau of Investigation (www.fbi.gov). Offers information and statistics on domestic and international crime
2. The National Institute of Justice, the research arm of the U.S. Department of Justice (www.ojp.usdoj.gov/nij). An informative site regarding research and projects of the NIJ in many areas, including violence against women, drug laws, and community policing
3. The Justice Information Center (www.ncjrs.org). Provides information and statistics regarding adult and juvenile crime worldwide
4. Site providing numerous links to other crime-related sites: (www .fsu.edu/~crimdo/cj.html)
5. The U.S. Sentencing Guidelines Manual (www.ussc.gov)
6. Crime rate data by ZIP code (www.capindex.com/zipcode.htm)
7. National Fraud Information Center (www.fraud.org). A project of the National Consumers League, this site provides a daily report and other information on fraud, as well as the opportunity to report fraud.
8. Benamati, Dennis C., *Criminal Justice Information: How to Find It, How to Use It.* Phoenix, AZ: Oryx House, 1998 (www.oryxpress.com)

17. CORPORATE AND BUSINESS INFORMATION

A. DIRECTORIES AND OTHER PUBLICATIONS

(The most likely place to locate these paper publications is the reference desk of a good library. However, many of these publications are now available directly online or through online database vendors. Many are also available from the publishers in CD-ROM format.)

1. *Business Periodical Index* (annual). New York: H.W. Wilson (800) 367-6770 (www.hwwilson.com). Excellent guide to hundreds of periodicals on business, finance, manufacturing, etc.

2. *Charitable Organizations of the United States* (sketches almost 800 fund-raising charities and evaluates expenses for administration), *Directories in Print,* 14th ed. (a comprehensive listing of directories for searching companies, individuals, and products), *Encyclopedia of Associations,* 34th ed. (comprehensive listings of international, national, regional, and local organizations), *Gale Directory of Publications and Broadcast Media* and *Gale's Biographical Index* (biographical data on owners and officers in many different businesses), and *Owners and Officers of Private Companies.* Detroit, MI: Gale Research, Inc. (800) 877-4253 (www.gale.com). (Many of Gale's publications are available on CD-ROM.)

3. Daniels, Lorna, *Business Information Sources.* Berkeley, CA: University of California Press, 1993

4. *Directory of American Research and Technology,* 31st ed. New Providence, NJ: R.R. Bowker, 1996, (800) 521-8110

5. *Directory of Corporate Affiliations: Who Owns Whom.* New Providence, NJ: National Register Publishing (5 vol.) (800) 521-8110. Provides data on parent, subsidiary, and affiliate relationships

6. *Dun & Bradstreet Ratings.* Bethlehem, PA: Dun & Bradstreet Information Services (800) 526-0651 (www.dbisna.com). Credit reports on thousands of businesses

7. *Foundation Grants Index* (provides information on grants to particular nonprofit organizations), *National Data Book* (contains descriptions of most U.S. private foundations), and *Source Book* (contains detailed profiles of the 1,000 largest foundations). New York: The Foundation Center (800) 424-9836 (www.fdncenter.org)

8. *Hoovers Handbook of Private Companies.* Austin, TX: Hoovers Business Press, 1998 (512) 374-4500 (www.hoovers.com)

9. *International Directory of Corporate Histories.* Detroit, MI: St. James Press, 1994

10. *Moody's Industry Review* and *Moody's Manuals.* New York: Moody's Investor Services, Inc. (a division of Dun & Bradstreet) (212) 553-0300. Financial and operating information on thousands of companies

11. *National Trade and Professional Associations of the United States,* 32d ed. New York: Columbia Books, 1997. Trade and professional associations listed alphabetically and by subject matter

12. *Standard & Poor's Register of Corporations, Standard & Poor's Corporation Records,* and *Standard & Poor's Register of Directors and Executives.* New York: McGraw-Hill (212) 208-8581 or (212) 924-6825. Information on thousands of corporations, corporate records, and corporate officers and directors

13. *Thomas's Register of American Manufacturers, Food Industry Register, Thomas's Regional Register,* and *Register of European Manufacturers.* New York: Thomas Publishing Co. (800) 647-1908 (www.thomasregister.com). Guides to products and product makers

14. Tracy, John A., *How to Read a Financial Report: Wringing Cash Flow and Other Vital Signs out of the Numbers,* 4th ed. New York: John Wiley, 1994

15. *U.S. Industrial Directory* and *U.S. Export Directory.* Stamford, CT: Reed International/Cahners (203) 328-2500

16. *Value Line Investment Survey.* New York: Value Line Publishing, Inc. (800) 634-3583 (www.valueline.com)

17. *Walkers Corporate Directory of U.S. Public Companies.* San Mateo, CA: Walker Research, LLC

18. *Who's Who Among Top Executives.* Tempe, AZ: Kaleo Publications, 1997, (800) 965-2536

19. *Who's Who In America.* New Providence, NJ: Marquis Publications (800) 521-8110. Detailed information on wealthy individuals and many other persons of note due to corporate affiliations, profession, or hobby. One of a series of *Who's Who* directories by Marquis.

B. ONLINE RESOURCES

1. American Bankruptcy Institute (ABI) (www.abiworld.org). Contains a daily and weekly summary of important bankruptcy news affecting American businesses

2. American Business Information (www.abii.com). Provides access to numerous databases including yellow pages, business profiles, and credit reporters (there is a fee for some information)

3. American Federation of Labor-Congress of Industrial Organizations (AFL-CIO) (www.aflcio.org). Links to sites with information on ongoing business activities affecting organized labor and employee rights

4. Annual Reports (www.prars.com). Annual reports on more than 3,000 corporations

5. Antitrust Division of the U.S. Department of Justice (www.usdoj .gov)

6. Better Business Bureau (www.bbb.org). The BBB also has a new site devoted to information on businesses operating online. (www .bbbonline.org)

7. The Big Book (www.bigbook.com). Addresses, phone numbers, and other information about businesses and individuals as well as maps to the addresses

8. Business Research in Information and Technology (www.brint.com)

9. Center for the Study of Responsive Law (www.csrl.org). This public interest center sponsors research and educational projects to encourage political, economic, and social institutions to be more responsive to the needs of consumers. Provides access to a multitude of reports dealing with companies of all kinds.

10. BizJournal (www.bizjournals.com)

11. Companies Online (www.companiesonline.com)

12. Chamber of Commerce (www.uschamber.org)

13. Consumer Product Safety Commission (www.cpsc.gov). Provides information on regulated products and businesses as well as access to publications

14. Corporate Salary Information (www.paywatch.org) or (www.wage web.com)

15. Corporate Information (www.corporateinformation.com)

16. Credit Reports (www.fool.com) or (www.thestreet.com)
17. EDGAR—Electronic Data Gathering Analysis and Retrieval System of the Securities Exchange Commission (www.sec.gov/edgarhp.htm). Substantial amounts of corporate financial and other information is available in the EDGAR database, including initial public offerings, proxy statements, annual corporate reports, and registration statements. Also try Edgar's private sector competitor, FreeEdgar (www.Free.Edgar.com)
18. Environmental Protection Agency (www.epa.gov). The EPA also maintains a site combining data from a variety of different EPA programs, including Superfund, the release of toxic chemicals, water-discharge permits, etc. (www.epa.gov/enviro/html/ef_home. html)
19. Federal Trade Commission (www.ftc.gov)
20. Food and Drug Administration (www.fda.gov)
21. Hoover's Online (www.hoovers.com). Provides financial, personnel, and business data on more than 1,500 corporations
22. Internet Non-Profit Center, a project of the American Institute of Philanthropy (www.nonprofits.org). Provides information on numerous philanthropic organizations in the United States
23. Initial Public Offering (IPO) Data (www.ipodata.com) or (www.ipocentral.com)
24. National Fraud Information Center (www.fraud.org). A project of the National Consumers League, this site provides a daily report and other information on fraud, as well as the opportunity to report fraud.
25. Price Waterhouse Technology Center (bamboo.tc.pw.com/cgi-bin/edgarscan_html). Filters and sorts the companies and types of SEC filings available through EDGAR. A more user-friendly format than the SEC site for EDGAR.
26. Progressive Business Web Pages (envirolink.org). Provides information on "socially responsible" businesses, including environmentally conscious firms
27. Company Sleuth (www.companysleuth.com)
28. Thomas Register of American Manufacturers (www.thomasregister.com). Provides free access to comprehensive data on American and European manufacturers and links to a number of other helpful sites
29. U.S. Business Advisor (www.business.gov/). This federal government program provides access to business-related government information and services.
30. Wall Street Research Network (www.wsrn.com)
31. Corporate Press Release (www.prnewswire.com)
32. Virtual Chase (www.virtualchase.com/coinfo/)

18. MEDICAL RESOURCES ONLINE

1. American Medical Association (www.ama-assn.org)
2. U.S. Center for Disease Control (www.cdc.gov)
3. National Institute for Health (www.nih.gov)
4. National Association for Public Health Statistics and Information Systems (NAPHSIS) (www.naphsis.org)

5. National Center for Health Statistics (www.cdc.gov/nchswww/default.htm)
6. Medical Resources (www.healthgate.com)
7. Doctor's Guide to the Internet (www.pslgroup.com/docguide.htm)
8. National Library of Medicine (www.nlm.nih.gov)
9. Medical Links for Laypersons (www.pobox.com/~subhas/health.html)
10. AMA Physician Online Doctor Finder (www.ama-assn.org/aps/amahg.htm)
11. Hospital Locator (www.hospital.select.com)
12. Healthgate (www.healthgate.com)
13. American Association of Physicians Assistants (www.aapa.org)
14. American Association of Nurses Assistants (www.aana.org)
15. American Physical Therapy Association (www.apta.org/apta)
16. Health Hippo (www.winternet.com/~hippo)
17. MEDLINE (www.nlm.nih.gov/databases/freemedl.html)
18. Medscape (www.medscape.com)
19. Medical Search (www.mwsearch.com). Medical information search engine
20. Medicare (www.medicare.gov)
21. Doctors on Call (www.doctorsoncall.com). A medical directory
22. Board Certified Directory (certifieddoctor.org/verify.html)
23. *How to Find Health Information on the Internet*, Alexandria, VA: CQ Press (800) 638-1710 (books.cq.com)
24. Achoo (www.achoo.com)
25. National Library of Medicine (www.ncbi.nlm.gov/PubMed)
26. Mayo Clinic (www.mayohealth.org)
27. American Council on Science and Health (www.acsh.org)
28. Health on the Net (www.hon.com)
29. The Healing Spectrum (www.thehealingspectrum.com/medical)
30. American Society of Health System Pharmacists (www.safemedication.com)
31. Dr. Koop (www.drkoop.com)
32. Department of Health and Human Services Health Finder (www.healthfinder.gov)
33. The Baby Center (www.babycenter.com)
34. Health A to Z (www.healthatoz.com)
35. Web MD (www.webmd.com)
36. Health Information (www.medem.com)(sponsored by the American Medical Association and six other physician groups)
37. Intellihealth (www.intellihealth.com)
38. Healtheon (www.healtheon.com)
39. Pharmaceutical Information (www.drugstore.com) or (www.rxlist.com) or (www.planetrx.com)
40. PDR Nurses Handbook (www.Nurses.PDR.com/members/database/index.html)
41. Gray's Anatomy (www.cancerweb.ac.uk/omd)
42. Nutrition (www.navigator.tufts.edu)
43. Alternative medicine (www.altmedicine.com)
44. Health Shop (www.healthshop.com)

45. Onhealth (www.onhealth.com)
46. Web Clinic (www.oshu.edu/cliniweb/)
47. American Cancer Society (www.cancer.org)
48. Obstetrics (www.babycenter.com)

19. MEDIA RESOURCES ONLINE

A. NATIONAL NEWSPAPERS ONLINE

Los Angeles Times (www.LATimes.com)

New York Times (www.nytimes.com)

USA Today (www.usatoday.com)

Wall Street Journal (www.wsj.com)

Washington Post (www.washingtonpost.com)

B. DIRECTORIES OF NEWSPAPERS ONLINE

1. Associated Press Internet Service (wire.ap.org). Lists all newspapers that are online and that make the AP wire service available online
2. Electronic Clipping Services (customnews.cnn.com/cnews/pna_auth. welcome) and (www.my.yahoo.com). These sites will sort and customize news for you and even e-mail highlights to you. CNN's site allows the user to identify key words to be searched to prepare the customized presentation.
3. Online Newspapers (www.naa.org/hot/). Provides access to hundreds of newspapers around the country with user-friendly interface
4. News Index and Total News (www.niu.edu/newsplace). A search engine devoted to locating numerous different news sources on the Internet
5. American Journalism Review (www.newslink.org/menu.html)
6. Newsgroups Directory (www.liszt.com) or (www.newsville.com/news/groups/)

C. PERIODICALS ONLINE

1. Law Journal Extra (www.ljx.com). Provides a great deal of law-related news and summaries of major stories in the National Law Journal, New York Law Journal, and Law Technology Product News
2. National Law Journal (www.nlj.com)
3. Time-Warner Online (www.pathfinder.com). The Time-Warner family of periodicals including Time, Fortune, Life, People, and Money magazines is accessible here.
4. Legal Online (www.legalonline.com)
5. Lawyers Weekly (www.lweekly.com)
6. Magazine Online Directory (www.enews.com)
7. Money Online (www.money.com/). Provides daily business news

D. TELEVISION NETWORKS ONLINE

www.abcnews.com
www.cbs.com
www.cnn.com
www.c-span.org
www.msnbc.com
www.pbs.org
Local stations (TV and radio) online. Try www.(station's 4-letter call sign).com

20. PEOPLE LOCATOR RESOURCES

A. PUBLICATIONS

1. Gunderson, Ted L., and Roger McGovern, *How to Locate Anyone Anywhere Without Leaving Home,* rev. ed., New York: Penguin Press, 1996
2. Johnson, Richard S., *How to Locate Anyone Who Is or Has Been in the Military,* 6th ed. Burlington, NC: MIE Publishing, 1995
3. King, Dennis, *Get the Facts on Anyone,* 2d ed. New York: McMillan, 1995
4. Lapin, Lee, *How to Get Anything on Anybody: Book II.* San Mateo, CA: ISECO, Inc., 1991
5. Riddle, Kelly, *Computer and Internet Investigating.* Austin, TX: Thomas Investigative Publications, 1998
6. Thomas, Ralph D., *How to Find Anyone Anywhere,* 4th ed. and *How to Investigate by Computer.* Austin, TX: Thomas Investigative Publications, 1998
7. Tillman, Norma Mott, *How to Find Almost Anyone Anywhere.* Nashville, TN: Rutledge Hill Press

B. SKIP-TRACING COMPANIES

1. Infoquest, 101 N. Fourth St., Suite 105, Sandpoint, ID 38364, (800) 562-7547 (www.infoquest.com)
2. Old Friends Information Service, 1 Camino Sobrante, No. 21, Orinda, CA 94563, (800) 841-7938
3. 1-800-USSearch (www.1800ussearch.com)

C. ONLINE PEOPLE SEARCH SERVICES

1. Stalkers Home Page (www.glr.com/stalk.html)
2. Rominger Legal Online People Finder (www.romingerlegal.com/)
3. American Research Bureau (www.heirfinder.com)
4. WhoWhere (www.whowhere.com)
5. International Genealogical Search (www.heirsearch.com)
6. Military on the Internet (www.refdesk.com)

D. CLUBS AND PROFESSIONAL ASSOCIATIONS

1. *Encyclopedia of Associations,* and *The Encyclopedia of International Associations.* Detroit, MI: Gale Research, Inc. (an ITP company) (800) 877-4253 (www.gale.com)
2. Internet Public Library's Association on the Net (www.ipl.org/ref/AON)
3. Yahoo (www.yahoo.com/Business_and_Economy/Organizations/Professional)

E. GENEALOGICAL RESOURCES—ONLINE

1. Family History Centers (www.deseretbook.com/famhis/). More than 2,000 computerized centers operated worldwide by the Church of Jesus Christ of Latter Day Saints (LDS) (Mormon), connected to the Family History Library of the LDS at 35 NW Temple Street, Salt Lake City, Utah 84150, (801) 531-2331. Among the computerized records maintained are a Social Security Death Index, a Military Index, an International Genealogical Index, and a Family History Library Catalog. For the Family History Center nearest you, consult the FHC home page above or contact Family History Support at (800) 346-6044.
2. LDS Family Search (www.familysearch.com). This site, owned by the Church of Jesus Christ of Latter Day Saints (LDS) (Mormon) and operated by IBM, is billed as "the world's biggest genealogical Web site." It is a free site, providing access to the LDS's massive International Genealogical Index begun after World War II and added to daily.
3. National Archives and Records Administration (www.archives.gov)
4. Online Genealogical Database (www.gentree.com/gentree.html)
5. National Genealogical Society (www.ngsgenealogy.org)
6. Miscellaneous (www.rootsweb.com) or (www.ancestory.com) or (www.genealogy.com)

F. GENEALOGICAL RESOURCES—PUBLICATIONS

1. *Everton's Genealogical Helper,* bimonthly journal, 3223 South Main St., Nibley, UT 84321.
2. Luebking, Sandra H., and Loretto D. Szucs, eds., *The Source: A Guidebook of American Genealogy,* rev. ed. Salt Lake City, UT: Ancestry Incorporated, 1995
3. The Handbook of Genealogists, 9th ed. Nibley, UT: Everton Publishers.

G. TELEPHONE AND ADDRESS DIRECTORIES ONLINE AND ON CD-ROM

1. The Big Book (www.bigbook.com)
2. Telephone Directory and Reverse Directories (www.anywho.com) and (www.whowhere.com)
3. Infospace (www.infospace.com)
4. 555 (www.555-1212.com)

5. ATT (www.att.com/tollfree/index.html)
6. GTE Superpages (www.superpages.com)
7. Switchboard, USA (www.switchboard.com)
8. Toll Free Numbers (att.net/dir800)
9. Yellow Pages on the Web (www.bigyellow.com)
10. Reverse Look-up Service (www.findlaw.com/directories/reverse.html)
11. Look Up USA (www.lookupusa.com)
12. Four11 (411.com)
13. Zip Code Directory—regular and reverse (www.usps.gov)

H. E-MAIL DIRECTORIES ONLINE

1. Four11 (www.four11.com)
2. Who-Where (www.whowhere.com)
3. IAF (www.iaf.net)
4. To access e-mail servers at large companies try nic@vnet.ibm.com (IBM) or sun.com (Sun Microsystems) or att.com (AT&T)

I. MAP, DIRECTION, AND CITY INFORMATION SERVICES ONLINE

1. Maps On Us (www.MapsOnUs.com)
2. Mapquest (www.mapquest.com)
3. Online City Search (www.citysearch.com).
4. MapList (www.maplist.com)
5. World Maps (www.lib.utexas/LIBS/PCL/MAP_collection/html)

21. SOCIAL SECURITY INDEX OF ASSIGNED NUMBERS

Alabama 416-424	Louisiana 433-439
Alaska 574	Maine 004-007
Arkansas 429-432	Maryland 212-220
Arizona 526-527	Massachusetts 010-034
California 545-573	Michigan 362-386
Colorado 521-524	Minnesota 468-477
Connecticut 040-049	Mississippi 425-428
Delaware 221-222	Missouri 486-500
Florida 261-267	Montana 505-508
Georgia 252-260	Montana 516-517
Hawaii 575-576	Nevada 530
Idaho 518-519	New Hampshire 001-003
Illinois 318-336	New Jersey 135-158
Indiana 303-317	New Mexico 525, 585
Iowa 478-483	New York 050-134
Kansas 509-515	North Carolina 237-246
Kentucky 400-407	North Dakota 501-502

Ohio 268-302
Oklahoma 440-448
Oregon 540-544
Pennsylvania 159-211
Rhode Island 035-039
South Carolina 247-251
South Dakota 503-504
Tennessee 408-415
Texas 449-467
Utah 528-529

Vermont 008-009
Virginia 223-231
Washington 531-539
Washington, DC 577-579
West Virginia 232-236
Wisconsin 387-399
Wyoming 520
Virgin Islands 580
Puerto Rico, Guam, Samoa, and
Philippine Islands 581-585

22. CREDIT REPORTING COMPANIES

1. Equifax, P.O. Box 740241, Atlanta, GA 30374-0241, (800) 685-1111 www.equifax.com
2. Experian, P.O. Box 2104, Allen, TX 75013-2104, (888) 397-3742 www.experian.com
3. Trans Union, P.O. Box 403, Springfield, PA 19064, (800) 888-4213 www.transunion.com
4. Online (www.icreditreport.com)

23. PUBLIC RECORDS SEARCH COMPANIES

A. NATIONAL SEARCH COMPANIES

1. Ameri-Search, Sacramento, CA (800) 877-2877 (www.amerisearch.com)
2. Attorneys Corporation Service, Inc., North Hollywood, CA (800) 462-5487
3. Capitol Services, Inc., Austin, Texas (800) 345-4647
4. CCH Washington Service Bureau, Washington, DC (800) 289-1057
5. CDB Infotek, Santa Ana, CA (800) 427-3747 (www.cdb.com/public)
6. CorpAmerica, Dover, DE (800) 622-6414 (www.LawService.com)
7. Corpex Banknote Co., Inc., Bayshore, NY (800) 221-8181
8. Corporation Trust Co., Wilmington, DE (302) 658-7581
9. Corporation Service Co., Wilmington, DE (800) 872-4636 (www.incspot.com)
10. CT Corporation System, New York, NY (800) 624-0909 (www.cchlis.com)
11. Dow Jones News/Retrieval Service, New York, NY (800) 369-7466 (www.djnr.com)
12. Experian (formerly Metromail), Schuamburg, IL (800) 316-2637 (www.experian.com/smallbusiness)
13. History Associates, Inc., Rockville, MD (301) 670-0076 (www.historyassociates.com)
14. Information America, Atlanta, GA (800) 235-4008 (owned by West law) (www.infoam. com)
15. Parasec, Sacramento, CA (800) 603-5868 (www.parasec.com)
16. Prentice-Hall Corporation System, Dover, DE (800) 866-0221

17. The Company Corporation, Wilmington, DE (800) 542-2677
18. USSearch (www.USSearch.com)
19. Washington Document Service, Washington, DC (800) 728-5201 (www.wdsdocs.com)

B. LOCATING SEARCH COMPANIES

1. *The Source Book of Public Records Providers: The National Guide to Companies That Furnish Automated Public Record Information, Search Services and Investigative Services,* 3d ed. The Public Record Research Library, Tempe, AZ: BRB Publications, 1995 (800) 929-3811 (www.brbpub.com)

24. ONLINE DATABASE VENDORS

1. American Information Network, Lansing, MI (517) 484-5221 (www.ameri.com)
2. Commerce Clearing House (CCH) Electronic Legislative Search Service (ELISS), New York, NY (800) 835-5224 (www.cch.com)
3. CT Corporation System, New York, NY (800) 624-0909 (www.cch-lis.com) (Included among database vendors as well as search companies because it offers, as an alternative, its CT Advantage System (www.ctadvantage.com), an electronic desk-top system that allows you to perform searches from your own desk.)
4. Database America, Montvale, NJ (www.databaseamerica.com) (Offers CD-ROM products as well.)
5. DataStar, Cary, NC (southeastern U.S. Office) (800) 334-2564 (www.datastarweb.com) Billed as "Europe's leading information resource," this London-based vendor specializes in business, scientific, and technical news from Eastern and Western Europe.
6. Dialog, Palo Alto, CA (800) 334-2564 (www.dialog.com)
7. Dow Jones Business Information Service, New York, NY (800) 369-7466 (bis.dowjones.com)
8. Dun & Bradstreet Information Services, Parsippany, NJ (800) 234-386 (www.dnb.com)
9. European Information Network Service (no U.S. office) (www.eins.org) Specializing in scientific and technical information in Europe
10. Experian (formerly Metromail), Schuamburg, IL (800) 316-2637 (www.experian.com/smallbusiness)
11. info USA, Omaha, NE (800) 321-0869 (www.abii.com)
12. Law Office Information Systems (LOIS), Professional Information Technology Access (PITA) (800) 364-2512 (www.pita.com) (Offers CD-ROM products as well.)
13. Lexis-Nexis, Reed Elsevier, Dayton, OH (800) 34NEXIS (www.lexis-nexis.com)
14. Moody's Investor Services, Inc., New York, NY (212) 553-1658 (www.moodys.com)
15. Online Computer Library Center, Inc. (OCLC), Dublin, OH (800) 848-5878 (www.oclc.org). Created for library subscribers, provides

search and retrieval and document databases from libraries in the United States and more than 60 other countries.

16. Ovid Technologies, Inc, Murray, UT (800) 950-2371 (www.ovid. com) Provides access to more than 90 databases in allied health, biomedical, business, general reference, humanities, science and technology, and social services.
17. Questel-Orbit, Inc., France Telecom Group, McClean, Virginia (U.S. office) (800) 456-7248 (www.orbit.com). This France-based service specializes in intellectual property, scientific, technical, chemical, and business information and news from around the world.
18. Westlaw: West Group, St. Paul, MN (800) 762-5272 (www.westlaw .com)

25. VITAL RECORDS

A. PUBLICATIONS

1. The U.S. Department of Health and Human Services (www.hhs.gov) has issued a pamphlet obtainable through the Government Printing Office (online at www.access.gpo.gov) entitled *Where to Write for Vital Records: Births, Deaths, Marriages and Divorces,* which provides the address of each state vital records office.
2. *American Jurisprudence 2d, Desk Book.* Rochester, NY: Lawyers Co-Operative Publishing Co.
3. Philo, Harry M., *Lawyer's Desk Reference,* 9th ed. St. Paul, MN: West Group, 2001

B. ONLINE SOURCES OF INFORMATION

1. Consumer Education Research Center (www.cerc.com)
2. National Association for Public Health Statistics and Information Systems (NAPHSIS) (www.naphsis.org/)
3. U.S. Department of Health and Human Services (www.hhs.gov); Center for Disease Control and Prevention (www.cdc.gov); and National Center for Health Statistics (www.cdc.gov/nchswww/default.htm)
4. Vital Records Resource (www.vitalcheck.com)

Glossary

Active listening: Listening not just to record the exact words spoken, but to catch meanings as well, by observing body language of the speaker and by noticing things like voice inflection, volume, grammar, enunciation, and accent. See *Body language*.

Administrative agency: See *Agency*.

Administrative law: The area of law dealing with administrative agencies and their functions. See *Agency*; *Agency rule or regulation*; and *Enabling legislation*.

Administrative Procedures Act: A statute governing the procedures by which agency action may be challenged or appealed.

Admission by party opponent: Any statement made by or on behalf of a party to the suit, or which has been adopted by the party as true. Is admissible at trial if offered against that party.

Adversarial system of justice: The system that allows disputing parties who are unable to resolve the dispute themselves to present their dispute as adversaries or contestants before a court or tribunal empowered to resolve the dispute for them.

Affidavit: A sworn and signed statement. Also called a declaration.

Affirmative defense: A defense raised by a defendant in a civil or criminal action which, if proven, will cause the defendant to prevail over one or all the claims of the plaintiff or prosecution (e.g., statute of limitations, release, or assumption of risk in a civil case; insanity or privilege in a criminal prosecution). The defendant has the burden of proof on the affirmative defense. See *Burden of proof*.

Agency: A governmental body created by state or federal legislation and charged with administering legislation in specific areas. Governmental agencies are engaged in rulemaking, investigation, and adjudication. See *Administrative law*; *Agency rule or regulation*; and *Enabling legislation*.

Agency rule or regulation: A rule or regulation promulgated by a state or federal agency to carry out the administrative responsibility delegated to that agency by the legislative body that created the agency. See *Agency*.

Agent: See *Principal-agent*.

Alternative dispute resolution (ADR): The process of resolving a legal dispute without pursuing litigation. Most popular forms of ADR are negotiation, mediation, and arbitration. See *Arbitration*; *Mediation*; and *Negotiation*.

Arbitration: A process in which disputing parties agree to submit their dispute to a disinterested person (or panel of persons) other than a judge or jury. The arbitrator(s) will listen to both sides and then render a decision which may be binding or non-binding depending on the agreement of the parties or a controlling statute. See *Alternative dispute resolution*; *Mediation*; and *Negotiation*.

Attorney-client privilege: An evidentiary privilege preventing the disclosure in a court or other formal proceeding, without the client's consent, of confidential communications between the attorney and client related to the matter in which the client is represented by the attorney; also the broader duty of the attorney to not disclose, without the client's consent or for any purpose, the confidences and secrets of the client.

Authentication: Establishing that a document, object, or voice to be offered in evidence at trial is genuine, i.e., it is in fact what it purports to be. See *Chain of custody*.

Bench trial: A trial conducted without a jury. See *Jury trial*.

Bias: Any reason a witness might have to favor or disfavor one side or another in a dispute; used to impeach a witness. See *Impeaching a witness*; *Interest*.

Bill of particulars: A disclosure the prosecution makes in a criminal case, upon request by the defendant and order of the court, the purpose of which is to make general allegations contained in the indictment or information more specific.

Body language: A person's posture, gestures, facial expressions, eye contact, clothes, or environment that communicate information to others.

Brady doctrine: Rule based on Supreme Court case of *Brady v. Maryland* requiring the prosecution in both state and federal proceedings to provide to the defense all exculpatory evidence in its possession, custody, or control.

Burden of proof: The obligation imposed on the party asserting a civil cause of action against another or an affirmative defense to such a cause of action, and on the government in a criminal prosecution and on the criminal defendant asserting an affirmative defense to such criminal prosecution, to prove all of the necessary elements of the cause of action or affirmative defense asserted by the requisite degree of proof. See *Affirmative defense*; *Cause of action*; *Civil law*; *Criminal law*; and *Degree of proof*.

Business records: Records in written or electronic form of a business's activities that are maintained in the ordinary course of the business's operations; such records are admissible in court over a hearsay objection. See *Hearsay*; *Records custodian*.

Canvass: In investigating, the physical inspection of the scene of an incident which normally includes locating and interviewing persons nearby as to their knowledge of the incident.

Cause of action: In the civil law, a recognized theory of liability on which one party may sue another. For example, negligence, breach of contract, etc.

Chain of custody: Establishing the continuous custody of an object to be offered in evidence at trial from the time of a relevant incident until trial; part of the required authentication of some items of evidence. See *Laying the foundation; Evidence.*

Chinese wall: See *Invisible wall.*

Circumstantial evidence: Indirect evidence that requires an inference or conclusion to prove a relevant fact.

City-county directory: A publication of many cities and counties setting out individual and business names, addresses, and phone numbers in a reverse directory format. See *Reverse directory.*

Civil law: The area of the law dealing with the determination and enforcement of all private or public rights, essentially all law that is not a criminal matter. Civil disputes involve claims between persons that one has engaged in conduct injurious to the person, property, or personal rights of the other as, for example, in the areas of torts, contracts, civil and Constitutional rights, business associations, and real property. Rules of civil procedure govern the civil process. See *Criminal law.*

Closed-ended questions: Questions that call for a specific, narrow answer that requires few words and little or no explanation.

Code of Federal Regulations (CFR): Official publication of the U.S. government containing the current federal regulations for each federal agency and department.

Colloquialisms: Words or phrases which are used incorrectly but which have gained widespread use in informal conversation.

Common law: A court decision in a contested case creating a precedent in the jurisdiction. See *Agency rule or regulation; Court rule;* and *Statute.*

Compensatory damages: Money damages sought in a civil lawsuit which *compensate* the plaintiff or make the plaintiff whole. Compensatory damages may be general (compensation for pain and suffering) or specific (out-of-pocket expenses such as medical bills, lost wages, etc.).

Conflict of interest: Anything that compromises or which could reasonably appear to compromise the objectivity or loyalty of the attorney or paralegal to the client.

Congressional Record: Official publication of the U.S. government containing the official proceedings of the Congress.

Consulting expert: See *Expert.*

Contingency agreement: A type of fee agreement in which the attorney agrees to take a designated percentage, usually a third, of what is recovered for the client as a fee for services.

Court rule: A rule of procedure or practice adopted by a federal or state court. See *Agency rule or regulation; Common law;* and *Statute.*

Credit report: See *Credit reporting agencies.*

Credit reporting agencies: Companies that collect and disseminate information for a fee on the credit history and credit worthiness of individuals; currently the three largest are *Equifax, Trans Union* and *Experian.* The information is disseminated as a *credit report.*

Criminal law: The area of the law dealing with prosecution by the state or federal government of persons accused of violating societal laws codified in criminal statutes that allow the government to seek punishment by fine or imprisonment or both. Criminal statutes are typically classified as crimes against the person, crimes against property, and crimes against the public. Rules of criminal procedure govern the prosecution process. See *Civil law.*

Criss-cross directory: See *Reverse directory.*

Cross examination: The questioning of a witness at trial by attorneys who did not call that witness to testify; cross examination follows the direct examination of that witness; leading questions may be used. See *Direct examination; Leading questions.*

Curriculum vitae: A person's written *resume* or *biography* setting forth their business or professional qualifications and accomplishments.

Database vendors: Commercial businesses that make various libraries of information and search engines available for subscribers. Nexis/Lexis and Westlaw are the two best known. Such vendors accessible to subscribers online are called *online database vendors.*

Declaration: See *Affidavit.*

Declaratory judgment: A judgment sought from a court that will declare the rights of the parties in some property or situation; a type of equitable relief. See *Equitable relief; Injunction;* and *Legal remedy.*

Defendant: The party who is sued in a civil lawsuit. The party who is prosecuted by the government in a criminal prosecution. See *Plaintiff.*

Degree of proof: The extent to which a party having the burden of proof in a civil lawsuit or criminal prosecution must convince the finder of fact in order to prevail; the most common are (1) by a preponderance of the evidence; (2) by clear and convincing evidence; and (3) beyond a reasonable doubt.

Demonstrative evidence: Evidence in the form of properly admitted charts, graphs, diagrams, etc. that illustrate something for the court. See *Documentary evidence; Real evidence;* and *Testimonial evidence.*

Deposition: A type of formal discovery authorized by Federal Rules of Civil Procedure 27-32, and analogous state rules of civil procedure, in which a lawyer asks questions of a party or witness (the deponent) who answers under oath. See *Interrogatories; Request for production of documents and things; Requests for admissions.*

Deposition summary or **index:** A summary of the transcript of a deposition and arranged by subject matter, selected topic, chronology, or narrative.

Direct examination: Questioning of a witness by the attorney who called the witness to testify; normally leading questions cannot be used. See *Cross examination; Leading questions.*

Docket control system: A law office system pursuant to which all deadlines are calendared and responsible persons in the office reminded (tickled) as a deadline approaches.

Documentary sources: In investigating, documents that are sources of information whether public records, business records, medical records, educational records, employment records, or personal records.

Document production: See *Request for production of documents and things.*

Documentary evidence: Evidence received from properly admitted documents. See *Demonstrative evidence; Real evidence;* and *Testimonial evidence.*

EDGAR: The Electronic Data Gathering Analysis and Retrieval system operated by the Securities Exchange Commission allows the accessing and copying of filings by publicly traded companies.

E-Government Act of 2002: A federal statute (found at 44 U.S.C. §3601, et. seq.) intended to make more information held by federal agencies available on the Internet.

Empathy: The capacity to participate in another's feelings.

Enabling legislation: In agency law, the statute that created and controls the agency. See *Agency*; *Agency rule or regulation*; and *Administrative law*.

Equitable relief: A type of remedy sought primarily in civil lawsuits that is based on what is fair and just rather than on what the plaintiff is legally entitled to. Two of the most common forms are injunctive relief and declaratory judgment. See *Declaratory judgment*; *Injunction*; and *Legal remedy*.

Evidence log: A paper or computerized record of all items of potential evidence accumulated in a case.

Exemplary damages: See *Punitive damages*.

Expert: One qualified by knowledge, skill, experience, training or education to have more knowledge on a topic than one not so qualified. When an expert testifies at trial they become an *expert witness*. An expert who consults with an attorney on a case but does not testify is a *consulting expert*. See *Lay witness*.

Explanatory question: A question that asks the person to explain an answer or expound further on it.

Factual analysis: A critical thinking skill; the process of taking information, making sure that you understand it, evaluating it in order to determine if it is reliable, and then applying it to determine the impact or difference it makes on your legal question.

Fair Credit Reporting Act: A federal statute, found at 15 U.S.C. §§1681, et seq., which regulates credit reporting agencies and the use of credit reports. See *Credit reporting agencies*.

Federal Financial Modernization Act: A Federal statute commonly known as the Gramm-Leach-Bliley Act found at 15 U.S.C. §§6801, et. seq., which regulates the disclosure of non-public information on consumers by financial institutions.

Federal Register: Official daily publication of the U.S. government, containing information regarding the status of proposed new or amended regulations.

Federalism: The division of power between the U.S. government and the various state governments.

Fee agreement: The agreement between an attorney and a client that sets out how the attorney is to be paid. Typical types include the hourly rate plus expenses agreement, the flat fee agreement, and the contingency fee agreement. See *Contingency agreement*.

Felony: A crime punishable by more than one year in jail. See *Misdemeanor.*

Fiduciary duty: The high duty of care, competence, trust, loyalty, and confidentiality that the attorney and paralegal owe to the client.

Field interview: An interview conducted outside the interviewer's office.

Finder of fact: In a trial the person(s) charged with deciding contested issues of fact based on the evidence presented at trial. In a jury trial the jury is the finder of fact. In a bench trial it is the trial judge. See *Bench trial.*

Formal discovery: Discovery governed by rules 26-37 of the rules of the federal or state civil procedure or by applicable rules of federal or state criminal procedure. Such discovery, with very limited exceptions, occurs after a civil lawsuit has been filed or a formal criminal prosecution begun, and requires notice to and the right to participation by all parties to the lawsuit or their legal representatives. See *Informal investigation.*

Freedom of Information Act: Federal statute found at 5 U.S.C. §552, (FOIA) that allows anyone to access certain files, documents, records, and other information in the possession of federal government agencies. See *Open records acts*; and *Privacy Act.*

Fundamental right: In constitutional law, a right deemed essential to an ordered liberty.

Gramm-Leach-Bliley Act: See *Federal Financial Modernization Act.*

Grand jury: A group usually consisting of sixteen to twenty-three people selected from the community to hear evidence of alleged criminal conduct and having the power to issue an indictment based on a finding of probable cause.

Header information: In the information brokerage trade, personal or financial information about consumers and businesses collected and organized in various ways to make it more usable, e.g., by geographic region, age, gender, education level, income level, trade or profession, then sold to merchandisers wishing to solicit such individuals or businesses. See *Information broker.*

Hearsay: A statement, other than the one made by the declarant (the one making the statement) while testifying at the trial or hearing (i.e., an out-of-court statement) and offered in evidence to prove the truth of the matter asserted. Hearsay statements are inadmissible at trial unless a recognized exception is found.

Homeland Security Act of 2002: A federal statute, found at 6 U.S.C. §101, et. seq., that dramatically consolidates a number of federal agencies and agency functions into a single federal agency.

Hypothetical questions: Questions that ask the client to assume some set of facts on which to premise an answer.

Immunity: Being free of the threat of criminal prosecution; normally granted by the government. Includes *transactional immunity* which is full immunity from prosecution on all charges related to the witness's testimony and *use immunity* which prohibits the government from using the witness's testimony or any evidence derived from it to prosecute the witness but not evidence independently obtained. See *Privileges; Self-incrimination.*

Impeaching a witness: Attacking the credibility of a witness, usually by showing bias or interest.

Indemnity: A legal doctrine pursuant to which one found to be legally responsible for an obligation is able to place the obligation on another either pursuant to a contract between the parties (contractual indemnity) or to the nature of the relationship between the parties (implied indemnity), e.g., as between principal and agent. See *Principal-agent.*

Indictment: The formal charge issued by the grand jury in a criminal prosecution.

Informal investigation: Private factual investigation that may be undertaken by an attorney on behalf of a client either before or after a lawsuit is commenced and which need not follow the formal rules set forth in the rules of civil or criminal procedure. See *Formal discovery.*

Information: The formal charging instrument filed by prosecutors in a criminal prosecution.

Information broker: A company, sometimes called an information wholesaler, in the business of collecting header information on individuals or businesses and selling it to those wishing to solicit those individuals or businesses. See *Header information.*

Injunction: A court order directing a party to do or refrain from doing something; a type of equitable relief. See *Declaratory judgment; Equitable relief;* and *Legal remedy.*

Intake sheet: A pre-printed checklist of questions used in a new client interview.

Interest: Any self-serving reason a witness might have to not be objective in her testimony; used to discredit a witness. See *Bias; Impeaching a witness.*

Interrogatories: A method of formal discovery pursuant to which written questions are submitted by one party to another which must be answered in writing and under oath by the party being interrogated. See *Deposition*; *Document request*; and *Request for admissions*.

Interview summary: A written summary of an interview.

Invisible wall: A set of procedures established in a law office to insure that a designated person in the office, due to a real or potential conflict of interest, will not view files related to a particular legal matter or otherwise become involved in it; sometimes called a *Chinese wall*.

Jencks Act: Federal statute found at 18 U.S.C. §3500 that requires the prosecution to provide the defense, upon request, with prior written or recorded statements of witnesses after they have testified.

Judgment proof: Description of a defendant who has insufficient assets to pay any judgment that may be rendered against him.

Jury trial: A trial conducted in the presence of a trial judge with a jury present to serve as the finder of fact.

Lay witness: A witness who is not an expert. See *Expert*.

Laying the foundation: Establishing a required factual basis as a prerequisite for the admission of certain evidence; often involving showing a chain of custody or genuiness. See *Authentication*; *Chain of custody*.

Leading questions: Questions which call for a yes or no response.

Legal assistant: A paralegal. See *Paralegal*.

Legal malpractice: When an attorney breaches the fiduciary duty owed to a client in a material way. See *Professional malpractice*.

Legal remedy: The relief that a plaintiff in a civil lawsuit is entitled to by law, usually measured in money damages. See *Compensatory damages*; *Equitable relief*; *Punitive damages*.

Legal services agreement: See *Fee agreement*.

Legally relevant: Information that matters, impacts, or makes a difference on the legal issues being considered.

Lexis/Nexis: A leading commercial database vendor. See *Database vendor*; *Westlaw*.

Long-arm statute: A state statute that sets forth the factual criteria for determining when a non-resident defendant has sufficient minimum contacts with a forum state to satisfy due process and justify the assertion of personal jurisdiction. See *Personal jurisdiction.*

Mediation: The process of attempting to resolve a legal dispute by using a neutral third party (the mediator) who acts as a communicator between the disputing parties, listening to both sides, trying to get both sides to be reasonable and realistic with a goal of helping the parties reach a voluntary settlement that both feel is fair. See *Alternative dispute resolution; Arbitration;* and *Negotiation.*

Misdemeanor: A crime punishable by up to a year in jail. See *Felony.*

Motion: An oral or written application made by a party to a lawsuit to the court asking for some kind of relief.

Motion in limine: A pretrial motion requesting the court to prior order a party to not question a witness about certain matters or to not allow a witness to mention certain inadmissible things while testifying.

Motion to suppress evidence (sometimes called a **motion to exclude evidence**): A pretrial motion used in a criminal prosecution asking the court to act before trial to disallow the admission of some evidence by the opponent.

Multiple-choice questions: Questions that invite the person to choose among two or more options offered by the interviewer.

Negotiation: The process by which the adverse parties, either before or during the litigation process, meet or talk informally, usually through their attorneys, to try and work out a compromise settlement to resolve the dispute. See *Alternative dispute resolution; Arbitration;* and *Mediation.*

Nonverbal communication: The impression we convey to others by body language. See *Body language.*

Online database vendor: See *Database vendors.*

Open-ended questions: Questions that encourage the witness to provide a narrative of events or a detailed explanation in their answer.

Open records acts: State statutes allowing access to information held by state and local governments. See *Freedom of Information Act; Privacy Act.*

Opinion questions: Questions that ask the person to express their opinion about something or even to speculate.

PACER: The Public Access to Court Electronic Records is a system, created and administered by the Administrative Office of the U.S. Courts that allows any subscriber to dial in by modem to a particular federal district or bankruptcy court clerk's office and quickly retrieve case information and dockets.

Paralegal: A person qualified by education, training, or work experience who is employed or retained by a lawyer, law office, corporation, governmental agency, or other entity and who performs specifically delegated substantive legal work for which a lawyer is responsible. Also referred to as *Legal assistant.*

Personal jurisdiction (also called *in personam* jurisdiction): Legal doctrine dealing with the power of a court to enter an order binding on a particular defendant. See *Long-arm statute*; *Subject matter jurisdiction.*

Plaintiff: The party that initiates a civil lawsuit against another. The government in a criminal prosecution. See *Defendant.*

Plan of investigation: The written plan made by an investigator before undertaking a factual investigation.

Pretext calling: An unscrupulous tactic used by some information brokers and private investigators whereby the caller pretends to be someone they are not in order to obtain financial or other information on the target.

Pressure questions: Questions that challenge the interviewee directly or indirectly and compel a response involving emotion or feeling as well as fact.

Principal-agent: Legal doctrine recognizing that one person (agent) may be acting on behalf of another (principal) in such a way that the principal is legally bound by the actions of the agent. See *Respondeat superior*; *Vicarious liability.*

Privacy Act: A federal statute found at 5 U.S.C. §552(a) that allows an individual to obtain access to certain information maintained by federal agencies about themselves. See *Freedom of Information Act*; *Open records acts.*

Private sources of information: Information of any kind that is in the possession of private individuals, businesses, educational institutions, or any other non-governmental custodian. See *Public sources of information.*

Privileges: An area of the law that declares that certain information should not be subject to disclosure in informal investigation, formal discovery, or in sworn testimony at trial. Examples include the attorney-client privilege, physician-patient privilege, spousal privilege, and the marital privilege. See also *Self-incrimination*; *Work product.*

Procedural law: The law that defines the manner in which substantive legal rights and duties may be enforced. Examples of substantive law include constitutional law, contract law, the law of business associations, tort law, criminal law, real property law, and so on. See *Substantive law.*

Professional malpractice: When an attorney breaches the fiduciary duty owed to a client in a material way. See *Legal malpractice.*

Public sources of information: Information of any kind that is in the possession of a federal, state, or local agency or department. See *Private sources of information.*

Punitive damages: Damages (sometimes called exemplary damages) sought in a civil action which are meant to "punish" the wrongdoer for his conduct rather than to compensate the plaintiff. See *Compensatory damages; Exemplary damages.*

Real evidence: Evidence (also called physical evidence) in the form of properly admitted objects (e.g., the weapon in a murder case). See *Demonstrative evidence; Documentary evidence;* and *Testimonial evidence.*

Records authorizations: Written authorizations allowing attorneys or others to obtain the medical, educational, or employment records of another.

Records custodian: The person designated as the custodian of records by a business or government agency; the proper person to testify as an authenticating witness for such records. See *Authentication; Business records.*

Request for production of documents and things: A method of formal discovery pursuant to which a party to a civil lawsuit request the other party to the lawsuit to produce documents or tangible things for inspection, copying, or testing, and the entry on land or property for inspection and testing. See *Deposition; Interrogatory; Requests for admissions;* and *Requests for physical or mental examination.*

Requests for admissions: A method of formal discovery in a civil lawsuit pursuant to which one party requests the opposing party to admit the truth of some factual allegation of a document or thing. See *Deposition; Interrogatories; Requests for production of documents and things;* and *Requests for physical or mental examination.*

Requests for physical or mental examination: A method of formal discovery in a civil lawsuit pursuant to which one party requests that the court order the opposing party or a witness to undergo a physical or mental examination. See *Deposition; Interrogatories; Requests for production of documents and things;* and *Requests for admissions.*

Respondeat superior: (Latin for "Let the master respond"): See *Vicarious liability.* When legal responsibility is placed on one for the acts of another.

Retainer: An advance payment made by a client to an attorney. See *Fee agreement*.

Reverse directory: A written or electronic directory maintained by many local communities that lists residences and businesses first by street address, then again by telephone numbers numerically.

Rules of appellate procedure: Body of rules that govern the filing and processing of an appeal of a court ruling to a higher court in a civil lawsuit or a criminal prosecution in state or federal court.

Rules of civil procedure: Body of rules that govern the filing and processing of a civil lawsuit in the federal or state courts.

Rules of criminal procedure: Body of rules that govern the filing and processing of a criminal prosecution in the federal or state courts.

Rules of evidence: Body of rules that govern the admission and exclusion of proof before the court in the trial of civil and criminal cases.

Search company: A company that, for a fee, will search federal, state, and local records.

Self-incrimination: Admitting to criminal activity by one's self. The Fifth Amendment to the U.S. Constitution grants individuals a privilege against being compelled to testify if such testimony would tend to self-incriminate the speaker. See *Immunity; Privilege*.

Simultaneous representation: The legal representation by an attorney of more than one party in a single legal matter; often the origin of a real or potential conflict of interest. See *Conflict of interest*.

Skip-tracing: The activity of locating a missing person; often performed for a fee by private investigators and other businesses.

Slang: Words or phrases used to mean something other than their standard definition; sometimes referred to as **street talk.**

Statement against interest: A statement made against the speaker's pecuniary (money), proprietary (ownership), or culpability (civil or criminal) interests. Admissible at trial as an exception to the hearsay rule.

Statute: An act of the U.S. Congress or a state legislature. See *Agency rule or regulation; Common law;* and *Court rule*.

Statute of limitation: A statute stating the time in which a lawsuit must be commenced against a defendant or be forever barred.

Statute of repose: A statute that places an absolute limit on the time in which a lawsuit must be commenced against a defendant without regard to when the cause of action arose.

Subject matter jurisdiction: Legal doctrine dealing with the question of the power of a court to hear a particular kind of case. See *Personal jurisdiction.*

Subpoena: A document issued by the court clerk ordering a person to appear at a deposition or trial. A subpoena that not only compels the presence of a witness but directs that witness to bring documents or things with him to the deposition is called a **subpoena** *duces tecum.*

Substantive law: The law that defines the rights and duties of persons with respect to each other. See *Procedural law,* which defines the manner in which those rights and duties may be enforced. Examples of substantive law include constitutional law, contract law, the law of business associations, tort law, criminal law, real property law, and so on.

Telephone interview: An interview conducted over the telephone rather than in person.

Testimonial evidence: Evidence received from the sworn testimony of witnesses. See *Demonstrative evidence*; *Documentary evidence*; and *Real evidence.*

Timeline: A drawing made by a witness showing the chronology of events.

Trust accounts: Bank accounts established by attorneys where the funds of clients or third parties are deposited.

Unauthorized practice of law: Practicing law without a license.

United States Government Manual: Official publication of the U.S. government containing basic who, what, and where information on the federal government and its agencies.

Venue: A legal doctrine dealing with the most appropriate geographic location (county or federal district) for the case to be heard.

Vicarious liability: Legal doctrine placing legal responsibility on one person for the acts of another. See *Respondeat superior.*

Vital statistics: Records maintained by local and state governments including information and certificates for births, deaths, marriages, and divorces.

Westlaw: A leading commercial database vendor. See *Database vendor*; *Lexis/Nexis.*

Witness statement: The written statement of a witness taken or made during or following an interview.

Work product: Material containing the mental impressions, conclusions, opinions, or legal theories of an attorney or other representative of a party concerning the litigation; normally subject to an absolute privilege.

Index